Developing Effective and High-Performing Teams in Higher Education

Tashieka Simone Burris-Melville
University of Technology, Jamaica

Shalieka Tiffia Burris
University of Technology, Jamaica

Published in the United States of America by
IGI Global
701 E. Chocolate Avenue
Hershey PA, USA 17033
Tel: 717-533-8845
Fax: 717-533-8661
E-mail: cust@igi-global.com
Web site: https://www.igi-global.com

Copyright © 2025 by IGI Global. All rights reserved. No part of this publication may be reproduced, stored or distributed in any form or by any means, electronic or mechanical, including photocopying, without written permission from the publisher.
Product or company names used in this set are for identification purposes only. Inclusion of the names of the products or companies does not indicate a claim of ownership by IGI Global of the trademark or registered trademark.

Library of Congress Cataloging-in-Publication Data

CIP Data Pending
ISBN: 979-8-3693-3852-0
eISBN: 979-8-3693-3853-7

Vice President of Editorial: Melissa Wagner
Managing Editor of Acquisitions: Mikaela Felty
Managing Editor of Book Development: Jocelynn Hessler
Production Manager: Mike Brehm
Cover Design: Phillip Shickler

British Cataloguing in Publication Data
A Cataloguing in Publication record for this book is available from the British Library.

All work contributed to this book is new, previously-unpublished material.
The views expressed in this book are those of the authors, but not necessarily of the publisher.

Editorial Advisory Board

Tony Bridwell, *The Encompass Group, USA*
Delroy Chevers, *Caribbean Maritime University, Jamaica*
Nola P. Hill-Berry, *University of Technology, Jamaica*
Lonnie Morris, Jr., *The Chicago School of Professional Psychology, USA*
Jana Roberts, *Trevecca Nazarene University, USA*
Sakhi Aggrawal, *Purdue University, USA*
Kristin Bledsoe, *Trevecca Nazarene University, USA*
Nicole Cameron, *University of Technology, Jamaica*
Rhonda Dookwah, *University of the Commonwealth Caribbean, Jamaica*
Kadia Hylton-Fraser, *Portmore Missionary Preparatory, Jamaica*
Henry Lewis, *University of Technology, Jamaica*
Dejon Lingo, *The University of the West Indies, Mona, Jamaica*
Andrew Melville, *Trevecca Nazarene University, USA*
Israel Oyedare, *Virginia Tech, USA*
Veronica Reid-Johnson, *University of the Commonwealth Caribbean, Jamaica*
Ryan Will, *Fort Hays State University, USA*

Table of Contents

Foreword xix

Preface xxii

Acknowledgment viii

Section 1
Cultivating Psychological Safety: The Foundation of Thriving Teams

Chapter 1
Safety Nets of Success A Deep Dive Into Team Climate and Psychological Safety 1
    Shalieka T. Burris, University of Technology, Jamaica
    Tashieka S. Burris-Melville, University of Technology, Jamaica
    Oprah D. Burris, Clan Carthy High School, Jamaica

Chapter 2
Promoting Trust and Psychological Safety in Team Environments Insights for Universities 29
    Memory Deredzai, University of Zimbabwe, Zimbabwe
    Pedzisai Goronga, University of Zimbabwe, Zimbabwe

Chapter 3
Empowering Students for Working in Culturally Rich and Psychologically Nourishing Work Environments 57
    Sara Redondo-Duarte, Universidad Complutense de Madrid, Spain
    Sonia Escorial Santa-Marina, UNIE Universidad, Spain

Section 2
Leadership and Teamwork: A Synergistic Approach

Chapter 4
Building Champions: Leadership as the Keystone of Team Performance 91
    Saptarshi Kumar Sarkar, Brainware University, India
    Sanchita Ghosh, Brainware University, India
    Piyal Roy, Brainware University, India
    Nobhonil Roy Choudhury, Brainware University, India

Chapter 5
Steering the Ship How Leadership Styles Shape Team Development and Performance 115
    Tara M. Knight, Trevecca Nazarene University, USA

Section 3
Building High Impact Teams for Teaching and Learning

Chapter 6
Building Collaboration Among Teacher Candidates in Higher Education: Developing Lesson Planning Competencies With Lesson Study (LS) Teams .. 145
    Tolgahan Ayantaş, Ankara University, Turkey
    Gürcan Gürgen, Ankara University, Turkey

Chapter 7
Embracing Collaborative Learning: Innovative Teaching Methods at Tertiary Level 187
    Morine Matongo, University of Zimbabwe, Zimbabwe
    Pedzisai Goronga, University of Zimbabwe, Zimbabwe

Chapter 8
Using Google Docs for Enhancing Collaboration in Academic Writing Instruction 217
    Nekiesha Reid, University of Guyana, Guyana

Chapter 9
Utilising Digital Tools to Enhance Teamwork Among Adult Learners in a Postgraduate Course 251
    Leesha Nicole Roberts, University of Trinidad and Tobago, Trinidad and Tobago

Chapter 10
Avatars of Academia: Exploring Virtual Collaboration's Tapestry 285
    Andi Asrifan, Universitas Negeri Makassar, Indonesia
    Anita Candra Dewi, Universitas Negeri Makassar, Indonesia
    Vivit Rosmayanti, Universitas Negeri Makassar, Indonesia
    Syamsuardi Saodi, Universitas Negeri Makassar, Indonesia
    Badruddin Kaddas, Universitas Islam Makassar, Indonesia
    Mulyadi Mulyadi, Universitas Islam Makassar, Indonesia

Chapter 11
Fostering Effective Communication and Information Sharing in Higher
Education Institutions 313
    Hlompho Cynthia Letsie, Limkokwing University of Creative
        Technology, Lesotho
    Tsepiso Claurina Mncina, Limkokwing University of Creative
        Technology, Lesotho
    Sekoai Elliot Nkhi, Limkokwing University of Creative Technology,
        Lesotho
    Mofana Mongali Mofana, Limkokwing University of Creative
        Technology, Lesotho

Section 4
Enhancing Research Impact Through Collaboration

Chapter 12
Perceptions of Faculty on Research Productivity: Developing Competencies
Through Teamwork, Mentorship, and Collaboration 339
    Cynthia Onyefulu, University of Technology, Jamaica

Chapter 13
Fusion Femme: Exploring Virtual Collaboration Among Women in
Academic Spaces 367
    Eraldine S. Williams-Shakespeare, University of Technology, Jamaica
    Sharlene M. Smith, Georgian Court University, USA
    Taneisha Wright-Cameron, University of Technology, Jamaica
    Joyce Esi Tawiah-Mensah, University of Cape Coast, Ghana
    Natasha G. Swann, University of Bahamas, Bahamas
    Adhwaa Alahmari, King Khalid University, Saudi Arabia

Chapter 14
Interrogating the Third Space in Collaborative Research: A Critical Narrative
Discourse 401
    Hope Mayne, University of Technology, Jamaica
    Shermaine Barrett, University of Technology, Jamaica
    Dwaine Hibbert, University of Technology, Jamaica

Section 5
Cracking the Code of Team Dynamics Success

Chapter 15
The Teamwork Equation: Why 1 + 1 = Much More Than 2 in Academic
Union Success 419
 Eraldine S. Williams-Shakespeare, University of Technology, Jamaica
 Tashieka S. Burris-Melville, University of Technology, Jamaica
 Clavery O. Allen, University of Technology, Jamaica
 Nadine A. Barrett-Maitland, University of Technology, Jamaica
 Denise Allen, University of Technology, Jamaica
 Atherine Anneth Marie Salmon, University of Technology, Jamaica
 Joan L. Lawla, University of Technology, Jamaica
 Robert A. Johnson, University of Technology, Jamaica
 Meredith Williams, University of Technology, Jamaica

Chapter 16
Sculpting Educational Excellence Brand Building Approaches for Higher
Education Institutions 449
 Remi John Thomas, Vishwakarma University, India
 Madhuri Sawant, Dr. Babasaheb Ambedkar Marathwada University, India

Section 6
The Ongoing Journey Towards Diversity and Inclusion

Chapter 17
Leveraging Diversity and Inclusion for Enhanced Team Outcomes in Higher
Education 479
 Muhammad Usman Tariq, Abu Dhabi University, UAE & University College Cork, Ireland

Compilation of References 513

About the Contributors 613

Index 629

Detailed Table of Contents

Foreword xix

Preface xxii

Acknowledgment viii

Section 1
Cultivating Psychological Safety: The Foundation of Thriving Teams

Chapter 1
Safety Nets of Success A Deep Dive Into Team Climate and Psychological Safety 1
    Shalieka T. Burris, University of Technology, Jamaica
    Tashieka S. Burris-Melville, University of Technology, Jamaica
    Oprah D. Burris, Clan Carthy High School, Jamaica

With the increasing challenges confronting higher education institutions (HEIs), encouraging a positive team climate that encourages psychological safety is crucial for developing high-performing and thriving teams. This study explored the differences in team climate perceptions and psychological safety between academic and administrative staff at a higher education institution. Employing a quantitative survey research design, the research study investigated how the staff groups perceive various aspects of team climate and psychological safety. The study also explored the relationship between team climate and psychological safety. The data revealed that academic teams had a lower perception of the team climate and a slightly lower perception of psychological safety when compared to administrative teams. The relationship between team climate and psychological safety scores was weak and not statistically significant. These findings highlight the need for strategies to enhance psychological safety, particularly in academic settings where perceptions are less uniform.

Chapter 2
Promoting Trust and Psychological Safety in Team Environments Insights for Universities 29
    Memory Deredzai, University of Zimbabwe, Zimbabwe
    Pedzisai Goronga, University of Zimbabwe, Zimbabwe

This chapter examined the importance of trust and psychological safety in university team environments. Trust and psychological safety influence the overall success of educational institutions. A comprehensive overview of trust and psychological safety is provided, highlighting their significance in team dynamics and their impact on individual and collective performance since teamwork is at the core of academic excellence. Evidence-based strategies to promote trust and psychological safety in team environments such as open communication, inclusive governance and decision-making processes, supportive and nurturing culture, clear goals and clear expectations among others are discussed. threats to trust and psychological safety within team environments are discussed. In essence, the chapter provides valuable insights for educators, administrators, policymakers and institutional leaders seeking to create inclusive and effective team environments that foster trust and psychological safety, ultimately enhancing and shaping the overall educational experience for both staff and students.

Chapter 3
Empowering Students for Working in Culturally Rich and Psychologically Nourishing Work Environments 57
    Sara Redondo-Duarte, Universidad Complutense de Madrid, Spain
    Sonia Escorial Santa-Marina, UNIE Universidad, Spain

The aim of this chapter is to explore university practices that contribute to the creation of diverse and inclusive work teams in a psychologically safe environment. To this end, the first section explores the implications of VUCA environments for student learning, as well as the relevance of the concepts of diversity and inclusion in work teams. In this context, experiential learning is presented as a powerful methodological approach to strengthen the links between education, work and personal development. The second section addresses the importance of fostering a collaborative and healthy working environment in student teams. In this regard, a proposed team model and some constructive feedback strategies are included. Finally, some examples of initiatives to promote diversity and inclusion in the university context are described.

Section 2
Leadership and Teamwork: A Synergistic Approach

Chapter 4

Building Champions: Leadership as the Keystone of Team Performance........... 91
 Saptarshi Kumar Sarkar, Brainware University, India
 Sanchita Ghosh, Brainware University, India
 Piyal Roy, Brainware University, India
 Nobhonil Roy Choudhury, Brainware University, India

This paper explores the role of leadership in team development and performance in organizations. It reviews literature on leadership theories, team dynamics, and performance outcomes, examining the impact of different leadership styles on team cohesion, motivation, and productivity. The paper analyzes effective leadership strategies and best practices, providing insights on how organizations can empower and nurture leaders. Empowered leaders can harness team potential, maximizing effectiveness and paving the way for sustainable growth. The findings emphasize the importance of understanding and implementing nuanced leadership approaches, fostering a culture of excellence, and achieving enduring success.

Chapter 5

Steering the Ship How Leadership Styles Shape Team Development and Performance 115
 Tara M. Knight, Trevecca Nazarene University, USA

Purpose: This research explores the importance of leadership style on team performance and development. This research will answer the question: How do different leadership styles impact the development and performance of a team? Design/Methodology Approach: qualitative systemic literature review. Findings: There is not one leadership style that is perfection. Therefore, a hybrid of leadership styles is needed to develop employees and improve performance effectively. The most successful leaders will be the ones who are most flexible and can wear many hats. Theory: Contingency Theory of Leadership Keywords: leadership, employee performance, leadership style, employee development, work environment, Authoritarian Leadership, Autocratic Leadership, Directive Leadership, Transformational Leadership, Transactional Leadership, Servant Leadership, Paternalistic Leadership

Section 3
Building High Impact Teams for Teaching and Learning

Chapter 6
Building Collaboration Among Teacher Candidates in Higher Education:
Developing Lesson Planning Competencies With Lesson Study (LS) Teams .. 145
Tolgahan Ayantaş, Ankara University, Turkey
Gürcan Gürgen, Ankara University, Turkey

This study aims to unveil teacher candidates' progress in lesson planning using the Lesson Study (LS) approach. Through action research, lesson plans generated by teacher candidates underwent content analysis and subsequent interviews. The findings revealed that collaborative work among social studies teacher candidates led to more feasible and content-rich lesson plans. The study underscores the efficacy of collaborative work in producing more viable and content-rich lesson plans. These outcomes underscore the potential of LS Teams to contribute to the professional growth of teacher candidates and deepen their understanding of their field.

Chapter 7
Embracing Collaborative Learning: Innovative Teaching Methods at Tertiary Level.. 187
Morine Matongo, University of Zimbabwe, Zimbabwe
Pedzisai Goronga, University of Zimbabwe, Zimbabwe

This chapter explores innovative teaching methods that incorporate collaborative learning at higher education level. The discussion critically interrogates benefits, challenges and strategies for successful implementation of collaborative methodologies. Also known as cooperative learning, collaborative learning is a pedagogical technique that promotes active engagement, participatory learner engagement in learning in emancipatory epistemological spaces, contact, and mutual assistance among students.

Chapter 8
Using Google Docs for Enhancing Collaboration in Academic Writing
Instruction 217
    Nekiesha Reid, University of Guyana, Guyana

Collaborative learning is a powerful method to fostering engagement and meaningful learning experiences within academic writing instruction, promoting participation critical thinking & skill development. In this vein, computer-mediated collaborative writing has been increasingly integrated into the classroom using tools like Google Docs. However, there is still limited research focused on understating the benefits and challenges of Google Docs for academic writing instruction, especially outside the second language learning classroom. Based on quantitative survey data from tertiary students in Guyana, this chapter explores the benefits and challenges associated with using Google Docs in academic writing instruction. The results show that that Google Docs offers a versatile platform that aligns with the evolving needs of modern educational practices, contributing to learning and academic writing skill development. However, for maximal impact, educators must also confront challenges that may surface, such as ensuring equitable participation and overcoming resistance to new technologies.

Chapter 9
Utilising Digital Tools to Enhance Teamwork Among Adult Learners in a
Postgraduate Course 251
    *Leesha Nicole Roberts, University of Trinidad and Tobago, Trinidad and
       Tobago*

This chapter provides an in-depth examination of the role of digital tools in enhancing virtual teamwork among adult learners in higher education, focusing on the "Fundamentals of Educational Technology" course within the Master of Education in Innovative Learning Technologies (MEILT) Programme at the Advanced Learning Institute (ALI). Through a qualitative narrative inquiry, the chapter explores how digital platforms such as Learning Management Systems (LMS), video conferencing, and social media facilitate communication, collaboration, and learning outcomes among part-time students. The analysis highlights the benefits of these tools in promoting flexibility, real-time collaboration, and distributed cognition while addressing challenges such as digital etiquette and technological fluency. Additionally, the chapter offers practical recommendations for improving the use of digital tools to support teamwork in adult education within the context of Trinidad and Tobago.

Chapter 10
Avatars of Academia: Exploring Virtual Collaboration's Tapestry 285
    Andi Asrifan, Universitas Negeri Makassar, Indonesia
    Anita Candra Dewi, Universitas Negeri Makassar, Indonesia
    Vivit Rosmayanti, Universitas Negeri Makassar, Indonesia
    Syamsuardi Saodi, Universitas Negeri Makassar, Indonesia
    Badruddin Kaddas, Universitas Islam Makassar, Indonesia
    Mulyadi Mulyadi, Universitas Islam Makassar, Indonesia

The effects of COVID-19 on educational institutions, leadership, technology in the classroom, virtual reality, and collaborative learning are just a few of the topics covered in this extensive review of recent studies. It explores the pros and cons of virtual teams in educational contexts, focusing on knowledge work in virtual environments and how they could improve interdisciplinary partnerships. Setting clear goals, communicating effectively, and managing cultural differences are critical tactics outlined in the article for successful virtual collaboration. Additionally, it delves into how virtual collaboration tools might enhance teamwork and student engagement, as well as the changing function of avatars in educational environments. The paper highlights the potential of virtual reality, augmented reality, artificial intelligence, and gamification to revolutionize collaborative learning, build immersive environments, and enhance learning outcomes in the next quarter of a century. It predicts immense progress in education due to these technologies' incorporation.

Chapter 11
Fostering Effective Communication and Information Sharing in Higher
Education Institutions 313
> *Hlompho Cynthia Letsie, Limkokwing University of Creative
>   Technology, Lesotho*
> *Tsepiso Claurina Mncina, Limkokwing University of Creative
>   Technology, Lesotho*
> *Sekoai Elliot Nkhi, Limkokwing University of Creative Technology,
>   Lesotho*
> *Mofana Mongali Mofana, Limkokwing University of Creative
>   Technology, Lesotho*

Effective communication is crucial for cohesive team dynamics in higher education settings, going beyond individual interaction. This chapter discussed the effective communication and information sharing towards the development effective and high Performing teams in higher education. In higher education institutions, email, bulletin boards, messaging applications, and questionnaires are efficient means of communication in order for high performing teams. It is revealed that communication obstacles including language, cultural, psychological, emotional, environmental, and physical barriers are the main hindrance of effective communication. In order to surmount these challenges, the study proposes an emotional intelligence model of communication to overcome the identified obstacles because they have psychological impact on communicators and for the development of high performing teams. As a result, recommend that self-acknowledgment and positive interpersonal relationships, which are fundamental components of emotional intelligence be considered to develop high performing teams.

Section 4
Enhancing Research Impact Through Collaboration

Chapter 12
Perceptions of Faculty on Research Productivity: Developing Competencies
Through Teamwork, Mentorship, and Collaboration.. 339
    Cynthia Onyefulu, University of Technology, Jamaica

This study investigated lecturers' perceptions of research productivity, factors impacting research productivity, and how to develop lecturers' competencies through teamwork, mentorship, and collaboration to improve research productivity. Five research questions guided the study and were answered using an online questionnaire and document review. The sample size was 31 lecturers from a single university in Jamaica. The results revealed that the rate of research productivity among lecturers has been increasing over the years. The results showed that across the 17 years examined, conference abstracts, presentations, and proceedings were the highest. Peer-reviewed journal papers follow this, with books and book chapters being the least. Lecturers' perceptions of conducting research and publications were reported under motivation, assistance, and mandatory.

Chapter 13
Fusion Femme: Exploring Virtual Collaboration Among Women in
Academic Spaces 367
    Eraldine S. Williams-Shakespeare, University of Technology, Jamaica
    Sharlene M. Smith, Georgian Court University, USA
    Taneisha Wright-Cameron, University of Technology, Jamaica
    Joyce Esi Tawiah-Mensah, University of Cape Coast, Ghana
    Natasha G. Swann, University of Bahamas, Bahamas
    Adhwaa Alahmari, King Khalid University, Saudi Arabia

This intrinsic case study explored six women of colour in varying stages of their academic careers across five universities in the Caribbean, North America, Africa and Asia, reflecting on their experiences with virtual teamwork and its influence on research, teaching innovation and leadership. The chapter presents challenges experienced by early to mid-career academics and outlines opportunities that virtual collaborative engagement efforts may yield. The research question guiding this study was "how can women of colour in academia support each other virtually in areas of research, teaching excellence and leadership?" Data collected via a focus group discussion revealed several challenges related to each key area of interest and ranged from discrimination to lack of mentorship on the job. The findings highlight several factors that affect research (funding and time affordance), teaching (mentorship and support) and leadership (mindset of long-service over merit and gender and personal biases) progress for women of colour. The ability to collaborate virtually offered these women an avenue through which they can support each other while increasing research output, improving teaching skills and positioning themselves to excel in leadership.

Chapter 14
Interrogating the Third Space in Collaborative Research: A Critical Narrative Discourse.. 401
Hope Mayne, University of Technology, Jamaica
Shermaine Barrett, University of Technology, Jamaica
Dwaine Hibbert, University of Technology, Jamaica

In this research project, three researchers from three different research backgrounds and academic disciplines drew on Bhabha's third space theory to reflect on their experience conducting collaborative research. The collaborative research process created a third space where the researchers were able to share their perspectives and challenge ideas to achieve consensus. Utilising a critical narrative inquiry approach, the researchers shared their experiences of working with each other in a collaborative research project. They sought to explore: 1) How do three different perspectives of research contribute to the research process? 2) What does the collaborative research practice look like? 3) How can this process contribute to new positions in qualitative research? Narratives were analysed using a cross-case thematic analysis. The findings revealed that the research process was not linear and prescriptive but more so a descriptive process, which created a space for new understandings about collaborative research to emerge.

Section 5
Cracking the Code of Team Dynamics Success

Chapter 15
The Teamwork Equation: Why 1 + 1 = Much More Than 2 in Academic
Union Success 419
    Eraldine S. Williams-Shakespeare, University of Technology, Jamaica
    Tashieka S. Burris-Melville, University of Technology, Jamaica
    Clavery O. Allen, University of Technology, Jamaica
    Nadine A. Barrett-Maitland, University of Technology, Jamaica
    Denise Allen, University of Technology, Jamaica
    Atherine Anneth Marie Salmon, University of Technology, Jamaica
    Joan L. Lawla, University of Technology, Jamaica
    Robert A. Johnson, University of Technology, Jamaica
    Meredith Williams, University of Technology, Jamaica

This study examined the critical link between team dynamics and effectiveness within an academic staff union. The research underscores the importance of teamwork in achieving union success, particularly in an environment where workers' rights can be overshadowed. The investigation explored how strong team dynamics, characterized by dedication, collaboration, and strategic maneuvering, empower academic staff unions to secure and uphold faculty well-being. A convergent parallel mixed-methods approach was employed. The study's findings highlight the importance of team dynamics and collaboration within academic staff unions.

Chapter 16
Sculpting Educational Excellence Brand Building Approaches for Higher
Education Institutions 449
    Remi John Thomas, Vishwakarma University, India
    Madhuri Sawant, Dr. Babasaheb Ambedkar Marathwada University,
      India

This paper presents a comprehensive seven-stage conceptual framework for branding in higher education institutions, based on a study conducted in Maharashtra, India. It addresses research gaps in understanding the challenges faced by institutions in this diverse and dynamic setting. Drawing on personal experience, literature review, and marketing theories, the framework guides institutions in brand development and sustainability. The study emphasizes stages such as defining vision and purpose, creating a distinct brand identity, positioning the brand, enhancing awareness and performance, conducting brand audits, and sustaining brand equity. It offers valuable insights for institutions aiming to strengthen their brand presence in the competitive academic landscape.

Section 6
The Ongoing Journey Towards Diversity and Inclusion

Chapter 17
Leveraging Diversity and Inclusion for Enhanced Team Outcomes in Higher
Education 479
   Muhammad Usman Tariq, Abu Dhabi University, UAE & University
      College Cork, Ireland

This chapter examines the central role of diversity and inclusion in improving team outcomes in higher education. By leveraging the diverse perspectives, experiences, and talents of team members, colleges can foster innovation, promote collaboration, and promote academic excellence. The discussion will address key principles, strategies and practices for realizing the potential of diverse and inclusive teams, including communication, diverse leadership, intercultural competence and equity-focused initiatives. Through an analysis of case studies, best practices, and future trends, the chapter highlights the transformative impact of diverse and inclusive teams on research, teaching, and institutional culture. In addition, it explores the challenges and opportunities associated with building and maintaining diverse teams and the continued importance of diversity and inclusion as drivers of academic excellence in a rapidly changing global environment.

Compilation of References 513

About the Contributors 613

Index 629

Foreword

In today's rapidly evolving higher education landscape, the ability to foster effective teams and collaborative environments is more crucial than ever. Academic excellence, student success, and innovative research are all deeply rooted in the ability of institutions to cultivate high-performing teams. At the University of Technology, Jamaica (UTech, Ja.), we recognize that our transformation and growth depend on visionary leadership and creating environments where teamwork can thrive. Throughout my career, both in academia and industry, I have consistently seen how successful teams drive not only operational excellence but also innovation and long-term strategic goals. Leading teams at UTech, Ja. as well as in my previous role at Rolls-Royce, has shown me the power of collaboration in delivering complex, high-stakes projects and achieving institutional goals.

This book, *Developing Effective and High-Performing Teams in Higher Education,* is an invaluable resource that speaks directly to the need for fostering teamwork in academia. Written and edited by Dr. Tashieka Burris-Melville and Dr. Shalieka T. Burris, both esteemed scholars at UTech, Ja., this book presents a deep understanding of the complexities involved in building successful teams within academic institutions. Having led teams at Rolls-Royce—where I was responsible for large, cross-functional teams tasked with developing cutting-edge aerospace technologies—I have seen firsthand the significance of collaboration, trust, and shared goals in driving successful outcomes. The same principles apply in higher education, where diverse teams must work together to meet ambitious academic and research objectives.

The authors of this book delve into the intricacies of team dynamics, leadership, and collaboration, offering strategies that resonate with my own experience in managing teams both in the private sector and in academia. At Rolls-Royce, where I served as Technology Project Lead, I was tasked with overseeing multi-million-dollar projects that required meticulous coordination among engineers, researchers, and project managers across the globe. The success of these projects hinged not only on technical expertise but on fostering an environment where every team member felt empowered to contribute ideas, take risks, and collaborate freely. This is a key concept the authors explore, particularly in their discussion of psychological safety—an essential component of any high-performing team.

As President of UTech, Ja., I have the privilege of leading a diverse institution with ambitious goals. One of my primary objectives is to ensure that our faculty and staff work together as a cohesive unit, united in our mission to deliver the highest quality education to our students. The challenges of leading a university through times of change require the same level of strategic leadership that I applied in industry. At Rolls-Royce, I led teams in the development of the UltraFan demonstrator engine, a next-generation project that required collaboration across multiple teams, departments, and even external partners. The success of this project depended on a leadership approach that was adaptable, inclusive, and responsive to the needs of each team member—principles that are essential for fostering high-performing teams in higher education as well.

This book emphasizes the importance of leadership styles that promote collaboration and trust, qualities that have been central to my leadership approach throughout my career. As I guide UTech, Ja., toward achieving new heights in academic and research excellence, it is imperative that we embrace leadership models that are flexible and adaptive, capable of addressing the unique challenges and opportunities that arise in higher education. In my own experience, leadership is not about rigidly adhering to one style but about understanding the needs of the team and adapting accordingly—a key takeaway from this book that resonates deeply with my own philosophy.

At UTech, Ja., our goal is to create a student-centered institution where collaboration is at the heart of everything we do. This is particularly important in fostering a culture of excellence in teaching and learning, where educators must work together to develop innovative pedagogical approaches that enhance student outcomes. My experience leading research and development teams at Rolls-Royce has shown me that innovation is often the result of diverse perspectives coming together to tackle complex problems. Similarly, in higher education, collaboration between faculty members can lead to groundbreaking research and more effective teaching strategies that benefit both students and the broader academic community.

One of the key strengths of this book is its focus on actionable strategies for building high-performing teams. As someone who has been involved in both academic and corporate leadership, I understand the importance of not just having a vision but creating a roadmap to achieve that vision. At UTech, Ja., we are actively working to implement many of the best practices outlined in this book, particularly in relation to fostering a culture of trust, accountability, and shared responsibility. These principles were critical in my work leading global teams at Rolls-Royce, and they are equally important in the context of higher education.

The book also underscores the value of mentorship and collaboration in enhancing research outcomes, another area where UTech, Ja., is committed to making strides. Throughout my career, I have seen how mentorship plays a crucial role in developing the next generation of leaders, both in academia and industry. At Rolls-Royce, I had the opportunity to mentor young engineers and researchers, helping them navigate the challenges of working in a fast-paced, high-tech environment. Similarly, at UTech, Ja., we are dedicated to creating opportunities for faculty to collaborate on research projects, share knowledge, and mentor emerging scholars, thereby enhancing our research impact.

In conclusion, *Developing Effective and High-Performing Teams in Higher Education* is an essential resource for anyone in academic leadership. It provides not only theoretical insights but also practical strategies for fostering teamwork, collaboration, and leadership within higher education institutions. As President of UTech, Ja., I have experienced firsthand the transformative power of high-performing teams, and I am confident that the insights in this book will be invaluable as we continue to build a university that is not only a beacon of academic excellence but also a model of collaboration and innovation. I highly recommend this book to educators, administrators, and policymakers who are committed to driving the future of higher education through effective teamwork and leadership.

Kevin Brown
University of Technology, Jamaica

Dr. Kevin Brown *was appointed as the fifth President of the University of Technology, Jamaica in September 2023. With over 18 years of experience in academia and the aerospace industry, Dr. Brown has been a leader in complex aerospace structural system design, transport systems, and engineering materials. He previously served as Technology Project Lead at Rolls-Royce, overseeing global teams and strategic initiatives. A published researcher and patent holder, Dr. Brown has also led high-value technology programmes in collaboration with top universities. Committed to community engagement, he has worked closely with government and private sector entities and has been a radio broadcaster for over 12 years. An alumnus of UTech, Jamaica, Dr. Brown holds a Master's and PhD from the University of Nottingham and is dedicated to driving UTech's mission of excellence and empowerment.*

Preface

What if the greatest innovation in higher education is not a new technology or research breakthrough, but the ability to unlock the full potential of teams? This question invites us to reconsider the foundations of success in academia. Universities and colleges around the world are grappling with shifts in pedagogical practices, technological advances, and an increasingly diverse student population. Effective and high-performing teams have become central to addressing these demands, promoting environments where collaboration, creativity, and accountability can thrive. The notion that higher education operates in silos is increasingly being dismantled, as institutions recognize that success in academia is not solely the result of individual accomplishments but the product of cohesive, well-structured teams working towards common goals (Kezar & Lester, 2009). This book, *Developing Effective and High-Performing Teams in Higher Education*, emerges from the understanding that the dynamics of team-based work within academic environments are both complex and essential to institutional success.

The concept of teamwork is not new to higher education, but the depth and breadth of team structures have expanded in recent years. No longer confined to project groups or academic departments, teams in universities now span various disciplines, departments, and even institutions. These cross-functional collaborations, whether through curriculum design, research initiatives, or student support services, require a more significant understanding of what makes teams successful. Research has shown that team effectiveness in higher education is not merely a matter of assembling individuals with complementary skills. Instead, it requires a deliberate and thoughtful approach to leadership, communication, and cultivating a shared vision (Kezar et al., 2019; Sessa & London, 2006). This book seeks to comprehensively explore the key principles, strategies, and challenges associated with developing high-performing teams within the unique context of higher education. The diverse contributors offer insights grounded in theory and practice, drawing on case studies, empirical research, and experiential knowledge to create a practical and rigorous resource.

PSYCHOLOGICAL SAFETY

A central theme throughout this work is the importance of psychological safety, which has been recognized as a critical factor in fostering team success (Edmondson, 1999). Psychological safety allows members to engage in open dialogue, share ideas without fear of judgment, and collaborate more effectively. This concept is particularly relevant in academic settings, where exchanging ideas and intellectual risk-taking are paramount to innovation and progress. Psychological safety plays an integral role in building high-performing teams. When team members are confident that they will not be punished or humiliated for speaking up, they are more likely to engage in open dialogue, take risks, and offer creative solutions to problems (Edmondson, 2018). This trust and openness contribute to higher levels of engagement and accountability, which, in turn, improve overall team performance and drive the achievement of collective goals (Edmondson & Lei, 2014).

THE ROLE OF LEADERSHIP

Additionally, this book addresses the need for leaders in higher education to adopt a more collaborative leadership style, shifting away from traditional hierarchical structures towards models that encourage inclusivity and shared decision-making (Kezar & Holcombe, 2017). Leadership is frequently conceptualized within a formal framework—department heads, deans, and administrators occupying positions of authority. However, when the objective is to cultivate high-performance teams, authentic leadership extends beyond mere titles. What is crucial is that leadership and teamwork are interdependent. Effective leadership requires a strong, motivated team to realize a leader's vision, while a high-performing team needs wise leadership for direction and success (Sohmen, 2013). Thus, the leader's role in developing a psychologically safe environment is critical for the team's success. Leaders set the tone for the team by showing vulnerability. Acknowledging and admitting mistakes signal that it is safe for others to do the same. Providing feedback in a way that focuses on growth rather than blame helps maintain psychological safety. Leaders should frame challenges as learning opportunities rather than failures. In this book, readers will gain insights into the leader's critical role in shaping team dynamics and driving success. There is also an opportunity for readers to reflect on the type of leader they hope to become.

TARGET AUDIENCE

This book is intended for a broad range of readers within higher education, particularly those who are directly involved in the formation, management, or participation in teams. Academic leaders such as department heads, deans, and administrators will find valuable insights into sustaining high-performing teams, especially in environments where collaboration can often be challenging. The strategies outlined will also benefit faculty members who lead research groups, curriculum committees, or interdisciplinary projects to work with diverse colleagues toward common goals.

Additionally, this book is a useful resource for higher education professionals outside of traditional faculty roles, including support staff, student services coordinators, and academic advisors. These individuals often work in teams to enhance student success, and the frameworks provided can help them strengthen communication and inclusivity and enhance overall team performance. Whether you are leading a team, contributing to one, or aspiring to create a culture of collaboration, this book offers practical tools and guidance for maximizing the potential of teams in a university setting.

ORGANIZATION OF THE BOOK

The book is organized into six sections and a total of seventeen chapters. A concise overview of each part and chapter is provided. **Part 1** focuses on the critical role that psychological safety plays in developing high-performing and resilient teams in higher education. Effective teamwork relies on a foundation of psychological safety, as individuals will feel empowered to contribute and collaborate without hesitation.

In Chapter 1, *Safety Nets of Success: A Deep Dive into Team Climate and Psychological Safety*, Shalieka T. Burris, Tashieka S. Burris-Melville, and Oprah D. Burris examine how team climate influences psychological safety among academic and administrative staff at a higher education institution. Their quantitative study reveals that academic teams tend to have lower perceptions of psychological safety compared to administrative teams.

In Chapter 2, *Promoting Trust and Psychological Safety in Team Environments: A Focus on Higher Education*, Pedzisai Goronga and Memory Deredzai explore the significance of trust and psychological safety in promoting successful university team environments. The authors emphasize that strategies such as inclusive governance, clear communication, and supportive cultures are essential in nurturing these environments.

Chapter 3, focusing on *Empowering Students for Working in Culturally Rich and Psychologically Nourishing Work Environments* by Sara Duarte and Sonia Santa-Marina, addresses the importance of having a psychologically safe and culturally inclusive work environment for students, with experiential learning highlighted as a key approach to building collaborative and resilient student teams.

Part 2 explores how leadership styles influence the development and success of teams in higher education.

Chapter 4: *Building Champions: Leadership as the Keystone of Team Performance*, written by Saptarshi Kumar Sarkar and Sanchita Ghosh, dives into the role of leadership in empowering teams, drawing on literature that connects leadership theories to team cohesion and productivity. The authors advocate for leadership strategies that inspire and motivate, emphasizing the pivotal role leaders play in unlocking team potential.

In chapter 5: *Steering the Ship: How Leadership Styles Shape Team Development and Performance*, Tara Knight builds on this discussion by examining the impact of various leadership styles—ranging from authoritarian to transformational—on team development and performance. Through a literature review, it concludes that a hybrid leadership approach is often the most effective, which allows leaders to adapt to different team dynamics and challenges.

As education shifts toward more collaborative and technology-driven methods, it is vital to rethink how teamwork is integrated into teaching and learning practices. **Part 3** of this book addresses this theme through a series of innovative case studies and research.

Chapter 6: *Building Collaboration Among Teacher Candidates: Developing Lesson Planning Competencies With Lesson Study Teams*, by Tolgahan Ayantaş and Gürcan Gürgen discusses how lesson study teams improve lesson planning competencies among teacher candidates. The findings suggest that collaborative efforts lead to more effective and content-rich lesson plans.

In Chapter 7: *Embracing Collaborative Learning: Innovative Teaching Methods at the Tertiary Level*, Morine Matongo, Pedzisai Goronga, and Francis Muchenje examine the benefits and challenges of collaborative learning at the tertiary level. It also discusses strategies for successfully implementing collaborative methodologies to enhance student engagement and learning outcomes.

Chapter 8: *Using Google Docs for Enhanced Collaboration in Academic Writing Instruction*, by Nekiesha Reid, explores how digital tools like Google Docs can enhance collaboration in academic writing instruction. It provides practical insights into how technology facilitates teamwork in higher education.

In chapter 9: *Utilizing Technology and Digital Tools to Enhance Virtual Teamwork Among Adult Learners in a Master of Education Programme Course: A Narrative Inquiry*, Leesha Nicole Roberts focuses on the role of digital platforms in promoting virtual teamwork among adult learners. It offers recommendations for improving teamwork through digital tools in online education environments.

Chapter 10: *Avatars of Academia: Exploring Virtual Collaboration's Tapestry* by Andi Asrifan, Anita Candra Dewi, Vivit Rosmayanti, Syamsuardi Saodi, Badruddin Kaddas, and Mulyadi Mulyadi examines the effects of virtual collaboration on education. It explores how tools such as avatars, virtual reality, and artificial intelligence are transforming teamwork and learning outcomes in higher education.

Part 5 emphasizes the role of team dynamics in achieving high performance, particularly in unionized academic settings.

Chapter 15: *The Teamwork Equation: Why 1 + 1 = Much More Than 2 in Academic Union Success* by Eraldine Williams-Shakespeare, Tashieka Burris-Melville, Clavery Allen, Nadine Maitland, Denise Allen, Atherine Lee, Joan Lawla, and Robert Johnson examines the role of teamwork in academic union success. It highlights how collaboration and strategic maneuvering empower academic staff unions to uphold faculty well-being.

Chapter 16: *Sculpting Educational Excellence: Brand Building Approaches for Higher Education Institutions* by Remi Thomas and Madhuri Sawant presents a seven-stage conceptual framework for branding. It explores key stages like defining vision, establishing a unique brand identity, and positioning in a competitive market while addressing challenges faced by institutions in diverse settings. The chapter emphasizes the importance of collaborative efforts from all stakeholders to build and sustain brand equity, offering valuable strategies for higher education institutions seeking to strengthen their brand presence and impact.

Part 6 describes the journey towards diversity and inclusion.

In chapter 17: *Leveraging Diversity and Inclusion for Enhanced Team Outcomes in Higher Education*, Muhammad Tariq discusses the role of diversity and inclusion in enhancing team outcomes. Through case studies and best practices, it highlights how diverse teams drive academic success through collaboration.

CONCLUSION

This volume aspires to elevate the ongoing discourse on the transformation of higher education by offering a synthesis of pragmatic strategies and scholarly insights. Through these contributions, we endeavor to empower academic institutions with the frameworks and tools necessary to cultivate the highly skilled and cohesive teams demanded by the complexities of the twenty-first century. Our deepest appreciation is extended to the esteemed contributors whose rigorous research and innovative thinking have shaped this work. We trust that this compilation will serve as an indispensable resource for academic leaders, faculty, and administrators who are committed to advancing the development of high-performing teams and driving institutional excellence.

For faculty members, administrators, or department chairs who are tasked with managing or participating in teams, this book serves as both a guide and a resource. Whether you are forming a new team, revitalizing an existing one, or simply looking to enhance your leadership skills, the tools and strategies presented here will provide valuable insights. Teams in higher education can be powerful vehicles for change, innovation, and academic excellence when managed effectively, and it is our hope that this book will contribute to that mission.

As we embark on this journey together, we encourage you to keep in mind that team building is not a one-time event, but an ongoing process. The real work of creating effective teams happens over time, through intentional actions, reflection, and a commitment to growth. With the right tools, mindset, and strategies, we believe that any team in higher education can achieve extraordinary outcomes.

Tashieka Burris-Melville
University of Technology, Jamaica

Shalieka Burris
University of Technology, Jamaica

REFERENCES

Edmondson, A. (1999). Psychological safety and learning behavior in work teams. *Administrative Science Quarterly*, 44(2), 350–383. DOI: 10.2307/2666999

Edmondson, A. C. (2018). *The fearless organization: Creating psychological safety in the workplace for learning, innovation, and growth*. Wiley.

Edmondson, A. C., & Lei, Z. (2014). Psychological safety: The history, renaissance, and future of an interpersonal construct. *Annual Review of Organizational Psychology and Organizational Behavior*, 1(1), 23–43. DOI: 10.1146/annurev-orgpsych-031413-091305

Kezar, A., Dizon, J. P. M., & Scott, D. (2019). Senior leadership teams in higher education: What we know and what we need to know. *Innovative Higher Education*, 45(2), 103–120. DOI: 10.1007/s10755-019-09491-9

Kezar, A., & Holcombe, E. (2017). *Shared leadership in higher education: Important lessons from research and practice*. American Council on Education.

Kezar, A., & Lester, J. (2009). *Organizing higher education for collaboration: A guide for campus leaders*. Jossey-Bass.

Sessa, V. I., & London, M. (2006). *Continuous learning in organizations: Individual, group, and organizational perspectives*. Lawrence Erlbaum Associates.

Sohmen, V. S. (2013). Leadership and teamwork: Two sides of the same coin. *Journal of IT and Economic Development*, 4(2), 1–18.

Acknowledgment

We give all thanks and praise to God, the source of wisdom and strength, whose guidance has been instrumental in the completion of this volume. This project would not have been possible without His divine inspiration and grace.

We extend heartfelt gratitude to the team at IGI Global for the invitation to produce this volume and for their unwavering support throughout the publication process. Their professionalism and commitment have been invaluable.

We would also like to express our deep appreciation to all the contributing authors for their insightful work, dedication, and collaboration. Your contributions have enriched this volume significantly. To the editorial advisory board members and the reviewers, thank you for your expertise, critical feedback, and thoughtful guidance, which have elevated the quality of this work.

To our family, friends, and colleagues, your encouragement, patience, and support have sustained us throughout this journey. We are truly blessed to have you by our side, and we share this success with you.

Thank you all for making this project a reality.

Section 1
Cultivating Psychological Safety: The Foundation of Thriving Teams

Chapter 1
Safety Nets of Success
A Deep Dive Into Team Climate and Psychological Safety

Shalieka T. Burris
https://orcid.org/0009-0002-1343-277X
University of Technology, Jamaica

Tashieka S. Burris-Melville
https://orcid.org/0000-0002-5321-8877
University of Technology, Jamaica

Oprah D. Burris
Clan Carthy High School, Jamaica

ABSTRACT

With the increasing challenges confronting higher education institutions (HEIs), encouraging a positive team climate that encourages psychological safety is crucial for developing high-performing and thriving teams. This study explored the differences in team climate perceptions and psychological safety between academic and administrative staff at a higher education institution. Employing a quantitative survey research design, the research study investigated how the staff groups perceive various aspects of team climate and psychological safety. The study also explored the relationship between team climate and psychological safety. The data revealed that academic teams had a lower perception of the team climate and a slightly lower perception of psychological safety when compared to administrative teams. The relationship between team climate and psychological safety scores was weak and not statistically significant. These findings highlight the need for strategies to enhance psychological safety, particularly in academic settings where perceptions are less uniform.

DOI: 10.4018/979-8-3693-3852-0.ch001

INTRODUCTION

During the latest faculty workshop, a familiar frustration bubbled up. This was the issue of quality education for students and adequately compensating faculty for the extra workload. Shelly hovered over the microphone on Zoom to share her thoughts on the grappling issue, but there was unease. Shelly is usually bursting with ideas. However, she noticed a growing culture of hesitation within the team. New ideas were met with skepticism, even hostility. Mistakes were met with icy stares and hushed whispers. The fear of looking foolish, of being blamed, hung heavy in the air. It was a common belief that to speak out against the system was to paint a target on your back. She discovered this truth the hard way. In a previous meeting, she presented her perspectives on policies that affected the organization's performance. The room fell into an uncomfortable silence; her voice was met not with nods of agreement but with averted eyes.

"You're starting to sound disgruntled, Shelly. This negativity isn't a good look." "Disgruntled? I wasn't disgruntled; I was passionate!" Her attempts to address the high-class size and compensation issues were met with reprimands. She was "disruptive," "disgruntled," they said. A surge of punishments followed; her projects were reassigned, her proposals dismissed, and her growth within the company stunted. Sitting in her cubicle, she realized the extent of her isolation. Whispers of her so-called insubordination spread through the office like a chilling breeze, and the weight of an unacknowledged truth bore down upon her. A culture that touted values of unity and progress had shown its true face—one resistant to the introspection that begets true advancement. She, who had once burned with a passion for improving and innovating, now wrestled with the reality that her environment was anathema to vulnerability and change.

Have you ever felt like your perceived safety net had holes in it? Experiencing this uncertainty can be incredibly unsettling. It is akin to standing on shaky ground or realizing that what you thought was solid support may not be as reliable as you once believed. These moments often prompt introspection and a reassessment of the people, systems, or structures you have relied on for security. This chapter, therefore, takes a deep dive into the perceptions of team climate and psychological safety among staff groups at a higher education institution.

In the 21st century, organizations have transitioned from traditional hierarchical models to team-based structures, reflecting a broader trend toward collaboration and teamwork. This shift is mirrored in higher education settings, where academic, technical, and administrative pursuits increasingly rely on collective efforts. However, team climate and psychological safety emerge beyond mere collaboration as fundamental pillars for team survival and success (Edmondson, 1999). For teams to excel, a positive team climate and ensuring psychological safety are no longer optional – they are essential ingredients for team success. Team climate and psychological safety have garnered scholarly attention in the organizational behavior literature. However, there is a paucity of empirical studies measuring team climate and psychological safety in higher education institutions (HEIs) in the Caribbean.

TEAM CLIMATE

Team climate refers to the shared perceptions team members hold about the characteristics of their work environment (MacInnes et al., 2020). It consists of factors like leadership style, decision-making processes, workload distribution, recognition practices, and the level of collaboration among workers. Studies show that climate is connected to individual job attitudes like organizational commitment and turnover intentions, as well as job performance (Buttner & Lowe, 2017; Guenter et al., 2017; McKay et al., 2008). The literature underscores the significant influence of team climate on faculty motivation and job satisfaction (Kumar, 2023; Ong et al., 2020; Sahito & Vaisanen, 2017). A supportive climate characterized by open communication, trust, and respect encourages belonging and knowledge sharing. According to Kumar (2023), employees who perceive their work environment as supportive and collegial are more likely to feel valued and motivated, resulting in higher levels of job satisfaction. Increased satisfaction fuels collaborative research endeavors and innovative teaching practices (Edmondson, 1999).

Team Climate and Performance

According to organizational theory, the prevailing climate within a workplace is a crucial intermediary factor that influences the relationship between the overall work environment and the attitudes and behaviors of employees (Campbell et al., 1970; Kopelman et al., 1990). Moreover, the social exchange theory (SET) is a prominent framework for understanding behavior in the workplace, with roots dating back to the 1920s. In SET, interactions are viewed as interdependent and contingent on the actions of others (Blau, 1964). The theory emphasizes the role of perceived fairness in shaping individuals' reactions to their social exchanges. When employees perceive that their contributions are valued and equitably rewarded within the team context, they are more likely to reciprocate with commitment, effort, and loyalty. This stresses the significance of organizational policies and practices that promote fairness and equity, as they can influence the quality of social exchanges and ultimately impact organizational effectiveness.

A positive team climate is a well-established factor contributing to high-performing teams. Numerous studies have documented this correlation across various industries, including HEIs. A supportive environment where team members consistently support each other will boost the morale of the team, which will subsequently promote a more functional and effective team (Holmes, 2005; Nelson, 1997; Salas et al., 2000). This environment fosters trust and open communication, which enables team members to share ideas and collaborate more effectively. Additionally, a positive climate can reduce stress and increase job satisfaction, further enhancing team performance. As a result, teams are better equipped to navigate challenges and achieve their objectives efficiently. Moreover, a positive team climate sets the tone for psychological safety to exist.

Psychological Safety

Harrison (2022) argued that a strong correlation exists between a favourable team climate and psychological safety—they are interdependent. Within a positive team environment, individuals exhibit concern for one another, appreciate each other's skills and efforts, and regard each other's perspectives on the team's tasks as valuable. This is only possible through psychological safety. Psychological safety plays a pivotal role in human interactions. The idea of feeling safe to take risks and be one's self can be traced back as far as the early 1950s. However, the concept of psychological safety has gained significant traction since 2004, reflected by its increasing popularity and importance in workplace discourse. Using Google Trends to analyze the trajectory of psychological safety since 2004, Geraghty (2024), an expert in safety cultures and psychological safety, highlights several activities that led to a steady rise in interest. Figure 1 captures Geraghty's plot and annotated chart of key events on psychological safety from 2004 to 2024.

Figure 1. Google search frequency on psychological safety from 2004-2024(Geraghty, 2024)

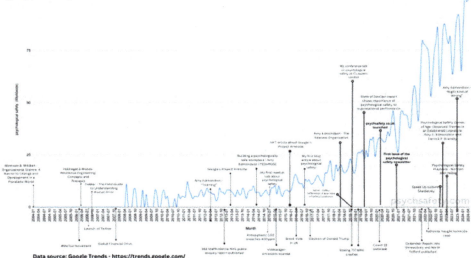

This trend aligns with several key developments.

1. Research and Publications Amy Edmondson's seminal work and subsequent publications have contributed to a growing body of research on the importance of psychological safety in high-performing teams (Edmondson, 1999, 2018, 2023).
2. High-Profile Case Studies: Companies like Google, Pixar Animation Studios, IDEO, and Microsoft have cultivated a culture of psychological safety to promote innovation, collaboration, and overall organizational success (Amabile et al., 2014; Prakash et al., 2021; Woolf, 2024).
3. Increased Focus on Workplace Culture: As organizations recognize the link between employee well-being, innovation, and performance, psychological safety has become a focal point in enhancing workplace culture.
4. Global Events and Movements: Events like the COVID-19 pandemic and social justice movements have underscored the need for inclusive and supportive work environments, further propelling discussions around psychological safety.

The growing trend on Google Trends suggests a broader awareness and recognition of psychological safety's impact, driving more organizations to prioritize it as a key component of their leadership and team-building strategies. Figure 2 outlines a comprehensive development of psychological safety in organizational teams.

Figure 2. Development of psychological safety

1940'S
- Joseph Schumpeter - creative destruction
- Abraham Maslow - safety and belonging
- Herbert Simon - organizations are learning entities

1950 & 1960'S
- Carl Rogers - creativity is best nurtured in a psychologically safe atmosphere
- Douglas McGregor - nonphysical "security needs"

1965
- Edgar Schein and Warren Bennis - introduced the term "psychological safety"

1990-1999
- William Kahn - identified psychological safety as a critical condition for employee engagement.
- Amy Edmondson - expanded and popularized the concept of psychological safety

2012
- Google - conducted a comprehensive study known as "Project Aristotle," identifying psychological safety as the most critical factor for high-performing teams.

2018
- Amy Edmondson - provided practical guidance for leaders on fostering psychological safety.

2020-2024
- Timothy Clark - stages of psychological safety
- Psychological safety has become a mainstream topic in leadership development.

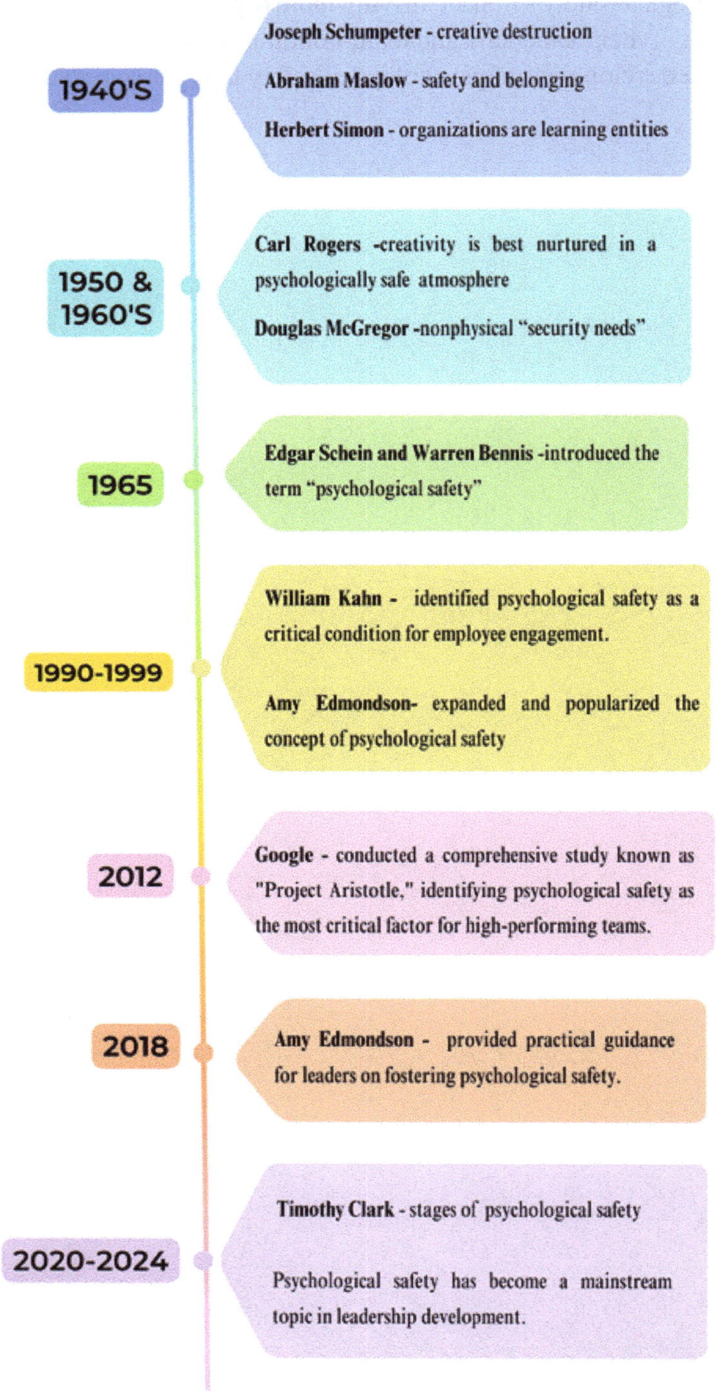

Scholars like Joseph Schumpeter, Abraham Maslow, Herbert Simon, Carl Rogers, and Douglas McGregor laid the groundwork for understanding this concept, though they did not use the term psychological safety itself (LeaderFactor, 2023). The term psychological safety was coined by organizational scholars Edgar Schein and Warren Bennis. In their work, *Personal and Organizational Change Through Group Methods: The Laboratory Approach*, they described it as a group climate that encourages trying new things and tolerates failure without punishment.

Psychological safety was later popularized in the 1990s by Dr. Edmondson, a professor at Harvard Business School, and since then, there has been a resurgence of interest in the concept. Edmondson added to the definition of psychological safety to mean having confidence that one will be free of embarrassment, rejection, or punishment when one speaks (Andreatta, 2018; Edmondson, 1999). Psychological safety gives teams a sense of security in interpersonal risk-taking, understanding that their ideas or mistakes will not be held against them (Bariso, 2018; Edmondson, 1999). Edmondson (1999) noted that a team's ability to provide psychological safety increases team efficacy and performance. Edmondson further posited that teams with high psychological safety exhibit greater learning behaviors and a willingness to explore new approaches. This fosters a growth mindset within teams, allowing them to adapt to challenges and continuously improve their performance. Psychological safety is an avenue that allows for trust to take place (Morgan, 2022). The environment is no longer safe without this level of comfort and opportunity to share and express emotions (Morgan, 2022).

Google, in its quest to build the perfect team and determine why some work teams are more successful than others, embarked on a two-year research initiative. The study, dubbed "Project Aristotle," aimed to identify the key factors that contribute to successful teams within the company (Duhigg, 2016). The researchers analyzed a massive dataset encompassing over 180 Google teams, including information on team composition, work practices, and individual performance. Project Aristotle highlighted the importance of group norms and dynamics over individual characteristics (Tamiru, 2023). Therefore, a collection of highly skilled individuals does not guarantee success if the team environment discourages collaboration and open communication. Moreover, factors traditionally associated with success, like individual talent or team size, were not the most significant predictors. Instead, the research revealed that psychological safety was the most defining characteristic of high-performing teams (Duhigg, 2016; Tamiru, 2023). Overall, Project Aristotle's findings shifted the focus from individual talent to a collaborative and psychologically safe environment as the recipe for building successful teams.

Dimensions and Stages of Psychological Safety

Amy Edmondson's framework for psychological safety comprises four key dimensions, which include inclusion and diversity, attitude to risk and failure, willingness to help, and open conversation (see Figure 3). These dimensions collectively create an environment where team members feel safe to engage, innovate, and support one another. For an organization or workplace to be psychologically safe, it must meet all four dimensions.

The inclusion and diversity dimension emphasizes the importance of creating an inclusive environment where diverse perspectives are not only welcomed but valued. Psychological safety ensures that all team members feel accepted and respected regardless of their background. Edmondson (2018) argued that when psychologically safe, diverse teams are more innovative and better at problem-solving because they can draw on a wider range of experiences and viewpoints.

A psychologically safe workplace encourages a healthy attitude toward risk-taking and views failure as a learning opportunity rather than a setback. Edmondson (2018) highlighted that when employees are not afraid of the consequences of failing, they are more likely to experiment, take initiative, and innovate. This attitude is crucial for continuous improvement and adaptability in dynamic environments.

The willingness to help dimension focuses on the importance of a collaborative environment where team members are ready to support each other. Psychological safety nurtures a culture of mutual assistance, where individuals feel comfortable asking for help and offering it without fear of being judged or penalized. Such an environment enhances team cohesion and effectiveness (Edmondson, 2018).

Finally, open and honest communication is a cornerstone of psychological safety. Edmondson (2018) noted that when employees feel safe to speak up, share ideas, and voice concerns without fear of retribution, it leads to better decision-making and problem-solving. Open conversation promotes transparency and trust within the team (Edmondson, 2018). These dimensions are interrelated and collectively contribute to a psychologically safe environment, which is essential for fostering innovation, resilience, and high performance in organizations.

Timothy Clark developed a framework in 2020 for psychological safety that mirrors Edmondson's four dimensions. Clark (2020) outlined four progressive stages that teams experience as they build trust and comfort with one another. These stages illuminate the developing dynamic of feeling safe to be oneself and contribute fully within a team environment. Figure 4 captures the four stages of psychological safety.

Figure 4. The four stages of psychological safety

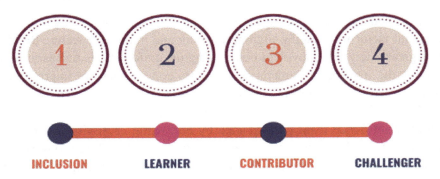

The first stage, inclusion safety, focuses on the basic need to feel like you belong. According to Clark (2020), team members feel comfortable being present, accepted for who they are, and valued for their contributions. This initial sense of security is crucial for building a foundation of trust. Learner safety, the second stage proposed by Clark (2020), emphasizes the freedom to learn and grow without fear of judgment. Team members feel comfortable asking questions, experimenting with ideas, and admitting mistakes (Clark, 2020). This encourages a growth mindset and allows for individual development, ultimately benefiting the team. The third stage, contributor safety, represents the confidence to share ideas and expertise openly. As posited by Clark (2020), this stage facilitates team members to feel safe to express their opinions, propose solutions, and take calculated risks without fear of embarrassment or retaliation. Moreover, this stage unlocks the team's collective intelligence and allows for innovative solutions to emerge. The final stage, challenger safety, is the most advanced level and signifies the ability to question the status quo and offer constructive criticism. Team members feel empowered to challenge assumptions, voice dissent, and advocate for alternative approaches (Clark, 2020), creating an environment where even the most established ideas are open to improvement. This leads to benefits such as continuous learning and adaptation.

These stages are not necessarily linear. Teams may move back and forth between stages depending on the situation and dynamics. However, by understanding these stages and actively promoting psychological safety, leaders can nurture a team environment where members feel comfortable contributing their best selves; an environment like this can create a more innovative, engaged, and successful team.

Psychological Safety for Teams

It is paramount to note that psychological safety is not just a feel-good notion but a crucial factor for building high-performing and innovative teams. Building psychological safety often involves confronting uncomfortable conversations and challenging the status quo. Sometimes necessary conversations or improvements may involve questioning current practices or raising diverging views. Bradley et al. (2012) postulated that high psychological safety climates allow task conflict to positively influence team performance by enhancing creativity and rigorous decision-making without harmful interpersonal dynamics. If difficult conversations are never welcomed or addressed, who will feel secure in speaking up in the future? Thus, team leaders have to be careful about the environment they encourage and refrain from shutting down uncomfortable conversations. Nonetheless, while it is important to embrace candor, discussions must be productive and respectful. For instance, team leaders and members should focus on the issue instead of the person, practice active listening, set ground rules for respective discourse, and guide the conversations toward solutions.

Building psychological safety must be a conscious endeavor, as it requires constant reinforcement and attention to create a space where vulnerability is strength, not weakness. People are often afraid to speak up if they think their ideas might be ridiculed or rejected; if team members are unsure of what kind of behavior is acceptable, they will be less likely to take risks, and teams can fall into a groupthink mentality, where everyone feels pressure to agree with the majority, even if they have doubts. In these instances, it is the responsibility of team leaders to establish the norms and expectations of the team and emphasize that differing ideas provide more positives than negatives to the group.

We have encountered situations where leaders, through their actions, inadvertently reinforced a lack of psychological safety within their teams. One notable instance involved a team member to whom the team leader assigned a crucial task with minimal notice. Despite her readiness to contribute, the last-minute instructions left her feeling unprepared and flustered. When she voiced her frustration and concern about the inadequate preparation time, the team leader responded dismissively. The leader's response did not acknowledge the difficulties caused by the rushed instructions. Instead, it dismissed the team member's valid need for clarity and adequate preparation. This dismissive attitude had severe repercussions–the team member felt unsupported and undervalued, which in turn eroded her trust in the team leader. The overall atmosphere of the team became one where employees felt their concerns were not taken seriously, diminishing their sense of psychological safety. This highlights the importance of creating a work environment where employees feel safe to express their concerns without fear of being dismissed.

Leaders, therefore, play a crucial role in creating a psychologically safe environment by being responsive and supportive. Most importantly, leadership styles play a pivotal role in shaping the psychological safety of teams within higher education. Transformational, consultative, and participative leadership styles are particularly effective in facilitating such an environment (Edmondson, 1999; Rabiul et al., 2024; Selander et al., 2023). Transformational leaders inspire and motivate their teams by providing individualized support and encouraging open communication, which builds trust and respect (Edmondson, 1999; Northouse, 2022; Rabiul et al., 2024; Selander et al., 2023). Participative leaders, by involving team members in decision-making, create a sense of ownership and value diverse perspectives, further enhancing a supportive climate. Servant leadership, with its focus on serving and prioritizing team members' needs, nurtures a sense of care and support that is crucial for psychological safety (Edmondson, 1999; Rabiul et al., 2024; Selander et al., 2023).

On the other hand, authoritarian leadership, characterized by centralized decision-making and limited team input, can hinder psychological safety by creating an atmosphere of fear and constraint, discouraging team members from voicing their ideas or concerns (Edmondson, 1999; Wang et al., 2022; Wu et al., 2019). Therefore, adopting leadership approaches that emphasize trust, inclusion, and support is essential for nurturing a psychologically safe and thriving team environment in higher education. Figure 5 demonstrates the relationship between leadership behaviours and their influence on team climate and psychological safety.

Figure 5. Relationship between leadership behaviors and outcomes (McKinsey and Company, 2021)

Benefits of a Psychologically Safe and Positive Team Climate

The relationship between team climate and psychological safety is not unidirectional. A positive team climate, characterized by trust and respect, lays the groundwork for psychological safety to flourish. Conversely, a team environment where individuals feel psychologically safe is more likely to develop a supportive and collaborative climate. This interactive relationship creates a powerful dynamic that fuels team effectiveness.

PURPOSE OF THE STUDY

This quantitative survey research aimed to investigate team climate and psychological safety perceptions within teams at a higher education institution. It explored the views of staff regarding psychological safety and identified factors contributing to or hindering psychological safety. By understanding these factors, the study seeks to provide valuable insights that can inform the development of organizational policies and practices within higher education institutions.

RESEARCH QUESTIONS

The following research questions were used to guide the study:

1. What differences were observed in team climate perceptions when comparing staff groups?
2. What differences were observed in perceived psychological safety when comparing staff groups?
3. Is there a relationship between the perceived team climate and the level of psychological safety scores?

SIGNIFICANCE OF THE STUDY

Psychological safety is a critical element of high-performing teams in all sectors, and higher education is no exception. When individuals feel safe to take risks, share ideas openly, and learn from mistakes, teams become more innovative, adaptable, and, ultimately, more effective in achieving their goals. This study has the potential to make significant contributions in several ways, including understanding staff perceptions, identifying areas for improvement, and informing best practices.

This knowledge can inform efforts to create a more supportive and empowering work environment for staff. The study can also identify specific faculties or colleges' team dynamics where psychological safety might be lower. This information can be used to develop targeted interventions and strategies to promote greater psychological safety across the institution. Moreover, a psychologically safe environment fosters collaboration, innovation, and intellectual risk-taking. This, in turn, can lead to the development of more engaging and effective teaching practices, ultimately benefiting student learning outcomes. Finally, this study can contribute to a growing body of research on psychological safety in higher education. By sharing the findings, the study can inform best practices for promoting a culture of psychological safety at institutions across the educational space.

RESEARCH DESIGN

The researchers utilized a quantitative survey design to achieve the research objectives. This method involved the collection of numerical data through structured surveys. Survey research involves using structured questionnaires or interviews to collect data systematically (Creswell & Creswell, 2018). This approach allows researchers to describe a population's trends, attitudes, or opinions by studying a sample of that population (Creswell & Creswell, 2018). A cross-sectional survey collects data at a single point in time and provides the advantage of collecting the data quickly (Mills & Gay, 2019). Additionally, the researchers were interested in understanding the current trends and opinions of the population; thus, the cross-sectional survey was appropriate to use (Mills & Gay, 2019). Participants were classified into academic and administrative groups. This comparative approach allowed for an examination of differences in perceptions of team climate and perceived psychological safety between the two staff categories. Correlational analysis was also employed to investigate the relationships between variables of interest, specifically examining the associations between team climate perceptions and perceived psychological safety scores.

PARTICIPANTS

The study's participants comprised 71 staff members from a higher education institution, classified into two groups– academic and administrative. The participants were selected using convenience sampling. This method allowed the researchers to access readily and include individuals who were available, though it may limit the generalizability of the findings (Mills & Gay, 2019). Prior to the start of the study, the researchers received approval from the university's ethics committee, ensuring that it adhered to ethical guidelines concerning informed consent, confidentiality, and participant welfare.

DATA COLLECTION

A cross-sectional survey was utilized to collect quantitative data on participants' perceptions of team climate and psychological safety within teams at the higher education institution. The survey instrument collectively measures aspects of psychological safety and team climate within an organization. The shortened version of the Team Climate Inventory (TCI) was developed by Kivimaki and Elovainio (1999). The TCI measures four constructs using a 5-point Likert scale across 14 items. Cronbach's alpha was used to determine the internal consistency for the TCI, showing good reliability, $\alpha = .88$, with a lower bound of .85 and an upper bound of .92. The Psychological Safety Scale is based on the work of Edmondson (1999). This scale measures six psychological safety constructs using a 5-point Likert scale across seven items. A Cronbach alpha coefficient was calculated for the Psychological Safety scale. The items for Psychological Safety have a Cronbach's alpha coefficient of .77, indicating acceptable reliability, with a lower bound of .69 and an upper bound of .84.

The survey was distributed electronically to all eligible participants via Google Forms. Participants were provided with clear instructions on how to complete the survey and information regarding the voluntary nature of participation and the confidentiality of their responses. At least three reminder emails were sent to encourage participation and maximize response rates.

DATA ANALYSIS

Comparative analyses were conducted using one-way analysis of variance (ANOVA) to answer the first two research questions, which tested whether differences occurred between the staff groups' scores on team climate perceptions and perceived psychological safety, respectively. Factorial ANOVAs were also used to analyze the groups' team climate and psychological safety perceptions based on their age, gender, and years employed at the university. The third research question was answered using a Pearson correlation to explore the relationship between team climate perceptions and perceived psychological safety scores.

RESULTS

The demographic profile of the 71 participants is summarized in Table 1. Participants were predominantly female ($n = 54$, 76.1%). Most participants belong to the academic group ($n = 38$, 53.5%), the age category of 41-50 ($n = 26$, 36.6%), and the 13-20 years employed category ($n = 23$, 32.4%).

Table 1. Participants' demographics

Variable	n	%
Gender		
Male	17	23.9
Female	54	76.1
Age Categories		
30 years and under	6	8.5
31-40 years	18	25.4
41-50 years	26	36.6
51 and above	21	29.6
Condition		
Academic	38	53.5
Administrative	33	46.5
Years Employed		
1-5 years	21	29.6
6-12 years	14	19.7
13-20 years	23	32.4
More than 20 years	13	18.3

Note. Due to rounding, percentages may not equal 100%.

The survey results for the familiarity with the concept of psychological safety in a work environment show that a significant portion of respondents, 33.8%, are not familiar with the concept at all. Meanwhile, 38% of the respondents are somewhat familiar with psychological safety, representing the largest group. Those who consider themselves familiar account for 16.9% of the participants. A smaller percentage, 7%, indicated they are very familiar with the concept, and only 4.2% are extremely familiar. These findings suggest that while a majority have at least some awareness of psychological safety, a notable portion of the group lacks familiarity with the concept.

Research Question 1: What differences were observed in team climate perceptions when comparing staff groups?

The perceptions of the staff groups were measured using four constructs from the Team Climate Inventory (vision, participative safety, task orientation, and support for innovation). The administrative staff group scored higher in all instances (see Table 2).

Table 2. Descriptive statistics for team climate inventory

Variable	M	SD	n
Vision			
Academic	15.00	3.39	38
Administrative	16.52	2.82	33
Support for Innovation			
Academic	9.18	2.84	38
Administrative	10.42	2.99	33
Task Orientation			
Academic	46.89	11.82	38
Administrative	51.67	10.12	33
Participative Safety			
Academic	12.97	4.31	38
Administrative	13.85	3.62	33

A one-way ANOVA was conducted to determine whether differences existed in the staff groups' team climate perceptions. The ANOVA was examined based on a significance level of .05. The results of the ANOVA revealed that a significant difference existed in the academic and administrative groups' perceptions of vision, $F(1, 69) = 4.11, p < .05$. However, no significant difference was found in the groups' perceptions of support for innovation, $F(1, 69) = 3.21, p = .078$, task orientation, $F(1, 69) = 3.15, p = .080$, or participative safety, $F(1, 69) = 0.84, p = .362$, indicating those responses are all similar.

The staff groups' team climate scores were also compared by gender and age using a factorial ANOVA. The main effect of gender was not significant, $F(1, 63) = 2.01$, nor was the main effect of age significant, $F(3, 63) = 0.28$. The interaction between the variables was also not significant, $F(3, 63) = 1.61$.

Research Question 2: What differences were observed in perceived psychological safety when comparing staff groups?

To address this question, the staff groups were compared on their perceived psychological safety using a one-way ANOVA. The ANOVA was examined based on a significance level of .05. Although the administrative group ($M = 21.36, SD = 2.84$) outscored the academic group ($M = 20.84, SD = 4.37$), the difference was not significant, $F(1, 69) = 0.34$. However, the difference was close to being significant, $p = .560$.

A factorial ANOVA was also run to compare the staff groups' perceptions of psychological safety on their condition and years employed at the university (see Table 5). No significant difference was found.

Table 3. Factorial ANOVA results for psychological safety perceptions

Variable	F	df	p
Condition	0.43	1,63	.516
Years employed	0.29	3,63	.836
Condition*Years employed	0.69	3,63	.563

Research Question 3: Is there a relationship between the perceived team climate and the level of psychological safety scores?

A Pearson r correlation was conducted to determine the relationship between the participants' team climate ($M = 49.11$, $SD = 11.24$) and psychological safety scores ($M = 21.08$, $SD = 3.72$). The relationship between the variables was weak and positive, which was not statistically significant, $r(69) = .232$, $p = 0.52$.

DISCUSSION

A positive team climate and a high psychological safety level are essential for higher education teams to thrive, innovate, and reach their full potential. This study investigated the perceptions of team climate and psychological safety at a higher educational institution in Jamaica. The first research question explored the differences in team climate perceptions when comparing staff groups. The results yielded insightful findings. The study found that administrative staff generally perceive a more favorable team climate compared to their academic counterparts. The administrative staff consistently scored higher across all four constructs of the Team Climate Inventory—vision, support for innovation, task orientation, and participative safety—indicating a more favorable perception of the team climate within this group. This finding is not consistent with the literature. In a study conducted by Arabaci (2010), it was found that academics generally perceive a more positive climate of organizational culture. Moreover, this finding was also corroborated by Cameron and Quinn (2011) and Kezar and Eckel (2002).

While the administrative staff outscored the academic staff across all constructs, it is important to note that there was only one statistically significant difference. The significant difference in perceptions of vision highlights a potential area of concern that could impact overall team cohesion and effectiveness. It suggests the need for better communication and alignment regarding the organizational vision to ensure all staff groups feel equally connected to and motivated by the vision. The higher perception of team climate among administrative staff, compared to academic staff, may be attributed to the fact that academics, while functioning within units, often have personal goals that compete with the collective goals of their units. This is supported by literature indicating that academic staff frequently juggle individual research agendas and professional aspirations, which can sometimes conflict with the collaborative objectives of their departments (Brew, 2017; Gonzales et al., 2013).

On the other hand, the similarity in perceptions of support for innovation, task orientation, and participative safety suggests a consistent organizational culture in these areas. The lack of significant differences from the factorial ANOVA implies that the organizational efforts to promote an inclusive and cohesive team environment are effective across different demographic segments. Both male and female staff and staff members of varying ages experience the team climate similarly.

Differences in Perceived Psychological Safety between Staff Groups

The second research question aimed to identify differences in perceived psychological safety between academic and administrative staff. Although the administrative staff reported higher average psychological safety scores than the academic staff, the difference was not statistically significant. This result aligns with research by Edmondson (2018), who found that psychological safety varies within different organizational contexts and is often influenced by leadership styles and group dynamics rather than by functional roles alone.

The lack of significant differences between groups could suggest that both academic and administrative staff face similar challenges regarding psychological safety. However, the slight edge observed in the administrative staff's scores may reflect a more structured environment, often characterized by clearer hierarchies and communication channels, which can foster a sense of security. In contrast, academic environments, known for their autonomy and individualism, may pose unique challenges to cultivate a uniformly safe psychological climate (Ong et al., 2020). The findings suggest that psychological safety interventions should be tailored to address the specific needs and cultural characteristics of academic teams, where the less hierarchical nature of work might require different approaches to fostering a supportive and open environment (Kumar, 2023).

Relationship Between Team Climate and Psychological Safety

The third research question explored the relationship between team climate and psychological safety. The Pearson correlation analysis revealed a weak, positive relationship between these variables, which was not statistically significant. This finding contrasts with much of the existing literature, which typically indicates a stronger connection between team climate and psychological safety (Edmondson, 1999; Clark, 2020). For example, Edmondson (1999) posited that a positive team climate, characterized by trust, mutual respect, and open communication, is fundamental to developing psychological safety within teams.

Several factors could explain the weak relationship observed in this study. The context of higher education institutions in the Caribbean, where hierarchical and rigid structures often prevail, may inhibit the natural development of a supportive team climate that nurtures psychological safety. Additionally, the absence of a statistically significant relationship may reflect the complex interplay of other variables, such as leadership behaviour, organizational culture, and individual personality traits, which were not fully captured in this study (Selander et al., 2023).

Despite the weak correlation, the positive direction of the relationship suggests that efforts to improve team climate could still positively impact psychological safety over time. This underscores the importance of holistic interventions that simultaneously address multiple aspects of team dynamics, including leadership, communication, and collaboration, to cultivate an environment conducive to psychological safety (Guenter et al., 2017).

Implications for Higher Education Institutions

The results of this study highlight several critical implications for HEIs aiming to encourage a positive team climate and enhance psychological safety. One key approach to achieving these goals is through the application of Edmondson's Right Kind of Wrong framework. Edmondson (2023) argued that organizations should strive to cultivate a culture where the right kind of wrong is embraced—meaning that not all failures are detrimental. Instead, organizations should differentiate between blameworthy and praiseworthy failures, the latter being those stemming from thoughtful experimentation, learning, and innovation. This approach is particularly relevant for HEIs, where the pursuit of knowledge often involves trial and error. By adopting this framework, HEIs can create an environment where staff feel safe to take risks, make mistakes, and learn from them without fear of retribution.

Edmondson's framework provides a structured way for HEIs to improve psychological safety. HEIs should establish clear guidelines that distinguish between different types of failures. Failures that result from intentional neglect or ethical breaches should be addressed differently from those that occur as part of the learning process or innovative efforts. This distinction can help reduce the stigma associated with failure and encourage a culture of open communication and continuous improvement (Edmondson, 2023). HEIs should also consider revising their policies and procedures to emphasize learning from failures rather than punishing them. This could involve integrating failure analysis into regular team meetings, where staff can openly discuss what went wrong in a non-punitive environment. By normalizing these discussions, HEIs can reduce the fear of failure, thereby enhancing psychological safety and fostering a more innovative and adaptive organizational culture.

Moreover, there is a clear need for targeted interventions to improve the team climate, particularly among academic staff. Strategies could include leadership development programs emphasizing inclusive decision-making and innovation support (Taylor & Brownell, 2017; Sugiyama et al., 2016). Additionally, promoting open communication and trust within academic teams could help bridge the gap in perceptions of team climate (Kozlowski & Ilgen, 2006).

Finally, enhancing psychological safety across all staff groups should be a priority. This can be achieved through professional development initiatives promoting understanding and applying psychological safety principles (Edmondson, 2018). Creating forums for open dialogue where staff can express concerns without fear of retribution is essential. For instance, initiatives like peer support groups or regular team-building activities could reinforce a culture of mutual respect and support (Kozlowski & Ilgen, 2006; Ozigbo et al., 2020).

CONCLUSION

This study highlights the critical role of a positive team climate and psychological safety in facilitating high-performing teams within higher education institutions (HEIs). The findings reveal that while administrative staff often experience a more favorable team climate, the need for targeted strategies to enhance psychological safety across all staff groups is evident. To create an environment where all staff members can be heard, feel valued, and be safe, HEIs must implement comprehensive measures that address low psychological safety and an unfavourable team climate.

RECOMMENDATIONS

Therefore, we recommend these specific measures be put in place to build a more supportive and high-performing work environment, which will enhance psychological safety and create a favorable team climate.

1. Implement training programs designed to educate all staff groups about the importance of psychological safety. These programs should focus on strategies for creating an open, supportive environment where staff feel comfortable sharing ideas and concerns without fear of judgment or reprisal.
2. Establish and promote clear, open communication channels across all staff groups. Encourage regular feedback sessions and create anonymous reporting mechanisms for staff to voice their concerns and suggestions. This will help identify areas where psychological safety may be lacking and address them promptly.
3. Perform regular assessments of team climate and psychological safety across different staff groups. Then, use the data to identify areas of improvement and measure the effectiveness of implemented strategies, which can help maintain a positive and supportive team environment and address any emerging issues proactively.
4. Train leaders and managers to model behaviors that support psychological safety and a positive team climate. Leaders should be equipped to handle conflicts constructively, provide constructive feedback, and create an environment where staff feel respected and heard. This top-down approach can significantly influence the overall team climate.

REFERENCES

Amabile, T. M., Fisher, C. M., & Pillemer, J. (2014). IDEO's culture of helping: By making collaborative generosity the norm, the design firm has unleashed its creativity. *Harvard Business Review.* https://hbr.org/2014/01/ideos-culture-of-helping

Andreatta, B. (2018, November 21). Leading with emotional intelligence [Video]. *LinkedIn.* https://www.linkedin.com/learning/leading-with-emotional-intelligence-3/lead-with-emotional-intelligence?resume=false&u=43761300

Arabacı, I. B. (2010). Academic and administration personnel's perceptions of organizational climate (Sample of Educational Faculty of Fırat University). *Procedia: Social and Behavioral Sciences, 2*(2), 4445–4450. DOI: 10.1016/j.sbspro.2010.03.709

Bariso, J. (2018). *EQ applied: The real-world guide to emotional intelligence: How to make emotions work for you, instead of against you.* Borough Hall.

Blau, P. (1964). *Exchange and power in social life.* Routledge.

Bradley, B. H., Postlethwaite, B. E., Klotz, A. C., Hamdani, M. R., & Brown, K. G. (2012). Reaping the benefits of task conflict in teams: The critical role of team psychological safety climate. *The Journal of Applied Psychology, 97*(1), 151–158. DOI: 10.1037/a0024200 PMID: 21728397

Brew, A. (2017). *Research and teaching: Beyond the divide.* Bloomsbury Publishing.

Buttner, E. H., & Lowe, K. B. (2017). Addressing internal stakeholders' concerns: The interactive effect of perceived pay equity and diversity climate on turnover intentions. *Journal of Business Ethics, 143*(3), 621–633. DOI: 10.1007/s10551-015-2795-x

Cameron, K. S., & Quinn, R. E. (2011). *Diagnosing and changing organizational culture: Based on the competing values framework.* Jossey-Bass.

Campbell, J. P., Dunnette, M. D., Lawler, E. E., & Weick, K. E. (1970). *Managerial behaviour, performance and effectiveness.* McGraw Hill., DOI: 10.2307/2521540

Clark, T. R. (2020). *The 4 stages of psychological safety: Defining the path to inclusion and innovation.* Berrett-Koehler Publishers, Inc.

Creswell, J. W., & Creswell, J. D. (2018). *Research design: Qualitative, quantitative, and mixed methods approaches* (5th ed.). Sage publications.

Duhigg, C. (2016, February 25). What Google learned from its quest to build the perfect team. The Work Issue. The New York Times Magazine. https://www.nytimes.com/2016/02/28/magazine/what-google-learned-from-its-quest-to-build-the-perfect-team.html

Edmondson, A. (1999). Psychological safety and learning behavior in work teams. *Administrative Science Quarterly*, 44(2), 350–383. DOI: 10.2307/2666999

Edmondson, A. C. (2018). *The fearless organization: Creating psychological safety in the workplace for learning, innovation, and growth*. Wiley.

Edmondson, A. C. (2023). *Right kind of wrong: The science of failing well*. Simon and Schuster.

Geraghty, T. (2024, May 3). Psychological safety: A timeline. Psychological Safety. https://psychsafety.co.uk/psychological-safety-a-timeline/

Gonzales, L. D., Martinez, E., & Ordu, C. (2013). Exploring faculty experiences in a striving university through the lens of academic capitalism. *Studies in Higher Education*, 39(7), 1097–1115. DOI: 10.1080/03075079.2013.777401

Guenter, H., Gardner, W. L., Davis McCauley, K., Randolph-Seng, B., & Prabhu, V. P. (2017). Shared authentic leadership in research teams: Testing a multiple mediation model. *Small Group Research*, 48(6), 719–a765. DOI: 10.1177/1046496417732403 PMID: 29187779

Harrison, O. (2022, December 12). *Building a positive team climate for better performance: How to bring psychological safety to tech teams*. Forbes.https://www.forbes.com/sites/forbestechcouncil/2022/12/12/building-a-positive-team-climate-for-better-performance-how-to-bring-psychological-safety-to-tech-teams/?sh=7bd0258fdcc4

Holmes, T. (2005). Ten characteristics of a high performance team. In Silberman, M. (Ed.), *The 2005 ASTD team and organization development sourcebook* (pp. 179–182). ASTD Press.

Kezar, A., & Eckel, P. D. (2002). The effect of institutional culture on change strategies in higher education: Universal principles or culturally responsive concepts? *The Journal of Higher Education*, 73(4), 435–460. DOI: 10.1080/00221546.2002.11777159

Kivimaki, M., & Elovainio, M. (1999). A short version of the team climate inventory: Development and psychometric properties. *Journal of Occupational and Organizational Psychology*, 72(2), 241–246. DOI: 10.1348/096317999166644

Kopelman, R. E., Brief, A. P., & Guzzo, R. A. (1990). The role of climate and culture in productivity. In Schneider, B. (Ed.), *Organizational climate and culture* (pp. 282–318). Jossey-Bass.

Kozlowski, S. W. J., & Ilgen, D. R. (2006). Enhancing the effectiveness of work groups and teams. *Psychological Science in the Public Interest*, 7(3), 77–124. DOI: 10.1111/j.1529-1006.2006.00030.x PMID: 26158912

Kumar, P. (2023). Organisational climate and its impact on job satisfaction. *International Journal of Advances in Engineering and Management*, 5(1), 1060–1071.

LeaderFactor. (2023). *The complete guide to psychological safety.* https://www.leaderfactor.com/resources/what-is-psychological-safety

MacInnes, J., Gadsby, E., Reynolds, J., Mateu, N. C., Lette, M., Ristl, C., & Billings, J. (2020). Exploring the team climate of health and social care professionals implementing integrated care for older people in Europe. *International Journal of Integrated Care*, 20(4), 3. Advance online publication. DOI: 10.5334/ijic.5467 PMID: 33132788

McKay, P. F., Avery, D. R., & Morris, M. A. (2008). Mean racial-ethnic differences in employee sales performance: The moderating role of diversity climate. *Personnel Psychology*, 61(2), 349–374. DOI: 10.1111/j.1744-6570.2008.00116.x

McKinsey and Company. (2021, February 11). Psychological safety and the critical role of leadership development. https://www.mckinsey.com/capabilities/people-and-organizational-performance/our-insights/psychological-safety-and-the-critical-role-of-leadership-development

Mills, G. E., & Gay, L. R. (2019). *Educational research: Competencies for analysis and applications* (12th ed.). Pearson.

Morgan, R. P. (2022). *Team work: Why some teams work, while others fail and how to build a team that succeeds. The awesome leader's guide.* Choose Awesome Company.

Ong, C. H., Shi, C. H., Kowang, T. O., Fei, G. C., & Ping, L. L. (2020). Factors influencing job satisfaction among academic staffs. *International Journal of Evaluation and Research in Education*, 9(2), 285–291. DOI: 10.11591/ijere.v9i2.20509

Ozigbo, A. M., Idegbesor, M., Ngige, C. D., & Nwakoby, N. P. (2020). Team building and performance in organizations: An exploration of issues. *International Journal of Management and Entrepreneurship*, 2(1), 184–199.

Prakash, D., Bisla, M., & Rastogi, S. G. (2021). Understanding authentic leadership style: The Satya Nadella Microsoft approach. *Open Journal of Leadership*, 10(2), 95–109. DOI: 10.4236/ojl.2021.102007

Rabiul, M. K., Rashed, K., & Rashid, H. O. (2024). Transformational leadership style and psychological safety to meaningful work: Moderating role customer incivility. *Journal of Management Development*, 43(1), 49–67. DOI: 10.1108/JMD-09-2023-0292

Sahito, Z., & Vaisanen, P. (2017). Factors affecting job satisfaction of teacher educators: Empirical evidence from the Universities of Sindh Province of Pakistan. *Journal of Teacher Education and Educators*, 6(1), 5–30. DOI: 10.5430/ijhe.v6n4p122

Selander, K., Korkiakangas, E., Toivanen, M., Yli-Kaitala, K., Kangas, H., Nevanperä, N., & Laitinen, J. (2023). Engaging leadership and psychological safety as moderators of the relationship between strain and work recovery: A cross-sectional study of HSS employees. *Health Care*, 11(7), 1045. DOI: 10.3390/healthcare11071045 PMID: 37046972

Sugiyama, K., Cavanagh, K. V., van Esch, C., Bilimoria, D., & Brown, C. (2016). Inclusive leadership development. *Journal of Management Education*, 40(3), 253–292. DOI: 10.1177/1052562916632553

Tamiru, N. (2023, June). *Team dynamics: Five keys to building effective teams*. https://www.thinkwithgoogle.com/intl/en-emea/consumer-insights/consumer-trends/five-dynamics-effective-team/

Taylor, L. D.Jr, & Brownell, E. (2017). Building inclusive leaders: A critical framework for leadership education. In Boitano, A., Schockman, H. E., & Dutra, R. L. (Eds.), *Breaking the zero-sum game: Transforming societies through inclusive leadership* (pp. 323–340). Emerald Publishing Limited. DOI: 10.1108/978-1-78743-185-020171033

Wang, D., Wang, L., Wei, S., Yu, P., Sun, H., Jiang, X., & Hu, Y. (2022). Effects of authoritarian leadership on employees' safety behavior: A moderated mediation model. *Frontiers in Public Health*, 10, 846842. Advance online publication. DOI: 10.3389/fpubh.2022.846842 PMID: 35655454

Woolf, J. (2024, March 25). How Pixar fosters a culture of vulnerability at work. *Harvard Business Review*. https://hbr.org/2024/03/how-pixar-fosters-a-culture-of-vulnerability-at-work

Wu, T., Liu, Y., Hua, C., Lo, H., & Yeh, Y. (2019). Too unsafe to voice? Authoritarian leadership and employee voice in Chinese organizations. *Asia Pacific Journal of Human Resources*, 58(4), 527–554. DOI: 10.1111/1744-7941.12247

Chapter 2
Promoting Trust and Psychological Safety in Team Environments
Insights for Universities

Memory Deredzai
University of Zimbabwe, Zimbabwe

Pedzisai Goronga
https://orcid.org/0000-0001-9066-7498
University of Zimbabwe, Zimbabwe

ABSTRACT

This chapter examined the importance of trust and psychological safety in university team environments. Trust and psychological safety influence the overall success of educational institutions. A comprehensive overview of trust and psychological safety is provided, highlighting their significance in team dynamics and their impact on individual and collective performance since teamwork is at the core of academic excellence. Evidence-based strategies to promote trust and psychological safety in team environments such as open communication, inclusive governance and decision-making processes, supportive and nurturing culture, clear goals and clear expectations among others are discussed. threats to trust and psychological safety within team environments are discussed. In essence, the chapter provides valuable insights for educators, administrators, policymakers and institutional leaders seeking to create inclusive and effective team environments that foster trust and psychological safety, ultimately enhancing and shaping the overall educational experience for both staff and students.

DOI: 10.4018/979-8-3693-3852-0.ch002

INTRODUCTION

The world is turbulent and experiencing fast-paced alterations in all sectors of life due to many factors. The education sector has been hit hard as it is also experiencing unprecedented changes (Zhu et al., 2019). Navigating these changes in educational institutions such as universities is achievable through teamwork, hence universities are called upon to change tact. In this view, fostering trust and psychological safety in academic environments has been considered paramount in propelling the institutions forward. According to Shahid and Din (2021), trust and psychological safety are considered the most important conditions for team learning and are linked to improved institutional outcomes. In a higher education institution such as a university for example, trust and psychological safety can collectively be taken to build a safe work atmosphere that guarantees team members the freedom to work autonomously without trepidation (Ming et al., 2015). Since universities run on team effort, it is important to build a climate that allows team members to trust each other, and take risks without fear of negative consequences (Shahid & Din, 2021; Edmondson, 2019). Universities are by nature team environments which thrive on team effort and performance as teamwork promotes collaboration and allows team members to share their diverse perspectives and experiences. For teamwork to flourish, the need for trust and psychological safety cannot be overstated. The two psychological attributes are vital for fostering effective teamwork and maximizing team performance. According to Gerlach and Gockel (2018), trust and psychological safety are 'resources' that are utilized by team members to benefit educational institutions. The focus of this chapter is to explore the significance of trust and psychological safety in university environments which thrive on team cohesion. The presence of trust and psychological safety in universities empower educators, faculty and administrators with the tools and knowledge necessary to cultivate inclusive and supportive team environments thereby enhancing the overall educational experience of stakeholders where collaboration is nurtured and growth flourishes (Zhu et al., 2019).

LITERATURE REVIEW

Understanding Trust and its Importance

The concept of trust is receiving increasing attention in education and has begun to experience heightened interest in many organizations including education (Dzimiriska et al., 2018; Tierney, 2006). According to Van Houtte (2007), trust is the confidence that expectations will be met and is made up of five dimensions which are competence, honesty, openness, reliability, and benevolence. As elucidated by Kelloway et al. (2012), in the context of universities, trust is the belief that a leader has the necessary positive attributes to lead, advise, protect, and support subordinates to do what they are supposed to. One of the major causes of mistrust is the belief that others are incompetent to do what is required (Bryk & Schneider, 2002). As such, it was found that threats to trust are caused by a lack of respect, personal regard for others and integrity (Vidovich & Currie, 2011). This means that in the absence of trust there is no team cohesion implying that trust is a critical variable in organizational functioning.

According to Rehman et al. (2017), trust comprises an affective component which carries the emotional bond between an individual and the institution to which one is a member. The bond here referred to develops over a long time. According to Hanson (2019), trust between and among team members and their leaders contributes to psychological safety and is considered foundational for the development of psychological safety in educational institutions (Creed, 2023). In their actions, leaders are required to actively demonstrate trust, empathy, consistency, and transparency by acting morally and responsibly at all times (Kelloway et al., 2012). Trust is earned, not sold, bought, or transferred. It takes a long time to build but is fragile implying that it can be destroyed easily (Edmondson, 2019; Rehman et al., 2017). Overall, it can be argued that trust is the belief that one can rely on the actions, decisions, and integrity of others and reflects team members' perceptions of an organization's trustworthiness (Kelloway et al., 2012).

Conceptualizing Psychological Safety in University Settings

The belief shared by team members that they are safe to undertake institutional tasks without fear of being blamed for making mistakes is referred to as psychological safety. Sher et al. (2019) and Edmondson (1999), concur that psychological safety refers to a work environment that does not have psychological violence and where members interact with each other freely and are able to take risks without fear of being blamed. In the context of university, a psychologically safe environment is one where individual team members feel included in the culture, or subculture and are safe to learn, contribute and challenge the status quo (Edmondson, 2019). Similar to the attribute of trust, psychological safety is important in team environments as it is a means to adaptation and innovation. According to Levine and Van Pelt (2021) and Musto (2021), psychological safety has become a prerequisite in the fast-changing educational landscape which is impacting universities in significant ways. In addition, Sher et al. (2019) weighs in by explaining the importance of psychological safety as its presence in university environments contributes to team members' growing trust, effective communication, and a sense of belongingness.

Because of the plural character of universities, team members encounter complex and challenging issues such as interpersonal conflict and uncertainty. The existence of misunderstandings as well as conflict can influence members' cognition, behavior and emotions which can consequently reduce trust and psychological safety between and among members (Thau et al., 2009; Chen et al., 2014). Discord has a serious impact on trust and institutional psychological safety thereby mutilating team cohesion leading to inefficiency and lack of meaningful productivity. Ideally, in university team settings, members should be part of the solution to institutional challenges. A psychologically safe workplace should allow members to share their perspectives, seek and provide feedback, take risks and collaborate in a manner that overcomes threats (Edmondson, 1999). Securing effective teams requires new work relations to be formed to facilitate the integration of different perspectives, sharing of ideas and information and collaborating with organizational members to realize shared institutional goals (Edmondson & Lei, 2014).

This discussion points to the fact that a safe and trustworthy environment is an important driver of team members' psychological safety and institutional leaders are vital cogs in this regard (De Smet et al., 2023). Leaders are important because the responsibility of creating a positive institutional team climate rest on their actions since they are positioned to influence others' behaviors (Robinson et al., 2023; Lu et al., 2019). In this view we point out that leaders who engage in authoritative behaviors run the risk of destroying trust and psychological safety within their organizations while those who are consultative and supportive create a positive institutional team climate (De Smet et al., 2023). This implies that trust and psychological safety result from social interactions between and among team members and their leadership in which doing good is reciprocal (Chan & Mak, 2014). Taken together, trust and psychological safety can contribute to increased communication, collaboration, and innovation within universities in which robust, dynamic, innovative and inclusive institutional culture is nourished.

Strategies for Building Trust and Psychologically Safety

Involving all institutional members in governance issues as a way of building responsible social capital and a culture of trust in team environments is highlighted in literature (Robinson et al., 2023; Tierney, 2006). Trust is considered the glue that binds relationships together, therefore fostering it is crucial for building strong relationships that enhance team cohesion and create avenues for developing psychologically safe work environments (Vidovich & Currie, 2011). Various strategies can be implemented in order to build a culture of trust within university settings. In order to implement the strategies successfully, institutional leaders are required to possess certain principles in their work-related knowledge and skills (Palmer, 2021). Among the strategies is openly sharing their fears, worries, and hopes to create an environment of authenticity and connection with subordinates. The act of sharing concerns encourages others to do the same thereby encouraging formation of trust and development of psychologically safe work environments for team members. According to Palmer (2021), leaders who create a culture that emphasizes trust are themselves trusted by their subordinates. It is one of the leader's responsibilities to communicate clearly to followers to help build trust and psychological safety in universities.

Unambiguous Communication

Effective communication flowing from both directions allows universities to run efficiently. According to Palmer (2021), effective communication is the hallmark for creating trustworthy and psychologically safe institutional environments. This means that institutional leaders are required to model transparency in sharing information (Kelloway et al., 2012) as well as listen actively to ensure that subordinates' voices and concerns are heard (Palmer, 2021). Robinson et al. (2023) suggest maintaining open channels of communication, being truthful, providing opportunities for feedback and making effort to communicate face to face in real time as important for building trust and enhancing psychological safety in institutions. Real time communication is important insofar as it ensures that proper communication occurs, and that leaders hear for themselves the concerns of subordinates. According to Shahid and Din (2021), face to face communication provides leaders with a rare learning opportunity, seen as leading by example, and trusted by subordinates. It is thus important to point out that leadership practices should allow open communication where all stakeholders are part of the institutional culture (Dziminska et al., 2018). This explains that leadership is critical for creating and fostering trust and psychological safety in university contexts (Shahid & Din, 2021).

Leading With Compassion

According to Palmer (2021), one powerful way of building trust and psychological safety in universities is leading with compassion. Genuinely responding to others' needs by focusing on what they can accomplish for the institution is being compassionate. Compassion refers to loving, caring, helping, and understanding others with their problems selflessly (Palmer, 2021; Shahid & Din, 2021). As a way of enhancing trust, leaders should be humble, humorous, as well as show a genuine interest in others and their individual and collective contributions. Leaders should also demonstrate respect, appreciation, and liking for members in the entire organization. This means that leaders should be approachable and show genuine care for their team members to create an atmosphere of trust and rapport leading to creating psychologically safe work environments. Kottmann et al. (2016) support this by stating that being exemplary in behavior boosts the leader's credibility and acceptance by subordinates. (Bouckenooghe et al. (2015) add that a leader should be able to guide subordinates in ways that uplift their morale and contribute to their resiliency. As perceived by Shahid and Din (2021), a people-oriented institution's valuable assets are its employees who are instrumental in achieving its goals, hence leaders should create opportunities for building trust and fostering psychological safety (Smith, 2013).

Being Appreciative and Grateful

It is important to show appreciation for others and what they contribute towards institutional growth and development (Palmer, 2021). Leaders who recognize and appreciate the contributions that team members make can build trust in the institution and enhance psychological safety in their institutions (Hopkins, 2017; Owens & Hekman, 2012). One way of fostering trust is regularly acknowledging and reinforcing positive behaviors and outcomes. This approach holds immense potential for fostering a sense of value and respect, thereby strengthening trust among team members (Palmer, 2021). There is need for organizational leaders to acknowledge and show appreciation for achievements made by incentivizing subordinates' efforts (Dahleez & Aboramadan, 2022). It is counterproductive to achieving higher levels of functionality and productivity and psychologically damaging to demean institutional members (Rehman et al., 2017). May et al. (2004) noted that there is a positive relationship between interpersonal relationships, trust and psychological safety. In building trust, institutional leaders are obliged to empower members by providing them with chances to develop leadership skills ultimately strengthening trust within the teams (Hopkins, 2017). In order to lead institutions effectively, leadership functions should not be limited to a single individual in a formal leadership position (Lambert, 2002). Educational leaders can garner trust if they can trust others, share leadership responsibilities and make way for others to develop their leadership talents (Palmer, 2021).

The Power of Collaboration

The challenges confronting higher educational systems in the 21st century require collective effort to address them. According to Dahleez and Aboramadan (2022), through collaborative effort, people can accomplish more. Trust can be realized by working together as a team. Creating a collaborative environment where individual members' ideas and contributions are genuinely recognized can foster trust and a sense of collective ownership (Palmer, 2021; Travis, 2016). Fostering trust within team environments requires a combination of open communication, psychological safety, appreciation, strong and authentic leadership (Shahid & Din, 2021; Robinson et al., 2023). Addressing challenges will lead to positive results such as increased confidence levels and enhanced cordial relationships culminating to better team cohesion and increased productivity (Clark, 2020). Through the positive influence by authentic leadership, teams can cultivate an atmosphere of collaboration, mutual support and trust, leading to enhanced performance and overall organizational success.

Intersectionality of Leadership, Trust, and Psychological Safety

Leadership plays a critical role in promoting trust and psychological safety within their institutions. According to Aranzamendez et al. (2015), building an institution where faculty, staff, lecturers, and students are psychologically safe requires leaders with certain essential leadership qualities including inclusiveness, trustworthiness and honesty among others. Leaders who possess such qualities are exemplary and model the behaviors they want team members to exhibit in their organizations. Effective communication is the lifeblood of efficient functioning of universities; leaders are encouraged to allow open communication among team members (Creed, 2023). It is important for leaders to be approachable, open to new ideas and receptive to feedback. Effective leaders should be known for welcoming and valuing team members' opinions, contributions, and concerns. There is also needed to forge trustworthy educational environments that enable team members to share their knowledge, skills, and ideas. This can be possible when leaders foster collaboration among members by creating opportunities for multidisciplinary projects and promoting a sense of shared purpose (Robinson et al., 2023).

In order to foster trust and psychological safety among team members, institutional leaders should have high personal moral integrity (Robinson et al., 2023) and that they should able to publicly admit their mistakes and value diverse perspectives. By doing this, leaders will be able to forge safe environments for members (Creed, 2023). In order to have productive institutions, leaders must ensure that individuals trust each other. In support, Robinson et al. (2023) point out that leadership is not solely responsible and accountable for building a psychologically safe work environment; it is also the collective responsibility of all stakeholders to cultivate contexts that are psychologically safe for everyone. The presence of trust and psychological safety in universities allows members to view their institutions as emotionally supportive, free from life pressure, and having pleasant interpersonal relationships (Bondarchuk et al., 2022). This implies that leaders should focus on building interpersonal relationships with team members based on the principles of trustworthiness, respectfulness, and empathy in order to build a psychologically safe work environment which will ultimately permit social interaction (Soares & Lopez, 2020). Trust is forged through ongoing communication, transparency and keeping commitments where team members are allowed time to share their thoughts and seek clarity by asking questions (Creed, 2023). According to Robinson et al. (2023), recognizing and rewarding collaborative efforts are considered critical for building trust and psychological safety in higher education institutions such as universities.

As a way of fostering trust and psychological safety in university contexts, leadership need to provide the necessary support and resources for team members to excel (Wang et al. 2018). This involves offering guidance, mentorship and coaching to help individuals develop their skills and overcome challenges. Leadership have to ensure that team members have access to the tools, training and information they need to perform their roles effectively and succeed as a team. Ensuring the growth of trust and psychological safety requires that leadership and team members embrace mistakes as learning opportunities (Creed, 2023; Owens & Hakman, 2012). Leaders are required to create a culture where mistakes are not blamed on individuals but are taken as opportunities for learning and growth (Creed, 2023; Owens & Hakman, 2012) as genuine leaders encourage team members to take risks, experiment, and learn from failures without fear of blame or punishment (Qian et al., 2020; Yaffe & Kirk, 2011). In addition, leaders are required to provide constructive feedback and help team members reflect on their experiences to foster continuous improvement since leadership entails influencing others to realize common goals (Cherkowski et al., 2021).

The issue of team members' well-being is at the heart of any genuine institutional leader. According to Deredzai et al. (2024), team members' mental and psychological well-being is of utmost importance and should be prioritized. Under the guidance of genuine leadership institutions need to create a work-life balance, recognizing and addressing stressors and promoting a positive and supportive work environment (Cherkowski et al., 2021; Cook et al., 2022). Leaders should be sensitive to the emotional needs of team members by providing resources for mental health support to enhance their overall well-being (Cherkowski et al., 2021).

Team members' motivation to work hard can be fostered when team effort is recognized. It has been found that leaders who demonstrate positive emotions impact members by inspiring them through the contagion process thereby enhancing collegiality (Owens & Hakman, 2012). Recognition of team effort can be achieved when leaders celebrate success and make an effort to foster a positive culture of belonging and their collective ability to support one another (Ayo & Fraser, 2008). This means that leaders must recognize and celebrate the achievements and contributions of team members in order to build trust. Team members who have no trust for their leaders expend both their cognitive and emotional energy safeguarding themselves from their leaders and depleting their physical resources in the process (Kelloway et al., 2012). Opportunities for creating a positive and inclusive team culture, where individuals feel valued, appreciated and motivated should therefore be prioritized. Leaders need to encourage a sense of camaraderie and teamwork by promoting a supportive and uplifting atmosphere where trust and psychological safety are part of the environment (Robinson et al., 2023). In this regard, it can be argued that, if leaders implement these strategies, they are on a path to promoting trust and psychological safety within their teams ultimately leading to inclusive and innovative members.

Threats To Trust and Psychological Safety In Universities

Universities face many threats to established trust and psychological safety to team members. These threats tend to affect the way people relate as well as their effort to collaborate and innovate. Communication is critical to institutional efficiency (Palmer, 2021). Given the centrality of communication, its absence in universities is a serious threat. When members are not allowed to communicate openly and honestly, the attributes of trust and psychological safety is seriously compromised (Palmer, 2021). If there are inadequate feedback opportunities, psychological safety is hindered when members are not allowed adequate feedback opportunities leading to fear of expressing their opinions, ideas, or concerns leading to a toxic academic environment (Edmondson, 2019). Fear can arise from a hierarchical or authoritarian leadership culture, where power dynamics discourage open dialogue among members (Shahid & Din, 2021). Furthermore, trust and psychological safety is compromised when individual members do not feel included, supported or valued in the organizations in which they are part (Sher et al., 2019). This means that lack of inclusion, support and being valued pose a threat to the establishment of trust and psychological safety in university environments.

By their composition, universities are generally plural and multicultural organizations that are characterized by diversity (Hudzik, 2015). When diverse perspectives are not respected, members may hesitate to contribute fully to enrich the experience. According to Dziminiska et al. (2018), an institutional culture that focuses on blame and punishment rather than learning from mistakes poses a threat to the development of trust and psychological safety. Reprimanding or penalizing members for making and admitting mistakes, sharing ideas or taking initiatives is detrimental to the establishment of a trustworthy and psychologically safe team environments (Edmondson & Lei, 2014). It therefore implies that universities must leverage diversity that characterize such institutions and harness the potential of multiple perspectives.

For institutions such as universities to prosper, team members must be aware of their expectations. However, if members are unsure about their roles, responsibilities, or the expectations placed upon them, trust and psychology become elusive. According to Smith (2013), the absence of clear roles leads to confusion, misunderstandings, conflict, and lack of psychological safety. Similarly, lack of support and recognition of effort made by other members and leadership can dampen the spirit of collaboration, innovation, forward-looking and hard work thereby posing a threat to the nourishment of trust and enhancement of psychological safety (Edmondson, 1999, 2019). Furthermore, trust and psychological safety in institutions like universities are undermined when team members do not feel supported or recognized for their contributions (Liu et al., 2016). Therefore, it is important for leadership to recognize and celebrate members' achievements as a way of showing appreciation for efforts made by individuals and teams (Dahleez & Aboramadan, 2022). It is critical to note that addressing these among other threats to trust and psychological safety requires effort and commitment. Thus, in order to foster a positive team climate, members should be allowed to engage in open and transparent communication, creating a culture that values inclusivity and diverse perspectives, providing constructive feedback, encouraging risk-taking, and recognizing, celebrating and appreciating members' contributions (Kelloway et al., 2012). In view of these issues, we point out that, if these threats to promoting trust and psychological safety are addressed, a collaborative and innovative climate can be created where individuals can take risks and collectively contribute to the achievement of shared institutional goals.

Sustaining Trust and Psychological Safety in Universities

Universities experience challenges that impact trust and psychological safety of members (Robinson et al., 2023). The challenges require a kind of leadership that will steer the institution towards adaptation in order to continue serving their clientele and take their part in national development (Levine & Van Pelt, 2021; Musto, 2021). This is because psychological safety has evolved to become important for fostering inclusion, enhancing learning, and promoting change and innovation (Clark, 2020). Universities are characterized as human interaction-intensive organizations that undertake challenging interpersonal work hence the importance of forging trust and psychological safety (Edmondson et al., 2016).

There are many factors that influence the development of trust and psychological safety in universities. Musto (2021) notes that innovation can only happen when institutions have built trust in their employees and created psychologically safe environments. The presence of trust and psychological safety in universities is instrumental to inclusion and intellectual curiosity among team members. This can be exhibited by team members' willingness to listen, learn from each other and challenge the status quo (Sher et al., 2019; Robinson et al., 2023; Edmondson, 2019). Regular team meetings, open forums, and anonymous feedback channels can be employed to sustain psychological safety in universities.

Research indicates that contemporary educational environments increasingly require institutional members to contribute to improving organizational practices (Creed, 2023; Edmondson, 1999). This is because leaders have important responsibilities in developing trust and psychological safety which increases institutional effectiveness (Wang et al., 2018). Specifically, humble leadership has a significant influence on subordinates' attitudes and behaviors such as job satisfaction, psychological strength, and work engagement (Ou et al., 2017; Jeung & Yoon, 2016; Owens et al., 2013). The reason is that academic leaders have a major role to fulfill in the administration and management of a complex web of stakeholders through effective planning, organizing, leading, and controlling (Coco, 2011).

Important lessons can be drawn from the social information processing theory. The theory indicates that individuals within organizations rely on information cues from both their team members and their leaders to understand their work environments and accordingly regulate their behaviors (Qian et al., 2020). Thus, in this regard, leaders serve as critical sources of information in view of their social standing and their direct involvement and interactions with subordinates (Chiu et al., 2016). We therefore argue that trust and psychological safety work to influence the relationship between leadership and creative, collaborative and motivated team members (Wang et al., 2018). This is so because leadership plays a critical role in setting the tone for trust and psychological safety by establishing clear expectations in their organizations (Robinson et al., 2023; Roussin & Webber, 2012), providing support (Dahleez & Aboramadan, 2022), and modelling vulnerability (Edmondson, 1999). Team norms such as open and respectful communication, inclusivity and accountability also contribute significantly to fostering the attributes of trust and psychological safety. These norms have been found to positively influence creativity among team members (Jiang & Gu, 2016; Liu et al., 2016). In a trustworthy and psychologically safe environment, team members are more likely to take risks and willingly share new ideas because of the absence of anxiety and fear because they do not exist in a safe climate (Frazier et al., 2016).

RESEARCH METHODOLOGY

This chapter adopted a qualitative research methodology where data was collected at the site where participants were experiencing the phenomenon under exploration as advised by Creswell (2015). As defined by Gray (2011), qualitative research is a research approach that seeks to understand phenomena in their natural living spaces and uses multiple theoretical lenses and methods such as observations, document analysis and interviews. Data was gathered by way of talking to lecturers at their university campus, which is a major aspect of qualitative research, that of studying individuals in their natural environments. An exploratory multiple case study which focuses on participants as separate individuals was used. The multiple case study design focused on selected lecturers as independent knowledge experts on issues of their experiences of trust and psychological safety in the university. The design was adopted because it allowed the researchers to examine a relatively new subject of interest (Babbie, 2020). Given that the phenomena of trust and psychological safety have become subjects of interest and relatively new in universities, an exploratory case study was appropriate. It allowed for flexibility in application as well as in-depth exploration of trust and psychological safety, providing a rich, contextual understanding that can inform both theory and practice and add to the existing knowledge base. This method was particularly useful as it facilitated the exploration of lecturers' experiences regarding trust and psychological safety in their university.

CONTEXT AND PARTICIPANTS

The study was carried out at one Zimbabwean university in which only one faculty was involved. The sample comprised twenty-four lecturers drawn from a population of seventy lecturers. Four lecturers from each of the six departments were selected on the basis of availability and willingness to take part in the study. They all agreed on an individual basis to be interviewed. The transferability and trustworthiness of the findings and conclusions were increased through participant triangulation as data was gathered from multiple participants. As described by Gray (2011), an interview is a purposive conversation between two or more people in which one of them assumes the role of the researcher. Interviews have long been the most common qualitative method of data collection used in case studies (Sunzuma & Kakoma, 2023), because most of them are human issues that can provide insights into a multifaceted situation (Biggam, 2011). In-depth semi-structured interview questions were used to allow lecturers an opportunity to express themselves and clarify their responses without restrictions. Interviews were preferred because they allowed researchers to gather data that could not be gathered through other means (Sunzuma & Kakoma, 2023). A researcher-made semi-structured interview guide was used as a tool for data gathering.

DATA ANALYSIS

Thematic analysis was utilized to make sense of data collected from lecturers through in-depth interviews. The technique is a process of finding patterns or themes that are found in qualitative data and reducing it to a story and its interpretation (Maguire & Delahint, 2017; Neuendorf, 2019). According to Kiger and Varpio (2020), thematic analysis is a qualitative practical data analysis technique applicable to many qualitative methods through data coding, searching for, and refining themes. The analysis process involved reducing and organizing the data by way of summarization and identification of themes (Castleberry & Nolen, 2018). The qualitative analysis process involved reading and re-reading the transcripts for familiarity and understanding as advised by Braun and Clarke, 2006). The approach is flexible and is not tied to any theoretical or epistemological perspective hence it was utilized (Braun & Clarke, 2006).

FINDINGS AND DISCUSSION

An analysis of the interview data from lecturers resulted in the following themes: lecturers' understanding of concept trust, conceptualizing psychological safety and its significance, perspectives on experiencing trust by lecturers in university, ensuring psychological safety for team members in universities, leadership role in building trust and fostering psychological safety, views on threats to building trust and psychological safety, and strategies to sustain trust and psychological safety. Data was presented following these themes.

Lecturers' Understanding of the Concept of Trust

Trust is a fundamental aspect that must be available in team environments such as universities. It is important because it enables effective collaboration, promotes ethical behavior, and enhances productivity and morale (Shahid & Din, 2021). By fostering trust within teams, an environment that encourages open communication, innovation, and high-quality work can be created. Additionally, trust is a crucial element in team environments as it fosters collaboration, enhances communication, and promotes a positive work culture (Dziminska et al., 2018). In response to question about their understanding of the concept trust, and its importance in university team environments, the following are some of the interviewees' extracts:

Trust is the foundation of effective teamwork and collaboration within a team environment. It creates an atmosphere where members feel safe to express their ideas, share information, and take risks without fear of judgment or negative consequences. Trust does not solely dependent on the behaviour of others but can be influenced by leaders' actions. If their behaviours are positive, they are able to foster an environment of trust and strengthen the subordinates' dynamics and overall performance (LR 14).

Trust is essential in team environments because it establishes a sense of reliability and integrity among team members. It enables individuals to work together towards common goals, knowing that their colleagues will act honestly and ethically. Trustworthiness is demonstrated when team members can rely on each other, even in challenging situations and involves being honest and transparent (LR 2).

Within a university context, trust has a direct impact on productivity, morale, and the quality of work produced. When team members trust each other, they feel comfortable collaborating, sharing ideas, and supporting one another. Trust creates an environment where team members can focus on their work without worrying about backstabbing or negative interactions allowing for increased creativity, improved problem-solving, and a stronger sense of unity (LR 11).

The three extracts presented definitions of trust in different ways but the responses showed an understanding of the concept trust. Their definitions mainly focused trust being an enabler of teamwork and collaboration and how it has direct impact on creativity, problem-solving and, team cohesion. This is consistent with the definition by Van Houtte (2007) which presents trust is the confidence that expectations will be met in view of working together. The definitions also mention the dimensions of relying on other team members and leaders who should act in morally responsible ways (Shahid & Din, 2021). These issues are explained by Kelloway et al. (2012), who aver that trust is the belief that a leader has the necessary positive attributes to lead, advise, protect, and support team members. This means that in the absence of trust there is no team cohesion implying that trust is a critical variable in organizational functioning (Vidovich & Currie, 2011).

Conceptualizing Psychological Safety and its Significance

Psychological safety refers to creating an environment where team members feel safe to take risks, share ideas, and express their opinions without fear of negative consequences or judgment (Sher et al., 2019; Edmondson, 1999). Psychological safety in university team environments is crucial for fostering learning, well-being, effective communication, collaboration, and innovation (Sher et al., 2019). It creates an atmosphere where students and faculty members feel safe to express themselves, share ideas, and engage in open discussions. By prioritizing psychological safety, universities can create a supportive and inclusive environment that enhances the overall educational and academic experience for all.

> *Psychological safety is of utmost importance as it fosters a culture of learning, innovation, and collaboration. When students and faculty members feel psychologically safe, they are able to engage in open discussions, ask questions, and explore new ideas. It encourages members to take risks, challenge existing knowledge regimes, and contribute to the overall growth and development of the team. It creates an atmosphere where different perspectives are valued and nurtured, leading to a richer university pedagogical experience (LR 24).*
>
> *In university environments, psychological safety is crucial for the well-being of students. It involves creating an atmosphere where students feel comfortable expressing themselves, seeking help, and sharing their concerns. Psychological safety also plays a significant role in reducing anxiety and stress levels among students and lecturers, allowing them to focus and participate actively in team activities (LR 13).*
>
> *When individuals feel psychologically safe, they are more likely to share their thoughts, ask questions, and engage in constructive discussions. This leads to better decision-making, problem-solving, and overall team performance (LR 10).*

Participants' responses indicated their understanding of what psychological safety entails. Important in the responses is the articulation that the concept involves creation of an atmosphere in which different stakeholders feel secure. Such an atmosphere is necessary for enabling members to engage in their various activities without fear of retribution (Edmondson, 2019). Interviewees mentioned that the presence of psychological safety reduces anxiety and stress among both students and lecturers. The definitions of psychological safety given by interviewees are in agreement with those in literature. For example, Sher et al. (2019) and Edmondson (1999) concur that psychological safety refers to a work environment that does not have psychological violence and that members interact with each other freely and are able to take risks without fear of being blamed. Thus, in the context of university, a psychologically safe environment is one where individual team members feel included in the culture, or subculture and are safe to learn, contribute and challenge the status quo (Edmondson, 2019)

Perspectives on Experiencing Trust by Lecturers In University

The experience of trust by team members in a university may differ based on each individual's perspective. For some, trust may be experienced through open communication and support (Sher et al., 2019), while for others it may be built on accountability and reliability (Edmondson, 1999). Additionally, trust can also be established through collaboration and empowerment (Dahleez & Aboramadan, 2022). These different perspectives highlight the multifaceted nature of trust and how it can be nurtured in various ways within university environments.

> *As a member in the university, I have experienced trust through open communication and the support I have received from colleagues. I have experienced it during workshops when members are encouraged to ask questions, contribute and participate actively. Trust is built when team members are willing to listen, understand, and respect each other's ideas and perspectives. It is nurtured when team members provide support, guidance, and constructive feedback to help each other grow professionally. This creates a sense of comradeship and mutual respect within members. I have personally experienced (LR 23).*
>
> *In my experience as a team member in the university, trust has been established through accountability and reliability. Trust is built when team members take ownership of their responsibilities, meet deadlines, and fulfill their commitments. This has been particularly useful to me as I can confidently say that I benefited a lot from how we work at our institution (LR 4).*
>
> *Trust, in my experience as a team member in the university, is established through collaboration and empowerment. Trust is built when team members are encouraged to contribute their ideas, share their expertise, and participate actively in decision-making processes. This was evident during the time when we were changing our programmes. Members were allowed to contribute based on their area of expertise. In my view this worked transform our institution focusing on programmes that would impact people's lives (LR 9).*

Evidence from participants' responses demonstrates that they were consulted and encouraged to part on issues to do with curriculum changes. This may serve to show that they were enjoying trust and psychological safety that prevailed in the university. Based on the prevailing conditions, participants took part and contribute to developing people-oriented programs with a national impact through collaborative effort (Dahleez & Aboramadan, 2022). This is supported by the view that trust is the glue that binds relationships together. It also explains why fostering trust and psychological safety is crucial in universities. It emerged from participants' responses that building strong relationships enhances team cohesion and creates avenues for developing psychologically safe work environments (Vidovich & Currie, 2011). In the case of this study, the availability of trust enabled team members to work together for the accomplishment of common goals. Literature demonstrates that the presence of trust and psychological safety in work environments increases work commitment consequently leading to increased productivity and inclusivity (Cherkowski et al., 2021; Edmondson & Lei, 2014).

Ensuring Psychological Safety for Team Members In Universities

The need to ensure psychological safety for team members in universities requires fostering open communication, supportive leadership, inclusion, and psychological support mechanisms (Palmer, 2021; Robinson et al., 2023). Members enjoying psychological safety will exhibit behaviors such as active participation, risk-taking, collaboration, and seeking help when needed. By prioritizing psychological safety, universities can create an environment that promotes well-being, innovation, and overall team effectiveness (Cherkowski et al., 2021; Deredzai et al., 2024). In response to the question on how universities can guarantee psychological safety for members, some participants had the following to say:

In order to guarantee psychological safety for team members in universities, I think it is important to foster a culture of open communication and support. This can be achieved by encouraging team members to express their thoughts and ideas freely. Members enjoying psychological safety in a university setting can be observed through their willingness to contribute ideas, engage in discussions and take risks without fear of retribution. They would also demonstrate trust in their colleagues by seeking to collaborate, and feel comfortable seeking guidance or assistance when needed (LR 9).

Building trust and psychological safety can involve setting clear expectations, providing resources for skill development and fostering a sense of belonging. Encouraging collaboration, recognizing and celebrating achievements and addressing conflicts proactively can also contribute to a psychologically safe university environment (LR 1).

It is also important to encourage a culture of psychological support, such as mentorship programmes, counselling services and wellness initiatives. These can contribute to a psychologically safe environment. There is also need to create work-life balance and addressing issues of stress and burnout to further enhance psychological safety for members (LR 12).

The verbatim statements above show present participants' views about what universities can do to sustain trust and psychological safety to enhance team cohesion and maximize productivity. The issues of adopting efficient communication, allowing members to express their concerns freely, setting clear expectations and balancing work and life to stand out clearly are important for sustaining trust and psychological safety. The issue of open communication is strongly highlighted in literature where effective communication has been dubbed as the hallmark for creating trustworthy and psychologically safe institutional environments (Palmer, 2021). This means that institutional leaders are required to model transparency in sharing information (Kelloway et al., 2012) as well as listening actively to ensure that subordinates' voices and concerns are heard (Palmer, 2021). Being able to balance work and life is also very important in order to reduce stress and burnout among members (Deredzai et al., 2024).

Role of Leadership in Building Trust and Fostering Psychological Safety

The role of university leadership in building trust and fostering psychological safety can be seen from different perspectives. Whether as role models and facilitators, advocates of inclusion and support, or enablers of communication and growth, university leaders play a vital role in creating an environment where team members feel safe, empowered, and valued (Aranzamendez et al., 2015). It has been documented that by prioritizing trust and psychological safety, leaders can promote collaboration, innovation, and overall team effectiveness within the university settings (Creed, 2023; Robinson et al., 2023). The participants were asked during interviews about what they considered to be roles of university leaders with regard to trust and psychological safety. Below are some of their excerpts showing their responses:

In my view, it is the responsibility of leaders to actively promote a culture of trust. This can be done by listening attentively, valuing diverse perspectives and above all to be approachable. They can also facilitate team-building activities, provide opportunities for feedback and address conflicts promptly. They serve as role models, setting the tone for open communication, transparency and respect. Regardless of age, human beings need to be respected (LR 18).

Leaders should create environments that promote trust by ensuring that team members feel valued, respected, and included. They should also provide resources for professional development, mentorship opportunities and support services to address the well-being of team members as well as create a team environment that fosters growth, collaboration and overall success (LR 6).

In order to foster psychological safety, leaders should make effort to promote a growth mindset and provide opportunities for continuous learning and development- professional development to be exact. This can include offering training programmes, creating platforms for exchange of ideas. Leaders should also be able to recognise and celebrate achievements by their subordinates (LR 21).

Participants' responses show that the establishment of trust and psychological safety almost entirely hinges on institutional leaders. This is because, for institutional functionality, a lot is expected of them. For example, creating a climate that builds trust and fosters psychological safety is their overall responsibility. This is echoed by Musto (2021) and Levine and Van Pelt (2021) who argue that universities require a kind of leadership that can lead the institution towards adaptation in order to continue serving their clientele and take their part in national development. This is because, according to Clark (2020), psychological safety is important for fostering inclusion, enhancing learning, and promoting change and innovation. Effective communication is the lifeblood of efficient functioning of universities; leaders are encouraged to allow open communication among team members (Creed, 2023). This is only possible leaders are approachable, open to new ideas and receptive to feedback. Effective leaders should be known for welcoming and valuing team members' opinions, contributions and concerns as well as celebrating members' achievements (Dahleez & Aboramadan, 2022).

Views on Threats to Building Trust and Psychological Safety

While universities make an effort to build trust and psychological safety in their institutions, they also meet challenges during the process. Threats to building trust and psychologically safe team environments in universities can vary in origin and level of intensity. They may include a lack of communication and transparency, fear of failure and negative consequences, and a lack of diversity and inclusion. These threats can be mitigated by allowing open communication, creating a culture that embraces learning from failures, and fostering diversity and inclusion. These mechanisms can help build trusting and psychologically safe team environments that enhance collaboration, innovation, and increase team effectiveness. The participants were interviewed on their knowledge of the threats to trust and psychological safety in universities. The following are some of the interviewees' extracts:

One threat to building trust and psychologically safe team environments in universities is a lack of communication and transparency. Some leaders withhold information. When this happens it can lead to rumours, misunderstandings and a breakdown in trust among team members. This can cause institution to run inefficiently (LR 16).

Some leaders have a tendency to scold or shout at individual for making even small mistakes. When team members are afraid of making mistakes or facing repercussions for taking risks, they may become hesitant to share ideas, express concerns, let alone speak against the traditional normative standards (LR 2).

A university campus in which there is a lack of diversity and inclusion can be a threat to building trust and psychologically safety in universities. When team members do not feel represented or valued, it can lead to feelings of exclusion, lower engagement, and reduced trust among team members (LR 5).

The responses indicate that there are many factors that militate against building trust and fostering psychological safety in university environments as observed by Palmer (2021). As already indicated effective communication is essential in the running of institutions. When for some reason members are not allowed to communicate openly and honestly, trust and psychological safety is seriously compromised (Palmer, 2021). If there are inadequate feedback opportunities, psychological safety is hindered. Edmonson (2019) points out that when members are not allowed adequate feedback opportunities it can lead to fear of expressing their feelings, leading to a toxic academic environment. According to Shahid and Din (2021), fear can arise from a hierarchical or authoritarian leadership culture, where power dynamics discourage open dialogue among members. Furthermore, trust and psychological safety are compromised when individual members do not feel included, supported or valued in the organizations in which they are part (Sher et al., 2019). This agrees with an observation made by Hadzik (2015) that universities are generally plural and multicultural organizations that are characterized by diversity. When diverse perspectives are not respected, members may hesitate to contribute fully to enrich the academic experience. To address this threat, leaders should actively promote diversity and inclusion, ensure equitable opportunities for all team members, and create a culture that embraces different perspectives. This can involve implementing diversity initiatives, providing training on cultural competence, and fostering an inclusive environment where everyone feels respected and valued.

Strategies to Sustain Trust and Psychological Safety in Universities

Sustaining trust and psychological safety in universities can be achieved by employing a number of strategies. These may include among others, encouraging open communication and appreciation, emphasizing learning from mistakes, and creating space for feedback, and promoting inclusion and establishing clear expectations. When implemented, these strategies can foster a supportive and inclusive team environment that enhances trust, psychological safety, and improved team performance. The participants were interviewed on what strategies can be employed to sustain trust and psychological safety in team environments. Below are some of the responses given by participants:

I can mention a few ways making sure trust is sustained and psychological is fostered. I think it is important to pay attention to team members' concerns, acknowledging their opinions, and appreciating the contributions they make. This can foster a sense of psychological safety. This can be done by providing regular feedback, recognising achievements and creating opportunities for open dialogue between and among members (LR 2).

I think encouraging team members to share their ideas, concerns, and suggestions without fear of negative consequences can enhance psychological safety. Creating platforms for feedback, such as anonymous suggestion boxes or regular feedback sessions, can provide opportunities for open and honest communication (LR 17).

Establishing clear expectations and norms, along with transparent communication, can help minimise ambiguity and build trust. Clearly communicating goals, roles and responsibilities can create a sense of psychological safety and enable team members to work collaboratively and effectively (LR 7).

An analysis of participants' responses indicates that there are quite a handful of strategies that can be employed to sustain trust and psychological safety in universities. Data contained in excerpts identified many ways of sustaining trust including effective communication, inclusivity appreciating, and recognizing and celebrating members' achievements. This is supported by Sher et al. (2019) who say that team members' willingness to listen and learn from each other. Robinson et al. (2023) and Edmondson (2019) also indicate that holding regular team meetings, open forums, and anonymous feedback channels can be useful in efforts to sustain psychological safety in universities. Participants' responses to the question about strategies demonstrate that universities can do something to create environments in which trust, and psychological safety can be experienced.

CONCLUSION

This discourse has interrogated the significance of trust and psychological safety in university team environments. Through examination of relevant literature, it became clear that no institution can function meaningfully in a trust and psychological safety-starved environment. The attributes of trust and psychological safety have immense influence on fostering inclusivity, collaboration, innovation, and institutional growth. Thus, by emphasizing trust and psychological safety, educators and administrators can create inclusive and supportive university environments in which team members feel valued, respected and empowered to contribute their unique perspectives to the development of their institutions. Strategies to cultivate trust and psychological safety, such as allowing open communication, encouraging diverse viewpoints, and establishing clear expectations were discussed. The need to address power dynamics inherent in university leadership setups and creating a culture of accountability and continuous improvement has been stressed. We pointed out that environments that are characterized by trust and psychological safety have the capacity to foster resilience, creativity, critical thinking, and prepare individuals to thrive in a dynamic world. We call upon readers to appreciate that it is an ongoing process to promote trust and psychological safety in institutions. It requires effort, reflection, and adaptation to the evolving needs of diverse teams. The centrality of leadership in creating a climate for nurturing trust and psychological safety in university campuses has been chronicled. It emerged that promoting trust and psychological safety requires committed, humble and transformative leadership, continuous communication, and a genuine dedication to team well-being (Deredzai et al., 2024). It is the contention of this chapter that when the attributes of trust and psychological safety are fostered in university environments, collaboration and personal growth can blossom. Together, team members can unlock the full potential of universities through fostering inclusive environments that empower and uplift individuals and groups. It is expected that the insights deriving from this discourse will catalyze change and inspire team members, educators, students, and administrators to champion the development of trust and psychological safety in university spaces.

REFERENCES

Aranzamendez, G., James, D., & Toms, R. (2015). Finding antecedents of psychological safety: A step toward quality improvement. *Nurse Forum, 50* (3), 171-178. DOI: 10.1111/nuf.12084

Ayo, L., & Frazer, C. (2008). The four constructs of collegiality. *International Journal of Evidence Based Coaching and Mentoring*, 6(1), 57–65.

Babbie, E. (2020). *The practice of social research.* Cengage.

Biggam, J. (2011). Succeeding with your masters dissertation: A step-by-step handbook. New Open University Press and McGraw Hill.

Bondarchuk, O. I., Balakhtar, V. V., Ushenko, Y. O., Gorova, O. O., Osovska, I. M., Pinchuk, N. I., Yakubovskam, N. O., Balakhtar, K. S., & Moskalov, M. V. (2022). The psychological safety of the educational environment of Ukrainian higher education institutions in a pandemic: Empirical data of a comparative analysis of participants' assessments studying online. In *Proceedings of the 1st Symposium on Advances in Educational Technology*, 1, 14-31. Doi:DOI: 10.5220/0010920100003364

Bouckenooghe, D., Zafar, A., & Raja, U. (2015). How ethical leadership shapes employees' job performance: The mediating role of goal congruence and psychological capital. *Journal of Business Ethics*, 129(2), 251–264. DOI: 10.1007/s10551-014-2162-3

Braun, V., & Clarke, V. (2006). Using thematic analysis in psychology. *Qualitative Research in Psychology*, 3(2), 77–101. DOI: 10.1191/1478088706qp063oa

Bryk, A., & Schneider, B. (2002). *Trust in schools: A core resource for improvement.* Russell Sage Foundation.

Castleberry, A., & Nolen, A. C. (2018). Thematic analysis of qualitative research data: Is it as easy as it sounds? *Currents in Pharmacy Teaching & Learning*, 10(6), 807–815. DOI: 10.1016/j.cptl.2018.03.019 PMID: 30025784

Chan, S. C. H., & Mak, W. (2014). The impact of servant leadership and subordinates' organisational tenure on trust in leader and attitudes. *Personnel Review*, 43(2), 272–287. DOI: 10.1108/PR-08-2011-0125

Chen, C., Liao, J., & Wen, P. (2014). Why does formal mentoring matter? The mediating role of psychological safety and the moderating role of power distance orientation in the Chinese context. *International Journal of Human Resource Management*, 25(8), 1112–1130. DOI: 10.1080/09585192.2013.816861

Cherkowski, S., Kutsyuruba, B., Walker, K., & Crawford, M. (2021). Conceptualising leadership and emotions in higher education: Well-being as wholeness. *Journal of Educational Administration and History*, 53(2), 158–171. DOI: 10.1080/00220620.2020.1828315

Chiu, C. Y. C., Owens, B. P., & Tesluk, P. E. (2016). Initiating and utilising shared leadership in teams: The role of leader humility, team proactive personality and team performance capability. *The Journal of Applied Psychology*, 101(12), 1705–1720. DOI: 10.1037/apl0000159 PMID: 27618409

Clark, L. (2020). Leadership imperatives for success: Cultivating trust. https://www.harvardbusiness.org/leadership-imperatives-for-success-cultivating-trust-2-of-3/

Coco, C. M. (2011). Emotional intelligence in higher education: Strategic implications for academic leaders. *Journal of Higher Education Theory and Practice*, 11(2), 112–117.

Cook, A., Keyte, R., Sprawson, I., Matharu, A., & Mantzios, M. (2022). Mental health first aid experiences: A qualitative investigation into the emotional impact of mental health first aid responsibilities. Doi: DOI: 10.21203/rs.3.rs-1393314/v1

Creed, A. (2023). Empowering change: Psychological safety in higher education project teams. Available at https://www.linkedin.com/pulse/fostering-psychological-safety-university-learning-creed-ph-d-7zbrc/ accessed 23 March 2024

Creswell, J. W. (2015). *A concise introduction to mixed methods research*. Sage Publications.

Dahleez, K., & Aboramadan, M. (2022). Servant leadership and job satisfaction in higher education: The mediating roles of organisational justice and organisational trust. *International Journal of Leadership in Education*, •••, 1–22. DOI: 10.1080/13603124.2022.2052753

De Smet, A., Rubenstein, K., & Schrah, G. (2023). Psychological safety and the critical role of leadership development. https://www.mckinsey.com/capabilities/people-and-organisational-performance/our-insights/psychological-safety-and-the-critical-role-of-leadership-development#/

Deredzai, M., Goronga, P., & Maupa, B. (2024). Mental health and well-being of students and faculty: Enhancing quality mental health and well-being of female students and faculty in colleges. In Kayyali, M. (Ed.), *Building resiliency in higher education: Globalisation, digital skills, and student wellness* (pp. 332–353). IGI Global., DOI: 10.4018/979-8-3693-5483-4.ch018

Dziminska, M., Fijalkowska, J., & Sulkowski, L. (2018). Trust-based quality culture conceptual model for higher education institutions. *Sustainability (Basel)*, 10(8), 1–22. DOI: 10.3390/su10082599

Edmondson, A. C. (1999). Psychological safety and learning behaviour in work teams. *Administrative Science Quarterly*, 44(2), 350–383. DOI: 10.2307/2666999

Edmondson, A. C. (2019). *The fearless organisation: Creating psychological safety in the workplace for learning, innovation and growth.* John Wiley and Sons.

Edmondson, A.C., Higgins, M., Singer, S.J., & Weiner, J. (2016). Promoting psychological safety in healthcare organisations and education organisations: A comparative perspective. Res Hum Dev, 13 (1), 65-83. Htttps://doi,org/DOI: 10.1080/15427609.2016.114128

Edmondson, A. C., & Lei, Z. (2014). Psychological safety: The history, renaissance, and future of an interpersonal construct. *Annual Review of Organizational Psychology and Organizational Behavior*, 1(1), 23–43. DOI: 10.1146/annurev-orgpsych-031413-091305

Frazier, M. L., Fainshmidt, S., Klinger, R. L., Pezeshkan, A., & Vracheva, V. (2016). Psychological safety: A meta-analytic review and extension. *Personnel Psychology*, 70(1), 113–165. DOI: 10.1111/peps.12183

Gerlach, R., & Gockel, C. (2017). We belong together: Belonging to the principal's in-group protect teachers from the negative effects of task conflict on psychological safety. *School Leadership & Management*. Advance online publication. 101080/13632434.2017.1407307

Gray, D. E. (2011). *Doing research in the real world.* Sage Publications, Inc.

Hopkins, G. (2017). What makes effective teaching teams tick? Education World, https://www.educationworld.com/a admin/admin/admin408 a.shtml

Hudzik, J. (2015). Leading internationalisation in higher education. What matters most? *Journal of Studies in International Education*, 19(1), 6–21.

Jeung, C. W., & Yoon, H. J. (2016). Leader humility and psychological empowerment: Investigating contingencies. *Journal of Managerial Psychology*, 31(7), 1122–1136. DOI: 10.1108/JMP-07-2015-0270

Jiang, W., & Gu, Q. (2016). How abusive supervision and abusive supervisory climate influence salesperson creativity and sales team effectiveness in China. Mang. *Management Decision*, 54(2), 455–475. DOI: 10.1108/MD-07-2015-0302

Kelloway, E. K., Turner, N., Barling, J., & Loughlin, C. (2012). Transformational leadership and employee psychological well-being: The mediating role of employee trust in leadership. *Work and Stress*, 26(1), 39–55. DOI: 10.1080/02678373.2012.660774

Kiger, M. E., & Varpio, L. (2020). Thematic analysis of qualitative data: AMEE guide No 131. *Medical Teacher*, 42(8), 846–854. DOI: 10.1080/0142159X.2020.1755030 PMID: 32356468

Kottman, A., Huisman, J., Brockerhoff, L., Cremonini, L., & Mampaey, J. (2016). How can one create a culture for quality enhancement: Final report. Ghent University: Ghent, Belgium.

Lambert, L. (2002). A framework for shared leadership. *Educational Leadership*, 59, 37–40. http://www.ascd.org/publications/educational-leadership/may02/vol59/num08/toc.aspx

Levine, A., & Van Pelt, S. (2021). *The great upheaval: Higher education's past, present and uncertain future*. Johns Hopkins University Press.

Liu, W., Zhang, P., Liao, J., Hao, P., & Mao, J. (2016). Abusive supervision and employee creativity: The mediating of psychological safety and organisational identification. *Management Decision*, 54(1), 130–147. DOI: 10.1108/MD-09-2013-0443

Lu, J., Zhang, Z., & Jia, M. (2019). Does servant leadership affect employees' emotional labor? A social information-processing perspective. *Journal of Business Ethics*, 159(2), 507–518. DOI: 10.1007/s10551-018-3816-3

May, D. R., Gilson, R. L., & Harter, L. M. (2004). The psychological conditions of meaningfulness, safety and availability and the engagement of the human spirit at work. *Journal of Occupational and Organizational Psychology*, 77(1), 11–37. DOI: 10.1348/096317904322915892

Ming, C., Xiaoying, G., Huizhen, Z., & Bin, R. (2015). A review on psychological safety: Concepts, measurements, antecedents and consequences variables In *Proceedings of the 2015 International Conference on Social Science and Technology Education*, (pp.433-440) Atlantis Press. DOI: 10.2991/icsste-15.2015.118

Musto, R. G. (2021). *The attack on higher education: The dissolution of the American university*. Cambridge University Press. DOI: 10.1017/9781108559355

Neuendorf, K. A. (2019). Content analysis and thematic analysis. In Brough, P. (Ed.), *Research methods for applied psychologists: Design analysis and reporting* (pp. 211–223). Routledge.

Ou, A. Y., Seo, J., Choi, D., & Hom, P. W. (2017). When can humble top executives retain middle managers? The moderating role of top management team faultiness. *Academy of Management Journal*, 60(5), 1915–1931. DOI: 10.5465/amj.2015.1072

Owens, B. P., & Hekman, D. R. (2012). Modelling how to grow: An examination of humble leader behaviours, contingencies and outcomes. *Academy of Management Journal*, 55(4), 787–818. DOI: 10.5465/amj.2010.0441

Owens, B. P., Johnson, M. D., & Mitchell, T. R. (2013). Expressed humility in organisations: Implications for performance, teams and leadership. *Organization Science*, 24(5), 1517–1538. DOI: 10.1287/orsc.1120.0795

Palmer, R. (2021). Building a culture of trust: An imperative for effective school leadership. Faculty Publications, 4246 https://digitalcommons.anderws.edu/pubs/4246

Qian, X., Zhang, M., & Jiang, Q. (2020). Leader humility and subordinates' organisational citizenship behaviour and withdrawal behaviour: Exploring the mediating mechanisms of subordinates' psychological capital. *International Journal of Environmental Research and Public Health*, 17(7), 1–14. DOI: 10.3390/ijerph17072544

Rehman, S. U., & Cao, Q. (2017). Rise in level of trust and trustworthiness with trust building measures: A mathematical model. *Journal of Modelling in Management*, 12(3), 17–34. DOI: 10.1108/JM2-09-2015-0076

Robinson, E. T., Jones, C., & Brazeau, G. A. (2023). Addressing an uncertain future with a culture of psychological safety. *American Journal of Pharmaceutical Education*, 87(7), 100032. Advance online publication. DOI: 10.1016/j.ajpe.2022.11.005 PMID: 37380278

Roussin, C. J., & Webber, S. S. (2012). Impact of organisational identification and psychological safety on initial perceptions of coworker trustworthiness. *Journal of Business and Psychology*, 27(3), 317–329. DOI: 10.1007/s10869-011-9245-2

Shahid, S., & Din, M. (2021). Fostering psychological safety in teachers: The role of school leadership, team effectiveness and organisational culture. *International Journal of Educational Leadership and Management*, 9(2), 122–149. DOI: 10.17583/ijelm.2021.6317

Sher, A., Gul, S., Riaz, M. K., & Naeem, M. (2019). Psychological safety: A cross-level study of a higher educational institute (HEI). *Journal of Management Sciences*, 6(1), 30–49. DOI: 10.20547/jms.2014.1906103

Smith, H. R. (2013). The role of trust in religious education. *Religious Education (Chicago, Ill.)*, 14(2). https://rsc.byu.edu/vol-14.no-2-2013/role-trust-religious-education

Soares, A. E., & Lopez, M. P. (2020). Are students safe to learn? The role of lecturer's authentic leadership in the creation of psychologically safe environments and their impact on academic performance. *Active Learning in Higher Education*, 21(1), 65–78. DOI: 10.1177/1469787417742023

Sunzuma, G., & Kakoma, L. (2023). Zimbabwean mathematics pre-service teachers' implementation of the learner-centred curriculum during teaching practice. *Eurasia Journal of Mathematics, Science and Technology Education*, 19(5), em2258. Advance online publication. DOI: 10.29333/ejmste/13131

Thau, S., Bennett, J., Mitchel, M. S., & Marrs, M. B. (2009). How management style moderates the relationship between abusive supervision and workplace deviance: An uncertainty management theory perspective. *Organizational Behavior and Human Decision Processes*, 108(10), 79–92. DOI: 10.1016/j.obhdp.2008.06.003

Tierney, W. (2006). *Trust and the public good*. Peter Lang.

Travis, T. A. (2016). Four ways to approach difficult conversations and build trust. TrustED: The bridge to school improvement. https://trustedschool.org/2016/05/14/4-ways-to-approach-difficult-converstations-build-trust/

Van Houtte, M. (2007). Exploring teacher trust in technical/vocational secondary schools. *Teaching and Teacher Education*, 23(6), 826–839. DOI: 10.1016/j.tate.2006.03.001

Vidovich, L., & Currie, J. (2011). Governance and trust in higher education. *Studies in Higher Education*, 36(1), 43–56. DOI: 10.1080/03075070903469580

Wang, Y., Liu, J., & Zhu, Y. (2018). Humble leadership, psychological safety, knowledge sharing and follower creativity: A cross-level investigation. *Frontiers in Psychology*, 9, 1727. DOI: 10.3389/fpsyg.2018.01727 PMID: 30283379

Yaffe, T., & Kark, R. (2011). Leading by example: The case of leader OCB. *The Journal of Applied Psychology*, 96(4), 806–826. DOI: 10.1037/a0022464 PMID: 21443315

Zhu, J., Yao, J., & Zhang, L. (2019). Linking empowering leadership to innovative behaviour in professional learning communities: The role of psychological empowerment and team psychological safety. *Asia Pacific Education Review*, 20(4), 657–671. DOI: 10.1007/s12564-019-09584-2

Chapter 3
Empowering Students for Working in Culturally Rich and Psychologically Nourishing Work Environments

Sara Redondo-Duarte
https://orcid.org/0000-0003-2012-8784
Universidad Complutense de Madrid, Spain

Sonia Escorial Santa-Marina
UNIE Universidad, Spain

ABSTRACT

The aim of this chapter is to explore university practices that contribute to the creation of diverse and inclusive work teams in a psychologically safe environment. To this end, the first section explores the implications of VUCA environments for student learning, as well as the relevance of the concepts of diversity and inclusion in work teams. In this context, experiential learning is presented as a powerful methodological approach to strengthen the links between education, work and personal development. The second section addresses the importance of fostering a collaborative and healthy working environment in student teams. In this regard, a proposed team model and some constructive feedback strategies are included. Finally, some examples of initiatives to promote diversity and inclusion in the university context are described.

DOI: 10.4018/979-8-3693-3852-0.ch003

Copyright © 2025, IGI Global. Copying or distributing in print or electronic forms without written permission of IGI Global is prohibited.

1. PREPARING STUDENTS TO NAVIGATE VUCA AND DIVERSITY CONTEXTS

In recent years there has been a change in the role of universities, which no longer focus exclusively on teaching and research, but also on the generation of social value. This aspect is especially linked to the essential purposes of a university: to generate and disseminate knowledge, promote training and professional development, and intervene in social transformation.

Universities have a dual challenge in preparing students. On the one hand, they must create opportunities for students to experience what it means to work in a VUCA environment and discover the main opportunities and challenges it presents. On the other hand, universities must be able to foster learning environments that value diversity and promote inclusion. In this sense, there are many initiatives that can be carried out both at curricular and extracurricular level in the universities. The teacher must create safe environments in which students can express their opinions, suggest ideas, ask questions, raise concerns, speak up and admit mistakes without fear of negative consequences (Cote, 2024). Likewise, university life departments can promote diversity, inclusion and safe psychological environments through the various extracurricular activities and services they offer to students.

1.1. Experiential Learning: More Necessary Than Ever in VUCA Contexts

Universities must find new methodologies that respond to the social and professional training demands of the different labor sectors. For this reason, it is appropriate to address the term VUCA (standing for volatility, uncertainty, complexity, and ambiguity), used as an attempt to describe the new environment in which our students will work in the future (Baran and Woznyj, 2020). This context is characterized by frequent, rapid, and important changes; the uncertainty generated by the impossibility of knowing what effects specific issues will have; the complexity of assuming that we do not know enough about an issue; and finally, the ambiguity and lack of clarity that makes it difficult to understand a situation accurately. VUCA environments require creating strong and resilient teams, with diverse talents, who can prepare for the unpredictable, with an open attitude, who are willing to experiment and generate new ideas for problem solving, as well as to recover from crises at a higher level than before.

Thus, universities are challenged to adapt to the labor market in VUCA contexts, which implies that students acquire and develop relevant skills for the future. Therefore, the question that arises is: What are the implications of these VUCA contexts in the holistic development of university students? What teaching methodologies may be more appropriate to prepare them for VUCA contexts?

Horstmeyer (2020) suggests that in the current VUCA environment, the relevance of hard skills is short-lived, which in turn increases the demand for soft skills such as advanced social, emotional, and cognitive competencies (p.3). According to Soemitra et al (2023), preparing students to work in VUCA situations means to develop relevant competencies for the 21st century, such as openness to accept change, adaptation, inspirational motivation, innovation, vision, passion, strategic thinking, collaboration, flexibility, communication, accountability, among others. Navigating in VUCA environments requires the ability to quickly and effectively anticipate or respond to external changes (Troise et al., 2022). Hartwig et al. (2020) state that workplace resilience is a potential key asset to maintain performance and well- being in the face of adversity.

The VUCA environment also demands that future professionals be able to make ethical decisions in ambiguous situations and face moral dilemmas responsibly. As Gonzalez-Mulé and Cockburn (2021) state, companies that promote critical thinking and ethical decision making among their employees are more likely to succeed in VUCA environments. To this end, universities must foster a culture of integrity and accountability on campus, incorporate into their curricula ethical contents, and invite professionals and experts to share their experiences (p. 276).

In a global world, we need a globalized view that allows us to analyze problems in a contextualized way, in their globality. It necessarily requires connecting the disciplines. Soemitra et al. (2023) state that "interdisciplinary learning that integrates content knowledge and understanding in the world of Education with relevant skills in the job industry is an important solution for VUCA contexts" (p.1). Interdisciplinarity requires interaction, exchange and mutual enrichment between disciplines. According to Elizondo (2020), the globalized concept is not a concrete methodology but a view that allows a better understanding of the world. The professional world requires interdisciplinary collaboration, combining methodologies to achieve shared goals. At a higher stage we can speak of transdisciplinarity, where disciplines are approached transversally. In a transdisciplinary project, teams of professionals from various fields collaborate to address a common problem. They also develop a unified conceptual framework for understanding the issue, which integrates and goes beyond the scope of their individual disciplines (Henao et al., 2017). For our students, working in an interdisciplinary and transdisciplinary way implies coordinating the knowledge of different specialties to solve social, technological and scientific problems effectively.

Undoubtedly, experiential or experience-based learning is a very useful approach for developing the competencies demanded by VUCA environments. Experiential learning has its foundations in constructivism, as it seeks to construct knowledge and meaning through immersion in and reflection on real-world experiences. According to Gleason and Rubio (2020), strategies and teaching methods that generate experiential experiences foster active learning and holistic and multidimensional student development. To implement these active methodologies, it is necessary to expose students to real-world problems in which they can put their knowledge and skills into practice. For Piaget, "the key to learning lies in the mutual interaction of the process of accommodation of concepts or schemas to experience in the world and the process of assimilation of events and experiences from the world into existing concepts and schemas" (Kolb, 2014, p. 23).

In experiential learning, the social process of collaborative knowledge construction is key. Two main theories associated with collaborative learning are Piaget's social-cognitive conflict and Vygotsky's social interaction (Redondo-Duarte, 2012). According to the Piagetian theory of social-cognitive conflict, our own conflict encounters others and can create a state of disequilibrium within the group members. It results in the construction of new conceptual structures and understanding. From this point of view, new knowledge takes place in the individual mind and can be brought back to the level of social interaction. On the other hand, the Vygotskian theory of social interaction has two interpretations. The more traditional is based on the concept of the zone of proximal development of Vygotsky and assumes that, due to participation in collaborative activities, individuals can master something they could not do before. That is, collaboration is interpreted as a facilitator of individual cognitive development. A second interpretation states that learning comes from the negotiation of meaning and the sharing of multiple perspectives, which, consequently, modify our own representations. According to this perspective, learning is more a social process than an individual effort.

For the experiential learning theory, "ideas are not fixed and immutable elements of thought but are formed and re-formed through experience" (Kolb, 2014, p. 26). Thus, learning is conceived as a process, not in terms of outcomes. Necessarily, the process of learning requires the resolution of conflicts, combining action and reflection. Thus, knowledge is conceived as a transformation process, not as an independent content to be acquired. Through experiential learning students construct information, learn by doing, and critically reflect on their own learning. According to Li and Li (2020, p. 509), learners in modules taught through experiential learning demonstrated "better multicultural comprehension and sensitivity, and they are well-prepared to connect theory with practice, and they have greater levels of confidence".

Three main benefits of experiential learning can be pointed out. First, the increase of student motivation and involvement, both in the definition of the problem being addressed and, in the process, used to solve it (Fidalgo et al., 2017). Second, it connects learning with the professional context (Gleason & Rubio, 2020), allowing the students to get closer to the reality of their community and to establish a network of relationships who contribute to their professional growth. Third, experiential learning facilitates the achievement of relevant learning and improve learners' workplace execution by building transversal competencies such as initiative, critical thinking, creativity, problem-solving, teamwork, communication, decision making, as well as the ability to address multi-faceted problems (Butler et al., 2019; Gezuraga and García, 2020).

Experiential learning can be applied to higher education through a variety of methodologies such as problem-based learning, project-based learning, service-learning, challenge-based learning, etc. The objective is the search for a concrete solution or the generation of a final product in response to a predefined real problem. The main components of experiential learning are usually the following (Fidalgo et al., 2017; Llorens- Largo, 2021):

- A case, problem or project that is meaningful to the student and has a connection to his or her environment.
- The students should search for a concrete solution or the generation of a final product in response to a real predefined problem.
- A real work environment: students work collaboratively in small groups solving more complex problems. Different student profiles are involved in a work team that will be oriented towards the same goal.
- A learning-by-doing approach in which students can make decisions based on the new knowledge they discover as they advance in the process.
- The teacher's role as mediator to promote appropriate circumstances for learning, making the student increasingly autonomous.

However, experiential learning also has some limitations. Among them, it should be noted that this type of learning is not suitable for exercising memory, or for basic and introductory learning (Ertmer and Newby, 1993). The fact that the focus of the learning process is a real situation or problem poses a certain difficulty. In addition, the contents are not as predetermined as in conventional teaching (Redondo-Duarte, 2012). On the other hand, students tend to focus more on the test than on the learning itself (Fidalgo et al., 2017).

The role of the teacher is essential for the successful implementation of experiential learning. It is the designer and facilitator of didactic situations, who, as an expert in the discipline, guides students to apply knowledge, providing appropriate and timely feedback for them to develop their competencies (Gleason and Rubio, 2020). However, the teacher should not only be a mediator of communication between students, but also a designer of the interactions so that students achieve the learning outcomes. In other words, the teacher must play the role of "orchestrator" regulating the interactions and adapting in real time the activities to what is happening in the classroom (Lipponen, 2023).

Thus, experiential learning is a very powerful framework for strengthening the links between education, work and personal development. On the one hand, it contributes to developing the skills demanded by the labor market, and, on the other hand, it responds to educational objectives, making it possible to integrate work in the classroom with the real world.

Two examples of experiential learning activities to promote diversity and inclusion at university are described below. The first of them is the initiative undertaken by Unie University in collaboration with The Core (School of Audiovisual Studies). During the academic year 2023-24, students from the Psychology and Audiovisual Communication programs were challenged to create an audiovisual piece about Autism at the University. This project resulted in the documentary "El Día a Día con Ana," which portrays the university experiences of Ana, a student with autism. The entire project was executed by students under the supervision of a faculty member from The Core Labs and the Diversity and Inclusion Unit. Eight students from various degree programs participated in this project, showcasing a multidisciplinary approach to experiential learning.

Figure 1. Documentary "El día a Día con Ana" (Unie Universidad)

Another example of experiential learning can be found in an educational innovation project conducted at the Faculty of Education at Universidad Complutense de Madrid during the 2022-2023 academic year. Faculty and students collaborated in designing and developing micro- videos[1] focused on student diversity and effective inclusive practices at the university (Macías et al., 2023). Each micro-video provides concrete and feasible guidelines for faculty to implement measures that address diversity and inclusion.

1.2. How Should the University Prepare Students to Work in a Diverse and Psychologically Healthy Environment?

Diversity and inclusion are key concepts in the management of modern work teams. Bassett-Jones et al. (2005), define it as a voluntary corporate strategy to address the demographic diversity experienced in the workplace. Diversity is defined as the visible and invisible differences that make individuals unique, such as gender, age, ethnicity, nationality, sexual orientation, disability, or professional experience. These differences include not only demographic aspects but also factors such as work styles, ways of thinking, and approaches to problem-solving.

The debate about inclusion is not centered on effectiveness or the improvement of practices, but rather on the ideological foundations underlying these practices. In this sense, Chinchilla and Cruz (2016) refer to diversity management as a voluntary strategy, not just a reaction to a particular legal framework. An inclusive climate promotes a sense of belonging, mutual respect, and values the contributions of each person to the organization. This requires policies that promote equal opportunities, flexible work arrangements, and open communication channels where all voices are heard. However, the mere presence of diversity does not guarantee its benefits if there is no authentic inclusive culture. Currently, 58% of companies do not consider this aspect relevant (Page Group, 2022).

Having teams composed of diverse individuals brings numerous advantages to organizations. First, diversity stimulates innovation and creativity by exposing team members to new perspectives. Each person brings his or her own life experiences, enriching the exchange of ideas. This translates into higher levels of productivity and ideas that drive the development of more competitive products and services. Nine percent of companies expect diversity to bring greater innovation, along with six percent who find it useful for entering new markets (Page Group, 2022). In this sense, a report elaborated by Boston Consulting Group (2018), concluded that companies in the top percentile for gender diversity achieve a 15% higher profitability than the industry average. In addition, diverse teams are usually more representative of the different clients and markets that companies serve. More than 35% of companies have adapted their selection processes to attract more diverse talent (Page Group, 2022).

Effectively managing diversity in the workplace is crucial to leveraging the competitive advantages that a diverse team brings and fostering an inclusive culture. According to Nishii and Mayer (2009), "diversity in work teams can enhance creativity and decision making, provided it is managed appropriately" (p. 1412). Students must develop cross-cultural and conflict resolution skills to successfully navigate diverse and multicultural work environments. A work environment where all individuals feel valued and respected, regardless of their differences, is crucial.

According to the McKinsey study "Why Diversity Matters" (2015), companies with greater diversity in their top management tend to be more profitable. Similarly, Novacek et al (2021) states that as many as 50% of employees have left a job because of diversity, equity and inclusion (hereinafter, DEI) issues. Conversely, when DEI is viewed as a tool to maximize people's advantage, inclusiveness extends to all employees. Companies have a once-in-a-lifetime opportunity to reinvent the workplace and become more resilient than ever.

Understanding diversity in higher education is an added value for the holistic development of the student. The exclusion of certain groups is often marked by a lack of knowledge of what is different, which causes distance, uncertainty, fear, unease or insecurity towards those who, in theory, are not like you (Tortosa & Pineda, 2021). Addressing diversity in higher education has become a regulatory requirement to which universities must respond and offer a commitment on the part of all those involved in education (Álvarez-Pérez et al., 2023). Therefore, these institutions must promote greater equity and equal opportunities, as well as social respect for the rights of all people.

Universities play a key role in the implementation of Sustainable Development Objective (SDG) 4 of the 2030 Agenda, promoting inclusive, equitable and quality education. In this context, García-Sánchez and Mulero-Mendigorri (2020) emphasize that the commitment of educational institutions to training professionals who are cognizant of socio-environmental challenges and to generating knowledge that addresses global issues is essential for achieving sustainable development. According to Pendones et al. (2021), the current dynamics of globalization and economic structural changes demand a higher level of academic preparation to access improved opportunities.

Schwab (2016), founder of the World Economic Forum, recently coined the term Fourth Industrial Revolution to describe society and the dawn of the future. The author points out that this latest revolution will not only change what we do, but also who we are, which affects our identity and all related areas. In this context, the university constitutes a constantly improving organization, whose key function is the production and dissemination of knowledge through qualified graduates. This enterprising institution focuses on the preparation of professionals of high value in the labor market, with new visions, high innovative development, capable of creating competitive proposals and developing qualitatively superior research (Cabrera et al., 2021). Herrera (2006) reflects on the process of refining a didactic approach that meets these high aspirations within the framework of the university-industry relationship. These ideas are based on the premise that within the instruction-education unit, education enhances the effectiveness and efficiency of instruction.

It is therefore evident that the gap between university and industry must be increasingly narrowed, creating a simulation space for students to adequately prepare them for the professional world. At a technical level, the use of simulation accelerates the learning process and contributes to improving its quality. The training can be repeated as many times as necessary to acquire the skills that will later be applied in practice. In addition, it allows real time feedback from teachers and peers, and reflection on the action, which allows a formative assessment (López, 2021). In this binomial, it is essential not to overlook the importance of competency preparation, ensuring that students can adapt optimally to their professional roles.

This approach leads to the effective performance of all professionals, fostering adaptability to changes in response to the demands of the global working world. In this borderless context, professionals must utilize new languages, respect cultural diversity, and engage in ongoing training in the use of ICTs, among other aspects, to ensure a climate of well-being (Romero et al., 2022).

2. BUILDING CONFIDENCE AND PSYCHOLOGICAL SAFETY IN STUDENT TEAMS

This section addresses the importance of fostering a collaborative and safe working environment in student teams. It emphasizes that, to achieve effective learning and development, it is crucial to create an environment of trust and openness where students feel comfortable expressing their ideas, share their perspectives and take risks.

2.1. Creating Psychological Safety at Work Starts at University

The topic of mental health in the professional setting has gained significant relevance and scholarly attention in recent years. The work environment can have both positive and negative impacts on an individual's well-being. On the one hand, a fulfilling job that contributes to personal growth and self-actualization can provide beneficial effects. On the other hand, stressful work conditions, inadequate work schedules, and potential situations of abuse or harassment can lead to detrimental impacts on the mental health of the employee (Allande-Cussó et al., 2022). Some data and findings related to mental health in the workplace are the following:

- Prevalence of mental health problems: According to the World Health Organization (2022), it is estimated that over 264 million people worldwide suffer from depression, and many others experience anxiety and other mental disorders. These problems also impact work environments and can have a significant impact on employees' productivity and well-being.

- Work-related stress: Work-related stress is a common issue in many work teams. A study conducted by the European Agency for Safety and Health at Work (2022) found that approximately 50% of European workers reported feeling stressed by their work. Chronic stress can have negative effects on employees' mental and physical health.
- Economic impact: Mental health problems in work teams also have a significant economic impact. The World Health Organization (2022) reports that mental and neurological disorders are estimated to cost the global economy approximately $1 trillion annually in lost productivity.
- The importance of promoting mental health in the workplace: More and more organizations are recognizing the significance of addressing mental health concerns within the professional setting. Cultivating a healthy work environment that encourages trust, open communication, and mutual support can help prevent the development of mental health problems and enhance overall employee well-being.

According to Allande-Cussó et al., (2022), "a negative work situation can trigger the development of serious mental disorders such as psychotic disorders, neurotic disorders, cognitive disorders, work stress disorders, psychoactive substance abuse disorders and self-injurious disorders" (p.1). Thus, from the universities, we must work so that our students are able to generate work environments where there is psychological security. This concept is defined as the ability to show feelings without fear of negative consequences to a team member's self-image, status or career (Arias, 2014). Psychological safety is a key determinant of high-quality communication, trust and decision making in a team (O'donovan & McAuliffe; 2020a; Kim et al., 2020), and is related to intrinsic motivation and innovative work behavior (Wu et al., 2021).

Creating a psychologically safe environment in the workplace has a direct influence on work performance. Some of its benefits include more effective conflict management by team members, acceptance of more risks, taking on new roles and responsibilities, and even having fun at work. According to Bring et al (1998), when individuals face psychological threats or feel psychologically insecure, they are more inclined to exhibit defensive tendencies rather than demonstrate innovative behaviors. Thus, it is a key mission for the universities to train change-oriented leaders that enable psychological safety (O'Donovan and McAuliffe, 2020b).

2.2. A Team Role Model to Foster Psychological Safety in Student Teams

Self-esteem directly influences the behavior of individuals and affects the promotion of psychological well-being, since the way in which the individual evaluates him/herself has repercussions in all areas of social, emotional, intellectual, behavioral and academic development (Pendones, 2021). From the universities, we should prepare professionals capable of successfully solving social problems and directing their lives to progress in their university career. Likewise, it is essential to train leaders that promote psychological safety through inclusive leadership behaviors, good interpersonal relationships and supportive organizational practices (O'Donovan and McAuliffe, 2020b).

To this end, we propose a team role model to foster psychological safety in student teams. This model is based on collaborative work as a fundamental pillar to promote psychological safety and effective learning. Thus, students are no longer passive receivers of knowledge, but are required to actively participate in their learning process, share ideas, solve problems and work together towards common goals (Almendros et al., 2021). Educational research corroborates how collaborative learning promotes the principles of democratic education, fosters the active participation of students and allows progress towards the postulates of inclusive education (Sanahuja et al., 2023).

The team role model developed by Meredith Belbin has become a widely used and recognized tool in the field of teamwork and organizational development. This model provides a solid framework for understanding the dynamics and performance of work teams (Belbin, 2013):

- The need to have a variety of profiles and complementary skills within a team.
- The importance of self-awareness and self-knowledge of team members. By identifying and understanding their own tendencies and preferences, team members can better adapt to the roles they play and maximize their strengths.
- The development and evolution of teams through their different stages: formation, storming, normalization and performance.

This model is often used in the business context from Human Resources departments or leadership training, but it is perfectly transferable to the university classroom.

Belbin (2013) argues that a team role refers to the way of behaving, contributing and relating to other people at work. Although some of the roles are natural, other ones may be adopted by the individual, and some may even be discovered after being adopted. The types and subtypes of roles proposed by Belbin are shown below in Figure 2.

Figure 2. Belbin's model roles (Own elaboration based on Belbin, 2013)

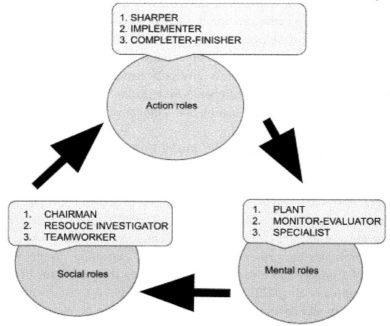

Based on Belbin's and Johnson et al (1997) research, we propose a team role model to foster psychological safety in student teams (see Figure 2 below). **Self-esteem** is at the center of the model. Different studies have shown the existence of a close relationship between the degree of self-esteem and academic performance (Rice, 2000). According to Ferradás et al., (2015) the student's beliefs about their competence to perform certain academic activities is a factor that derives from self-esteem and self-efficacy. These concepts form a virtuous circle when they allow students to obtain good results, but they become a brake on learning when students do not have a good assessment of themselves. This will lead to a higher level of emotional maladjustment and a high tendency to depression and anxiety (González, 2018).

The **role of the team leader** (or driver, according to Belbin's model) is fundamental in the model. He or she must be able to perform multiple roles within the team, acting as a facilitator who balances and coordinates the different contributions of the group members. An effective leader, according to Belbin (2013), must know how to identify and leverage the strengths of each team member, assigning responsibilities in a way that complements each other and maximizes the collective potential. Additionally, the leader must be flexible and adapt to the changing needs of the project, fostering collaboration and open communication among team members.

Within the framework of a preventive culture of psychological safety, it is important to establish a **clear role definition** where each team member knows what he/she must do, how to do it and what is expected of him/her. The team must jump from "knowing" to "asking", accepting that they do not have all the answers. To this end, it is essential to be clear about the roles that the students will play in the activity.

The **feeling of belonging** and usefulness within a peer group helps to establish the self-concept. According to Luna and Molero (2013), self-concept is very important in the formation of personality, because by developing a positive self-concept from adolescence, psychological and pedagogical problems are avoided. Íñiguez (2016) determined that young people with a high self-concept will have greater independence. It will be easier for them to assume responsibilities and they will have more resistance to frustration, so their relationships with others will be healthier and more balanced. On the other hand, people with a low self-concept will find it difficult to trust their personal skills and abilities, so they will feel undervalued by others and their way of acting will be defensive.

Subsequently, **co-creation** must be cultivated by seeking input from others and understanding an idea before reacting to it. The leader must also create opportunities for co-creation. This process means a profound democratization, decentralization of value creation, which will no longer be centered on the company, but will include interactions with customers, suppliers, partners and employees (Gouillart and Ramaswamy, 2012).

Figure 3. Team role model to foster psychological safety in student teams (Own elaboration)

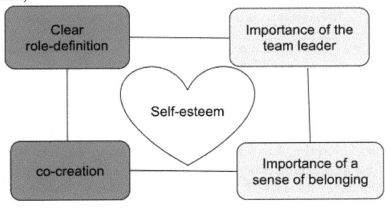

2.3. Constructive Feedback Strategies to Promote Psychological Safety in Student Teams

A major obstacle in collaborative work is that people find it difficult to deal with critical comments about themselves. Many of our students are reluctant to teamwork because they are not comfortable providing and/ or receiving feedback from their peers. Some of the problems they face are related to the fact that they do not know how to call their peers' attention to situations they are unhappy with without appearing aggressive or rude. In the workplace these situations are not much different. In fact, some workers are completely unaware of others' perceptions and have a difficult time dealing with critical feedback about themselves. At the heart of the matter is the fact that our students do not know how to give constructive feedback to their peers or how to receive it.

Positive feedback gives us specific information to help us improve. Among its benefits, it can be highlighted the following (Flanagan, 2017): It creates enthusiasm, makes expectations clear from the start, strengthens relationships, builds confidence and self-esteem, demonstrates care and involvement, and gives us specific information to help us improve. It is important that teachers provide guidelines for students to be able to give constructive and effective feedback to their peers. Table 1 shows some examples of constructive feedback according to different dimensions of collaborative work.

Table 1. Constructive feedback examples

Dimension	Example of feedback
Expectation	"Let's distribute the tasks to be performed by each one of us. What aspects of the task would you like to develop?"
Observation	"During the last two meetings, you barely said anything. We are sure you have very interesting ideas to contribute, and we would like to hear about them".
Assessment	"I have reviewed all the work and I think there are some areas that we need to improve. For example, in section 1 there is a lack of examples".
Consequence	"The delivery date is approaching, and section 5 has not yet been prepared. Please, can you finish it? It should be ready tomorrow".

Source: own elaboration.

Giving and receiving feedback is not an easy task. In this sense, the SARA feedback model (Surprise, Annoyance, Anger and Rejection) can help the students understand the natural progression of their reactions when giving and receiving feedback. The stages of the SARA model are described below (Flanagan, 2017):

- Shock: The initial reaction to receiving feedback is often surprising, especially if the feedback is unexpected or not aligned with the individual's self-

perception. Some of the feelings can be: "What?" "I don't understand how they could feel this way about me".
- Anger: surprise is replaced by anger or anxiety. "How dare they?" or "I'm frustrated that my hard work isn't being recognized, and instead, I'm being criticized".
- Resistance: during this stage, we try to make sense of the feedback. We can experience a period of resistance and denial.
- Acceptance: it is the final stage of the SARA model. As we process the feedback, we come to a point of acceptance. At this point, the student can think about what they need to change. Some questions students may ask themselves are: What do I need to consider? What can I do? Who could help me?

In the process of providing and receiving feedback it is very important to know ourselves, as our level of self-knowledge can greatly influence our interactions with others. The Johari Window, created by Joseph Luft and Harrington Ingham, can be a good feedback tool to improve the effectiveness of group interactions. The model is based on two ideas: (1) confidence can be acquired by revealing information about yourself to a group; (2) self-knowledge can be developed with team feedback. The Johari window illustrates the process of giving and receiving feedback. As it is shown in Figure 3, it consists of four areas (Luft, 1961):

- Open area. It corresponds to what each person knows about him/herself and is also known to others.
- Hidden area. This includes what each person knows about him/herself but does not deliberately make known to others. It is possible for others to pick it up indirectly, but not by each person's own will.
- Blind area. It corresponds to the aspects that a person does not know about him/herself, but that others do know or, at least, perceive. In general, it includes unconscious behaviors.
- Unknown area. Those elements that a person is unaware of him/herself and that others are also unaware of. Through self-discovery and mutual exploration, some of this unknown information can move to the open area.

Figure 4. Johari window(Luft, 1961, p.1)

	Known to Self	Not Known to Self
Know to Others	I Area of Free Activity	II Blind Area
Not Known to Others	III Avoided or Hidden Area	IV Area of Unknown Activity

By sharing information and being open to feedback, students can increase their open area, reduce the blind spot and hidden area, and enhance mutual understanding and trust within a group. To use the Johari Window with our students in the classroom, it is important that they first conduct a self- reflection to identify characteristics they believe are known to themselves and others (open area) and those know only to themselves (hidden area). Subsequently, it is necessary to organize activities where students give and receive feedback from their peers. At this point, it is important that they share their observations in a constructive and respectful manner.

3. ACTIVITIES TO PROMOTE DIVERSE AND INCLUSIVE TEAMS AT UNIVERSITY

Inclusive education in higher education institutions is an ethical and social imperative that promotes equal opportunities and respect for diversity (Escorial, 2023). According to Williams et al. (2020), the effective implementation of diversity and inclusion initiatives in higher education institutions requires a participatory approach that involves multiple stakeholders. Attention to diversity should focus on promoting real equality, removing barriers and implementing the necessary support to ensure the academic success of all students. The following is a set of activities and programs to promote diverse and inclusive team building at the university.

a) Hackathons

Hackathons are collaborative events where participants gather in teams to find solutions to complex, real problems or to improve a certain product or service in a given space and time. This generates a very attractive climate of knowledge, since all participants will be able to learn from each other. The common goal of the challenge is something that all participants will pursue, although each one will approach it in different ways. Thus, it opens the door to debates about the pros and cons of what they are trying to develop. Cristóbal and Rubio (2022) point out the advantages of participating in this type of space as a challenging and enriching personal experience, promoting creative freedom in a context of horizontality, encouraging open collaboration, decision making and the generation of new community networks and peer learning, among others.

Hackathons can promote experience learning and a diverse culture since participants are generally of different profiles and ages so that there is a diversity of perspectives and opinions. To this end, they are usually formed in small work teams, and each one contributes what they know how to do and learns to work collaboratively by sharing knowledge. The hackathons also allow students to approach a project from the STEM (Science, Technology, Engineering and Math) approach in which Science, Technology, Engineering and Mathematics are worked as a single discipline allowing to go deeper into the essence of the problem to be solved. The following are two examples of hackathons carried out in Spanish universities.

The Faculty of Economics and Business at Universidad de León (Spain), in collaboration with the General Foundation of the University of León and Business (FGULEM), organized the second edition of Idea-T ULE. This event is part of the University-Business Knowledge Transfer Plan 2023-2024 (TCUE Plan) and aims to foster innovation, university entrepreneurship, and multidisciplinary experimentation. Four large companies are participating by presenting business challenges that the competing teams will need to address.

Another case in point is that of the Chair of Commercial Innovation at the University of Zaragoza (Spain), in collaboration with the Zaragoza Chamber of Commerce, organized a Commercial Innovation Hackathon. The primary objective of this event is to cultivate creativity, entrepreneurship, and innovation among students, with the specific aim of promoting and revitalizing local commerce within the autonomous community of Aragon. Students from diverse academic disciplines are encouraged to collaborate in teams to devise innovative solutions to enhance commercial activities. The hackathon is strategically designed to stimulate the local economy while providing students with invaluable hands-on learning experiences. Participants will be awarded diplomas, and the top three projects will receive a monetary prize of €500 each, in addition to elective academic credits.

b) Buddy Programs

Buddy Programs are based on a cooperative, student-centered active and experiential learning methodology. According to Moliner and Alegre (2020), "the social implications of peer tutoring are also valuable, as they foster student inclusion and improve the classroom climate" (p.1). Different psychological variables have been widely addressed in this field, such as anxiety or attitude towards different subjects. Peer mentoring programs and successful academic outcomes have been associated with student success. Therefore, many institutions have allocated significant resources to new student adjustment programs (Arco-Tirado et al., 2019).

We strongly recommend the implementation of mentoring or Buddy Programs in universities. Freshmen, in addition to being assisted by university services, have a reference figure among the students of previous years. These programs should focus mainly on two aspects. On the one hand, the possibility for freshmen to receive academic support from another student in a higher course (Buddy student) who is taking the same degree, and who can serve as a guide, support and consultation on specific doubts. Second, freshmen can receive social support to better integrate into the university, get to know the university's spaces and facilities, meet other students, etc. It is important that the Buddy student be competent in active listening, empathy, social and communication skills, as well as having conflict resolution tools.

Our proposal suggests providing training for Buddy students on three fundamental axes: (1) academic support among peers, (2) active listening and empathy, and (3) conflict resolution. In addition, the participants can be provided with a script sheet and a template to be filled in at the beginning and end of the course, so that they have one or two clear objectives to work on throughout the year.

Common features of these buddy programs include the awarding of university credits for participation, a duration of one academic year, and the requirement to complete mandatory activities, including training sessions. There are many universities that offer buddy programs to international students. For example, at Linnaeus University (Sweden), every year, approximately 800-900 international students enroll in the Buddy program. Buddies and newbies are matched in two rounds each semester to create a diverse environment. It is also worth mentioning the buddy program of Universidad Carlos III (Spain), which offers numerous benefits to both international and veteran students, including credit recognition for veteran students who provide support.

c) Blind Soccer Tournament

Sport should be understood as a normalizing and social inclusion tool (Pérez-Tejero et al., 2012). Sport in the university context allows the promotion of social relations among students, promotes the spirit of self-improvement, and contributes to the adaptation of students to the fulfillment of a series of rules for its practice (Fuentes, 2015). In this sense, we strongly recommend the participation of the university community in an interuniversity blind soccer tournament. This is an inclusive activity, in which students with visual impairment or blindness can participate, as well as students who do not have this condition.

This is a playful way to raise awareness of the experiences that a blind person could live. As an example, Unie Universidad (Spain) participated in the II Blind Soccer Tournament organized by Universidad Politécnica de Madrid and the Special Employment Center (CEE), Integra. The satisfaction of the students who attended was 9.75 out of 10 and 100% would recommend a colleague to participate in this activity next year. Some qualitative impressions of the students were the following: "We have tried a different sport and it has helped us to empathize and understand the world of the blind. In addition, we have bonded as a team". "Learning and getting to know something new and meeting new teammates! I loved it!".

d) Commemoration of Diversity Days

Doria and Manjarrés-Rodelo (2020) found that, after concluding an awareness program, 100% of teachers and administrators, respectively, considered it important to talk about inclusion in schools and were more interested in the elimination of barriers presented by students. According to Escorial (2023), awareness-raising through programs for teaching staff and the broader university community is essential to promote the real inclusion of all students. Awareness-raising should enable: (1) Inclusive and quality education; (2) Bio-psycho-social vision of disability (awareness of the comprehensive perspective on disability); (3) Breaking Negative Beliefs and Stereotypes; (4) Encouraging positive attitudes towards diversity and equal opportunities; (5) Facilitating tools and methods for educational adaptation.

One of the key strategies for transforming a university into an inclusive space is to foster awareness. Celebrating significant days, such as International Disability Day (December 3), Women's Day (March 8), and the Day Against Homophobia, Biphobia, and Transphobia (March 17), among others, serves as an effective approach. These celebrations provide opportunities to unite, inspire, and continue working together towards a more equitable future.

One of the earliest experiences in Latin American universities is from the Universidad Pedagógica Experimental Libertador, specifically the Pedagogical Institute of Caracas (Venezuela). A notable success story is the conference held on December 3, 2013, titled "Breaking Barriers, Opening Doors: For an Inclusive Society." This event, organized by the Special Education Department of the Caracas Pedagogical Institute, featured twelve interactive sessions designed to facilitate encounters between people with disabilities and the university community.

An illustrative example is the celebration of Women's Day on March 8, 2024, at Unie University (Spain). This event not only underscored the progress made but also prompted critical reflection on the ongoing challenges in achieving gender equality. The event was meticulously organized by students from the Buddy Program and various university clubs, and it featured Alicia Rouco, a researcher from the European Space Agency, who engaged in an informal yet profound discussion with the students. The primary objective of the event was to cultivate an environment where all women felt empowered and supported. The event witnessed substantial participation, with over 75 students attending, and it garnered an average satisfaction rating of 9.3 out of 10. Additionally, 100% of the respondents indicated they would recommend such awareness talks to their peers, demonstrating the event's success in fostering awareness and engagement.

On December 3, 2023, in commemoration of the International Day of Disability, the Universidad Autónoma de Madrid (Spain) hosted an event titled "Leave Your Mark." This event aimed to promote the rights and well-being of individuals with disabilities across various societal and developmental spheres. Additionally, the event sought to raise awareness regarding the conditions and challenges faced by people with disabilities in political, social, economic, and cultural contexts.

e) Safe Points

Camas (2015) argues that in contemporary democratic societies, equality is a fundamental principle for coexistence. It is a principle that binds all people in dignity, respect and rights, regardless of their condition or circumstance. Thus, from the universities we must create safe spaces so that the entire university community develops their activity within the values of respect, tolerance, pride, and inclusion.

To this end, we propose to create a network of safe points. These would be like the violet points that offer tools and spaces for reporting and preventing gender violence, but extended to anyone who may feel bad, harassed or violated. This initiative can be accompanied by information so that the affected person can know the next steps. It is also recommendable to carry out training actions for the prevention of harassment in all its aspects. Thus, associations or experts in this field should be involved to share with the university community tools to deal with bullying, strategies to identify and report it, etc. This would be another measure in the framework of the bullying protocol and coexistence plan of universities.

The implementation of violet dot initiatives in leading international universities demonstrates effective strategies for addressing gender-based violence. For example, at Stanford University, the SPECTRA program offers a comprehensive array of services, including mandatory violence prevention training for all students, accessible reporting facilities, and counseling and support groups. For its part, the "Our Strength Is" program at Harvard University is a pioneering initiative that includes comprehensive training for all students, open dialogues with student leaders, awareness campaigns, and well-defined reporting and support protocols. Finally, it is worth mentioning Oxford University, with a holistic approach that encompasses education, early intervention, victim support, and policy reforms. The introduction of their program has led to an increase in reporting, suggesting heightened awareness and a greater propensity to report incidents.

The "Espacio Violeta" of the University of Valencia (Spain) is a resource established by the Equality Unit to prevent gender violence within the university community and to respond to incidents as necessary. These preventive and intervention measures are outlined in the III Plan for Equality and are executed by a technical team comprising a psychologist and a lawyer, with support from the University Security Department and coordination by the Equality Unit. The initiative also benefits from the collaboration of a network of volunteers (students, faculty, and staff), who play a crucial role in raising awareness among the university population, as well as informing and supporting individuals affected by gender violence across different campuses.

The IV Equality Plan of the University of Málaga (Spain), specifically in its seventh axis, includes six measures related to the prevention of gender violence. One of the notable actions taken in 2020 was the establishment of violet points on all university campuses, creating spaces free from gender violence. At these violet points, members of the university community who are victims of abuse, harassment, aggression, or sexist discrimination can receive assistance, information, and support.

4. LESSONS LEARNED

According to Bauman (2003), liquid modernity, whose axis is no longer the work ethic but the aesthetics of consumption, has supplanted the institutional structures of the previous stage, which provided security and confidence in the future. These structures have been replaced with others that are much more transitory and less solid, and therefore incapable of orienting and giving long-term meaning to individual and collective life.

In this context of liquid modernity, where transitory structures and the aesthetics of consumption prevail, higher education institutions play a key role in preparing students for diverse and psychologically healthy working environments. This responsibility is approached from different perspectives. Firstly, it is crucial to promote an inclusive organizational culture within universities, fostering a sense of belonging and mutual respect. This will enable students to develop holistically and acquire competences to maximize the benefits of diversity in work teams. Academic institutions should also create simulation spaces that replicate the demands of the professional world, providing not only technical skills, but also adaptive competences for dynamic and globalized work contexts.

Second, it is essential to foster trust and psychological safety in student teams, creating learning environments where individuals feel comfortable to express ideas, share perspectives and take risks. This will lay the foundation for the effective development of the skills required for professional success. In the workplace, mental health is an increasingly relevant and globally studied issue. Mental health problems, such as depression, anxiety and chronic stress, have a significant impact on the productivity and well-being of employees, as well as representing an important economic cost for organizations and society in general.

Given this situation, it is crucial that universities prepare future professionals to create healthy work environments, with psychological safety, open communication and mutual support. This is the only way to create workplaces that protect and promote the mental health of employees, maximizing their well-being and performance.

REFERENCES

Allande- Cussó, R., García, J. J., Facundo, J., Navarro, Y., Climent, J.A., Gómez, J. (2022). Salud mental y trastornos mentales en los lugares de trabajo. *Revista Española de Salud Pública*, 96, 1–11.

Almendros, P., Montoya, M., & Pablo-Lerchundi, I. (2021). Flipped classroom and collaborative learning in chemistry. *Educación en la Química*, 32(4), 142–153. DOI: 10.22201/fq.18708404e.2021.5.78412

Álvarez-Pérez, P. R., González-Benítez, N., & López-Aguilar, D. (2023). Perspectivas y retos de una universidad inclusiva desde un enfoque psicopedagógico. *Revista Costarricense de Orientación*, 2(2), 1–15. Advance online publication. DOI: 10.54413/rco.v2i2.34

Arco-Tirado, J. L., Fernández-Martín, F. D., & Hervás-Torres, M. (2020). Evidence-based peer-tutoring program to improve students' performance at the university. *Studies in Higher Education*, 45(11), 2190–2202. DOI: 10.1080/03075079.2019.1597038

Arias, M. I. B. (2014). Efectos del conocimiento compartido y la seguridad psicológica en la eficacia de los equipos de trabajo. *Criterio Libre*, 12(20), 185–198. DOI: 10.18041/1900-0642/criteriolibre.2014v12n20.232

Baran, B. E., & Woznyj, H. M. (2020). Managing VUCA: The human dynamics of agility. *Organizational Dynamics*, 100787(Aug), DOI: 10.1016/j.orgdyn.2020.100787 PMID: 32843777

Bassett-Jones, N. (2005). The paradox of diversity management, creativity and innovation. *Creativity and Innovation Management*, 14(2), 169–175. DOI: 10.1111/j.1467-8691.00337.x

Bauman, Z. (2003). *Modernidad líquida*. Fondo de Cultura Económica.

Belbin, M. (2013). *Roles de Equipo en el trabajo*. Belbin Spain & Latam.

Boston Consulting Group. (17th May of 2018). It's time to Reimagine Diversity, Equity & Inclusion. https://www.bcg.com/press/1june2021-necessary-redefine-the-diversity-policies-equity-and-inclusion-in-companies

Butler, M. G., Church, K. S., & Spencer, A. W. (2019). Do, reflect, think, apply: Experiential education in accounting. *Journal of Accounting Education*, 48, 12–21. DOI: 10.1016/j.jaccedu.2019.05.001

Cabrera, H., Rodríguez Pérez, B., León González, J. L., & Medina León, A. (2021). Bases y oportunidades de la vinculación universidad-empresa. *Revista Universidad y Sociedad, 13*(1), 300-306. https://rus.ucf.edu.cu/index.php/rus/article/view/1926

Camas, F. (2015). La emergencia de la igualdad de género. Cambios y persistencias de las actitudes de las y los jóvenes en España (1994-2010). [Doctoral thesis, Universidad de Granada, Granada, Spain].

Carmona, C. E. (2021). *Ámbitos para el aprendizaje: una propuesta interdisciplinar.* Ediciones Octaedro.

Chinchilla, N., & Cruz, H. (2016). Diversidad y paradigmas de empresa: Un nuevo enfoque. *Revista Empresa y Humanismo*, 14(1), 47–79. DOI: 10.15581/015.14.4259

Cote, C. (28th of March, 2024). How to build a psychologically safe workplace. https://online.hbs.edu/blog/post/psychological-safety-in-the-workplace

Cox, T., Griffiths, A. J., & Rial-González, E. (2000). *Research on work-related stress.* Agencia Europea para la Seguridad y la Salud en el Trabajo. Oficina de Publicaciones Oficiales de las Comunidades Europeas. http://agency.osha.eu.int/publications/reports/stress

Cristóbal, E. P., & Rubio, L. A. (2022). Los hackathones como herramientas para trabajar las competencias de emprendimiento en economía azul fuera de las aulas: Experiencia de la universidad de Cádiz a través del laboratorio social Coedpa. In C. Hervás-Gómez; C. Corujo; A.M., de la Calle and L. Alcántara (Eds). *Formación del profesorado y metodologías activas en la educación del siglo XXI* (pp. 1008-1029). Dykinson.

Doria Dávila, D. P., & Manjarrés-Rodelo, M. M. (2020). Educación inclusiva: programa de sensibilización en una institución educativa de Sincelejo-Sucre. *RHS-Revista Humanismo Y Sociedad, 8*(1), 6–21. https://doi.org/DOI: 10.22209/rhs.v8n1a01

Elizondo Carmona, C. (2022). *Ámbitos para el aprendizaje.* Octaedro., DOI: 10.47916/9788418615221

Ertmer, P. A., & Newby, T. J. (1993). Conductismo, cognitivismo y constructivismo: Una comparación de los aspectos críticos desde la perspectiva del diseño de la instrucción. *Performance Improvement Quarterly*, 6(4), 50–72. DOI: 10.1111/j.1937-8327.1993.tb00605.x

Escorial, S. (25th-27th October 2023). *La universidad en el s.XXI: La educación inclusiva como eje estratégico.* VI Congreso Discapacidad y Universidad. Universidad de Salamanca y Fundación ONCE, Salamanca, Spain.

Ferradás, M. M., Freire, C., Regueiro, B., Piñeiro, I., Rodríguez, S., & Valle, A. (2015). Estrategias de self-handicapping en estudiantes universitarios. Diferencias entre cursos [Self-handicapping strategies in university students. Differences between courses]. *Revista de Estudios e Investigación en Psicología y Educación. Extr.*, 1, 63–66. DOI: 10.17979/reipe.2015.0.01.345

Fidalgo, A., Sein-Echaluce, M. L., & García, J. (2017). Aprendizaje basado en Retos en una asignatura académica universitaria. *Revista Iberoamericana de Informática Educativa*, 25, 1–8.

Flanagan, S. (2017). *Penn State Performance Management: Giving and receiving feedback*. Penn State University. https://hr.psu.edu/sites/hr/files/GivingAndReceivingFeedbackIndividualContributor.pdf

Fuentes-Guerra, F. J. (2015). *El deporte en el marco de la Educación Física*. Wanceulen.

Fundación Universia. (2017). *Universidad y discapacidad. IV Estudio sobre el grado de inclusión del sistema universitario español respecto de la realidad de la discapacidad.* Comité Español de Representantes de Personas con Discapacidad-CERMI. http://riberdis.cedid.es/handle/11181/5632

García-Sánchez, I. M., & Mulero-Mendigorri, E. (2020). La Agenda 2030 y los Objetivos de Desarrollo Sostenible: Retos y oportunidades para las universidades españolas. *Revista Española del Tercer Sector*, 45, 175–190.

Gezuraga, M., & García, A. (2020). Recepciones de la pedagogía experiencial de Dewey en diversos enfoques metodológicos: El valor añadido del aprendizaje-servicio. *Educatio Siglo XXI*, 38(3), 295–316. DOI: 10.6018/educatio.452921

Gleason, M. A., & Julio, E. (2020). Implementación del aprendizaje experiencial en la universidad, sus beneficios en el alumnado y el rol docente. *Review of Education*, 44(2), 2215–2644. DOI: 10.15517/revedu.v44i2.40197

González, B. (2018). ¿Cómo mejorar el aprendizaje? Influencia de la autoestima en el aprendizaje del estudiante universitario. *Revista Complutense De Educación*, 30(3), 781–795. DOI: 10.5209/rced.58899

Gonzalez-Mulé, E., & Cockburn, B. S. (2021). Worked to death: The relationships of work hours and worked outcomes with mortality. *Academy of Management Journal*, 64(1), 276–302. DOI: 10.5465/ambpp.2015.10934abstract

Gouillart, F., & Ramaswamy, V. (2012). *La co-creación de valor y experiencias*. Temas Grupo Editorial.

Hartwig, A., Clarke, S., Johnson, S., & Willis, S. (2020). Workplace team resilience: A systematic review and conceptual development. *Organizational Psychology Review*, 10(3-4), 169–200. DOI: 10.1177/2041386620919476

Henao-Villa, C. F., García-Arango, D. A., Aguirre-Mesa, E. D., González-García, A., Bracho-Aconcha, R., Solorzano-Movilla, J. G., & Arboleda-Lopez, A. P. (2017). Multidisciplinariedad, interdisciplinariedad y transdisciplinariedad en la formación para la investigación en ingeniería. *Revista Lasallista de Investigacion*, 14(1), 179–197. DOI: 10.22507/rli.v14n1a16

Herrera, J. (2006). El vínculo universidad – empresa en la formación de los profesionales universitarios. *Actualidades Investigativas en Educación*, 19(2), 1–30. DOI: 10.15517/aie.v6i2.9208

Hidalgo, D. A. Z., & Román, F. Q. (2023). El aula invertida en el trabajo colaborativo en estudiantes de una universidad pública peruana. *Horizontes.Revista de Investigación en Ciencias de la Educación*, 7(31), 2433–2447. DOI: 10.33996/revistahorizontes.v7i31.675

Horstmeyer, A. (2020). The generative role of curiosity in soft skills development for contemporary VUCA environments. *Journal of Organizational Change Management*, 33(5), 737–751. DOI: 10.1108/JOCM-08-2019-0250

Hunt, V., Layton, D., & Prince, S. (2015). *Why Diversity Matters*. McKinsey & Company. https://www.mckinsey.com/capabilities/people-and-organizational-performance/our-insights/why-diversity-matters

Iñiguez Fuentes, M. S. (2016). *Influencia de la familia en el autoconcepto y la empatía de los adolescentes* [Doctoral thesis, Universitat de València, Spain]. https://www.educacion.gob.es/teseo/imprimirFicheroTesis.do?idFichero=v%2Bt%2FRFMi%2Fbc%3D

Johnson, D. W., Johnson, R. T., & Smith, K. A. (1997). *El Aprendizaje Cooperativo regresa a la Universidad: ¿qué evidencia existe de que funciona?* Retrieved from: https://www.researchgate.net/publication/267940683_El_Aprendizaje_Cooperativo_regresa_a_la_Universidad_que_evidencia_existe_de_que_funciona#fullTextFileContent

Kim, S., Lee, H., & Connerton, T. P. (2020). How psychological safety affects team performance: Mediating role of efficacy and learning behavior. *Frontiers in Psychology*, 11, 1581. DOI: 10.3389/fpsyg.2020.01581 PMID: 32793037

Kolb, D. (2014). *Experiential Learning: Experience as the Source of Learning and Development*. Pearson Education.

Li, J., & Li, Y. (2021). The role of grit on students' academic success in experiential learning context. *Frontiers in Psychology*, 12, 774149. DOI: 10.3389/fpsyg.2021.774149 PMID: 34733225

Lipponen, L. (2023). Exploring foundations for computer-supported collaborative learning. In Stahl, G. (Ed.), *Computer support for collaborative learning* (pp. 72–81). Routledge. DOI: 10.4324/9781315045467-12

López Esquivel, N. G. (2021). Simulación clínica como método innovador de enseñanza-aprendizaje en las carreras de Medicina de la Universidad del Pacífico. *Revista Multidisciplinar UP, 2*(2), 13–23. https://www.upacifico.edu.py:8043/index.php/Rev_MUP/article/view/199

Luft, J. (1961). The johari window. *Human relations training news, 5*(1), 6-7.

Luna, M., & Molero, D. (2013). Revisión teórica sobre el autoconcepto y su importancia en la adolescencia. (2013). *Revista Electrónica de Investigación y Docencia (REID), 10*. https://revistaselectronicas.ujaen.es/index.php/reid/article/view/991

Macías, M. E., ... (2023). Proyecto de innovación y mejora de la calidad docente. Convocatoria 2022/2023. Diseño de micro vídeos para el profesorado sobre diversidad y buenas prácticas inclusivas para el alumnado universitario. https://docta.ucm.es/rest/api/core/bitstreams/3d46fb73-1da8-4aa5-9843-4f646ddd0e56/content

Martínez Cantos, J. (2020). Políticas de igualdad y diversidad. In F. J. García Castaño, M. C. López Sánchez & C. Torrego Seco (dirs.), *Educación inclusiva* (pp. 727-745). Ediciones Pirámide.

Moliner, L., & Alegre, F. (2020). Efectos de la tutoría entre iguales en el autoconcepto matemático de los estudiantes de secundaria. *PLoS One*, 15(4), E0231410. DOI: 10.1371/journal.pone.0231410 PMID: 32275730

Nishii, L. H., & Mayer, D. M. (2009). Do inclusive leaders help to reduce turnover in diverse groups? The moderating role of leader–member exchange in the diversity to turnover relationship. *The Journal of Applied Psychology*, 94(6), 1412–1426. DOI: 10.1037/a0017190 PMID: 19916652

Novacek, G., Lee, J., & Krentz, M. (2021). *It's time to reimagine diversity, equity, and inclusion. Leading in the new reality. Resilience.* Boston Consulting Group. https://web-assets.bcg.com/0b/c4/c45a07e54f48ae0dc784667a66dd/bcg-its-time-to-reimagine-diversity-equity-and-inclusion-may-2021-r.pdf

O'donovan, R., & McAuliffe, E. (2020a). A systematic review exploring the content and outcomes of interventions to improve psychological safety, speaking up and voice behavior. *BMC Health Services Research*, 20(1), 1–11. DOI: 10.1186/s12913-020-4931-2 PMID: 32041595

O'donovan, R., & Mcauliffe, E. (2020b). A systematic review of factors that enable psychological safety in healthcare teams. *International Journal for Quality in Health Care : Journal of the International Society for Quality in Health Care*, 32(4), 240–250. DOI: 10.1093/intqhc/mzaa025 PMID: 32232323

Organización Mundial de la Salud. (20th May 2024). Salud mental. https://www.who.int/es/health-topics/mental-health

Page Group. (20th May 2024). *Estudio sobre diversidad e inclusión 2022*. https://www.michaelpage.es/sites/michaelpage.es/files/2022-06/MP_ES_Estudio_Diversidad_Inclusi%C3%B3n_2022.pdf

Pendones, J. A., Flores, Y., Espino, G., & Durán, F. A. (2021). Autoconcepto, autoestima, motivación y su influencia en el desempeño académico. Caso: Alumnos de la carrera de Contador Público. *RIDE Revista Iberoamericana para la Investigación y el Desarrollo Educativo*, 12(23). Advance online publication. DOI: 10.23913/ride.v12i23.1008

Pérez-Tejero, J., Ocete, C., Ortega-Vila, G., & Coterón, J. (2012). Diseño y aplicación de un programa de intervención de práctica deportiva inclusiva y su efecto sobre la actitud hacia la discapacidad: El Campus Inclusivo de Baloncesto. *Revista Internacional de Ciencias del Deporte, 8*(29), 258– 271. https://doi.org/http://dx.doi.org/10.5232/ricyde2012.0 2905

Redondo- Duarte. S. (2012). *Evaluación de la aplicación del modelo pedagógico de UEM personal a estudios universitarios de grado y postgrado en modalidad online* [Doctoral dissertation, Universidad Europea de Madrid, Spain]. https://abacus.universidadeuropea.com/handle/11268/1342

Rice, P. (2000). *Adolescencia. Desarrollo, relaciones y cultura*. Prentice Hall.

Romero Carrión, V.L., Bedón Soria, Y.T., & Franco Medina, J. L. (2022). Meta-análisis de competencias transversales en la empleabilidad de los universitarios. *Revista gestión de las personas y tecnología, 15*(43), 20-42. http://dx.doi.org/DOI: 10.35588/gpt.v15i43.5464

Sanahuja Ribés, A., Cantos Aldaz, F. J., & Moliner Miravet, L. (2023). *¿Trabajamos en equipos cooperativos? Percepciones de estudiantes de bachillerato*. Proceedings 2nd International Congress: Education and Knowledge. Universitat Jaume I. Octaedro.

Schwab, K. World Economic Forum, & Sala-i-Martín, X. (2013). *The Global Competitiveness Report 2013–2014: Full Data Edition*. World Economic Forum.

Skrtic, T. M., Sailor, W., & Gee, K. (1996). Voice, collaboration, and inclusion: Democratic themes in educational and social reform initiatives. *Remedial and Special Education*, 17(3), 142–157. DOI: 10.1177/074193259601700304

Soemitra, A., Lubis, A. S., Dewi, R. S., & Ovami, D. C. (2023). Essential Hard skill For Students in VUCA Era: Literature Study. *Journal of Trends Economics and Accounting Research*, 3(4), 605–610. DOI: 10.47065/jtear.v3i4.634

Tortosa, A. J. P., & Pineda, J. A. S. (2021). *Challenge-Based Learning: un puente metodológico entre la Educación Superior y el mundo profesional*. ARANZADI/CIVITAS.

Troise, C., Corvello, V., Ghobadian, A., & O'Regan, N. (2022). How can SMEs successfully navigate VUCA environment: The role of agility in the digital transformation era. *Technological Forecasting and Social Change*, 174, 121227. DOI: 10.1016/j.techfore.2021.121227

Williams, D. A., Wade-Golden, K. C., & Stevens, F. I. (2020). *Making diversity work on campus: A research-based perspective*. Stylus Publishing, LLC.

Wu, A., Roemer, E. C., Kent, K. B., Ballard, D. W., & Goetzel, R. Z. (2021). Mejores prácticas organizacionales que apoyan la salud mental en el lugar de trabajo. *Journal of Occupational and Environmental Medicine*, 63(12), E925–E931. DOI: 10.1097/JOM.0000000000002407 PMID: 34840320

KEY TERMS AND DEFINITIONS

CEE: A special employment center is a company or institution that aims to provide employment and training to people with disabilities or particular difficulties in accessing the labor market. These centers offer an adapted work environment with specialized support to help workers develop their professional skills and abilities.

Coeducation: It is an educational model that aims to promote equal opportunities between women and men in all areas of life. It is based on the joint education of male and female students, fostering respect, cooperation, and the rejection of any type of discrimination based on sex. Some key characteristics of coeducation: It involves the elimination of stereotypes and gender roles traditionally assigned to each sex; It values the abilities and aptitudes of boys and girls equally, without discrimination; It promotes the integral development of the person, regardless of their sex; It encourages coexistence, dialogue, and coll among students of both genders; It seeks to create an educational environment free of sexist biases and prejudices; It contributes to the formation of more free and autonomous citizens who respect diversity.

Diversity, Equity, and Inclusion (DEI): The practices, policies, and programs that promote representation and meaningful participation of diverse groups of individuals, including those of different ages, races, ethnicities, genders, sexual orientations, disabilities, and socioeconomic backgrounds. The key elements of DEI are the following: Diversity: presence and representation of people from varied backgrounds and experiences within an organization or community; Equity: fair treatment, access, opportunity, and advancement for all people, while identifying and eliminating barriers that have prevented the full participation of some groups; Inclusion: creation of an environment where all individuals feel welcomed, respected, supported, and valued.

Holistic Approach: in education refers to a framework that seeks to view the student in a comprehensive manner, considering not only academic aspects, but also the emotional, social, physical and spiritual dimensions of the individual.

Leadership: can be defined as the ability to influence, inspire and motivate other people to work towards the achievement of common goals. Some key characteristics of leadership include: Vision and the capacity to establish a clear direction; Effective communication skills and the ability to mobilize people; Emotional intelligence and the capacity to empathize and connect with the team; Effective decision-making and problem-solving; Delegation of responsibilities and empowerment of collaborators; Inspiration, motivation and the ability to generate commitment; Integrity, consistency between values and actions; Adaptability and flexibility in the face of change.

Liquid Society: is a concept developed by the sociologist Zygmunt Bauman to describe the characteristics of the current postmodern society. Some of the main ideas of this concept are: Fluidity and constant change: The liquid society is characterized by fluidity, uncertainty, and accelerated change, as opposed to the solidity and stability of modernity. Social structures, roles, relationships, etc. are becoming increasingly ephemeral and unstable; Individualization: individuals have increasingly more responsibility in constructing their own biographies and life trajectories, in a context of growing fragility of social ties; Consumerism and transience: the liquid society promotes consumerism and transience as ways of life, where objects, experiences, and relationships have a passing character; Weakening of traditional institutions: institutions such as the family, work, politics, etc., are losing their ability to guide and structure the lives of individuals in a stable manner; Insecurity and risk: the growing uncertainty and unpredictability generates a sense of permanent insecurity and risk in individuals.

Peer Tutoring: A teaching and learning strategy that involves students teaching other students. Students who serve as peer tutors work one-on-one or in small groups with other students to provide academic support, practice skills, and reinforce learning.

Self-Efficacy: it is defined as the beliefs and convictions that a person has about their own capacity to organize and execute the necessary actions to achieve certain results or successfully perform a specific task.

Violet Points: they are physical or virtual spaces where information, guidance, and support are provided to women who have suffered gender-based violence. Their objective is to make this type of violence visible and to fight against it, offering resources and support to the victims.

Zone of Proximal Development (ZDP): It is a concept developed by Vigotksy, defined as the distance between the current level of development, determined by the ability to independently solve a problem development level, determined by the ability to solve a problem independently, and the level of potential developmental potential, determined by solving a problem under the guidance of adults or in collaboration with more capable adults or in collaboration with more capable peers.

Endnote

[1] The micro-videos are available at https://www.youtube.com/channel/UCgO PuUr1KzsCHnXiNCdhrQg

Section 2
Leadership and Teamwork: A Synergistic Approach

Chapter 4
Building Champions:
Leadership as the Keystone of Team Performance

Saptarshi Kumar Sarkar
Brainware University, India

Sanchita Ghosh
Brainware University, India

Piyal Roy
Brainware University, India

Nobhonil Roy Choudhury
https://orcid.org/0009-0009-1046-7492
Brainware University, India

ABSTRACT

This paper explores the role of leadership in team development and performance in organizations. It reviews literature on leadership theories, team dynamics, and performance outcomes, examining the impact of different leadership styles on team cohesion, motivation, and productivity. The paper analyzes effective leadership strategies and best practices, providing insights on how organizations can empower and nurture leaders. Empowered leaders can harness team potential, maximizing effectiveness and paving the way for sustainable growth. The findings emphasize the importance of understanding and implementing nuanced leadership approaches, fostering a culture of excellence, and achieving enduring success.

DOI: 10.4018/979-8-3693-3852-0.ch004

Copyright © 2025, IGI Global. Copying or distributing in print or electronic forms without written permission of IGI Global is prohibited.

1. INTRODUCTION

This article investigates the critical function of leadership in encouraging team growth and enhancing organizational performance. It examines literature on leadership theories, team dynamics, and performance outcomes to better understand the impact of various leadership styles on essential aspects such as team cohesiveness, motivation, and productivity. The modern corporate environment is defined by dynamic challenges, fast technical breakthroughs, and constantly changing market needs. Effective leadership drives teams toward attaining corporate goals, cultivating an excellence culture, and being adaptable in the face of rapid change. Transformational leadership focuses on inspiring vision, promoting cooperation, and empowering team members to realize their greatest potential. It helps team members achieve common goals, encourages innovation, and instils a feeling of purpose and ownership. Transactional leadership emphasizes setting clear goals, rewarding employees, and resolving performance difficulties through corrective measures. However, its long-term effects on team growth and motivation may be limited. Servant leadership stresses empathy, ethical decision-making, and meeting the needs of others, which leads to increased trust, collaboration, and intrinsic motivation within teams. This research focuses on the interaction of various leadership styles and team dynamics, since different styles can have diverse effects on team cohesiveness, motivation, and productivity. Organizations may pick and apply leadership techniques that are most appropriate for their settings and objectives by examining the influence of leadership styles on five important features. Effective leadership strategies and best practices include fostering open communication, providing opportunities for skill development, recognizing and rewarding achievements, promoting a culture of collaboration, and encouraging continuous learning and improvement. In conclusion, this chapter underscores the critical role of leadership in driving team development and performance in organizational settings.

1.1 Background and Context

Leadership has been thoroughly researched in many fields, including psychology, sociology, and management. Leadership theories have developed over time, from attribute theories, which focus on leaders' natural traits, to contingency theories, which highlight situational elements that influence leadership effectiveness. Transformational leadership is distinguished from other leadership theories by its emphasis on inspiring and encouraging followers to go beyond their personal self-interests for the greater benefit of the company (Bass et al. 1985). In contrast, transactional leadership emphasizes trade connections between leaders and followers, with incentives and penalties used to promote performance (Reid et al. 2018). Furthermore, servant leadership has received attention for its emphasis on meeting the needs of others and cultivating an environment of empathy and empowerment (Greenleaf et al. 1977). Tuckman's phases of group growth offer a framework for comprehending the numerous stages that teams go through as they form, storm, norm, perform, and adjourn (Tuckman et al. 1965). Hackman's team effectiveness model highlights the role of task design, team makeup, and leadership in obtaining high-performance results (Mathieu et al. 2017).

1.2 Problem Statement

Despite a wealth of knowledge on leadership and team dynamics, many companies and educational institute fail to successfully use leadership to enhance team performance. The difficulty is the disconnect between theoretical understanding and actual implementation. While leadership theories give useful insights into the characteristics and actions of good leaders, many companies still struggle to put theory into practice. Furthermore, the dynamic nature of teams, as well as the growing needs of the corporate environment, necessitate a more in-depth understanding of how leadership can adapt to changing situations.

1.3 Objectives of the Study

This study delves into the critical role leadership plays in shaping team development and performance. Here's a breakdown of the specific objectives:

This study explores the impact of leadership styles on team dynamics and performance outcomes, focusing on communication, decision-making, and morale. It also explores leadership strategies for team motivation, such as setting clear goals, providing recognition, and fostering a growth mindset. The study also investigates the relationship between leadership effectiveness and key team performance indicators like cohesion, collaboration, and innovation. The goal is to understand how strong leadership fosters unity, encourages teamwork, and stimulates creative problem-solving. The study also aims to identify best practices for organizations to develop and empower leaders, such as leadership development programs, mentorship opportunities, and tools. By examining these objectives, this study aims to provide valuable insights into the crucial role leadership plays in maximizing team effectiveness within organizations.

1.4 Significance of the Study

This chapter provides a detailed study and at the same time, is not an attempt at merely identifying the correlation between leadership and team performance. Not only does it expand on the different types of leadership and their effects on interactions involving the collective and its members, but it also goes into the specifics of how leadership methods influence collaboration, information exchange, and decision-making. Therefore, it is the objective of this study to provide enriched understanding of leadership and team work dynamics by investigating the aforementioned facets in depth.

In addition, the research aims at making conclusions and recommendations to relevant organizations to encourage them to grow and expand while avoiding fatal mishaps to their development. It defines how the occupants of leadership positions may be trained on how to lead, and how organizations can be availed with the necessary resources to create thus essential leadership development and mentorship programs which need to be instituted within organizations. All the aforesaid recommendations are expected to provide a direct improvement on the performance of the teams.

In envisioning the contribution this study makes in empowering organizations with leadership strategies for high-performance teamwork, it looks forward to a positive ripple effect fallout. It is essential to understand that harmonious work relationships and creative approaches are the key success drivers in the teams led by managers. Thus, the present work creates the basis for building such an environment, which in turn will enhance the competitive advantage of an organization. In the current world economy, organizations that are more conscious of leadership programs are most likely to thrive and foster productive teams. Hence the significance of the research, as it holds valuable recommendations for organizations in their pursuit of increased success in a competitive market.

In conclusion, this study's significance lies not only in expanding our understanding of leadership and team dynamics but also in offering practical tools for organizations to cultivate strong leadership and achieve lasting success through high-performing teams.

2. LITERATURE REVIEW

A strong understanding of leadership theories and team development models is crucial for examining the dynamics of leadership within teams and its impact on performance. This literature review explores key theoretical frameworks that shed light on leadership in team contexts. One prominent area of research delves into leadership styles. Trait theories, for instance, identify specific characteristics associated with effective leadership, while behavioural theories categorize leadership styles such as directive, participative, or transformational. These styles can significantly influence team dynamics. For example, a directive leader might dictate tasks, leading to a team that lacks initiative. Conversely, a participative leader might encourage team involvement in decision-making, fostering a more engaged and collaborative environment. Another important area of study focuses on team development models. Tuckman's model, for example, proposes stages that teams progress through, including forming, storming, norming, and performing. Understanding these stages helps leaders navigate potential conflicts during the "storming" phase and foster an environment conducive to high performance in the "performing" stage. Furthermore, contingency theories recognize that the effectiveness of a leadership style is contingent on factors like the maturity of the team, the task at hand, and the organizational context. A leader might need to adapt their style to best suit the specific needs of the team and situation. By examining these various theoretical frameworks and models, this study aims to develop a comprehensive understanding of the interplay between leadership styles, team dynamics, and team performance. This understanding can then be used to identify best practices for leaders to foster high-performing teams within organizations.

2.1 Leadership Theories

Leadership theories provide valuable insights into the traits, behaviours, and styles that make leaders effective. Three prominent theories that offer distinct perspectives on leadership include transformational, transactional, and servant leadership.

Table 1. Overview of prominent leadership theories

Leadership Theory	Description
Transformational Leadership	Emphasizes a leader's ability to inspire and motivate followers to achieve extraordinary results. Transformational leaders raise aspirations, challenge conventional thinking, and create a shared vision for the future. They act as role models, foster trust, and encourage innovation within the team.
Transactional Leadership	Focuses on an exchange-based relationship between leader and follower. Leaders set clear goals and expectations, offering rewards or punishments based on performance. This style is effective in maintaining efficiency and achieving objectives, particularly in well-defined tasks or situations requiring clear direction.
Servant Leadership	Takes a service-oriented approach, prioritizing the needs and well-being of followers. Servant leaders foster a collaborative environment, encourage growth and development, empower teams, delegate tasks effectively, and provide necessary resources and support. They act as mentors, placing the needs of the team above their own.

While each theory offers a distinct viewpoint, they are not mutually exclusive. Effective leaders may exhibit characteristics from all three styles, adapting their approach based on the situation and the needs of their team.

2.2 Team Development Models

The development of team usually has a clear framework that can help fully comprehend it and distinguish the stages that a team passes through on its way to becoming effective. Among the most well-known models that can be found in the literature, Forming-Storming-Norming-Performing (FSNPA) created by Tuckman is one of the most famous models, which describes the four stages of team development.

The Forming stage involves the first part where people know each other and identify the list of working rules and regulation. In this stage, the leaders need to establish clear communication channels and to set realistic expectations as well as ensure people feel connected to the groups.

It is followed by the Storming stage, and this is a efficient if well managed stage. This phase promotes advocation and collaboration and gives team members opportunity to share their opinions and work on controversies. This is one of the most critical phases where leaders are required to assist the team in going through differences and coming up with useful solutions for addressing them.

During the Norming stage, the rest of the strategies are created, communication becomes more openly structured, and there is a mutual understanding of the roles and responsibilities within the team. This stage should also be supported by the leaders through encouraging collaboration, rewarding the team, and creating ways through which the team members may interact.

Therefore, the final stage, which is the Performing stage, is a culmination of the ultimate optimal level that a team enjoys. The aims focus of this stage is characterized by mutual cooperation, as well as work and efficient communication. When it comes to motivating the team, leaders ensure that they assign responsibilities, give authorities, and support them constantly.

Thus, when confronted with challenges in motivation and team dynamics, it is vital to recognize and apply the stages of team development in the given community as well as address the employees' needs and boosting the FSNPA model to foster encouragement, open communication and drive teams to perform at their best.

2.2.1 Tuckman Stages of Group Development

Unveiling Team Dynamics: A Deep Dive into Tuckman's Forming-Storming-Norming-Performing Model

Tuckman's Forming-Storming-Norming-Performing (FSNPA) model, developed by Bruce Tuckman in 1965, is a widely recognized framework for understanding the stages that teams typically progress through as they evolve from a collection of individuals into a high-performing unit. Let's delve deeper into each stage and explore its significance for leaders:

i. Forming Stage: Laying the Foundation

Imagine the first team meeting. This initial stage, "forming," is characterized by introductions, establishing ground rules, and team members getting acquainted with their roles and responsibilities within the project or team.

Leaders play a crucial role at this stage. Setting clear expectations, fostering open communication, and creating a welcoming environment are essential for building trust and psychological safety within the team.

ii. Storming Stage: Weathering the Storm

As the team dives deeper into their work, inevitable disagreements and conflicts may arise. This "storming" stage can be a healthy sign of individual engagement, but it needs to be managed constructively to prevent hindering progress.

Leaders can act as facilitators during this stage. Encouraging healthy debate, fostering open communication, and helping the team navigate differences to arrive at solutions are key. By guiding the team through these conflicts, leaders can help them emerge stronger and more unified.

iii. Norming Stage: Building Cohesion

Through open communication, collaboration, and navigating the "storming" stage effectively, the team enters the "norming" stage. Here, norms are established, roles and responsibilities become solidified, and a sense of cohesion starts to develop.

Leaders can solidify this stage by actively encouraging teamwork, recognizing team achievements (both big and small), and providing opportunities for team bonding activities. This fosters a sense of shared purpose and motivates the team to work together effectively.

iv. Performing Stage: Reaching Peak Performance

The ideal outcome – the "performing" stage. Here, the team functions as a well-oiled machine. Team members communicate effectively, collaborate seamlessly towards shared goals, and demonstrate a high level of trust and understanding. Leaders can empower the team at this stage by delegating tasks effectively, providing autonomy, and offering ongoing support. Recognizing individual and team contributions further motivates the team to maintain this high level of performance.

v. Beyond the Stages: Adaptability is Key

It's important to remember that team development is not always a linear process. Teams may regress to earlier stages due to changes in membership, leadership shifts, or unforeseen challenges. Leaders who understand these models can anticipate potential roadblocks and guide the team back on track. By fostering a supportive environment, open communication, and a focus on team development throughout these stages, leaders can empower their teams to achieve exceptional results.

2.2.2 Hackman's Model of Team Effectiveness

J. Richard Hackman's model, proposed in 1987, takes a different approach to understanding team effectiveness. While Tuckman's model focuses on the stages of team development, Hackman emphasizes the importance of specific conditions that need to be in place for a team to thrive. Let's explore these key factors and how they contribute to high-performing teams:

1. Foundational Elements: Task Design and Team Composition:

Task Design: Hackman argues that the nature of the task itself significantly impacts team success. Effective tasks require a clear goal or purpose that motivates the team. They should also involve a degree of task interdependence, meaning team members rely on each other's skills and contributions to achieve the goal. Tasks that are too simple or lack interdependence can lead to boredom and disengagement.

Team Composition: The right people with the right skills are crucial. Teams need a diverse range of skills and experiences to tackle complex challenges. However, simply having talented individuals isn't enough. Team members should also be compatible and willing to work collaboratively.

2. Cultivating a Supportive Environment: Norms and Leadership:

The second element of a wealthy inventory of team resources that it is crucial to create entails a clear understanding of the nature of norms as a framework that supports effective team behaviour: the norms of a team refer to expectations for behaviour. These norms usually include diversity of communication, respect for each other and honoring organizational objectives. These norms are very important and are developed by leaders to ensure that they have set example for other members of the organization as well as ensuring that every member complies to those norms. Management is likewise critical in the process in order to steer the group towards triumph. The knowledge of Hackman's model allows a leader to ensure a certain environment that encourages team development, generate mechanisms for effective communication and establish how to deal with conflict issue. It is crucial in the case of management and leadership as such principles will improve the performance of the working team massively.

Hackman's model provides valuable insights for leaders and organizations seeking to build high-performing teams. By carefully considering task design, team composition, fostering supportive norms, and providing effective leadership, organizations can create an environment where teams can thrive and achieve their full potential.

2.3 Interplay Between Leadership and Team Dynamics

The relationship between leadership and team dynamics is a fascinating and intricate dance. Leaders, through their styles and behaviours, significantly influence the way teams' function, ultimately impacting performance outcomes. Here's a closer look at this dynamic interplay:

Leadership Styles Shape Team Dynamics

Leadership can be defined in many ways but generally it has the propensity of having differing effects on team communication, decision making, and indeed spirits. For instance, a directive leadership style where a leader prescribes how subordinates should perform their tasks and closely supervises them leads to lack of teamwork and discourage subordinates from expressing their ideas. On the other hand, a person with participative nature of workplace leadership is more likely to increase the employees' engagement because he or she promotes decision-making involvement of the workers. These contrasting examples play an important role in realization of the fact that leadership styles can influence the dynamics and productivity of the team formed.

Leadership Impacts Team Performance

Managers also fully understand the crucial role they play in building a positive working atmosphere within their teams. Thus, they seldom sit idly, and are always trying to create the best atmosphere within the working team where people would feel wanted, appreciated, and heard. This approach is helpful in establishing confidence between the leaders and led since it aligns them well, provides a platform for integrated working and thus creates innovative teams (Yukl et al., 2010). On the other hand, weak leadership presents negative consequences in this case, organisation penalties are diminished. The major negative leadership behaviors are micromanaging the employees, not giving clear directions and vision, and cultivating the culture of fear and blame; these behaviors negatively impact the teams and employees by demotivating them, hindering innovation and reducing efficiency (Avolio et al., 2009).

Building a Thriving Team Environment

It is essential to make sure that the above president/manager provides her/his subordinates with goals and expectations, and feedback to foster a direction and suggest purpose in what they do. In the way they relate to their team members, they befriend them in furthering the cause of the team by listening to them, accepting their suggestions, and being willing to take necessary risks. Managers also assign tasks correctly; give so much freedom, but also provide necessary assistance and tools for it to be most efficient. Also, leaders who can address conflict and effectively regulate conflicts contribute to the assurance that the team or members will stay ahead and focusing on the objectives.

Understanding the intricate relationship between leadership and team dynamics is crucial for building successful teams. By adopting effective leadership styles and fostering a supportive environment, leaders can empower their teams to collaborate effectively, innovate, and achieve extraordinary results.

2.4 Impact of Leadership Styles on Team Performance

Leadership Styles: The Orchestra Conductor of Team Performance

Leadership styles play a central role in determining how well teams perform. Just as an orchestra conductor influences the sound and quality of the music, leaders shape team dynamics and ultimately impact results. Here's a breakdown of how various leadership styles influence team performance:

Transformational Leadership: Igniting Passion and Innovation

Transformational leaders are the visionaries who inspire and motivate teams to achieve extraordinary results. They set ambitious goals, challenge the status quo, and create a shared sense of purpose within the team. This fosters strong team cohesion, motivates individuals to go above and beyond, and encourages innovation. Research suggests that teams under transformational leaders experience higher levels of performance and job satisfaction (Bass et al. 1994).

Transactional Leadership: Delivering Results Through Structure and Rewards

Transactional leaders provide clear direction, establish performance expectations, and offer rewards or incentives for achieving goals. This style is effective in achieving short-term performance objectives, particularly in situations requiring well-defined tasks and a focus on efficiency. Transactional leadership can help teams stay organized and motivated to achieve specific outcomes.

Servant Leadership: Investing in People for Long-Term Success (Liden et al. 2008)

Servant leadership takes a more people-centric approach. Servant leaders prioritize the well-being and growth of their team members. They empower individuals, delegate tasks effectively, and provide the resources and support necessary for success. This fosters a sense of trust, loyalty, and commitment within the team, leading to long-term sustainable success (Podsakoff et al. 1990).

Choosing the Right Style: Context Matters

The most effective leadership style is not a one-size-fits-all approach. The ideal style depends on various factors, including the maturity of the team, the nature of the task at hand, and the overall organizational culture.

A complex project requiring innovation might benefit from a transformational leader who can inspire creative solutions. A team facing tight deadlines and needing clear direction might thrive under a transactional leader's guidance. A team needing long-term development and a focus on employee well-being might excel under a servant leader.

The Takeaway: A Symphony of Styles for Peak Performance

Understanding these different leadership styles and their impact on team performance empowers leaders to adapt their approach based on the specific situation. By incorporating elements from different styles and fostering trust, clear communication, and a focus on growth, leaders can create a harmonious and high-performing team, leadership theories and team development models offer valuable insights for maximizing team effectiveness. By understanding the unique strengths of transformational, transactional, and servant leadership styles, leaders can create an environment where teams are motivated, engaged, and empowered to achieve remarkable results.

3. RESEARCH DESIGN

This study adopts a mixed-methods research design to gain a rich and nuanced understanding of the relationship between leadership and team development and performance. This approach leverages the strengths of both quantitative and qualitative methods (Creswell & Plano Clark, 2018). The quantitative component will involve surveying a large sample of participants. This survey will gather data on leadership styles used by team leaders, team dynamics experienced by team members, and performance outcomes achieved by the teams. By analyzing this quantitative data, we can identify trends and potential correlations between leadership styles and team performance. The qualitative component will involve in-depth interviews with a smaller, targeted group of participants. These interviews delved deeper into the lived experiences of team members and leaders. By collecting their opinions and perceptions, we can acquire crucial information that surveys alone may not provide. This mixed-methods approach, which combines the breadth of quantitative data with the depth of qualitative data, provides for a more thorough investigation of the intricate interplay between leadership and team dynamics in performance. By collecting their opinions and perceptions, we can acquire crucial information that surveys alone may not provide. This mixed-methods approach, which combines the breadth of quantitative data with the depth of qualitative data, provides for a more thorough investigation of the intricate interplay between leadership and team dynamics in performance.

3.1 Data Collection Methods

To acquire information for the study, a variety of data gathering approaches were used.

A structured questionnaire was utilized to assess participants' perceptions of leadership styles (transformational, transactional, and servant), team dynamics (cohesion, communication, collaboration), and performance outcomes (productivity, innovation, work satisfaction). The survey was sent online to a diverse sample of individuals working in a variety of industries and organizational settings. Semi-structured interviews were conducted with a subset of survey respondents to better understand their perspectives and experiences. The interviews enabled open-ended discussions regarding leadership effectiveness, team dynamics, and corporate culture. The interviews were recorded and transcribed for further examination.

3.2 Sampling Techniques

The study's participants were selected using a combination of probability and non-probability sampling methods. A representative sample of participants from the target population was chosen by a random selection approach. This technique ensures that every person in the population has an equal chance of being picked, decreasing bias and increasing the generalizability of the findings (Babbie et al. 2020)

Both convenience sampling and probability sampling were employed to enroll research participants. This technique comprises choosing persons who are readily available and enthusiastic to take part in the study. While convenience sampling may introduce bias, it is often more practical and cost-effective in studies with limited resources or time (Creswell et al. 2017).

4. THE ROLE OF LEADERSHIP IN TEAM DEVELOPMENT

Effective leadership is critical for developing high-performance teams capable of meeting corporate objectives. This section delves into the numerous facets of leadership's involvement in team development, such as inspiring a common vision, establishing trust and collaboration, empowering and growing team members, and resolving disagreements and managing problems. Inspiring a common vision is an essential component of good leadership. Leaders develop a compelling vision that is consistent with business goals and motivates team members to work together (Kouzes & Posner, 2007). It offers direction and purpose, inspiring team members to contribute their skills and abilities toward a common goal of achievement.

4.2 Building Trust and Fostering Collaboration

Trust is the basis for good team connections. Leaders help to develop trust by encouraging open communication, openness, and honesty (Dirks & Ferrin, 2002). Trust allows team members to feel secure expressing their ideas, taking risks, and working efficiently toward common goals (Mayer et al., 1995). Transactional leaders foster trust through consistent and equitable interactions in which promises are maintained and rewards are provided properly depending on performance (Bass et al. 1994). Servant leaders build trust by emphasizing their team members' well-being and growth, resulting in a supportive and inclusive work environment (Greenleaf et al. 1977).

4.3 Empowering and Developing Team Members

Empowering and developing team members is critical to building a culture of development and creativity within teams. Leaders empower team members by distributing responsibility, creating chances for skill growth, and providing constructive feedback and support (Conger & Kanungo, 1988). Empowered team members feel respected and driven to put up their best efforts to achieve team goals. Transformational leaders empower their teams by challenging people to think creatively, giving chances for growth and development, and cultivating a culture of continual learning and improvement (Bass, 1990). Servant leaders empower their teams by acting as mentors and facilitators, providing chances for personal and professional development, and removing barriers to achievement (Spears, 1996).

4.4 Resolving Conflicts and Managing Challenges

Conflicts and problems are unavoidable in every team environment. To sustain team cohesiveness and productivity, effective leaders must resolve disagreements and manage difficulties in a timely and efficient manner (De Dreu & Weingart, 2003). Leaders must be proficient in conflict resolution, communication, and problem-solving in order to handle issues before they escalate and disrupt team dynamics. Conflicts should be viewed as opportunities for growth and learning, with open discourse and cooperation supporting mutually beneficial solutions (Bass et al. 1985). Transactional leaders settle disagreements by following established rules and conventions to keep the team organized (Avolio, Bass, & Jung, 1999). Servant leaders stress understanding all parties' underlying needs and interests in order to support a settlement based on empathy, respect, and fairness (Greenleaf et al. 1977). To summarize, good leadership inspires a common vision, fosters trust and collaboration, empowers and develops team members, and resolves disagreements and manages problems. Leaders that exemplify these leadership traits and behaviours foster an environment favourable to creativity, productivity, and success within their teams.

5. LEADERSHIP STYLES AND THEIR IMPACT ON TEAM PERFORMANCE

Leadership styles such as transformational, transactional, and servant leadership have a substantial influence on team dynamics and performance. Transformational leadership fosters team cohesion and motivation by appealing to higher-order needs and values, resulting in a shared sense of purpose and vision among teammates. This method instils intellectual curiosity, ingenuity, and a sense of trust, respect, and devotion among followers. It promotes enhanced engagement, inventiveness, and job satisfaction, resulting in improved performance outcomes. Transactional leadership emphasizes the exchange of incentives and penalties between leaders and followers in order to improve performance and assure task completion. It establishes clear expectations, performance goals, and rewards for meeting targets, while also implementing corrective measures for departures from norms. This strategy has been associated to higher job completion rates and team conformity.

Servant leadership puts team members' well-being and advancement first, emphasizing empathy, humility, and ethical decision-making. It encourages both individual and group growth by providing mentoring, coaching, and chances for skill development and advancement. Servant leaders actively listen to their team members' needs and concerns, offer guidance and support, and remove roadblocks to success. In summary, transformational, transactional, and servant leadership styles all have different effects on team dynamics and performance. Transformational leadership fosters team cohesion and motivation by creating a shared vision; transactional leadership promotes task completion and compliance by providing clear expectations and rewards; and servant leadership fosters both individual and community growth.

6. STRATEGIES FOR DEVELOPING EFFECTIVE LEADERSHIP

Effective leadership is critical to high-performance teams and organizational success. Leadership development programs, mentoring and coaching efforts, feedback and performance management systems, and fostering a culture of continual learning and growth are all effective strategies for building leadership talents. These programs seek to improve the knowledge, skills, and capacities of present and rising leaders in companies. They frequently concentrate on critical skills like as communication, decision-making, problem solving, conflict resolution, and emotional intelligence. Simulations, case studies, role-playing exercises, and group discussions may help participants apply leadership ideas in real-world situations. According to research, leadership development programs have a major influence on leadership effectiveness and organizational performance, resulting in enhanced self-awareness, confidence, and the capacity to effectively manage teams, all of which boost team morale, productivity, and creativity.

6.1 Mentoring and Coaching Initiatives

Mentoring and coaching activities connect leaders with experienced mentors or coaches who provide guidance, support, and feedback to help them develop as leaders (Eby et al., 2013). Mentors serve as role models and counsellors, sharing their expertise, skills, and insights to assist mentees in issue solving, goal setting, and professional development. Coaches, on the other hand, help leaders identify their strengths and areas for improvement, set development goals, and carry out action plans to improve their leadership abilities (Grant, 2019). Coaching sessions may involve one-on-one conversations, goal-setting exercises, and skill-building activities tailored to the leader's specific needs. Mentoring and coaching are excellent ways to develop leadership skills, raise self-awareness, and promote continuous learning and advancement (Kram et al. 1988). Mentors provide individualized help and direction.

6.2 Feedback and Performance Management Systems

Feedback and performance management systems are important components of leadership development because they assist leaders recognize their own strengths, weaknesses, and areas for improvement (London et al. 2002). These methods include regular performance assessments, goal-setting discussions, and constructive feedback sessions to assess leadership effectiveness and growth over time. 360-degree feedback assessments, for example, are frequently used in leadership development programs to gather feedback from a wide range of sources, including peers, subordinates, and supervisors (Bracken et al. 2001). Leaders gain a comprehensive understanding of their impact on others and areas for growth by obtaining feedback from a range of sources.

Effective feedback and performance management systems build a culture of accountability, transparency, and continuous improvement inside firms. Leaders receive actionable feedback on their performance.

6.3 Creating a Culture of Continuous Learning and Improvement

A culture of continuous learning and growth is critical for leadership development and organizational success. Organizations that value learning invest in resources, infrastructure, and activities that foster professional development and skill progression at all levels. Leaders are encouraged to seek out new challenges, take risks, and experiment with creative approaches. This culture fosters adaptability, resilience, and agility, helping businesses to thrive in rapidly changing environments. Leaders have a growth mindset, viewing setbacks and mistakes as opportunities to learn and advance. Leadership development programs, mentoring and coaching initiatives, feedback and performance management systems, and building a culture of continuous learning and improvement are all examples of effective leadership practices. Investing in leadership development enables businesses to cultivate competent leaders that drive innovation, engagement, and success.

7. CASE STUDIES AND EXAMPLES

In this part, we give two case studies that demonstrate the use and impact of various leadership styles in real-world organizational settings. Case Study 1 studies the effective application of transformational leadership in a technology start-up, whereas Case Study 2 investigates the role of servant leadership in developing high-performing healthcare teams.

7.1 Case Study 1: Successful Implementation of Transformational Leadership in a Tech Start up

Background: XYZ Tech is a rapidly developing start-up that specializes in software development for e-commerce platforms. The firm was started five years ago by a group of ambitious entrepreneurs who wanted to transform the online buying experience. As the firm grew fast, the founders understood the importance of excellent leadership to manage the obstacles of increasing operations and promoting innovation.

Leadership Challenge: The founders of XYZ Tech were confronted with the difficulty of overseeing a vibrant and varied team of software engineers, designers, and marketers in a competitive sector. They wanted to install creativity, teamwork, and dedication in team members while remaining focused on attaining business goals.

Solution: The founders used transformational leadership to empower their staff and accelerate organizational growth. They concentrated on communicating a compelling vision for the company's future, cultivating an environment of creativity and experimentation, and allowing people to take ownership of their work.

Results: The adoption of transformational leadership has a significant influence on XYZ Tech's organizational culture and performance. Team members were inspired and involved, which resulted in enhanced productivity, creativity, and teamwork. The firm enjoyed significant market expansion and success, establishing itself as a leader in the e-commerce software sector.

Lessons learned: The story of XYZ Tech highlights how transformational leadership can enable teams to accomplish ambitious goals and promote innovation. Leaders may develop a culture of innovation, inspire a common vision, and empower people to create a dynamic and high-performing organizational culture that is favourable to success.

7.2 Case Study 2: The Role of Servant Leadership in Building High-Performing Healthcare Teams

Background: ABC Healthcare is a large hospital network dedicated to providing high-quality patient care across all specialties. The company employs a diverse group of healthcare professionals, including doctors, nurses, technicians, and support staff. With the healthcare industry's growing demands and complexities, ABC Healthcare realized the need of strong leadership in guaranteeing patient safety and satisfaction.

Leadership Challenge: ABC Healthcare faced the challenge of establishing cohesive, high-performing healthcare teams capable of providing excellent patient care in a fast-paced and demanding environment. Leaders must foster teamwork, communication, and trust while prioritizing patient-centered care and safety.

Solution: ABC Healthcare's leadership team used a servant leadership strategy to handle the healthcare industry's specific difficulties. They prioritized addressing the needs of patients, staff, and the community, emphasizing empathy, compassion, and ethical decision-making throughout their leadership practices.

Results The adoption of servant leadership had a revolutionary effect on ABC Healthcare's corporate culture and performance. Leaders focused their team members' well-being and growth, resulting in higher employee satisfaction, engagement, and retention. Patients benefited from enhanced communication, cooperation, and treatment quality, which led to increased satisfaction and better health outcomes. The story of ABC Healthcare demonstrates the importance of servant leadership in developing high-performing healthcare teams and encouraging patient-centered care. Leaders may build a friendly and inclusive work environment where both workers and patients thrive by emphasizing the needs of others, establishing an empathy and cooperation culture, and setting a good example.

Table 2. A concise overview of the case studies

Case Study	Context	Leadership Challenge	Solution	Results	Lessons Learned
1	XYZ Tech, a fast-growing tech startup specializing in e-commerce software development	Leading a dynamic and diverse team of software engineers, designers, and marketers in a competitive industry	Adopting a transformational leadership approach to inspire creativity, collaboration, and commitment among team members	Increased productivity, creativity, and collaboration; rapid growth and success in the market	Transformational leadership empowers teams to achieve ambitious goals and drive innovation
2	ABC Healthcare, a large hospital network dedicated to providing quality patient care	Building cohesive and high-performing healthcare teams capable of delivering exceptional patient care	Embracing a servant leadership approach to serve the needs of patients, staff, and the community	Increased job satisfaction, engagement, and retention among staff; improved patient communication, teamwork, and quality of care	Servant leadership fosters a supportive and inclusive work environment and promotes patient-centered care

These case studies highlight the importance of effective leadership in driving organizational success and fostering a positive work environment. Whether through transformational leadership in a tech start-up or servant leadership in healthcare, leaders play a crucial role in inspiring, motivating, and empowering their teams to achieve excellence.

8. ANALYSIS AND DISCUSSION

In this section, we delve into the analysis and discussion of the key findings from the literature review and case studies presented earlier. We synthesize the insights gained from both the academic literature and real-world examples to explore practical implications for organizations and identify gaps and areas for future research.

8.1 Synthesizing Key Findings from Literature and Case Studies

The literature review and case studies reveal common themes and insights about leadership's role in team development and performance. Transformational, transactional, and servant leadership styles emerged as prominent styles with distinct effects on team dynamics and outcomes. Transformational leadership, characterized by vision, inspiration, and empowerment, is associated with higher levels of team cohesion, motivation, and innovation. Transactional leadership, focused on task accomplishment and compliance through rewards and punishments, is effective in structured situations. The case study of ABC Healthcare highlighted the importance of transactional leadership in ensuring patient safety and satisfaction through clear expectations and performance standards. Finally, servant leadership, characterized by empathy, humility, and ethical decision-making, promotes individual and collective growth and well-being within organizations. By understanding the strengths and limitations of different leadership styles and adapting their approach to suit their teams and organizations, leaders can create a culture of excellence and achieve sustainable results.

8.2 Exploring Practical Implications for Organizations

Organizations should invest in leadership development programs to enhance team performance and inspire, motivate, and empower their teams. These programs should include training workshops, coaching sessions, and experiential learning opportunities to enhance leadership competencies and capabilities. This will create a pipeline of skilled leaders who drive innovation, engagement, and success. Organizations should also prioritize a positive organizational culture that values empathy, collaboration, and continuous learning. Leaders should lead by example and demonstrate servant leadership behaviours that prioritize team members' well-being. Feedback and performance management systems should be implemented to provide leaders with actionable feedback on their performance and areas for improvement. This fosters a culture of transparency and accountability, empowering leaders to excel in their roles and drive organizational growth. Lastly, organizations should encourage a culture of experimentation and innovation, where leaders take risks, challenge the status quo, and embrace change. By fostering a growth mindset and embracing failure as an opportunity for learning, organizations can create an environment where creativity thrives and innovation flourishes.

8.3 Identifying Gaps and Areas for Future Research

The role of leadership in team development and performance has been well-understood, but there are still gaps that need further investigation. One area of focus is the study of boundary conditions and contextual factors that moderate the effectiveness of different leadership styles. This could include examining how cultural differences affect the effectiveness of transformational, transactional, and servant leadership in diverse organizational contexts. Understanding these cultural nuances can help organizations tailor their leadership approach to maximize effectiveness and align with organizational values and objectives. Longitudinal research could also explore the long-term effects of different leadership styles on team dynamics and performance. Emerging leadership concepts, such as authentic, ethical, and shared leadership, could also be explored to advance our understanding of effective leadership practices and inform organizational strategies for leadership development. In conclusion, the analysis and discussion of key findings from literature review and case studies offer valuable insights into leadership's role in team development and performance.

9. CONCLUSION

The study of leadership's impact on team development and performance has identified three key styles: transformational, transactional, and servant leadership. Transformational leadership fosters innovation and collaboration, transactional leadership ensures efficiency and goal attainment, and servant leadership promotes growth and well-being. These styles have practical implications for organizations, such as investing in leadership development programs, cultivating a positive organizational culture, implementing feedback and performance management systems, and encouraging continuous learning and improvement. Despite progress in understanding leadership, there are still areas for future research. Future research should focus on understanding the boundary conditions and contextual factors that moderate the effectiveness of different leadership styles, investigating the long-term effects of leadership on team dynamics and performance, and exploring emerging leadership concepts. In conclusion, effective leadership is crucial for driving organizational success and fostering a culture of excellence. By understanding different leadership styles and implementing evidence-based practices, organizations can cultivate skilled leaders who inspire, motivate, and empower their teams to achieve extraordinary results.

REFERENCES

Argyris, C., & Schön, D. A. (1978). *Organizational learning: A theory of action perspective*. Addison-Wesley.

Avolio, B. J., Bass, B. M., & Jung, D. I. (1999). Re-examining the components of transformational and transactional leadership using the Multifactor Leadership. *Journal of Occupational and Organizational Psychology*, 72(4), 441–462. DOI: 10.1348/096317999166789

Avolio, B. J., Walumbwa, F. O., & Weber, T. J. (2009). Leadership: Current theories, research, and future directions. *Annual Review of Psychology*, 60(1), 421–449. DOI: 10.1146/annurev.psych.60.110707.163621 PMID: 18651820

Babbie, E. R. (2020). *The practice of social research*. Cengage AU.

Bass, B. M. (1985). *Leadership and performance beyond expectations*. Free Press.

Bass, B. M. (1985). *Leadership and performance beyond expectations*. Free Press.

Bass, B. M. (1990). From transactional to transformational leadership: Learning to share the vision. *Organizational Dynamics*, 18(3), 19–31. DOI: 10.1016/0090-2616(90)90061-S

Bass, B. M., & Avolio, B. J. (1994). *Improving organizational effectiveness through transformational leadership*. Sage Publications.

Bass, B. M., & Riggio, R. E. (2006). *Transformational leadership* (2nd ed.). Psychology Press. DOI: 10.4324/9781410617095

Bracken, D. W., Timmreck, C. W., & Church, A. H. (2001). *The handbook of multisource feedback*. Jossey-Bass.

Burns, J. M. (1978). *Leadership*. Harper & Row.

Conger, J. A., & Kanungo, R. N. (1988). The empowerment process: Integrating theory and practice. *Academy of Management Review*, 13(3), 471–482. DOI: 10.2307/258093

Creswell, J. W., & Creswell, J. D. (2017). *Research design: Qualitative, quantitative, and mixed methods approach*. Sage publications.

Day, D. V., Harrison, M. M., & Halpin, S. M. (2014). *An integrative approach to leader development: Connecting adult development, identity, and expertise*. Routledge.

De Dreu, C. K., & Weingart, L. R. (2003). Task versus relationship conflict, team performance, and team member satisfaction: A meta-analysis. *The Journal of Applied Psychology*, 88(4), 741–749. DOI: 10.1037/0021-9010.88.4.741 PMID: 12940412

Dirks, K. T., & Ferrin, D. L. (2002). Trust in leadership: Meta-analytic findings and implications for research and practice. *The Journal of Applied Psychology*, 87(4), 611–628. DOI: 10.1037/0021-9010.87.4.611 PMID: 12184567

Eby, L. T., Allen, T. D., Hoffman, B. J., Baranik, L. E., Sauer, J. B., Baldwin, S., Morrison, M. A., Kinkade, K. M., Maher, C. P., Curtis, S., & Evans, S. C. (2013). An interdisciplinary meta-analysis of the potential antecedents, correlates, and consequences of protégé perceptions of mentoring. *Psychological Bulletin*, 139(2), 441–476. DOI: 10.1037/a0029279 PMID: 22800296

Garvin, D. A., Edmondson, A. C., & Gino, F. (2008). Is yours a learning organization? *Harvard Business Review*, 86(3), 109–116. PMID: 18411968

Grant, A. M. (2019). The third 'generation' of workplace coaching: Creating a culture of quality conversations. *Coaching (Abingdon, UK)*, 12(2), 117–134.

Greenleaf, R. K. (1977). *Servant leadership: A journey into the nature of legitimate power and greatness*. Paulist Press.

Judge, T. A., & Piccolo, R. F. (2004). Transformational and transactional leadership: A meta-analytic test of their relative validity. *The Journal of Applied Psychology*, 89(5), 755–768. DOI: 10.1037/0021-9010.89.5.755 PMID: 15506858

Kluger, A. N., & DeNisi, A. (1996). The effects of feedback interventions on performance: A historical review, a meta-analysis, and a preliminary feedback intervention theory. *Psychological Bulletin*, 119(2), 254–284. DOI: 10.1037/0033-2909.119.2.254

Kouzes, J. M., & Posner, B. Z. (2007). *The leadership challenge* (4th ed.). Jossey-Bass.

Kram, K. E. (1988). *Mentoring at work: Developmental relationships in organizational life*. University Press of America.

Liden, R. C., Wayne, S. J., Zhao, H., & Henderson, D. (2008). Servant leadership: Development of a multidimensional measure and multi-level assessment. *The Leadership Quarterly*, 19(2), 161–177. DOI: 10.1016/j.leaqua.2008.01.006

London, M., & Smither, J. W. (2002). Feedback orientation, feedback culture, and the longitudinal performance management process. *Human Resource Management Review*, 12(1), 81–100. DOI: 10.1016/S1053-4822(01)00043-2

Mathieu, J. E., Hollenbeck, J. R., van Knippenberg, D., & Ilgen, D. R. (2017). A century of work teams in the Journal of Applied Psychology. *The Journal of Applied Psychology*, 102(3), 452–467. DOI: 10.1037/apl0000128 PMID: 28150984

Mayer, R. C., Davis, J. H., & Schoorman, F. D. (1995). An integrative model of organizational trust. *Academy of Management Review*, 20(3), 709–734. DOI: 10.2307/258792

Podsakoff, P. M., MacKenzie, S. B., Moorman, R. H., & Fetter, R. (1990). Transformational leader behaviours and their effects on followers' trust in leader, satisfaction, and organizational citizenship behaviours. *The Leadership Quarterly*, 1(2), 107–142. DOI: 10.1016/1048-9843(90)90009-7

Podsakoff, P. M., MacKenzie, S. B., Moorman, R. H., & Fetter, R. (1990). Transformational leader behaviors and their effects on followers' trust in leader, satisfaction, and organizational citizenship behaviors. *The Leadership Quarterly*, 1(2), 107–142. DOI: 10.1016/1048-9843(90)90009-7

Reid, W. M., & Dold, C. J. (2018). Burns, Senge, and the study of leadership. *Open Journal of Leadership*, 7(01), 89–116. DOI: 10.4236/ojl.2018.71006

Spears, L. C. (1996). Reflections on Robert K. Greenleaf and servant-leadership. *Leadership and Organization Development Journal*, 17(7), 33–35. DOI: 10.1108/01437739610148367

Spears, L. C. (1996). Reflections on Robert K. Greenleaf and servant-leadership. *Leadership and Organization Development Journal*, 17(7), 33–35. DOI: 10.1108/01437739610148367

Tuckman, B. W. (1965). Developmental sequence in small groups. *Psychological Bulletin*, 63(6), 384–399. DOI: 10.1037/h0022100 PMID: 14314073

Van Dierendonck, D., & Nuijten, I. (2011). The servant leadership survey: Development and validation of a multidimensional measure. *Journal of Business and Psychology*, 26(3), 249–267. DOI: 10.1007/s10869-010-9194-1 PMID: 21949466

Walumbwa, F. O., Hartnell, C. A., & Oke, A. (2010). Servant leadership, procedural justice climate, service climate, employee attitudes, and organizational citizenship behavior: A cross-level investigation. *The Journal of Applied Psychology*, 95(3), 517–529. DOI: 10.1037/a0018867 PMID: 20476830

Yukl, G. (2006). *Leadership in Organizations. Prentice Hall. Inc.* Erylewood Cliffs.

Chapter 5
Steering the Ship
How Leadership Styles Shape Team Development and Performance

Tara M. Knight
https://orcid.org/0009-0005-1211-7446
Trevecca Nazarene University, USA

ABSTRACT

Purpose: This research explores the importance of leadership style on team performance and development. This research will answer the question: How do different leadership styles impact the development and performance of a team? Design/Methodology Approach: qualitative systemic literature review. Findings: There is not one leadership style that is perfection. Therefore, a hybrid of leadership styles is needed to develop employees and improve performance effectively. The most successful leaders will be the ones who are most flexible and can wear many hats. Theory: Contingency Theory of Leadership Keywords: leadership, employee performance, leadership style, employee development, work environment, Authoritarian Leadership, Autocratic Leadership, Directive Leadership, Transformational Leadership, Transactional Leadership, Servant Leadership, Paternalistic Leadership

INTRODUCTION

Leadership presence and active engagement are essential for developing a team and improving performance. The type of leader is just as important as a leader's presence. Effective leaders demonstrate skills such as influencing, strategic thinking, delegation, coaching and mentoring, executive presence, resilience, communication, involvement, and impact. To be successful, an organization must align the right combination of team members and leaders who have "the determination of a right working mentality with high dedication and loyalty to their work, providing guidance, direction, motivation and proper working coordination from a leader to his subordinates" (Paais & Pattiruhu, 2020, p. 577).

It is suggested that organizations emphasize aligning the right leaders according to their company culture and the team they will lead. Frequently, a leader is chosen because of tenure or a need for someone to take the role. This routine comes to the workers' detriment. Work motivation and organizational culture positively affect team member performance (Paais & Pattiruhu, 2020). An effective leader influences the organizational culture and, depending on the leadership style, can motivate team members to embrace their vision (Northouse, 2022).

An effective leader is also critical to an organization's competitiveness because they have the ability to influence workers to achieve company goals (Paais & Pattiruhu, 2020). A great leader understands the type of motivation that a team member needs. Leaders have the referent power to motivate team members by forming a corporate culture where employees feel seen. Team members who receive authentic encouragement and attention regarding their excellent work are satisfied with their work environment and work harder, which increases performance results (Paais & Pattiruhu, 2020). Work motivation and organizational culture positively affect team performance (Paais & Pattiruhu, 2020). An effective leader influences the organizational culture and, depending on the leadership style, can motivate team members to embrace their vision (Northouse, 2022).

So, where do we begin? Most leaders want to be the difference-maker leaders that Bridwell (2022) discusses in his blog, *Leading With Authentic - Influence*, but how? An individual needs to take an honest inventory of the type of leader they are now and then consider the leader they desire to be. To the organizational leaders and decision-makers, I pose a question. When seeking leaders for your organization, do you consider the leadership style that would be complementary to the company's culture and vision in your hiring process? An honest assessment of the current company climate and the kind of leadership required to realign it with the company culture and vision is a must. This chapter will use a qualitative systematic literature review to explore how leadership style shapes team development and performance.

RATIONALE

Leadership considerably impacts employee engagement, performance, and development. According to research conducted by Paais and Pattiruhu (2020), leadership, motivation, and culture variables have a 57.4% impact on job satisfaction, and the same variables have a 73.5% impact on job performance. When comparing management to leadership, Northouse (2022) highlights that leaders create a vision, build teams, and motivate and inspire others.

Leadership, motivation, and company culture are a package that works together to allow team members to be their best selves. Removing one variable negatively impacts job satisfaction and performance, resulting in a loss for the organization. The right type of leader can be in the wrong organizational culture. For example, a transformational leader and the direct reports will struggle if the organization's culture does not encourage innovation and out-of-the-box thinking.

According to the Global Leadership Forecast of 2023 by Development Dimensions International, Inc. (DDI), leader quality ratings decreased significantly (Neal et al., 2023). In 2020, 48% of managers rated their organization's senior leadership quality as 'very good or excellent,' but in 2022, that number dropped to 40% (Neal et al., 2023). Subordinate findings show that only 32% trust senior leadership, and 46% trust their direct manager (Neal et al., 2023). Neal et al. (2023) found there is a gap in the top five skills leadership should have:

1. Identifying and developing future talent,
2. Strategic thinking,
3. Managing successful change,
4. Decision-making priorities,
5. and influencing others.

Only 12% of leaders rated themselves adequate in all five essential skills, and only 29% of organizations train their leaders on those critical skills (Neal et al., 2023). The organization is responsible for ensuring the leadership team has the skills to perform their duties effectively (Pontefract, 2023).

Gallup has studied employees and managers for five decades (Beck & Harter, 2014). They use talent-based assessments, in-depth structured interviews, and web-based assessments to predict performance. Gallup reports that companies fail to choose the right managerial candidate for the job 82% of the time (Beck & Harter, 2014). "Managers account for at least 70% of the variance in team employee engagement" (*State of the Global Workplace: 2024 report*, n.d., p. 2). Executives struggle to understand why team performance varies in different departments, regardless of the industry, size, or location (Beck & Harter, 2014). Many individuals are promoted to leadership positions because they deserve it or there is a need, not because they are the best individuals for the job (Beck & Harter, 2014).

Gallup finds that great managers have the following talents: they can motivate every employee, they are assertive and create a culture of responsibility, genuine relationships are built due to their transparency and trustworthiness, and they make executive decisions based on the need of the team and not politics (Beck & Harter, 2014). Gallup estimates that organizations achieve 147% higher earnings per share on average when they successfully increase employee engagement and quality leadership (Beck & Harter, 2014).

Gallup's 2024 State of the Global Workplace annual report reports the 2023 results of global employees and the role of work in their mental health and well-being. Employee teams that are engaged directly influence the positive outcomes in organizations. Low employee team engagement has cost the global economy 9% of the GDP or USD 8.9 trillion. Gallup found that 23% of employees classify themselves as engaged, 62% are not engaged, and 15% are actively disengaged (*State of the Global Workplace: 2024 report*, n.d.). Focusing solely on the United States, Gallup reports the following results about employee engagement: "51% are not engaged, and 16% are actively engaged" (*State of the Global Workplace: 2024 report*, n.d., p. 34).

Leadership directly impacts employee engagement, team performance, development, and work environment. Radha and Aithal's (2023) study on the performance of employees in the banking center and its impact on organizational health found that a positive work environment can increase employee performance. Sugiharjo et al. (2023) found that "work environment as a mediator of leadership style influences employee performance positively and significantly" (Sugiharjo et al., 2023, p. 1). Canavesi and Minelli (2022) found that high-pressure work environments with poor work-life balance severely hindered employee engagement.

As stated previously, leadership considerably impacts employee engagement, team performance, and development. A leader that focuses on engagement and performance increases the strength of the team.

RESEARCH QUESTIONS

The following research questions guided the study:
RQ1: How does leadership style impact team development?
RQ2: How does leadership style impact team performance?

THEORETICAL FRAMEWORK

Fred Fiedler's *Contingency Theory of Leadership* recognizes that the best or most effective leadership style for a given situation is the one that best aligns with that situation (Asana, 2024; da Cruz et al., 2011; Miner, 2005; Peters et al., 1985). First established as a formal theory in 1964, this approach differs from a *Structural Model* that examines the impact of leadership styles, leader motivation, and relationship quality on employee attitude and team performance (Asana, 2024; Miner, 2005). The contingency theory of leadership also differs from the situational leadership model because the situational approach focuses on the team members' characteristics (Asana, 2024). Leadership style is adjusted to the maturity and readiness of the team members (Northouse, 2022).

Theoretical Principles

Influential leaders can adjust their leadership style for the situation at hand and the team members who follow them (Asana, 2024; Northouse, 2022). The leadership style of each prospective leader should be examined to ensure that the situation is a good fit (Peters et al., 1985). Though the *Contingency Theory of Leadership* has been heavily criticized, it has successfully increased knowledge about leadership (da Cruz et al., 2011). Other leadership theories focus on finding the best leadership style, whereas Fiedler focuses on the relationship between leadership style and different situations (da Cruz et al., 2011; Dias et al., 2023).

Situational Leadership Model, developed by Dr. Paul Hersey and Dr. Ken Blanchard, understands that leaders must adapt to different circumstances (Dugan, 2017; Greenwood, 1996; Northouse, 2022). This theory requires leaders to thoroughly examine the team's competency and commitment to completing tasks (Northouse, 2022). Both theories are relevant to the current study as they support the argument that organizations should attempt to hire the right leader for the situation and the company culture.

Core Concepts

The core concept of the present study is the impact of leadership style on team performance and development. Evidence suggests that different leadership styles are more effective in developing teams and increasing performance. For example, a transformational leadership style may be effective when an organization performs well and resources are high. However, a transactional leadership style may be more effective when the organization is in a deficit, and quick action is needed to get back in the green. For this study, the independent variables are the five core leadership styles and three subordinate leadership styles found in Figure 1, and the dependent variables are team development and team performance.

Figure 1. Leadership styles and team performance and development (Author's own work)

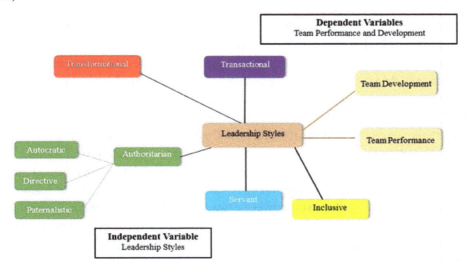

METHODOLOGY

This study uses a qualitative systematic literature review to focus on how leadership style impacts team development and performance. Peer-reviewed studies and articles were identified using academic databases and reviewing references from other literature reviews. An Excel spreadsheet was created as a literature matrix to report the collected data containing the primary subjects, themes, findings, source citations, and source type. Relevant themes were then used to categorize and synthesize each article with the research questions.

LITERATURE REVIEW

Often, leaders have a presence in an organization, but the effect of their leadership style negatively impacts teams. Some organizations have placed so much emphasis on having a leadership presence that they neglect to consider if the leadership style of a potential candidate will complement the company culture. Leadership style is vital in an organization. At times, a tenured person is assumed to be a leader and thus placed in a leadership position only to find out they do not have the qualifications to motivate and empower others effectively. Leadership style matters because not all are equipped to encourage others effectively. A hands-off approach to leadership may work in some settings but not others. When considering who should lead, an organization must assess the culture, values, and team members. At times, a versatile leader who can adapt to the different needs of the team is best.

Employees observe other employees, so a lack of fairness hinders a team's effectiveness and development. This type of hindrance further emphasizes the reason why the type of leadership style is so important. Without trust, a team will fail (Lencioni, 2002). It is up to the organization to insert the right leaders with the appropriate leadership style based on the dynamics of their organization and the team's needs (Paais & Pattiruhu, 2020). A strong leader can adapt to the needs of the team. This type of leadership style is essential to an organization and the development of teams.

A study conducted by Arifuddin et al. (2023) analyzed the effect of leadership style and work motivation on employee performance. The results of their quantitative analysis proved that motivation has a positive influence on employee performance (Arifuddin et al., 2023). Their testing also proved that leadership style positively influences employee performance. When comparing the two results, motivation had a greater influence on employee performance. An effective leadership style can combine the needs of employees and the company's interests (Arifuddin et al., 2023). "The leadership style of a leader and the motivation given by the leader greatly impacts the performance of employees" (Arifuddin et al., 2023, p. 207).

Leadership Theories and Historical Perspective

Landis et al. (2014) described leadership as the dynamic exchange of actions and interactions between leaders and followers, culminating in accomplishing collective objectives. As such, leadership is the most critical element of an organization (Landis et al., 2014). It constantly evolves; therefore, leadership styles and behaviors must be analyzed often. As societal norms and cultural dynamics change, leaders must quickly adapt and shift their behaviors to the team's needs (Dugan, 2017). Leaders have become more culturally aware and emotionally intelligent, increasing their effectiveness in motivating teams and increasing performance (Dias et al., 2023). Effective leadership creates a positive work environment and assists with the commitment of followers to the organization's vision and mission (Dias et al., 2023).

There are several theories regarding leadership and team performance. Various theories show just how essential the leader-team dynamic is for organizations. Leadership is not a new concept, having existed for centuries. The great leaders of old played a vital role in developing social order (Landis et al., 2014).

History of Leadership and Leadership Theories

Throughout history, great leaders left their footprints for others to follow. Moses was one of the first leaders to make an impact on society. He led a culturally diverse and, at times, irate group of people through uncertainty (Landis et al., 2014). He tried many ways to motivate them and retain order. Confucious was a prominent moral leader in Chinese history. He was a servant leader, for he believed it was a leader's duty to serve the people (*Confucius' Three Keys to Successful Leadership*, 2013). He also believed leaders should think before they act. Ford Motor Company successfully closed an entire distribution center without laying off employees. Henry Ford pioneered the five-day, 40-hour work week and believed in empowering his employees by setting them up for success (Jlittle, 2023).

Though the term 'leader' emerged around the 1300s, leadership did not evolve until the 1800s (Badshah, 2012). Leadership theory began as a trait theory, and in the 1960s, an urgency to find the best form of leadership occurred (Greenwood, 1996). The most cited theory between 1900 and 2023 is transformational leadership, with 41 percent of the citations, and contingency theory is the second most cited theory at 15 percent (Dias et al., 2023). From 1900 to 1949, leadership theories were predominantly based on personal traits, skills and values (Dias et al., 2023). Individual leadership styles were dominant from 1950 to 1969 (Dias et al., 2023). The focus switched to leadership styles and situational leadership from the 1970s to the 1980s, with motivational and transformational theories following in the 90s (Dias et al., 2023). By the 2000s, leadership theories had become heavily influenced by communication and information technology.

Trait Theory. Trait theory was the most widely respected leadership theory in the early 1900s (Greenwood, 1996). It focuses on a leader's physical and behavioral characteristics (Greenwood, 1996; Horner, 1997; Northouse, 2022). Trait theory was initially coined the 'Great Man' theory because researchers identified attributes from influential political, social, and military leaders (Horner, 1997; Landis et al., 2014; Northouse, 2022). Trait theorists studied the attributes of those strong leaders and determined there are 14 traits that leaders are born with that allow them to surpass their peers (Horner, 1997; Landis et al., 2014; Northouse, 2022). They perceived the following characteristics personified a leader: intelligence, scholarship, dependability, social participation, socio-economic status, initiative, persistence, know-how, self-confidence, insight, cooperativeness, popularity, adaptability, and verbal facility (Badshah, 2012; Northouse, 2022).

Trait theory has extensively documented research spanning a century, giving it credibility that others do not have (Northouse, 2022). It identifies the required components of a leader, which assists organizations in screening and selecting candidates for leadership training (Northouse, 2022).

Criticism. In the 1940s, Ralph M. Stogdill challenged trait theory in his research when he found that a leader in one circumstance may not be a leader in another circumstance (Greenwood, 1996; Northouse, 2022). Stogdill determined that leadership varies according to the situation, the followers, and the leader; therefore, no leadership style is superior to the other (Greenwood, 1996; Northouse, 2022). Researchers criticize that though many traits were identified as attributes of a strong leader, the findings were not consistent, and factors such as environment and situation were completely ignored (Horner, 1997; Northouse, 2022). Additionally, trait theory does not account for organizational training; a trait is not easily taught or learned (Northouse, 2022). Lastly, this theory does not describe how the leadership traits impact team performance and engagement (Northouse, 2022).

Contingency Theory of Leadership: Fiedler's contingency theory infers that "leadership effectiveness is a function of the interaction between the leader and the leadership situation" (da Cruz et al., 2011; Peters et al., 1985, p. 274). Fiedler contends that team performance is contingent upon the leader's leadership style and level of control over a situation (da Cruz et al., 2011). Under this theory, attributes, behavior, and style do not determine if an individual is a leader (da Cruz et al., 2011). According to Fiedler, a leader's personality determines their leadership style (da Cruz et al., 2011). The theory uses a scale to classify leadership style called the 'Least Preferred Co-Worker (LPC) Scale' to categorize each leader as either task-oriented or person-oriented (da Cruz et al., 2011; Peters et al., 1985). Leadership situations are categorized by their levels of favorableness: leader-member relations, task structure, and position power (Peters et al., 1985). There are eight leadership situations once all parameters are combined (Peters et al., 1985). The most favorable leadership situation is the leader-member relations, high task structure, and strong position-power combination (Peters et al., 1985).

Contingency leadership theory is beneficial for identifying favorable situations for the leader-team dynamic (da Cruz et al., 2011). The LPC scale can assist organizations with candidate selection for leadership positions (da Cruz et al., 2011). Extensive research supports this theory and finds it valid and reliable (da Cruz et al., 2011). The theory contributes to research by extending the knowledge about leadership and the impact of situations on the leader (da Cruz et al., 2011). It is a predictive and valuable theory that provides detailed information on the various leadership styles and the optimal situations for each.

Criticism: Contingency leadership theory is criticized for its complexity, with researchers finding it challenging to identify the correct situation-behavior combination (da Cruz et al., 2011; Mitchell et al., 1970). The interpretation of the theory has been updated four times since its inception, and some critics do not see the point of the process of classifying the scores in the LPC (da Cruz et al., 2011). The most compelling criticism is that it fails to explain why certain leadership styles are more effective than others (da Cruz et al., 2011). Lastly, the theory does not guide organizations on how to adapt their styles to various situations (da Cruz et al., 2011).

Situational Leadership Theory: Hersey and Blanchard based their situational leadership theory on Bill Reddin's 3-D management style theory (Northouse, 2022). Blanchard upgraded the original theory model and created the SLII model. The SLII model urges leaders to utilize directive and supportive behaviors for each situation (Northouse, 2022). The 'situation' is the attitudes, motivation, emotional intelligence, and team skill set they will lead (Northouse, 2022). For this theory to succeed, leaders must adjust their behavior, focusing on their directing style and coaching and supporting and delegating approaches (Indeed Editorial Team, 2024; Northouse, 2022). The coaching approach is team-focused and concentrates on the skill-building of each team member and establishing a healthy team environment (Indeed Editorial Team, 2024; Northouse, 2022). Directing and delegating concentrate on a high output and accountability from the team while empowering each individual (Indeed Editorial Team, 2024).

Situational leadership theory benefits leaders because it has a track record of success (Northouse, 2022). The theory is easy to understand and provides guidelines on what should and should not be carried out by the leader (Northouse, 2022). Due to the nature of situational leadership, diversity, inclusion, and engagement are incorporated. Adjusting behaviors regarding team culture and norms builds team trust and cohesiveness (Northouse, 2022).

Criticism: Situational leadership theory is criticized for lacking studies on the SLII model and whether the model is intended for employees or teams (Northouse, 2022). There is ambiguity regarding how "commitment is combined with confidence" and the theoretical basis for each development level (Northouse, 2022, p. 116). Lastly, situational leadership theory does not address how the leader or followers' demographics impact the model

Path-Goal Theory of Leadership Styles. In the 1970's, the path-goal theory of leadership styles emerged as one of the first motivational theories on leadership (Northouse, 2022). This theory provides guidelines on how leaders can motivate employees and teams to achieve goals (Dugan, 2017; Horner, 1997; Northouse, 2022). The path-goal theory of leadership styles focuses on team tasks, team motivation, and the confidence level of individual contributors (Horner, 1997; Northouse, 2022). The primary goal is to increase team performance and job satisfaction. The path-goal theory of leadership styles is one of the first theories to concentrate exclusively on the benefit of the followers and not the leader (Northouse, 2022). Instead of the leader focusing on adapting to the skillset and behaviors of the team as in situational leadership theory, it focuses on leadership style and the characteristics of the team (Northouse, 2022; Pacia & Guevarra, 2023). The ultimate strategy of the leader is to adjust the leadership style to the motivational needs of the team (Horner, 1997; Northouse, 2022).

In common with the path-goal theory of leadership styles, expectancy performance management theory and expectancy motivation theory are based on the assumption that followers are motivated by the belief that they can achieve a goal (Indeed Editorial Team, 2024; Northouse, 2022). The leader defines the goals, clarifies the path for each member of the team, and then provides support (Horner, 1997; Northouse, 2022). Expectancy performance management theory also helps leaders understand why some team members outperform others (Indeed Editorial Team, 2024). It focuses on the follower's belief they will achieve their goals (expectancy), a belief they will be rewarded for achieving goals (instrumentality), and the team member's attitude toward taking on more responsibility (valence) (Indeed Editorial Team, 2024). The strength of the path-goal theory of leadership styles is its practical model and clear theoretical framework that directs leaders on motivating teams and enhancing performance (Northouse, 2022).

Criticism: The path-goal theory of leadership styles is criticized for its complexity and overload of leadership style levels, such as the degrees of structure, authority, and clarity (Northouse, 2022). There is not enough supporting research on the success of this theory. A concern for some critics is that the theory has a one-way effect in that the leader affects the follower, which can lead to dependency (Northouse, 2022). Lastly, it is assumed leaders can effectively communicate in all situations (Northouse, 2022).

In pursuing quality education in the Philippine educational system, Pacia and Guevarra (2023) evaluated the moderating effect of task structure in leadership and the path-goal theory of leadership styles on teachers' motivation, performance, and satisfaction. In this study, teachers perceived their school leadership to have directive, supportive, participatory, and achievement-oriented leadership styles (Pacia & Guevarra, 2023). The study comprised 579 junior high school teachers in the Division of San Pablo City. The researchers found a significant positive relationship between the path-goal theory of leadership styles and teacher work motivation and performance (Pacia & Guevarra, 2023). There was no significant correlation between the path-goal theory of leadership styles, leadership task structure, and teacher job satisfaction (Pacia & Guevarra, 2023). The direct influence of the path-goal theory of leadership styles positively impacts teacher work motivation and work performance. The findings support their hypothesis that, to enhance teacher motivation, a positive, encouraging work environment is essential (Pacia & Guevarra, 2023).

McGregor Theory. Douglas McGregor believed employees must be supervised, avoid responsibility, and be coerced to perform their duties; he labeled those employees as Theory X assumptions (Kopelman et al., 2008; Landis et al., 2014; Sahin, 2012). Theory Y assumptions are the group of employees who are motivated to work and accept responsibility (Landis et al., 2014; Sahin, 2012). The McGregor theory has been around for over 50 years, and it is still used and respected by researchers (Ďuricová & Šugereková, 2017). The theory is credited with providing an understanding of management (Ďuricová & Šugereková, 2017).

Criticism: The theory is criticized for assuming all employees are lazy, and it does not consider the changing nature of organizations, employees, or cultural environments (Gannon & Boguszak, 2013; Kopelman et al., 2008). Critics also state that the theory is harsh for individuals who need additional guidance with their tasks (Gannon & Boguszak, 2013).

A study conducted by Sahin (2012) examined if there was a relationship between McGregor's Theory X and Theory Y leadership styles and effective communication with the Leader-Member Exchange (LMX) theory as a mediator. They found that the Theory Y management style enhanced the quality of LMX and employees' commitment to the organization; however, Theory X had no significant impact (Sahin, 2012).

Leader-Member Exchange Theory. In leader-member exchange theory (LMX), the leader receives status for accomplishing a goal (Landis et al., 2014). LMX focuses on the leader-follower and the differences between the leader and the team (Dias et al., 2023; Landis et al., 2014; Northouse, 2022; Sahin, 2012). Two groups are classified LMX: in-group and out-group (Northouse, 2022). Members of the in-group work well with the leader; their personalities are compatible with them, and they are willing to take on additional responsibilities (Northouse, 2022). In exchange, the in-group team member receives more accolades, empowerment, and attention from the leader (Landis et al., 2014; Northouse, 2022). In-group members are highly motivated achievers, reliable, and expressive (Northouse, 2022). The out-group team members are less compatible with the leader; they do what is required but do not go above and beyond (Landis et al., 2014; Northouse, 2022).

Researchers found that LMX teams had less turnover, favorable performance evaluations, greater job satisfaction, and career progression (Northouse, 2022). A large body of research backs LMX, which has proven to be cross-cultural (Northouse, 2022). LMX accurately describes typical leader-team dynamics, and it is the only theory that explicitly outlines the leader-follower relationship emphasizing communication. Leaders' are reminded to treat each team member fairly and to remove all biases toward different genders, religions, and ages (Northouse, 2022).

Criticism: LMX creates division in the team, and its fairness is questionable (Northouse, 2022). The presence of in-group and out-group takes away from the cohesiveness of the team and borders very closely to discrimination (Northouse, 2022). Out-group members who may potentially want to take on more responsibility may not because of their initial exclusion from the in-group (Northouse, 2022).

LEADERSHIP STYLES AND THEIR IMPACT ON TEAM PERFORMANCE AND DEVELOPMENT

Transactional and Transformational Leadership

Bucic et al. (2010) take a deep-dive approach to examining how leadership style impacts team development. Their approach was to research the impact of leadership style on employee growth by taking a team-level perspective. Doing so gave insight into how impactful leadership style is to employee learning (Bucic et al., 2010). The main objective of their study was to identify the most common leadership style used by top management team leaders and to reveal how leadership style influences employee learning (Bucic et al., 2010).

Two processes incorporate team learning: feedback learning and feed-forward learning (Bucic et al., 2010). Feedback learning monitors how institutionalized learning affects a person, whereas feed-forward learning incorporates the intuition and interpretation of a team member into institutionalized parts of collective team learning (Bucic et al., 2010). The feed-forward process is a conglomerate of individual perceptions, reasoning, and intuition shaped by risk-taking, innovation, and group experiments. Because of the variations in team learning, leadership must closely monitor "team learning to maximize the expected payoffs from team performance and output" (Bucic et al., 2010, p. 231). Some leadership styles are best for team learning: democratic, servant, and transformational, to name a few (Northouse, 2022).

Transactional leaders exercise feedback learning and emphasize exploitation (Bucic et al., 2010; Northouse, 2022). They motivate teams by giving team members promotions when they surpass their goals (Northouse, 2022). A transactional leadership style is the traditional style of leadership where an exchange is made between leaders and team members to meet their self-interests (Bucic et al., 2010; Northouse, 2022). Team members do not find this leadership style trustworthy (Northouse, 2022). Transactional leaders like routines and the refinement of learning (Northouse, 2022). Anything that falls outside of what the leader puts in place can be unsettling, resulting in corrective action.

Transformational leaders emphasize exploration. This approach impacts feed-forward learning, identifying "how team members contribute personal knowledge to team learning" (Bucic et al., 2010, p. 5). Team members tend to respond to leaders who empower them and encourage creativity and an entrepreneurial mindset (Northouse, 2022). Team members adopt an entrepreneurial mindset due to a transformational leader's encouragement to be innovative and develop new ideas and methods. The team earns the most significant learning opportunity when this method is in place (Bucic et al., 2010; Northouse, 2022).

Transformational leaders interact with all team members regardless of their skill set. They motivate them by leading by example and explaining how to increase achievement (Northouse, 2022). They are skilled in providing a vision that team members find attainable and give them a sense of pride. The transactional leader earns the respect and trust of the team as a result (Northouse, 2022). Since a transformational leader encourages creativity and risk-taking, they are better suited to recognize the team's value and integrate new knowledge with existing knowledge to facilitate team further learning (Bucic et al., 2010).

Some researchers believe that both transactional and transformational leadership are required depending on the shifts in the organization's needs (Bucic et al., 2010; Northouse, 2022). As a result, an effective leader will need the flexibility and discernment to know which hat to wear (Northouse, 2022). A strong and wise leader can identify and adjust their style to the organization's current and emerging climate changes.

The organizational leadership style at the top directly impacts how team leaders perform (Northouse, 2022). Bucic et al. (2010) theorize that low-level leaders mirror the leadership style of upper management. If the organization maintains a distant leadership style, the vision and expectation of all lower-level leads and team members is to operate within the company strategies, processes, and structures (Bucic et al., 2010). In this example, transactional leaders provide detailed instructions for team members to adhere to within the boundaries of the organization's vision, and a reward-based system is used to motivate them (Northouse, 2022). An innovative leader who encourages team members to think outside the box would not thrive in this leadership climate because of the limitations. In contrast, a transformational leader can operate freely in an organizational culture where the decision-makers encourage exploration initiations (Northouse, 2022).

Bucic et al. (2010) identified key leadership behaviors, styles, and decision-making in their research:

1. Leaders of a team encompass both transformational and transactional leadership styles.
2. There is a positive relationship between transactional leadership and feedback learning.
3. Transformational leadership has a positive impact on feed-forward learning.
4. Dual leadership provides structure and procedures and simultaneously encourages innovative ideas.
5. Leadership style, whether transactional, transformational, or both, impacts team and employee performance and development.

Authoritarian Leadership Styles

Pizzolitto et al. (2023) focus on the authoritarian leadership style in their study. Three leadership styles fall under the authoritarian leadership umbrella: autocratic, directive, and paternalistic (Pizzolitto et al., 2023). Authoritarian leadership exudes a high level of control over subordinates, and absolute obedience is required (Oh et al., 2023; Pizzolitto et al., 2023). There is a distancing between who is in charge and who is not, and collaboration is not encouraged (Pizzolitto et al., 2023).

Pizzolitto et al. (2023) state, "Authoritarian leadership exercises control and authority over followers, limiting their autonomy and self-determination, and is often associated with the "dark side" of leadership" (Chiang et al., 2021; McIntosh & Rima, 2007). Team members' self-efficacy and proactivity are stifled, ultimately limiting innovation and creativity (Oh et al., 2023; Pizzolitto et al., 2023). There is a high level of distrust among teams exposed to authoritarian leadership (Chiang et al., 2021; Pizzolitto et al., 2023). Pizzolitto et al.'s (2023) findings regarding the effects authoritarian leadership has on team performance show an adverse effect on team members. Further studies show that authoritarian leadership styles lead to suppressed feelings, adverse team performance, and negative employee retention (Oh et al., 2023; Wang et al., 2019).

The authoritarian leader's suppressed emotions tend to create a tense environment where the team members are exhausted and unmotivated (Chiang et al., 2021; Oh et al., 2023; Wang et al., 2019). Wang et al. (2019) found the more dependent a subordinate is, the stronger the authoritarian domination of the leader. Though there is a negative stigma around this leadership style, this style is helpful in some situations. Teams with low power struggle and high participation are successful under an authoritarian leader (Pizzolitto et al., 2023). Authoritarians positively affect team communication when authority is not abused, and leadership effectiveness improves significantly when authoritarian behaviors are reduced (Chiang et al., 2021).

The autocratic leadership style findings show team members are more accepting of this leadership style because it is less damaging and more goal-oriented (Pizzolitto et al., 2023). In their research, Pizzolitto et al. (2023) found that autocratic leadership positively and negatively affected team member performance. It differed according to the situation. Autocratic leadership had positive results on performance, but because of the elevated stress conditions, it had a negative effect on team member satisfaction. Compromising the team's self-confidence adversely impacts performance (Pizzolitto et al., 2023).

In their study, Fiaz et al. (2017) found a negative relationship between autocratic leadership style and team members' motivation. Autocratic leaders place more emphasis on performance and less on development; all of the power is in their hands (Fiaz et al., 2017). The leader assumes employees are naturally lazy and cannot be trusted, teamwork does not exist, and communication is poor under autocratic leadership (Fiaz et al., 2017). On a positive note, autocratic leaders ensure that procedures are clearly defined.

A directive leadership style trains team members to be disciplined by guiding and coaching (Pizzolitto et al., 2023). This leadership style reduces ambiguity and increases team members' trust and motivation. "Research suggests that who the leader is and what the leader is directing can fundamentally alter the impact of directive leadership" (Krause et al., 2024, p. 661). In their study, Pizzolitto et al. (2023) found that directive leadership was the most effective during project implementation because this leadership style has strong strategy and performance skills. Directive leaders show a sincere interest in team members and aspire to high productivity (Krause et al., 2024). This type of leadership is more accepted in Eastern countries than in Western countries, though Eastern country scholars agree that directive needs fine tuning to increase performance (Pizzolitto et al., 2023).

When comparing a directive leadership style to an empowering one, Pizzolitto et al. (2023) found that directive leadership is highly effective in stressful conditions with adaptation and performance. However, under calmer conditions, empowering leadership positively affected team performance. Under adverse, unstable environments, directive leadership positively impacted team cohesiveness when upper management was heterogeneous while empowering leadership positively impacted performance when upper management was homogeneous (Pizzolitto et al., 2023). Homogeneous leaders achieve higher team member performance when the team has similar abilities and is like-minded (Pizzolitto et al., 2023). However, the reverse is true in the United States.

The paternalistic leadership style includes three styles: authority, morality, and benevolence (Pizzolitto et al., 2023). They are genuinely interested in the team's well-being, privately and professionally. They are like a father figure, hence the name (Qin, 2022). The benevolent side of a paternalistic leader is very strong (Pizzolitto et al., 2023; Qin, 2022). Though this leadership style is typically associated with positive performance, it has an authoritarian and benevolent side; therefore, performance can vary. Qin (2022) found that paternalistic leaders positively impacted team member performance at the middle and senior leadership levels. They influence their subordinates through "reverence and obedience, recognition and emulation, and gratitude" (Qin, 2022, p. 126). Paternalistic leaders thrive in organizations with strict order and stable work environments (Qin, 2022).

Authoritarian leadership is the least desirable style for team member performance, hence why it is called a dark-side trait. The paternalistic leadership style is the most balanced of authoritarian leadership styles (Pizzolitto et al., 2023).

Servant Leadership Style

A servant leader acts with high moral standards and great concern for the organization's stakeholders. The qualities of a servant leader include humility, team and individual development, listening, empowerment of individuals and the team, shared decision-making, ethical behavior, and a sense of community (Canavesi & Minelli, 2022; Northouse, 2022). They engage the team emotionally, relationally, and ethically, bringing out their best selves. Canavesi and Minelli (2022) define employee engagement as a series of positive attitudes.

Canavesi and Minelli (2022) found that servant leadership positively influences employee engagement. Engaged employees are more loyal and productive. Moral-based leadership promotes integrity and priorities that support the development of employees (Northouse, 2022). Instead of leaders pursuing their self-interest, they put energy or efforts into relationships with stakeholders to increase loyalty, trust, and employee commitment (Canavesi & Minelli, 2022; Northouse, 2022).

Though there have been over 20 years of research regarding servant leadership theory, it has been criticized for its name (Northouse, 2022). The name of the theory implies servitude and followership, which is perceived to be the opposite of leadership (Northouse, 2022). Servant leadership theory empowers followers and teams, but it is unclear how organizational enhancements are made. Lastly, there is a lack of consensus on the theoretical framework. Servant leadership theory is solely employee-focused, which implies neglecting other leadership duties such as forecasting, delegating, coaching, and production (Northouse, 2022).

Leadership Style Misalignment and Consequences

Dysfunctional leadership spreads organizational misalignments (Heracleous & Werres, 2016; Juliana et al., 2021). Leadership has the responsibility and the authority to make decisions, allocate resources, and maintain the corporate culture (Heracleous & Werres, 2016). Misaligned leaders can negatively impact the corporate culture with how they communicate, develop, and treat their subordinates (Heracleous & Werres, 2016; Juliana et al., 2021). The wrong alignment of leaders can lead to low motivation, disorganization, poor communication, weak employee retention, and decreased morale (Heracleous & Werres, 2016; Juliana et al., 2021).

A study by Heracleous and Werres (2016) examined the organization's behaviors and leadership in two prominent companies: Worldcom and Nortel Networks. They found that the CEO of Worldcom focused on acquisitions and tight cost control but neglected human resource development (Heracleous & Werres, 2016). The CEO also exercised an autocratic leadership style by which they had total authority over the board of directors and subordinates (Heracleous & Werres, 2016). Additionally, large loans and bonuses were given to senior executives at the demand of the CEO. The downfall of the organization was poor business dealings, "internal misalignments due to problematic corporate culture and human resource practices," and "ineffective leadership and corporate governance" (Heracleous & Werres, 2016, pp. 7-8).

The role and alignment of leadership are vital in an organization (Briker et al., 2020; Heracleous & Werres, 2016). A dominant autocratic CEO and a passive board of directors led to aggressive growth, large debt, and unsupported subordinates, ultimately becoming the organization's demise (Heracleous & Werres, 2016).

Correcting Leadership Misalignment

Healthy teams have strong, mindful leaders who balance organizational, team, and individual needs (Zackrison, 2021). There are steps leaders can take to help them create healthy teams. Zackrison (2021) suggests the following:

1. First, leaders want to do a self-examination, note their strengths and weaknesses, and assess their emotional intelligence.
2. They should then determine what they need to be successful at work and in their personal life. This will include career progression, work-life balance, education, developing leaders on the team, etc.
3. Next, write down the goals and the steps required to get there.

After leaders build themselves, they need to build their team (Zackrison, 2021).

4. Identify each team member's strengths and weaknesses to help them develop and achieve their goals while balancing the leader's and team member's goals to avoid burnout. Sometimes, the team's needs are more significant than the leader's and individual team member's, so it is vital to remain flexible.
5. Next, coach and lead the team as a team and not as individuals.
6. Lastly, ensure that the team's and individuals' goals align with the organization's needs. The leader is a member of a group of leaders in the organization and leads a team; therefore, maintaining a balance between the two is essential.

SUMMARY

It is beneficial for organizations to create a culture based on ethics and collaborate with teams to achieve organizational goals (Canavesi & Minelli, 2022). Servant leadership is hindered by high pressure, poor working conditions, and a lack of proper work-life balance (Canavesi & Minelli, 2022). When an organization's top leadership is servant-led, authoritative and positional power is not imposed, team members' opinions are welcomed and valued, and there is low supervision (Canavesi & Minelli, 2022). Unfortunately, without guidance, some employees are unclear about their tasks (Northouse, 2022). It is evident from the literature that there is no one leadership style that is best suited for team performance and development. Instead, a hybrid, adaptable form of leadership that encompasses empowerment, direction, communication, and morality is ideal.

DIVERSITY AND INCLUSION: THE ROLE OF THE LEADER

What is an Inclusive Leadership Style?

Inclusive leadership is a rapidly growing leadership style that encompasses many different approaches and has a proven track record of success for employees, the team, the organization, and society. The 1987 Workforce 2000 report motivated organizations to diversify, specifically with women and people of color, to gain a competitive advantage (Northouse, 2022). As a result of that report, several diversity programs and management diversity training ensued (Northouse, 2022). Later, it was determined that diversity alone was not sufficient. The addition of inclusion allows diversity to acquire the benefits it needs for the organization, and inclusive leadership's role is to replace discriminatory and oppressive policies and behaviors in the organization (Northouse, 2022).

The lack of a theoretical foundation and strategies for incorporating inclusion in organizations has prevented organizations from fully implementing inclusive leadership in their corporate training (Northouse, 2022). Cambridge Dictionary defines inclusion as "the act of including someone or something as part of a group" (Cambridge University Press & Assessment, n.d., Inclusion). Inclusion is a basic need, along with affection (Northouse, 2022). Inclusive leadership brings and maintains a sense of shared identity to the team (Radicioni, 2023). Leaders ensure that each team member knows that everyone brings value, and the leader's behavior encourages unity and respect for one another (Northouse, 2022; Oh et al., 2023; Radicioni, 2023). Under the guidance of an inclusive leader, status differences in teams decrease, and all members are encouraged to participate. (Northouse, 2022; Radicioni, 2023). Open communication in the team increases trust in the decision-making process (Oh et al., 2023).

Despite the many benefits of the role of inclusive leaders, researchers find that the concepts of inclusive leadership are often used interchangeably with Leadership-Member Exchange (Northouse, 2022). Many leadership styles define behaviors related to healthy leader-follower relationships that coincide with those of inclusive leadership (Northouse, 2022). The lack of variability makes measuring inclusivity and linking specific behaviors to outcomes challenging (Northouse, 2022).

Inclusive Leader Team Behaviors

According to Harvard Business Review, leaders account for 70% of total points allocated regarding employees feeling they belong and feel psychologically safe (Zheng et al., 2023). Inclusive leaders experience a "17% increase in team performance, 20% increase in decision-making quality, and 29% increase in team collaboration" (Radicioni, 2023; Zheng et al., 2023, para. 1). Inclusive leader-led organizations reap the benefits of innovation revenue and are 50% more likely to make better decisions (Zheng et al., 2023).

Zheng et al. (2023) interviewed 40 DEI award winners or peer-nominated exemplary inclusive leaders from various sectors to discover key strategies, successes, and behaviors for inclusive leadership. The common traits found among the participants are humility, curiosity, and empathy (Northouse, 2022; Radicioni, 2023; Zheng et al., 2023). They identified five behaviors the leaders used:

(1) The leaders strive for authenticity and psychological safety because they are both essential for creating an environment where people can be themselves and share their opinions without backlash (Northouse, 2022; Radicioni, 2023; Zheng et al., 2023). They display an example of curiosity, humility, and vulnerability to their teams by openly sharing their vulnerabilities instead of hiding them, revealing their weaknesses, and sharing failures and successes (Radicioni, 2023; Zheng et al., 2023).

(2) They redefine rules instead of mindlessly following them without question (Radicioni, 2023; Zheng et al., 2023). Inclusive leaders challenge long-standing rules and practices such as dress codes, hair standards, and tattoos, which inherently target African American women and young adults (Zheng et al., 2023). Some leaders advocated removing full-time or part-time status criteria from candidate applications not to penalize working mothers (Zheng et al., 2023).

(3) Zheng et al. (2023) discovered that inclusive leaders embrace and consistently implement active learning (Radicioni, 2023). The leaders agreed that it is human nature to have biased habits or tendencies; therefore, self-examination and reflection on those behaviors are required to change those habits (Radicioni, 2023; Zheng et al., 2023). Inclusive leaders are intentional about educating themselves on different cultures and underrepresented groups. Instead of hoping to recruit more underrepresented groups, they proactively create a process to recruit them (Zheng et al., 2023).

(4) Inclusive leaders ensure equal opportunity and fair outcomes for each team member (Northhouse, 2022; Radicioni, 2023; Zheng et al., 2023). They accomplish this by paying close attention to each member's needs, especially those of the underrepresented groups, to help remove potential barriers (Zheng et al., 2023).

(5) Inclusive leaders view inclusivity as everyone's job, not just HR (Radicioni, 2023). Many leaders believe HR handles diversity equity and inclusion (DEI) initiatives, so they do not need to get involved (Zheng et al., 2023). When an organization makes DEI initiatives part of its organizational values, it becomes part of the company culture; therefore, if a leader leaves the organization, they do not take the inclusive initiatives out the door with them (Zheng et al., 2023).

DEI may look different in various organizations. Some incorporate DEI into recruitment, compensation, and retention, while others have built it into their organizational strategy (Zheng et al., 2023). Inclusive leadership is powerful because it causes individuals to step out of their comfort zone and work with someone different from them, thus benefiting from creative collaboration and new innovative ways of completing tasks (Northouse, 2022; Zheng et al., 2023). Inclusivity is a vital part of leadership, and although there are advancements, more work is needed (Radicioni, 2023). For example, per the 2022 Women CEO in America report, only 8.8% of Fortune 500 CEOs are women, and only 1% are women of color (Radicioni, 2023). DEI executive leadership is a model for teams; therefore, more representation is needed for buy-in (Radicioni, 2023).

LEADERSHIP STYLES AND THEIR IMPACT ON HIGHER EDUCATION

Researchers vary in their perspective of what type of leadership is most effective in higher education. However, they agree that the shortage of influential leaders to drive change and reform within institutions, adapt to the ever-evolving landscape of innovative technologies like artificial intelligence, and effectively strategize for long-term goals is a pressing issue (Paais & Pattiruhu, 2020; Pellitteri, 2021; Posthuma & Al-Riyami, 2012). Using emotional intelligence to analyze leadership styles can help educational leaders become more successful and transformative by highlighting the unique emotional dynamics of each style (Pellitteri, 2021; Zackrison, 2021).

In Table 1, Pellitteri (2021) examines three case studies and their frequency of using certain leadership styles in higher education. The most commonly used leadership styles were then examined through emotional intelligence. The theory is that higher education leaders with high emotional intelligence are more likely to consider the culture of the school environment and the staff (Pellitteri, 2021). The findings suggest that balancing several leadership styles increases a leader's effectiveness in team development and performance, which aligns with the findings from the literature review (Pellitteri, 2021). Senior leaders of higher education institutions can further establish teams of academic leaders by creating leadership development programs that encourage collaborative efforts and distribute leadership responsibilities across diverse groups and people (Posthuma & Al-Riyami, 2012).

Table 1. The impact of leadership styles in higher education

	Case Studies
Participants	(1) Educational leaders at a Polytechnical educational organization in Ghana; 214 leaders in teaching and non-teaching roles. (2) Educational settings in Somaliland. (3) 42 administrators in medical educational settings across three hierarchical levels of authority.
Findings/Results	(1) Most frequent styles used: coaching, pacesetting, democratic, and affiliative. A mix of styles was used in varying situations. Author concluded that each style is critical and that leadership style should be aligned to a particular task. (2) The autocratic leadership style resulted in lower performance levels, whereas egalitarian, transformative, and transactional styles had higher performance and engagement. (3) Low-level management was primarily participative. Middle management used coaching styles, and senior management used multiple styles of leadership.
Cited Literature	(Pellitteri, 2021)
Supporting Literature	(Bucic et al., 2010; Chiang et al., 2021; Pizzolitto et al., 2023; Zackrison, 2021)

CONCLUSION

This chapter discusses the impact of leadership style on team development and performance, the consequences of misalignments, and the steps leaders can take to create a healthy team. The findings gathered in this study reveal that leaders are on the front line, and what they do or do not do significantly impacts the organization and the team. Creating a culture of inclusivity empowers the team and creates growth. This study successfully answered the research questions on how leadership style impacts team performance and development. A leader's style can empower the team, increase performance, and develop a team with an entrepreneurial mindset, or it can stagnate growth and diminish autonomy and self-determination. Since employees are essential to the success of an organization, it is in the organization's best interest to invest time and money into developing strong leaders who align with its vision.

REFERENCES

Arifuddin, A., Lita, W., Catherine, S., & Yingxiang, S. (2023). The influence of leadership style and work motivation on employee performance. *Journal Markcount Finance*, 1(3), 206–215. DOI: 10.55849/jmf.v1i3.116

Asana, T. (2024, May 24). *Fiedler's contingency theory: Why leadership isn't uniform*. Asana. https://asana.com/resources/fiedlers-contingency-theory

Badshah, S. (2012). Historical study of leadership theories. *Journal of Strategic Human Resource Management*, 1(1), 49–59.

Beck, R., & Harter, J. (2014). Why great managers are so rare. *Gallup Business Journal*, 25.

Bridwell, T. (2022, March 10). Leading with authentic-influence. Tony Bridwell. com. https://www.tonybridwell.com/resources/leading-with-authentic-influence

Briker, R., Walter, F., & Cole, M. S. (2020). The consequences of (not) seeing eye-to-eye about the past: The role of supervisor–team fit in past temporal focus for supervisors' leadership behavior. *Journal of Organizational Behavior*, 41(3), 244–262. DOI: 10.1002/job.2416

Bucic, T., Robinson, L., & Ramburuth, P. (2010). Effects of leadership style on team learning. *Journal of Workplace Learning*, 22(4), 228–248. DOI: 10.1108/13665621011040680

Cambridge University Press & Assessment. (n.d.). Inclusion. In *Cambridge Academic Content Dictionary*. Retrieved on August 9, 2024, from https://dictionary.cambridge.org/us/dictionary/english/inclusion#google_vignette

Canavesi, A., & Minelli, E. (2022). Servant leadership and employee engagement: A qualitative study. *Employee Responsibilities and Rights Journal*, 34(4), 413–435. DOI: 10.1007/s10672-021-09389-9

Chiang, J. T. J., Chen, X. P., Liu, H., Akutsu, S., & Wang, Z. (2021). We have emotions but can't show them! Authoritarian leadership, emotion suppression climate, and team performance. *Human Relations*, 74(7), 1082–1111. DOI: 10.1177/0018726720908649

Confucius' three keys to successful leadership. (2013, June 19). Forbes. https://www.forbes.com/2009/05/21/confucius-tips-wisdom-leadership-managing-philosophy.html

da Cruz, M. R. P., Nunes, A. J. S., & Pinheiro, P. G. (2011). Fiedler's contingency theory: Practical application of the least preferred coworker (LPC) scale. *IUP Journal of Organizational Behavior*, 10(4), 7–26.

Dias, M., Vieira, P., Pereira, L., Quintão, H., & Lafraia, J. (2023). Leadership theories: A systematic review based on bibliometric and content analysis methods. *GPH-International Journal of Business Management, 6*(05), 01-16.

Dugan, J. P. (2017). *Leadership theory: Cultivating critical perspectives*. John Wiley & Sons.

Ďuricová, L., & Šugereková, T. (2017). A Managers self-concept in the context of their leadership style within McGregors theory. *Človek a spoločnosť, 20*(1), 36-44.

Fiaz, M., Su, Q., & Saqib, A. (2017). Leadership styles and employees' motivation: Perspective from an emerging economy. *Journal of Developing Areas*, 51(4), 143–156. https://doi-org.trevecca.idm.oclc.org/10.1353/jda.2017.0093. DOI: 10.1353/jda.2017.0093

Gannon, D., & Boguszak, A. (2013). Douglas McGregor's theory x and theory y. *CRIS - Bulletin of the Centre for Research and Interdisciplinary Study, 2013*(2), vol. 85-93.

Greenwood, R. G. (1996). Leadership theory: A historical look at its evolution. *The Journal of Leadership Studies*, 3(1), 3–16. DOI: 10.1177/107179199600300102

Heracleous, L., & Werres, K. (2016). On the road to disaster: Strategic misalignments and corporate failure. *Long Range Planning*, 49(4), 491–506. DOI: 10.1016/j.lrp.2015.08.006

Hewlett, S. A. (2024, January 23). *The new rules of executive presence*. Harvard Business Review. https://hbr.org/2024/01/the-new-rules-of-executive-presence

Horner, M. (1997). Leadership theory: Past, present and future. *Team Performance Management*, 3(4), 270–287. DOI: 10.1108/13527599710195402

Indeed Editorial Team. (2024, June 28). *What are theories of performance management? (With benefits)*. Indeed Career Guide. https://uk.indeed.com/career-advice/career-development/theories-of-performance-management

Jlittle. (2023, May 1). *Ford's five day workweek. May 1st 1926. Today in Ford Motor Company history*. Gary Crossley Ford. https://www.garycrossleyford.com/blog/today-in-ford-history/fords-five-day-workweek-may-1st-1926/

Juliana, C., Gani, L., & Jermias, J. (2021). Performance implications of misalignment among business strategy, leadership style, organizational culture and management accounting systems. *International Journal of Ethics and Systems*, 37(4), 509–525. DOI: 10.1108/IJOES-02-2021-0033

Kopelman, R. E., Prottas, D. J., & Davis, A. L. (2008). Douglas McGregor's theory X and Y: Toward a construct-valid measure. *Journal of Managerial Issues*, ●●●, 255–271.

Krause, R., Withers, M. C., & Waller, M. J. (2024). Leading the board in a crisis: Strategy and performance implications of board chair directive leadership. *Journal of Management*, 50(2), 654–684. https://doi-org.trevecca.idm.oclc.org/10.1177/01492063221121584. DOI: 10.1177/01492063221121584

Landis, E. A., Hill, D., & Harvey, M. R. (2014). A synthesis of leadership theories and styles. *Journal of Management Policy and Practice*, 15(2), 97.

Lencioni, P. M. (2002). *The five dysfunctions of a team: A Leadership Fable, 20th Anniversary Edition*. John Wiley & Sons.

McIntosh, G. L., & Rima, S. D. (2007). *Overcoming the dark side of leadership: How to become an effective leader by confronting potential failures*. Baker Books.

Miner, J. B. (2005). *Essential theories of motivation and leadership*. M.E. Sharpe.

Mitchell, T. R., Biglan, A., Oncken, G. R., & Fiedler, F. E. (1970). The contingency model: Criticism and suggestions. *Academy of Management Journal*, 13(3), 253–267. DOI: 10.2307/254963

Neal, S., Rhyne, R., Boatman, J., Watt, B., & Yeh, M. (2023). *Global leadership forecast 2023: DDI*. DDI. https://www.ddiworld.com/global-leadership-forecast-2023

Northouse, P. G. (2022). *Leadership: theory and practice* (9th ed.). SAGE Publications.

Oh, J., Kim, D. H., & Kim, D. (2023). The impact of inclusive leadership and autocratic leadership on employees' job satisfaction and commitment In sport organizations: The mediating role of organizational trust and the moderating role of sport involvement. *Sustainability (Basel)*, 15(4), 3367. DOI: 10.3390/su15043367

Paais, M., & Pattiruhu, J. R. (2020). Effect of motivation, leadership, and organizational culture on satisfaction and employee performance. *The Journal of Asian Finance. Economics and Business*, 7(8), 577–588. DOI: 10.13106/jafeb.2020.vol7.no8.577

Pacia, D. R., & Guevarra, P. M. (2023). Influence of path-goal theory of leadership styles and the moderating role of task structure in leadership on teachers' satisfaction, motivation, and performance. *International Journal of Multidisciplinary: Applied Business & Education Research*, 4(7), 2330–2345. https://doi-org.trevecca.idm.oclc.org/10.11594/ijmaber.04.07.15. DOI: 10.11594/ijmaber.04.07.15

Pellitteri, J. (2021). Emotional intelligence and leadership styles in education. *Psychology & its Contexts/Psychologie a Její Kontexty, 12*(2).

Peters, L. H., Hartke, D. D., & Pohlmann, J. T. (1985). Fiedler's contingency theory of leadership: An application of the meta-analysis procedures of Schmidt and Hunter. *Psychological Bulletin*, 97(2), 274–285. https://doi-org.trevecca.idm.oclc.org/10.1037/0033-2909.97.2.274. DOI: 10.1037/0033-2909.97.2.274

Pizzolitto, E., Verna, I., & Venditti, M. (2023). Authoritarian leadership styles and performance: A systematic literature review and research agenda. *Management Review Quarterly*, 73(2), 841–871. DOI: 10.1007/s11301-022-00263-y

Pontefract, D. (2023, February 8). New research suggests an alarming decline in high-quality leaders. *Forbes*. https://www.forbes.com/sites/danpontefract/2023/02/08/new-research-suggests-an-alarming-decline-in-high-quality-leaders/

Posthuma, R., & Al-Riyami, S. (2012). Leading teams of higher education administrators: Integrating goal setting, team role, and team life cycle theories. *Higher Education Studies*, 2(3), 44–54. DOI: 10.5539/hes.v2n3p44

Qin, M. (2022). The impact of middle and senior leadership styles on employee performance--evidence from Chinese enterprises. *Informing Science: The International Journal of an Emerging Transdiscipline, 25*, 123-142. https://doi-org.trevecca.idm.oclc.org/10.28945/4936

Radha, P., & Aithal, P. S. (2023). A study on the performance of employees in the banking sector and its impact on the organizational health. *International Journal of Management* [IJMTS]. *Technology and Social Sciences*, 8(4), 119–127.

Radicioni, B. (2023, December 15). *What is inclusive leadership?* Babson Thought & Action. https://entrepreneurship.babson.edu/what-is-inclusive-leadership/

Rahman, S., & Alam, M. (2019). Leadership style and its impact on employee performance: An empirical study on private commercial banks in Bangladesh. *International Journal of Human Resource Management*, 8(3), 1–10.

Rivaldo, Y., & Nabella, S. D. (2023). Employee performance: Education, training, experience and work discipline. *Calitatea*, 24(193), 182–188.

Sahin, F. (2012). The mediating effect of leader–member exchange on the relationship between Theory X and Y management styles and affective commitment: A multilevel analysis. *Journal of Management & Organization*, 18(2), 159–174. DOI: 10.5172/jmo.2012.18.2.159

State of the global workplace: 2024 report. (n.d.). Gallup, Inc. https://www.gallup.com/workplace/349484/state-of-the-global-workplace.aspx

Sugiharjo, R. J., Purbasari, R. N., Rahmat, A., & Paijan, P. (2023). The role of the work environment as a mediation for the effect of leadership style on the performance of banking institution employees. *Dinasti International Journal of Management Science*, 5(1), 1–14. DOI: 10.31933/dijms.v4i6.1976

Wahdiniawati, S. A., & Sarinastiti, N. (2023). Employee development: Analysis organization culture, competence and mentoring: A literature review. *International Journal of Business and Applied Economics*, 2(2), 295–308. DOI: 10.55927/ijbae.v2i2.2798

Wang, Z., Liu, Y., & Liu, S. (2019). Authoritarian leadership and task performance: The effects of leader-member exchange and dependence on leader. *Frontiers of Business Research in China*, 13(1), 19. Advance online publication. DOI: 10.1186/s11782-019-0066-x

Zackrison, E. (2021, March 10). Leading Strategically [Video]. LinkedIn Learning. https://www.linkedin.com/learning/leading-strategically/aligning-needs?u=43761300

Zheng, W., Kim, J., Kark, R., & Mascolo, L. (2023, September 28). *What makes an inclusive leader?* Harvard Business Review. https://hbr.org/2023/09/what-makes-an-inclusive-leader

KEY TERMS AND DEFINITIONS

Employee Development: Employee development analyzes the areas which an individual needs improvement and skills that can be enhanced. Management focuses on teaching in the areas that need improvement and building upon the skills that are present to strengthen them.

Employee Engagement: Employee engagement is an individual's display of passion and dedication to their career and the company they work for.

Employee Performance: Employee performance is an individual's ability to attain goals and fulfill responsibilities and duties.

Executive Presence: **It is the combination of the following traits:** gravitas (inclusiveness, respecting others, and listening to learn), communication, and appearance.

Leader: A leader is an individual who can influence, motivate, coach, support, and empower subordinates to achieve goals, perform their assignments in accordance with the company objectives, and ultimately lead others.

Leadership Style: Leadership style is the specific behaviors, skills, and emotional intelligence a leader uses when interacting with subordinates.

Referent Power: Based upon power a leader obtains from being liked by followers.

Section 3
Building High Impact Teams for Teaching and Learning

Chapter 6
Building Collaboration Among Teacher Candidates in Higher Education:
Developing Lesson Planning Competencies With Lesson Study (LS) Teams

Tolgahan Ayantaş
https://orcid.org/0000-0003-4348-0975
Ankara University, Turkey

Gürcan Gürgen
Ankara University, Turkey

ABSTRACT

This study aims to unveil teacher candidates' progress in lesson planning using the Lesson Study (LS) approach. Through action research, lesson plans generated by teacher candidates underwent content analysis and subsequent interviews. The findings revealed that collaborative work among social studies teacher candidates led to more feasible and content-rich lesson plans. The study underscores the efficacy of collaborative work in producing more viable and content-rich lesson plans. These outcomes underscore the potential of LS Teams to contribute to the professional growth of teacher candidates and deepen their understanding of their field.

DOI: 10.4018/979-8-3693-3852-0.ch006

INTRODUCTION

Societies employ various teacher training approaches to promote sustainable development, enhance the quality of education, and gain a competitive advantage in international rankings. To achieve this, teachers show an interest in professional development (PD) based on collaborative work, inquiry-based teaching, effective communication, critical thinking, problem-solving skills, knowledge construction, guiding students, integrating research, using analytical skills, and achieving high productivity (Afdal & Spernes, 2018; Burns, 2011; Van Driel, et al., 2012; Voogt & Roblin, 2012). PD has garnered increasingly more attention, and the growing experimental evidence has shown that PD is a crucial strategy of modern-day instructional practices (Garet et al., 2016; Gore et al., 2021; Opfer, 2016; Wei et al., 2010). It seems that PD has been functional in generating more culturally sensitive instructional practices among teachers, with teachers reporting significant and transformative development as a result of taking part in PD (Nakajima & Goode, 2019; Penner-Williams et al., 2019; Zhang et al., 2021). Researchers have revealed that teachers new to the profession experience difficulties in areas such as planning, implementation, and classroom management; lacking practical experience and the opportunity to collaborate and share their experiences. As such, newly qualified teachers need to learn the approaches that can best provide an environment in which they might undertake effective collaborative works. However, the effectiveness of teacher education is somewhat controversial in this area, and some current PD approaches are deemed insufficient because the unity of theory and practice is lacking and they seem to fail to be able to change deep-seated cultural beliefs and underlying behavioural patterns (Ball et al., 2009; Gong & Wang, 2017; Hennissen et al., 2017; Sykes et al., 2010).

It is not difficult to see that numerous philosophical approaches, models and techniques have been put forward for the development of teacher qualifications since the emergence of formal teacher education. Since the 19th century, many views have been published regarding how teacher education should be. However, these views have led to a considerable volume of research that effectively repeats itself and is not actually useful in practical terms since no revolutionary paradigm shift has occurred within teacher education. While some studies have focused on developing teachers on the job (i.e., 'inservice training'), others have aimed to develop them prior to their entry into the profession (i.e., 'preservice training') (Wei et al., 2010). Proposed professional development models for teachers include the development of teachers' field knowledge, professional knowledge, general cultural knowledge, and pedagogical content knowledge competencies. The focus remains on the basic aims, philosophy, curriculum structure, teaching tools, technology and materials, students' perception, success and learning styles, and the atmosphere of the teaching and learning environment. Therefore, debates about teacher competencies have a long history (Elliot, 1993; Shulman, 1987; Zeichner, 1983).

Traditional models of teacher professional development (PD) have been reported as teacher-centred and ineffective because they frequently consist of short workshops or seminars presented by academicians or 'experts' (Girvan et al., 2016; Kennedy, 2016). However, recent studies indicate significant changes within the scope of innovation or reform studies in teacher PD approaches. These transformations in teacher education are closely related to economic, political, and social changes. Some of these changes have occurred for previously mentioned reasons, while others have been influenced by the requirements of the 21st century. Consequently, a consensus has emerged in the literature that continual professional development for teachers is essential to promote and advance student learning (Hilton et al., 2015). Evaluations of PD suggest that the quality of teaching practices is likely to improve through a more collaborative approach (Mayrhofer, 2019).

In Finland, there has been a focus on research-oriented teacher education, whereas it has been the behavioural paradigm in Singapore, and the functional development of teachers in both the United Kingdom and in China (Shanghai). On another side, teachers' continuing professional development (CPD) has been afforded increasing importance in many countries worldwide (Westbury et al., 2005; Fraser et al., 2007; Gopinathan, 2008; Zeng & Day, 2019). Creating a collaborative, questioning, and self-directed learning environment according to PD approaches based on these newer models has provided important contributions for both inservice teachers and teacher candidates. However, in many studies, it has been clearly recognised that PD approaches generally have a 'prescriptive structure' and that existing paradigms are still being strictly adhered to, even though there is a clear need for autonomy and personalisation in the development of teachers (Opfer and Pedder, 2011; Kennedy, 2016; Gore et al., 2017; Noonan, 2019; Yurkofsky et al., 2019).

THE NECESSITY Of FOCUSING ON THE PRE-SERVICE PERIOD

The quality of education in any society is profoundly influenced by the effectiveness and preparedness of its teachers. Therefore, it is crucial to invest in the professional development of teachers right from their pre-service period. This formative stage is a critical time when prospective teachers develop foundational knowledge, skills, and attitudes that will shape their future teaching practices. Providing additional support to teacher candidates during their undergraduate education can significantly enhance their readiness and efficacy as future educators. Pre-service teacher education programmes are designed to equip future teachers with the necessary pedagogical knowledge and practical skills. However, these programmes often fall short of addressing the complex realities of contemporary classrooms. Teacher candidates frequently encounter challenges when transitioning from theoretical coursework to actual teaching practice. This gap between theory and practice can be bridged by offering targeted support, such as mentoring, specialised workshops, and hands-on teaching experiences. Mentoring, for instance, can provide pre-service teachers with personalised guidance and feedback from experienced educators. This support helps teacher candidates navigate the intricacies of lesson planning, classroom management, and student engagement. Specialised workshops focusing on current educational technologies, differentiated instruction, and inclusive practices can further enhance their preparedness. Moreover, hands-on teaching experiences, such as internships and practicum placements, allow teacher candidates to apply their learning in real-world settings, fostering confidence and competence. Enhanced support during the pre-service period not only benefits the teacher candidates but also has a positive impact on the overall educational system. Well-prepared teachers are more likely to implement effective teaching strategies, maintain high levels of student engagement, and contribute to improved student outcomes. Additionally, providing robust support to teacher candidates can reduce the attrition rates among new teachers, who often leave the profession due to lack of preparation and support. A focus on the pre-service period also ensures that future teachers are well-versed in the latest educational research and innovations. This knowledge empowers them to be adaptive and responsive to the evolving needs of their students. In the long term, such an approach contributes to the development of a more skilled and resilient teaching workforce.

One innovative approach that has shown significant promise in supporting practising teachers is the Lesson Study (LS) model. LS involves collaborative lesson planning, observation, and reflection, allowing teachers to learn from one another and continuously improve their teaching practices. Given its success with in-service teachers, it is worth considering the integration of LS into pre-service teacher education. Implementing LS with teacher candidates can provide numerous benefits. Firstly, it promotes a culture of collaboration and continuous improvement from the outset of their careers. Teacher candidates working together in LS groups can share diverse perspectives and strategies, enriching their learning experience. Secondly, the reflective nature of LS helps pre-service teachers develop critical thinking and problem-solving skills, which are essential for effective teaching. By engaging in cycles of planning, observing, and reflecting, teacher candidates can gain deeper insights into the teaching and learning process. Moreover, LS can help bridge the gap between theory and practice. By collaboratively planning and observing lessons, pre-service teachers can see how theoretical concepts are applied in real classroom situations. This hands-on approach reinforces their learning and prepares them for the complexities of actual teaching. In summary, focusing on the pre-service period and providing additional support to teacher candidates is essential for developing effective and resilient educators. Integrating the LS approach into pre-service teacher education can further enhance this process, fostering a collaborative and reflective mindset that will benefit teachers and their students throughout their careers. By investing in the pre-service period, we can ensure a stronger, more capable teaching workforce, ultimately leading to better educational outcomes for all students.

LESSON STUDY (LS) TEAMS

Lesson Study (LS) is a cyclical professional development model based on collaboration and experience sharing. It consists of four main stages: 1) study (goal setting), 2) planning, 3) implementation (research lessons and teaching), and 4) reflection (debrief) (Dudley, 2014). According to Cheung and Wong (2014), the LS teams originated in Japan in the early 1900s and began to be used in the United States during the late 1990s. This approach is now applied as a professional development model in many countries such as Singapore, the United States, the United Kingdom, Greece, Indonesia, Australia, Malaysia, China, Iran, Thailand, Spain, the Netherlands, and South Africa. In recent years, it has emerged as a model that continues to be enriched with different perspectives such as technological support (Joubert et al., 2020).

Historically, LS was designed to improve educational practices through collaborative lesson planning, teaching, observing, and reflecting. Its theoretical foundation is rooted in the belief that teacher collaboration and continuous improvement are key to effective teaching. By engaging in LS, teachers work together to identify educational goals, design detailed lesson plans, implement these plans while observing student responses, and reflect on the outcomes to refine their teaching practices. The impact of LS on lesson planning is profound, as it directly links historical and theoretical contexts to practical applications in the classroom. The cyclical nature of LS ensures that teachers constantly engage in a process of setting goals, planning, implementing, and reflecting, which leads to a deeper understanding of the teaching and learning process. This model fosters a collaborative environment where teachers can share their experiences and insights, leading to the development of more effective and comprehensive lesson plans. For example, in Japan, where LS originated, the focus has always been on improving student learning outcomes through meticulous lesson planning and collaborative reflection. This historical context highlights the importance of detailed and thoughtful lesson planning as a means to achieve educational excellence. Similarly, the theoretical underpinning of LS emphasizes the role of teacher collaboration in enhancing lesson quality. When teachers collectively plan and reflect on their lessons, they can incorporate diverse perspectives and strategies, which enriches the teaching process and ultimately benefits student learning. LS has been shown to be highly appropriate for both rural and urban locations since it does not necessitate an expansive substructure. This makes it accessible and practical for a wide range of educational settings. Studies have demonstrated that LS is a significant and powerful tool for use in teacher training, enhancing teachers' abilities to create effective lesson plans that are responsive to their students' needs (Cheung & Wong, 2014).

Why LS?

The Lesson Study (LS) approach stands out in teacher education for its emphasis on collaborative planning, implementation, and reflection within a team. Unlike other widely recognized models such as the Clinical Practice Model and the Reflective Teaching Model, LS prioritises teamwork and collective problem-solving, which are essential for addressing complex educational challenges.

One widely recognized model is the Clinical Practice Model, often employed in the United States. This model emphasizes extensive field experiences integrated throughout the teacher education program, rather than concentrating practical training solely in the final year. Candidate teachers engage in continuous, structured clinical experiences in partnership with schools, allowing for a deeper integration of theory and practice. This model is praised for providing candidates with sustained, authentic classroom experiences and opportunities for ongoing reflection and professional growth.

Another prevalent model is the Reflective Teaching Model, commonly used in the United Kingdom. This approach prioritises the development of reflective practitioners who critically analyse their teaching practices. Teacher candidates are encouraged to engage in self-reflection and peer collaboration to identify areas of improvement and adapt their instructional strategies accordingly. This model fosters a continuous cycle of feedback and adaptation, enhancing teachers' ability to respond to diverse classroom situations effectively.

Contrasting these models with LS highlights several key differences. While LS places a strong emphasis on collaborative planning, implementation, and reflection within a team, the Clinical Practice Model focuses on sustained individual experiences in real classroom settings. On the other hand, the Reflective Teaching Model emphasizes individual self-reflection and adaptability, whereas LS promotes collective analysis and peer-supported growth. LS offers distinct advantages in fostering a culture of democratic discussion and collaborative problem-solving. It allows teacher candidates to engage in iterative cycles of planning, teaching, observing, and reflecting, thus promoting a deep understanding of teaching practices and student learning processes. This collective approach not only enhances the quality of lesson planning but also builds a supportive professional community among teachers. The emphasis on teamwork in LS is crucial for several reasons. Collaborative efforts lead to a richer exchange of ideas and strategies, as teachers bring diverse perspectives and experiences to the table. This collective approach helps in addressing a wider range of classroom challenges and fosters a sense of shared responsibility for student learning outcomes. Team-based reflection and analysis ensure that teaching practices are continuously refined and adapted to meet the needs of all students. Moreover, LS promotes a supportive environment where teachers can learn from each other and grow professionally. By working together, teacher candidates develop essential skills such as communication, cooperation, and conflict resolution, which are vital for their future roles as educators. This collaborative culture also encourages innovation and creativity in lesson planning and implementation, leading to more effective and engaging teaching practices. While LS has its distinct strengths, integrating elements from the Clinical Practice Model and the Reflective Teaching Model can provide a more comprehensive approach to teacher education. The Clinical Practice Model's extensive field experience and the Reflective Teaching Model's emphasis on individual reflection can complement the collaborative framework of LS. By combining these approaches, teacher candidates can benefit from sustained, authentic classroom experiences, individual self-reflection, and collaborative planning and problem-solving. In conclusion, the LS approach, with its strong focus on teamwork and collective reflection, offers significant advantages in teacher education. It fosters a culture of collaborative problem-solving and continuous improvement, which is essential for addressing the complexities of modern classrooms. Integrating elements from other models can further enhance the effectiveness of LS, providing a well-rounded and robust framework for developing skilled and reflective educators.

Lesson Study (LS) is a powerful professional development tool that has been shown to enhance teacher practices and student outcomes through collaborative planning, observation, and reflection. Research highlights the effectiveness of LS in fostering continuous improvement and deepening teachers' pedagogical knowledge (Darling-Hammond & Richardson, 2009; Lewis et al., 2012). The approach, rooted in Japanese educational practices, encourages teachers to critically examine their teaching methods and collaboratively refine their lessons (Fernandez, 2002; Murata, 2011). Studies have demonstrated that LS not only supports the development of teaching strategies but also enhances teachers' abilities to assess and address student learning needs (Fischman & Wasserman, 2017; Giannakidou et al., 2013; Villalon, 2016). Furthermore, LS has been shown to be particularly beneficial in teacher education, providing a practical framework for pre-service teachers to develop their skills in a supportive, collaborative environment (Bjuland & Mosvold, 2015; Towaf, 2016). Effective implementation of LS requires robust knowledge management strategies and a clear understanding of its benefits and challenges (Cheng, 2020; Kanellopoulou & Darra, 2019). LS also emphasizes the importance of reflective practice and continuous professional growth, which are essential for maintaining high teaching standards (NSDC, 2011; Reeves, 2010). The integration of LS in various educational contexts has shown to significantly improve teaching practices and student outcomes by promoting a culture of collaboration and reflective practice (Stigler & Hiebert, 2016; Wood, 2018). This approach aligns with broader trends in professional development that emphasize sustained, collaborative learning opportunities for educators (Wessels, 2018; Bjuland & Mosvold, 2015). As such, LS can be a transformative approach to professional development, driving significant improvements in teaching quality and student achievement (Darling-Hammond & Richardson, 2009; Reeves, 2010).

The research stage, considered the first stage of the LS approach, reveals problems related to student learning, examines curricula comprehensively, and makes preliminary preparations to address target behaviours. The second stage, the planning stage, involves planning lessons according to the targeted behaviours, preparing the course subject with the contribution of stakeholders, and putting the course structure into written form. At this stage, teachers begin to develop themselves as they design the course learning outcomes. The third stage is implementation, where one teacher (or teacher candidate) in the group enacts the lesson while their peers participate as observers, after which the course plan is prepared. Supporting this stage with a video or audio recording is beneficial to aid the peer review and reflective process. The final stage of the LS approach is the reflection stage, where various stakeholders share their observations of the lesson (Fujii, 2016; Lewis, 2016; Takahashi & McDougal, 2016).

By its very nature, LS can be considered an action process. However, as can be clearly seen from the literature, a problem exists in that the relationship between practice and context cannot always be clearly demonstrated. It is for this reason that some studies have specifically discussed whether or not LS is really that effective and what the contribution of LS's action-based nature actually is (Hadfield & Jopling, 2016; Schipper et al., 2017). It seems that in the literature, LS research has, for several years, continued to try to understand what kind of contributions the action-based processes of LS create. It is also considered usual to stretch some aspects of the LS teams according to the context of the school environment. However, for groups that aim to implement LS for the first time, it must be introduced with a meeting and sample implications. Thus, the first dimension of the action-based process involves stakeholders needing to understand 'what LS is and how to implement it?'

LS' Limitations

However, it is essential to also consider the challenges and limitations associated with LS. Implementing LS can be time-consuming, requiring significant commitment from teachers to participate in planning, observing, and reflecting activities. This can be particularly challenging in educational settings where teachers already face heavy workloads and limited time. Additionally, the success of LS largely depends on the willingness and ability of teachers to collaborate effectively, which may not always be present in every school environment. There may also be resistance to change from educators who are accustomed to traditional teaching methods. Moreover, while LS has been shown to be highly appropriate for both rural and urban locations since it does not necessitate an expansive substructure, there can still be logistical challenges in terms of coordinating schedules and resources. In some cases, the necessary support from school administration and access to professional development opportunities may be limited, hindering the successful implementation of LS (Bjuland & Mosvold, 2015; Hervas, 2021; Sims & Walsh, 2009). Teachers may be hesitant to adopt LS due to concerns about increased workload, lack of time, or unfamiliarity with the process. Institutions might resist due to potential disruptions to established routines or scepticism about the model's effectiveness. To address these challenges, it is crucial to provide comprehensive professional development and support, highlighting the long-term benefits of LS for both teachers and students. Building a supportive school culture that values collaboration and continuous improvement can also mitigate resistance. Additionally, involving teachers in the initial planning and decision-making processes can foster a sense of ownership and commitment to the LS model, thereby facilitating smoother implementation.

LS's Variations

The Lesson Study (LS) model, which originated in Japan, has been adapted and implemented in various cultural and educational contexts worldwide. Each adaptation reflects the unique cultural, social, and educational values of the region, demonstrating the model's flexibility and broad applicability. In the United States, for instance, LS has been integrated with Professional Learning Communities (PLCs) to promote collaborative professional development among teachers. This integration allows for structured, ongoing collaboration and reflection, aligning with the American educational emphasis on professional development and accountability. In contrast, in the United Kingdom and other European countries, LS is often embedded within existing teacher training and development frameworks. Here, the focus is on reflective practice and continuous improvement. This approach fits well with the European educational tradition, which values ongoing professional development and reflective teaching practices. Further examples of LS adaptations include the Philippines and Denmark, where the model has been tailored to fit local contexts. In the Philippines, adaptations are necessary to address cultural differences between Japanese and Philippine teachers. These differences can include varying approaches to authority, collaboration, and educational priorities, requiring careful adjustment of the LS model to ensure its effectiveness. Similarly, in Denmark, the adaptation of LS by teachers has brought challenges related to work and power dynamics. Danish teachers have had to navigate cultural and power issues inherent in their educational system, which can influence how LS is implemented and perceived. These challenges highlight the need for sensitivity to local contexts when adapting LS, ensuring that it aligns with the cultural and social dynamics of the teachers and students involved (Ebaeguin & Stephens, 2014; Lim-Ratnam et al., 2019; Skott & Møller, 2020).

To enhance the clarity of the application of the LS model, practical examples and case studies from various educational settings are essential. For instance, in rural schools in Indonesia, LS has been effectively used to enhance teachers' pedagogical skills without requiring significant technological infrastructure. Similarly, in urban schools in the United States, LS has been integrated with digital tools to facilitate collaborative planning and reflection among teachers. In Singapore, case studies show how LS has been adapted to align with the national curriculum, resulting in improved student outcomes. These examples illustrate the versatility of the LS model and its ability to be tailored to different educational contexts, thereby demonstrating its broad applicability and effectiveness.

Although some studies in the literature mention examples where LS is terminated after completion of a single cycle, after maybe 1 day or a few hours, it should be clearly stated that these do not reflect the original LS studies undertaken in Japan. LS was originally designed to be implemented in Japan to include processes lasting for at least 5 weeks (Murata & Takahashi, 2002). Therefore, should the cyclical design of LS not be well understood, it be inevitable that certain problems would be experienced in its application. It should be clearly stated that the examples in which the first stage of the lesson study are not applied cannot be qualified as a correctly constructed lesson study (Takahashi & McDougal, 2016). In related studies, it is clearly emphasised that observation is of vital importance in terms of the basic dimensions of the lesson study. Therefore, one of the most important stages of action-based processes is observation, whilst another is reflection. Researchers can increase the contribution of the action-based dimensions of LS through their roles as facilitators. The action-based processes of LS provide a certain level of improvement such as stakeholders questioning and critiquing each other, observations and evaluations of students' learning and materials, collaborative learning, and teaching (Akiba et al., 2019; Lee & Tan, 2020; Schipper et al., 2020; Skott & Møller, 2020). In the area of mathematics, for example, to make teaching more effective, LS research studies are generally applied to develop an understanding of student learning, with the aim of subsequently improving teachers' teaching skills. In other words, LS research generally focuses upon the professional development of in-service teachers in its processes (Coenders & Verhoef, 2019; Rappleye & Komatsu, 2017; Schipper et al., 2017; Vrikki et al., 2017).

Resistance and Strategies: Overcoming Barriers to Implementing Lesson Study

Implementing new educational methods like Lesson Study (LS) often encounters resistance from teachers, administrators, and educational institutions. Understanding the common sources of this resistance and developing effective strategies to address them is crucial for the successful adoption of LS. This section analyses the common forms of resistance and provides strategies and real-world examples for overcoming these barriers.

Many teachers fear that implementing LS will add to their already heavy workload. This concern is particularly prevalent in environments where teachers are already overburdened with administrative tasks and large class sizes. Resistance can stem from a lack of familiarity with the LS process. Teachers who are accustomed to traditional methods may feel uncomfortable with the collaborative and reflective nature of LS. Educational institutions often have established routines and practices. Introducing LS requires a shift in these routines, which can meet with institutional resistance. Implementing LS effectively requires time, training, and resources. Schools with limited budgets or staff may resist adopting LS due to these constraints. In some educational cultures, the hierarchical nature of teacher-student relationships and the top-down approach to teaching can hinder the collaborative ethos of LS.

Providing comprehensive professional development and training can alleviate fears related to increased workload and unfamiliarity with LS. Workshops, seminars, and ongoing support can help teachers understand the benefits of LS and how to integrate it into their practices. In the United States, some school districts have implemented professional learning communities (PLCs) that incorporate LS principles. Teachers participate in regular training sessions to develop their understanding and skills in LS, easing the transition to this new method. Cultivating a supportive and collaborative school culture is essential. Encouraging open communication and providing opportunities for teachers to share their experiences and successes with LS can foster a positive attitude towards the method. In the United Kingdom, some schools have established LS as a core part of their professional development programmes. By embedding LS in the school culture and celebrating its successes, these schools have reduced resistance and promoted widespread adoption. Schools need to allocate dedicated time and resources for LS activities. This includes scheduling regular LS sessions during school hours and providing access to necessary materials and support. Japanese schools, where LS originated, allocate specific periods during the school day for teachers to engage in LS. This institutional support ensures that teachers have the time and resources needed to participate fully in the process. Digital tools and online platforms can help mitigate resource constraints and facilitate the LS process. Virtual meetings shared digital documents, and online feedback tools can make LS more accessible and manageable. In Singapore, some schools use digital platforms like Google Classroom and Zoom to conduct LS sessions. These tools enable teachers to collaborate and reflect without the need for extensive physical resources. Involving all stakeholders, including administrators, parents, and the wider community, can help build support for LS. When stakeholders understand the benefits of LS, they are more likely to support its implementation. In Finland, schools engage parents and the community in the LS process by sharing outcomes and inviting them to observe LS sessions. This transparency builds trust and support for the method.

Resistance to new educational methods like Lesson Study is common, but it can be effectively managed with targeted strategies. By providing professional development, building a supportive culture, allocating resources, leveraging technology, and engaging stakeholders, schools can overcome barriers and successfully implement LS. Real-world examples from various educational contexts demonstrate that these strategies can lead to the successful adoption and integration of LS, ultimately enhancing teaching practices and student learning outcomes.

LS and Digital Tools

The integration of digital tools and online platforms has significantly enhanced the Lesson Study (LS) process, providing new avenues for collaboration and reflection. These digital platforms, including video conferencing tools, collaborative document editing software, and specialised LS software, enable teachers to engage in LS activities asynchronously and across geographical boundaries. For example, teachers can record and share classroom lessons for collective analysis and feedback, facilitating a richer and more dynamic exchange of ideas. This ability to share and review lessons in a digital format allows for more detailed and constructive feedback, which can lead to improved teaching strategies and student outcomes. Furthermore, online platforms support the documentation and archiving of LS cycles, making it easier to track progress and revisit past reflections. This aspect of digital integration not only expands the reach of LS but also enhances its accessibility and efficiency, allowing for more inclusive participation and continuous professional development. Digital tools promote LS by enabling rigorous collaboration, synchronous observations, data collection, and feedback. These capabilities lead to a deeper understanding of teaching practices and their impacts on student learning. Online LS models have been shown to have positive effects on both teaching and learning. For instance, digital platforms like Zoom, WhatsApp, Google Classroom, Schoology, and Edmodo have been found to positively affect student learning outcomes by facilitating more interactive and engaging learning environments. Additionally, digital tools open new ways to conduct LS, supporting teacher professional development through various methods such as analysing videos, using external video resources, fictional animations, structured digital LS work, hybrid teacher collaboration, and digital teacher collaboration. By leveraging these technologies, teachers can participate in LS even if they are not in the same physical location, thus broadening the scope and reach of collaborative professional development. However, while the benefits of integrating digital tools into LS are clear, some studies have highlighted potential issues. For example, the reliance on technology requires a certain level of digital literacy and access to reliable internet connections, which may not be uniformly available to all teachers. Additionally, there can be challenges related to maintaining the personal and relational aspects of LS in an online environment. Despite these challenges, the overall impact of digital tools on LS is overwhelmingly positive, offering new opportunities for enhancing teaching practices and student learning outcomes. The integration of digital tools and online platforms into LS represents a significant advancement in educational practice. By facilitating collaboration, improving accessibility, and supporting detailed analysis and reflection, these technologies enhance the effectiveness of LS and contribute to the professional development of teachers. As digital tools continue to evolve, they will likely play an increasingly important role in the ongoing improvement of educational practices worldwide (Hrastinski, 2021; Huang et al., 2021; Tuanaya et al., 2022; Weaver et al., 2021).

LS and Evaluation

Effective assessment and evaluation are integral to the Lesson Study (LS) process, providing critical insights into the impact of collaborative practices on teaching and learning. Various methods and tools are employed to assess the effectiveness of LS cycles, ensuring a comprehensive evaluation of both teaching practices and student outcomes. Pre- and post-lesson observations are fundamental to the LS process. These observations involve teachers and peers systematically reviewing classroom interactions and instructional strategies before and after implementing lesson plans. This method allows for real-time feedback and provides a basis for reflective discussions on what worked well and what could be improved. Gathering student feedback is another crucial component. Students' perspectives on their learning experiences offer valuable qualitative data that can highlight the effectiveness of instructional strategies. This feedback can be collected through surveys, interviews, or informal discussions, providing teachers with insights into student engagement and comprehension. Teachers' reflective journals serve as a personal and professional development tool, encouraging continuous self-evaluation. By maintaining detailed accounts of their teaching experiences, teachers can document their observations, thoughts, and reflections on the LS process. These journals are valuable for identifying patterns, challenges, and successes over time. Quantitative data, such as student performance metrics, provide objective measures of educational outcomes. Standardised test scores, classroom assessments, and other performance indicators can be analysed to determine the impact of LS on student achievement. Combining these data with qualitative insights from teacher reflections and peer feedback allows for a more holistic evaluation of the LS process. Specialised LS software tools facilitate the systematic documentation and analysis of data. These tools can help track progress, organise observations, and support the reflective process, enabling a nuanced understanding of the outcomes. By leveraging technology, educators can streamline the assessment process and enhance the precision of their evaluations. The methodology used in evaluating LS often involves user-focused evaluation, multi-level logical models, and an 'improving rather than proving' approach. This philosophy emphasises the continuous improvement of teaching practices rather than merely demonstrating their effectiveness. Theory-based evaluation is particularly effective in assessing LS-based instructional programs, as it aligns with the iterative and reflective nature of LS. Assessment methods and tools in primary schools are adapted to the age group, situation, and curriculum, focusing on teacher-student interactions. For example, the Adapted Lesson Study Project (ALSP) has shown improvements in teaching efficacy and lesson quality through iterative collaborative and reflective practices. Continuous assessment and diagnosis-prescription evaluation are suggested approaches to enhance student learning evaluation methods, ensuring they are tailored to the specific needs of younger learners. Continuous assessment and evaluation not only ensure the effectiveness of LS but also contribute to the refinement and enhancement of teaching practices. This ongoing process leads to improved educational outcomes by enabling teachers to make data-driven decisions and adapt their instructional strategies to meet the evolving needs of their students. The robust and multi-faceted approach to assessment and evaluation within the LS framework is essential for understanding and enhancing the impact of collaborative teaching practices. By employing a variety of methods and tools, educators can gain comprehensive insights into the effectiveness of LS and continuously improve their teaching methodologies, ultimately leading to better educational outcomes for students (Bényei & Csernoch, 2022; Follmer et al., 2023; Godfrey et al., 2018; Jain & Brown, 2020).

Why Social Studies?

Social studies courses target the acquisition of behaviours originating from many different disciplines and covers the values and skills that individuals will most often need in their general social life. It is generally accepted that the underlying purpose of social studies teaching is to prepare students to become active democratic citizens. Social studies lessons attempt to achieve this purpose through numerous themes such as culture, time, continuity, change, people, places, environments, individual development, identity, individuals, groups, institutions, power, authority, governance, production, distribution, consumption, science, technology, society, global connections, as well as civic ideals and practices, etc. Social studies not only transmit societal values and norms, but also aim to change them as social studies claims to raise responsible, effective, sensitive, and democratic citizens of the future (Evans, 2004; Stanley, 2015; Stern, 2013). When social studies teachers engage students in discussions about controversial issues, they can create a learning environment where students develop a deep and multifaceted understanding of the hidden mechanisms at the heart of the relevant social, economic, or political discussion. Furthermore, building these discourses with students in the social studies classroom constitutes authentic democratic participation by helping students to learn the value of diverse opinion by engaging in deliberation or debate regarding the most important public issues, and by recognising the affordances and boundaries of individual freedom within a democratic society. However, many social studies lessons can lack adequate conversation about such fundamental issues (Hawley, 2012; Hostetler et al., 2018).

Research studies have mentioned some of the understandings that social studies teacher candidates are expected to develop, and the experiences that they should gain in order to nurture their civic identity as young people in a multicultural, pluralistic, and globally interdependent society. Also, preparing social studies teacher candidates to be proficient in technology has become a key issue, as social studies content becomes more linked to today's digital technologies. Social studies teacher education should be grounded in critical pedagogy and maintain a focus on several key components of humanising pedagogy including fostering a dialogic relationship between student and teacher, focusing on the student experience, facilitating a critique of knowledge, and framing critical questions through the introduction of subjugated knowledge. At the same time, social studies researchers have been all too aware of common and persistent patterns of instruction in social studies and lament the disconnect between the kind of social studies teaching that leads to powerful learning and that students and teachers actually experience in the classroom (Adler, 2006; Bolick et al., 2003; Crowe & Cuenca, 2016; Crowley & Smith, 2015; Crocco & Cramer, 2005; Dinkelman & Cuenca, 2020; King & Chandler, 2016).

In Turkey, social studies candidate teachers are trained within the education faculties of universities according to a 4-year undergraduate programme of education. Once trained and qualified, teachers can apply to work in public or private secondary schools subject to being successful in certain additional centralised exams as well as interviews. When we look at the training process of social studies teachers in Turkey, it can be seen that a simultaneous model-based approach is adopted in the teacher training programmes, with content knowledge and professional knowledge courses given within a simultaneous order. When we look specifically at applied courses, it can be seen that such courses come to the fore in the final year of the undergraduate teacher education programme. As a result, the courses that place teacher candidates in a real classroom environment in Turkey are deemed inadequate. The insufficiencies of the current approach and the gaps between research and practice in social studies teacher education have led to the prominent use of models in which teacher candidates take on the role of researchers to share their experiences. One of these is the Lesson Study (LS), which is a model of teacher development that has gained significant popularity in recent years. LS aims not only to improve the quality of teacher candidates, but also to help them understand the fundamental nature of their field, to maintain a focus on student learning, use effective educational technologies, create important teaching materials through collaborative work on controversial issues, and to experience a culture of democratic discussion and debate. Therefore, LS can help in the development of many different competencies that are required by today's social studies teachers.

There have been only a limited number of studies in the areas of history and social studies related to LS; whereas, it is more frequently applied within the fields of mathematics and science education (Hubbard, 2007). However, research on LS in the field of social studies has been increasing. For example, Halvorsen and Kesler (2013) conducted a study combining fifth-grade American History with LS experience. Howell and Saye (2016) examined fourth-grade social studies teachers' sharing their LS experiences. Faizah et al. (2020) explored the use of the LS approach in teaching economic issues in social studies. Wadi et al. (2020) investigated the contributions of LS to multicultural education practices in the social studies arena. Kohlmeier et al. (2020) stated that the LS practices of social studies teachers have the potential to instil permanent instructional change. Seemingly, these studies focus on the professional development of inservice teachers, not teacher candidates. However, LS studies focusing on the professional competencies of teacher candidates are also needed, because any aim to develop the teaching profession by necessity will include both preservice and inservice teaching elements.

LS is considered a challenging activity for teachers and teacher candidates, mostly due to their resistance to change in terms of traditionally held beliefs about the profession. According to Vermunt et al. (2019), teachers with less than 10 years of teaching experience in the LS action-based process, especially in creating meaning-oriented learning, are often considered to be more successful than teachers with 10 or more years of teaching experience. This research finding encouraged the authors of the current study to plan for LS teams with both inservice teachers and candidate teachers with minimal experience.

The research questions of the study are formulated as follows:

1. How do lesson planning and competency skills of social studies teacher candidates develop within the research and planning stages of the LS teams?
2. How do lesson planning and competency skills of social studies teacher candidates develop within the implementation stage of the LS teams?
3. How do lesson planning and competency skills of social studies teacher candidates develop within the reflection stage of the LS teams?

METHODOLOGY

An examination of the literature related to LS shows that case study and action research, two well-known qualitative research methods, were the most preferred. The current research was designed based on the practice-oriented action research model, a known qualitative research method. The practice-oriented action research model is a qualitative research method focused on improving practical skills and solving problems through collaborative, systematic activities. In this research, the LS teams have many different versions (Norwich, 2018), created with small groups in non-public places (i.e., university faculties and secondary schools), in the form of what would be considered a standard LS team (Chong et al., 2017). The LS cycle is compatible with all stages of practice-oriented action research as, by its very nature, it focuses on the improvement of current teaching practices. As known in action research, individuals can act collaboratively to resolve problems through systematic activities. In this context, the function of action research in the current study is to improve the practical skills of educators and inform them about the main problem areas and their solutions. In practice-oriented action research, the primary directive is to develop the application to be implemented (Glesne, 2016; Lune & Berg, 2017).

An examination of the literature related to LS shows that case study and action research, two well-known qualitative research methods, were the most preferred. The current research was designed based on the practice-oriented action research model, a known qualitative research method. This model focuses on improving practical skills and solving problems through collaborative, systematic activities. The LS cycle, involving planning, teaching, observing, and reflecting, aligns with all stages of practice-oriented action research, aiming to improve current teaching practices through collaborative efforts.

The research participants consisted of eight social studies teacher candidates (four female, four male) studying at a state university in Ankara, Turkey. Throughout the study, each teacher candidate is only referred to by an assigned nickname in line with recognised ethical considerations for human-based research (See Table 1).

Table 1. Participants

Nickname	Gender	Age (years)
Candan	Female	22
Derya	Female	25
Akın	Male	22
Baha	Male	23
Aylin	Female	22
Beril	Female	23
Cem	Male	22
Doruk	Male	22

The research participants consisted of eight social studies teacher candidates (four female, four male) studying at a state university in Ankara, Turkey. Ethical considerations were strictly followed, with participants referred to by assigned nicknames (e.g., Candan, Derya) to maintain confidentiality.

THE ROLE OF THE RESEARCHERS

In terms of LS sessions being mostly led by more experienced experts, the literature referred to these 'knowledgeable others' as significantly contributing to the LS teams (Bjuland and Helgevold, 2018; Wake et al., 2013; Walker, 2011). In the groups where the LS teams had been applied for the first time, it was seen as being of significant importance that the experienced stakeholders or knowledgeable others dealt with the participants on a one-to-one basis (Amador and Weiland, 2015; Elliott, 2016). In the current research, the researchers were in the role of 'knowledgeable others' in guiding the LS sessions and collecting data on the research problem. The kinds of support offered by the researchers during the planning and discussion stages included helping teachers understand the sense behind the learning outcomes, raising warnings from time to time regarding instructional gaps that may have occurred during the secondary school social studies lesson, encouraging the diversification of the methods and techniques used, reminding teachers of the readiness levels and developmental characteristics of the students, and offering recommendations on the use of textbooks and other resources. Throughout the LS research lesson, the researchers only made observations and took notes.

In this study, researchers acted as 'knowledgeable others', guiding LS sessions and collecting data. Their support included helping teachers understand learning outcomes, identifying instructional gaps, encouraging diverse methods, and advising on resources. Researchers observed and took notes during LS sessions, contributing to data collection and analysis.

DATA ANALYSIS

The collected data, in the form of written materials or audio recordings transcribed into written text, were subjected to content analysis to identify themes and meanings. This process was facilitated by the researchers, who were responsible for transcribing the recordings and conducting the content analysis. The process formed a careful, detailed, systematic evaluation and interpretation according to an interpretive, social anthropological, and collaborative social research approach. Typically, content analysis is performed on written documentation, photographs, film or video, and transcribed audio recordings (Lune and Berg, 2017). The content analysis process includes categorising, comparing, and concluding; with significant actions being the formation of meaningful categories, links established between categories, and the drawing of theoretical conclusions from the textual or other data forms (Cohen et al., 2007). During the content analysis process, identifying, categorising, and labelling patterns in the examined data were conducted, and then the emerging themes were reviewed. Since the data were only intended for use by the researchers, a more detailed classification was not required, and therefore, no analytical computer software was employed (Patton, 2002).

The collected data, in the form of written materials and transcribed audio recordings, were subjected to content analysis. This process involved categorising, comparing, and drawing theoretical conclusions from the data, following an interpretive, social anthropological, and collaborative social research approach.

TRUSTWORTHINESS AND CREDIBILITY

In this study, a detailed and systematic data collection process was employed to ensure the richness and depth of the qualitative data. The primary data collection methods included focus group discussions, participant observation, and written reflections from teacher candidates. The researchers facilitated focus group discussions to elicit in-depth insights into the participants' experiences and perceptions. Additionally, researchers observed the participants during the LS sessions, taking detailed notes to capture the dynamics and interactions. Written reflections from the participants were also collected to understand their individual viewpoints and self-assessed competencies.

To ensure the trustworthiness and credibility of the data collection tools employed, and to diversify the methods as much as possible, the methodological triangulation approach was adopted in the current study (Flick, 2004). The obtained data and emerging themes were presented in a review meeting held following the focus group sessions. The themes specified in the notes taken by the teacher candidates about each other, and their competencies were then subjected to verbal member checking (Merriam & Tisdell, 2015).

All data collection methods were conducted in accordance with the ethical principles of qualitative research to ensure the trustworthiness and credibility of the findings. Participants were fully informed about the study's purpose, procedures, and their rights, including the right to withdraw at any time without any consequence. Informed consent was obtained from all participants prior to data collection. Confidentiality was maintained throughout the study, with all data anonymized to protect the identity of the participants. The researchers ensured that the data collection process was respectful and non-intrusive, prioritizing the well-being and comfort of the participants. By adhering to these ethical standards, the study aimed to produce credible and trustworthy findings that accurately reflect the participants' experiences and perspectives.

A detailed and systematic data collection process was employed, including focus group discussions, participant observations, and written reflections. Methodological triangulation ensured the richness and depth of the data. Trustworthiness was further enhanced by obtaining informed consent, maintaining confidentiality, and adhering to ethical research principles.

FINDINGS

At the conclusion of the study, it was seen that the quality of the lesson plans had improved, and that the teaching environment had gained strength through the application of various teaching methods, techniques, tools, materials, and resources. The teacher candidates' mastery of the lesson plans was shown to have increased, and their lesson planning and lesson conducting competencies had improved. The teacher candidates themselves stated clearly that the LS teams positively affected their lesson planning and implementation competencies.

CONTRIBUTION OF RESEARCH AND PLANNING STAGES

The social studies teacher candidates' lesson planning competencies were found to have improved during the Research and Planning stages of the study. The research and planning stages significantly contributed to the improvement of lesson plans and the teaching environment. The diverse teaching methods, techniques, tools, materials, and resources applied during these stages strengthened the teaching environment. Additionally, teacher candidates' mastery of the lesson plans increased, and their competencies in lesson planning and conducting improved. The positive impact of LS teams on teacher candidates' lesson planning and implementation competencies was also clearly stated by the candidates themselves.

Akın, one of the teacher candidates, suggested that the development of opinions, brainstorming, and speech ring methods and techniques should form the focus of student learning whilst discussing choices. Akın noted, "The process of sharing our views on the learning outcomes of a course had not been previously experienced before being introduced to the LS teams. The LS teams helped us a lot during the research and planning stages."

Beril and Aylin showed that the students' in-class participation could be increased by using appropriate worksheets (materials specific to social studies). Beril said, "Planning a lesson with my classmates and being accompanied by an expert allowed me to better understand the lesson planning process and the characteristics of our students." Aylin added, "We performed better week by week. I achieved a level of efficiency in our research and planning processes."

Doruk suggested using materials appropriate to the level of the students (and with materials specific to social studies). Doruk reflected, "Before LS, I thought that I could manage the lesson thanks to my communication skills, but LS taught me that lesson planning is a serious process."

The teacher candidates gained experience through adopting the lesson plans, caring about the success or failure of the plan, internalising the multidisciplinary and interdisciplinary structure of the social studies field much better, and studying the development of teaching materials. In addition, creating a written lesson plan during the LS teams helped to increase their range and level of experience.

Candan, another of the candidate teachers, particularly suggested the use of informational diagrams, written materials, and literary works had diversified the materials used in her lessons (with materials specific to social studies). Candan mentioned, "Understanding and discussing the learning outcomes during the research stage of the LS, and sharing during the planning stage, helped me improve in attracting the students' attention to the lesson."

Derya suggested using social and academic networks to better attract the students' attention. Derya observed, "Preparing the plans by discussing with my peers helped make the lessons go well. I saw the LS teams as a development process that allowed us to self-assess and gain awareness."

Cem suggested that activities should be completed regularly for the evaluation of the students' learning. Cem noted, "Lesson plans were not the product of simply one person, but the product of all of us as a team. This responsibility made the process more effective."

Baha researched and presented informative cartoons especially for use in fifth-grade social studies lessons. Baha stated, "The research stage of LS allowed me to see different resources related to social studies. Cartoons, for example, could be used to attract the students' attention."

According to the coding realised during the content analysis, the areas where the teacher candidates developed the most are as presented in follows:

1. Specifying completely the teaching methods and techniques to be used in the lesson plan.
2. Enriching the lessons (content, teaching methods, materials, etc.).
3. Recognising the students' characteristics, gaining their attention, and anticipating their reactions.
4. Planning the assessment and evaluation of the students' learning.

CONTRIBUTIONS OF THE IMPLEMENTATION STAGE

During the implementation stage of the lesson study, the social studies teacher candidates were seen to have increased their performance. Problems such as the teacher candidates having not practiced the lesson plan correctly, not choosing the right teaching methods or techniques, and inadequate classroom management were mostly resolved. In applying the LS, the teacher candidates understood that the knowledge they acquired within the scope of numerous theoretical lessons at the College were able to be used in the field of practice, in real classroom life, and much more efficiently through collaborative working practices. In other words, they established a link between the theory and the practice.

Beril noted, "The video we decided to include in the lesson plan did not seem very necessary to me, but sticking to the lesson plan actually did work" (Week 8, self-evaluation). Candan observed, "Derya was making great efforts to stick to the lesson plan" (Notes in observation-evaluation form). Aylin reflected, "I guided them. On some points, I ignored the extracurricular behaviour of the students so they could have a rest. I empathised with them, and this approach worked" (Week 8, self-evaluation).

Akın shared, "After passing the attention-grabbing and informing parts, I distributed the case studies to the students. They seemed worried that they were like exams, so they were initially nervous. I told them not to be afraid and to relax" (Mentioned during LS sessions). Cem stated, "My ability to communicate with my students has increased. My peers suggested I use certain communication techniques in the LS sessions, and they worked" (Week 4, self-evaluation). Akın also mentioned, "The students became distracted whilst doing the activity I presented in the class. We had anticipated this situation during the LS teams and decided not to interfere too much" (Week 3, self-evaluation). Beril added, "When the pupils started not listening to me, I put the lecturing aside for a while and asked them questions from the lesson plan, and that change in approach worked" (Week 4, self-evaluation).

In the findings, it was seen that the LS implementation phase not only offered the teacher candidates the opportunity to combine theory and practice, but it also clearly increased their communication and classroom management skills.

CONTRIBUTIONS OF DISCUSSION/REFLECTION STAGE

During the reflection phase of the LS teams, the teacher candidates generally developed competencies as a result of sharing their experiences, observations, and comments. Unlike the previous LS stages, the reflection stage focused on the sharing of experiences, and both peer- and self-critique. The thoughts put forward by the teacher candidates and the discussions they held during the teaching process helped to improve their perspectives towards the lesson plans, as well as the overall teaching process.

Beril reflected, "In our discussions, I saw that my performance in the lesson was not perfect. My peers saw certain things that I had not noticed. Sharing our suggestions to correct our deficiencies was the most important aspect of the LS teams" (2nd research lesson).

Akın mentioned, "The students shared their positive thoughts about the process with us. The experience we gained from peer discussions had a great impact on the formation of this process" (3rd research lesson).

Derya noted, "I have developed the missing aspects of my field knowledge and teaching method knowledge, thanks to the sharing aspect of the discussion stages" (Focus group interview).

Baha stated, "I think that the LS teams strengthen communication between people. Supportive criticism during the discussion stage helped us to improve" (Focus group interview).

When the contributions of the discussion/reflection stage in the LS teams are evaluated, it can be easily noticed that it is difficult for teacher candidates to develop a different perspective on teaching processes. It is especially difficult for teacher candidates trained according to a classical education-teaching approach to develop a different perspective and to evaluate certain courses in a collaborative process based on the sharing of ideas and experiences. However, on this point, the 'facilitator' role of the researcher is very important. Encouraging participants to share their observations about lessons during the discussion stages was noted to contribute positively to the process.

Lesson Study (LS) has proven to be a vital tool for enhancing collaboration and increasing efficiency in higher education settings. By encouraging teamwork and the sharing of diverse perspectives, LS fosters a collaborative environment where teacher candidates can actively engage in the planning, implementation, and reflection stages of lesson development. This collaborative approach not only improves the quality of lesson plans but also enriches the teaching environment through the integration of various teaching methods, techniques, and resources. Moreover, LS helps bridge the gap between theoretical knowledge and practical application, allowing teacher candidates to apply what they have learned in real classroom settings more effectively. The experiences and insights gained through LS contribute significantly to the professional growth of teacher candidates, making it an essential model for promoting collaboration and efficiency in higher education.

DISCUSSION

The current study revealed a means of improving the lesson planning and implementation competencies of social studies teacher candidates. The LS teams implemented within the scope of this research provided the social studies teacher candidates with the opportunity to experience suitable competencies that were otherwise insufficiently developed according to the traditional approach to teacher education. Whilst applying LS, the participant teacher candidates developed the skills of finding and using course materials best able to attract their students' attention, and to develop activities appropriate to their students' improvable features and readiness levels. In the study, it was seen that LS practices increased the quality of lesson plans created by the participant social studies teacher candidates. Thus, the collaborative working environment was found to present a significant opportunity to empower the improved quality of their teaching practices. As a result, according to the study's findings, it was concluded that the teacher candidates' lesson planning and lesson implementation competencies had been notably enhanced through the application of the LS teams.

Prior to the implementation of LS groups, the participant social studies teacher candidates lacked sufficient opportunity to gain practical experience due to insufficient practice lessons. As shown, social studies teacher candidates in Turkey can gain more during their preservice education where their competencies regarding classroom management and teaching strategies are developed from the Teaching Practices Lesson and Teaching Principles and Methods Lesson. In the current study's approach, social studies teacher candidates presented their weekly individual lesson plans to their lecturer and mentor teacher prior to implementation. However, this situation was not found to be the same at every university in Turkey. Faculty members and mentor teachers often lack the opportunity or drive to provide adequate feedback to teacher candidates. This situation may be due in part to the high number of teacher candidates, as well as the workload of mentor teachers. As a result, teacher candidates prepare their lesson plans individually, and as such lesson plans rarely reflect the nature of the social studies field as it should be.

As a branch of teaching, social studies has a broad structure that includes multidisciplinary, interdisciplinary, and effective citizenship skills that include complex procedures, values, and skills dimensions. Social studies curricula offer many opportunities to develop a critical perspective on controversial issues such as imperialism, separation of powers, language, religion, culture, society, democracy, migration, economic crisis, and social classes. It is clear, therefore, that social studies teacher candidates can experience the need for discussions in which they are able to share their knowledge, ideas, and experiences on the teaching of critical social issues in their chosen field. However, it is significantly challenging to come across good lesson samples that deal with these very issues. The compelling structure of social studies reveals the measures to be taken for the teaching of this field, and that they should start from the preservice period of teacher training. The fact that practice lessons are held only in the last semester of undergraduate education in Turkey, and within only a limited timeframe, seems to present the most significant obstacle to teacher candidates gaining adequate experience in the teaching of students in a live classroom environment. As such, the LS teams offer certain opportunities to overcome this deficiency in the teacher training process.

Information sharing between participants during the LS teams can help to improve teachers' lesson planning and implementation competencies, whilst making it easier for them to internalise the information about their field. The LS approach is somewhat different from others because teacher candidates are encouraged to establish empathy with their students, to identify any learning difficulties that their students may face, to support the teaching process with various methods and techniques, and to comprehensively examine the learning outcomes of lessons during the LS teams. In the current study, it was seen that the social studies teacher candidates' experience of creating a written lesson plan during the LS teams increased, and that their classroom lessons were enriched in terms of the methods, techniques, tools, and equipment used. The teacher candidates mostly preferred the teaching methods and techniques they were most accustomed to using and lacked sufficient motivation to further diversify and enrich the teaching process. Their individual efforts were seen to be inadequate, with low motivation and that they also experienced test anxiety. The knowledge gained during their undergraduate education in terms of the professional knowledge lessons they attended, and the school classroom practice lessons were not found to adequately represent real-life school classroom situations. For this reason, the teacher candidates experienced a somewhat lonely struggle between the expectations of their mentor teacher, their faculty teacher, and their own potential. It was clear that they needed some form of collaborative working exercise. The LS teams led to them using not only the lecturing method along with question-and-answer sessions (i.e., classical teaching methods), but also simulation, micro-teaching, educational gaming, drama, and oral history. In this respect, the experiences reported in the current study appear compatible with the findings of previous research in the LS literature (e.g., Cheng, 2020; Wood, 2018).

The most significant purpose of the LS teams is not the creating of a perfect lesson plan, but to deliver improvements to teachers' competencies in practical classroom teaching. The most important contributions of the LS teams, therefore, can be said to be supporting cooperation between teachers, ensuring the professional development of teacher candidates (e.g., lesson planning skills), enabling teacher candidates to reflect upon their teaching processes, and to conduct significant discussions. Teachers can therefore experience active learning, planning, implementation, observation, and feedback processes thanks to the LS teams. The collaborative nature of LS teams facilitates teamwork by bringing together diverse perspectives and expertise, thereby enhancing the overall learning experience. In the context of higher education, teamwork is essential for increasing efficiency and productivity. The LS teams exemplify this by allowing teachers to work collaboratively, share insights, and support each other through the various stages of lesson planning and implementation. This collaborative approach not only helps in identifying and addressing instructional gaps but also fosters a sense of community and shared responsibility among teachers. By working together, teachers can leverage each other's strengths, leading to improved lesson quality and a more effective teaching-learning environment. The feedback and reflection sessions within the LS teams ensure continuous improvement and professional growth, which are crucial for maintaining high standards in education. This integration of teamwork into the LS process aligns perfectly with the book's main theme of enhancing productivity in higher education through collaborative efforts. The collaborative nature of LS teams not only boosts individual teacher performance but also contributes to a more cohesive and supportive educational environment, ultimately leading to better learning outcomes for students.

As such, teacher candidates can strengthen their awareness of reviewing and planning lessons during the LS teams, by engaging in collaborative planning efforts. This collaboration makes the teaching process more understandable for both teachers and teacher candidates. The current study aligns with previous research in the LS literature, highlighting the benefits of such collaborative efforts. In the context of professional development (PD) and social studies, teamwork is crucial. The challenges faced in social studies education, such as insufficient practical experience and the need for improved lesson planning, can be effectively addressed through the collaborative approach of LS teams. By working together, teacher candidates and experienced teachers can share insights, provide mutual support, and develop more comprehensive and effective lesson plans. This teamwork not only enhances individual competencies but also fosters a supportive community that is essential for professional growth. The integration of teamwork into LS is an appropriate intervention to address the deficits in social studies education. It allows for the pooling of diverse experiences and perspectives, leading to richer and more effective teaching strategies. Furthermore, the collaborative nature of LS ensures that feedback and reflection are integral parts of the process, promoting continuous improvement and higher standards in education. Thus, emphasizing teamwork within LS is not only compatible with the findings of previous research but also aligns with the overarching goal of enhancing productivity and effectiveness in higher education through collaborative efforts (e.g., Kanellopoulou & Darra, 2019; Lee, 2019; Murata, 2011; Stigler & Hiebert, 2016).

The teacher candidates notably developed an understanding of their students' learning when they worked together during the LS teams. They also increased their level of literacy regarding the preservice curricula of social studies teacher candidates, which in turn led them to consider the cognitive, affective, and psychomotor learning outcomes of the curricula. In many studies, unlike other approaches, the LS teams clearly emphasised there being a dimension of developing an understanding of the target students' learning for both serving teachers and teacher candidates. The LS teams also help in the design of assessment and evaluation processes that places student thinking at the centre from the beginning to the end of the teaching-learning process. According to the results of the current study, the findings of previous studies in the LS literature were also confirmed (e.g., Bjuland & Mosvold, 2015; Fernandez, 2002; Fischman & Wasserman, 2017; Towaf, 2016).

As known, the LS teams help teacher candidates to not only develop appropriate strategies for their classroom lesson and reach the goals set for the lesson, but also to improve their self-confidence as teachers. The literature indicates that LS teams enhance teaching development, ultimately benefiting students by providing a higher quality of education. Research on LS has significantly shown that the teaching environment of the LS emphasises transformative effects on the qualifications of both teachers and teacher candidates, as well as improving teacher candidates' critical thinking skills. During the LS teams, teacher candidates share both spatial and pedagogical knowledge during the planning and reflection process, and thereby exhibit collaborative efforts focused on how students actually learn, and not how their teacher just happens to teach. This situation develops student-centred thinking skills, and in this respect, the current study also appears consistent with the LS literature (e.g., Darling-Hammond & Richardson, 2009; Giannakidou et al., 2013; Lewis et al., 2012; NSDC, 2011; Reeves, 2010; Villalon, 2016; Wessels, 2018).

The scientific value of the current study, which aims to reveal how best to improve the LS process, lesson planning, and implementation competencies of social studies teacher candidates, lies in highlighting the benefits of the collaborative experience provided by the LS process. By including the outputs of the LS process applied with teacher candidates, the study underscores the importance of teamwork in enhancing educational practices.

This collaborative experience emphasises the importance of teamwork in enhancing productivity in higher education. By working together, teacher candidates develop a deeper understanding of lesson planning and implementation, benefiting from the diverse perspectives and feedback of their peers. This not only improves their individual competencies but also fosters a supportive learning community. It is recommended to promote such teamwork approaches that increase the likelihood of achieving the goals of higher education. The LS process exemplifies how collaborative efforts can lead to higher quality education by promoting continuous improvement and professional growth. Emphasising teamwork within the LS framework highlights the significant impact of collaborative practices on the efficiency and effectiveness of education.

The implementation of Lesson Study (LS) teams has demonstrably enhanced the competencies of social studies teachers. Through the structured and collaborative nature of LS, teachers engaged in systematic cycles of planning, observing, and reflecting on lessons. This process facilitated the development of advanced pedagogical skills and deeper content knowledge. By collaboratively designing lesson plans, teachers shared best practices and innovative teaching strategies, which were subsequently tested and refined. The iterative nature of LS allowed teachers to receive continuous feedback, fostering a reflective practice that is essential for professional growth. As a result, social studies teachers reported increased confidence in their instructional methods and a greater ability to engage students in meaningful learning experiences.

Teamwork is a central theme of this book, and its significance cannot be overstated within the context of LS. The collaborative framework of LS provides a supportive environment where teachers work together towards common educational goals. This collective effort not only enhances individual teaching practices but also builds a strong professional community. Teamwork encourages the sharing of diverse perspectives, fostering a culture of mutual respect and cooperation. By working in teams, teachers can pool their expertise, address common challenges, and develop cohesive instructional strategies. This collaborative spirit is fundamental to the success of LS and underscores the importance of teamwork in achieving educational excellence.

The LS process inherently reflects the principles of teamwork. From the initial planning stages to the final reflection sessions, collaboration is at the core of LS activities. Teachers come together to identify learning objectives, design detailed lesson plans, and discuss anticipated challenges. During lesson observations, team members actively engage in data collection and provide constructive feedback. The subsequent reflection sessions are crucial for collective analysis, where teachers discuss the outcomes, share insights, and propose adjustments. This continuous cycle of collaborative inquiry not only improves lesson quality but also strengthens the professional bonds among team members. The manuscript provides specific examples of how teamwork was integrated into each phase of the LS process, highlighting its critical role in fostering educational improvements.

In conclusion, the positive outcomes achieved through LS can be largely attributed to the effective teamwork among teachers. The collaborative efforts within LS teams led to significant improvements in teaching practices, resulting in enhanced student engagement and learning outcomes. The shared responsibility and collective problem-solving approach fostered by LS teams created a dynamic and supportive learning environment. By working together, teachers were able to implement more effective instructional strategies, address individual student needs, and continuously improve their teaching methods. The manuscript concludes by emphasising that the successes observed in the LS process are a testament to the power of teamwork, reinforcing its importance as a cornerstone of educational practice.

ACKNOWLEDGEMENT

This study was conducted by drawing on a portion of the master's thesis research carried out by the first author under the academic supervision of the second author at Ankara University's Institute of Educational Sciences.

REFERENCES

Adler, S. (Ed.). (2006). *Critical issues in social studies teacher education*. IAP.

Afdal, H. W., & Spernes, K. (2018). Designing and redesigning research-based teacher education. *Teaching and Teacher Education*, 74(1), 215–228. DOI: 10.1016/j.tate.2018.05.011

Akiba, M., Murata, A., Howard, C. C., & Wilkinson, B. (2019). Lesson study design features for supporting collaborative teacher learning. *Teaching and Teacher Education*, 77, 352–365. DOI: 10.1016/j.tate.2018.10.012

Amador, J., & Weiland, I. (2015). What preservice teachers and knowledgeable others professionally notice during LS. *Teacher Educator*, 50(2), 1–18. DOI: 10.1080/08878730.2015.1009221

Ball, D. L., Sleep, L., Boerst, T. A., & Bass, H. (2009). Combining the development of practice and the practice of development in teacher education. *The Elementary School Journal*, 109(5), 458–474. DOI: 10.1086/596996

Bényei, R., & Csernoch, M. (2022). PEDAGOGICAL EVALUATION PHASES – LESSON STUDY SURVEY. *Education and New Developments 2022 – Volume I.* https://doi.org/.DOI: 10.36315/2022v1end122

Bjuland, R., & Helgevold, N. (2018). Dialogic processes that enable student teachers' learning about pupil learning in mentoring conversations in a LS field practice. *Teaching and Teacher Education*, 70, 246–254. DOI: 10.1016/j.tate.2017.11.026

Bjuland, R., & Mosvold, R. (2015). LS in teacher education: Learning from a challenging case. *Teaching and Teacher Education*, 52, 83–90. DOI: 10.1016/j.tate.2015.09.005

Bolick, C., Berson, M., Coutts, C., & Heinecke, W. (2003). Technology applications in social studies teacher education: A survey of social studies methods faculty. *Contemporary Issues in Technology & Teacher Education*, 3(3), 300–309. https://www.learntechlib.org/primary/p/19913/

Burns, M. (2011). *Distance education for teacher training: Modes, models and methods.* Education Development Center Inc. Scribbr. http://library.uog.edu.gy/eBooks/Distance_Education_for_Teacher_Training_by_Mary_B urns_EDC.pdf

Cheng, E. C. (2020). Knowledge management strategies for sustaining Lesson Study. *International Journal for Lesson and Learning Studies*, 9(2), 167–178. DOI: 10.1108/IJLLS-10-2019-0070

Cheung, W. M., & Wong, W. Y. (2014). Does LS work? *International Journal for Lesson and Learning Studies.*, 3(2), 137–149. DOI: 10.1108/IJLLS-05-2013-0024

Chong, J. S. Y., Han, S. H., Abdullah, N. A., Chong, M. S. F., Widjaja, W., & Shahrill, M. (2017). Utilizing LS in improving year 12 students' learning and performance in mathematics. *Mathematics Education Trends and Research*, 2017(1), 1–8. DOI: 10.5899/2017/metr-00095

Coenders, F., & Verhoef, N. (2019). LS: Professional development (PD) for beginning and experienced teachers. *Professional Development in Education*, 45(2), 217–230. DOI: 10.1080/19415257.2018.1430050

Cohen, L., Manion, L., & Morrison, K. (2007). *Observation. Research methods in education.* Routledge. Scribbr. https://www.researchgate.net/

Creswell, J. W. (2013). *Research Design Qualitative, Quantitative, and Mixed Method Approaches* (4th ed.). SAGE Publications.

Crocco, M., & Cramer, J. (2005). Technology use, women, and global studies in social studies teacher education. *Contemporary Issues in Technology & Teacher Education*, 5(1), 38–49. https://www.learntechlib.org/primary/p/5951/

Crowe, A. R., & Cuenca, A. (Eds.). (2016). *Rethinking social studies teacher education in the twenty-first century.* Springer International Publishing. DOI: 10.1007/978-3-319-22939-3

Crowley, R. M., & Smith, W. (2015). Whiteness and social studies teacher education: Tensions in the pedagogical task. *Teaching Education*, 26(2), 160–178. DOI: 10.1080/10476210.2014.996739

Darling-Hammond, L., & Richardson, N. (2009). Research review/teacher learning: What matters. [Scribbr. https://outlier.uchicago.edu/]. *Educational Leadership*, 66(5), 46–53.

Dinkelman, T., & Cuenca, A. (2020). A turn to practice: Core practices in social studies teacher education. *Theory and Research in Social Education*, 48(4), 583–610. DOI: 10.1080/00933104.2020.1757538

Dudley, P. (2014). *LS: A handbook.*

Ebaeguin, M., & Stephens, M. (2014). Cultural Challenges in Adapting Lesson Study to a Philippines Setting. *Mathematics Teacher Education and Development, 16.*

Elliot, J. (1993). Three Perspectives on Coherence and Continuity in Teacher Education. Reconstructing Teacher Education. London: Falmer Press.

Elliott, J. (2016). The mentoring process and LS: Are they compatible? Open Online Journal for Research and Education, Special Issue 5. Scribbr. http://journal.ph-noe.ac.at

Evans, R. W. (2004). *The social studies wars: What should we teach the children?* Teachers College Press.

Faizah, N., Chotimah, C., & Mukhlis, I. (2020). The Implementation of LS in Economic Subjects to Improve Student's Learning Motivation. [CARJO]. *Classroom Action Research Journal*, 4(1), 44–52. DOI: 10.17977/um013v4i12020p048

Fernandez, C. (2002). Learning from Japanese Approaches to Professional Development: The Case of LS. *Journal of Teacher Education*, 53(5), 393–405. DOI: 10.1177/002248702237394

Fischman, D., & Wasserman, K. (2017). Developing Assessment through LS. *Mathematics Teaching in the Middle School*, 22(6), 344–351. DOI: 10.5951/mathteacmiddscho.22.6.0344

Flick, U. (2004). Triangulation in qualitative research. *A companion to qualitative research, 3*, 178-183.

Follmer, D., Groth, R., Bergner, J., & Weaver, S. (2023). Theory-based Evaluation of Lesson Study Professional Development: Challenges, Opportunities, and Lessons Learned. *The American Journal of Evaluation.* Advance online publication. DOI: 10.1177/10982140231184899

Fraser, C., Kennedy, A., Reid, L., & Mckinney, S. (2007). Teachers' continuing professional development: Contested concepts, understandings and models. *Journal of In-service Education*, 33(2), 153–169. DOI: 10.1080/13674580701292913

Fujii, T. (2016). Designing and adapting tasks in lesson planning: A critical process of Lesson Study. *ZDM Mathematics Education*, 2016(48), 411–423. DOI: 10.1007/s11858-016-0770-3

Garet, M. S., Heppen, J. B., Walters, K., Parkinson, J., Smith, T. M., Song, M., . . . Borman, G. D. (2016). Focusing on Mathematical Knowledge: The Impact of Content-Intensive Teacher Professional Development. NCEE 2016-4010. National Center for Education Evaluation and Regional Assistance.

Giannakidou, E., Gioftsali, K., & Tzioras, E. (2013). The reflective action of teacher candidates when implementing an appied version of the LS model. *Hellenic Journal of Research in Education, 1*, 30-58. Scribbr. https://ejournals.epublishing.ekt.gr/index.php/hjre/article/view/8791/9012

Girvan, C., Conneely, C., & Tangney, B. (2016). Extending experiential learning in teacher professional development. *Teaching and Teacher Education*, 58, 129–139. DOI: 10.1016/j.tate.2016.04.009

Glesne, C. (2016). *Becoming qualitative researchers: An introduction*. Pearson. One Lake Street, Upper Saddle River, New Jersey 07458.

Godfrey, D., Seleznyov, S., Anders, J., Wollaston, N., & Barrera-Pedemonte, F. (2018). A developmental evaluation approach to lesson study: Exploring the impact of lesson study in London schools. *Professional Development in Education*, 45(2), 325–340. DOI: 10.1080/19415257.2018.1474488

Gong, X., & Wang, P. (2017). A Comparative Study of Pre-Service Education for Preschool Teachers in China and the United States. *Current Issues in Comparative Education, 19*(2), 84-110. Scribbr. https://files.eric.ed.gov/fulltext/EJ1144805.pdf

Gopinathan, S. (2008). *Transforming teacher education: Redefined professionals for 21st century schools.*https://repository.nie.edu.sg/bitstream/10497/22550/1/Transforming-Teacher-Education_Report.pdf

Gore, J., Lloyd, A., Smith, M., Bowe, J., Ellis, H., & Lubans, D. (2017). Effects of Professional development on the quality of teaching: Results from a randomised controlled trial of Quality Teaching Rounds. *Teaching and Teacher Education*, 68, 99–113. DOI: 10.1016/j.tate.2017.08.007

Gore, J. M., Miller, A., Fray, L., Harris, J., & Prieto, E. (2021). Improving student achievement through professional development: Results from a randomised controlled trial of Quality Teaching Rounds. *Teaching and Teacher Education*, 101, 103297. DOI: 10.1016/j.tate.2021.103297

Hadfield, M., & Jopling, M. (2016). Problematizing lesson study and its impacts: Studying a highly contextualised approach to professional learning. *Teaching and Teacher Education*, 60, 203–214. DOI: 10.1016/j.tate.2016.08.001

Halvorsen, A. L., & Kesler Lund, A. (2013). LS and history education. *Social Studies*, 104(3), 123–129. DOI: 10.1080/00377996.2012.698326

Hawley, T. S. (2012). Purpose as content and pedagogy: Rationale-development as a core theme of social studies teacher education. *Journal of Inquiry and Action in Education*, 4(3), 1. https://digitalcommons.buffalostate.edu/cgi/viewcontent.cgi?article=1041&context=jiae

Hennissen, P., Beckers, H., & Moerkerke, G. (2017). Linking practice to theory in teacher education: A growth in cognitive structures. *Teaching and Teacher Education*, 63, 314–325. DOI: 10.1016/j.tate.2017.01.008

Hervas, G. (2021). Lesson Study as a Faculty Development Initiative in Higher Education: A Systematic Review. *AERA Open*, 7, 2332858420982564. Advance online publication. DOI: 10.1177/2332858420982564

Hilton, A., Hilton, G., Dole, S., & Goos, M. (2015). School leaders as participants in teachers' professional development: The impact on teachers' and school leaders' professional growth. *The Australian Journal of Teacher Education*, 40(12), 8. DOI: 10.14221/ajte.2015v40n12.8

Hostetler, A., Sengupta, P., & Hollett, T. (2018). Unsilencing critical conversations in social-studies teacher education using agent-based modeling. *Cognition and Instruction*, 36(2), 139–170. DOI: 10.1080/07370008.2017.1420653

Howell, J. B., & Saye, J. W. (2016). Using LS to develop a shared professional teaching knowledge culture among 4th grade social studies teachers. *Journal of Social Studies Research*, 40(1), 25–37. DOI: 10.1016/j.jssr.2015.03.001

Hrastinski, S. (2021). *Digital tools to support teacher professional development in lesson studies: a systematic literature review*. International Journal for Lesson and Learning Studies., DOI: 10.1108/IJLLS-09-2020-0062

Huang, R., Helgevold, N., & Lang, J. (2021). Digital technologies, online learning and lesson study. *International Journal for Lesson and Learning Studies*, 10(2), 105–117. DOI: 10.1108/IJLLS-03-2021-0018

Hubbard, J. (2007). LS: Teachers Collaborate in Lesson Development. *Social Studies and the Young Learner*, 19(4), 25–29.

Jain, P., & Brown, A. (2020). Using an Adapted Lesson Study with Early Childhood Undergraduate Students. *Teaching Education*, 33(2), 154–174. DOI: 10.1080/10476210.2020.1826424

Joubert, J., Callaghan, R., & Engelbrecht, J. (2020). LS in a blended approach to support isolated teachers in teaching with technology. *ZDM Mathematics Education*, 52(5), 907–925. DOI: 10.1007/s11858-020-01161-x

Kanellopoulou, E.-M., & Darra, M. (2019). Benefits, Difficulties and Conditions of LS Implementation in Basic Teacher Education: A Review. *International Journal of Higher Education*, 8(18), 18. Advance online publication. DOI: 10.5430/ijhe.v8n4p18

Kennedy, M. M. (2016). How does professional development improve teaching? *Review of Educational Research*, 86(4), 945–980. DOI: 10.3102/0034654315626800

King, L. J., & Chandler, P. T. (2016). From non-racism to anti-racism in social studies teacher education: Social studies and racial pedagogical content knowledge. In *Rethinking social studies teacher education in the twenty-first century* (pp. 3–21). Springer. DOI: 10.1007/978-3-319-22939-3_1

Kohlmeier, J., Howell, J., Saye, J., McCormick, T., Shannon, D., Jones, C., & Brush, T. (2020). Investigating teacher adoption of authentic pedagogy through LS. *Theory and Research in Social Education*, 48(4), 492–528. DOI: 10.1080/00933104.2020.1751761

Lee, L. H. J., & Tan, S. C. (2020). Teacher learning in Lesson Study: Affordances, disturbances, contradictions, and implications. *Teaching and Teacher Education*, 89, 102986. DOI: 10.1016/j.tate.2019.102986

Lee, M. Y. (2019). The development of elementary pre-service teachers' professional noticing of students' thinking through adapted LS. *Asia-Pacific Journal of Teacher Education*, 47(4), 383–398. DOI: 10.1080/1359866X.2019.1607253

Lewis, C. (2016). How does LS improve mathematics instruction? *ZDM Mathematics Education*, 48(4), 571–580. DOI: 10.1007/s11858-016-0792-x

Lewis, C. C., Perry, R. R., Friedkin, S., & Roth, J. R. (2012). Improving Teaching Does Improve Teachers: Evidence from LS. *Journal of Teacher Education*, 63(5), 368–375. DOI: 10.1177/0022487112446633

Lim-Ratnam, C., Lee, C., Jiang, H., & Sudarshan, A. (2019). Lost in adaptation? Issues of adapting Japanese lesson study in non-Japanese contexts. *Educational Research for Policy and Practice*, 18(3), 263–278. DOI: 10.1007/s10671-019-09247-4

Lune, H., & Berg, B. L. (2017). *Qualitative research methods for the social sciences*. Pearson.

Mayrhofer, E. (2019). LS and teachers' beliefs. *International Journal for Lesson and Learning Studies.*, 8(1), 19–33. DOI: 10.1108/IJLLS-11-2018-0091

Merriam, S. B., & Tisdell, E. J. (2015). *Qualitative research: A guide to design and implementation*. John Wiley & Sons.

Murata, A. (2011). Introduction: Conceptual overview of lesson study. In Alston, A., Hart, L., & Murata, A. (Eds.), *Lesson-study research and practice in mathematics: Learning together* (pp. 1–12). Springer. DOI: 10.1007/978-90-481-9941-9_1

Murata, A., & Takahashi, A. (2002). *Vehicle to Connect Theory, Research, and Practice: How Teacher Thinking Changes in District-Level LS in Japan.* Proceedings of the Annual Meeting [of the] North American Chapter of the International Group for the Psychology of Mathematics Education (24th, Athens, GA, October 26-29, 2002). Volumes 1-4; see SE 066887.

Nakajima, T. M., & Goode, J. (2019). Transformative learning for computer science teachers: Examining how educators learn e-textiles in professional development. *Teaching and Teacher Education*, 85, 148–159. DOI: 10.1016/j.tate.2019.05.004

Noonan, J. (2019). An affinity for learning: Teacher identity and powerful professional development. *Journal of Teacher Education*, 70(5), 526–537. DOI: 10.1177/0022487118788838

Norwich, B. (2018). Making Sense of International Variations in LS and LS-like Practices: An Exploratory and Conceptual Perspective. *International Journal for Lesson and Learning Studies*, 7(3), 201–216. DOI: 10.1108/IJLLS-02-2018-0007

NSDC (National Staff Development Council). (2011). *Standards for professional learning*. Scribbr. www.nsdc.org

Opfer, D. (2016). *Conditions and practices associated with teacher professional development and its impact on instruction in TALIS 2013*.

Opfer, V. D., & Pedder, D. (2011). The lost promise of teacher professional development in England. *European Journal of Teacher Education, 34*(1), 3e24. https://doi.org/DOI: 10.1080/02619768.2010.534131

Patton, M. Q. (2002). *Qualitative research and evaluation methods* (3rd ed.). Sage.

Penner-Williams, J., Diaz, E. I., & Worthen, D. G. (2019). Sustainability of teacher growth from professional development in culturally and linguistically responsive instructional practices. *Teaching and Teacher Education*, 86, 102891. DOI: 10.1016/j.tate.2019.102891

Rappleye, J., & Komatsu, H. (2017). How to make LS work in America and worldwide: A Japanese perspective on the onto-cultural basis of (teacher) education. *Research in Comparative and International Education*, 12(4), 398–430. DOI: 10.1177/1745499917740656

Reeves, D. B. (2010). Transforming Professional Development into Student Results (Alexandria, VA: Association for Supervision and Curriculum Development, 2010). (Washington, DC: Council of Chief State School Officers, April 2011). *Journal of School Psychology*, 38(3), 277–298.

Schipper, T., Goei, S. L., de Vries, S., & van Veen, K. (2017). Professional growth in adaptive teaching competence as a result of Lesson Study. *Teaching and Teacher Education*, 68, 289–303. DOI: 10.1016/j.tate.2017.09.015

Schipper, T. M., van der Lans, R. M., de Vries, S., Goei, S. L., & van Veen, K. (2020). Becoming a more adaptive teacher through collaborating in Lesson Study? Examining the influence of Lesson Study on teachers' adaptive teaching practices in mainstream secondary education. *Teaching and Teacher Education*, 88, 102961. DOI: 10.1016/j.tate.2019.102961

Shulman, L. S. (1987). Knowledge and teaching: Foundations of the new reform. *Harvard Educational Review*, 57(1), 61–77. https://eric.ed.gov/. DOI: 10.17763/haer.57.1.j463w79r56455411

Sims, L., & Walsh, D. (2009). Lesson Study with preservice teachers: Lessons from lessons. *Teaching and Teacher Education*, 25(5), 724–733. DOI: 10.1016/j.tate.2008.10.005

Skott, C. K., & Møller, H. (2020). Adaptation of lesson study in a Danish context: Displacements of teachers' work and power relations. *Teaching and Teacher Education*, 87, 102945. DOI: 10.1016/j.tate.2019.102945

Stanley, W. B. (2015). Social studies and the social order: Transmission or transformation? In *Social studies today* (pp. 17–24). Routledge.

Stern, B. S. (2013). *Social studies: Standards, meaning, and understanding*. Routledge. DOI: 10.4324/9781315851204

Stigler, J. W., & Hiebert, J. (2016). LS, improvement, and the importing of cultural routines. *ZDM Mathematics Education*, 48(4), 581–587. DOI: 10.1007/s11858-016-0787-7

Sykes, G., Bird, T., & Kennedy, M. (2010). Teacher education: Its problems and some prospects. *Journal of Teacher Education*, 61(5), 464–476. DOI: 10.1177/0022487110375804

Takahashi, A., & McDougal, T. (2016). Collaborative lesson research: Maximizing the impact of LS. *ZDM Mathematics Education*, 48(4), 513–526. DOI: 10.1007/s11858-015-0752-x

Towaf, S. M. (2016). Integration of LS in Teaching Practice of Social Study Student Teachers to Improve the Quality of Learning and Promote a Sustainable LS. *Journal of Education and Practice*, 7(18), 83–91. https://iiste.org/Journals/index.php/JEP

Tuanaya, R., Manggaberani, A., Safitri, R., & Ramadan, S. (2022). Meta-analysis study: Analysis of the Effect of Digital Platforms on Learning Outcomes. *Materials of International Practical Internet Conference "Challenges of Science"*. https://doi.org/DOI: 10.31643/2022.17

Van Driel, J. H., Meirink, J. A., van Veen, K., & Zwart, R. C. (2012). Current trends and missing links in studies on teacher professional development in science education: A review of design features and quality of research. *Studies in Science Education*, 48(2), 129–160. DOI: 10.1080/03057267.2012.738020

Vermunt, J. D., Vrikki, M., van Halem, N., Warwick, P., & Mercer, N. (2019). The impact of Lesson Study professional development on the quality of teacher learning. *Teaching and Teacher Education*, 81, 61–73. DOI: 10.1016/j.tate.2019.02.009

Villalon, J. J. Julio J. Villalon. (2016). LS: Its influence on planning, instruction, and self-confidence of pre- service mathematics teachers. *US-China Education Review B*, 6(7), 429–439. DOI: 10.17265/2161-6248/2016.07.003

Voogt, J., & Roblin, N. P. (2012). A comparative analysis of international frameworks for 21st century competences: Implications for national curriculum policies. *Journal of Curriculum Studies*, 44(3), 299–321. DOI: 10.1080/00220272.2012.668938

Vrikki, M., Warwick, P., Vermunt, J. D., Mercer, N., & Van Halem, N. (2017). Teacher learning in the context of LS: A video-based analysis of teacher discussions. *Teaching and Teacher Education*, 61, 211–224. DOI: 10.1016/j.tate.2016.10.014

Wadi, H., Suryanti, N. M. N., & Sukardi, S. (2020, August). *The Collaborative Learning for Multicultural of Social Science with LS Pattern for Strengthening Student Character Education*. In 1st Annual Conference on Education and Social Sciences (ACCESS 2019) (322-326). Atlantis Press.

Wake, G., Foster, C., & Swan, M. (2013, July). A theoretical lens on LS: Professional learning across boundaries. In *Proceedings of the 37th Conference of the International Group for the Psychology of Mathematics Education* (Vol. 4, 369-376).

Walker, E. (2011). How "Language-Aware" Are Lesson Studies İn An East Asian High School Context. *Language and Education*, 25(3), 187–202. DOI: 10.1080/09500782.2011.555557

Weaver, J., Matney, G., Goedde, A., Nadler, J., & Patterson, N. (2021). *Digital tools to promote remote lesson study*. International Journal for Lesson and Learning Studies., DOI: 10.1108/IJLLS-09-2020-0072

Wei, R. C., Darling-Hammond, L., & Adamson, F. (2010). *Professional development in the United States: Trends and challenges* (Vol. 28). National Staff Development Council.

Wessels, H. (2018). *Noticing in Pre-service Teacher Education: Research Lessons as a Context for Reflection on Learners' Mathematical Reasoning and Sense-Making*. In G. Kaiser et al. (Eds.), Invited Lectures from the 13th International Congress on Mathematical Education. ICME-13 Monographs. DOI: 10.1007/978-3-319-72170-5_41

Westbury, I., Hansen, S.-E., Kansanen, P., & Björkvist, O. (2005). Teacher Education for Research-Based Practice in Expanded Roles: Finland's Experience. *Scandinavian Journal of Educational Research*, 5(5), 475–485. DOI: 10.1080/00313830500267937

Wood, K. (2018). The many faces of LS and learning study. *International journal for lesson and learning studies*. 7(1), 2018. 2–7. https://doi.org/DOI: 10.1108/IJLLS-10-2017-0047

Yurkofsky, M. M., Blum-Smith, S., & Brennan, K. (2019). Expanding outcomes: Exploring varied conceptions of teacher learning in an online Professional development experience. *Teaching and Teacher Education, 82*, 1e13. https://doi.org/DOI: 10.1016/j.tate.2019.03.002

Zeichner, K. M. (1983). Alternative Paradigms of Teacher Education. *Journal of Teacher Education*, 34(3), 3–9. https://eric.ed.gov/. DOI: 10.1177/002248718303400302

Zeng, Y., & Day, C. (2019). Collaborative teacher professional development in schools in England (UK) and Shanghai (China): Cultures, contexts and tensions. *Teachers and Teaching*, 25(3), 379–397. DOI: 10.1080/13540602.2019.1593822

Zhang, L., Basham, J. D., Carter, R. A.Jr, & Zhang, J. (2021). Exploring Factors associated with the implementation of student-centered instructional practices in US classrooms. *Teaching and Teacher Education*, 99, 103273. DOI: 10.1016/j.tate.2020.103273

ADDITIONAL READINGS

Baumfield, V., Bethel, A., Boyle, C., Katene, W., Knowler, H., Koutsouris, G., & Norwich, B. (2022). How lesson study is used in initial teacher education: An international review of literature. *Teacher Development*, 26(3), 356–372. DOI: 10.1080/13664530.2022.2063937

Hervas, G. (2021). Lesson Study as a Faculty Development Initiative in Higher Education: A Systematic Review. *AERA Open*, 7, 2332858420982564. Advance online publication. DOI: 10.1177/2332858420982564

Hervas, G., & Medina, J. (2020). Key components of lesson study from the perspective of complexity: A theoretical analysis. *Teachers and Teaching*, 26(1), 118–128. DOI: 10.1080/13540602.2020.1745174

Jansen, S., Knippels, M., & Joolingen, W. (2021). Lesson study as a research approach: a case study. *International Journal for Lesson & Learning Studies*. https://doi.org/.DOI: 10.1108/IJLLS-12-2020-0098

Kihwele, J. (2020). Affordances and Constraints of Implementing Lesson Study for Teachers' Professional Development. *RE:view*, 9, 49–69. Advance online publication. DOI: 10.21083/ajote.v9i0.5731

Rodrigues, M., & Arroio, A. (2020). Lesson Study In Pre-Service Physics Teachers' Education: A Case In Brazil. *Gamtamokslinis Ugdymas. Natural Sciences Education*, 17(2), 139–152. Advance online publication. DOI: 10.48127/gu-nse/20.17.139

Rozimela, Y. (2020). Developing Teachers' Professionalism through School Initiative-Based Lesson Study. *European journal of educational research*, 9, 1513-1526. https://doi.org/.DOI: 10.12973/eu-jer.9.4.1513

Wati, I., & Dayal, H. (2022). *Exploring possibilities and challenges of Lesson Study: A case study in a small island developing state*. Waikato Journal of Education., DOI: 10.15663/wje.v27i3.812

KEY TERMS AND DEFINITIONS

Lesson Study (LS): Lesson Study is a process in which a group of teachers collaboratively plan, implement, and evaluate a specific lesson. This process enables teachers to develop a deep understanding and continually revise their lessons to enhance learning outcomes.

Professional Development (PD): Professional Development refers to structured activities designed to enhance the knowledge and skills of teachers, administrators, or other education professionals, aimed at improving pedagogical practices and increasing student achievement. These activities may target various goals such as enhancing individual teaching skills, learning new pedagogical approaches, or expanding professional networks.

Social Studies: Social Studies is an educational field that enables individuals to acquire and understand information about the societal, cultural, economic, and political worlds. In this field, students explore interdisciplinary subjects such as history, geography, sociology, economics, and politics, developing a profound understanding of how society operates.

Teacher Candidates' Professional Competencies: Teacher Candidates' Professional Competencies refer to the knowledge, skills, and attitudes required for future teachers to effectively support student learning. These competencies may encompass various areas such as pedagogical knowledge, classroom management, student assessment, professional ethics, and cultural sensitivity.

Teacher Training Approaches: Teacher Training Approaches refer to the methods and strategies used to support teachers' professional development and help them embrace effective pedagogical practices. These approaches encompass a wide range of techniques, from traditional classroom-based training to distance learning, mentorship programs, and simulations.

Teamwork: Teamwork refers to the collaborative efforts of a group to achieve common goals, particularly in educational settings. It involves sharing ideas, resources, and responsibilities to enhance teaching practices and student learning outcomes. In the context of LS, teamwork is crucial as it fosters a supportive environment where teachers can collaboratively develop, implement, and refine lesson plans, thereby improving educational efficiency and effectiveness.

Chapter 7
Embracing Collaborative Learning:
Innovative Teaching Methods at Tertiary Level

Morine Matongo
University of Zimbabwe, Zimbabwe

Pedzisai Goronga
University of Zimbabwe, Zimbabwe

ABSTRACT

This chapter explores innovative teaching methods that incorporate collaborative learning at higher education level. The discussion critically interrogates benefits, challenges and strategies for successful implementation of collaborative methodologies. Also known as cooperative learning, collaborative learning is a pedagogical technique that promotes active engagement, participatory learner engagement in learning in emancipatory epistemological spaces, contact, and mutual assistance among students.

INTRODUCTION

The pedagogical landscape of higher education has undergone a transformative shift in recent decades, with collaborative learning emerging as a cornerstone of modern instructional practice (Laal & Ghodsi, 2012; Roschelle & Teasley, 1995). This interactive approach to teaching and learning has gained widespread acclaim for its ability to foster a range of desirable student outcomes, including enhanced critical thinking, problem-solving aptitude, and teamwork skills (Barkley et al., 2014; Zhu,

DOI: 10.4018/979-8-3693-3852-0.ch007

2012). This chapter offers a comprehensive exploration of collaborative learning methodologies in the higher education context, critically examining their benefits, challenges, and strategies for successful implementation. Collaborative learning, also commonly referred to as cooperative learning, is a pedagogical technique that encourages active student engagement and mutual assistance in the construction of knowledge (Dillenbourg, 1999; Smith & MacGregor, 1992). In contrast to traditional teacher-centered models that prioritise the unidirectional transmission of information, collaborative learning empowers students to work together in small groups, leveraging their collective intellect to develop a deeper understanding of the subject matter (Laal & Ghodsi, 2012; Roschelle & Teasley, 1995). This shift in epistemological orientation is particularly crucial at the higher education level, where students are expected to cultivate advanced critical thinking and independent research skills to navigate the challenges of the modern workforce (Barkley et al., 2014; Zhu, 2012).

CONCEPTUALIZATION OF COLLABORATIVE LEARNING IN MODERN EDUCATION

The traditional, teacher-centric model of education has been challenged in recent decades by a growing emphasis on student-centered learning. Collaborative learning, a pedagogical approach that prioritises active student engagement and mutual support in the construction of knowledge, has emerged as a cornerstone of this shift (Sawyer & Obeid, 2017). This chapter explores the conceptualisation of collaborative learning in modern education, examining its theoretical underpinnings, practical applications, and the role of technology in facilitating its implementation.

Collaborative learning finds its theoretical foundation in constructivist learning theory, which posits that learners actively construct their understanding of the world through social interaction and collaboration (Sawyer & Obeid, 2017). This perspective emphasises the importance of active participation, peer interaction, and the negotiation of meaning in the learning process. Collaborative learning aligns with this theory by providing students with opportunities to engage in dialogue, share perspectives, and work together to solve problems, thereby fostering deeper understanding and knowledge construction.

In the 21st-century educational landscape, collaborative learning manifests in diverse forms, including group discussions, cooperative projects, peer teaching, problem-solving tasks, and collaborative online learning environments (Sawyer & Obeid, 2017). These approaches emphasize the development of essential skills for navigating the interconnected and rapidly changing world, such as teamwork, effective communication, critical engagement with issues, and problem-solving abilities (Sawyer & Obeid, 2017).

The integration of technology has significantly impacted the implementation of collaborative learning in modern education (Sawyer & Obeid, 2017). Online platforms, video conferencing tools, collaborative document editors, and social media networks provide opportunities for students to connect, share ideas, and work together regardless of geographical distances (Sawyer & Obeid, 2017). These technological tools enable seamless collaboration, both in-person and virtually, promoting active engagement and knowledge construction among students (Sawyer & Obeid, 2017).

The benefits of collaborative learning extend beyond the acquisition of knowledge. Studies have shown that collaborative learning environments can foster a sense of community, enhance student motivation, and improve academic performance (Barkley et al., 2014). Furthermore, the development of communication, teamwork, and critical thinking skills through collaborative learning are highly valued in the contemporary workforce (Zhu, 2012).

However, the successful implementation of collaborative learning requires careful consideration of potential challenges. Ensuring equitable participation within groups, managing group dynamics, and providing appropriate scaffolding are crucial for maximising the benefits of this approach (Barkley et al., 2014). Additionally, instructors must be adept at designing collaborative activities that align with learning objectives and provide clear guidelines for student collaboration (Zhu, 2012).

In inference, the conceptualisation of collaborative learning in modern education represents a fundamental shift towards a more student-centered, constructivist approach to teaching and learning (Sawyer & Obeid, 2017). This approach emphasises the importance of teamwork, communication, critical thinking, and problem-solving skills, which are increasingly crucial in the interconnected and rapidly changing world (Sawyer & Obeid, 2017). The integration of technology further enhances the opportunities for collaborative learning, enabling students to engage in meaningful, cross-boundary interactions and knowledge construction (Sawyer & Obeid, 2017). As research continues to explore the nuances of collaborative learning, educators are well-equipped to leverage its potential for fostering a dynamic and engaging learning environment that prepares students for the challenges of the 21st century.

SITUATING CONSTRUCTIVIST THEORY OF LEARNING INTO COLLABORATIVE LEARNING

The constructivist theory of learning, with its emphasis on active knowledge construction, provides a compelling theoretical framework for understanding the effectiveness of collaborative learning in modern education. This chapter examines the intersection of constructivism and collaborative learning, exploring how this pedagogical approach aligns with and reinforces core constructivist principles.

Constructivism, as a learning theory, posits that learners actively build their understanding of the world through their experiences, interactions, and reflections (Mcleod, 2024). This contrasts with traditional transmissionist models, where knowledge is viewed as a passive entity transferred from teacher to student. Collaborative learning, with its emphasis on student-centered, experiential, and interactive approaches, aligns perfectly with this constructivist perspective (Palincsar, 1998; Elliott et al., 2000).

Central to constructivism is the notion that social interaction plays a crucial role in learning. Collaborative learning environments, such as group projects, discussions, or problem-solving activities, provide fertile ground for this social interaction (Palincsar, 1998; Elliott et al., 2000). When students collaborate, they engage in discussions, share ideas, and negotiate meaning with others, leading to a deeper understanding of the subject matter (Enest, 1994; Phillips, 1995). This process of collaborative negotiation challenges students' existing beliefs, exposes them to diverse perspectives, and encourages them to refine their understanding through constructive dialogue.

Lev Vygotsky's concept of the Zone of Proximal Development (ZPD) further underscores the importance of social interaction in learning, a concept that aligns seamlessly with the constructivist framework (Vygotsky, 1978). The ZPD refers to the gap between what a learner can achieve independently and what they can achieve with guidance and support from others (Vygotsky, 1978; Rogoff, 1994). Collaborative learning environments provide a space for students to operate within their ZPD, as they scaffold each other's learning through peer support, feedback, and encouragement (Vygotsky, 1978).

Collaborative learning also fosters active engagement and participation, empowering students to construct knowledge together (Fox, 2001). Instead of passively receiving information from a teacher or textbook, students actively contribute to the creation of knowledge through their interactions with peers, their communities, and their environments (Fox, 2001). This active engagement allows students to integrate new information with their prior knowledge and experiences, leading to deeper understanding and conceptual development (Fox, 2001).

Furthermore, collaborative learning can lead to cognitive dissonance, a phenomenon where students encounter discrepancies between their existing understanding and new information or perspectives (von Glasersfeld, 2013). Resolving this cognitive dissonance can lead to cognitive consonance and growth, resulting in a more nuanced and sophisticated understanding (Driscoll, 2000). This process of cognitive conflict resolution, facilitated by collaborative dialogue and negotiation, is a key mechanism for knowledge construction within the constructivist framework.

Collaborative learning also encourages students to take ownership of their learning process, fostering motivation and engagement (Oliver, 2000). By actively participating in group tasks, setting goals, making decisions, and evaluating their own and others' contributions, students become active agents in their own learning journey (Oliver, 2000). This sense of ownership and agency is a cornerstone of constructivist learning, where students are not passive recipients of knowledge but active constructors of their own understanding.

In inference, the constructivist theory of learning provides a strong theoretical foundation for understanding the effectiveness of collaborative learning. By emphasizing active knowledge construction, social interaction, and the importance of the ZPD, constructivism highlights the key elements that make collaborative learning a powerful pedagogical approach. As educators continue to explore the potential of collaborative learning, a deep understanding of the constructivist framework will be essential for designing and implementing effective and engaging learning experiences that foster student growth and development.

A GLIMPSE AT INNOVATIVE PEDAGOGICAL METHODS

With the advent and proliferation of disruptive technologies, it is imperative to use innovative pedagogical approaches that respond to global best practices. There are various methods that qualify to be described as innovative teaching methods. Among many others, these include problem-based learning, blended learning, and flipped classrooms and have been shown to improve student learning. These approaches assist students grasp and apply concepts more effectively, as well as increase their interest in and access to learning material (Salma, 2020). The flipped classroom model is based on the idea that there are more effective uses of instructional time than lecture or direct instruction (Arfstrom, 2014). Instead it takes the traditional lecture-based method and delivers educational content outside of class via online modes such as videos, books, or multimedia tools powered by technology. The remainder of class time is spent on collaborative activities like group discussions, problem-solving, and project-based learning. This strategy allows students to work through course materials at their own pace while actively applying their knowledge in a collaborative environment that brings sensitivity to inclusive practices that respects cultural differences and diversity. Innovative teaching methods represent a departure from traditional instructional approaches to emphasising creative, student-centered, and technology-enhanced strategies to enhance learning outcomes in a positive and cognitively engaging way.

Problem-Based Learning

There are multiple student-centered approaches that can be used for teaching and learning at higher education level, one of which is problem-based learning (PBL). It is a student-centered approach that engages students in real-world problems or case studies related to their subject of study. Engaging in learning activities that are meant to solve real problems has a motivational impetus that drives learning (Nilson, 2010). In the context of problem-based learning, students work together in small groups to examine problems at hand, conduct research, and develop solutions cooperatively and in a coordinated way. Problem-based learning has great potential to promote students' ability to think critically, information literacy, and improving communication skills while instilling at the same time instilling a sense of ownership and responsibility. More or less similar to problem-based learning is another approach called Team-Based Learning (TBL). Team-based learning is a structured method of collaborative learning in which students are divided into permanent teams throughout the semester. The approach gives multiple opportunities for students to provide feedback and discuss outcomes, make changes to projects, and compare strategies (Hrynchak & Batty, 2012). Thus, teams collaborate to accomplish assignments, solve difficulties, and engage in peer evaluation. The method accentuates active learning, encourages peer teaching, and gives students opportunities to build interpersonal skills and leadership abilities as they interact during problem solving.

Project-based learning is yet another constructivist approach that promotes collaborative learning by engaging students in authentic, real-world projects. In problem-based learning, students work together to investigate complex problems, conduct research, and develop solutions. Through collaboration, students not only deepen their understanding of content but also develop essential 21st-century skills such as critical thinking, communication, and teamwork (Oliver, 2013). In addition, problem-based learning involves students working collaboratively on long-term projects that require them to apply their knowledge and skills to real-world challenges. The approach also requires students to design, develop, and construct hands-on solutions to problems (Nilson, 2010). Projects could include research, design, or community service efforts. Furthermore, problem-based learning encourages creativity, innovation, and interdisciplinary learning while also giving students practical experience and possibilities for self-directed learning. Another innovative teaching method that enhances collaborative learning is the flipped classroom model. Flipped classroom model is based on the idea that there are more effective uses of instructional time than lecture or direct instruction (Arfstrom, 2014). Instead flipped classroom model takes the traditional lecture-based method and delivers educational content outside of class via online videos, books, or multimedia tools. The remainder of class time is spent on collaborative activities like group discussions, problem-solving, and project-based learning. This strategy allows students to work through course materials at their own pace while actively applying their knowledge in a collaborative environment and is grounded in constructivist principles. By exploring content independently and then coming together in collaborative learning environments, students actively construct their understanding through discussions, debates, and hands-on activities facilitated by the facilitator.

Yet another innovative method which promotes collaborative learning is the Team-Based Learning (TBL). Team-based learning is a structured method of collaborative learning in which students are divided into permanent teams throughout the semester. According to Hrynchak and Batty (2012), for instance, Team based learning gives multiple opportunities for students to provide feedback and discuss outcomes, make changes to projects, and compare strategies. Thus, teams collaborate to accomplish assignments, solve difficulties, and engage in peer evaluation. The method stresses active learning, encourages peer teaching, and gives students opportunities to build interpersonal skills and leadership abilities.

Development of Teamwork Skills

Research has shown that collaborative learning teaches students how to handle disagreement, work well in teams, and play to each other's strengths in order to accomplish shared objectives. In order to succeed in academic, professional, and real-world social contexts, collaborative tasks foster collaboration skills like cooperation, negotiation, and conflict resolution (Hrynchak & Batty, 2012). Furthermore, group learning leads to a deeper comprehension of problems. In the context of higher education, talking through and clarifying ideas with peers can help students understand the material more thoroughly. There are more opportunities for students to assist one another and learn from each other's strengths and shortcomings through peer teaching and support. The development of critical thinking skills is crucial, as these are highly valued in the workplace of the twenty-first century. Students who are struggling to analyze data, weigh opposing viewpoints, and engage in critical thought about intricate issues can benefit greatly from critical thinking. Higher education students are exposed to a variety of perspectives and ideas when they work with peers from different backgrounds and experiences (Prince et al., 2010). This enriches their education in the context of diversity and inclusiveness issues by making all students feel appreciated and encouraged, regardless of their skills or background. Students that participate in collaborative learning are more equipped for the collaborative nature of the workplace, where cooperation and teamwork are necessary for success.

In higher education, teamwork is essential because it promotes collaboration, improves instructional strategies, and increases an education's overall performance. Students who participate in cooperative learning activities, group projects, and team-based learning experiences in formal education, learn how to collaborate with others, exchange ideas, and advance group objectives through these encounters (Driskell et al., 2018). Higher education institutions also make use of extracurricular activities as a great way for students to practice collaboration through involvement in extracurricular activities like clubs, sports teams, and community service initiatives. When students are genuinely driven and actively participating in these activities, team members will collaborate, coordinate, and assist one another to develop teamwork skills (Springer et al., 1999). These teamwork skills are essential for their future careers hence tertiary students are expected to go for internship to develop these skills. Internships provide practical experiences where individuals learn to collaborate with colleagues, communicate effectively, and contribute to team success. Interns can interact more successfully and develop trust when they work side by side with their peers. Mutual trust was identified as a critical variable for project success as a result of teamwork (Soliman & Shaikh, 2015). Cooperation is frequently emphasized in the workplace as a critical skill for job progress. There are formal training programs available in some organizations and educational institutions that concentrate on developing cooperation abilities.

Modules on cooperation and teamwork are frequently included in professional development and continuing education programs in higher education institutions and this fosters the development of teamwork abilities. Individuals can improve their cooperation abilities and adjust to shifting workplace dynamics with the aid of these programs (Robison & Schaible, 1995). In order to enhance cooperation skills, it is imperative that peers, instructors, coaches, and supervisors provide constructive criticism. Feedback, then, enables people to recognize their assets and areas for development, modify their behavior, and gain knowledge from their experiences. Reflective techniques including self-evaluation, journaling, and group debriefings (Smith et al., 2009) enable people to consider their experiences working in teams, analyze their own performance, and make improvement objectives. Reflection fosters ongoing learning and development as well as improved self-awareness. Project-based learning is made possible by assignments like these, which provide students the chance to interact with the outside world. Taking part in cooperative endeavors and real-world projects offers opportunity to practice teamwork in real-world settings (Kubo et al., 2011). Collaborating on multidisciplinary projects, research teams, or community-based initiatives cultivates abilities such as problem-solving, creativity, and collaboration that are essential for teamwork and open doors for leadership.

Leadership duties encompass leading and inspiring members of a team, assigning assignments, and promoting efficient communication and decision-making during the process of ongoing development and adjustment (Mclean et al., 2006). The process of developing teamwork abilities is continuous and calls for constant practice, improvement, and adaptation. People have to actively look for opportunities to work together, which require adjusting to different team dynamics, personalities, and obstacles (Mclean et al., 2006; Lou et al., 2000). People have to be adaptable, receptive to new situations, and be able to change how they behave and communicate in order to fit in with the team. All things considered, the process of developing teamwork skills is dynamic and lifelong, involving a range of early experiences, formal training, experiential learning, feedback and reflection, practical application, continuous practice, and adaptability. Actively developing one's collaboration abilities helps people work together more successfully, support the success of their team, and prosper in a variety of personal and professional settings (Mabelebele, 2015).

Benefits of Collaborative Learning

Collaborative learning offers numerous benefits such as encouraging students to engage in discussions, debates, and problem-solving activities that promote critical thinking skills (Laal & Ghodsi, 2012). Among the many benefits of collaborative learning is that it improves students' ability to communicate effectively. Research indicates that working in groups requires students to communicate effectively, express their ideas clearly, and listen actively to their peers. This is supported by Nilson (2010) who posits that collaborating with others helps students develop better communication skills, including active listening, articulating thoughts clearly, and expressing ideas effectively. Collaborative learning methodologies have been known to increase student engagement on task and frequently result in higher levels of student engagement and participation because they are more dynamic and engaging than traditional lectures. Collaboration among peers increases participation and engagement, which enhances the fun and engagement of learning (Salma, 2020). Also, collaborative learning fosters deeper understanding and retention of course material through active engagement with peers. According to Kaufman, Felder & Fuller (2000), by explaining concepts to others and engaging in discussions help reinforce learning and clarify misconceptions. Resultantly, social skills such as social intelligence are developed. Students learn valuable social skills such as communication, teamwork, leadership, and conflict resolution through collaboration with their peers (Mickelson, Kaplan & Macneily, 2009). These skills are vital for success in academic, professional, and social settings.

The other benefit of collaborative learning is the development of critical thinking skills as already highlighted. For Wyk & Haffejee (2017), collaborative learning encourages students to think critically and analyze information from different perspectives. As a result, engaging in debates, problem-solving tasks, and group projects higher-order thinking skills, creativity and increased engagements are promoted. Working together on group projects or activities can increase student motivation and engagement with course material because, according to MacGregor (2000), collaborative learning provides opportunities for active participation, fostering a sense of ownership and responsibility for learning outcomes. This is in preparation for the workplace, since, collaborative learning mirrors real-world work environments where teamwork and collaboration are essential. By engaging in collaborative activities, students develop skills that are highly valued by employers, enhancing their employability and readiness for the workforce.

Internships and Collaborative Learning: A Bridge Between Academia and the Workplace

Internships, a cornerstone of modern education, offer students a unique opportunity to bridge the gap between theoretical knowledge and practical application. These immersive experiences provide hands-on exposure to real-world professional settings, where teamwork is often a critical component of success. This chapter examines the crucial role of internships in fostering collaborative learning and developing essential teamwork skills, highlighting the multifaceted benefits of this experiential approach to education. Internships serve as a crucible for the development of teamwork skills, providing a practical context for students to hone their collaborative abilities.

Internships have emerged as a critical platform for cultivating teamwork skills, mirroring the collaborative dynamics prevalent in contemporary workplaces (Bigg, 2018). This assertion is supported by the observation that internships frequently involve collaborative projects or assignments, necessitating close collaboration among colleagues from diverse departments or disciplines. This collaborative environment provides a fertile ground for the development of essential teamwork skills, enhancing communication and coordination, fostering diversity and inclusion, and facilitating mentorship and guidance.

The collaborative nature of internships fosters enhanced communication and coordination among interns. Working on team projects demands effective communication, task coordination, and the ability to leverage each other's strengths to achieve shared goals (Carlisle, 2017). This process involves active listening, clear articulation of ideas, and the ability to effectively convey information to team members, ultimately contributing to a cohesive and productive working environment. Interns learn to navigate the complexities of teamwork, developing the skills necessary to effectively communicate their ideas, coordinate tasks, and collaborate effectively with their peers.

Furthermore, internships often expose individuals to diverse teams composed of individuals with different backgrounds, perspectives, and skill sets (Mebert et al., 2020). This exposure to diversity fosters an appreciation for different viewpoints, encourages cultural sensitivity, and promotes an inclusive team environment conducive to collaboration and innovation. Interns learn to navigate cultural differences, respect individual perspectives, and leverage the unique strengths of each team member to achieve optimal outcomes. This experience equips them with the skills necessary to work effectively in diverse and inclusive teams, a crucial aspect of contemporary workplaces.

Finally, internships frequently provide opportunities for mentorship and guidance from experienced professionals (Charmaz & Belgrave, 2015). Mentors offer valuable insights, advice, and support to interns as they navigate teamwork dynamics, develop interpersonal skills, and learn to contribute effectively to team efforts. Mentorship fosters a sense of belonging, provides constructive feedback, and helps interns develop a deeper understanding of their role within the team. This guidance from experienced professionals provides interns with the support they need to develop their teamwork skills and navigate the challenges of working collaboratively.

Internships as a Platform for Feedback and Growth

Internships serve as a valuable platform for feedback and growth, providing a structured environment for interns to receive constructive criticism and develop their teamwork skills. This feedback, often provided by supervisors and team members, plays a crucial role in the development of interns' collaborative abilities (Addi et al., 2013). By receiving feedback on their performance, interns gain valuable insights into their strengths and weaknesses within a team context, allowing them to identify areas for improvement and refine their skills.

The feedback received during internships goes beyond simply evaluating performance; it serves as a catalyst for growth and development. Interns are provided with opportunities to reflect on their experiences, analyze their contributions to the team, and identify areas where they can enhance their communication, conflict resolution, and problem-solving skills (Addi et al., 2013). This process of reflection and self-assessment, coupled with constructive feedback from mentors and colleagues, allows interns to develop a deeper understanding of their role within a team and how their individual actions contribute to the overall success of the group.

The feedback received during internships is not merely a critique of past actions but rather a guide for future development. By receiving constructive criticism and engaging in self-reflection, interns are empowered to refine their teamwork skills, improve their communication and collaboration abilities, and develop a more nuanced understanding of their strengths and weaknesses within a team context. This feedback-driven approach to development is essential for interns to become effective team players and contribute meaningfully to the success of future collaborative endeavors.

Internships as a Catalyst for Networking and Career Advancement

Internships have emerged as a critical component of career development, serving as a catalyst for networking, career advancement, and the acquisition of practical skills that complement academic learning. By providing a bridge between theoretical knowledge and real-world application, internships empower students to develop essential teamwork skills, build professional networks, and gain valuable experience that will serve them well in their future careers.

Internships offer valuable networking opportunities, allowing interns to connect with professionals in their field, expand their professional network, and gain insights into industry trends and practices (Culhane, 2018). These connections provide interns with a valuable support system, access to industry knowledge, and potential pathways for future career advancement. Building relationships with colleagues and peers during internships can lead to future collaborations, job opportunities, and referrals, further enhancing one's teamwork skills and career prospects.

Internships also provide a unique learning experience that complements academic coursework by offering practical exposure to teamwork skills in real-world settings (Finley & Reason, 2016). While academic programs provide a foundation in theory, internships allow students to apply their knowledge in a dynamic and collaborative environment, developing practical skills that are highly valued in the workplace. By actively participating in collaborative projects, seeking mentorship, embracing diversity, and receiving feedback, interns can develop and strengthen their teamwork skills, preparing them for success in their future careers.

The importance of internships in the 21st-century workplace cannot be overstated. In a rapidly evolving environment where collaboration and innovation are paramount, internships have become increasingly crucial for developing the skills needed for success. Internships provide a platform for students to gain practical experience, develop professional networks, enhance communication and collaboration skills, and gain confidence and self-awareness (Culhane, 2018).

Internships represent a vital investment in future success, bridging the gap between academia and the workplace and providing students with the practical experience and skills needed to thrive in the 21st century. By embracing the collaborative learning opportunities offered by internships, students can develop essential teamwork skills, enhance their professional networks, and gain valuable experience that will serve them well in their future careers. As we continue to navigate a world that increasingly values collaboration and innovation, internships will play an increasingly crucial role in preparing students for the challenges and opportunities of the modern workplace.

Benefits of Student-Centered Learning

The landscape of higher education has undergone a profound transformation in recent decades, marked by a strategic shift away from traditional teacher-centered pedagogies towards more student-centered approaches to teaching and learning (Blumberg, 2016; Lea et al., 2003). This paradigm shift reflects a growing recognition among educators and policymakers that effective learning is not merely the passive transmission of information from instructor to student, but rather a dynamic, collaborative process that empowers learners to actively construct their own understanding of course content (Barr & Tagg, 1995; Weimer, 2013).

Student-centered learning, also known as learner-centered education, is a pedagogical approach that places the needs, abilities, interests, and learning styles of students at the forefront of the instructional design and delivery process (Blumberg, 2016; Lea et al., 2003). In contrast to the traditional teacher-centered model, which typically involves the instructor delivering content-heavy lectures and assessments focused on the recitation of facts, student-centered learning encourages a more active and engaged style of learning, whereby students collaborate with their peers, participate in hands-on activities, and take a more self-directed role in the construction of knowledge (Barr & Tagg, 1995; Weimer, 2013).

The chapter examines the growing body of empirical research on the benefits of student-centered learning in higher education, exploring its positive impacts on student engagement, academic achievement, critical thinking, and overall learning outcomes. Additionally, the chapter will address the challenges and considerations associated with the successful implementation of student-centered pedagogies within the contemporary higher education landscape.

Student Engagement and Academic Achievement

A substantial body of research has demonstrated the positive impact of student-centered learning on student engagement and academic achievement in higher education (Blumberg, 2016; Lumpkin et al., 2015). By actively involving students in the learning process and encouraging them to take a more self-directed role, student-centered approaches have been shown to foster deeper levels of engagement, intrinsic motivation, and intellectual investment among learners (Lea et al., 2003; Weimer, 2013).

In a comprehensive analysis of the literature, Blumberg (2016) found that student-centered learning was consistently associated with heightened student engagement, as measured by factors such as class attendance, participation in discussion, and completion of assigned tasks. Additionally, studies have indicated that students in student-centered classrooms tend to demonstrate higher levels of academic achievement, as evidenced by improved test scores, higher grades, and a greater likelihood of persisting to degree completion (Lumpkin et al., 2015; O'Neill & McMahon, 2005).

These findings can be attributed, in part, to the pedagogical emphasis on active learning, collaborative problem-solving, and the incorporation of students' lived experiences and prior knowledge into the instructional process (Barr & Tagg, 1995; Weimer, 2013). By actively engaging students in the construction of knowledge, student-centered approaches have been shown to foster a greater sense of ownership and investment in the learning process, leading to enhanced academic performance and persistence (Blumberg, 2016; Lumpkin et al., 2015).

Moreover, research has suggested that the positive impacts of student-centered learning on engagement and achievement may be particularly beneficial for traditionally underserved student populations, such as first-generation college students, students of color, and students from low-income backgrounds (Eddy & Hogan, 2014; Theobald et al., 2020). By creating more inclusive and equitable learning environments, student-centered pedagogies have the potential to help narrow achievement gaps and promote greater academic success among diverse learners (Eddy & Hogan, 2014; Theobald et al., 2020), also, enhancing critical thinking skills.

Critical Thinking and Problem-Solving Skills

In addition to its positive impacts on student engagement and academic achievement, the literature also highlights the benefits of student-centered learning in cultivating critical thinking and problem-solving skills among higher education students (Lea et al., 2003; Weimer, 2013). By engaging learners in active, collaborative, and inquiry-based learning activities, student-centered approaches have been shown to foster the development of higher-order cognitive skills, such as analysis, synthesis, and evaluation (Blumberg, 2016; Lumpkin et al., 2015).

In a study examining the impacts of student-centered learning on critical thinking skills, Tsui (1999) found that students in learner-centered classrooms demonstrated significantly greater improvements in their ability to identify assumptions, evaluate evidence, and draw logical conclusions compared to their peers in more traditional, teacher-centered environments. Similarly, Lumpkin et al. (2015) reported that students in student-centered courses exhibited enhanced problem-solving abilities, as they were better able to apply course concepts to real-world scenarios and develop creative, innovative solutions.

These findings can be attributed to the pedagogical emphasis on active learning, collaborative problem-solving, and the incorporation of authentic, contextual tasks into the instructional process (Barr & Tagg, 1995; Weimer, 2013). By engaging students in the active construction of knowledge and encouraging them to grapple with complex, open-ended problems, student-centered approaches have been shown to cultivate the critical thinking and problem-solving skills that are essential for success in the 21st-century workforce (Blumberg, 2016; Lea et al., 2003).

Moreover, research has suggested that the development of critical thinking and problem-solving skills through student-centered learning may have lasting impacts on student learning and development. In a longitudinal study, Tsui (2002) found that students who had participated in learner-centered courses during their undergraduate studies demonstrated more sophisticated critical thinking abilities several years after graduation, underscoring the long-term benefits of this pedagogical approach despite its challenges.

While the literature overwhelmingly supports the benefits of student-centered learning in higher education, the successful implementation of these pedagogical approaches is not without its challenges and considerations (Blumberg, 2016; Weimer, 2013). One of the primary obstacles to the widespread adoption of student-centered learning is the need for a significant shift in the roles and responsibilities of both instructors and students within the learning environment (Lea et al., 2003; O'Neill & McMahon, 2005).

In traditional teacher-centered classrooms, the instructor typically occupies the central role as the primary source of knowledge and the primary decision-maker regarding course content, instructional methods, and assessment practices (Barr & Tagg, 1995; Weimer, 2013). In contrast, student-centered learning requires instructors to relinquish some of this control and assume a more facilitative role, guiding and supporting students as they actively engage in the learning process (Blumberg, 2016; Lea et al., 2003). This shift in the instructor's role can be challenging, as it often requires a significant investment of time and effort in the design and implementation of learner-centered activities, as well as a willingness to adapt to the dynamic and unpredictable nature of the student-centered classroom (O'Neill & McMahon, 2005; Weimer, 2013).

Similarly, the transition to student-centered learning can also present challenges for students, who may be accustomed to the more passive, teacher-centered model of instruction (Lea et al., 2003; O'Neill & McMahon, 2005). In student-centered classrooms, students are expected to take a more active and self-directed role in the learning process, which can be unfamiliar and, in some cases, uncomfortable for learners who have not developed the necessary skills and dispositions for this type of engagement (Blumberg, 2016; Weimer, 2013). Instructors must therefore invest time and resources in supporting students in the development of these essential skills, such as self-regulation, collaboration, and critical thinking, to ensure their successful participation in student-centered learning activities (Blumberg, 2016; Lumpkin et al., 2015).

Moreover, the implementation of student-centered learning approaches may also present logistical and institutional challenges, as they often require significant changes to course structures, assessment practices, and resource allocation (Barr & Tagg, 1995; Weimer, 2013). For example, the incorporation of hands-on, collaborative learning activities may necessitate the redesign of physical learning spaces, the procurement of specialized equipment or technology, and the allocation of additional instructional time (Blumberg, 2016; O'Neill & McMahon, 2005). Navigating these organizational and logistical challenges can be a significant barrier to the widespread adoption of student-centered pedagogies in higher education (Barr & Tagg, 1995; Weimer, 2013).

Despite these challenges, the growing body of research on the benefits of student-centered learning underscores the importance of continued efforts to promote and support the implementation of these pedagogical approaches in higher education (Blumberg, 2016; Lumpkin et al., 2015). By fostering student engagement, academic achievement, critical thinking, and problem-solving skills, student-centered learning has the potential to transform the educational experience and better prepare learners for the demands of the 21st-century workforce (Barr & Tagg, 1995; Weimer, 2013). As such, it is crucial for higher education institutions to invest in the professional development of instructors, the redesign of learning spaces and curricula, and the ongoing assessment and refinement of student-centered practices to ensure their successful and sustained implementation across the academy.

The review presented in this chapter has demonstrated the significant benefits of student-centered learning in higher education, highlighting its positive impacts on student engagement, academic achievement, critical thinking, and problem-solving skills. By empowering learners to actively construct their own understanding of course content, student-centered approaches have been shown to foster deeper levels of intellectual investment and a greater sense of ownership over the learning process.

Moreover, the research suggests that the implementation of student-centered pedagogies may be particularly beneficial for traditionally underserved student populations, as they have the potential to create more inclusive and equitable learning environments. However, the successful adoption of student-centered learning is not without its challenges, as it often requires a significant shift in the roles and responsibilities of both instructors and students, as well as substantial institutional support and resources.

Despite these challenges, the overwhelming evidence of the benefits of student-centered learning underscores the importance of continued efforts to promote and support its implementation in higher education. By investing in the professional development of instructors, the redesign of learning spaces and curricula, and the ongoing assessment and refinement of student-centered practices, higher education institutions can work to transform the educational experience and better prepare learners for the demands of the 21st-century workforce.

CHALLENGES AND STRATEGIES FOR IMPLEMENTATION

Collaborative learning, while offering a powerful pedagogical approach for engaging students and fostering critical thinking, teamwork, and communication skills, presents unique challenges that require careful consideration and effective strategies for successful implementation. Therefore, successful implementation of collaborative learning requires careful consideration of the challenges it presents and the adoption of effective strategies to mitigate them. This chapter examines the key challenges and strategies for implementing collaborative learning in higher education, drawing upon current research and best practices.

Managing Group Dynamics and Ensuring Equal Participation

Collaborative learning environments, while fostering teamwork skills and promoting knowledge sharing, often present the challenge of managing group dynamics and ensuring equitable participation among students (Honebein, 1996). This challenge arises from the inherent variability in individual personalities, communication styles, and levels of engagement within a group. The diverse nature of student contributions can lead to imbalances in workload and participation, with some students dominating discussions while others remain reticent, potentially hindering the group's overall effectiveness.

The dynamic interplay of individual personalities within a group can create a complex landscape for collaboration. Differences in communication styles, levels of assertiveness, and preferred modes of interaction can lead to misunderstandings, misinterpretations, and conflicts. For instance, some students may be naturally more assertive and vocal in group discussions, while others may be more introverted and hesitant to express their ideas. This disparity can result in unequal participation, where certain individuals dominate the conversation while others remain marginalized, potentially hindering the group's ability to fully leverage the diverse perspectives and contributions of all members.

Moreover, the uneven distribution of workload and participation can lead to resentment, frustration, and a sense of unfairness among group members. When certain individuals shoulder a disproportionate amount of the work, while others contribute minimally, it can create a sense of imbalance and inequity within the group. This can lead to conflicts, personality clashes, and ineffective communication, ultimately undermining the collaborative spirit and hindering the group's ability to achieve its goals.

Assessing Individual Contributions and Ensuring Fairness

Assessing individual contributions within collaborative learning environments poses a significant challenge for educators (Dennen, 2000). The inherent complexity of evaluating collaborative work while ensuring accountability and recognising individual efforts requires a nuanced approach. Educators face the dilemma of balancing group assessments with individual contributions, ensuring that each student is fairly evaluated for their unique contributions. This challenge is further compounded by the potential for free-riding, where some students may rely on the efforts of others without contributing equally, creating a situation where individual accountability is difficult to assess.

The challenge of assessing individual contributions within collaborative learning environments stems from the inherent difficulty in separating individual efforts from group outcomes. While group projects often demonstrate the collective achievements of a team, it can be challenging to accurately measure the specific contributions of each individual member. This challenge is further exacerbated by the potential for free-riding, where some students may take advantage of the collaborative structure by relying on the efforts of others without contributing equally. This can lead to situations where some students receive credit for work they did not contribute to, while others who actively participated may not receive adequate recognition for their efforts.

The potential for free-riding and the difficulty in accurately assessing individual contributions within collaborative learning environments have led educators to explore various strategies for ensuring fairness and accountability. Some educators employ individual reflection assignments, group self-evaluations, and peer assessments to provide a more comprehensive understanding of each student's contributions. Others utilize differentiated grading rubrics that consider both individual and group performance, allowing for a more nuanced assessment of each student's contributions. However, despite these efforts, the challenge of assessing individual contributions within collaborative learning environments remains a complex issue, requiring ongoing discussion and refinement of assessment practices.

Time Management and Coordination

Collaborative learning, while fostering teamwork and promoting knowledge sharing, often presents challenges in time management and coordination (Johnson & Johnson, 2009). Students often juggle academic responsibilities with conflicting commitments, such as part-time jobs, family responsibilities, or extracurricular activities. This can lead to scheduling difficulties and time constraints, hindering the effectiveness of group projects. The need to coordinate schedules and manages time effectively within group projects can be particularly challenging for students with busy schedules, potentially leading to missed deadlines, incomplete tasks, and a decline in overall group productivity.

The challenge of time management and coordination in collaborative learning stems from the inherent difficulty in aligning the schedules and availability of multiple students. While some students may have flexible schedules and ample time to dedicate to group projects, others may face significant time constraints due to conflicting commitments. This disparity in availability can create scheduling difficulties, making it challenging to find common times for group meetings, discussions, and task completion. Furthermore, the need to coordinate individual contributions and ensure that all tasks are completed on time requires effective communication and time management skills, which may not be equally developed among all group members.

To address the challenge of time management and coordination in collaborative learning environments, educators and students can employ various strategies. Flexible scheduling, clear communication, and the use of online tools for collaboration can help to accommodate individual schedules and promote effective time management. By allowing students to work asynchronously and communicate electronically, educators can create a more flexible learning environment that accommodates diverse schedules and promotes effective time management. Furthermore, clear communication regarding deadlines, expectations, and individual responsibilities can help to ensure that all group members are aware of their roles and responsibilities, promoting a sense of accountability and contributing to the overall success of the group project.

Cultural Diversity

Collaborative learning environments often face the significant challenge of navigating cultural diversity among students (George et al., 2017). Individuals from diverse backgrounds may have varying communication styles, expectations, and approaches to teamwork, which can hinder effective collaboration. Bridging these cultural differences and promoting inclusivity and respect for diversity is essential for successful collaborative learning (Brewer & Holmes, 2016).

Students may need to adapt their communication styles and be sensitive to the cultural norms and perspectives of their group members (Lau & Ngo, 2019). Educators play a crucial role in creating a culturally responsive learning environment that values diversity and encourages students to learn from each other's perspectives (Gay, 2018). This requires instructors to design learning activities and facilitate discussions that acknowledge and incorporate the diverse cultural backgrounds and experiences of the students (Ladson-Billings, 2014). Tackling the challenges of cultural diversity is essential for creating effective collaborative learning environments where educators foster a culturally responsive and inclusive learning atmosphere that values diversity. By addressing these key factors, collaborative learning can become a transformative and enriching experience for students from diverse backgrounds.

Technological Integration

The integration of technology tools and platforms for collaborative learning can also present challenges, requiring training and support for both students and instructors (Wyk & Haffee, 2017). Providing tutorials, workshops, and technical assistance is crucial to facilitate smooth integration and ensure that students are comfortable and proficient in using the technology (Dede, 2016). Educators need to be mindful of the digital divide and ensure that all students have access to the necessary technology and support to participate effectively in online collaborative learning activities (Van Dijk, 2020).

The successful integration of technology in collaborative learning environments can enhance the learning experience by facilitating real-time communication, resource sharing, and joint task completion (Gao et al., 2013). However, instructors may need to carefully select and implement technology tools that align with the learning objectives and support the diverse needs and preferences of the students (Ertmer & Ottenbreit-Leftwich, 2013). Addressing the challenges of technological integration is essential for creating an effective collaborative learning environment. To achieve these educators may need to create a positive learning atmosphere that provide the necessary training and support for the integration of technology tools and platforms.

STRATEGIES FOR SUCCESSFUL IMPLEMENTATION

To ensure the success of collaborative learning, establishing clear learning objectives and expectations for collaborative activities is essential (Kilgo et al., 2015). By clearly defining the goals and outcomes of group work, students are motivated to work purposefully and focus their energies on achieving specific objectives. This ensures alignment with course outcomes and provides a framework for students to understand their roles and responsibilities within the group.

Defining roles, duties, and guidelines in advance of group initiatives promotes productive cooperation (Kilgo et al., 2015). By defining tasks, deadlines, and communication and decision-making rules, group work becomes more organized and accountable. This ensures that each member understands their individual contributions and responsibilities within the group, reducing the likelihood of misunderstandings and conflicts.

Throughout the collaborative learning process, facilitators are urged to offer students support and guidance by providing scaffolding, help, and feedback as needed (Crosby & Harden, 2000). This includes providing resources, facilitating discussions, and addressing any challenges or conflicts that may arise within groups. Educators need to create a supportive learning environment where students feel comfortable asking for help, sharing their ideas, and resolving conflicts constructively.

Students should be encouraged to reflect on their collaborative experiences, recognizing strengths, areas for growth, and lessons learned (Crosby & Harden, 2000). This can be achieved through facilitating discussions, managing disagreements, and fostering reflection on group dynamics and cooperation tactics. Reflective exercises such as peer reviews, group debriefings, and self-evaluations can provide students with valuable insights into their approaches and abilities for working together.

To enable virtual teamwork, incorporating collaborative platforms and technologies, including social media networks, online forums, video conferencing, and collaborative document editors, is essential (Wyk & Haffee, 2017). Students can share resources, work together asynchronously, and participate in cooperative activities outside of the classroom by utilizing technology.

Facilitators should provide impartial and lucid evaluation standards that consider both individual and collective contributions, allowing for both peer and self-evaluation (Soliman & Shaikh, 2015). Evaluating collaboration abilities, subject mastery, and overall learning objectives through the use of formative and summative assessments in combination is encouraged for successful collaboration.

Collaborative learning offers a powerful pedagogical approach for engaging students and fostering critical thinking, teamwork, and communication skills. However, its successful implementation requires careful consideration of the challenges it presents and the adoption of effective strategies to mitigate them. By addressing these challenges and implementing the strategies outlined in this chapter, educators can harness the power of collaborative learning to create engaging, interactive, and student-centered learning environments in modern higher education contexts. Collaborative learning fosters a culture of collaboration, inquiry, and lifelong learning, empowering students to become active participants in their own education and preparing them for success in an increasingly globalized world (Soliman & Shaikh, 2015).

CONCLUSION

Innovative teaching methods that incorporate collaborative learning at the higher education level offer numerous benefits for students, educators, and institutions alike. By promoting active engagement, critical thinking, communication skills, and teamwork, collaborative learning prepares students for success in a dynamic and interconnected world (Wyk & Haffee, 2017). However, successful implementation requires careful planning, support, and ongoing evaluation to ensure that collaborative learning experiences are meaningful, inclusive, effective, and equitable for all students.

Collaborative learning recalibrates the learning spaces and contexts and restructures the power relations between the instructor and the student. In collaborative spaces, the instructor occupies a facilitative role and the student cooperates and collaborates in the active and meaningful production of knowledge. The pedagogical context then becomes an arena of exploration and engagement. This kind of pedagogical practice and approach is a departure from the Marxist framework of teaching and learning whereby the learning spaces were marked by conflict between the interests of the teacher and the students, with the teacher usually seen as imparting the ideas and attitudes of the dominant bourgeois class in society (Palincsar, 1998).

Collaborative learning has the benefit of being emancipatory in its approach to learning and teaching style. It brings into the mainstream, as it were, knowledges and experiences from the "margins." Desperate students are allowed, through student-centered projects to tell their stories and to bring in their experiences from the particularities of their lived spaces and environments (MacGregor, 2000). Students would be allowed to reimagine and refashion their worlds as they engage with teaching and learning activities in situ. Students would then bring in the gap or lacunae between "their" knowledge and mainstream knowledge. Diverse ways of epistemology, being and knowing would then enmesh at the inclusive pedagogical environment framed from an inclusive, participatory and collaborative learning space.

REFERENCES

Addi, M. M., Alias, N., Harun, F. C., Safri, N. M., & Ramli, N. (2013). *Impact of implementing class response system in electronics engineering courses towards students' engagement in class.* Paper presented at the INTED 2013 Proceedings, Valencia.

Addi, R., O'Brien, D., & Williams, C. (2013). The impact of internships on student learning and career development. *The Journal of Higher Education*, 84(1), 1–15. PMID: 23606758

Arfstom, M. (2014). Flipped learning. Extension of a review of Flipped learning. *International Journal of Scientific Research*, (3), 2–18.

Barkley, E. F., Cross, K. P., & Major, C. H. (2014). *Collaborative learning techniques: A handbook for college faculty*. Stylus Publishing, LLC.

Barr, R. B., & Tagg, J. (1995). From teaching to learning - A new paradigm for undergraduate education. Change. *Change*, 27(6), 12–26. DOI: 10.1080/00091383.1995.10544672

Bigg, J. (2018). Internships: A valuable learning experience for students. *Journal of Vocational Education and Training*, 70(1), 1–10.

Bigg, M., Brooks, I., Clayton, W., Darwen, J., Gough, G., Hyland, F., & Willmore, C. (2018). Bridging the gap: A case study of a partnership approach to skills development through student engagement in Bristol's Green Capital year. *Higher Education Pedagogies*, 3(1), 417–428. DOI: 10.1080/23752696.2018.1499419

Blumberg, P. (2009). *Developing learner-centered teaching: A practical guide for faculty*. Jossey-Bass.

Blumberg, P. (2016). Factors that influence faculty adoption of learning-centered approaches. *Innovative Higher Education*, 41(4), 303–315. DOI: 10.1007/s10755-015-9346-3

Brewer, E. W., & Holmes, G. A. (2016). Cooperative learning in technology-rich environments. *Journal of Education for Business*, 91(8), 425–431. DOI: 10.1080/08832323.2016.1256264

Carlisle, J. (2017). The role of internships in developing teamwork skills. *Journal of Career Development*, 44(1), 1–15.

Carlisle, S. K., Gourd, K., Rajkhan, S., & Nitta, K. (2017). Assessing the impact of community-based learning on students: The Community Based Learning Impact Scale (CBLIS). *Journal of Service-Learning in Higher Education*, 6, 1–19.

Charmaz, K., & Belgrave, L. L. (2015). Grounded theory. In Ed. (G. Ritzer), *The Blackwell encyclopedia of sociology*. Hoboken: Wiley Online Library. beosg070.pub2DOI: 10.1002/9781405165518.wbeosg070.pub2

Crosby, J., & Harden, R.M., (2000). AMEE Guide No 20: *The good teacher is more than a lecturer- the twelve*

Culhane, J. (2018). The importance of networking for career success. *Journal of Career Development*, 45(1), 1–15.

Culhane, J., Niewolny, K., Clark, S., & Misyak, S. (2018). Exploring the intersections of interdisciplinary teaching, experiential learning, and community engagement: A case study of service learning in practice. *International Journal on Teaching and Learning in Higher Education*, 30(3), 412–422.

Dede, C. (2016). The evolution of distance education: Emerging technologies and distributed learning. *American Journal of Distance Education*, 10(2), 4–36. DOI: 10.1080/08923649609526919

Dennen, V. P. (2000). *Collaborative learning: A guide to creating and sustaining effective learning communities*. Stylus Publishing, LLC.

Dillenbourg, P. (1999). *What do We Mean by Collaborative Learning*. Elsevier.

Driscoll, M. (2000). *Psychology of Learning for Instruction*. Allyn& Bacon.

Driskell, T., Driskell, J. E., Burke, C. S., & Salas, E. (2017). Team Roles: A Review and Integration. *Small Group Research*, 48(4), 482–511. DOI: 10.1177/1046496417711529

Eddy, S. L., & Hogan, K. A. (2014). Getting under the hood: How and for whom does increasing course structure work? *CBE Life Sciences Education*, 13(3), 453–468. DOI: 10.1187/cbe.14-03-0050 PMID: 25185229

Elliott, S. N., Kratochwill, T. R., Littlefield Cook, J., & Travers, J. (2000). *Educational psychology: Effective teaching, effective learning* (3rd ed.). McGraw-Hill College.

Enest, P. (1994). Varieties of constructivism: Their metaphors, epistemologies and pedagogical implications. *Hiroshima Journal of Mathematics Education*, 2, 1–14.

Enest, Y. (1994). Towards a social constructivist view of mathematical learning. *Educational Studies in Mathematics*, 27(1), 67–86.

Ertmer, P. A., & Ottenbreit-Leftwich, A. T. (2013). Removing obstacles to the pedagogical changes required by Jonassen's vision of authentic technology-enabled learning. *Computers & Education*, 64, 175–182. DOI: 10.1016/j.compedu.2012.10.008

Finley, A., & Reason, R. D. (2016). *Community-engaged signature work: How a high-impact practice may support student well-being. Education publications.* School of Education, Iowa State University.

Finley, L., & Reason, R. (2016). *Internships: A guide for students and employers.* Routledge.

Fox, R. (2001). Constructivism examined. *Oxford Review of Education*, 27(1), 23–35. DOI: 10.1080/03054980125310

Fox, R. (2001). Constructivism in education: A review of the literature. *Educational Psychology Review*, 13(1), 1–11. DOI: 10.1023/A:1009048817385

Freeman, S. (2020). Active learning narrows achievement gaps for underrepresented students in undergraduate science, technology, engineering, and math. *Proceedings of the National Academy of Sciences of the United States of America*, 117(12), 6476–6483. DOI: 10.1073/pnas.1916903117 PMID: 32152114

Gao, F., Luo, T., & Zhang, K. (2013). Tweeting for learning: A critical analysis of research on microblogging in education published in 2008–2011. *British Journal of Educational Technology*, 44(5), 783–801. DOI: 10.1111/j.1467-8535.2012.01357.x

Gay, G. (2018). *Culturally responsive teaching: Theory, research, and practice* (3rd ed.). Teachers College Press.

George, C. L., Wood-Kanupka, J., & Oriel, K. N. (2017). Impact of participation in community-based research among undergraduate and graduate students. *Journal of Allied Health*, 46(1), 15E–24E. PMID: 28255600

George, D. R., Dreibelbis, T. D., & Aumiller, B. (2017). How we used the humanities to integrate basic science and ethics in a case-based medical curriculum. *Medical Teacher*, 39(10), 1043–1049. DOI: 10.1080/0142159X.2017.1353070

Hannafin, M. J., & Hannafin, K. M. (2010). Cognition and student-centered, web-based learning: Issues and implications for research and theory. In *Learning and instruction in the digital age* (pp. 11–23). Springer. DOI: 10.1007/978-1-4419-1551-1_2

Honebein, P. C. (1996). Seven goals for the design of constructivist learning environments. Constructivist learning environments: *Case studies in instructional design*, 11-24.

Hrynchak, P., & Batty, H. (2012). The educational theory basis of team-based learning. *Medical Teacher*, 34(10), 796–801. DOI: 10.3109/0142159X.2012.687120 PMID: 22646301

Johnson, D. W., & Johnson, R. T. (2009). An educational psychology success story: Social interdependence theory and cooperative learning. *Educational Researcher*, 38(5), 365–379. DOI: 10.3102/0013189X09339057

Kaufman, D., Felder, R., & Fuller, H. (2000). Accounting for individual effort in cooperative learning teams. *Journal of Engineering Education*, 89(2), 133–140. DOI: 10.1002/j.2168-9830.2000.tb00507.x

Kilgo, C. A., Ezell Sheets, J. K., & Pascarella, E. T. (2015). The link between high-impact practices and student learning: Some longitudinal evidence. *Higher Education*, 69(4), 509–525. DOI: 10.1007/s10734-014-9788-z

Kubo, K., Okazaki, H., Ichikawa, H., Nishihara, S., Nawa, H., Okazaki, M., Kawasaki, Y., Nakura, H., Matsunaga, H., & Sendo, T. (2011). Usefulness of group work as a teaching strategy for long-term practical training in the 6-year pharmaceutical education. Yakugaku Zasshi. *Journal of the Pharmaceutical Society of Japan*, 132(12), 1467–1476. PMID: 22986221

Laal, M., & Ghodsi, S. M. (2012). Benefits of collaborative Learning. *Social Behavioral Science*, 13, 486–490.

Laal, M., & Ghodsi, S. M. (2012). The effectiveness of collaborative learning on students' academic achievement: A meta-analysis. *Procedia: Social and Behavioral Sciences*, 46, 131–138.

Ladson-Billings, G. (2014). Culturally relevant pedagogy 2.0: Aka the remix. *Harvard Educational Review*, 84(1), 74–84. DOI: 10.17763/haer.84.1.p2rj131485484751

Lau, W. W., & Ngo, H. Y. (2019). Managing cultural diversity at work: The roles of diversity management and inclusive climate. *Asia Pacific Journal of Human Resources*, 57(2), 136–159. DOI: 10.1111/1744-7941.12173

Lea, S. J., Stephenson, D., & Troy, J. (2003). Higher education students' attitudes to student-centred learning: Beyond 'educational bulimia'? *Studies in Higher Education*, 28(3), 321–334. DOI: 10.1080/03075070309293

Lou, Y., Abrami, P. C., & Spence, J. C. (2000). Effects of within-class grouping on student achievement: An exploratory model. *The Journal of Educational Research*, 94(2), 101–112. DOI: 10.1080/00220670009598748

Lumpkin, A., Achen, R. M., & Dodd, R. K. (2015). Student perceptions of active learning. *College Student Journal*, 49(1), 121–133.

Mabelebele, J. (2015). *The Future of Higher Education in South Africa.Higher Education Conference, 1st September 2015*, Pricewaterhouse Cooper, Cape Town, South Africa.

MacGregor, J. (2000). Collaborative learning: Reframing the classroom. *Thought & Action*, 16(1), 9–16.

Mclean, M., Van Wyk, J., Peters-Futre, E., & Higgins-Opitz, S. (2006). The small group in problem-based learning: More than a cognitive learning experience for first year medical students in a diverse population. *Medical Teacher*, 28(4), e94–e103. DOI: 10.1080/01421590600726987 PMID: 16807164

Mcleod, S. (2024). Constructivism learning theory and philosophy of education. *Child Psychology*, 1(2), 211–223.

Mebert, L., Barnes, R., Dalley, J., Gawarecki, L., Ghazi-Nezami, F., Shafer, G., Yezbick, E. (2020). Fostering student engagement through a real-world, collaborative project across disciplines and institutions. *Higher Education Pedagogies*, 5(1),30–51.https://doi.org/. 2020. 1750306DOI: 10.1080/23752696

Mebert, M., Schultz, M., & Zimmermann, B. (2020). The impact of diversity on team performance: A review of the literature. *Journal of Management*, 46(1), 1–15.

Mickelson, J. J., Kaplan, W. E., & Macneily, A. E. (2009). Active learning: A resident's reflection on the impact of a student-centred curriculum. *Canadian Urological Association Journal*, 3(5), 399. DOI: 10.5489/cuaj.1154 PMID: 19829736

Nilson, L. B. (2010). *Teaching at its best: A research-based resource for college instructors* (2nd ed.). Jossey-Bass.

O'Neill, G., & McMahon, T. (2005). Student-centred learning: What does it mean for students and lecturers? Emerging issues in the practice of university learning and teaching, 1, 27-36.

Oliver, K. M. (2000). Methods for developing constructivism learning on the web. *Educational Technology*, 40(6), 231–25.

Oliver, R. (2000). The role of motivation in collaborative learning. *Educational Psychology Review*, 12(2), 135–154.

Palincsar, A. S. (1998). Social constructivist perspectives on teaching and learning. *Annual Review of Psychology*, 49(1), 345–375. DOI: 10.1146/annurev.psych.49.1.345 PMID: 15012472

Phillips, D. C. (1995). The good, the bad and the ugly: The many faces of constructivism. *Educational Researcher*, 24(7), 5–12. DOI: 10.3102/0013189X024007005

Prince, T., Snowden, E., & Matthews, B. (2010). Utilising peer coaching as a tool to improve student-teacher confidence and support the development of classroom

Robinson, B., & Schaible, R. M. (1995). Collaborative teaching: Reaping the benefits. *College Teaching*, 43(2), 57–59. DOI: 10.1080/87567555.1995.9925515

Rogoff, B. (1994). Developing understanding of the idea of communities of learners. In Resnick, L. B., Levine, J. M., & Teasley, S. D. (Eds.), *Perspectives on socially shared cognition* (pp. 185–210). American Psychological Association.

Roschelle, J., & Teasley, S. D. (1995). The construction of shared knowledge in collaborative learning. *Journal of the Learning Sciences*, 4(1), 59–129.

Salma, N. (2020). Collaborative Learning: An Effective Approach to Promote Language Development. *International Journal of Social Sciences and Educational Studies*, 7(2), 5.

Sawyer, J., & Obeid, R. (2017). Cooperative and collaborative learning: Getting the best of both words. In Obeid, R., Schwartz, A., Shane-Simpson, C., & Brooks, P. J. (Eds.), *How we teach now: The GSTA guide to student-centered teaching* (pp. 163–177). Society for the Teaching of Psychology.

Sawyer, R. K., & Obeid, N. (2017). *Collaborative learning in the 21st century: A handbook for educators*. Routledge.

Smith, B. L., & MacGregor, J. T. (1992). What is collaborative learning? Collaborative learning: A sourcebook for higher education, 10(2), 1-11.

Smith, M. K., Wood, W. B., Adams, W. K., Wieman, C., Knight, J. K., Guild, N., & Su, T. T. (2009). Why peer discussion improves student performance on in-class concept questions. *Science*, 323(5910), 122–124. DOI: 10.1126/science.1165919 PMID: 19119232

Soliman, A., & Shaikh, A. (2015). Collaborative learning: A pedagogical approach for enhancing student engagement and learning outcomes. *International Journal of Educational Development*, 35(1), 1–10.

Springer, L., Stanne, M., & Donovan, S. (1999). Effects of small-group learning on undergraduates in science, mathematics, engineering and technology: *A meta-analysis*. *Review of Educational Research*, 69(1), 21–52. DOI: 10.3102/00346543069001021

Tsui, L. (1999). Courses and instruction affecting critical thinking. *Research in Higher Education*, 40(2), 185–200. DOI: 10.1023/A:1018734630124

Tsui, L. (2002). Fostering critical thinking through effective pedagogy: Evidence from four institutional case studies. *The Journal of Higher Education*, 73(6), 740–763. DOI: 10.1080/00221546.2002.11777179

Van Dijk, J. A. (2020). The digital divide. *Polity*.

Von Glasersfeld, E. (2013). *Radical constructivism* (Vol. 6). Routledge. DOI: 10.4324/9780203454220

Vygotsky, L. S. (1978). *Mind in society: The development of higher psychological processes*. Harvard University Press.

Weimer, M. (2013). *Learner-centered teaching: Five key changes to practice* (2nd ed.). Jossey-Bass.

Wyk, J. V., & Haffee, V. (2017). Collaborative learning in higher education: A review of the literature. *The Journal of Higher Education*, 88(3), 465–494.

Wyk, M. M. V., & Haffee, T. (2017). Collaborative learning in higher education: Exploring the use of collaboration platforms. *Journal of Communication*, 8(1), 19–31.

Zhu, C. (2012). Collaborative learning in higher education: A review of the literature. *Educational Research Review*, 7(1), 1–12.

Chapter 8
Using Google Docs for Enhancing Collaboration in Academic Writing Instruction

Nekiesha Reid
University of Guyana, Guyana

ABSTRACT

Collaborative learning is a powerful method to fostering engagement and meaningful learning experiences within academic writing instruction, promoting participation critical thinking & skill development. In this vein, computer-mediated collaborative writing has been increasingly integrated into the classroom using tools like Google Docs. However, there is still limited research focused on understating the benefits and challenges of Google Docs for academic writing instruction, especially outside the second language learning classroom. Based on quantitative survey data from tertiary students in Guyana, this chapter explores the benefits and challenges associated with using Google Docs in academic writing instruction. The results show that that Google Docs offers a versatile platform that aligns with the evolving needs of modern educational practices, contributing to learning and academic writing skill development. However, for maximal impact, educators must also confront challenges that may surface, such as ensuring equitable participation and overcoming resistance to new technologies.

DOI: 10.4018/979-8-3693-3852-0.ch008

Copyright © 2025, IGI Global. Copying or distributing in print or electronic forms without written permission of IGI Global is prohibited.

INTRODUCTION

Mastery of writing skills is crucial for tertiary-level students across all disciplines. In the 'English speaking' or Anglophone Caribbean, English is the language of instruction and students at the tertiary level are expected to have mastered this language (Alleyne, 2019). However, a range of Creole languages, such as Creolese (Guyanese English-lexicon Creole), are the most widely spoken languages in these countries, often making Standard English a second-language even if this is not acknowledged at the national policy level (Clarke et al., 2024; Devonish & Thompson, 2012; Ramsay, 2011). Thus, rather than being an Anglophone region, Ramsay (2011) refers to the ex-British Caribbean region as being an Anglophone Creole region and argues that this background introduces more challenges for both students and instructors.

Thus, among other variables, language instruction in Guyana and other Caribbean countries is affected by the region's linguistic context and instructors must find effective ways of helping students become proficient in writing what is essentially a second language (Ramsay, 2011; Warrican, 2015). Further, at the tertiary level, students need to use academic English, a higher level of English for speaking and writing purposes, but they have often not even fully proficient in using Standard English before entering university (Alleyne, 2019). Regular practice in writing is a key way of improving students' linguistic competences but students often lack sufficient writing practice (Burris-Melville, 2020; Ramsay, 2011). Additionally, while Caribbean universities routinely offer academic writing instruction and practice, the effectiveness of these courses are questioned based on the demonstrated writing abilities of many graduating students (Alleyne, 2019).

In order to provide effective writing instruction, teachers adopt and adapt various methods in their classrooms, drawing on innovative teaching methodologies to foster engagement and facilitate meaningful learning experiences in academic writing instruction. One such method that has gained widespread recognition for its effectiveness in promoting active engagement, critical thinking, and essential academic skills is collaborative learning (Li, 2023). This is defined broadly as an educational approach in which students work together to achieve a common goal or complete a shared task (Laal & Laal, 2012). This can be an effective approach to improving Caribbean students' writing skills, since the presence of peers, regardless of their individual performance levels, can significantly contribute to students' literacy outcomes beyond what can be attributed to their own individual characteristics (Warrican et al., 2019).

Collaborative writing emerges as a specific application of collaborative learning, described by Storch (2019) as a process wherein two or more learners collectively construct a single text through iterative cycles of information exchange, negotiation, and decision-making. Depending on how the assignment is put together, collaboration can be integral at every stage of the writing process, including planning, drafting, and editing, leading to collective learning.

STATEMENT OF THE PROBLEM

Collaborative writing has been shown to be effective in improving academic English writing skills (Teng, 2021). Research also indicates that online collaborative writing instruction significantly enhances writing performance, motivation, and self-efficacy among university-level learners (Li, 2023). However, the majority of the research in this area focuses on English as a foreign language (EFL) students (see, for example, Andrade & Roshay, 2023 and Teng, 2021). This narrow focus indicates a significant gap in the literature, necessitating studies that evaluate the effectiveness of online collaborative writing instruction across diverse student demographics to enrich and broaden the understanding of its pedagogical impact.

Specifically, this chapter explores the integration of collaborative learning principles into academic writing instruction, specifically examining the benefits and challenges of using Google Docs as a tool to facilitate this collaborative learning. Google Docs is a widely-used cloud-based software application developed by Google, offering a comprehensive suite of tools for document creation, editing, and collaboration (Google, 2024). It is one tool that is used for computer-supported collaborative learning, which is an educational approach where shared learning processes, such as knowledge building and group cognition, and shared learning activities, such as elaboration, co-elaboration, and argumentation, occur in a computer-supported setting (Kaliisa et al., 2022; Lämsä et al., 2021).

As a free web-based word processor, Google Docs offers a versatile platform that enables students to create, revise, and edit documents seamlessly (Mills, 2013). As part of the Google Workspace (formerly G Suite) platform, Google Docs allows users to create a variety of documents, including text documents, reports, letters, and articles, along with some basic spreadsheet and presentation functionalities, all stored and accessed online. By incorporating Web 2.0 technology, multiple persons can write, format, and edit a single document simultaneously from different locations (Google, 2024). This has led to Google Docs to be touted as a valuable tool for collaboration among students (Mills, 2013; Oleson, 2020; Revere, & Kovach, 2011).

Information and Communication Technologies (ICTs) have been shown to foster collaboration in learning environments, facilitating ubiquitous and asynchronous processes while ensuring accessibility (Herrera-Pavo, 2021). In this context, Google Docs stands out as a prime example, being both free to use and accessible offline. These features not only make it affordable but also widely available, empowering learners to engage in collaborative work and learning activities regardless of geographical or connectivity constraints. However, there is the question as to whether this cloud-based tool is well-suited to contributing to collaborative learning in the area of academic writing. To date, research indicates that Google Docs is useful for collaborative writing, for example, as an effective tool for providing feedback and teaching peer feedback skills in a university-based Intensive English Programme (Andrade & Roshay, 2023). Further, Google Docs can be used to promote mutual collaboration and autonomous participation, as well as active communication and dynamic interaction in the classroom (Ali, 2021; Jeong, 2016). Moreover, regular collaborative activities via Google Docs have been shown to significantly enhance students' overall academic writing skills (Hoang & Hoang, 2022). However, these results are again primarily based on collaborative learning in the EFL classroom. In contrast, this research focuses on native English speakers in order to broaden the understanding of collaborative learning dynamics across different student populations.

RESEARCH QUESTIONS

Through a review of relevant literature and data from an exploratory case study conducted among tertiary students in Guyana, this chapter examines how the learning space afforded by Google Docs affects collaborative activity in academic writing, focusing on the benefits and challenges associated with using Google Docs for enhancing collaboration in academic writing instruction. In contrast to previous studies focusing primarily on EFL students, this research includes native English speakers to offer insights into the efficacy of online collaborative writing instruction across a broader spectrum of student demographics. Specifically, this research answers three questions:

a) What are the benefits and challenges for tertiary students using Google Docs for online collaborative academic writing?
b) How effective is Google Docs as a collaborative academic writing tool for tertiary students?
c) What are the features of Google Docs that make it an effective tool for collaborative academic writing for tertiary-level students?

The next section initiates this inquiry by reviewing central theoretical concepts, then outlines the methodology for the exploratory case study. This is followed by the results from the exploratory case study conducted among undergraduate students who undertook a one-semester (three-month) course in Technical Communication in Spring 2024. This analysis provides valuable insights into the effectiveness of

Google Docs as a collaborative writing tool and how collaborative academic writing activity is affected using this computer-supported collaborative learning tool.

LITERATURE REVIEW

Online Collaborative Writing

As described by Storch (2019), collaborative writing is a process wherein two or more learners collectively construct a single text through iterative cycles of information exchange, negotiation, and decision-making. Depending on how the assignment is put together, collaboration can be integral at every stage of the writing process, including planning, drafting, and editing, leading to collective learning. This is instructional approach has gained traction in recent years (Bikowski and Vithanage, 2016; Cho, 2017; Storch, 2019), arguably offering distinct advantages over traditional face-to-face collaborative writing instruction (Abrams, 2019; Hsu, 2020). First, students can much more easily communicate and collaborate in real-time, irrespective of their geographical locations (Hsu, 2020; Storch, 2019). This flexibility allows students to collaborate and receive feedback from peers, regardless of physical proximity, thereby expanding the range and possibilities of collaborative writing experience.

Second, using online tools for collaborative writing instruction opens up a plethora of online writing resources to students, including dictionaries, grammar checkers, and writing communities (Lai et al., 2016; Abrams, 2019). These resources can bolster learners' writing development since students can use them to improve their writing skills and effectively address common writing challenges (Li & Zhu, 2013; Hoang & Hoang, 2022). Overall, existing research indicates that online collaborative writing tools can be used by educators can contribute to the development of dynamic and inclusive learning environments in which where students engage in meaningful collaboration, leverage diverse resources, and refine their writing skills. Further, this approach can also cultivate essential collaborative and digital literacy skills essential for success in today's interconnected world (Storch, 2019).

Why Use Google Docs for Online Collaborative Writing?

Google Docs stands out as a versatile platform that is well- suited for collaborative writing activities in academic settings. In particular, its accessibility across various devices and platforms makes it a convenient tool for students to collaborate from anywhere with internet access (Ebadi & Rahimi, 2017). Moreover, Google Docs seamlessly integrates with other Google Workspace applications, such as Google

Drive, Sheets, and Slides, enhancing productivity and enabling the incorporation of multimedia elements into writing projects effectively (Jeong, 2016). Based on the description of the app by Google (2024), the primary features supporting collaboration in Google Docs are:

1. Shared Access: Allows multiple users to view or edit the document, essential for joint efforts.
2. Real-Time Editing: Enables multiple users to work on the document simultaneously, fostering immediate feedback and dynamic interaction.
3. Offline Editing: Allows users to work on their sections without an internet connection and sync changes later, supporting asynchronous cooperation.
4. Commenting and Suggesting: Allows users to leave comments and suggestions, facilitating detailed discussions and collective refinement of the document.
5. Version History: Keeps track of all changes made to the document, allowing users to review and revert to previous versions, ensuring transparency and manageability.
6. Presence Indicators: Shows who is currently viewing or editing the document, enhancing team awareness and fostering a sense of working together

These features facilitate joint efforts, immediate feedback, detailed discussions, transparency, and team awareness, which are essential for effective collaborative work. Among these features, among the most important is Google Docs' ability to maintain a comprehensive version history, allowing both students and instructors to track changes made by individual students (Woodard & Babcock, 2014). This transparency promotes accountability, enabling instructors to monitor each student's contribution to collaborative writing projects (Kurniawati, 2022; Mills, 2013). Additionally, Google Docs' commenting and feedback tools facilitate constructive dialogue among students and between students and instructors (Ishtaiwa & Aburezeq, 2015; Kurniawati, 2022). Through comments and suggestions, students can engage in peer feedback, discussions, and collaborative writing refinement.

More features have been added since the app's release to further enhance collaborative working, including (Google, 2024):

1. In-Document Chat: Provides a platform for direct communication within the document, aiding quick discussions and clarifications.
2. Task Lists and Checklists: Helps track tasks and responsibilities, useful for organising collaborative projects.

3. Notification Alerts: Users receive alerts when changes are made, keeping everyone updated and engaged in the collaborative process.
4. Integration with Google Meet (video conferencing): Facilitates video meetings directly within the document, enabling real-time discussion and collaborative decision-making.

These additional features contribute to streamlining communication, task management, and decision-making processes, thereby providing more technological affordances that open up more room for improved collaboration among users of Google Docs. Technological affordances refer to the ability of a technological tool or system to enable users to accomplish the necessary tasks efficiently and effectively, meeting their needs and expectations (Kirschner et al., 2004). When designing instructional experiences, it is essential for educators to consider how these affordances can enhance learning outcomes (Herrera-Pavo, 2021). In designing academic writing tasks, selecting the appropriate tools is crucial for promoting interaction and collaborative learning since each tool possesses unique characteristics suited to specific educational purposes.

Google Docs falls within the category of tools for 'collaborative authoring,' meaning that is allows multiple users to write and edit text online simultaneously (Biasutti, 2017). It shares common features with other collaborative tools, including speed, simplicity, convenience, open-source accessibility, and maintainability (Lomas et al., 2008). Specifically, there are three key features that set collaborative tools apart from communication tools in general: strong communication capability, easy-to-understand capability, and capability and expectation of collaboration (Lomas et al., 2008). Google Docs effectively meets all three of these criteria:

1. Facilitating communication and interaction among participants through various features discussed above, including real-time editing and ability to comment on specific sections of the document;
2. An intuitive and user-friendly interface as the design mimics traditional word processors, making it familiar and easy to navigate for most users. This familiarity significantly reduces the learning curve, allowing users to quickly adapt to the tool without extensive training; and
3. Clearly supports and encourages collaboration with features like shared access, presence indicators, and version history that signal to users that their input is both expected and valued. The tool is designed to facilitate turn-taking and collective editing, reinforcing the collaborative nature of the workspace.

These technological affordances make it evident when and how users should interact, ensuring that collaboration is structured and effective. By leveraging these affordances, educators can create engaging, interactive learning environments that enhance students' collaborative skills and seek to improve learning outcomes (Alshammary & Alhalafawy, 2022; Biasutti, 2017; Moonma, 2021). In contrast, when using other word processing tools, collaborating on a document generally involves passing it back and forth between authors. Each author takes turns improving the work, often correcting, modifying, or building on the contributions of others. Despite features like track changes, this process is likely to be tedious and error-prone, frequently leading to version-control issues, formatting problems, and the loss of information about who made specific changes (Lomas et al., 2008).

Google Docs has significantly improved the ability to collaborate by addressing these challenges. Its features aim to make collaboration more efficient, effective, and user-friendly, transforming how documents are co-authored. In line with, Susilawati et al. (2023) found that Google Docs has been seen as a user-friendly platform by students based on high perceived ease of use. Correspondingly, students reported being satisfied with using Google Docs and provided positive feedback on this tool, in particular highlighting its usefulness for writing anytime and anywhere (Moonma, 2021). In general, students perceived Google Docs as highly useful, recognising its value in aiding their writing process and enhancing their writing skills (Susilawati et al., 2023). Similarly, Google Docs has been deemed more useful for feedback than Microsoft Word (Mohammed & AL-Jaberi, 2021), indicating that Google Docs is useful for allowing both instructors and peers to provide constructive feedback, engage in discussions, and refine writing collaboratively (Ali, 2021; Kurniawati, 2022). For example, interviews with students underscore the perceived usefulness of Google Docs in enhancing English academic writing skills, although opinions on the enjoyment of collaborating on the platform are mixed (Hoang & Hoang, 2022). Overall, empirical studies indicare that students generally hold positive perceptions of Google Docs as an online writing tool and value the collaborative peer-editing experience it offers (Jeong, 2016; Moonma, 2021).

However, Google Docs has been criticised for a clunky commenting system, a difficult-to-navigate revision history feature, and a less-than-easy-to-use system of tracking changes and revisions as documents get longer (Ishtaiwa & Aburezeq, 2015). These technological challenges in using Google Docs may impede students' progress, such as a lack of familiarity with helpful features and difficulty in following instructions (Ebadi & Rahimi, 2017). Still, Google Docs for collaborative writing has been linked to improved student performance. For example, Moonma (2021) found that academic writing students performed better in co-producing texts in the online mode (using Google Docs) compared to the face-to-face setting. Other studies showed that significant improvements were made in certain aspects of academic writing, such as task response and lexical resources, through the use of Google Docs (Hoang & Hoang, 2022). This indicates that students become better at addressing the given writing prompts effectively and using a richer vocabulary.

Still other aspects of academic writing, like cohesion, coherence, and grammatical accuracy, showed less pronounced improvements in Hoang and Hoang's (2022) study. This indicates that, while Google Docs supports collaborative editing and discussion, which can improve content and vocabulary, it may not be as effective in helping students improve the logical flow of ideas (cohesion and coherence) and correct grammatical errors. These findings are further supported by research demonstrating the significant benefits of peer-editing on learners' academic writing skills (Ebadi and Rahimi, 2017). Interestingly, the study highlights that Google Docs surpasses traditional methods in both short- and long-term effectiveness for peer-editing. This underscores the platform's superiority in enhancing certain facets of writing proficiency. Despite its limitations in addressing some aspects of academic writing skills, Google Docs appears to be a valuable tool for collaborative writing, offering distinct advantages over traditional methods.

Benefits and Challenges of Online Collaborative Writing

Several studies reveal promising advantages of online collaborative learning but also underscore notable challenges. Importantly, online collaborative learning can serve as a catalyst for enhancing academic performance while nurturing essential soft skills including collaboration, communication, problem-solving, and critical thinking (Alshammary & Alhalafawy, 2022). Collaborative learning draws on a number of pedagogical elements like integrating synchronous and asynchronous learning, problem-based learning, cooperative activities, and formative assessment, which are the aspects that are pivotal in augmenting learning outcomes within collaborative frameworks (Akoto, 2021Biasutti, 2017; Kaliisa et al., 2022).

Empirical evidence corroborates the efficacy of online collaborative learning in enhancing student outcomes, with Talan's (2021) meta-analysis indicating a positive and moderate impact on academic achievement. Additionally, findings from a quantitative survey involving over 1000 German university students across 44 universities indicate that online collaborative learning can lead to improved individual learning experiences (Knopf et al., 2021). More in-depth examination of online study groups by Chiong and Jovanovic (2012) identified key advantages of online collaborative work as perceived by students to include social learning, getting peer assistance, and providing peer support. The opportunity to improve grades through group participation was also a significant motivator among students for participating in these collaborative activities (Chiong & Jovanovic, 2012). Students needs to be motivated to actively engage in the tasks since active interaction within collaborative settings fosters critical thinking skills as students to articulate their ideas and justify their positions (Hussin et al., 2019). Collaborative learning activities have thus been shown to provide students with opportunities for the development of social and higher-order thinking skills (Gonzales et al., 2023).

The online aspect is also important in facilitating collaborative learning, as evidenced in the academic writing domain. For example, in their study comparing online and face-to-face environments for collaborative writing, Özdemir (2021) used data from texts generated in both settings, alongside video recordings of face-to-face writing sessions and group interviews. The findings indicate that the online setting offered distinct advantages in terms of time management, flexibility, and support for creativity through multimedia tools. Notably, the texts produced using online collaborative work were deemed more successful overall compared to those produced in the face-to-face context, indicating a potentially higher level of achievement perception among students in the online environment compared to the face-to-face setting.

However, online collaborative work requires a substantial investment of time and effort, often surpassing the demands of individual learning (Capdeferro & Romero, 2012; Knopf et al., 2021). This can present a problem for students, particularly for those juggling personal and professional commitments (Chiong & Jovanovic, 2012). This leads to one of the central challenges of any collaborative task, which is difficulty in fostering active participation because students may be unable (e.g. due to time constraints or lack of self-confidence) or unwilling (e.g. stemming from low participation of other group members) to engage fully in group work (Chiong & Jovanovic, 2012; Gonzales et al., 2023). These constraints impede students' capacity and willingness to participate effectively, thereby compromising the quality of group interactions and outcomes (Hirokawa, 1983).

Disparities in participation levels are common in collaborative settings, where not all students contribute equally (Gonzales et al., 2023). The concept of differential participation acknowledges this variation, recognising that not all students participate equally in the collaborative process (González-Lloret, 2020; Revere & Kovach, 2011). Beyond variations in participation levels, the concept of asymmetrical engagement highlights a deeper issue, which is the imbalance in the level of engagement among group members (Ramble, 2017; Revere & Kovach, 2011). It refers to the fact that some individuals may be significantly more engaged or invested in the collaborative process compared to others, leading to an uneven distribution of effort or contribution (Chiong & Jovanovic, 2012; Ramble, 2017). This term implies a more pronounced contrast between the levels of engagement among participants, often resulting in one or a few individuals carrying a disproportionate share of the workload or responsibility. In other words, asymmetric collaboration implies that some individuals are not fully committed to the collaborative process.

This imbalance is likely to both undermine group cohesion and hampers the achievement of the group's objectives (González-Lloret, 2020; Revere & Kovach, 2011). Further, this imbalance in the level of commitment and quality of individual contributions is a major driver of frustration in collaborative work (Capdeferro & Romero, 2012). When some members (perceive that they) contribute significantly more than others, it creates a sense of imbalance and unfairness within the group. This can lead to frustration among those who feel they are shouldering a disproportionate share of the workload or who perceive others as not pulling their weight (Capdeferro & Romero, 2012; Gonzales et al., 2023). Lack of real collaboration leads to shallow collaborative engagements, which focuses on the quality of interactions and these would be lacking depth or substance and would be generally characterised by superficial discussions or minimal engagement (Cashman et al., 2014; Ramble, 2017). Overall, shallow collaborative engagements, differential participation and asymmetrical engagement have been shown to accompany student adoption of emerging technologies (Ramble, 2017).

However, it is essential to acknowledge that these challenges are not isolated but interconnected. Students also complains about differing perspectives, difficulties in group organisation, lack of shared goals, and communication gaps that all contribute to a sense of disconnection within groups and undermine effective collaboration (Capdeferro & Romero, 2012; Gonzales et al., 2023). These issues exacerbate shallow collaborative engagements, differential participation, and asymmetrical engagement, leading to inefficiencies and frustrations within collaborative efforts. For example, poor group communication inhibits meaningful exchange of ideas and coordination within the group, leading to misunderstandings, misalignment, and ultimately, ineffective collaboration (Abdullah Alharbi & Mohammed Hassan Al-Ahdal, 2024; Fushino, 2010; Hirokawa, 1983).

Developing Effective Online Collaborative Learning

The effectiveness of online collaborative learning will depend on technological, social, and educational affordances of the teaching and learning context (Kirschner et al., 2004). Thus, alongside the technological affordances provided by platforms like Google Docs or other collaborative authoring tools, consideration of educational and social affordances is crucial in the academic writing classroom (Herrera-Pavo, 2021; Kirschner et al., 2004). To begin, educational affordances refer to the opportunities or possibilities for learning provided by the learning environment (Kirschner et al., 2004). In other words, the features and characteristics of the learning environment determine the feasibility and effectiveness of different learning behaviours. Technological tools can contribute to educational affordances as their functionalities can enrich engagement, efficiency, and presence, thus augmenting educational quality

(Bower & Sturman, 2015). They can also be used pedagogically for feedback, gamification, communication, recording, and other purposes contingent upon the technology type (Bower & Sturman, 2015).

However, Kirschner et al. (2004) argue that the chosen educational paradigm and teacher mediation and are particularly influential in terms of the enactment of learning behaviours within the educational context. The chosen educational paradigm, such as constructivism or social constructivism, dictates the pedagogical approach and strategies employed in collaborative learning environments (Herrera-Pavo, 2021; Kirschner et al., 2004). For instance, under a constructivist paradigm, which emphasises active engagement and knowledge construction, educational affordances may prioritise learner-centred activities and opportunities for exploration and discovery (O'Connor, 2022). On the other hand, in a social constructivist paradigm that emphasises social interaction, educational affordances may focus on facilitating collaborative problem-solving tasks, fostering peer-to-peer learning, and creating platforms for knowledge sharing and co-construction (Carless, 2022; Felder & Brent, 2007). In line with this, collaboration can be seen as one mechanism of student 'co-working' and is based on social constructivist notions of knowledge being created and mutually shared in social relations (Oleson, 2020). Additionally, effective teacher mediation can enhance the affordances of the learning environment by providing scaffolding, feedback, and resources tailored to support collaborative learning activities (Kaendler et al., 2015). In general, teacher mediation refers to the guidance, support, and facilitation provided by instructors in guiding students' learning processes (Kaendler et al., 2015).

As it relates to educational affordances, Razali et al. (2015) identified three main groups of factors that influence the effectiveness of online collaborative learning: learning environment, learning design, and learning interaction. First, the *Learning Environment* encompasses aspects related to the environment in which learning takes place. This includes:

1. Usability: how user-friendly and intuitive the online platform or tools are for learners;
2. Accessibility: ensuring that all learners, including those with disabilities, can access and engage with the learning materials and activities; and
3. Stability: the reliability and consistency of the online platform or technology used for collaborative learning.

> Second, *Learning Design* involves the design and structure of the learning experience. It encompasses the following elements:
>
> 1. Content: the material or information presented to learners;

2. Process: the methods and strategies used to facilitate learning and collaboration;
3. Evaluation: how learning outcomes are assessed and measured; and
4. Time constraints: any limitations or deadlines imposed on collaborative activities.

Third, *Learning Interaction* focuses on the interactions that occur within the learning environment, including both learner-learner and learner-teacher interactions. Effective interaction fosters engagement, participation, and knowledge exchange among learners.

Overall, these three categories intersect with the educational affordances discussed by Kirschner et al. (2004) in that they collectively contribute to shaping the learning environment and opportunities for learning. For example, elements of learning design such as the process by which collaborative writing is facilitated and the evaluation methods employed, all contribute to the educational affordances available. Assigning group writing tasks that require peer review and feedback is one way to foster collaborative interaction and knowledge exchange (Tan & Chen, 2022; Trengove, 2017). Similarly, the online collaborative writing learning environment encompasses the digital platforms and tools used for collaboration. Ensuring these platforms are user-friendly (usability), accessible to all participants, including those with disabilities (accessibility), and reliable (stability) contributes to an environment conducive to effective collaborative writing.

Some of the potential drawbacks of using technology in education are the risks of overreliance and prioritising technology over pedagogy (Bower & Sturman, 2015). This emphasises the need for meticulous planning and consideration of various variables before implementation (Ignacio et al., 2022). The final critical aspect for educators to consider in developing effective online collaborative learning is social affordances, which refers to the properties of the environment that facilitate social interaction and collaboration among learners (Kirschner et al., 2004). Specifically, these properties act as social-contextual facilitators that are essential for effective social interaction within a learning context (Kirschner et al., 2004; Kreijns et al., 2003). This is one of the most important issues that students bring up when identifying challenges (González-Lloret, 2020; Ramble, 2017; Revere & Kovach, 2011), which is unsurprising since social interaction is key to the efficacy of collaborative learning (Kreijns et al., 2003). Thus, although technological tools like Google Docs offer technological and educational affordances that can support communication and collaboration, their effectiveness is not guaranteed.

Two major pitfalls that impede achieving the desired results include assuming that participants will automatically socially interact simply because the environment makes it possible and neglecting the social (psychological) dimension of the desired social interaction (Kreijns et al., 2003). First, it is a common misconception that providing a collaborative platform will naturally lead to effective social interaction among participants. However, this assumption often leads to differential participation, asymmetrical engagement, and shallow collaboration as discussed above. Such imbalance can hinder the depth and quality of collaboration, as meaningful exchange of ideas and coordinated efforts are critical for successful outcomes (Abdullah Alharbi & Mohammed Hassan Al-Ahdal, 2024; Fushino, 2010;).

Second, the social and psychological aspects of interaction are crucial for effective collaboration, yet they are often overlooked. Effective collaboration requires more than just the availability of communication tools; it necessitates an environment where participants feel psychologically safe and motivated to engage. If students do not feel comfortable or confident, they may be unwilling to contribute fully, leading to uneven participation (Chiong & Jovanovic, 2012; Gonzales et al., 2023). Additionally, social loafing, where individuals exert less effort because they feel less accountable in a group, can further reduce the effectiveness of collaborative learning (González-Lloret, 2020; Revere & Kovach, 2011). Therefore, understanding and fostering the psychological aspects of social interaction, such as building trust and encouraging equitable participation, are essential.

To address these pitfalls, educators must design and facilitate online collaborative environments that actively promote and support meaningful interaction, ensuring that technological, educational and social affordances are effectively integrated (Herrera-Pavo, 2021; Kirschner et al., 2004). Thus, in addition to using Google Docs, this involves creating structured activities that require equitable participation, providing clear guidelines and expectations, and ensuring ongoing support and feedback (Dooley & Bamford, 2018; Kirschner, 2001).

METHODOLOGY

Method

A pragmatic approach was chosen to guide the exploratory case study undertaken. As a research philosophy, pragmatism "sidesteps the contentious issues of truth and reality, accepts… that there are singular and multiple realities that are open to empirical inquiry and orients itself toward solving practical problems in the 'real world'" (Feilzer, 2010, p. 8). Rooted in the belief that knowledge should not only reflect reality but also serve practical purposes, pragmatic researchers navigate the tension between theoretical accuracy and practical relevance. By prioritising the pursuit of solutions that address tangible needs and challenges faced by individuals, organisations, or communities, pragmatism ensures that research findings are not only academically rigorous but also have real-world applications (Feilzer, 2010).

Within this paradigm, the exploratory case study was chosen to support the chapter's aim to provide an in-depth exploration of an example of a group working with Google Docs. The case study is ideal for providing particular, evidence-based and holistic insights into the complexities of single cases within their real-life context, and holds potential for being compared to other cases (Flyvbjerg, 2011). This method allows for a detailed examination of the group's interactions, practices, and outcomes in using Google Docs, shedding light on how this tool can enhance collaborative learning and writing skills in an academic setting.

An exploratory research design was used because it is "the type of inquiry related to discovery, which takes place when a researcher examines a new interest or in instances where the study subject is relatively new" (Babbie, 2020, p. 88). Given that the use of Google Docs for collaborative work in academic writing instruction is still a relatively new area of study, an exploratory case study is particularly justified since it allowed for flexibility in application as well as in-depth exploration of this specific instance, providing a rich, contextual understanding that can inform both theory and practice. Overall, this method facilitated the exploration of the experiences, perceptions, and outcomes of students regarding the use of Google Docs in collaborative writing instruction.

The Setting and Participants

The setting for this study is a one-semester (three-month) course in Technical Communication, specifically designed for first-year undergraduate students enrolled in the Science and Technical programmes at the University of Guyana, such as Health Sciences, Agriculture and Forestry, and Earth and Environmental Sciences The course aims to develop essential communication skills for students to function competently in professional, scientific, or technical environments. According to the course outline, it focuses on enhancing students' proficiency in writing reports that clearly understand the procedures and methods used in acquiring and analysing data. The course is a fundamental component of the curriculum, reflecting the institution's commitment to equipping students with the necessary skills for their future careers. Over 1000 students enrol in this course annually, delivered by various lecturers. For the Spring semester, 265 students participated in the researcher's section of the course, distributed across six tutorial sessions. These were all students enrolled in the Associates of Science programmes in Engineering, Computer Science/IT, and Agriculture.

In this course, students are required to use Google Docs to create and edit online documents collaboratively with their peers in real-time. The primary assignment involves writing an analytical report based on primary research conducted over the two months. Each team, consisting of 3-5 students, had to compile their report using Google Docs. They were directed to share the document link with the lecturer, ensuring that the lecturer has editing privileges for providing feedback and consultation on their drafts.

Using a convenience sampling approach, the study involved 109 students who attended class on the day of the survey. While the data was collected on a single day, the respondents were from all six tutorial sessions under the researcher's instruction. To encourage participation, a participation grade of 5% was awarded to students who completed the survey. All students present that day completed the survey, representing approximately 41.1% of the students enrolled in the lecturer's section of the course for the Spring semester. The demographic information of the participants is shown in Table 1. The sample is skewed towards males, with more than twice as many males as females included in the sample. This reflects the greater enrolment of males in the Engineering, IT, and Agriculture departments at the University of Guyana, and generally the greater representation of men in in science, technology, engineering, and math (STEM) fields globally (Chiang et al., 2024; Kwak & Ramirez, 2019). The age composition is equally split between students under 20 and between 20 and 24, reflecting the typical age range of first-year undergraduate students. This distribution suggests that the sample represents a diverse range of students who are at the early stages of their academic journey. It aligns with the demographic characteristics commonly associated with first-year undergraduates enrolled in STEM programs.

Table 1. Demographic description of the sample

	Characteristic	**Number**	**Percentage**
Gender	Female	35	32%
	Male	74	68%
Age Group	Under 20 years	53	49%
	20-24 years	55	51%
	25-35 years	0	0
	36-45 years	1	0

Instruments and Procedure

A survey instrument was administered online (using Google Forms) to students enrolled in the Technical Communication course at the end of the course in April 2024 to capture students' perceptions of the effectiveness, benefits, and challenges associated with using Google Docs for academic writing. The questionnaire generated quantitative information from two sections. The first section contained 15 closed-ended questions using Likert scale responses. Eight of these questions were taken from Woodrich and Fan's (2016) self-report questionnaire and one question taken from Akoto (2021). The remaining six questions were developed by the researcher. The questions used a 5-point Likert scale in which 5 is strongly agree and 1 is strongly disagree. The second section had 7 closed ended (yes/no) questions.

One drawback of utilizing data from self-completion surveys is the absence of a conversational aspect, leading to a lack of opportunity for follow-up or probing questions from an interviewer (Oates et al., 2022). Consequently, surveys are often perceived to lack the depth and richness of data obtained through interviews, as evidenced by research indicating a significantly higher quantity of data generated when qualitative data is collected through verbal modes compared to text-based modes like qualitative surveys (Guest et al., 2023; Oates et al., 2022). provided significant insights into the respondents' perceptions, enabling a comprehensive understanding of their perspectives on the effectiveness, benefits, and challenges associated with using Google Docs for academic writing.

Data Analysis

The quantitative survey data from Sections 1 and 2 was analyzed using descriptive statistics to summarize students' perceptions and experiences with collaborative learning using Google Docs. This involved compiling all responses into an Excel spreadsheet and calculating totals, means and standard deviations to provide a general overview of learners' perceptions and opinion of the benefits and challenges associated with using Google Docs for collaborative academic writing. This approach offered valuable initial insights into the perceived effectiveness of Google Docs as a collaborative writing tool, its perceived impact on student learning outcomes in academic writing, and challenges that have arisen from the students' perspectives.

RESULTS

Benefits and Challenges of Google Docs for Online Collaborative Academic Writing

The first set of results from the yes/no questions show significant consensus among respondents regarding their experiences with and perceptions of Google Docs (Table 2). First, the results show that the students found Google Docs helpful for writing the report (n=100), likely because it made the writing of the report easier (n=95) and made collaborating/cooperating with team members easier (92). The students also thought that Google Docs is largely advantageous for doing collaborative/cooperative group work (n=104), even though they faced challenges using Google Docs for their project (n=37) and identified disadvantages of using this tool in the assignment (n=38). Finally, an important finding is that students largely did not think that using Google Docs changed how they approached doing collaborative/cooperative group work (n=70).

Table 2. Responses to quantitative survey questions (Section 2)

Questions	YES (n)	NO (n)
1. Was Google Docs helpful for writing the investigative report/feasibility study?	100	9
2. Was writing the investigative report/feasibility study easier with Google Docs?	95	14
3. Did using Google Docs make it easier for you to work together with others?	92	17
4. Do you think there are advantages of using Google Docs for collaborative writing?	104	5
6. Has using Google Docs changed how you approach collaborative work?	70	39
7. Did you face any challenges using Google Docs for your writing project?	37	72
8. Do you think there are disadvantage(s) of using Google Docs for collaborative writing?	38	71

Effectiveness of Google Docs for Online Collaborative Academic Writing

These findings above are supported by the students' responses on Section 1 of the survey (mean responses shown in Table 3) that in general showed strong and consistent agreement in terms of the perceived usefulness and helpfulness of Google Docs for collaborating/cooperating with team members for their project. First, there was strong agreement among the students on the effectiveness of Google Docs in various aspects such as improving efficiency (M=4.15; SD=1.00), its usefulness for organizing and managing group writing tasks (M=4.21; SD=0.94), and its contribution to improved collaboration with group members (M=4.05; SD=1.05). This is reflected in a moderately high preference for collaborating on writing assignments using Google Docs (M=4.04; SD=1.03). There was also moderate agreement that Google Docs improved communication with group members (M=3.76; SD=1.17), encouraged active participation in the group work (M=3.88; SD=1.12), and contributed to learning from their team members (M=3.70; SD=1.12). Still, the higher level of standard deviation, along with the lower means, indicates more diversity in students' opinions in these areas.

Students also liked Google Docs for providing and receiving feedback, strongly agreeing that Google Docs was useful for receiving feedback from lecturers (M=4.31; SD=0.88), commenting and revising documents online (M=4.25; SD=0.86), and allowing students to provide feedback to their group members (M=4.19; SD=1.00). There was also moderate agreement that this tool made it easier for my group members to provide feedback (M=3.95; SD=1.12). In sum, the students agreed that Google Docs helped create better final assignments (M = 4.12; SD = 0.91) and they expressed a strong preference for using Google Docs for future assignments (M=4.26; SD=0.96).

Table 3. Mean responses to quantitative survey questions (Section 1)

Questions	M	SD
1. Google Docs improved collaboration with my group members when completing the investigative report/feasibility study.	4.05	1.05
2. Using Google Docs improved the efficiency of the group when completing the investigative report/feasibility study.	4.15	1.00
3. Everyone in my team contributed more when using Google Docs.	3.56	1.17
4. Google Docs improved communication with my group members when completing the investigative report/feasibility study.	3.76	1.17
5. I had something to contribute to my team on these assignments.	4.60	0.77
6. Google Docs made it easier for me to receive feedback from my lecturer.	4.31	0.88
7. I learned from my team members when using Google Docs.	3.70	1.12
8. Google Docs made it easier for me to provide feedback to my group members.	4.19	1.00
9. Google Docs encouraged active participation from my group members when completing the investigative report/feasibility study.	3.88	1.12
10. Google Docs helped us to better organize and manage the group writing tasks.	4.21	0.94
11. Google Docs helped my group create a better final assignment.	4.12	0.91
12. I liked being able to comment and revise the document online.	4.25	0.86
13. Google Docs made it easier for my group members to give me feedback.	3.95	1.12
14. I prefer to collaborate on writing assignments using Google Docs.	4.04	1.03
15. I would like to use Google Docs for more assignments in the future.	4.26	0.96

DISCUSSION

Benefits of Using Google Docs for Online Collaboration in Academic Writing

The benefits identified by students in utilizing Google Docs for collaborative tasks are primary linked to its technological and educational affordances. Specifically, Google Docs serves as a robust platform that actively supports and fosters collaboration (Lomas et al., 2008), facilitating interaction among peers and educators alike. The survey findings affirm this, with a notable consensus indicating that Google Docs significantly enhanced collaboration among group members during the completion of their collaborative investigative report/feasibility assignment. Additionally, the ability to comment and revise documents online and the preference for collaborating on writing assignments using Google Docs were rated highly, underscoring the perceived benefits of Google Docs in facilitating effective collaboration and continuous improvement. Further, students recognized Google Docs as a valuable tool for organizing and managing group writing tasks, indicating its effectiveness in structuring collaborative work and contributing to the attainment of higher-quality outcomes. This sentiment is reinforced by respondents' agreement that Google Docs increased the efficiency of group tasks. These results reflect a consensus on its ability to streamline collaborative efforts, indicating positive experiences and affirming its value in facilitating productive collaboration. Overall, the technological functionalities of Google Docs contributed to educational affordances since these functionalities contributed to increased engagement, efficiency, and presence, thus enhancing educational quality (Bower & Sturman, 2015).

Effectiveness of Google Docs for Online Collaborative Academic Writing

The survey results strongly suggest that most respondents found Google Docs to be an effective platform for collaborative work, again linked to its contribution in terms of technological and educational affordances. Specifically, Google Docs effectively facilitated communication and interaction among students (Lomas et al., 2008). Survey respondents expressed that Google Docs notably enhanced communication with group members. Additionally, the platform's functionality in facilitating feedback exchange between lecturers and group members was highly rated, indicating its utility in feedback processes. In particular, students highlighted the platform's effectiveness in enabling group members to provide feedback, reflecting a positive experience with peer feedback mechanisms. Effective peer feedback is essential for successful collaboration, enabling team members to exchange insights, identify areas for improvement, and enhance overall work quality (Malecka et al., 2022; Tan & Chen, 2022). The ability to give and receive feedback in real-time can help in maintaining a continuous dialogue, ensuring that all group members are aligned and contributing to the project's goals. By contributing to both learner-learner and learner-teacher interactions, Google Docs facilitates meaningful exchanges of ideas, feedback, and insights among users, contributing to an enriched learning experience (Razali et al., 2015). This underscores how technology can support and enhance social interactions in the learning process, ultimately contributing to a richer and more effective educational experience (Bower & Sturman, 2015; Herrera-Pavo, 2021).

In terms of the overall impact, respondents highlighted that Google Docs notably enhanced the quality of their final assignments. This suggests that the platform plays a significant role in improving the educational outcomes of collaborative tasks. Additionally, survey results indicated that users perceived learning from their team members during the collaborative process facilitated by Google Docs. Also telling is that there is a clear preference among students to use Google Docs in future assignments. Using Google Docs or other collaborative writing technology may thus improve students' attitude towards writing, which is a necessary input to improving writing itself (Alleyne, 2019) because this will likely decrease students' fear of writing and reduce push back to doing more writing (Burris-Melville, 2020). Together, these results show a number of benefits of using Google Docs, which served as a multifaceted tool that not only addresses technological requirements for effective collaboration but also aligns with the educational affordances necessary for promoting meaningful learning experiences in collaborative online writing.

Challenges of Using Google Docs for Online Collaboration in Academic Writing

The key challenge identified by the students is related to the social affordances of working online collaboratively. Specifically, students found challenges with equitable participation, indicating problems gaps in terms of how the learning environment has been structured to facilitate social interaction and collaboration among learners (Kirschner et al., 2004). Asking students to use a platform like Google Docs does not automatically result in effective collaboration, which is reflected in the participants' respondents. On one hand, students' responses indicated moderate agreement that active participation from group members was encouraged by Google Docs, reflecting a generally positive impact on engagement. In line with this, the response with the highest mean across from all questions indicates that students felt confident in their contributions to the group assignments, suggesting a sense of involvement and engagement in the collaborative process. On the other hand, the response with the lowest mean was whether everyone in the team contributed more when using Google

Docs. This discrepancy suggests an important issue: while students feel confident about their own contributions, they perceive a lack of equitable participation among team members.

Both of these perceptions cannot be objectively true simultaneously, highlighting a common challenge in collaborative online learning environments. First, students report high confidence in their own contributions, which could be influenced by the self-enhancement effect, where individuals perceive their input more favorably than it might objectively be (Dufner et al., 2019). This self-enhancement effect is seen in research from Alleyne (2019) among students at UWI Mona in which they concluded that students overestimate their own writing ability. Specifically, the students' responses indicated that they saw academic writing instruction as more important for other students than for themselves. Importantly, students who believe they contribute more to a group (high relative self-enhancement) may reduce on their effort, weakening group performance (Hoorens, 2011). It can also lead to reduced group performance if these students feel the group is dependent on them and take on even more responsibility, potentially frustrating others and taking away learning opportunities (Hoorens, 2011).

Additionally, the self-report nature of the survey may further amplify this bias, calling into question the reliability of these responses. Overall, it is important to acknowledge that self-perception may not always align with the actual dynamics and contributions within the group. Nonetheless, it is important to understand students' perceptions since they play a crucial role in understanding their experiences and perspectives within collaborative learning environments, providing valuable insights that can inform educators' approaches to fostering more equitable participation and engagement among all group members.

Further, the low mean response regarding equal contribution points to an underlying issue of uneven participation within groups. Some members may have felt more engaged and productive than others. This raises concerns about the inclusivity and equitability of collaborative tools like Google Docs, indicating that simply providing a collaborative platform does not ensure balanced participation without roles and responsibilities of team members being outlined (González-Lloret, 2020; Revere & Kovach, 2011). This discrepancy underscores the complexities of online collaboration, where individual perceptions of contribution and actual group dynamics do not always align.

The high level of individual contribution reported might also be attributed to the affordances provided by tools like Google Docs, which facilitate individual input and visibility. However, these tools alone do not guarantee balanced participation. The (perceived) lack of equal contribution suggests that some team members may be dominating the work, while others may be less engaged or contributing less frequently. This imbalance can stem from several factors, including differences in confidence, time management, or willingness to engage (González-Lloret, 2020; Revere & Kovach, 2011).

Furthermore, the assumption that providing a collaborative platform like Google Docs will automatically result in equitable participation is flawed (Kreijns et al., 2003). Research indicates that technology must be complemented with intentional design and facilitation to promote meaningful interaction and ensure balanced contributions (Revere & Kovach, 2011). Without clear roles, responsibilities, and structured activities, some students may not fully engage, leading to differential participation and asymmetrical engagement (Dooley & Bamford, 2018; Kirschner, 2001; Ramble, 2017).

CONCLUSION

Integrating collaborative learning principles into academic writing instruction holds immense potential for enhancing student engagement, critical thinking skills, and writing proficiency. Google Docs emerges as a powerful ally in this endeavor, offering a platform where students can collaborate, communicate, and co-create knowledge effectively. By embracing methods such as collaborative peer review and revision, students not only refine their writing skills but also foster a sense of community and teamwork within the classroom.

As Caribbean educators explore innovative teaching approaches, Google Docs stands out as a valuable tool for facilitating collaborative learning experiences in academic writing instruction. However, its efficacy hinges on both teachers' and students' adeptness in leveraging its features. Therefore, pedagogical support and active student engagement are vital for maximizing the benefits of technological tools like Google Docs (Ali, 2021; Ebadi & Rahimi, 2017; Li, 2023).

Despite the potential of tools like Google Docs to enhance engagement and individual contributions in online collaborative learning, they do not inherently address the challenge of equitable participation. To ensure balanced and effective collaboration, educators must in particular take account of the social affordances of their teaching environment, design online collaborative activities that explicitly promote inclusivity and active involvement from all group members (Kirschner, 2001). Thus, technological, educational, and social affordances must all be taken into account in order to effectively address the social and psychological factors that shape group dynamics and individual engagement.

To tackle these challenges, educators should design and facilitate online collaborative environments that foster meaningful interaction. This involves structuring activities for equitable participation, providing clear guidelines and expectations, and offering ongoing support and feedback (Dooley & Bamford, 2018; Kirschner,

2001). Additionally, creating a conducive social environment by fostering a sense of community, encouraging positive group dynamics, and acknowledging the contributions of all members is crucial.

Facilitators must also ensure ample opportunities for interaction within the learning environment to promote collaborative learning. This includes providing dedicated spaces for group work equipped with the necessary collaboration tools (Kirschner, 2001). Moreover, implementing peer-review processes and offering continuous feedback mechanisms can further enhance the effectiveness of online collaborative learning (Dooley & Bamford, 2018). By addressing these aspects, educators can mitigate the risks of shallow engagement and neglect of social-psychological dimensions, thereby optimizing the overall effectiveness of collaborative learning experiences.

REFERENCES

Abdullah Alharbi, M., & Mohammed Hassan Al-Ahdal, A. A. (2024). Communication barriers in the EFL classroom: Is poor listening the culprit that obstructs learning? *Interactive Learning Environments*, 32(2), 772–786. DOI: 10.1080/10494820.2022.2098776

Akoto, M. (2021). Collaborative multimodal writing via Google Docs: Perceptions of French FL learners. *Languages (Basel, Switzerland)*, 6(3), 140. DOI: 10.3390/languages6030140

Ali, A. D. (2021). Using Google Docs to enhance students' collaborative translation and engagement. *Journal of Information Technology Education*, 20, 503–528. Advance online publication. DOI: 10.28945/4888

Alleyne, M. L. (2019). Academic writing in the Caribbean: Attitudes matter. In Milson-Whyte, V., & Oenbring, R. (Eds.), *Creole composition: Academic writing and rhetoric in the Anglophone Caribbean* (pp. 125–154). Parlor Press LLC.

Alshammary, F. M., & Alhalafawy, W. S. (2022). Sustaining enhancement of learning outcomes across digital platforms during the COVID-19 pandemic: A systematic review. *Journal of Positive School Psychology*, 6(9), 2279–2301. http://mail.journalppw.com/index.php/jpsp/article/view/12650/8202

Andrade, C., & Roshay, A. (2023). Using Google Docs for collaborative writing feedback with international students. *The CATESOL Journal*, 34(1), 1–8. http://www.catesoljournal.org/wp-content/uploads/2023/06/CJ34-1_Andrade-Roshay_Formatted.pdf

Babbie, E. (2020). *The practice of social research*. Cengage.

Biasutti, M. (2017). A comparative analysis of forums and wikis as tools for online collaborative learning. *Computers & Education*, 111, 158–171. DOI: 10.1016/j.compedu.2017.04.006

Bower, M., & Sturman, D. (2015). What are the educational affordances of wearable technologies? *Computers & Education*, 88, 343–353. DOI: 10.1016/j.compedu.2015.07.013

Burris-Melville, T. S. (2020). An investigation into the challenges undergraduate students face in academic writing at a Jamaican University [Doctoral dissertation, Trevecca Nazarene University]. ProQuest Dissertations and Theses Global.

Capdeferro, N., & Romero, M. (2012). Are online learners frustrated with collaborative learning experiences? *International Review of Research in Open and Distance Learning*, 13(2), 26–44. DOI: 10.19173/irrodl.v13i2.1127

Carless, D. (2022). From teacher transmission of information to student feedback literacy: Activating the learner role in feedback processes. *Active Learning in Higher Education*, 23(2), 143–153. DOI: 10.1177/1469787420945845

Cashman, J., Linehan, P. C., Purcell, L., Rosser, M., Schultz, S., & Skalski, S. (2014). *Leading by convening: A blueprint for authentic engagement*. Idea Partnership. https://eric.ed.gov/?id=ED584148

Chiang, F. K., Tang, Z., Zhu, D., & Bao, X. (2024). Gender disparity in STEM education: A survey research on girl participants in World Robot Olympiad. *International Journal of Technology and Design Education*, 34(2), 629–646. DOI: 10.1007/s10798-023-09830-0 PMID: 37359821

Chiong, R., & Jovanovic, J. (2012). Collaborative learning in online study groups: An evolutionary game theory perspective. *Journal of Information Technology Education*, 11(1), 81–101. https://www.learntechlib.org/p/111494/. DOI: 10.28945/1574

Clarke, C., Daynauth, R., Wilkinson, C., Devonish, H., & Mars, J. (2024). Guylingo: The Republic of Guyana Creole corpora. arXiv preprint arXiv:2405.03832. https://doi.org//arXiv.2405.03832 DOI: 10.18653/v1/2024.naacl-short.70

Devonish, H., & Thompson, D. (2012). Guyanese Creole. In Kortmann, D., & Lunkenheimer, K. (Eds.), *The Mouton world atlas of variation in English* (pp. 265-278). de Gruyter Mouton. https://doi.org/DOI: 10.1515/9783110280128.265

Dooley, L. M., & Bamford, N. J. (2018). Peer feedback on collaborative learning activities in veterinary education. *Veterinary Sciences*, 5(4), 90. DOI: 10.3390/vetsci5040090 PMID: 30336578

Dufner, M., Gebauer, J. E., Sedikides, C., & Denissen, J. J. (2019). Self-enhancement and psychological adjustment: A meta-analytic review. *Personality and Social Psychology Review*, 23(1), 48–72. DOI: 10.1177/1088868318756467 PMID: 29534642

Ebadi, S., & Rahimi, M. (2017). Exploring the impact of online peer-editing using Google Docs on EFL learners' academic writing skills: A mixed methods study. *Computer Assisted Language Learning*, 30(8), 787–815. DOI: 10.1080/09588221.2017.1363056

Feilzer, M. Y. (2010). Doing mixed methods research pragmatically: Implications for the rediscovery of pragmatism as a research paradigm. *Journal of Mixed Methods Research*, 4(1), 6–16. DOI: 10.1177/1558689809349691

Felder, R. M., & Brent, R. (2007). Cooperative learning. In Mabrouk, P. (Ed.), *Active learning: Models from the Analytical Sciences, ACS Symposium Series 970* (pp. 34-53). American Chemical Society. DOI: 10.1021/bk-2007-0970.ch004

Flyvbjerg, B. (2011). Case study. In Denzin, N. & Lincoln, Y. (Eds.), *The Sage handbook of qualitative research,* 4 (pp. 301-316). Sage.

Fushino, K. (2010). Causal relationships between communication confidence, beliefs about group work, and willingness to communicate in foreign language group work. *TESOL Quarterly*, 44(4), 700–724. DOI: 10.5054/tq.2010.235993

Gonzales, G., Despe, K. B., Iway, L. J., Genon, R., Intano, J. O., & Sanchez, J. (2023). Online collaborative learning platforms in science: Their influence on attitude, achievement, and experiences. *Journal of Educational Technology and Instruction*, 2(2), 1–16. https://ijeti-edu.org/index.php/ijeti/article/view/55. DOI: 10.70290/jeti.v2i2.55

González-Lloret, M. (2020). Collaborative tasks for online language teaching. *Foreign Language Annals*, 53(2), 260–269. DOI: 10.1111/flan.12466

Google. (2024). About Google Docs. https://www.google.com/docs/about/

Guest, G., Namey, E., O'Regan, A., Godwin, C., & Taylor, J. (2020). Comparing interview and focus group data collected in person and online. Patient-Centred Outcomes Research Institute (PCORI), Washington, DC. https://www.ncbi.nlm.nih.gov/books/NBK588708/

Herrera-Pavo, M. Á. (2021). Collaborative learning for virtual higher education. *Learning, Culture and Social Interaction*, 28, 100437. DOI: 10.1016/j.lcsi.2020.100437

Hirokawa, R. Y. (1983). Group communication and problem-solving effectiveness: An investigation of group phases. *Human Communication Research*, 9(4), 291–305. DOI: 10.1111/j.1468-2958.1983.tb00700.x

Hoang, D. T. N., & Hoang, T. (2022). Enhancing EFL students' academic writing skills in online learning via Google Docs-based collaboration: A mixed-methods study. *Computer Assisted Language Learning*, ●●●, 1–23. DOI: 10.1080/09588221.2022.2083176

Hoorens, V. (2011). The social consequences of self-enhancement and self-protection. In Alicke, M., & Sedikides, C. (Eds.), *Handbook of self-enhancement and self-protection* (pp. 235–257). Guilford Press.

Hussin, W. N. T. W., Harun, J., & Shukor, N. A. (2019, July). Online tools for collaborative learning to enhance students' interaction. In *2019 7th International Conference on Information and Communication Technology (ICoICT)* (pp. 1-5). IEEE. https://doi.org/DOI: 10.1109/ICoICT.2019.8835197

Ignacio, J., Chen, H. C., & Roy, T. (2022). Advantages and challenges of fostering cognitive integration through virtual collaborative learning: A qualitative study. *BMC Nursing*, 21(1), 251. DOI: 10.1186/s12912-022-01026-6 PMID: 36076227

Ishtaiwa, F. F., & Aburezeq, I. M. (2015). The impact of Google Docs on student collaboration: A UAE case study. *Learning, Culture and Social Interaction*, 7, 85–96. DOI: 10.1016/j.lcsi.2015.07.004

Jeong, K. O. (2016). A study on the integration of Google Docs as a web-based collaborative learning platform in EFL writing instruction. *Indian Journal of Science and Technology*, 9(39). Advance online publication. DOI: 10.17485/ijst/2016/v9i39/103239

Kaendler, C., Wiedmann, M., Rummel, N., & Spada, H. (2015). Teacher competencies for the implementation of collaborative learning in the classroom: A framework and research review. *Educational Psychology Review*, 27(3), 505–536. DOI: 10.1007/s10648-014-9288-9

Kaliisa, R., Rienties, B., Mørch, A. I., & Kluge, A. (2022). Social learning analytics in computer-supported collaborative learning environments: A systematic review of empirical studies. *Computers and Education Open*, 3, 100073. DOI: 10.1016/j.caeo.2022.100073

Kirschner, P., Strijbos, J. W., Kreijns, K., & Beers, P. J. (2004). Designing electronic collaborative learning environments. *Educational Technology Research and Development*, 52(3), 47–66. DOI: 10.1007/BF02504675

Kirschner, P. A. (2001). Using integrated electronic environments for collaborative teaching/learning. *Learning and Instruction*, 10, 1–9. DOI: 10.1016/S0959-4752(00)00021-9

Knopf, T., Stumpp, S., & Michelis, D. (2021). How online collaborative learning leads to improved online learning experience in higher education. In Karpasitis, C. (Ed.), *ECSM 2021 8th European Conference on Social Media 2021* (No. July, pp. 119-127).

Kreijns, K., Kirschner, P. A., & Jochems, W. (2003). Identifying the pitfalls for social interaction in computer-supported collaborative learning environments: A review of the research. *Computers in Human Behavior*, 19(3), 335–353. DOI: 10.1016/S0747-5632(02)00057-2

Kurniawati, A. (2022). Google Docs to manage an EFL writing class: How it helps and what to prepare. [JEE]. *Journal of English and Education*, 8(2), 97–109. DOI: 10.20885/jee.v8i2.25740

Kwak, N., & Ramirez, F. O. (2019). Is engineering harder to crack than science? A cross-national analysis of women's participation in male-dominated fields of study in higher education. *Annual Review of Comparative and International Education*, 2018(37), 159–183. DOI: 10.1108/S1479-367920190000037014

Laal, M., & Laal, M. (2012). Collaborative learning: What is it? *Procedia: Social and Behavioral Sciences*, 31, 491–495. DOI: 10.1016/j.sbspro.2011.12.092

Lämsä, J., Hämäläinen, R., Koskinen, P., Viiri, J., & Lampi, E. (2021). What do we do when we analyse the temporal aspects of computer-supported collaborative learning? A systematic literature review. *Educational Research Review*, 33, 100387. DOI: 10.1016/j.edurev.2021.100387

Li, Y. (2023). The effect of online collaborative writing instruction on enhancing writing performance, writing motivation, and writing self-efficacy of Chinese EFL learners. *Frontiers in Psychology*, 14, 1165221. DOI: 10.3389/fpsyg.2023.1165221 PMID: 37441335

Lomas, C., Burke, M., & Page, C. L. (2008). Collaboration tools. *Educause Learning Initiative*, 2(11). http://www.ccti.colfinder.org/sites/default/files/PreService_International/resources/KD/M4/U4/Collaboration%20Tools.pdf

Malecka, B., Boud, D., & Carless, D. (2022). Eliciting, processing and enacting feedback: Mechanisms for embedding student feedback literacy within the curriculum. *Teaching in Higher Education*, 27(7), 908–922. DOI: 10.1080/13562517.2020.1754784

Mills, M. S. (2013). Collaborative presentations using Google Docs. In *The Plugged-In Professor* (pp. 151–163). Chandos Publishing. DOI: 10.1016/B978-1-84334-694-4.50012-0

Mohammed, M., & AL-Jaberi, M. A. (2021). Google Docs or Microsoft Word? Master's students' engagement with instructor written feedback on academic writing in a cross-cultural setting. *Computers and Composition*, 62, 102672. DOI: 10.1016/j.compcom.2021.102672

Moonma, J. (2021). Comparing collaborative writing activity in EFL classroom: Face-to-face collaborative writing versus online collaborative writing using Google Docs. *Asian Journal of Education and Training*, 7(4), 204–215. DOI: 10.20448/journal.522.2021.74.204.215

O'Connor, K. (2022). Constructivism, curriculum and the knowledge question: Tensions and challenges for higher education. *Studies in Higher Education*, 47(2), 412–422. DOI: 10.1080/03075079.2020.1750585

Oates, M., Crichton, K., Cranor, L., Budwig, S., Weston, E. J., Bernagozzi, B. M., & Pagaduan, J. (2022). Audio, video, chat, email, or survey: How much does online interview mode matter? *PLoS One*, 17(2), e0263876. DOI: 10.1371/journal.pone.0263876 PMID: 35192659

Olesen, M. (2020). Cooperative collaboration in the hybrid space of Google Docs-based group work. *Education Sciences*, 10(10), 269. DOI: 10.3390/educsci10100269

Özdemir, O. (2021). A case study regarding the comparison of collaborative writing in digital and face-to-face environments. *International Journal of Psychology and Educational Studies*, 8(2), 246–258. DOI: 10.52380/ijpes.2021.8.2.425

Rambe, P. (2017). Spaces for interactive engagement or technology for differential academic participation? Google Groups for collaborative learning at a South African University. *Journal of Computing in Higher Education*, 29(2), 353–387. DOI: 10.1007/s12528-017-9141-5

Ramsay, P. A. (2011). Much writing begets good writing: Some considerations for teaching writing in an Anglophone Creole context. *Caribbean Curriculum*, 18, 27-42. https://journals.sta.uwi.edu/ojs/index.php/cc/article/view/577

Razali, S. N., Shahbodin, F., Hussin, H., & Bakar, N. (2015). Factors affecting the effective online collaborative learning environment. In Abraham, A., Muda, A., & Choo, Y. H. (Eds.), *Pattern analysis, intelligent security and the Internet of Things: Advances in intelligent systems and computing* (Vol. 355). Springer., DOI: 10.1007/978-3-319-17398-6_20

Revere, L., & Kovach, J. V. (2011). Online technologies for engaged learning: A meaningful synthesis for educators. *Quarterly Review of Distance Education*, 12(2), 13–124, 149–150. https://www.proquest.com/openview/ee56bfc90cac37ad96a4f6be61918f02/1?pq-origsite=gscholar&cbl=29705

Storch, N. (2019). Collaborative writing as peer feedback. In Hyland, K., & Hyland, F. (Eds.), *Feedback in second language writing: Contexts and issues* (pp. 143–161). Cambridge University Press. DOI: 10.1017/9781108635547.010

Susilawati, S., Fajriah, Y. N., & Yunita, S. (2023, July). Google Docs in English for Business Purposes courses: The exploration of students' acceptance. In *ELT Forum: Journal of English Language Teaching* (Vol. 12, No. 2, pp. 98-109). https://doi.org/ DOI: 10.15294/elt.v12i2.67253

Talan, T. (2021). The effect of computer-supported collaborative learning on academic achievement: A meta-analysis study. [IJEMST]. *International Journal of Education in Mathematics, Science, and Technology*, 9(3), 426–448. DOI: 10.46328/ijemst.1243

Tan, J. S., & Chen, W. (2022). Peer feedback to support collaborative knowledge improvement: What kind of feedback feed-forward? *Computers & Education*, 187, 104467. DOI: 10.1016/j.compedu.2022.104467

Teng, M. F. (2021). The effectiveness of incorporating metacognitive prompts in collaborative writing on academic English writing skills. *Applied Cognitive Psychology*, 35(3), 659–673. DOI: 10.1002/acp.3789

Trengove, E. (2017). Peer interaction as mechanism for providing timely and accessible feedback to a large undergraduate class. *International Journal of Electrical Engineering Education*, 54(2), 119–130. DOI: 10.1177/0020720916688486

Warrican, S. J. (2015). Fostering true literacy in the Commonwealth Caribbean: Bridging the cultures of home and school. In Smith, P., & Kumi-Yeboah, A. (Eds.), *Handbook of research on cross-cultural approaches to language and literacy development* (pp. 367–392). IGI Global. DOI: 10.4018/978-1-4666-8668-7.ch015

Warrican, S. J., Alleyne, M. L., Smith, P., Cheema, J., & King, J. R. (2019). Peer effects in the individual and group literacy achievement of high-school students in a bi-dialectal context. *Reading Psychology*, 40(2), 117–148. DOI: 10.1080/02702711.2019.1571545

Woodard, R., & Babcock, A. (2014). Designing writing tasks in Google Docs that encourage conversation: An inquiry into feedback and revision. In Anderson, R., & Mims, C. (Eds.), *Handbook of research on digital tools for writing instruction in K-12 settings* (pp. 1–29). IGI Global. DOI: 10.4018/978-1-4666-5982-7.ch001

Woodrich, M. P., & Fan, Y. (2017). Google Docs as a tool for collaborative writing in the middle school classroom. *Journal of Information Technology Education*, 16, 391–410. http://jite.informingscience.org/documents/Vol16/JITEv16ResearchP391-410Woodrich3331.pdf. DOI: 10.28945/3870

ADDITIONAL READING

Fromm, J., Radianti, J., Wehking, C., Stieglitz, S., Majchrzak, T. A., & vom Brocke, J. (2021). More than experience? On the unique opportunities of virtual reality to afford a holistic experiential learning cycle. *The Internet and Higher Education*, 50, 100804. DOI: 10.1016/j.iheduc.2021.100804

Norman, D. (2014). *Turn signals are the facial expressions of automobiles*. Diversion Books.

Norman, D. A. (1988). *The design of everyday things*. Basic Books.

KEY TERMS AND DEFINITIONS

Academic Writing Instruction: The process of teaching students how to write effectively in academic contexts, focusing on skills such as research, critical analysis, and proper citation.

Asynchronous Collaboration: The ability for multiple users to contribute to a document or project at different times, allowing them to provide feedback, make revisions, and add contributions to the shared work at their own convenience.

Collaborative Learning: An educational approach where students work together in groups to achieve shared learning goals, promoting active participation, critical thinking, and knowledge construction.

Collaborative Writing: The joint effort of two or more individuals to create a single written document, pooling their ideas, expertise, and contributions throughout the writing process to achieve a common goal.

Computer-Supported Collaborative Learning: An educational approach where shared learning processes, such as knowledge building and group cognition, and shared learning activities, such as elaboration, co-elaboration, and argumentation, occur in a computer-supported setting.

Digital Literacy: The ability to effectively navigate, evaluate, and create information using digital technologies, encompassing skills such as information literacy, media literacy, and technological proficiency.

Peer Editing: A collaborative process in which students review and provide feedback on each other's writing, offering suggestions for improvement and helping to refine the clarity, coherence, and effectiveness of the written work.

Synchronous (or Real-Time) Collaboration: The ability for multiple users to work together on a document or project simultaneously, allowing for immediate feedback, revisions, and contributions.

Online Collaborative Learning: An educational approach where shared learning processes, such as knowledge building and group cognition, and shared learning activities, such as elaboration, co-elaboration, and argumentation, occur in a computer-supported setting.

Chapter 9
Utilising Digital Tools to Enhance Teamwork Among Adult Learners in a Postgraduate Course

Leesha Nicole Roberts
https://orcid.org/0000-0001-7881-0087
University of Trinidad and Tobago, Trinidad and Tobago

ABSTRACT

This chapter provides an in-depth examination of the role of digital tools in enhancing virtual teamwork among adult learners in higher education, focusing on the "Fundamentals of Educational Technology" course within the Master of Education in Innovative Learning Technologies (MEILT) Programme at the Advanced Learning Institute (ALI). Through a qualitative narrative inquiry, the chapter explores how digital platforms such as Learning Management Systems (LMS), video conferencing, and social media facilitate communication, collaboration, and learning outcomes among part-time students. The analysis highlights the benefits of these tools in promoting flexibility, real-time collaboration, and distributed cognition while addressing challenges such as digital etiquette and technological fluency. Additionally, the chapter offers practical recommendations for improving the use of digital tools to support teamwork in adult education within the context of Trinidad and Tobago.

DOI: 10.4018/979-8-3693-3852-0.ch009

Copyright © 2025, IGI Global. Copying or distributing in print or electronic forms without written permission of IGI Global is prohibited.

INTRODUCTION

Global challenges have shifted higher education towards virtual learning, necessitating advanced digital tools. Abedini et al. (2021) highlight the effectiveness of digital platforms in promoting adult learning within online communities by enhancing engagement and outcomes. This chapter analyses Learning Management Systems (LMS), video conferencing, and social media in facilitating teamwork among adult learners in the "Fundamentals of Educational Technology" course. This foundational course in the Master of Education in Innovative Learning Technologies (MEILT) at the Advanced Learning Institute (ALI) targets part-time students. Using a qualitative narrative inquiry approach during the September 2023 teaching period, it captures the experiences of both the instructor and learners, evaluating digital tools' effectiveness in improving group dynamics, collaboration, communication efficiency, and learning outcomes. Practical recommendations for using digital tools in Trinidad and Tobago adult education are provided.

Virtual Teamwork in Adult Education Using Digital Tools

The use of practical digital tools like Canvas, WhatsApp, and ZOOM has significantly transformed communication practices among university students globally, including those in Trinidad and Tobago. These tools facilitate immediate and asynchronous communication, allowing for more flexible interaction that suits the schedules of adult learners. WhatsApp groups, in particular, have become a staple in student communication, offering a platform for quick updates, sharing class materials, and peer support. This immediacy helps maintain a continuous flow of communication that is crucial for effective teamwork, especially when face-to-face meetings are not possible.

The Importance of Teamwork in Adult Learning Environments

Advancements in ICT mirror the shifting nature and needs of adult learners. An adult learner within the context of this chapter is defined as a learner beyond the usual school-going age who needs education for personal and professional development. The main characteristics of these learners are self-direction, life experience, readiness to learn, a problem-centered orientation, and internal motivation. Adult learners come with rich experiences that enhance their learning and, therefore, favour flexible, relevant, and practical educational programs (Brookfield, 1985; Connolly, 2008; Knowles et al., 2005; Merriam & Baumgartner, 2020; Owusu-Agyeman, 2019; Schunk, 2012). Theoretical frameworks in adult education, such as andragogy, self-directed learning, and transformative learning, provide essential insights into how adults learn most effectively. Knowles (1975) defines Andragogy as adult learners who are self-motivated and bring valuable life experiences to their learning process. Knowles (1975) further states that in self-directed learning, adults take responsibility for their learning and seek out resources and opportunities independently. Additionally, Mezirow (2018) Transformative learning theory refers to the fundamental shift at the level of basic premises in thought, feelings, and actions toward a more open, inclusive, and discerning perspective. These theoretical perspectives are highly pertinent for adult learners who use digital tools to help them undertake virtual teamwork and facilitate critical reflection on collaborative problem-solving, resulting in a transformative shift in their personal and professional growth through meaningful, technology-enhanced interactions (Makri & Vlachopoulos, 2020).

With the shift towards digital learning, virtual teamwork has become a cornerstone of adult education. It is not just a replication of traditional teamwork in an online setting but a fundamental transformation in education (Varhelahti & Turnquist, 2021). The use of technology is now seen as vital in adult education for flexible, accessible, and individual learning, corresponding to the diversity of schedules and needs of adult learners. In this manner, it is a catalyst for adults to enhance engagement and collaboration using these virtual platforms for teamwork. Tools like Office 365 and Google Docs have revolutionised teamwork, enabling real-time interaction and supporting adults who juggle education with work and family responsibilities (Bellare et al., 2023). The flexibility of asynchronous collaboration allows teams to engage at their convenience, fostering dynamic interaction, community, and accessibility. This ensures that teamwork remains inclusive and attainable, regardless of their personal or professional commitments. This collaborative experience in teamwork via the use of digital tools in adult education aligns with Vygotsky's social development theory, which emphasises peer interactions in learning (Barnett, 2019). These environments use social interaction, tailored scaffolding, peer learning, and culturally relevant tools to engage learners. Digital tools in virtual teams facilitate and enrich this interaction, promoting Discovery Learning and Distributed Cognition among adult learners (King, 1998; Rogers, 2006).

Challenges of Digital Tools in Virtual Teamwork

In a team environment, adult learners might struggle to find common free time between different schedules and balance their personal and professional lives with school, which can make it difficult for them to adjust to expectations that may arise within the team environment (Brandenburger & Janneck, 2021; Jony & Serradell-López, 2021). To address these issues, virtual tools allow team members to create flexible scheduling, establish clear communication protocols, and resolve conflicts more efficiently, which could enhance teamwork in adult education.

Furthermore, virtual teamwork in adult education presents challenges. It requires team members to learn new skills in digital etiquette and online communication, and fostering a sense of community without face-to-face interaction is difficult. Nonverbal cues are missing, leading to misunderstandings and weaker interpersonal connections. In Trinidad and Tobago, where social interactions are highly valued, this is particularly challenging. Diverse cultural backgrounds enrich teamwork but complicate communication styles (Homan et al., 2020). To alleviate these challenges, educators can use strategies that enhance virtual presence and cohesion, emphasising teamwork and collaboration. Recognising and accommodating cultural differences within digital platforms is crucial, supported by structured guidelines and team-building activities to improve digital collaboration skills (Baviera et al., 2022; Bhargava & Sharma, 2024).

BACKGROUND

Advanced Learning Institute (ALI) started as a higher education institution in 2004 with a primary focus on the development of Trinidad and Tobago in engineering and technology. Over the years, Advanced Learning Institute expanded its focus to align with the United Nations Sustainability Development Goals (SDG) in education, the humanities, environmental studies, agriculture, and food security. In 2008, the Advanced Learning Institute was locally accredited initially for five years by the Accreditation Council of Trinidad and Tobago (ACTT), seven years in 2017, and is currently preparing to renew its accreditation. As a twelve-year-old accredited academic institution, Advanced Learning Institute has a fair amount of the nation's citizens and some Caribbean neighbours seeking tertiary education at the full-time and part-time programs within the age groups of 15 to over 45 years at nine campuses in Trinidad and Tobago.

This chapter is positioned within the Faculty of Education (FoE), Master of Education at the Advanced Learning Institute. The academic staff consists of over 40 faculty members ranging from Instructor 1 to Associate Professors. The FoE graduates approximately 1500 students yearly and is one of the prominent programs within the Advanced Learning Institute. Younger students within this program are usually registered full-time, and older students are generally part-time. The FoE accepts students desirous of attaining a Bachelor of Education, Diploma in Education, or Master of Education, and there is typically a mixture of teaching and non-teaching students.

Specifically, the MEILT Programme is a two-year taught degree for teachers, corporate trainers, administrators, and anyone seeking advanced knowledge and training in technology-based instruction to explore careers in areas such as educational leadership, instructional software/games developers, E-Learning consultants, instructional designers, and technology support specialists.

This study focused on Fundamentals of Educational Technology, an introduction to the basic principles and practices of instructional technology. It is a foundation course in the MEILT Programme and is offered primarily to year one part-time students during the September semester. The cohort used for this study is the 2023 year one group, which consisted of twelve students and the course instructor.

THEORETICAL FRAMEWORK

For the context of this study, "Digital Tools" are defined as any Information Communication Technology (ICT) devices and software applications that can be used for teaching and learning experiences by teachers and students within and outside of the classroom settings (Moorhouse, 2023; Moorhouse & Yan, 2023; Ovcharuk et al., 2020). The integration of digital tools such as LMS, social media, and video conferencing platforms in tertiary education has significantly transformed traditional andragogy approaches. This transformation is particularly evident among adult learners who balance studies with professional commitments. Moreover, the discourse has demonstrated that these tools enhance productivity, foster teamwork, and improve collaboration in educational settings (Moorhouse & Yan, 2023; Ovcharuk et al., 2020; Rahmadi, 2020). Specifically, digital tools support effective teamwork and enrich adult learning experiences at the university level, particularly when integrated into flipped learning models and grounded in theoretical frameworks such as conversation theory, distributed cognition, discovery learning, and connectivism. Furthermore, the Community of Inquiry (COI) framework underscores the benefits of these digital tools in digital learning: blended learning and online learning, also known as virtual learning (Hughes & Roblyer, 2023).

Use of Digital Tools in Tertiary Education

Learning Management Systems (LMS)

LMS platforms, such as Canvas, have become integral to delivering structured educational content. Notably, they offer flexible access to course materials, thus enabling asynchronous learning, which is crucial for adult learners. Moreover, research indicates that LMS platforms facilitate virtual learning approaches, effectively supporting the diverse lifestyles of working students by allowing them to access learning at their convenience (Al Rawashdeh et al., 2021; Chaubey & Bhattacharya, 2015; Garcia et al., 2021; Shurygin et al., 2021).

Social Media

Social media tools, such as WhatsApp, are increasingly employed to create informal learning environments that facilitate peer interaction and collaboration. These platforms enable adult learners to form networks extending beyond traditional classroom boundaries, thereby fostering a sense of community and shared learning. Consequently, social media has emerged as a vital component in modern educational strategies, enhancing the overall learning experience by promoting connectivity and engagement among learners (Naghdipour & Manca, 2023; Venter, 2020).

Video Conferencing

Platforms such as ZOOM and Microsoft Teams have revolutionised real-time, synchronous learning and collaboration. For adult learners, video conferencing closely mimics classroom interactions, thereby helping to overcome the isolation often experienced in online learning environments. Consequently, these platforms play a crucial role in enhancing the engagement and effectiveness of remote education for adult learners (Mpungose, 2023).

The integration of digital tools like LMS, social media, and video conferencing has transformed tertiary education. LMS platforms provide flexible access to course materials, supporting adult learners. Social media and video conferencing enhance peer interaction and collaboration, fostering community and reducing online learning isolation. Educational theories, such as the Community of Inquiry framework, ensure these tools effectively support virtual teamwork and enhance learning outcomes.

THEORETICAL FOUNDATIONS

Adult Learning Theory, Virtual Teamwork and Communities of Practice (CoP)

Knowles' principles of andragogy underscore the self-directed nature of adult learning, positing that adults are intrinsically motivated learners with a strong inclination to apply their knowledge practically (Knowles, 1975). Digital tools align with these principles by offering practical, real-world applications and facilitating learning that seamlessly integrates with the learners' professional and personal lives.

Moreover, the incorporation of digital tools in higher education fosters teamwork, a critical component of adult learning. Virtual teamwork in online higher education focuses on specific factors that influence successful collaboration. These factors are motivation, communication, knowledge sharing, performance, coordination, cohesion, and trust (Jony & Serradell-López, 2021). Thereby fostering a CoP because of the social learning within groups and the shared common educational interest (Wenger, 1998). Collaborative platforms enable adult learners to engage in team-based projects, thereby enhancing their ability to work effectively in group settings and apply theoretical knowledge in practical, cooperative contexts. This integration not only supports self-directed learning but also reinforces the development of essential teamwork skills, which are vital in both academic and professional environments (Henschke, 2020).

Figure 1. Theoretical framework (Roberts, 2024)

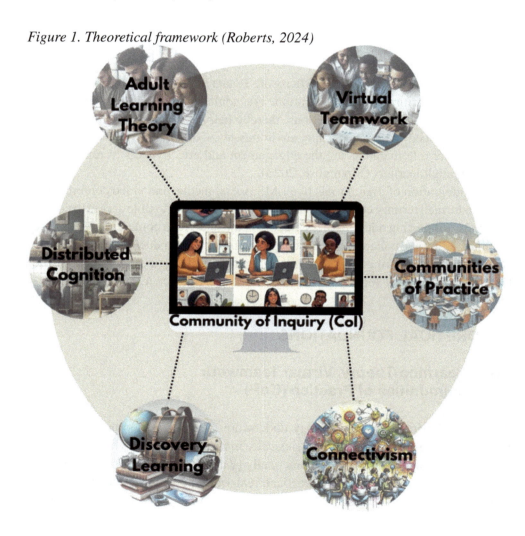

Instructional Theory

Community of Inquiry (COI) Framework and Connectivism

The COI framework is at the center of this theoretical framework and posits that effective online learning requires cognitive, social, and teaching presence (Garrison et al., 2001). It is used to assess the quality of online and blended learning environments. Additionally, Connectivism is a theory that can be used in the learning and instructional context to explain how people learn in the digital age (AlDahdouh et al., 2015). It emphasizes the impact of the Internet on creating new learning opportunities (Baque et al., 2020). Digital tools facilitate these presences by enabling interactions that are crucial for deep and meaningful learning experiences. For instance, video conferencing can enhance social presence, making the learning experience more engaging for adults. This type of holistic approach not only supports the individual learner's journey but also enhances the collective experience, leading to more successful teamwork and better learning outcomes.

Discovery Learning and Flipped Learning

Ozdem-Yilmaz and Bilican (2020) describe Discovery Learning as a cognitive process in which students actively engage in exploring and understanding concepts, shaping their minds to learn and internalize cultural knowledge. Additionally, Flipped Learning reverses the traditional educational paradigm by delivering instructional content, often online, outside of the classroom setting (Muzyka & Luker, 2016). This model empowers adult learners to engage with material at their own pace, thereby enhancing their understanding and retention of the content (Bergmann & Sams, 2012; Muzyka & Luker, 2016). Using Discovery Learning with the Flipped learning strategy allows for the more effective use of classroom time, which can be dedicated to discussions and collaborative activities. Such an approach is particularly beneficial in higher education and the application of digital tools usage because it promotes teamwork and group work, essential components of adult learning. By using digital tools to engage in collaborative tasks, adult learners can apply theoretical concepts in practical contexts, develop critical thinking skills, and enhance their ability to work effectively in diverse group settings in an online environment (Lakkala et al., 2021). These models not only adhere to the principles of andragogy but also equip adult learners with the necessary skills to meet the collaborative demands of professional environments (Butcher, 2020; Knowles, 1975; Marcut & Chisiu, 2018).

Conversation Theory and Distributed Cognition

Developed by Pask, conversation theory emphasizes learning through dialogue and understanding diverse perspectives (Heinze et al., 2007). Digital tools, particularly social media and forums integrated within LMSs, facilitate these meaningful conversations, which are crucial for knowledge construction among adult learners (Blau et al., 2020; Lacka et al., 2021). In higher education, such platforms promote teamwork and collaborative learning, enabling students to engage in group discussions, share insights, and critically analyze different viewpoints. Perry (2003) defined Distributed Cognition as a framework that "allows researchers to consider all of the factors relevant to the task, bringing together the people, the problem, and the tools used into a single unit of analysis" (p. 196). The combination of digital tools and interactive learning processes that include digital tools not only enhances comprehension and retention but also prepares adult learners for the collaborative and communicative demands of professional environments, reinforcing the principles of andragogy (Goñi et al., 2020; Henschke, 2020).

As a whole, incorporating digital tools in adult education, aligned with Knowles' andragogy principles, enhances self-directed, practical learning. This approach integrates seamlessly into learners' professional and personal lives. Flipped learning and conversation theory further support this by allowing learners to control their interactions and fostering rich dialogues, which are crucial for comprehension and collaboration. This synergy not only improves knowledge retention and application but also develops critical teamwork and communication skills. Thus, applying these theories thoughtfully ensures that adult learners are prepared for the modern workforce, making digital tools indispensable in higher education.

THE STUDY DESIGN

This inquiry used qualitative methodology and narrative inquiry research. Narrative Inquiry effectively captures human experiences in Indigenous contexts like Trinidad and Tobago through storytelling (Barkhuizen & Consoli, 2021). It amplifies Indigenous voices, preserves cultural heritage, and fosters community empowerment, supporting educational development, policy-making, and cultural preservation by respecting and understanding Indigenous epistemologies, such as the stories of the instructor and students in this inquiry (Patel, 2015; Smith, 2021).

THE CONTEXTUAL SETTINGS

The study is focused on a particular course in the MEILT Program. This course introduces the basic principles and practices of instructional technology. It is a foundation course and is offered primarily to year one part-time students during the September semester. The cohort used for this study is the 2023-year one group, which consisted of twelve students and the course instructor.

Using the theoretical framework as a guide, the research questions attempted to investigate the impacts of technology on facilitating or impeding effective teamwork and collaborative learning, examining both positive contributions and potential barriers encountered by students. This study focused on identifying the functionalities and features of the university's Learning Management Systems (LMS), video conferencing platforms, and popular social media applications that either support or hinder collaborative educational activities among adult learners. Additionally, it intended to uncover specific usability issues faced by adult learners when using digital tools for teamwork. It explored potential improvements or strategies for optimizing these tools for adult learning and collaboration, considering the cultural and educational contexts specific to the Caribbean.

The following research questions guided the study:

1. How do digital tools facilitate or challenge teamwork dynamics and collaborative learning among adult learners in higher education?
2. What specific features of digital tools like CANVAS, ZOOM, and WhatsApp enhance or hinder their effectiveness for collaborative learning in the Caribbean educational context?
3. Are there any distinct usability challenges that adult learners face when utilizing digital platforms for teamwork and collaborative purposes in higher education?
4. How can digital tools be better leveraged to support adult pedagogy and enhance collaborative learning environments in Trinidad and Tobago and similar Caribbean higher education settings?

The study period lasted eight weeks, beginning on September 26 and ending on December 15. The instructor used the first ZOOM session to ask students about their willingness to participate in the semester-long study and communicated with the class representative via WhatsApp to schedule the one-hour focus group sessions via the ZOOM application at the end of the semester from 13 to 15 December 2023. Since there were 12 students, there were three focus group sessions with four students in each group. The sessions were based on the research questions.

The utilization of focus group sessions in this segment of the study proved invaluable, as it enabled the researcher to comprehensively understand and document the diverse range of ideas, feelings, and perspectives held by students regarding the facilitative role of digital tools in their teamwork processes, both during and following the weekly class sessions throughout the semester. The focus group sessions were meticulously prepared following a structured protocol comprising nineteen questions. This protocol included five Likert scale questions and fourteen open-ended questions aligned with the study's research questions. The instructor systematically discussed the scheduling of focus group sessions, obtained informed consent to record, detailed the transcription process, and outlined the member-checking procedure with participants to ensure the accuracy and reliability of the data collected.

Richardson and Adams St. Pierre (2018) posited that triangulation uses different methods (for example, interviews, documents, etc.) to validate findings from the assumption that there is an object or point to be triangulated. However, qualitative researchers do not triangulate – they crystallize. "Crystallization provides us with a deepened, complex, and thoroughly partial understanding of the topic" (Richardson & Adams St. Pierre, 2018, p. 1417). Therefore, observations, field notes, ZOOM recordings, and focus group interviews were used to ensure Crystallization in this inquiry.

Each week, the students were given group work activities in the form of Flipped Learning, ZOOM Breakout Room activities, and a Final Group Project. The instructor journaled about the course activities each week, and at the end of the semester, students participated in focus group sessions.

This inquiry utilized the verification strategies Denzin and Lincoln (2018) outlined to ensure Trustworthiness. Trustworthiness refers to qualitative rigor (Denzin & Lincoln, 2018). This inquiry used Credibility and Transferability techniques. Prolonged observation and engagement of CANVAS and ZOOM for Semester 1, 2024, for the Fundamentals of Educational Technology course and Member Checking increased the inquiry's Credibility and the Crystallization of sources and methods.

DATA ANALYSIS AND RESULTS

The results are presented and discussed according to each theme that emerged from data analysis and aligned to each research question. There are examples of how the autoethnography method supported each theme (feelings of worry, eagerness, etc.) and the reflections of student experiences and insights into how participants utilized digital tools during their group work activities for the semester. Chang (2016) argued that even though chronicling and inventorying can be used to recall personal memory data, researchers can add their unique strategies based on the context of the inquiry. If the researcher wants to use the technique of self-observation to collect data, there are two options: field notes with self-reflection and self-analysis or a culture gram. The instructor used field notes for self-reflection and self-analysis. The focus group questions were used in the data analysis process, which led to the discovery of the emerging themes. Both sets of data were merged and used to answer the research questions.

> The analysis of the transcription from both the self-reflection and the focus group data followed the procedures outlined by Miles et al. (2014):

1. The first cycle of coding utilized In Vivo coding, which uses words or short phrases in the participant's jargon and dialect (Miles et al., 2014). For instance, a term used repeatedly throughout the interview sessions was "easy to use."
2. Operational Definitions of the Codes: The codes' list was determined based on the first cycle codes. Miles et al. (2014) posited that properly defining codes removes misconceptions during the analysis and reporting.
3. Emerging themes: The researcher can organize the data in themes for easy reference during reporting (Miles et al., 2014).

EMERGING THEMES

The field notes and the semi-structured interviews were analyzed using In Vivo and Axial coding methods (Saldaña, 2013). The participants are identified using pseudo-names to maintain the anonymity of the volunteers for the study. These emerging themes from the analysis were used to answer the research question for the study.

Analysis of Semi-Structured Interviews

First Cycle Coding: In-Vivo Codes

The data revealed responses based on the identified In Vivo codes, focusing on the most common categories of the phrases and words. This helped categorize the data and provide a more structured view of the participants' feedback. The students discussed their experiences with the LMS and video conferencing tools they used frequently for the course, as well as how social media tools such as WhatsApp were used for informal communication among peers and instructors. The categories are as follows:

1. User Experience
    a. "Great virtual campus experience."
    b. "Difficulty getting used to the interface at first."
2. Communication and Collaboration
    a. "Quick communication with classmates."
    b. "Helped maintain the personal touch in collaborations."
3. Learning and Organization
    a. "All course materials in one place made collaboration easier."
    b. "Outdated tutorials were not very helpful."
4. Instructor and Tool Usage
    a. "Discrepancy in how instructors integrate tools."
    b. "Inconsistent usage by some instructors."
5. Future Enhancements
    a. "AI integration would make the process more efficient."
    b. "Enhancing real-time features would be more effective."

Second Cycle Coding Themes: Axial Codes

The second coding cycle used the Axial coding method (Saldaña, 2013). Based on the categories above, the themes are organised according to the research questions:

Research Question 1

How do digital tools facilitate or challenge teamwork dynamics and collaborative learning among adult learners in higher education?

Facilitation

This theme emerged from the instructor's field notes and the data transcribed from the focus group sessions. The instructor reflected that digital tools are present in all of the University's sanctioned resources, and educational principles value innovation, learner-centeredness, collaboration and teamwork, internationalization, and inclusivity as part of the teaching and learning policy. The instructor also revealed *that since joining the FoE in 2006, I have been told about student-centeredness and the use of problem-based learning strategies. Now, in 2023, I can see that we have come a long way with respect to providing digital tools for instructors and students to communicate (Instructor field notes, 26 – 29 September 2023).*

Students' reflections indicated convenience and flexibility in the use of Digital Tools in the course. Most students expressed that digital tool like Canvas, ZOOM, and WhatsApp offered great convenience, enabling adult learners to attend classes and collaborate on projects without the need to be physically present, both formally and informally. This is particularly beneficial for those balancing work, family, and study commitments. One student stated, "Love the convenience of Canvas paired with ZOOM supported by WhatsApp, which offered me a great virtual campus experience"(Interview with Nyasha Davis, December 14, 2023). Another student said, "My experiences with digital tools have been very good, easy to use, and convenient" (Interview with Tariq Walker, December 15, 2023). Another student, when reflecting on the use of the university's LMS, stated, "Canvas: I found Canvas to be simple to navigate and very useful" (Interview with Amara Roberts, December 13, 2023).

Students in the course also stated that the use of Digital Tools facilitated ease of Communication when it came to both in-course and outside-course activities with group members. The instructor noted that "tools like WhatsApp and ZOOM facilitated quick and effective communication, allowing for immediate feedback and coordination among group members, especially when a Flipped Learning activity had to be prepared for class the next week" (Instructor field notes, 16 – 20 October 2023).

Zuri Williams, a student in the course, stated that "WhatsApp was great for quick communication with classmates." (Interview by author, December 15, 2023). Another indicated that "Using WhatsApp for group discussions was very effective" (Interview with Malik Brown, December 14, 2023). Imani Anderson added that "ZOOM meetings helped our group stay connected and discuss project details easily" (interview by author, December 13, 2023).

In the second week of classes, the instructor reflected on the CANVAS discussion given to the students after the weekly class session.

Students watched a YouTube video, responded in groups, and then collaborated class-wide via a discussion board. For me, this strategy, aligned with the COI framework, facilitated timely feedback and large-group interaction, highlighting the potential effectiveness of flipped learning activities for my next session. (Instructor field notes, 2 – 6 October 2023).

Challenges

However, while students indicated that these digital tools facilitated their online learning experience and fostered teamwork both inside and outside of the course, challenges included the steep initial learning curve for CANVAS. "It took a learning curve to know the expectation of how each tool applies to group work in my classes" (Aaliyah Dass, December 13, 2023). Another student stated that "Initially, navigating Canvas was a bit challenging" (Kwame Lewis, December 14, 2023, and Nia Clarke agreed that one of her challenges when using the LMS as a first-year student was "getting used to the interface of these tools were difficult at first" (Interview by author, December 14, 2023). One of the students described CANVAS as "clunky at first, but eventually, I learned it over time" (Omari Richards, December 15, 2023). Others indicated that they found some of the digital tools difficult to navigate initially, which disrupted their collaborative efforts. Zainab Samaroo stated that "the interface was not very intuitive at the beginning" (interview by author, December 15, 2023), and another student agreed by saying, "I found the layout of Canvas confusing at first" (Zuri Williams, December 15, 2023). The instructor expressed

This year's MEILT Program cohort includes educators, corporate professionals, and recent graduates from the FoE undergraduate program. I am eager to see how they integrate their diverse experiences into a course focused on the theoretical foundations of instructional technologies. Their varied backgrounds should provide rich insights and contribute to a dynamic learning environment for discussions and collaborative projects (Instructor field notes, 9 – 13 October 2023).

Research Question 2: What specific features of digital tools like CANVAS, ZOOM, and WhatsApp enhance or hinder their effectiveness for collaborative learning in the Caribbean educational context?

Enhancing Features

This theme had three subthemes: Organization of Content, Real-time Communication and Instant Messaging and Multimedia Sharing.

Organization of Learning Content: The course instructor reflects on the way she organizes her content in her postgraduate courses to facilitate more group work within the online environment. She notes that tools like CANVAS allow for organized access to course materials, which facilitates collaborative learning by keeping all members on the same page. The instructor revealed her process of developing the course page in CANVAS:

Using CANVAS has allowed me to design my course exactly as I have outlined it for my students. Each section is carefully chunked into modules, and resources are presented in a way that supports diverse learning styles and inclusivity. Still, even though the semester is in full swing, I have to go back and make minor changes based on the learners' context. The most beneficial aspect for me is the ability to organize students into groups for projects and discussions. This feature, combined with peer review using course rubrics, enhances the cognitive, social, and teaching presence in the course. It fosters active learning and communities of practice, emphasizing the importance of networks, interactions, and the use of tools and technology in the learning process (Instructor field notes, 9 – 13 October 2023).

Students had access to the course page for the entire semester. During focus group sessions, they reflected on their interactions with the course page during the third week. One student, previously an undergraduate at FoE, remarked, "I used Canvas throughout my years at UTT, and de way this course page was laid out it made me more organized, so I will say my experience improved over the years as the content was organized better" (Kwame Lewis, December 14, 2023). Another student noted, "Having all my course materials in one place on Canvas made it easier to collaborate" (Jabari Thompson, December 13, 2023). A third student stated, "Canvas helped me to keep meh assignments and things well-organized" (Omari Richards, December 15, 2023).

Another sub-theme that emerged was real-time communication. Students noted that ZOOM facilitated crucial weekly face-to-face interactions with the instructor. The instructor described that "breakout room activities enhanced engagement and clarified misconceptions during lectures. Some students preferred online learning for its efficiency in managing transport and work commitments" (Instructor field notes, 30 October – 3 November 2023).

These findings highlight the importance of real-time communication tools in fostering effective virtual teamwork and engagement. Aaliyah Dass stated that "ZOOM for online classes was very good for me because I travel to and from work and there are days when getting transport is difficult, such as on rainy days when town flood out" (interview by author, December 13, 2023). Another student agreed and stated,

ZOOM was great for live classes and discussions because I also travel, and many times I listened to the lecture while in the maxi and continued when I got home, but what makes it beneficial for me is whatever I miss I can go back and get the recording via CANVAS (Amara Roberts, December 13, 2023).

Another student favored real-time communication for interactivity and stated, "Using ZOOM for real-time meetings helped maintain the personal touch in our collaborations during the semester. Meeting classmates and working in the breakout rooms was important for me" (Nia Clarke, December 14, 2023). However, some students admitted that they had challenges with ZOOM during the semester in the area of internet use and bandwidth. One student, Zainab Samaroo, stated that sometimes she used up all her data for the month because she had to log into the class while at work on her phone or as she travelled home. She states

If I had to find myself in a face-to-face classroom, then that issue won't occur. Plus, many times, I get dropped and miss parts of the class or the electricity goes out, and I miss the entire class activity, but here is where I appreciate the group work because we have ways to work around it. I normally WhatsApp a group member, and they tell Miss my situation, or I send my part of the activity via WhatsApp. After I watch the recording, when I get back service (interview by author, December 15, 2023).

Instant messaging and multimedia were another frequently discussed sub-theme that emerged from the focus group sessions. The students in all three sessions indicated that they frequently use WhatsApp, which supports instant messaging and multimedia sharing, enabling quick dissemination of information and resources among group members. Tariq Walker, a student, stated, "Being able to contact my group member to ask for clarification on my part of the project is always an important factor for me, even though I don't like groups" (interview by author, December 15, 2023). This indicates that instant messaging and multimedia-sharing features have made it easier to communicate and collaborate outside of traditional learning situations. Another student stated that "WhatsApp was effective for quick sharing of class updates and resources" (Malik Brown, December 15, 2023). Another student stated, "Using WhatsApp, we could quickly discuss and share materials for group projects" (Zuri Williams, December 15, 2023).

Hindering Features

While students generally expressed positive views about using digital tools for group work during the semester, several challenges were also identified. The data revealed the theme of "Hindering Features," encompassing two sub-themes: outdated tutorials and inconsistent instructor usage. These sub-themes, as articulated by the students, are discussed in detail.

During the focus group sessions, students disclosed that while the ALI provided CANVAS and ZOOM for students and instructors, some of the tutorials offered needed to be updated. Several students, particularly those who had been out of academic schooling for over three years, expressed frustration with learning to use the sanctioned LMS and video conferencing tools. The discrepancy between the outdated tutorials and the current versions of the applications hindered their ability to learn and adapt. This challenge was especially pronounced among adult learners reentering the higher education system. Imani Anderson stated, "The video tutorials available use older versions that do not look like the CANVAS currently available" (interview by author, December 13, 2023). Another student agreed and stated, "The tutorials for using some tools were outdated and not very helpful" (Jabari Thompson, December 13, 2023). One student indicated that when she realized the tutorials provided were outdated, she went on her search and stated, "Finding current and relevant tutorials for these tools was a challenge" (Nia Clarke, December 14, 2023).

The next sub-theme that emerged from the data was "Inconsistent Use by Instructors." The instructor expressed that during a class session, some of the students indicated that there is often a discrepancy in how different instructors integrate tools like CANVAS into their courses, which can lead to confusion and inconsistent experiences for students. She further revealed

Some students are still asking about how to navigate CANVAS, which surprises me. One student inquired about the location of ZOOM recordings on the page, prompting me to share my ZOOM screen to demonstrate where to access the course recordings. During this demonstration, another student asked where the pre-class presentations were located, and I had to guide them to the modules section. I was quite shocked when several students revealed that, for their other courses, all materials are found in the files section, requiring them to search and download as needed. (Instructor field notes, 16 – 20 October 2023).

Some of the students stated, "There is a discrepancy among the lecturers and how much they integrate Canvas into their course, so I was shocked to see this course page well organized" (Kwame Lewis, December 13, 2023). Another agreed and stated, "Some instructors barely use the digital tools, which to me allows students to have inconsistent usage" (Malik Brown, December 14, 2023). Another student stated, "The varying levels of integration by different lecturers made it confusing, but I can say that this course really allowed me to experience the collaboration of the course virtually" (Zuri Williams, December 15, 2023).

Research Question 3: Are there any distinct usability challenges that adult learners face when utilizing digital platforms for teamwork and collaborative purposes in higher education?

Usability

This research focused on usability challenges faced by adult learners using digital tools for teamwork. Effective design ensures ease of navigation, reduces frustration, and enhances engagement. Three sub-themes emerged: steep learning curve, technology access, and familiarity, which the students discussed in detail.

Steep Learning Curve: Adult learners often face a significant learning curve when first introduced to digital tools, which can be a barrier to effective teamwork. This section is focused on students' perception of their user experiences while navigating the interface to interact in and out of classes. One student stated,

It took a learning curve to know the features of how each tool applies in CANVAS; for instance, I didn't realize that this course was awarding badges. I just used to see an email after I finished a module telling me I was awarded a badge, but I could never find where it was in CANVAS (Tariq Walker, December 15, 2023).

Another stated, "Initially, navigating Canvas was a bit challenging" (Amara Roberts, December 13, 2023). This confirms what students and the instructor revealed in the previous theme about hindering features. Another student stated, "Learning to use these tools effectively took some time" (Nia Clarke, December 14, 2023). However, students all agreed that WhatsApp groups were easy to use for their group meetings and to contact each other to discuss course content, which was frequently done whenever there was a Flipped learning activity. The instructor noted in the fourth week of the course in her journal:

I asked the students how they were accessing their learning resources if they were unsure of the navigation. One student explained that they formed a WhatsApp group for the class, where peers download and share the requested files. This indicates that while some students have adapted to using digital tools, others are still struggling, relying on peer assistance via WhatsApp to share notes before and after class. This collaborative approach underscores the importance of peer support in navigating educational technologies. (Instructor field notes, 16 – 20 October 2023).

Most of the students found the CANVAS interface difficult to navigate initially, which slowed down collaboration. For instance, when accessing the discussion peer review areas, one student stated, "Initially, the Canvas interface was difficult to use because the menus weren't obvious. I couldn't find the peer groups area or recognize that there was an icon to show we have one" (Zainab Samaroo, December 15, 2023). Another student remarked, "I found the interface of Canvas quite confusing at first" (Omari Richards, December 15, 2023). Nia Clarke commented, "The navigation in these tools was not very intuitive initially, and when you have group work and deadlines, it is frustrating" (interview by author, December 14, 2023).

Technology Access and Familiarity: During the focus group sessions, a few students indicated that they are not tech-savvy even though they have signed up for a technology-related postgraduate program. Some indicated that they struggled with the basic use of ZOOM, Canvas, and even WhatsApp. Several mature learners in the focus groups, like Amara, Nyasha, and Tariq, acknowledged that although they had previously used WhatsApp for personal communication, it was only upon joining the program that they fully utilized its features, including creating meeting events and conducting video conferences. Amara Roberts declared,

My experiences with digital tools are very good; I had to learn how to use all of them at first, which was the challenging part, but once I learned how to use them, it became easier. Like now I am a power WhatsApp user, and I know how to change my background on ZOOM so people cah see in meh house when we in class (Interview by author, December 13, 2023).

Another student noted,

I am not very tech-savvy, so using these tools was challenging at first, but with each Flipped Learning activity and for other courses when we had to meet up for group work, I learned them bit by bit. Now, at the end of the semester, I can say that I am competent in using CANVAS, ZOOM and WhatsApp for school. So I ready for next semester! (Tariq Walker, December 15, 2023).

Nyasha Davis commented,

Getting accustomed to the technology took some effort and patience, but I must say that working in a group where others knew how to use a particular digital tool was beneficial to me because my peers showed me when I didn't know (Interview with author, December 14, 2023).

Research Question 4: How can digital tools be better leveraged to support adult pedagogy and enhance collaborative learning environments in Trinidad and Tobago and similar Caribbean higher education settings?

The final research question aimed to assess students' perceptions of how digital tools could foster collaborative learning environments in higher education, particularly in Trinidad and Tobago, considering the digital divide challenges in ICT integration. The students' insights, as they perceived them, will be discussed in detail below through the identified sub-themes.

Provide Comprehensive and Updated Tutorials: Providing up-to-date and comprehensive tutorials and guides for using digital tools can help reduce the learning curve, especially for adult learners who need to know why they need to learn something before learning it, typically because they prefer to take charge of their learning process. Omari Richards asserted

If they know that working people are going back to school to get degrees, then they should create customized learning paths that are always updated and aligned to the version of the digital tool we are using. For example, I was really confused when the available video tutorials used older versions that did not look like the Canvas currently available (Interview with author, December 15, 2023).

Tariq Walker agreed and stated, "Yeah, updated tutorials would be very helpful in learning how to use these tools. I think Mobile-Friendly Platforms would also help because sometimes using ZOOM and CANVAS on your mobile is clumsy" (Interview with author, December 15, 2023). One student remarked,

based on the experience I had with this course, yuh know peer mentoring can be a way to support adult learners. I say this because when I got stuck, my group assisted; when some of them got stuck, and I could help, I helped, so yuh know, maybe tech-savvy students could assist those struggling with digital tools, and in that way, we all learn not just the digital tools but the course content (Nia Clarke, December. 14, 2023).

Standardized Digital Tool Usage Among Instructors is another theme that emerged from the data. One student observed, "There is a discrepancy among the lecturers regarding how much they integrate CANVAS into their course. To promote consistency, they can do professional development and encourage standardization among the lecturers" (Aaliyah Dass, December 13, 2023). Another stated, "Consistency in the use of these tools by all lecturers would be beneficial" (Nyasha Davis, December 14, 2023). Zuri Williams remarked, "I feel that a standardized approach to instructors' use of digital tools would reduce student confusion and promote better group work" (Interview with author, December 14, 2023). Overall, students felt that standardizing the use of digital tools across all instructors can provide a consistent experience for students.

Another sub-theme revealed is Leveraging AI For Personalized Learning. All of the students indicated that some AI use should be incorporated into their learning experience to ensure their group tasks are effectively completed. Jabari Thompson remarked, "The potential to use AI in the LMS can help students complete their tasks efficiently" (Interview with author, December 13, 2023). Another student mentioned,

"AI integration into learning tools would make the process more efficient" (Malik Brown, December 14, 2023). One student stated, "Using AI could provide personalized learning experiences and support" (Jabari Thompson, December 13, 2023).

Real-time communication and collaboration are other sub-themes that some students suggested to enhance the features of digital tools to improve the collaborative learning experience. Aaliyah Dass remarked, "ZOOM was very useful for video conferencing and online meetings for blended and online classes, so it should be available to students instead of us using things like GoogleMeet and Skype" (Interview with author, December 13, 2023). Another student stated, "Enhancing the real-time features would make these tools even more effective, like a live chat in CANVAS" (Jabari Thompson, December 13, 2023).

Informal Learning Communities is the final sub-theme. The instructor expressed that.

Tonight after class, I had an informal conversation with about 3 students regarding their group project. They shared that they have a WhatsApp group and have been progressing using that medium for the preliminary planning of the project. It is for that reason that they are seeking clarification on a part of the project because they all agreed via the group chat that they needed the clarification in order to move on. After speaking to them, it dawned on me that in adult learning, encouraging the use of tools like WhatsApp to create informal learning communities can foster better collaboration and peer support (Instructor field notes, 20 – 24 November 2023).

One student remarked, "WhatsApp was great for quick communication with classmates and coordinating group projects, so it should be encouraged in all classes" (Imani Anderson, December 13, 2023). Another stated, "Using WhatsApp for informal discussions and collaboration was very effective, and I was able to ask questions I was unclear about in class" (Nyasha Davis, December 14, 2023). Omari Richards asserted, "Informal learning communities on WhatsApp helped us stay connected and support each other" (Interview with author, December 15, 2023).

DISCUSSION

The qualitative feedback provided by the instructor and students offers valuable insights into the application of several educational theories and frameworks within the context of digital tools used in learning environments. Firstly, the principles of connectivism are evident in the participants' use of social media tools such as WhatsApp. These tools facilitate networked learning by enabling quick information sharing and maintaining connections with classmates and instructors. Similarly, video conferencing platforms like ZOOM also play a crucial role in real-time interactions, fostering a sense of community among learners during the semester for the course Fundamentals of Educational Technology (Lacka et al., 2021; Marcut & Chisiu, 2018).

Moreover, the Community of Inquiry (COI) framework was reflected in various aspects of the students' experiences. Cognitive presence is enhanced through digital tools that support interactive features and provide extensive online resources, aiding in a deeper understanding of course material. Additionally, social presence is promoted through discussion forums, group chats, and collaborative projects within CANVAS, ZOOM and WhatsApp, which encourage peer interaction. Furthermore, teaching presence is maintained through the structured guidance and availability of instructors on these digital platforms. (Moorhouse & Yan, 2023; Naghdipour & Manca, 2023)

In addition, distributed cognition was another prominent theme in the narratives. Students frequently mentioned the use of collaborative tools like CANVAS, Office 365, and Google Docs to complete assignments, which allowed for simultaneous editing and sharing of ideas, thus reflecting collective cognitive processes. The seamless integration of various digital tools within a single platform helps streamline group work and resource access, thereby enhancing collective problem-solving efforts (Hughes & Roblyer, 2023; Rogers, 2006; Sezer, 2024).

Furthermore, the students' comments align with adult learning theory, emphasizing the importance of self-directed learning and practical application. Students appreciated the flexibility of accessing learning materials at their convenience, enabling them to manage their learning pace. Additionally, instructional strategies such as Flipped Learning that facilitated real-world applications and collaborative discussion projects were particularly valued, as they resonate with the principles of adult learning (Henschke, 2020). Adult learners bring a wealth of experiences to their educational pursuits, enriching team interactions (Butcher, 2020). Tools like ZOOM enabled the sharing of these experiences by facilitating live discussions and presentations; WhatsApp facilitated informal, continuous communication and knowledge sharing, allowing adult learners to easily share insights and experiences, which is a key feature of user experience for applications of this nature (Abedini et al., 2021). Quick, on-the-go discussions via WhatsApp can help learners solve immediate problems or discuss topics relevant to their current course activities, making learning timely and directly applicable (Gachago et al., 2015; Rahmadi, 2020), as the instructor revealed,

Last week, I gave a Flipped learning activity, and students were required to complete the readings and the activity before class. The intention was for us to start the class with the activity and then discuss it. Each group presented their work, and

I could see that most of them worked as a team to complete it. It is easy to see those groups that collaborate to complete the task. Since this Flipped Learning Activity went well, I am going to continue doing these activities (Instructor field notes, 23 – 27 October 2023).

Similarly, teamwork is a recurring theme in the responses, with many students highlighting the effectiveness of collaborative digital tools. They provided specific examples of how these tools either enhanced or hindered their teamwork experiences. Challenges related to coordination and communication were noted, underscoring the importance of reliable digital tools in maintaining effective team dynamics (Fittipaldi, 2020; Rasiah, 2014). Adult learners often prefer a high degree of autonomy in their learning processes. In a teamwork context, this translates to managing roles, responsibilities, and deadlines with minimal external oversight. Canvas, as an LMS, supported this autonomy by allowing teams to manage projects through integrated features like assignment submissions, group forums, and calendar tools, helping to coordinate tasks and deadlines autonomously.

Lastly, the students' insights into shared learning goals and mutual engagement revealed the concept of communities of practice. These digital tools helped learners in the course achieve common academic objectives and foster a sense of belonging to a learning community. The weekly interactions through video conferencing in-class activities and continuous use of social media platforms outside of classes support ongoing engagement and knowledge exchange among peers. (Rahmadi, 2020)

In summary, the instructor and students' data collected from the focus group sessions underscores the crucial role of digital tools in supporting connected, collaborative, and self-directed learning environments. The integration of these tools effectively enhances learning outcomes and facilitates teamwork, reflecting the principles of various educational theories and frameworks.

FUTURE RESEARCH DIRECTIONS

While not generalizable, this study has emerged themes that can be further researched in the areas of teamwork, educational technology, and instructional design. This study focused on the use of digital tools like CANVAS, ZOOM, and WhatsApp for group work in one higher education institution using one postgraduate course in Trinidad and Tobago, which has revealed some research trends that can be further explored through research. Firstly, enhancing connectivity and collaboration tools among students is pivotal. Some of these tools already facilitate real-time communication, but future studies can explore their expanded role in bridging geographical gaps within small-state Caribbean countries like Trinidad and Tobago.

Moreover, the integration of artificial intelligence (AI) into digital learning platforms has emerged as a significant trend. AI has the potential to provide personalized learning experiences, and intelligent tutoring can support group work with tailored feedback. Consequently, further research can examine how AI can enhance adult learning outcomes in Trinidad and Tobago's unique context.

Additionally, digital literacy is becoming increasingly important as the use of digital tools becomes more prevalent. Future studies can evaluate the effectiveness of digital literacy programs, ensuring that both students and educators are proficient in using these technologies for group work and learning.

Furthermore, addressing the digital divide is crucial for equitable access to digital tools and resources. Further research can focus on solutions to ensure all students, regardless of socio-economic status, have access to necessary technology and connectivity.

Similarly, blended learning models, which combine online and face-to-face instruction, can be explored to determine the optimal mix for enhancing group work and learning outcomes. In Trinidad and Tobago, this includes considering cultural and infrastructural factors that influence blended learning adoption.

These emerging trends align with the Digital Transformation Framework Policy recently launched by the Ministry of Education (MOE). The policy emphasizes improving education quality through technology, promoting inclusivity and access, supporting innovative teaching methods, fostering collaboration, and leveraging data-driven decision-making (GORTT, 2022). By focusing on these areas, future research can contribute to the policy's goals, ensuring that the integration of digital tools in higher education supports broader educational transformation objectives in Trinidad and Tobago. This alignment ensures that technological advancements enhance learning experiences, promote equity, and improve overall educational outcomes in the country.

CONCLUSION

This study offers comprehensive insights into the ways various digital tools bolster educational theories and frameworks associated with employing group work in adult education learning contexts. Analysis of student experiences reveals that digital tools are pivotal in cultivating connected, collaborative, and self-directed learning environments. Moreover, the instructor's reflections highlight the significance of employing instructional and technological frameworks in alignment with adult education principles at the higher education level. The emergent themes from this study emphasize the critical importance of integrating digital tools effectively to enhance learning outcomes and foster teamwork in adult education.

Digital tools such as Canvas, Zoom, and WhatsApp exemplify resources that support andragogical principles by enhancing accessibility, flexibility, and relevance while leveraging the rich experiences of adult learners. These tools facilitate self-directed and experiential learning, addressing the orientation towards problem-solving and practical application inherent in group work. By thoughtfully integrating these digital tools, educators can create dynamic and effective learning environments that meet the intrinsic motivations and needs of adult learners engaged in group activities.

REFERENCES

Abedini, A., Abedin, B., & Zowghi, D. (2021). Adult learning in online communities of practice: A systematic review. *British Journal of Educational Technology*, 52(4), 1663–1694. DOI: 10.1111/bjet.13120

Al Rawashdeh, A. Z., Mohammed, E. Y., Al Arab, A. R., Alara, M., Al-Rawashdeh, B., & Al-Rawashdeh, B. (2021). Advantages and disadvantages of using e-learning in university education: Analyzing students' perspectives. *Electronic Journal of e-Learning*, 19(3), 107–117. DOI: 10.34190/ejel.19.3.2168

AlDahdouh, A., Osorio, A., & Caires, S. (2015). Understanding knowledge network, learning and connectivism. *International journal of instructional technology and distance learning, 12*(10).

Baque, P. G. C., Cevallos, M. A. M., Natasha, Z. B. M., & Lino, M. M. B. (2020). The contribution of connectivism in learning by competencies to improve meaningful learning. *International Research Journal of Management. IT and Social Sciences*, 7(6), 1–8.

Barkhuizen, G., & Consoli, S. (2021). *Pushing the edge in narrative inquiry* (Vol. 102). Elsevier.

Barnett, S. (2019). Application of Vygotsky's Social Development Theory. *Journal of Education and Practice*, 10(35), 1–4.

Baviera, T., Baviera-Puig, A., & Escribá-Pérez, C. (2022). Assessing Team Member Effectiveness among higher education students using 180 perspective. *International Journal of Management Education*, 20(3), 100702. DOI: 10.1016/j.ijme.2022.100702

Bellare, Y., Smith, A., Cochran, K., & Lopez, S. G. (2023). Motivations and barriers for adult learner achievement: Recommendations for institutions of higher education. *Adult Learning*, 34(1), 30–39. DOI: 10.1177/10451595211059574

Bergmann, J., & Sams, A. (2012). *Flip your classroom: Reach every student in every class every day*. International society for technology in education.

Bhargava, S., & Sharma, R. (2024). Student engagement through teamwork skills: The mediating role of psychological well-being. *Higher Education, Skills and Work-based Learning*, 14(2), 271–292. DOI: 10.1108/HESWBL-06-2022-0126

Blau, I., Shamir-Inbal, T., & Avdiel, O. (2020). How does the pedagogical design of a technology-enhanced collaborative academic course promote digital literacies, self-regulation, and perceived learning of students? *The Internet and Higher Education*, 45, 100722. https://doi.org/https://doi.org/10.1016/j.iheduc.2019.100722. DOI: 10.1016/j.iheduc.2019.100722

Brandenburger, J., & Janneck, M. (2021). A Teamwork Tool to Support Group Work in Online-based Higher Education: Exploring User Experience and the Use of Support Mechanisms by Students. WEBIST, Brookfield, S. (1985). A critical definition of adult education. *Adult Education Quarterly*, 36(1), 44–49.

Butcher, J. (2020). *Unheard: The voices of part-time adult learners*. Higher Education Policy Institute.

Chang, H. (2016). *Autoethnography as Method* (Vol. 1). Routledge. DOI: 10.4324/9781315433370

Chaubey, A., & Bhattacharya, B. (2015). Learning management system in higher education. *International Journal of Science Technology & Engineering*, 2(3), 158–162.

Connolly, B. (2008). *Adult learning in groups* (1st ed.). Open University Press.

Denzin, N. K., & Lincoln, Y. S. (Eds.). (2018). *The Sage handbook of qualitative research* (5th ed.). Sage.

Fittipaldi, D. (2020). Managing the dynamics of group projects in higher education: Best practices suggested by empirical research. *Universal Journal of Educational Research*, 8(5), 1778–1796. DOI: 10.13189/ujer.2020.080515

Gachago, D., Strydom, S., Hanekom, P., Simons, S., & Walters, S. (2015). Crossing boundaries: Lectures' perspectives on the use of WhatsApp to support teaching and learning in higher education. *Progressio*, 37(1), 172–187. DOI: 10.25159/0256-8853/579

Garcia, J. G., Gañgan, M. G. T., Tolentino, M. N., Ligas, M., Moraga, S. D., & Pasilan, A. A. (2021). Canvas adoption assessment and acceptance of the learning management system on a web-based platform. *arXiv preprint arXiv:2101.12344*.

Garrison, D. R., Anderson, T., & Archer, W. (2001). Critical thinking, cognitive presence, and computer conferencing in distance education. *American Journal of Distance Education*, 15(1), 7–23. DOI: 10.1080/08923640109527071

Goñi, J., Cortázar, C., Alvares, D., Donoso, U., & Miranda, C. (2020). Is Teamwork Different Online Versus Face-to-Face? A Case in Engineering Education. *Sustainability (Basel)*, 12(24), 10444. https://www.mdpi.com/2071-1050/12/24/10444. DOI: 10.3390/su122410444

GORTT. (2022). *Digital Transformation Programme*. Trinidad and Tobago: Ministry of Education Retrieved from https://www.moe.gov.tt/digital-transformation-policy-2023-2027/#:~:text=The%20vision%20of%20the%20MOE's,development%20of%20globally%20competitive%20citizens."&text=To%20promote%20a%20learner%20centred,system%20and%20among%20all%20stakeholders.

Heinze, A., Procter, C., & Scott, B. (2007). Use of conversation theory to underpin blended learning. *International Journal of Teaching and Case Studies*, 1(1-2), 108–120. DOI: 10.1504/IJTCS.2007.014213

Henschke, J. A. (2020). *Facilitating Adult and Organizational Learning Through Andragogy: A History, Philosophy, and Major Themes: A History, Philosophy, and Major Themes*. IGI Global. https://doi.org/https://doi.org/10.4018/978-1-7998-3937-8

Homan, A. C., Gündemir, S., Buengeler, C., & van Kleef, G. A. (2020). Leading diversity: Towards a theory of functional leadership in diverse teams. *The Journal of Applied Psychology*, 105(10), 1101–1128. DOI: 10.1037/apl0000482 PMID: 31971407

Hughes, J. E., & Roblyer, M. (2023). *Integrating educational technology into teaching: Transforming learning across disciplines* (9th ed.). Pearson Education, Inc.

Jony, A. I., & Serradell-López, E. (2021). Key factors that boost the effectiveness of virtual teamwork in online higher education. Research and Innovation Forum 2020: Disruptive Technologies in Times of Change, King, A. (1998). Transactive Peer Tutoring: Distributing Cognition and Metacognition. *Educational Psychology Review*, 10(1), 57–74. DOI: 10.1023/A:1022858115001

Knowles, M. (1975). *Self-Directed Learning: A Guide for Learners and Teachers* (Vol. 2). Association Press., DOI: 10.1177/105960117700200220

Knowles, M. S., Holton, E., & Swanson, R. (2005). *The adult learner: the definitive classic in adult education and human resource development* (6th ed.). Elsevier. DOI: 10.4324/9780080481913

Lacka, E., Wong, T. C., & Haddoud, M. Y. (2021). Can digital technologies improve students' efficiency? Exploring the role of Virtual Learning Environment and Social Media use in Higher Education. *Computers & Education*, 163, 104099. https://doi.org/https://doi.org/10.1016/j.compedu.2020.104099. DOI: 10.1016/j.compedu.2020.104099

Lakkala, S., Galkienė, A., Navaitienė, J., Cierpiałowska, T., Tomecek, S., & Uusiautti, S. (2021). Teachers Supporting Students in Collaborative Ways—An Analysis of Collaborative Work Creating Supportive Learning Environments for Every Student in a School: Cases from Austria, Finland, Lithuania, and Poland. *Sustainability (Basel)*, 13(5), 2804. https://www.mdpi.com/2071-1050/13/5/2804. DOI: 10.3390/su13052804

Makri, A., & Vlachopoulos, D. (2020). Applying adult learning theories in digital educational and training programs. EDULEARN20 Proceedings, Marcut, I. G., & Chisiu, C. M. (2018). Heutagogy–an appropriate framework for computer aided learning course with post-graduate teacher students. *Journal Plus Education*, 21, 203–215.

Merriam, S. B., & Baumgartner, L. M. (2020). *Learning in adulthood: A comprehensive guide*. John Wiley & Sons.

Mezirow, J. (2018). Transformative learning theory. In *Contemporary theories of learning* (pp. 114–128). Routledge. DOI: 10.4324/9781315147277-8

Miles, M. B., Huberman, A. M., & Saldana, J. (2014). *Qualitative data analysis: A method sourcebook*. Sage Publications.

Moorhouse, B. L. (2023). Teachers' digital technology use after a period of online teaching. *ELT Journal*, 77(4), 445–457. DOI: 10.1093/elt/ccac050

Moorhouse, B. L., & Yan, L. (2023). Use of Digital Tools by English Language Schoolteachers. *Education Sciences*, 13(3), 226. https://www.mdpi.com/2227-7102/13/3/226. DOI: 10.3390/educsci13030226

Mpungose, C. B. (2023). Lecturers' reflections on use of Zoom video conferencing technology for e-learning at a South African university in the context of coronavirus. *African Identities*, 21(2), 266–282. DOI: 10.1080/14725843.2021.1902268

Muzyka, J. L., & Luker, C. S. (Eds.). (2016). The Flipped Classroom: Vol. 1. *Background and Challenges*. Oxford University Press.

Naghdipour, B., & Manca, S. (2023). Teaching presence in students' WhatsApp groups: Affordances for language learning. *E-Learning and Digital Media*, 20(3), 282–299. DOI: 10.1177/20427530221107968

Ovcharuk, O., Ivaniuk, I., Soroko, N., Gritsenchuk, O., & Kravchyna, O. (2020). The use of digital learning tools in the teachers' professional activities to ensure sustainable development and democratization of education in European countries. *EDP Sciences, E3S Web of Conferences.* https://doi.org/https://doi.org/10.1051/e3sconf/202016610019

Owusu-Agyeman, Y. (2019). An analysis of theoretical perspectives that define adult learners for effective and inclusive adult education policies. *International Review of Education*, 65(6), 929–953. DOI: 10.1007/s11159-019-09811-3

Ozdem-Yilmaz, Y., & Bilican, K. (2020). Discovery Learning—Jerome Bruner. *Science education in theory and practice: An introductory guide to learning theory*, 177-190.

Patel, L. (2015). *Decolonizing educational research: From ownership to answerability*. Routledge. DOI: 10.4324/9781315658551

Perry, M. (2003). Distributed cognition. *HCI models, theories, and frameworks: Toward a multidisciplinary science*, 193-223.

Rahmadi, F. (2020). WhatsApp Group for Teaching and Learning in Indonesian Higher Education: What's Up? Rasiah, R. R. V. (2014). Transformative higher education teaching and learning: Using social media in a team-based learning environment. *Procedia: Social and Behavioral Sciences*, 123, 369–379.

Richardson, L., & Adams St. Pierre, E. (2018). Writing: A Method of Inquiry. In Denzin, N. K., & Lincoln, Y. S. (Eds.), *The SAGE handbook of qualitative research* (p. 1417). SAGE Publications Inc.

Rogers, Y. (2006). Distributed Cognition and Communication. In Brown, K. (Ed.), *Encyclopedia of Language & Linguistics* (2nd ed., pp. 731–733). Elsevier., https://doi.org/https://doi.org/10.1016/B0-08-044854-2/00862-2 DOI: 10.1016/B0-08-044854-2/00862-2

Saldaña, J. (2013). The Coding Manual for Qualitative Researchers. *Sage (Atlanta, Ga.).*

Schunk, D. H. (2012). *Learning theories an educational perspective*. Pearson Education, Inc.

Sezer, B. (2024). The effects of group-based personalized online teaching on learners' community of inquiry and achievement of a course. *Turkish Online Journal of Distance Education*, 25(2), 130–143. https://doi.org/https://doi.org/10.17718/tojde.1310963. DOI: 10.17718/tojde.1310963

Shurygin, V., Saenko, N., Zekiy, A., Klochko, E., & Kulapov, M. (2021). Learning management systems in academic and corporate distance education. [iJET]. *International Journal of Emerging Technologies in Learning*, 16(11), 121–139. DOI: 10.3991/ijet.v16i11.20701

Smith, L. T. (2021). *Decolonizing methodologies: Research and indigenous peoples*. Bloomsbury Publishing. DOI: 10.5040/9781350225282

Varhelahti, M., & Turnquist, T. (2021). Diversity and Communication in Virtual Project Teams. *IEEE Transactions on Professional Communication*, 64(2), 201–214. DOI: 10.1109/TPC.2021.3064404

Venter, A. (2020). Synchronising Informal and Formal Learning Spaces to Facilitate Collaborative Online Learning. *Africa Education Review*, 17(6), 1–15. DOI: 10.1080/18146627.2021.1954536

Wenger, E. (1998). Communities of practice: Learning as a social system. *The Systems Thinker*, 9(5), 2–3.

ADDITIONAL READING

Angeli, C. (2008). Distributed cognition: A framework for understanding the role of computers in classroom teaching and learning. *Journal of Research on Technology in Education*, 40(3), 271–279. DOI: 10.1080/15391523.2008.10782508

Borup, J., Graham, C. R., West, R. E., Archambault, L., & Spring, K. J. (2020). Academic communities of engagement: An expansive lens for examining support structures in blended and online learning. *Educational Technology Research and Development*, 68(2), 807–832. DOI: 10.1007/s11423-020-09744-x

Dincă, M., Luştrea, A., Craşovan, M., Onițiu, A., & Berge, T. (2023). Students' Perspectives on Team Dynamics in Project-Based Virtual Learning. *SAGE Open*, 13(1), 21582440221147269. DOI: 10.1177/21582440221147269

Marais, N. (2011). Connectivism as learning theory: The force behind changed teaching practice in higher education. *Education, Knowledge & Economy*, 4(3), 173–182.

Moore, J. L., & Rocklin, T. R. (1998). The distribution of distributed cognition: Multiple interpretations and uses. *Educational Psychology Review*, 10(1), 97–113. DOI: 10.1023/A:1022862215910

Rasiah, R. R. V. (2014). Transformative higher education teaching and learning: Using social media in a team-based learning environment. *Procedia: Social and Behavioral Sciences*, 123, 369–379. DOI: 10.1016/j.sbspro.2014.01.1435

Roberts, L. N., Solomon, F. N., & Cummings, R. (2024). Navigating the AI Landscape: Student and Teacher Perceptions of AI in Assessments in High School and College Settings. In *AI-Enhanced Teaching Methods* (pp. 268-285). IGI Global.

Skelton, K., Evans, R., & LaChenaye, J. (2020). Hidden communities of practice in social media groups: Mixed methods study. *JMIR Pediatrics and Parenting*, 3(1), e14355. DOI: 10.2196/14355 PMID: 32207693

KEY TERMS AND DEFINITIONS

Credibility: The degree of trust users place in the application, system, product, or service and the company behind it.

Desirability: The extent to which users find the application, system, product, or service appealing and satisfying to use.

Findability: How easily users can find the information they need within the application, system, product, or service.

Interdependence: The mutual reliance between two or more group members, where each member's actions and contributions affect the entire group's outcomes

Peer Feedback: Peers or group members provide constructive criticism and suggestions to help improve each other's work and learning outcomes. Peer feedback is an essential component of collaborative learning and helps individuals refine their ideas and approaches.

Real-time Communication: Communication that happens instantly, without any significant delay, allowing for immediate interaction and feedback.

Synergy: The increased effectiveness and efficiency that results when people or groups work together cooperatively.

Usability: The ease with which users can learn to use and interact with an application, system, product, or service.

Usefulness: The ability of the application, system, product, or service to fulfill users' needs and provide value.

User Experience (UX): the overall experience a person has when interacting with an application, product, system, or service. It is concerned with the user's perceptions and responses resulting from the use or anticipated use of an application, product, system, or service.

User Interface (UI): The part of the application, system, product, or service that users interact with directly, including visual design and interactive elements.

Chapter 10
Avatars of Academia:
Exploring Virtual Collaboration's Tapestry

Andi Asrifan
https://orcid.org/0000-0002-9934-6129
Universitas Negeri Makassar, Indonesia

Syamsuardi Saodi
https://orcid.org/0000-0001-8551-9300
Universitas Negeri Makassar, Indonesia

Anita Candra Dewi
Universitas Negeri Makassar, Indonesia

Badruddin Kaddas
https://orcid.org/0000-0003-1531-4558
Universitas Islam Makassar, Indonesia

Vivit Rosmayanti
https://orcid.org/0000-0002-3648-9878
Universitas Negeri Makassar, Indonesia

Mulyadi Mulyadi
Universitas Islam Makassar, Indonesia

ABSTRACT

The effects of COVID-19 on educational institutions, leadership, technology in the classroom, virtual reality, and collaborative learning are just a few of the topics covered in this extensive review of recent studies. It explores the pros and cons of virtual teams in educational contexts, focusing on knowledge work in virtual environments and how they could improve interdisciplinary partnerships. Setting clear goals, communicating effectively, and managing cultural differences are critical tactics outlined in the article for successful virtual collaboration. Additionally, it delves into how virtual collaboration tools might enhance teamwork and student engagement, as well as the changing function of avatars in educational environments. The paper highlights the potential of virtual reality, augmented reality, artificial intelligence, and gamification to revolutionize collaborative learning, build immersive environments, and enhance learning outcomes in the next quarter of a century. It predicts immense progress in education due to these technologies' incorporation.

DOI: 10.4018/979-8-3693-3852-0.ch010

1. INTRODUCTION

The forefront and creativity orientation of SL's user base means that this is where new possibilities for virtual world knowledge work are most likely to emerge as opposed to established and more static forms of web-mediated work (Chen & Kent, 2020) (Hosseini et al., 2022). Finally, our own experiences in exploratory "just playing around" uses of SL revealed intrigue and confusion that required explanation and exegesis.

Our past and current work focuses on SL for several reasons. First, the "basic" version of SL is free to educators and some other groups, thus making it potentially more cost-effective than other virtual worlds for research in organizational and workplace settings (Lorenzo-Alvarez et al., 2020) (Mikula et al., 2021) (Tlili et al., 2022). While costly for some organizations, step-up fees to access more land or capabilities provide further affordances (recalling Giddens' notion that resources must be expended) for design and research. This dual-tier pricing reverse of the normal situation where educational versions of products cost more may be an idea worth exploring in future research on how different virtual world "societies" emerge and how they may differentially support various forms of work.

This perspective is reflected in our choice to study existing work in virtual worlds rather than attempting to transfer activities from the real world, as is being done by many organizations exploring Second Life for purposes such as training and simulation (Zhao et al., 2021) (Haram et al., 2021) (Tlili et al., 2022). An overarching theme of this paper is that to understand and harness the potential of virtual worlds for knowledge work, it is necessary to push the envelope of what these worlds are and what they can be. This requires deep engagements with stakeholders, iterative design, and a willingness to take theoretical risks.

This chapter examines the capacity of virtual worlds, particularly Second Life (SL), in the academic setting, specifically emphasizing their ability to support knowledge process, collaboration, and professional involvement. The SL platform provides a cost-efficient and immersive setting for educators and researchers to replicate real-life situations and investigate innovative methods of teaching and collaboration. The chapter examines prominent developing technologies, including Virtual Reality (VR) and Artificial Intelligence (AI), and their capacity to revolutionize academic methodologies. An analysis of the development of avatars and their educational influence emphasizes the crucial function these technologies have in improving teaching, learning, and multidisciplinary collaboration in academic environments.

Second Life is an especially compelling site for professional activities due to the freedom and creativity afforded by 3D content creation and the potential to construct work environments that are more enjoyable and engaging than their "real world" counterparts (Richter & Richter, 2023) (Mystakidis et al., 2021) (Asad et al., 2021)

(Jovanović & Milosavljević, 2022). We have embarked on a long-term research program to understand how virtual worlds can best support distributed knowledge work. Our primary research approach is to engage as participant observers, eventually developing and testing design ideas in collaboration with sponsoring organizations.

At the nexus of Web 2.0 and virtual reality, Avatars of Academia explores the innovative use of web-based virtual worlds to support collaboration among knowledge workers at "The Ohio State University". Our current investigation is a growing interest in using virtual worlds to support various professional activities, from meetings to e-commerce. Specifically, we are exploring Second Life (SL). This widely used web-based virtual world has attracted the attention of various organizations interested in the possible cost and affordance advantages of virtual worlds over other, more traditional web-based communication tools.

1.1. Background

Since the closure of the Sojourner Truth Library at New Paltz due to the COVID-19 pandemic, there has been increased interest in creating a virtual library for SUNY New Paltz (Martinez et al., 2023) (Asumah & Nagel, 2024) (Lantz-Wagner, 2022). A task force of librarians and other academic technologists is considering this service's needs and possibilities (Mehta & Wang, 2020) (McGuire et al., 2020). Such resources will be crucial to undergraduate and graduate students' information literacy and on-going research needs. However, our entire SUNY community is scattered now, with some residing in New Paltz and others taking classes online from distant locales. It would be ideal to simulate a renovated and expanded version of the Sojourner Truth library on the New Paltz campus, accessible to the SUNY community. Yet, even with quiet and private areas in the virtual library, the possibility of meeting in teams for instruction, exploratory learning, and discussion has been raised. These days, it is often difficult to find a venue and time for group meetings to work on a research project. If a virtual library could satisfy these needs and variables, it would greatly interest many faculty and students. The task force for an NPVLC is considering the possibility of integrating and meshing three types of virtual environments that already exist or are under development. These include a 3D multi-user environment such as Second Life, a video game, Chimera's Project, developed for instruction and authentic learning in the sciences, and a more traditional web-based library tutorial or classroom environment (Jovanović & Milosavljević, 2022) (Suzuki et al., 2020) (Kruk, 2022) (Thompson et al., 2020). This is an exciting and ambitious idea, considering the possibilities of bridging or overlapping these environments and creating cyber-commons for the SUNY community to engage in information literacy and hands-on research. The level of success for such a project has yet to be determined. Still, discussions and inquiries with colleagues across several campuses have shown an interest and need for information literacy resources and virtual or distance education. This essay examines the roles and potentials of virtual collaboration, various types of virtual environments, and the creation of custom avatars to enhance instruction and exploration.

1.2. Purpose

Stephanie H. Waldal, a professor of comparative pathology from U.C. Davis and a colleague of PARC from a previous project, was very interested in learning where and how she could collaborate on such a platform. Her interests would involve easing political conflict in third-world countries and hoping to work with anthropologists or political scientists. Our research would also inform developers of virtual environments about the uptake in academic users and possibly identify areas needing further development. All of these are potential users of the information derived from the following research. Each is looking for a different way to collaborate, but all hope that a virtual environment could, in some way, facilitate their meeting with colleagues from other areas of expertise.

Our research aimed to understand how cross-disciplinary collaborations in both the sciences and humanities could occur in emerging media. Encouraging scientists and humanists to think outside their normal processes and consider working with colleagues in different fields could invoke new methodologies and directions of inquiry for both. Virtual environments, we hoped, would provide a platform where professionals in disparate fields can meet and find common ground. While we had plans for specific case studies in mind after finding out what virtual environment platforms were available, we decided that a broad, high-altitude survey research would be best to determine the lay of the land. With this information, we could, in turn, inform professionals in many different fields how and where they might collaborate with others.

1.3. Scope

The scope is limited to virtual worlds that permit synchronous communication to augment teaching and learning at a distance. We use virtual worlds to describe immersive, highly graphical, synchronous internet environments in which avatars represent participants. This implies a bounded space, simulated to represent the real world or an imaginary one, through which participants can move and interact with other participants and objects. This definition incorporates a wide range of platforms; for example, one of the most popular virtual worlds is Second Life, which can be accessed without charge and offers great flexibility. However, educators have also used simple game-based environments like Whyville and immersive 3D learning environments such as Quest Atlantis. We do not cover "desktop video-conferencing" systems and simple chat/browser-based platforms because these lack the necessary immersion and interactivity to substitute face-to-face interaction effectively. On the other hand, we do not rule out conventional e-learning platforms entirely, many of which have included 3D or virtual world components in recent years. If such platforms become more like the virtual worlds we have defined, we may consider them within the scope of this review.

2. VIRTUAL COLLABORATION IN ACADEMIA

Virtual collaboration enables academic communities in different geographical locations to collaborate in real-time or asynchronously. Researchers and students can participate in collaborative activities previously restricted to physical settings by utilizing technologies such as teleconferencing software and virtual worlds. Second Life provides a distinctive platform for users to utilize its immersive 3D environment to engage in virtual creation and interaction, enriching group conversations, research, and collaborative learning endeavors.

Virtual collaboration can consist of either a shared-space paradigm, based on teleconferencing software providing shared audio and video interfaces to same-place working, or a shared-time paradigm involving real-time interaction (or realistic simulation of it) in different places, e.g., using MUDs or an office suite enabling multiple users to animate and interact within the same virtual environment (McCollum, 2020) (Witherspoon et al., 2023) (Van et al., 2020). This research focuses on the shared-time paradigm, which is more complex due to added time coordination requirements and has greater potential to benefit academic activities involving group work and meetings. In such groups, the most basic attempts at virtual collaboration may be ad hoc discussions prompting email debates or traditional correspondence methods. More advanced and dedicated groups involved in research, teaching, or distance learning may be more organized and use net meetings and Second Life to hold scheduled discussions or lectures or simulate physical presence in 3-D environments (Mara et al., 2021) (Buhalis et al., 2023) (Mystakidis, 2022).

Virtual collaboration is the set of functionalities and practices that enable a group of individuals to collaborate in a (sometimes mixed-mode) synchronous or asynchronous manner in the shared environment of cyberspace, i.e., to communicate and interact, with the primary purpose of working together towards a common goal or shared intellectual endeavor (Broman et al., 2024) (Deschênes, 2024). Its many forms include teleconferencing, email, computer-mediated communication (CMC), chat, and multi-user domains (MUDs).

2.1. Definition

The recent push by educational institutions and scholarly researchers to offer distance education and conduct scientific inquiry over the Internet has important implications for the culture of academic work and the nature of the scholarship (Goudeau et al., 2021) (Beck et al., 2022) (Jogezai et al., 2021) (Crompton et al., 2021). One essential aspect of internet technology is the ability to interact with people at a distance or nearly in real-time. This can occur through the exchange of text messages, as in the classic example of Internet Relay Chat (IRC) or Usenet newsgroups, and through audio and video data. Audio/video data exchange may occur in a session with individuals participating at various times, as with the exchange of video mail, or in a session with real-time interaction between people at a distance, as with a "face-to-face" conversation over the Internet phone (Karam et al., 2021) (Ukoha, 2022). Textual interaction may occur in the same modes. In a virtual "meeting," many individuals may interact in real-time conversation. At the same time, in an asynchronous mode, various participants may, over an extended period, contribute messages that others read and respond to at later times. These communicative technologies are potentially of great importance for the conduct of scholarly research (Howlett, 2022) (Ray, 2023).

2.2. Benefits

Increased academic and social contact between faculty and students in separate institutions (Leal et al., 2021) (Sobaih et al., 2020) (Turnbull et al., 2021) (Mishra, 2020). The importance of external relationships, as suggested by the new accreditation criteria and technological advances, has increased the value of collaborative research. Virtual collaboration provides a cost-effective way to connect with colleagues and conduct projects with real-time interaction, the lifeblood of relationship-based research (Griffen, 2022). This is particularly relevant for researchers in developing nations, who may lack resources to travel for meetings with colleagues or cannot secure visas to travel to other countries. By allowing individuals to work with the full range of digital media from their own countries, virtual collaboration provides a way to level the playing field and increase the involvement and contributions of disenfranchised groups (Wang, 2021).

2.3. Challenges

Lack of technological pedagogical knowledge even assuming the hardware and connectivity problem is not an issue, many professors are often ignorant about the most effective use of technology in an educational context (Kaimara et al., 2021)

(Enochsson et al., 2022) (Reynolds et al., 2022) (Rasiah et al., 2020). These professors are often caught up in what is described as instrumental use of technology when adapting the technology to replicate an existing task rather than to enable some new teaching and learning with the affordances of new technology. An example of this might be the use of a forum in which the students merely post responses to a text-based question. This forum is used as a direct substitute for assessing a written assignment. It does not utilize a forum's unique characteristics, such as asynchronous discussion (Calderon & Sood, 2020). An education and training program to support these educators in developing their technological and pedagogical knowledge is critical to the success of any virtual collaborative initiative (Lei & Medwell, 2021).

Cost of high-tech equipment and connectivity In some virtual collaborative ventures, the cost of entry is very high (Jin & Wang, 2024) (Guofeng et al., 2020). Professors and schools intend to delve into high-tech and sometimes expensive virtual settings such as Massively Multiplayer Online Games (MMOGs) and real-time virtual environments. These environments often require a relatively high-performance computer and a broadband internet connection at home. A study of faculty members teaching in online programs at the tertiary education level reported that 63% of the respondents stated that cost was the primary obstacle to using new technology in teaching and learning (Polly et al., 2021) (Lassoued et al., 2020) (Hennessy et al., 2022). Over 50% of the respondents felt that not only was professional development essential for them to use technology to its full potential in teaching and learning, but they also wanted to see explicit evidence of the effectiveness of various technologies (other than email and web pages) in accomplishing various educational goals. In many situations, the cost-to-benefit ratio is insufficient to justify entering such virtual settings (Hämäläinen et al., 2021) (Mlambo et al., 2021) (Karakose et al., 2021).

3. Evolution of Avatars in Academia

Research in developing avatars has been underway for nearly four decades, and no review could do justice to the scope and variety of this work (Dwivedi et al., 2023) (Román et al., 2024). Current graphical and conversational interfaces used as avatars have been influenced by entities ranging from VRML objects to Eliza, a very early and elementary 'chatbot' program (Coleman, 2023). This section considers the historical evolution of avatars and associated technologies, followed by a discussion detailing the role of technology in the development of avatars. Using avatars in educational settings remains a contentious and often emotive issue (Zhang et al., 2022) (Butow & Hoque, 2020). This can be partially explained by examining the intense and sometimes conflicting views about the role of technology in education. This section seeks to redress the balance between technophiles and technophobes with a balanced assessment of the impact of avatars on education, which is a key issue.

3.1. Historical Overview

Evolution of Avatars in Academia Historical Overview Avatars have been defined as digital representations of people and have come a long way since their primarily text-based MUD (Multi-User Dungeon) beginnings (Ioannidis & Kontis, 2023) (Coleman, 2023). In a special issue of the Journal of Virtual Environments, Maxim and Sarah describe the first known study of avatars in a virtual world as a group of sketchpad objects composed of somewhat abstract graphical icons. The researchers interpreted the sketchpads differently as properties and text descriptions of the objects and the users as avatars. As technology and the internet have grown and enhanced, so have avatars. With most homes having easy access to a multimedia computer and a growing amount of people having high-speed internet access, the world of avatars is almost limitless (Alam and Mohanty2022). Avatars today can range from a simple chat bubble icon to a highly complex and polytheistically real-time 3D character (Alpala et al., 2022). They are used for many purposes, such as gaming, virtual worlds, social media, education, and simulations. This paper will look at the evolution of avatars and the growth of avatar communities and activities within modern virtual worlds and evaluate the influence and impact these communities have on our society.

3.2. Role of Technology

Avatars are quickly becoming a cost-effective method for students to explore the online world while interacting with others as if they were in the real world. Unwin and Smith (2009) state that "in an educational context, the idea is to provide a three-dimensional graphical environment which is engaging, interactive and provides a context for learning, within which students' learning activities can be situated." (Smith et al., 2024) (Oni et al.2020). Using avatars as an educational tool goes beyond meeting virtually to discuss assignments. A recent study found that of the 3085 undergraduates surveyed, 382 were assigned to use avatars to attend interview skills training sessions, using this data in comparison to 2703 who were assigned regular online training (Haginoya et al., 2020) (Haginoya et al., 2023) (Røed et al., 2023). It was found that those who used avatars were likelier to have used the taught skills at the interview six months post-intervention and reported increased self-efficacy in developing interview skills. This suggests that the use of avatars may be effective at creating a sense of presence, this being a social and emotional feeling of being involved in an environment, which is an important factor for e-learners as often dropout rates are high as students may feel isolated (Erickson-Davis et al., 2021) (Rus-Calafell et al., 2020) (Cadet & Chainay, 2021).

3.3. Impact on Education

This means that students can participate in subject matter far beyond the textbook. Discussions can involve past, present, and future social, scientific, and global issues, which could lead to a more politically, socially, or scientifically aware student and could better direct the decision-making roles they may embark on (O'Dowd, 2021). Immersive worlds also allow learning to become more interactive. This is not about treating students as consumers and making education more fun. It is about engaging the student more deeply in the learning process to build a better understanding and retention of knowledge (Enyedy & Yoon, 2021). For instance, a history class about Ancient Rome could involve the students taking on the roles of Roman citizens and engaging in various role-play scenarios. The students learn in context and will feel that they have better understood their subject by having 'lived' it (Limeri et al., 2020). This will reduce student apathy toward learning and gradually increase student proficiency. Moreover, Second Life allows for global connectedness by transcending the geographical barriers of traditional education.

This point is not specifically about education. However, almost everything in Second Life can teach us something about the real world. What is important is that the more informal learning that may take place in Second Life does not become a substitute for education. Younger generations are technologically savvy, and it may be important to install some guidance to ensure that all this informal learning is used most effectively (Hennessy et al., 2022).

4. VIRTUAL COLLABORATION TOOLS

A major behavior change largely fueled by the internet is the ability to work on group projects virtually. This can be considered one of the largest changes in sociology and technology that involves work (Whillans et al., 2021). It is noted by Terrence and Montressor (1992) that for a group to be considered working together, they must work cooperatively and construct shared goals that can be achieved under a cooperative effort (Pham, 2021). An argument against this is that it is just as effective for smaller groups of 2-3 students to meet face-to-face and work in the same physical location. While this can be true, it is not practical for meeting times, travel, and varying schedules. The same authors also point out that groups need to maintain moderate communication between meetings to be effective, and to facilitate this, there is often a need for frequent contact.

4.1. Communication Platforms

Through Gmail, Hangouts provides users a chat platform and a video calling platform (Hurst, 2020). Many apps are available to users, such as screen sharing and a whiteboard, which can also be used for video calling. The addition of a video call scheduling system and the ability to call any phone number via Google Voice are features that may later provide an advantage on Skype (Hurst, 2020). WebEx is another video call communications platform that can cater to 25 participants who want to discuss and share their ideas, with a feature to record the demonstration or a conversation. WebEx is a small part of a larger web conferencing service, which will be discussed in the next section (Hurst, 2020). Slack has been making its mark in universities in terms of messaging platforms. Slack is a cloud-based software capable of collaborating with teams and is also friendly for desktop and mobile devices. Slack is an alternative to email at times and a real-time messaging feature. It also integrates with third-party software and supports inline photos and video (Simon and Fierro, 2023). Yahoo Groups has also been a casual communications platform with the use of email and a webpage for information storage. However, Yahoo Groups will not offer a good idea to newcomers who have the mentality of Yahoo's disastrous state in this day and age. Email is the simplest form of communication and the most compatible with any person or group with an email address (Roberts et al., 2021) (Newman & Ford, 2021). It is also possible to communicate through SMS when you have a reminder for a meeting or a sudden change of group plans. Text messages do not offer good data retention, but it is possible to do so on an app like WhatsApp, where the chat history is saved on a mobile device.

According to the definition, a communication platform is a system used to convey an intended message to someone else (Hasal et al., 2021). Communication platforms allow you to send or receive a message through a technical device (Babun et al., 2021). The device may or may not be delivered through a messaging platform. Nowadays, there are so many different communications platforms that it is not easy to find the right one to fit specific needs. With communications platforms in terms of web conferencing, Google Hangouts was considered an advancement from Skype video calling due to its ability to carry out more than two connections and the added feature of broadcasting to a public audience (Hurst, 2020).

4.2. Virtual Meeting Software

Virtual meetings are a growing aspect of academic/industrial interactions and collaborations (Azizi et al., 2022) (Chen et al., 2022) (Vauterin & Virkki-Hatakka, 2021) (Rådberg & Löfsten, 2023). Such meetings can save the participating parties time and funds that would otherwise go into a physical meeting while providing a platform for effective communication. The qualitative data was collected from informants who participated in a virtual meeting and then interviewed by the researcher or simply by taking notes from a meeting attended by the interviewer. The researcher was the only outsider to the meeting in this particular setting. Thus, using an intuitive tool that required minimal technical maintenance was necessary for the meeting to succeed (Buerkle et al., 2023). This favored using Netmeeting or the Windows Messenger IM client for virtual meetings. These were a fortunate choice for the researcher as they were free, and there is a high probability that many people would already have these programs installed on their PCs. They provided a good platform for verbal discussion and shared viewing of an MS Word document in the same window as the discussion (Jing et al., 2021). An interesting aspect of this study is that two of the informants were disabled students. Virtual meetings could provide a unique opportunity to communicate more naturally with their lecturers/tutors, which is not always possible in a face-to-face meeting. This could particularly be the case for students who have hearing difficulties, deaf children of deaf parents, or students with serious speech impediments who can make full use of text-based communication and share a Word document for a written explanation of a topic.

4.3. Document Collaboration Tools

Document collaboration solutions are crucial for facilitating the participation of many users in the editing of shared documents, particularly in academic and professional environments. Software applications such as Google Docs and Microsoft SharePoint provide instantaneous modification, version management, and concurrent participation by many team members. These systems mitigate version conflicts and enhance the effectiveness of document workflows. Nevertheless, there are residual constraints, including sporadic version clashes and the requirement for a robust internet connection. Advanced systems provide citation management tools and history-tracking capabilities that considerably improve the transparency and structure of collaborative writing efforts (Rysavy & Michalak, 2020).

4.4. Project Management Systems

Project management systems are a focal point in structuring collaborative projects and allocating resources efficiently (Larsson & Larsson, 2020). Several types exist, ranging from simpler task management systems, such as the list-making and grouping website Hiveminder, to advanced collaborative virtual environments. Project management systems facilitate the planning and allocation of tasks, scheduling, development of resources, communication, and the ability to create controllable and observable project structures. They allow members to have an overarching view of the progress and current state of the project. This is an invaluable asset in distributed environments, as members are not always working simultaneously. Project management systems allow for continuity of work as each member can pick up at the precise point where they left off.

The project management implemented at any one time will depend on the inherent nature and requirements of the project itself (Ika & Pinto, 2022). There are often trade-offs between the time/effort required to learn the system versus the utility it will provide. A larger, more complex project will benefit from a well-defined system, though using advanced project management for shorter-term projects is not always appropriate. Attempting to implement a complex system in an inappropriate situation may even harm the project. For example, a simple task that is difficult to enter into the system may consume more time than the task is worth (Ostad-Ali-Askari, 2022) (Norton & Chambers, 2020).

5. FUTURE TRENDS IN VIRTUAL COLLABORATION

Augmented Reality (AR), where virtual lessons can be superimposed on an actual environment, has the potential to be a powerful tool for distance learning and teaching (Alzahrani, 2020) (Iqbal et al., 2022). Especially if it becomes affordable, it could be used to gain access to course elements through a mobile device, e.g., an architecture student could access accurate 3D building models in the comfort of their desired environment. It is also worth noting that AR can also be applied to mobile web and e-learning platforms to enhance the interactive experience through markers or GPS data.

According to Conoloff and Murphy (1999), distance educators have long sought to replicate the lectures close to the in-class experience so that learners can access course content and presentations, not only disjointed print media (Brainard & Watson, 2020). In the next millennium, it is hoped that virtual reality (VR) will be the technology to achieve this. Considering the rapid advancement in VR technology (special mention to Sony Playstations VR, HTC Vive, and Oculus Rift), there is a good chance that in 25 years, VR will be more accessible. Given its ability to completely immerse its users into its environment, it could be an alternative to the modern distance-learning course, implement collaborative/team-based activities, and perhaps provide apprenticeships in skilled virtual environments. Its uses could also extend into simulations and dramas, e.g., medical simulations or historical enactments. We will witness rapid technological advancement in the coming 25 years. This, in turn, will affect how we carry out day-to-day tasks and will also impact education, learning, and teaching methods.

5.1. Virtual Reality and Augmented Reality

Virtual reality (VR) and augmented reality (AR) are at the epicenter of current technology trends, and as the hardware becomes more accessible, interest in how VR and AR can be utilized is rapidly growing (Tegally et al., 2022). In the context of virtual collaboration and e-learning, although the technologies are still in their infancy, there is the potential for VR and AR to be a major contributor to the future of collaborative learning. Tal, Levenberg, and Naim (2017) identify VR as a possible solution for distance learning, creating an immersive environment where distance learners and on-campus learners can feel as though they are in the same physical space, which could go a long way to reducing the perceived isolation of distance learners (Al-Balas et al., 2020). Park et al. (2018) describe the benefits of an immersive VR environment for collaborative learning, detailing a case study where students were tasked with assembling a virtual jigsaw puzzle (Baker et al., 2022) (Madariaga et al., 2023). Interactions were observed as the students enacted gestures and non-verbal communication while attempting to solve the task. The case study concluded that the VR environment provided a greater sense of engagement and enhanced the student's perception of the task. This supports the idea that VR can be especially useful for group work. This activity is often difficult to coordinate online and is the focus of much of the current research on CSCL. This is also supported by Thongseiratch and Howes (2017), who discuss a prototype VR environment for a collaborative e-learning engineering design course. An interview with the students revealed that they felt the VR environment helped promote team awareness and unity and provided a sense of competition, which led to a better understanding of the design concepts (Umar & Ko, 2022) (Zhang et al., 2020). While VR remains out of reach for most students, these studies provide some evidence that VR has the potential to enhance the quality of courses and create a more cohesive and engaging learning environment.

5.2. Artificial Intelligence in Collaboration

Virtual Collaborative Environments (VCE) have the potential to provide agent-based support (Brissaud et al., 2022). The idea of having artificial entities representing real humans working in collaboration is attractive. In the future, it may become possible to have an intelligent agent replace a real person in a collaborative venture. It is reasonable to assume that if agent support is effective, creating an intelligent agent that can work instead of its human counterpart would also be effective (Kox et al., 2021). The cost savings of running a virtual team where an agent can represent each person could be substantial. This also ties in with the notion of perpetual organizations where transient human members come and go, but the organization itself lives on in its agents (Nilsen et al., 2022) (Dauenhauer, 2020). This may be ideal in situations where the project being worked on is digital, e.g., game development or software engineering. This could all come into place in the next 20 years. In the previous example, we see that VCE can help to automate some forms of collaboration. Some collaboration is inherently highly unstructured and hard to automate using current methods, e.g., a team of artists brainstorming to develop a concept for a new character or verifying a system design with a customer to see if it meets their implied requirements (Ardito et al., 2020). It is highly desirable to have support in these situations because the less structured the collaboration, the more difficult and error-prone it is.

5.3. Gamification of Virtual Learning

A study conducted by California State University, Los Angeles, suggests that with the rise of virtual worlds, educators need to be trained in using simulation and other virtual reality-based instruction (Sattar et al., 2020) (Seo et al., 2021) (Kuna et al., 2023). This indicates that there will soon be a greater push for learning tools that utilize virtual environments. Another reason that gamification is becoming so much more attractive is that the current generations of college students have been raised on various types of consoles and online games. Today's students are very tech-savvy and have a positive attitude towards games. Thus, gamification can be a very effective method of engagement to raise interest and learning outcomes (Bouchrika et al., 2021). This interest in virtual environments and the positive student attitudes toward games make gamification more desirable, and this technique has now been trickled down into various pedagogical practices. According to Becker, an effective program can increase motivation and engagement. Create a more enjoyable learning process, improve transfer, and increase learning time. These can be done by implementing game elements into the course to create a game or by gaming simulations (Huang et al., 2022).

6. CONCLUSION

Highlighting the revolutionary potential of cutting-edge technologies like gamification, virtual reality (VR), augmented reality (AR), and artificial intelligence (AI), the article offers a thorough examination of the changing terrain of virtual collaboration in education. By automating certain parts of collaboration and increasing student engagement, these technologies have the potential to improve collaborative learning greatly. The article traces the development of avatars in academic settings across time, focusing on their increasing importance in classrooms. According to the article, effective knowledge work and interdisciplinary partnerships can be facilitated by virtual collaboration tools such as communication platforms, virtual meeting software, document collaboration tools, project management systems, and avatars.

Experts anticipate that these technological developments will significantly impact the educational landscape of the future, leading to significant improvements in pedagogical practices within the next quarter of a century. There seems to be a trend towards more interactive and interesting educational experiences, with virtual environments and gaming components being especially well-received by tech-savvy pupils.

On the other hand, the article discusses the difficulties of virtual teams, namely how teachers often do not know enough about technology to teach their classes effectively. Continuous professional development and training are essential to close this knowledge gap and guarantee that teachers can use these resources well to foster more meaningful relationships between students and teachers at all levels of education. In conclusion, there are great potential benefits to transforming education through virtual collaboration technologies. However, this will only be possible if we overcome the obstacles associated with teachers' lack of technical competence. A more linked and participatory educational environment will result from a well-rounded strategy integrating cutting-edge tools with sufficient support and teacher training.

REFERENCES

Akour, M. & Alenezi, M. (2022). Higher education future in the era of digital transformation. Education Sciences. DOI: 10.3390/educsci12110784

Al-Balas, M., Al-Balas, H. I., Jaber, H. M., Obeidat, K., Al-Balas, H., Aborajooh, E. A., ... & Al-Balas, B. (2020). Distance learning in clinical medical education amid COVID-19 pandemic in Jordan: current situation, challenges, and perspectives. BMC medical education, 20, 1-7. DOI: 10.1186/s12909-020-02257-4

Alam, A., & Mohanty, A. (2022). Metaverse and Posthuman animated avatars for teaching-learning process: interperception in virtual universe for educational transformation. In *International Conference on Innovations in Intelligent Computing and Communications* (pp. 47-61). Springer, Cham. DOI: 10.1007/978-3-031-23233-6_4

Ali, S., Abuhmed, T., El-Sappagh, S., Muhammad, K., Alonso-Moral, J. M., Confalonieri, R., ... & Herrera, F. (2023). Explainable Artificial Intelligence (XAI): What we know and what is left to attain Trustworthy Artificial Intelligence. Information fusion, 99, 101805. DOI: 10.1016/j.inffus.2023.101805

Alpala, L. O., Quiroga-Parra, D. J., Torres, J. C., & Peluffo-Ordóñez, D. H. (2022). Smart factory using virtual reality and online multi-user: Towards a metaverse for experimental frameworks. Applied Sciences, 12(12), 6258. DOI: 10.3390/app12126258

Alzahrani, N. M. (2020). Augmented reality: A systematic review of its benefits and challenges in e-learning contexts. Applied Sciences. DOI: 10.3390/app10165660

Anggarista, S., & Wahyudin, A. Y. (2022). a Correlational Study of Language Learning Strategies and English Proficiency of University Students At Efl Context. Journal of Arts and Education.

Ardito, C., Desolda, G., Lanzilotti, R., Malizia, A., Matera, M., Buono, P., & Piccinno, A. (2020). User-defined semantics for the design of IoT systems enabling smart interactive experiences. Personal and Ubiquitous Computing, 24, 781-796. DOI: 10.1007/s00779-020-01457-5

Arnold, S., & Jeglic, E. L. (2024). Stereotypes and unconscious bias in institutional child sexual abuse: Barriers to identification, reporting and prevention. *Child Abuse Review*, 33(2), e2865. Advance online publication. DOI: 10.1002/car.2865

Asad, M. M., Naz, A., Churi, P., & Tahanzadeh, M. M. (2021). Virtual reality as pedagogical tool to enhance experiential learning: a systematic literature review. Education Research International, 2021, 1-17. DOI: 10.1155/2021/7061623

Asumah, S. N., & Nagel, M. (2024). *Reframing Diversity and Inclusive Leadership: Race*. Gender, and Institutional Change.

Azizi, T., De Araujo, L. C., Cetecioglu, Z., Clancy, A. J., Feger, M. L., Liran, O., ... & Lund, P. A. (2022). A COST Action on microbial responses to low pH: Developing links and sharing resources across the academic-industrial divide. New Biotechnology, 72, 64-70. DOI: 10.1016/j.nbt.2022.09.002

Babun, L., Denney, K., Celik, Z. B., McDaniel, P., & Uluagac, A. S. (2021). A survey on IoT platforms: Communication, security, and privacy perspectives. Computer Networks, 192, 108040. DOI: 10.1016/j.comnet.2021.108040

Baker, J., DeLiema, D., Hufnagle, A. S., Carlson, S. M., Sharratt, A., & Ridge, S. W. (2022, September). Impasses in the wild: Autonomy support in naturalistic, parent-child outdoor play. In Frontiers in Education (Vol. 7, p. 885231). Frontiers. DOI: 10.3389/feduc.2022.885231

Beck, S., Bergenholtz, C., Bogers, M., Brasseur, T. M., Conradsen, M. L., Di Marco, D., ... & Xu, S. M. (2022). The Open Innovation in Science research field: a collaborative conceptualisation approach. Industry and Innovation, 29(2), 136-185. DOI: 10.1080/13662716.2020.1792274

Bouchrika, I., Harrati, N., Wanick, V., & Wills, G. (2021). Exploring the impact of gamification on student engagement and involvement with e-learning systems. *Interactive Learning Environments*, 29(8), 1244–1257. DOI: 10.1080/10494820.2019.1623267

Brainard, R., & Watson, L. (2020). Zoom in the classroom: Transforming traditional teaching to incorporate real-time distance learning in a face-to-face graduate physiology course. *The FASEB Journal*, 34(S1), 1. Advance online publication. DOI: 10.1096/fasebj.2020.34.s1.08665

Brissaud, D., Sakao, T., Riel, A., & Erkoyuncu, J. A. (2022). Designing value-driven solutions: The evolution of industrial product-service systems. CIRP annals. DOI: 10.1016/j.cirp.2022.05.006

Broman, M. M., Finckenberg-Broman, P., & Bird, S. (2024). Cyberspace Outlaws– Coding the Online World. International Journal for the Semiotics of Law-Revue internationale de Sémiotique juridique, 1-31. DOI: 10.1007/s11196-023-10100-4

Bru-Luna, L. M., Martí-Vilar, M., Merino-Soto, C., & Cervera-Santiago, J. L. (2021, December). Emotional intelligence measures: A systematic review. In Healthcare (Vol. 9, No. 12, p. 1696). DOI: 10.3390/healthcare9121696

Buerkle, A., Eaton, W., Al-Yacoub, A., Zimmer, M., Kinnell, P., Henshaw, M., ... & Lohse, N. (2023). Towards industrial robots as a service (IRaaS): Flexibility, usability, safety and business models. Robotics and Computer-Integrated Manufacturing, 81, 102484. DOI: 10.1016/j.rcim.2022.102484

Buhalis, D., Leung, D., & Lin, M. (2023). Metaverse as a disruptive technology revolutionising tourism management and marketing. Tourism Management. DOI: 10.1016/j.tourman.2023.104724

Butow, P. & Hoque, E. (2020). Using artificial intelligence to analyse and teach communication in healthcare. The breast. DOI: 10.1016/j.breast.2020.01.008

Cadet, L. B. & Chainay, H. (2021). How preadolescents and adults remember and experience virtual reality: The role of avatar incarnation, emotion, and sense of presence. International Journal of Child-Computer Interaction. DOI: 10.1016/j.ijcci.2021.100299

Calderon, O. & Sood, C. (2020). Evaluating learning outcomes of an asynchronous online discussion assignment: a post-priori content analysis. Interactive Learning Environments.

Chen, H., Zhang, Y., Jin, Q., & Wang, X. (2022, August). Exploring Patterns of Academic-Industrial Collaboration for Digital Transformation Research: A Bibliometric-Enhanced Topic Modeling Method. In *2022 Portland International Conference on Management of Engineering and Technology (PICMET)* (pp. 1-9). IEEE. DOI: 10.23919/PICMET53225.2022.9882847

Chen, J. C. C., & Kent, S. (2020). Task engagement, learner motivation and avatar identities of struggling English language learners in the 3D virtual world. *System*, 88, 102168. Advance online publication. DOI: 10.1016/j.system.2019.102168

Coleman, B. (2023). Hello avatar: rise of the networked generation.

Crompton, H., Burke, D., Jordan, K., & Wilson, S. W. (2021). Learning with technology during emergencies: A systematic review of K-12 education. British journal of educational technology, 52(4), 1554-1575. DOI: 10.1016/j.system.2019.102168

Dauenhauer, B. P. (2020). Ricoeur and the tasks of citizenship. Paul Ricoeur and contemporary moral thought.

Deschênes, A. A. (2024). Digital literacy, the use of collaborative technologies, and perceived social proximity in a hybrid work environment: Technology as a social binder. Computers in Human Behavior Reports. DOI: 10.1016/j.chbr.2023.100351

Dinh, J. V., Reyes, D. L., Kayga, L., Lindgren, C., Feitosa, J., & Salas, E. (2021). Developing team trust: Leader insights for virtual settings. Organizational Dynamics, 50(1), 100846. DOI: 10.1016/j.orgdyn.2021.100846

Dwivedi, Y. K., Kshetri, N., Hughes, L., Slade, E. L., Jeyaraj, A., Kar, A. K., ... & Wright, R. (2023). "So what if ChatGPT wrote it?" Multidisciplinary perspectives on opportunities, challenges and implications of generative conversational AI for research, practice and policy. International Journal of Information Management, 71, 102642. DOI: 10.1016/j.ijinfomgt.2023.102642

Enochsson, A. B., Kilbrink, N., Andersén, A., & Ådefors, A. (2022). Obstacles to progress: Swedish vocational teachers using digital technology to connect school and workplaces. International Journal of Training Research, 20(2), 111-127. DOI: 10.1080/14480220.2021.1979623

Enyedy, N., & Yoon, S. (2021). Immersive environments: Learning in augmented+ virtual reality. International handbook of computer-supported collaborative learning, 389-405. DOI: 10.1007/978-3-030-65291-3_21

Erickson-Davis, C., Luhrmann, T. M., Kurina, L. M., Weisman, K., Cornman, N., Corwin, A., & Bailenson, J. (2021). The sense of presence: Lessons from virtual reality. Religion, brain & behavior, 11(3), 335-351. DOI: 10.1080/2153599X.2021.1953573

Goudeau, S., Sanrey, C., Stanczak, A., Manstead, A., & Darnon, C. (2021). Why lockdown and distance learning during the COVID-19 pandemic are likely to increase the social class achievement gap. Nature human behaviour, 5(10), 1273-1281. DOI: 10.1038/s41562-021-01212-7

Griffen, S. N. (2022). Collaborative Public Management in Two Police Departments to Address Cross-Jurisdictional Boundaries: A Descriptive Case Study.

Guofeng, M., Jianyao, J., Shan, J., & Zhijiang, W. (2020). Incentives and contract design for knowledge sharing in construction joint ventures. *Automation in Construction*, 119, 103343. Advance online publication. DOI: 10.1016/j.autcon.2020.103343

Haginoya, S., Ibe, T., Yamamoto, S., Yoshimoto, N., Mizushi, H., & Santtila, P. (2023). AI avatar tells you what happened: The first test of using AI-operated children in simulated interviews to train investigative interviewers. Frontiers in Psychology, 14, 1133621. DOI: 10.3389/fpsyg.2023.1133621

Haginoya, S., Yamamoto, S., Pompedda, F., Naka, M., Antfolk, J., & Santtila, P. (2020). Online simulation training of child sexual abuse interviews with feedback improves interview quality in Japanese university students. Frontiers in psychology, 11, 998. DOI: 10.3389/fpsyg.2020.00998

Hämäläinen, R., Nissinen, K., Mannonen, J., Lämsä, J., Leino, K., & Taajamo, M. (2021). Understanding teaching professionals' digital competence: What do PIAAC and TALIS reveal about technology-related skills, attitudes, and knowledge?. Computers in human behavior, 117, 106672. DOI: 10.1016/j.chb.2020.106672

Hameed, I., Hyder, Z., Imran, M., & Shafiq, K. (2021). Greenwash and green purchase behavior: An environmentally sustainable perspective. *Environment, Development and Sustainability*, 23(9), 1–22. DOI: 10.1007/s10668-020-01202-1

Hannan, E., & Liu, S. (2023). AI: New source of competitiveness in higher education. . *Competitiveness Review*, 33(2), 265–279. DOI: 10.1108/CR-03-2021-0045

Haram, M. H. S. M., Lee, J. W., Ramasamy, G., Ngu, E. E., Thiagarajah, S. P., & Lee, Y. H. (2021). Feasibility of utilising second life EV batteries: Applications, lifespan, economics, environmental impact, assessment, and challenges. Alexandria Engineering Journal, 60(5), 4517-4536. DOI: 10.1016/j.aej.2021.03.021

Hasal, M., Nowaková, J., Ahmed Saghair, K., Abdulla, H., Snášel, V., & Ogiela, L. (2021). Chatbots: Security, privacy, data protection, and social aspects. Concurrency and Computation: Practice and Experience, 33(19), e6426. DOI: 10.1002/cpe.6426

Hennessy, S., D'Angelo, S., McIntyre, N., Koomar, S., Kreimeia, A., Cao, L., ... & Zubairi, A. (2022). Technology use for teacher professional development in low-and middle-income countries: A systematic review. Computers and Education Open, 3, 100080. DOI: 10.1016/j.caeo.2022.100080

Hosseini, E., Saeida Ardekani, S., Sabokro, M., & Salamzadeh, A. (2022). The study of knowledge employee voice among the knowledge-based companies: The case of an emerging economy. *Revista de Gestão*, 29(2), 117–138. DOI: 10.1108/REGE-03-2021-0037

Howlett, M. (2022). Looking at the 'field'through a Zoom lens: Methodological reflections on conducting online research during a global pandemic. Qualitative Research. DOI: 10.1177/1468794120985691

Huang, Y. K., Chuang, N. K., & Kwok, L. (2023). To speak up or remain silent: The double-edged effects of trust and felt trust. *International Journal of Contemporary Hospitality Management*, 35(9), 3285–3304. DOI: 10.1108/IJCHM-05-2022-0676

Hurst, E. J. (2020). Web conferencing and collaboration tools and trends. *Journal of Hospital Librarianship*, 20(3), 266–279. Advance online publication. DOI: 10.1080/15323269.2020.1780079

Ika, L. A., & Pinto, J. K. (2022). The "re-meaning" of project success: Updating and recalibrating for a modern project management. *International Journal of Project Management*, 40(7), 835–848. Advance online publication. DOI: 10.1016/j.ijproman.2022.08.001

Ioannidis, S., & Kontis, A. P. (2023). The 4 Epochs of the Metaverse. Journal of Metaverse. DOI: 10.57019/jmv.1294970

Iqbal, M. Z., Mangina, E., & Campbell, A. G. (2022). Current challenges and future research directions in augmented reality for education. Multimodal Technologies and Interaction, 6(9), 75. DOI: 10.3390/mti6090075

Jin, J. L., & Wang, L. (2024). Design and governance of international joint venture innovation strategy: Evidence from China. . *International Business Review*, 33(3), 102277. Advance online publication. DOI: 10.1016/j.ibusrev.2024.102277

Jing, A., May, K., Lee, G., & Billinghurst, M. (2021). Eye see what you see: Exploring how bi-directional augmented reality gaze visualisation influences co-located symmetric collaboration. Frontiers in Virtual Reality. DOI: 10.3389/frvir.2021.697367

Jogezai, N. A., Baloch, F. A., Jaffar, M., Shah, T., Khilji, G. K., & Bashir, S. (2021). Teachers' attitudes towards social media (SM) use in online learning amid the COVID-19 pandemic: the effects of SM use by teachers and religious scholars during physical distancing. Heliyon, 7(4). DOI: 10.1016/j.heliyon.2021.e06781

Jovanović, A. & Milosavljević, A. (2022). VoRtex Metaverse platform for gamified collaborative learning. Electronics. DOI: 10.3390/electronics11030317

Kaimara, P., Fokides, E., Oikonomou, A., & Deliyannis, I. (2021). Potential barriers to the implementation of digital game-based learning in the classroom: Pre-service teachers' views. Technology, Knowledge and Learning, 26(4), 825-844. DOI: 10.1007/s10758-021-09512-7

Karakose, T., Polat, H., & Papadakis, S. (2021). Examining teachers' perspectives on school principals' digital leadership roles and technology capabilities during the COVID-19 pandemic. Sustainability. DOI: 10.3390/su132313448

Karam, M., Fares, H., & Al-Majeed, S. (2021). Quality assurance framework for the design and delivery of virtual, real-time courses. Information. DOI: 10.3390/info12020093

Kox, E. S., Kerstholt, J. H., Hueting, T. F., & de Vries, P. W. (2021). Trust repair in human-agent teams: the effectiveness of explanations and expressing regret. Autonomous agents and multi-agent systems, 35(2), 30. DOI: 10.1007/s10458-021-09515-9

Kruk, M. (2022). Dynamicity of perceived willingness to communicate, motivation, boredom and anxiety in Second Life: The case of two advanced learners of English. . *Computer Assisted Language Learning*, 35(1-2), 190–216. Advance online publication. DOI: 10.1080/09588221.2019.1677722

Kuna, P., Hašková, A., & Borza, Ľ. (2023). Creation of virtual reality for education purposes. Sustainability. DOI: 10.3390/su15097153

Lan, Y. J. (2020). Immersion into virtual reality for language learning. Psychology of learning and motivation.

Lantz-Wagner, S. (2022). Paths to Pathways: Exploring Lived Experiences of International Students to and Through Third-Party Pathway Programs.

Larsson, J. & Larsson, L. (2020). Integration, application and importance of collaboration in sustainable project management. Sustainability. DOI: 10.3390/su12020585

Lassoued, Z., Alhendawi, M., & Bashitialshaaer, R. (2020). An exploratory study of the obstacles for achieving quality in distance learning during the COVID-19 pandemic. Education sciences. DOI: 10.3390/educsci10090232

Leal Filho, W., Wall, T., Rayman-Bacchus, L., Mifsud, M., Pritchard, D. J., Lovren, V. O., ... & Balogun, A. L. (2021). Impacts of COVID-19 and social isolation on academic staff and students at universities: a cross-sectional study. BMC public health, 21(1), 1213. DOI: 10.1186/s12889-021-11040-z

Lee, M. H., Wang, C., & Yu, M. C. (2023). A Multilevel Study of Change-Oriented Leadership and Commitment: The Moderating Effect of Group Emotional Contagion. Psychology Research and Behavior Management, 637-650. DOI: 10.2147/PRBM.S385385

Lei, M. & Medwell, J. (2021). ... the COVID-19 pandemic on student teachers: How the shift to online collaborative learning affects student teachers' learning and future teaching in a Chinese .... Asia Pacific Education Review. DOI: 10.1007/s12564-021-09686-w

Limeri, L. B., Carter, N. T., Choe, J., Harper, H. G., Martin, H. R., Benton, A., & Dolan, E. L. (2020). Growing a growth mindset: Characterizing how and why undergraduate students' mindsets change. International Journal of STEM Education, 7, 1-19. DOI: 10.1186/s40594-020-00227-2

Lorenzo-Alvarez, R., Rudolphi-Solero, T., Ruiz-Gomez, M. J., & Sendra-Portero, F. (2020). Game-Based learning in virtual worlds: A multiuser online game for medical undergraduate radiology education within second life. . *Anatomical Sciences Education*, 13(5), 602–617. DOI: 10.1002/ase.1927 PMID: 31665564

Madariaga, L., Allendes, C., Nussbaum, M., Barrios, G., & Acevedo, N. (2023). Offline and online user experience of gamified robotics for introducing computational thinking: Comparing engagement, game mechanics and coding motivation. . *Computers & Education*, 193, 104664. DOI: 10.1016/j.compedu.2022.104664

Mara, M., Stein, J. P., Latoschik, M. E., Lugrin, B., Schreiner, C., Hostettler, R., & Appel, M. (2021). User responses to a humanoid robot observed in real life, virtual reality, 3D and 2D. Frontiers in psychology, 12, 633178. DOI: 10.3389/fpsyg.2021.633178

Martens, J. (2020). 12. Vocalizations and Speciation of Palearctic Birds. Ecology and evolution of acoustic communication in birds, 221-240. DOI: 10.7591/9781501736957-019

Martinez, A., Bellody, K., & Smith, E. (2023). Collaborative communication with library student workers in unexpected places: digital reference analysis.

McCollum, B. M. (2020). Online collaborative learning in STEM. Active learning in college science: The case for evidence-based practice, 621-637. DOI: 10.1007/978-3-030-33600-4_38

McGuire, A. L., Aulisio, M. P., Davis, F. D., Erwin, C., Harter, T. D., Jagsi, R., ... & COVID-19 Task Force of the Association of Bioethics Program Directors (ABPD). (2020). Ethical challenges arising in the COVID-19 pandemic: An overview from the Association of Bioethics Program Directors (ABPD) task force. The American Journal of Bioethics, 20(7), 15-27. DOI: 10.1080/15265161.2020.1764138

Mehta, D., & Wang, X. (2020). COVID-19 and digital library services–a case study of a university library. *Digital Library Perspectives*, 36(4), 351–363. Advance online publication. DOI: 10.1108/DLP-05-2020-0030

Mikula, K., Skrzypczak, D., Izydorczyk, G., Warchoł, J., Moustakas, K., Chojnacka, K., & Witek-Krowiak, A. (2021). 3D printing filament as a second life of waste plastics—a review. Environmental Science and Pollution Research, 28, 12321-12333. DOI: 10.1007/s11356-020-10657-8

Mishra, S. (2020). Social networks, social capital, social support and academic success in higher education: A systematic review with a special focus on 'underrepresented' students. . *Educational Research Review*, 29, 100307. Advance online publication. DOI: 10.1016/j.edurev.2019.100307

Mlambo, M., Silén, C., & McGrath, C. (2021). Lifelong learning and nurses' continuing professional development, a metasynthesis of the literature. BMC nursing. DOI: 10.1186/s12912-021-00579-2

Mystakidis, S. (2022). Metaverse. Encyclopedia. DOI: 10.3390/encyclopedia2010031

Mystakidis, S., Berki, E., & Valtanen, J. P. (2021). Deep and meaningful e-learning with social virtual reality environments in higher education: A systematic literature review. Applied Sciences. DOI: 10.3390/app11052412

Newman, S. A. & Ford, R. C. (2021). Five steps to leading your team in the virtual COVID-19 workplace. Organizational Dynamics. DOI: 10.1016%2Fj.orgdyn.2020.100802

Nilsen, M., Kongsvik, T., & Almklov, P. G. (2022). Splintered structures and workers without a workplace: how should safety science address the fragmentation of organizations?. Safety science. DOI: 10.1016/j.ssci.2021.105644

Norton, W. E. & Chambers, D. A. (2020). Unpacking the complexities of de-implementing inappropriate health interventions. Implementation Science. DOI: 10.1186/s13012-019-0960-9

O'Dowd, R. (2021). What do students learn in virtual exchange? A qualitative content analysis of learning outcomes across multiple exchanges. International Journal of Educational Research. DOI: 10.1016/j.ijer.2021.101804

Oni, T., Assah, F., Erzse, A., Foley, L., Govia, I., Hofman, K. J., ... & Wareham, N. J. (2020). The global diet and activity research (GDAR) network: a global public health partnership to address upstream NCD risk factors in urban low and middle-income contexts. Globalization and Health, 16, 1-11. DOI: 10.1186/s12992-020-00630-y

Ostad-Ali-Askari, K. (2022). Management of risks substances and sustainable development. Applied Water Science. DOI: 10.1007/s13201-021-01562-7

Parker, S. K. & Grote, G. (2022). Automation, algorithms, and beyond: Why work design matters more than ever in a digital world. Applied Psychology. DOI: 10.1111/apps.12241

Pham, V. P. H. (2021). The effects of collaborative writing on students' writing fluency: An efficient framework for collaborative writing. Sage Open. DOI: 10.1177/2158244021998363

Polly, D., Martin, F., & Guilbaud, T. C. (2021). Examining barriers and desired supports to increase faculty members' use of digital technologies: Perspectives of faculty, staff and administrators. . *Journal of Computing in Higher Education*, 33(1), 135–156. Advance online publication. DOI: 10.1007/s12528-020-09259-7

Rådberg, K. K. & Löfsten, H. (2023). The entrepreneurial university and development of large-scale research infrastructure: exploring the emerging university function of collaboration and …. The Journal of Technology Transfer. DOI: 10.1007/s10961-023-10033-x

Rasiah, R., Kaur, H., & Guptan, V. (2020). Business continuity plan in the higher education industry: University students' perceptions of the effectiveness of academic continuity plans during COVID-19 …. Applied System Innovation. DOI: 10.3390/asi3040051

Ray, P. P. (2023). ChatGPT: A comprehensive review on background, applications, key challenges, bias, ethics, limitations and future scope. Internet of Things and Cyber-Physical Systems. DOI: 10.1016/j.iotcps.2023.04.003

Reynolds, R., Aromi, J., McGowan, C., & Paris, B. (2022). Digital divide, critical-, and crisis-informatics perspectives on K-12 emergency remote teaching during the pandemic. Journal of the Association for Information Science and Technology, 73(12), 1665-1680. DOI: 10.1016/j.iotcps.2023.04.003

Richter, S. & Richter, A. (2023). What is novel about the Metaverse?. International Journal of Information Management. DOI: 10.1016/j.ijinfomgt.2023.102684

Roberts, J. K., Pavlakis, A. E., & Richards, M. P. (2021). It's more complicated than it seems: Virtual qualitative research in the COVID-19 era. International journal of qualitative methods, 20, 16094069211002959. DOI: 10.1177/16094069211002959

Røed, R. K., Powell, M. B., Riegler, M. A., & Baugerud, G. A. (2023). A field assessment of child abuse investigators' engagement with a child-avatar to develop interviewing skills. Child Abuse & Neglect. DOI: 10.1016/j.chiabu.2023.106324

Román, M. O., Justice, C., Paynter, I., Boucher, P. B., Devadiga, S., Endsley, A., ... & Wolfe, R. (2024). Continuity between NASA MODIS Collection 6.1 and VIIRS Collection 2 land products. Remote Sensing of Environment, 302, 113963. DOI: 10.1016/j.rse.2023.113963

Rus-Calafell, M., Ward, T., Zhang, X. C., Edwards, C. J., Garety, P., & Craig, T. (2020). The role of sense of voice presence and anxiety reduction in AVATAR therapy. Journal of Clinical Medicine, 9(9), 2748. DOI: 10.3390/jcm9092748

Rysavy, M. D. T. & Michalak, R. (2020). Working from home: How we managed our team remotely with technology. Journal of Library Administration.

Sattar, M., Palaniappan, S., Lokman, A., Shah, N., Khalid, U., & Hasan, R. (2020). Motivating medical students using virtual reality based education. International Journal of Emerging Technologies in Learning (iJET), 15(2), 160-174. DOI: 10.3991/ijet.v15i02.11394

Seo, H. J., Park, G. M., Son, M., & Hong, A. J. (2021). Establishment of virtual-reality-based safety education and training system for safety engagement. Education Sciences. DOI: 10.3390/educsci11120786

Sharp, G., Bourke, L., & Rickard, M. J. F. X. (2020). Review of emotional intelligence in health care: An introduction to emotional intelligence for surgeons. . *ANZ Journal of Surgery*, 90(4), 433–440. Advance online publication. DOI: 10.1111/ans.15671 PMID: 31965690

Simon, N., & Fierro, A. S. (2023). Information technology tools for coil virtual exchange. In *Implementing Sustainable Change in Higher Education* (pp. 312–332). Routledge. DOI: 10.4324/9781003445227-21

Smith, K., Mansfield, J., & Adams, M. (2024). Learning from a dilemma: The opportunities online teaching provided for teacher growth and development. The Australian Educational Researcher. DOI: 10.1007/s13384-024-00704-5

Sobaih, A. E. E., Hasanein, A. M., & Abu Elnasr, A. E. (2020). Responses to COVID-19 in higher education: Social media usage for sustaining formal academic communication in developing countries. Sustainability. DOI: 10.3390/su12166520

Suzuki, S. N., Kanematsu, H., Barry, D. M., Ogawa, N., Yajima, K., Nakahira, K. T., ... & Yoshitake, M. (2020). Virtual Experiments in Metaverse and their Applications to Collaborative Projects: The framework and its significance. Procedia Computer Science, 176, 2125-2132. DOI: 10.1016/j.procs.2020.09.249

Tegally, H., San, J. E., Cotten, M., Moir, M., Tegomoh, B., Mboowa, G., ... & Schubert, G. (2022). The evolving SARS-CoV-2 epidemic in Africa: Insights from rapidly expanding genomic surveillance. Science, 378(6615), eabq5358. DOI: 10.1126/science.abq5358

Thompson, A., Elahi, F., Realpe, A., Birchwood, M., Taylor, D., Vlaev, I., ... & Bucci, S. (2020). A feasibility and acceptability trial of social cognitive therapy in early psychosis delivered through a virtual world: the VEEP study. Frontiers in Psychiatry, 11, 219. DOI: 10.3389/fpsyt.2020.00219

Tlili, A., Huang, R., Shehata, B., Liu, D., Zhao, J., Metwally, A. H. S., ... & Burgos, D. (2022). Is Metaverse in education a blessing or a curse: a combined content and bibliometric analysis. Smart Learning Environments, 9(1), 1-31. DOI: 10.1186/s40561-022-00205-x

Turnbull, D., Chugh, R., & Luck, J. (2021). Transitioning to E-Learning during the COVID-19 pandemic: How have Higher Education Institutions responded to the challenge?. Education and Information Technologies. DOI: 10.1007/s10639-021-10633-w

Ukoha, C. (2022). As simple as pressing a button? A review of the literature on BigBlueButton. Procedia Computer Science. DOI: 10.1016/j.procs.2021.12.167

Umar, M. & Ko, I. (2022). E-learning: Direct effect of student learning effectiveness and engagement through project-based learning, team cohesion, and flipped learning during the .... Sustainability. DOI: 10.3390/su14031724

Valenzano, A., Scarinci, A., Monda, V., Sessa, F., Messina, A., Monda, M., ... & Cibelli, G. (2020). The social brain and emotional contagion: COVID-19 effects. Medicina, 56(12), 640. DOI: 10.3390/medicina56120640

Van den Beemt, A., Groothuijsen, S., Ozkan, L., & Hendrix, W. (2023). Remote labs in higher engineering education: engaging students with active learning pedagogy. Journal of Computing in Higher Education, 35(2), 320-340. DOI: 10.1007/s12528-022-09331-4

Van den Beemt, A., MacLeod, M., Van der Veen, J., Van de Ven, A., Van Baalen, S., Klaassen, R., & Boon, M. (2020). Interdisciplinary engineering education: A review of vision, teaching, and support. Journal of engineering education, 109(3), 508-555. DOI: 10.1002/jee.20347

Vauterin, J. J. & Virkki-Hatakka, T. (2021). Mentoring PhD students working in industry: Using hermeneutics as a critical approach to the experience. Industry and Higher Education. DOI: 10.1177/0950422220959233

Wang, C. L. (2021). New frontiers and future directions in interactive marketing: Inaugural Editorial. *Journal of Research in Interactive Marketing*, 15(1), 1–9. DOI: 10.1108/JRIM-03-2021-270

Whillans, A., Perlow, L., & Turek, A. (2021). Experimenting during the shift to virtual team work: Learnings from how teams adapted their activities during the COVID-19 pandemic. Information and Organization. DOI: 10.1016%2Fj.infoandorg.2021.100343

Winton, B. G. (2022). Emotional intelligence congruence: The influence of leader and follower emotional abilities on job satisfaction. . *Leadership and Organization Development Journal*, 43(5), 788–801. Advance online publication. DOI: 10.1108/LODJ-04-2021-0163

Witherspoon, D. P., White, R. M., Bámaca, M. Y., Browning, C. R., Leech, T. G., Leventhal, T., Matthews, S. A., Pinchak, N., Roy, A. L., Sugie, N., & Winkler, E. N. (2023). Place-based developmental research: Conceptual and methodological advances in studying youth development in context. *Monographs of the Society for Research in Child Development*, 88(3), 7–130. DOI: 10.1111/mono.12472 PMID: 37953661

Wu, T. (2022). Digital project management: Rapid changes define new working environments. . *The Journal of Business Strategy*, 43(5), 323–331. Advance online publication. DOI: 10.1108/JBS-03-2021-0047

Zhang, M., Ding, H., Naumceska, M., & Zhang, Y. (2022). Virtual reality technology as an educational and intervention tool for children with autism spectrum disorder: current perspectives and future directions. Behavioral Sciences. DOI: 10.3390/bs12050138

Zhang, T., Shaikh, Z. A., Yumashev, A. V., & Chłąd, M. (2020). Applied model of E-learning in the framework of education for sustainable development. Sustainability. DOI: 10.3390/su12166420

Zhang, Y., Zhao, R., & Yu, X. (2022). Enhancing virtual team performance via high-quality interpersonal relationships: Effects of authentic leadership. *International Journal of Manpower*, 43(4), 982–1000. Advance online publication. DOI: 10.1108/IJM-08-2020-0378

Zhao, Y., Pohl, O., Bhatt, A. I., Collis, G. E., Mahon, P. J., Rüther, T., & Hollenkamp, A. F. (2021). A review on battery market trends, second-life reuse, and recycling. Sustainable Chemistry, 2(1), 167-205. DOI: 10.3390/suschem2010011

Chapter 11
Fostering Effective Communication and Information Sharing in Higher Education Institutions

Hlompho Cynthia Letsie
Limkokwing University of Creative Technology, Lesotho

Tsepiso Claurina Mncina
Limkokwing University of Creative Technology, Lesotho

Sekoai Elliot Nkhi
https://orcid.org/0000-0001-7929-6550
Limkokwing University of Creative Technology, Lesotho

Mofana Mongali Mofana
Limkokwing University of Creative Technology, Lesotho

ABSTRACT

Effective communication is crucial for cohesive team dynamics in higher education settings, going beyond individual interaction. This chapter discussed the effective communication and information sharing towards the development effective and high Performing teams in higher education. In higher education institutions, email, bulletin boards, messaging applications, and questionnaires are efficient means of communication in order for high performing teams. It is revealed that communication obstacles including language, cultural, psychological, emotional, environmental,

DOI: 10.4018/979-8-3693-3852-0.ch011

and physical barriers are the main hindrance of effective communication. In order to surmount these challenges, the study proposes an emotional intelligence model of communication to overcome the identified obstacles because they have psychological impact on communicators and for the development of high performing teams. As a result, recommend that self-acknowledgment and positive interpersonal relationships, which are fundamental components of emotional intelligence be considered to develop high performing teams.

INTRODUCTION

In recent decades, higher education systems globally are considered organizations because they are collectives founded by individuals to achieve and maintain specific objectives (Lueg & Graf, 2021; Roy & El Marsafawy, 2020). Universities and higher education institutions have different interests but their operations depend on human cooperation. Academics are viewed as essential societal institutions that produce certain activities and work to teach and train people with knowledge and skills that are relevant to the society (Lueg & Graf, 2021). Scholars like Zorlu and Korkmaz (2021) emphasize that in order for employees in organizations to successfully complete tasks and negotiate the complexity of contemporary organizational structures, there has to be strong interdepartmental interactions within the institutions. Therefore, there is a growing need to promote efficient communication and information exchange amongst and within higher education institutions in order to ensure high performance and long-term growth. We therefore argue that performance amongst team members cannot be of high standard if communication from decision making departments is ineffective. For teams to perform to the best of their abilities, communication ought to be effective.

Organizational communication is seen as a dynamic social process that facilitates information sharing within departments and its external environment (Zorlu & Korkmaz, 2021). This distinction highlights how important channels of communication are to the development of coherent operational frameworks that support the accomplishment of institutional goals. Moreover, Welch and Jackson (2007) substantiate the significance of internal communication in strategic management's capacity to motivate staff members or teams to dedicate themselves to the organization's objectives by demonstrating the critical role that it plays in fostering organizational success. According to Morgan et al. (2021), especially in the context of higher education institutions, the importance of effective communication extends beyond individual interactions to include cohesive team dynamics. Prioritizing openness and using appropriate communication strategies can help the organizations to reap favorable results for sustainability. However, poor organizational communication can make it more difficult to achieve desired results (Lee & Queenie Li, 2021; Hargie 2016). Therefore, it is important to make a deliberate effort to maintain effective communication channels within higher learning institutions.

Furthermore, Aysha et al. (2016) posit that thorough assessment of management-employee conversations in higher education establishments is necessary to determine their impact on favourable results. The authors emphasize the importance of management's understanding of the organizational environment building stakeholder trust on institutional goals. Although existing literature dwells on effective communication tactics in an organization, there is still little to no research on the long-term process of promoting communication, especially in Lesotho's higher education institutions. As a result of this paucity, additional study into the process of fostering effective communication in the institutions of higher learning is necessary to bridge this knowledge gap and offer guidance on how to create communication cultures that are sustainable for organizational growth.

THEORETICAL ORIENTATION

The chapter espouses the Dialogic Theory (DT) coined in 1998 from the seminal work of Kent and Taylor on "Building dialogic relationships through the World Wide Web" (Kent & Taylor 1998). Dialogue in communication was explored by to religious philosopher Martin Buber in 1958 (Kent & Taylor, 2002). Buber suggests that dialogue involves an effort to recognize the value of the other participant and not merely see them as means to achieving a desired goal (Kent & Taylor, 2002). Kent (2017) adds that dialogue embodies a principle of communication aimed at facilitating interaction between individuals or small groups of people. Furthermore, Weller (2013) notes that dialogue builds and improves channels of communication and understanding between an organization and its stakeholders. In the context of this study, we believe that dialogic communication is crucial for the development of effective and high-performing teams in higher education. The theory established five principles of dialogue that include risk, empathy, mutuality, commitment and propinquity (Kent & Taylor, 2002: 22). Risk as the first principle implies that since organizations communicate in their own terms, their open communication exposes them to criticism and unpredicted consequences (Kent & Taylor, 2002; Brekke, 2015). We therefore contend that opening up to criticism and being vulnerable clearly reveals that the organization is willing to foster effective communication because concerns of its stakeholders will be taken into account. Furthermore, empathy suggests that communicators should sympathize with their audience to gain trust because once trust is earned, support to the organization is guaranteed, leading to a successful communication which is the foundation to good public relations (Kent

& Taylor 2002; Lane & Bartlett, 2016; Kent & Taylor, 2021). Moreover, mutuality emphasizes the importance of establishing a common ground and understanding in the relationship which are based on collaboration and mutual equality (Kent & Taylor, 2002). We therefore argue for mutual relationship and empathy because trust will be gained, and all parties will feel valued if they both agree on the terms of their relationship and engagement. Commitment as another principle of DT refers to the organization's ability during communication to strive for open, genuine and honest communication where exchange of ideas is feasible (Lane & Bartlett, 2016). Propinquity as the last principle, calls for thorough consultations with stakeholders on issues that affect them in order to get their opinions (Lane & Bartlett, 2016; Kent & Taylor, 2021). We therefore believe that consultations with relevant stakeholders will result in communication that would be seamless as their views will be incorporated.

The theory was further improved on by Megan Ward who added five other principles to the theory (Ward, 2013). First principle is dialogic loop, which calls for a two-way communication through the medium which will facilitate interaction between the organisation and its stakeholders (Ward, 2013). We therefore believe that if the organisation identifies suitable communication platform that facilitates two-way communication for better interactions, it stands a higher chance of developing effective and high-performing teams for growth. Usefulness of information as the second principle suggests that information shared should be informative and valuable to stakeholders. The third principle is return visits which places emphasis on regular interaction on platforms that facilitate engagement (Ward, 2013). We are of the opinion that if information shared is valuable to audience, they will return for more and this will result in better engagement. The fourth principle is ease of interface, which implies that technology that eases communication with stakeholders should be easily accessed for information. The last principle is conservation of visitors, which suggests that digital platforms used should have links for visitors to branch to other sources of information without leaving the platform (Ward, 2013). This means that if the platforms used have links, users will find no reason to wander around in search of information.

Looking into the idea of fostering effective communication and information sharing in higher education institutions, we felt a need to complement DT with the transactional model of communication illustrated below in figure 1, which signifies the importance of two-way communication and other elements while not ignoring the immense impact of noise in communication. The message, sender, recipient, their ability to encode and decode the massage as well as the body language, tone, and environment in which the message is delivered are the crucial elements (Turner, 2020). While active listening and providing feedback are both necessary for effective communication, building trust, solving problems and accomplishing shared objectives all depend on effective communication (Turner, 2020).

Figure 1. Transactional model of communication (adopted from Adler and Rodman, 2009)

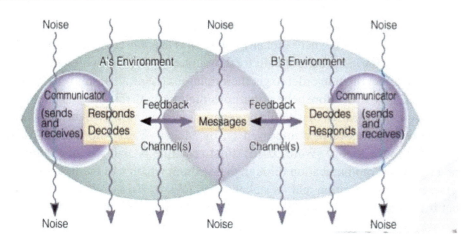

The above Barnlund's Transactional model of communication acknowledges the dynamic and interactive character of interpersonal communication. It also emphasizes the importance of a two-way communication in which messages and feedback are exchanged simultaneously between the sender and the recipient as stipulated by DT's dialogic loop (Jan-Mendoza, 2020; Baskin & Bruno, 1977). The model emphasizes the value of shared meaning in which both sides actively contribute to the interpretation and comprehension of the messages that are being communicated as well as the feedback (Tariq, 2023). This model is believed to be the most effective as it allows for immediate feedback from communicators who exchange their position (Mncina et al., 2024). According to this model, context and body language, in addition to spoken cues, are important means of meaningful communication (Barnlund, 1970). By encouraging attentive listening, compassion and an open mind, the model helps teams to communicate more effectively by building meaningful relationships, thus improving communication as well as having a deeper knowledge of others. The model takes into account the environment in which the communication takes place and recognizes that teams in the context of this study have a range of experiences including knowledge of communication in relational, social, psychological and physical contexts (Peate, 2021). The model further emphasizes the significance of contextual impacts outside of the single encounter notably social, cultural and relational contexts because it contends that communication forms a person's reality both before and after specific interactions occur (Barnlund, 1970). Therefore, we argue that the foundation for promoting efficient communication and information exchange is laid by the DT and Barnlund's Transactional model of communication.

EFFECTIVE COMMUNICATION

Effective communication is essential in institutions of higher learning and higher performing teams because it serves as a foundation for accomplishing objectives of the institutions (Turner, 2020). Mncina et al. (2023) and Zulch (2014) state that effective communication is about measuring the efficiency of communication which begins with understanding the capacity to communicate ideas clearly, accurately and by making sure that the receiver understands the message. This is done to facilitate mutual understanding within the institution as reflected in the mutuality principle of DT which acknowledges the importance of other team members. In general, communication is considered effective when it achieves objectives of the institution of higher learning and fulfills its intended purpose (Muszynska, 2018). However, determining the efficacy of communication can be difficult, particularly in higher education institutions because a detailed list of attributes that characterize the success of the communication process is needed (Muszynska, 2018). For the sake of cooperation and institutional development, we contend that effective communication is achievable if the institution pays more attention to these factors and integrates them into its communications. We also believe that reducing communication barriers is also necessary, particularly when it comes to the communicators' psychological well-being.

Among others, effective institutional communication relies heavily on clarity since its purpose is to ensure that the intended audience understands the messages (Muszynska, 2018). This is accentuated by the transactional model of communication during encoding and decoding stage. Furthermore, communicating in a clear and simple language, minimizing ambiguity and rationally arranging ideas for clarity renders communication effective (Olugbo et al., 2023). Active listening takes place when the message amongst team members within the institution is clear as stressed by the model. This indicates that participants pay close attention to the speaker, and they will actively participate within their teams as well as providing comments to show that they have understood messages intended for them (Phiri, 2021). In the context of this study, throughout meetings, seminars, and group discussions, faculty staff can all demonstrate active listening by keeping eye contact, nodding in agreement, and asking clarifying questions to ensure understanding. Incorporating nonverbal cues in institutional communication is vital because body language, gestures, and facial expressions emphasize what is being said as it conveys emotions and intentions (Dash, 2022). This notion is reflected in the transactional model's psychological factor and commitment principle of the DT.

Furthermore, feedback mechanisms also act as crucial conduits for measuring the efficacy of communication techniques and enabling continual development within an institution (Adu-Oppong, 2014). Additionally, adaptation emerges as a needed talent which enables team members to alter their communication tactics to varied contexts and staff and dynamic conditions intrinsic to institutions of higher learning (Uhl-Bien & Arena, 2018). Moreover, cultural sensitivity underlines the need to recognize and respect diverse cultural origins, traditions and communication styles prevalent among academic communities. We therefore argue that institutions may create a dynamic and inclusive communication environment that supports equitable involvement, creativity, and academic collaboration among staff and faculties by incorporating feedback loops, encouraging flexibility, and promoting cultural sensitivity (Baumgartner et al., 2015). Clarity of purpose is a guiding principle in the context of effective communication in higher education institutions because it guarantees that messages are communicated precisely and in line with overall goals, and thus maintaining mutuality principle of the theory whether in academic, support staff and administrative team members' communication (Olugbo, Obienu, & Frank 2023).

Similarly, civility and respect as supported by the commitment and propinquity principles of the DT set the ground rules for social interactions. This happens by creating a climate in which people of different backgrounds feel appreciated and encouraged to make significant contributions to discussions within the institution (Bonotti & Zech, 2021). Additionally, in order to facilitate ongoing evaluation, improvement and adaptation of communication strategies to meet the changing needs and preferences of stakeholders, feedback mechanisms and a dedication to continuous improvement are essential components of effective communication within academic settings (Phiri, 2021). Higher education institutions can foster a culture of effective communication where collaboration, innovation, and mutual respect among members are permanent features. We therefore uphold that this can be achieved by maintaining clarity of purpose, respect, and courtesy, as well as by embracing feedback-driven improvement cycles because team performance depends on communication, which Mckinney and Gammie (2004) relate to as a blood flow in the body. Therefore, any institution that understands the importance of communication prioritizes it at their workplace. Nonetheless, there are various types of communication within the institution that vary depending on the goal of communication, and they are expounded on below.

Types Of Communication in an Institution of Higher Education

Strong staff involvement is largely attributed to standardized internal communication techniques in high-achieving institutions with importance placed on teamwork, creativity, and overall institutional effectiveness (Lammers, 2011). We therefore argue that the efficacy of communication methods depends on the messages being sent as stipulated by the usefulness of information principle of the DT. The importance of formal communication for institutional effectiveness is emphasized, and formal channels of communication are used for training programs that provide employees with knowledge and skills to improve institutional productivity (Terzić, 2018; Letsie et al., 2023). One of the most common types of formal communication is vertical communication which consists of bottom-up; used commonly by subordinates to communicate to the management while top-down communication is primarily used by management to give instructions, direction, and supervision to subordinates (Olugbo, 2023). In horizontal communication, information and expertise are shared between employees who are at the same level of hierarchy or amongst peers of similar status (Abbott, 2012). This interpersonal communication promotes understanding, cooperation and effectiveness (Terzić, 2018). We therefore believe that the adoption of both horizontal and vertical communication channels can improve worker productivity, self-assurance, punctuality, and effectiveness because this two-way communication can improve organizational performance (Terzić, 2018). Letsie and Osunkule (2023) advocate for the sensible selection of communication routes tailored for the specific objectives of institutional communication endeavors by ensuring the accurate and relevant dissemination of information within the institution.

Effective Communication Channels in Higher Education

Good communication channels are essential in higher education institutions because they make it easier for different stakeholders to share important information as maintained by DT principle of commitment that emphasizes the importance of open and honest communication to share ideas and conservation of visitors where organizations are able to retain their visitors on their digital platforms. Email has remained a mainstay among these platforms, proving its effectiveness in reaching a large audience and informing staff members of critical updates (Hassini, 2006). The coordination of institutional activities and the regular distribution of updates are facilitated by the use of intranet and online platforms. Furthermore, in-person and virtual meetings are essential platforms used for important matters within the organization (Floyd, 2013). Additionally, notice boards placed in strategic locations on university campuses or on institutional websites function as physical platforms through which information relevant to all employees is disseminated (McConnell,

2007). Modern communication methods such as message apps provide direct and instantaneous contact between people or small groups and complement the conventional channels (Floyd, 2013). In addition, organizations use questionnaires and other feedback methods to ask staff about administrative concerns (Floyd, 2013). However, all of these depend on the nature of messages sent as purported by DT's ease of interface, return visits and conservation of visit principle. Within the framework of this study, easy communication helps to identify problems and facilitates solutions to them. As a result, we believe that in the context of higher education, this diverse approach to communication guarantees a smooth exchange of information, which encourages teamwork as well as improving institutional efficacy. However, we are aware that sharing of information does not only depend on the aforementioned channels and types of communication, we therefore expanded our arguments by looking closely at what can hinder effective communication and information sharing within institutions of higher learning.

Effective Communication Challenges in Institutions of Higher Education

Communication challenges such as culture, language, psychological, emotional, environmental, physical and technological barriers continually haunt the institutions of higher learning and strain relations among team members. Cultural barriers are eminent in academic institutions due to diverse nationalities, traditions and religions (Kapur, 2018). Similarly, Usha (2016) and Kapur (2018) add that when communicating with people from different cultural backgrounds, one has to be aware of the values, beliefs and attitudes that group holds and eventually move to the stage of acceptance of another person's culture. We believe that institutions of higher learning should be mindful of these subtle barriers because they can make or break the organization. In similar vein, language barriers are also major offenders that hamper effective communication and engagement. Usha (2016) and Kapur (2018) posit that language barriers often spring out if people do not share the same language, jargon and signs and symbols used globally. For example, academic staff members in different faculties are likely to use jargon in their field, and this could be confusing to the recipient. Furthermore, we argue for the use of a simple language to share information among team members that can break any semantic barrier, which is another factor hindering effective communication especially in multinational institutions. Semantic barrier, which refers to misunderstanding and wrong interpretation of meaning, often surfaces during encoding or decoding of message in the communication process (Gulam, n.d). It is particularly concerning when local languages are spoken on campus in front of international staff, or when languages are switched during staff meetings. This situation leaves them feeling overwhelmed and excluded as they struggle to comprehend the message being conveyed (Nkhi & Shange, 2024). This calls for shared meaning on interpretation of the messages to ensure smooth communication because failure to do so might result in tension and negative attitudes.

While effective communication is reliant on mental abilities of conversing parties, psychological factors can become obstacles to seamless communication among team members (Kannan & Meenakshi, 2022). Similarly, Kapur (2018) emphasizes the value of understanding the mental state and capacity of the team members as these elements make it easier to have a common understanding. This is in line with DT principle on mutuality, which stresses the need to establish a common ground during communication for better relations and collaboration (Kent & Taylor, 2002). In addition, Kannan and Meenakshi (2022) postulate that socio-psychological communication barriers affect the operation of organizations including education institutions. We believe that institutions of higher learning could find the common ground and nurture relationships if they engage in robust consultations with their stakeholders. This is substantiated by the DT principle, propinquity that advocates for consultations with members before making decisions. Moreover, psychological factors influence the emotional barriers emanating from either the sender or receiver that has potential to distort the communication (Sudhagar & Pradeep Gnanam, 2018; Kannan & Meenakshi, 2022). For example, emotions such as rage, sadness, stress, happiness affect the state of an individual, and all these can affect communication positively or negatively (Kannan & Meenakshi, 2022). We therefore contend that if institutions of higher learning are mindful of these emotions, team members will effectively engage leading to the attainment of organizational goals.

Another psychological barrier is hierarchical status in which junior colleagues become reluctant to engage with seniors and prefer to keep 'safe' distance. This is impersonal and also creates communication challenges, because colleagues will not be free to openly share their views (Sudhagar & Gnanam, 2018). Moreover, Usha (2016) opines that status or power within institutions of higher learning results in communication breakdown as some members would demand privileged treatment based on their perceived status. This also fuels the emotions of both the encoder and the decoder of the message. We believe that effective teams are built on effective communication, therefore team members should engage at all levels of the organization irrespective of hierarchical position as echoed by the propinquity principle that encourages thorough consultations and engagement with all stakeholders within the organization.

Communication takes place in the environment that is plagued by series of physical barriers such as noise, time and distance. Ineffectiveness of communication is closely linked to physical barriers, because communication in noisy environment, messages will be misunderstood or distorted, stating that place with lesser distractions could aid effective communication (Jelani & Nordin 2019, Kapur, 2018). We therefore argue that noise reflected in the Barnlund's Transactional model of communication could be a psychological barrier because it has potential to cause confusion, frustration, and anxiety among team members. In addition, different time zones, physical setting and distance between team members especially in international institutions have proven to be challenging, and this calls for all parties to adjust during communication (Usha, 2016; Jelani & Nordin, 2019). In the transactional model of communication, noise has the potential to disrupt any stage of the process. For instance, the sender, also known as communicator 1, may encounter challenges during encoding due to lack of clarity in their thoughts, resulting in an unclear message. Additionally, a lack of expertise in a specific subject matter or language barrier can lead to confusion. This can make it challenging for the receiver, or communicator 2, to fully grasp the intended message. Furthermore, noise can arise from a lack of necessary background information, leading to misinterpretation of the message. Biases held by the decoder towards the encoder or the message content can also contribute to noise. When it comes to the channel, noise may manifest when there is poor signal quality on the selected channel for transmitting the message. It is imperative for institutions to recognize that noise may arise at any stage of the communication process when messages are being exchanged between two parties.

Although communication takes place in different forms such as audio, video, oral and many others, Kapur (2018) writes that selecting the right medium of communication is critical for effective communication as it will facilitate interactions. Kim et al. (2017) add that effective communication channels which facilitate two-way communication are transparent and easily accessible and also open to all stakeholders. This is commensurate with DT principle on dialogic loop which advocates for two-way communication through the appropriate medium (Ward, 2013). If communication channels are not open, this could be a barrier because communication will be unidirectional, which means that the element of exchange and interaction will cease to exist. One-way communication is contrary to Barnlund's Transactional model of communication, which emphasizes the importance of a two-way communication (Jan-Mendoza, 2020; Baskin & Bruno, 1977). In the context of this study, we contend that institutions of higher learning should consider effective channels of communication that will foster effective communication and eliminate negative emotions and attitudes towards team members.

Technology enhances communication and interaction in the 21stcentury. However, challenges presented by these online communication platforms cannot be ruled out as some team members struggle to use the available platforms for interaction. Additionally, Arulele and Jere (2022) stated that some members may be technologically challenged. In order to close the digital gap, Kannan and Meenakshi (2022) advocate for access to technological information and relevant training targeting team members. Technology has also been criticized for enabling minimal face-to-face interactions and non-verbal cues, thus affecting the quality of communication because team members no longer engage in robust discussions to gain deeper understanding on issues around the organization (Medium, 2024; Husami, 2022). The use of technology in developing countries can also be a challenge due to the digital divide. For multinational organizations that have campuses in developing countries, some communities struggle to get access or keep up to speed of connectivity due to poor broadband infrastructure penetration (Aruleba & Jere, 2022). This means that some team members will not be easily reached, resulting in failure to communicate crucial messages.

Measures to Improve Communication in Institutions of Higher Education

In order to overcome challenges mentioned above, institutions of higher learning are tasked with the important instruction of clearly stating their expectations to ensure effective communication. It is important for organizations to eliminate cross-cultural barriers as they may be subtle or invisible at times. The first step is to develop cultural sensitivity or competence where individual team members have genuine respect and thorough understanding of different cultural norms, values and encourage mindfulness of those differences (Akkilinc, 2018). This view is supported by Jenifer and Raman (2015) that cross- cultural communication skills fosters effective communication among team members and this could result in seamless interaction among team members resulting in high performing teams. While communication is lifeblood of high performing teams, we believe that language should be prioritized to enable effective communication. We are of the view that language training should be mandatory for team members who use different languages and those likely to interact with foreigners (Letsie et al., 2023; Jenifer & Raman, 2015). In addition, Kapur (2018) suggests that simple language could be an answer in trying to minimize confusion in communication. Moreover, semantic hurdles and linguistic barriers can be eliminated by using inclusive language that is straightforward, avoids unnecessary jargon or technical terms, thus making sure that everyone understands, participate and provide the necessary explanations. This is consistent with the DT principle on commitment where all stakeholders are free to share their views (Steigerwald et al., 2022; Bullock, 2019).

Addressing the psychological barriers relies on team members' capacity to regulate their emotional intelligence, and this can help them transcend the psychological impact of their emotions in order to foster institutional teamwork and growth (Wollny et al., 2020). This view is consistent with Kannan and Meenakshi (2022) that emotions such as rage, sadness, stress and happiness have the potential to affect communication positively or negatively. We also propose that the speaker should be aware of the non-verbal cues as they might send mixed signals to the message recipients. We also suggest that institutions of higher learning should adopt an open door policy where all team members are able to interact freely. This will enable a healthy working environment where all team members will freely raise their opinions to relevant authorities within the institution. This is critical because Usha (2016) argues that status or power within institutions of higher learning results in communication breakdown. This is also echoed by DT principle on commitment, which calls for open, genuine and honest communication where exchange of ideas is feasible (Lane & Bartlett, 2016).

Having realized that environmental or physical barriers hugely impact team members' communication, it is important that institutions of higher learning are aware of the physical environment as distractions coming from the physical setting could be noise in communication, which could result in ineffective communication and poor productivity. This view is commensurate with Hargie (2016) that reducing outside distractions, managing noise, and dealing with any issues that could affect communication is critical. Equally important, international higher learning institution should also consider physical distance and different time zones to ensure effective communication. This view is confirmed by Usha (2016) and Jelani and Nordin (2019) that international institutions should adjust and adapt their communication to suit all team members.

We further suggest that institutions of higher learning should identify suitable channels and medium of communication that enable open communication. This is in line with transactional model of communication which emphasizes the importance of a channel of communication that permits two-way communication (Hargie, 2016). In addition, we believe that regular meetings and effective communication tools serve as vital platforms for the exchange of skills, ideas as well as the promotion of critical thinking and perspectives thereby nurturing open dialogue and collaborative problem-solving which promote active staff rather than passive recipients of information (Deysolong, 2023; Matošková, 2020). This is reflected in the dialogic loop tenet of the theory that emphasizes the importance of two-way communication through the medium which facilitates effective interaction (Ward, 2013).

Furthermore, this chapter calls for all-inclusive training for efficient use of technological devices and digital platforms for all members to ensure efficient use of relevant communication tools to facilitate virtual meetings and real-time communication thus encouraging information sharing and cooperative problem solving in a more constructive and participatory learning environment (Josué et al., 2023). This is in line with the dialogic loop principle which encourages the use of relevant tools of communication (Ward, 2023). In developing countries where digital divide is reality, we advocate for organizations to strike a balance between face-to-face interactions and use of technology in communication in order to reach all team members. This is substantiated by Aruleba and Jere (2022) that poor broadband infrastructure penetration in many developing countries could hamper effective communication for multinational organizations.

It is evident that all communication challenges identified above are closely linked to psychological barriers because culture, language, status, semantic, environmental and physical and technological barriers can evoke emotions leading to negative attitudes if the emotions of the sender are not in check. We therefore propose emotional intelligent model of communication illustrated below in figure 2, which emphasizes the importance of controlling emotions in stressful situations for effective institutional communication. This is because no matter what happens; there will always be a barrier that hampers effective communication. Our proposed model in figure 2 is an improvement of Barnlund's Transactional model of communication which incorporates two new tenets, which are emotions and attitudes of both the sender and the receiver as illustrated by two arrows pointing at opposite directions. The orange arrows indicate the impact that emotions have on communication. For instance, if an institution's management sends a vague message to various teams, even though it is sent through the appropriate channel and uses the appropriate type of communication, it may have a negative effect on teams because it lacks clarity, leading to confusion and misunderstanding amongst the employees. As a result, these employees may interpret the message differently and provide negative feedback or exude negative attitudes in response to the message. This also applies when the messages are positive; this will result in positive feedback and positive attitudes towards the sender as shown by the two orange arrows.

Figure 2. The emotional intelligent model of communication

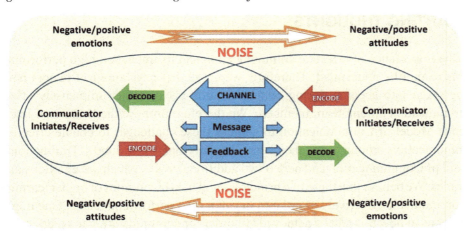

FUTURE DIRECTIONS

It is clear that psychological barriers have overarching effect on communication within the institutions of higher learning. While it is imperative to communicate both vertically and horizontally to share information among team members, communication offices within institutions should be central to all communication across different departments in order to eliminate misunderstanding, confusion and anxiety from unclear communication. We believe that self-acknowledgement and good associations with others are the core tenets of emotional intelligence because they include the ability to identify and categorize emotions, understand the underlying causes and consequences of those emotions, and regulate them in an adaptive manner (Goleman, 1995). Numerous components of developing emotional intelligence are also recognized to lessen stress in both staff and the institution. These components include lowering conflict, fostering better relationships, understanding, promoting harmony, stability, and continuity. People who dedicate themselves to developing practical competencies in the context of everyday settings have higher levels of emotional intelligence (Sinha & Sinha, 2007). The above submission cements our argument that emotional intelligence offers a fresh perspective on how to evaluate and comprehend people's behaviors, management styles, attitudes and interpersonal skills for high performing teams. This implies that whatever communication predicament the institution is facing, if emotions are subdued, the institution can foster effective communication and share necessary information amongst the relevant stakeholders. We strongly uphold the view that messages sent with negative emotions yield negative feedback as well as negative attitudes, but messages sent with positive emotions yield positive feedback and positive attitudes.

DEPARTING THOUGHTS

The importance of effective communication and its impact on high performing teams cannot be underrated. Therefore, we argue that psychological factors have to be taken into account during communication because they immensely affect communication among team members. We therefore propose the Emotional Intelligence Model of Communication to address these challenges to enable effective communication among team members. We developed Barnlund's Transactional Model of Communication and added two additional tenets which are emotions and attitudes. We believe that these two principles will help institutions of higher learning to communicate effectively in order to develop high performing teams. One might wonder as to how this can be achieved? In order for communication to be effective, we believe that emotions and attitudes should be considered for messages can be interpreted differently. A positive message is likely to be received with a positive attitude, while a negative message can be received with negative attitude. Therefore, the type of messages communicated can either trigger negative or positive emotions. Positive emotions suggest that teams will highly perform. Our point of departure is that while this model enhances effective communication as both parties are at liberty to initiate communication, we argue that communication in institutions of higher learning could be effective if each communicator is aware of their emotional state as this has net effect on the attitudes to be exuded by the message recipients. We have therefore contributed to theme of this book 'Developing Effective and High-Performing Teams in Higher Education' by coming up with strategies that can be employed for of effective communication geared towards the development of high performing teams. We even developed our model that we hope will strengthen effective communication in higher education.

REFERENCES

Adler, R. B., & Rodman, G. R. (2009). *Understanding human communication* (10th ed.). Oxford University Press.

Adu-Oppong, A. (2014). Communication In the Workplace: Guidelines for Improving Effectiveness. *Global Journal of Commerce & Management Perspectives.* 208-213.

Akkilinc, F. (2018). The importance of navigating cultural differences and comprehending cross-cultural communication. *Journal of International Social Research.*, 1(59), 607–613. DOI: 10.17719/jisr.2018.2666

Aruleba, K., & Jere, N. (2022). Exploring digital transforming challenges in rural areas of South Africa through a systematic review of empirical studies. *Scientific African*, 16, e01190. Advance online publication. DOI: 10.1016/j.sciaf.2022.e01190

Aysha, S., Berhannudin, M., Zulida, K., & Sazuliana, S. (2016). The relationship between organizational communication and employees productivity with new dimensions of effective communication flow. *Journal of Business and Social Review in Emerging Economies*, 2(93), 93–100. Advance online publication. DOI: 10.26710/jbsee.v2i2.35

Barnlund, D. C. (1970). A transactional model of communication. In Sereno, K. K., & Mortenson, C. D. (Eds.), *Foundations of communication theory* (pp. 83–92). Harper and Row.

Baskin, O., & Bruno, S. J. (1977). A Transactional Systems Model of Communication: Implications for transactional analysis. *Journal of Business Communication*, 15(1), 65–73. DOI: 10.1177/002194367701500106

Baumgartner, D., Bay, M., Lopez-Reyna, N. A., Snowden, P. A., & Maiorano, M. J. (2015). Culturally responsive practice for teacher educators: Eight recommendations. *Multiple Voices for Ethnically Diverse Exceptional Learners*, 15(1), 44–58. DOI: 10.56829/2158-396X.15.1.44

Bonotti, M., & Zech, S. T. (2021). *Understanding Ccvility. Recovering civility during COVID-19.* Palgrave Macmillan., DOI: 10.1007/978-981-33-6706-7

Brekke, T. S. K. (2015). Engaging publics through social Media: A study of how Netcom and Altibox communicate to create engagement on Facebook. (Publication no. 10852) [Masters dissertation, University of Oslo] University of Oslo e-Repository

Bullock, O., Colon, A. D., Shulman, H., & Dixon, G. (2019). Jargon as a barrier to effective science communication: Evidence from metacognition. *Public Understanding of Science (Bristol, England)*, 28(7), 096366251986568. DOI: 10.1177/0963662519865687 PMID: 31354058

Dash, B. (2022). *Significance of nonverbal communication and paralinguistic features in communication: A critical analysis.* https://doi.org/.DOI: 10.2015/IJIRMF/202204029

Deysolong, J. (2023). Assessing the benefits of cooperative learning or group work: Fostering collaboration and enhancing learning outcomes. *International Journal of e-Collaboration.* DOI: 10.6084/m9.figshare.23009159

Elo, S., Kääriäinen, M., Kanste, O., Pölkki, T., Utriainen, K., & Kyngäs, H. (2014). *Qualitative content analysis: A focus on trustworthiness.* Sage Publications. https://journals.sagepub.com/doi/pdf/10.1177/2158244014522633

Floyd, A. (2013). *Modern communication and intranets: Tools for effective internal communication.* https://doi.org/DOI: 10.101610.13140

Goleman, D. (1995). *Emotional intelligence.* Bantam Books, Inc. https://asantelim.wordpress.com/wp-content/uploads/2018/05/daniel-goleman-emotional-intelligence.pdf

Greenwood, S. (2020, November 9). Conducting qualitative secondary data analysis: PGT projects working document. Edshare UK. https://edshare.gla.ac.uk/867/5/conductingsecondary qualitative data analysis.pdf

Gulam, K. (nd). Business communication: Basic concepts and skills, chapter 4: *Barriers to Communication* [PowerPoint slides] https://www.gpnngr.org.in/lms/EXS-First%20year%20ECS%20Chapter%204%20Barriers%20to%20Communication.pdf

Hargie, O. (2016). The importance of communication for organisational effectiveness. In. Lobo, F. (Ed.) *Psicologia do Trabalho e das Organizações. Braga*, (pp. 15-32) Axioma.

Hassini, E. (2006). Student instructor communication: The role of email, computers and education. *Computers & Education*, 47(1), 29–40. DOI: 10.1016/j.compedu.2004.08.014

Husami, K. (2022, May 10). *How can technology be a barrier to communication?* Inside telecom. https://insidetelecom.com/how-can-technology-be-a-barrier-to-communication/

Jan-Mendoza, C. (2020). Communication and Communication Models. https://www.academia.edu/44018864/Communication_and_Communication_Models

Jelani, F., & Nordin, N. S. (2019). Barriers to effective communication at the workplace. *Universiti Teknologi MARA, 3*(2), 7-18 https://ir.uitm.edu.my/id/eprint/63597/1/63597.pdf

Jenifer, R. D., & Raman, G. P. (2015). Cross- cultural communication barriers in workplace. *International Journal of Management*, 6(1), 332–335. https://www.iaeme.com/IJM.asp

Josué, A., Bedoya-Flores, M., Mosquera-Quiñonez, E., Mesías-Simisterra, Á., & Bautista-Sánchez, J. (2023). Educational platforms: Digital tools for the teaching-learning process in education. *Ibero-American Journal of Education & Society Research*, 3(1), 259–263. DOI: 10.56183/iberoeds.v3i1.626

Kannan, M., & Meenakshi, S. (2022). An analysis of the socio-psychological barriers in the course of communicative competence in the English language. *International Journal of Social Science and Humanities Research*, 10(2), 115–122.

Kapur, R. (2018). *Barriers to effective communication.* Researchgate. https://www.researchgate.net/publication/323794732_barriers_to_effective_communication

Kent, M. L. (2017). *Principles of dialogue and the history of Dialogic Theory in public relations. Researchgate.*https://www.researchgate.net/publication/318509024_Principles_of_Dialogue_and_the_ History_of_Dialogic_Theory_in_Public_Relations

Kent, M. L., & Taylor, M. (1998). Building dialogic relationships through the World Wide Web. *Public Relations Review*, 24(3), 321–334. DOI: 10.1016/S0363-8111(99)80143-X

Kent, M. L., & Taylor, M. (2002). Toward a dialogic theory of public relations. *Public Relations Review*, 28(1), 21–37. DOI: 10.1016/S0363-8111(02)00108-X

Kent, M. L., & Taylor, M. (2021). Fostering dialogic engagement: Toward an architecture of social media for social change. *Social Media + Society*, 7(1), 1–10. DOI: 10.1177/2056305120984462

Kim, B., Park, E., & Camero, G. T. (2017). Transparent communication efforts inspire confident, even greater, employee performance. *Asian Journal of Public Relations*, 1(1), 9–31.

Korkmaz, F., & Zorlu, K. (2021). *Organizational communication as an effective Communication Strategy in Organisation and the Role of the Leader. In book: Management strategies to survive in a competitive environment*. How to Improve Company Performance., DOI: 10.1007/978-3-030-72288-3_21

Lammers, J. C. (2011). How institutions communicate: Institutional messages, institutional logics, and organizational communication. *Management Communication Quarterly*, 25(1), 154–182. DOI: 10.1177/0893318910389280

Lane, A. B., & Bartlett, J. (2016). Dialogic principles don't make it in Ppactice—And what we can do about It. *International Journal of Communication*, 10, 1–21.

Lee, Y., & Queenie Li, J. (2021). The role of communication transparency and organisational trust in publics' perception, attitudes and social distancing behaviour: A case study of the Covid 19 outbreak. *Journal of Contingencies and Crisis Management*, 29(4), 368–384. DOI: 10.1111/1468-5973.12354

Letsie, H., Nkhi, S. E., & Mncina, T. C. (2023). An investigation of the impact of non-formal education on sustainable development in Mafeteng, Lesotho. *Interdisciplinary Journal of Rural and Community Studies*, 5, 36–48. DOI: 10.38140/ijrcs-2023.vol5.04

Letsie, H., & Osunkule, O. (2024). An exploration of Pprticipatory communication practices in sustainable development and poverty alleviation: A case study of Lifajaneng village. *Journal of Asian and African Studies*, 00219096241235297. Advance online publication. DOI: 10.1177/00219096241235297

Lueg, K., & Graf, A. (2021, June 10). *The organization of higher education: An overview of sociological research into universities as organizations*. Elgaronline https://www.elgaronline.com/edcollchap/book/9781839103261/book-part-9781839103261-10.xml

Matošková, J. (2020). Communication tools as drivers of employees' knowledge sharing: Evidence from the Czech Republic. *Problems and Perspectives in Management*, 18(1), 415–427. DOI: 10.21511/ppm.18(1).2020.36

McConnell, J. (2007). Making intranets meaningful. *Communication World*, 24(3), 24–25.

McKinney, J. C., & Gammie, C. F. (2004). A measurement of the electromagnetic luminosity of a Kerr black hole. *The Astrophysical Journal*, 611(2), 977–995. DOI: 10.1086/422244

Medium. (2024). *How can technology be a barrier to communication?* https://medium.com/@shaifulhoquetoha2004/how-can-technology-be-a-barrier-to-communication-f954ed06e684

Mncina, T. C., Letsie, H., Nkhi, S. E., & Mofana, M. (2024). Effective communication in postgraduate supervision: Shaping experiences and overcoming challenges. *Interdisciplinary Journal of Education Research*, 6(13), 1–21. DOI: 10.38140/ijer-2024.vol6.13

Morgan, S., Ahn, S., Mosser, A., Harrison, T., Wang, J., Huang, Q., Ryan, A., Mao, B., & Bixby, J. (2021). The effect of Ttam communication behaviors and Ppocesses on interdisciplinary teams' research productivity and team satisfaction. Informing Science. *The International Journal of an Emerging Transdiscipline. 24.* 083-110. DOI: 10.28945/4857

Muszynska, K. (2018). A concept for measuring effectiveness of communication in project teams. *Journal of Economics and Management*, 33(3), 63–79. DOI: 10.22367/jem.2018.33.04

Nkhi, S. E., & Shange, T. (2024). The impact of pedagogical translanguaging in enhancing communicative competence of university students in Lesotho. *International Journal of Language Studies*, 18(1), 25–52. DOI: 10.5281/zenodo.10468177

Olugbo, M., Obienu, A. C., & Frank, A. (2023). Impact of effective communication on institutional performance: Case study in higher learning institutions. *Journal of Education. Society and Behavioural Science*, 36(10), 28–44. DOI: 10.9734/jesbs/2023/v36i101264

Park, Y. S., Konge, L., & Artino, A. (2019). The positivism paradigm of research. *Academic Medicine*, 95(5), 1. DOI: 10.1097/ACM.0000000000003093 PMID: 31789841

Peate, L. (2021). *The Nursing Associate's Handbook of Clinical Skills* (1st ed.). John Wiley & Sons Ltd., www.wiley.com/nursingassociate

Phiri, V. (2021). *Effective speaking and effective listening*. DOI: 10.13140/RG.2.2.31707.69922

Rossiter, M. P., & Bale, R. (2023). Cultural and linguistic dimensions of feedback: A model of intercultural feedback literacy. *Innovations in Education and Teaching International*, 60(3), 368–378. DOI: 10.1080/14703297.2023.2175017

Roy, R., & El Marsafawy, H. (2020). *Organizational structure for 21st century higher education institutions: Meeting expectations and crossing hallenges*.https://www.researchgate.net/publication/340685039_ORGANIZATIONAL_STRUCTURE_FOR_21ST_CENTURY_HIGHER_EDUCATION_INSTITUTIONS_MEETING_EXPECTATIONS_AND_CROSSING_CHALLENGES

Rupal, J. (nd). The barriers to effective communication https://www.peakwriting.com/UMUC/barriers_effective.pdf

Schensul, S. L., Schensul, J. J., & LeCompte, M. D. (1999). *Essential ethnographic methods, observations, interviews and questionnaire.* Rowan Altanura Publishers.

Shava, G., Hleza, S., Tlou, F., Shonhiwa, S., & Mathonsi, E. (2021). Qualitative content analysis. *International Journal of Research and Innovation in Social Science*, V(VII).

Sinha, S., & Sinha, D. (2007). Emotional intelligence and effective communication. In Kaul, A., & Kumar Gupta, S. (Eds.), *Management communication: Trends & strategies*. McGraw Hill.

Steigerwald, E., Ramírez-Castañeda, V., Brandt, D., Báldi, A., Shapiro, J., Bowker, L. & Tarvin, R. (2022). Overcoming language barriers in academia: Machine translation tools and a vision for a multilingual future. *Bio Science, 72.* htps://.DOI: 10.1093/biosci/biac062

Sudhagar, R., & Pradeep, S. (2018). Most common barriers to effective communication in the skill- based challenges about the lassroom situation. *International Journal of Trend in Research and Development*, 86-87, c.

Tariq, A. (2023, June 8). *Implementing the transactional model of Communication for better collaboration.* Chanty. https://www.chanty.com/blog/transactional-model-of-communication/

Terzić, E. (2018). The significance of vertical and horizontal communication for business effectiveness in sports organizations. *Sport Science (Travnik)*, 11, 110–118.

Turner, J. N. (2020). Communicating for change. In J, Tacchi & T. Tufte (Eds.*), Studies in communication for social change.* Palgrave. https://doi.org/DOI: 10.1007.978-3-030-42513-5_4

Uhl-Bien, M., & Arena, M. (2018). Leadership for organizational adaptability: A theoretical synthesis and integrative framework. *The Leadership Quarterly*, 29(1), 89–104. DOI: 10.1016/j.leaqua.2017.12.009

Usha, R. K. (2016). Communication barriers. *Journal of English Language and Literature*, 3(2), 74–76.

Ward, M. E. (2013). *Tools of the blogging trade: A study of how dialogic principles help organizations structure blogs to build relationships. Athens* [Masters dissertation, University of Georgia] Georgia

Welch, M., & Jackson, P. R. (2007). Rethinking internal communication: A stakeholder approach. *Corporate Communications*, 12(2), 177–198. DOI: 10.1108/13563280710744847

Weller, P. (2013). *Dialogue theories. Dialogue society.* London Great Britain. https://www.dialoguesociety.org/publications/Dialogue-Theories-Preview.pdf

Wollny, A., Jacobs, I., & Pabel, L. (2020). Trait emotional intelligence and relationship satisfaction: The mediating role of dyadic coping. *The Journal of Psychology*, 154(1), 75–93. DOI: 10.1080/00223980.2019.1661343 PMID: 31524567

Zorlu, K., & Korkmaz, F. (2021). Organizational communication as an effective communication strategy in organizations and the role of the leader. In Dincer, H., & Yüksel, S. (Eds.), *Management strategies to survive in a competitive environment: Contributions to management science.* Springer., DOI: 10.1007/978-3-030-72288-3_21

Zulch, B. G. (2014). Communication: The foundation of project management. *Procedia Technology*, 16, 1000–1009. DOI: 10.1016/j.protcy.2014.10.054

Section 4
Enhancing Research Impact Through Collaboration

Chapter 12
Perceptions of Faculty on Research Productivity:
Developing Competencies Through Teamwork, Mentorship, and Collaboration

Cynthia Onyefulu
University of Technology, Jamaica

ABSTRACT

This study investigated lecturers' perceptions of research productivity, factors impacting research productivity, and how to develop lecturers' competencies through teamwork, mentorship, and collaboration to improve research productivity. Five research questions guided the study and were answered using an online questionnaire and document review. The sample size was 31 lecturers from a single university in Jamaica. The results revealed that the rate of research productivity among lecturers has been increasing over the years. The results showed that across the 17 years examined, conference abstracts, presentations, and proceedings were the highest. Peer-reviewed journal papers follow this, with books and book chapters being the least. Lecturers' perceptions of conducting research and publications were reported under motivation, assistance, and mandatory.

INTRODUCTION

Academics in higher education and institutions of learning, such as colleges and universities, facilitate student learning, which helps them achieve personal development and train them for the workforce. In addition to teaching/training,

DOI: 10.4018/979-8-3693-3852-0.ch012

academics are involved in knowledge exchange, research, and innovation (United Nations Educational, Scientific & Cultural Organization [UNESCO], 2024). This is because academics are required to research, publish, and teach as part of their jobs (Niles et al., 2020; Zain et al., 2011). Despite what academics are required to do in higher education, research seems to be the main focus. Hence, Escotet (2012) saw the primary function as the "creation of knowledge and dissemination for the development of [the] world through innovation and creativity" (as cited in Weerasinghe et al., 2017, p. 533). Mehta et al. (2017) described research as "a tool for building knowledge and efficient learning" (p. 17), and Hiebert et al. (2022) shared the same view of why doing research.

Although academics are expected to teach and produce new knowledge through research (Iqbal & Mahmood, 2011; Probert & Sacs, 2015), studies have shown that some spend more time teaching (Sotodeh et al., 2014). Balancing these two essential activities depends on the type of universities where the academics are employed. For instance, some universities focus on teaching rather than research. The emphasis on research and publication is more for academics in research universities. Mohrman et al. (2008) described research universities as "institutions with a high priority on the discovery of new knowledge" (p. 5). Despite the classification of universities, people have different views and expectations about research productivity.

Conklin and Desselle (2006) defined research productivity as the number of original research and review publications submitted and accepted in peer-reviewed journals. Another definition of research productivity was provided by Iqbal and Mahmood (2011), who defined it as "publications of papers in professional journals, in [the] shape of books or presentation of research papers in conference proceedings" (p. 189). Abramo and D'Angelo (2014) argued that research productivity cannot be defined solely based on "the number of publications per researcher" (p. 1129). This is because it provides a narrow definition. A much broader definition was provided by Iqbal and Mahmood (2011), who stated that research productivity includes (a) writing such as books or chapters, (b) collecting and analyzing data, (c) supervising students' dissertations and projects, (d) obtaining research grants, (e) doing editorial duties, (f) obtaining patents and licenses, (g) writing of monographs, (h) conducting experimental studies, (i) producing artistic or creative works, (j) participating in public debates and commentaries (Iqbal & Mahmood, 2011). By expanding the meaning of research productivity, Iqbal and Mahmood have accounted for more research activities that would have contributed to academics' production of new knowledge.

Furthermore, Abramo and D'Angelo (2014) described research activity as a production process that consists of human inputs (instruments & materials), intangible resources such as knowledge and social networks, and outputs such as new knowledge in tangible (publications, patents, & conference presentations) and intangible (tacit knowledge & consulting activity) forms. Based on the description of research activities (outputs), academics' production of new knowledge could be multi-input and multi-output (Abramo et al., 2014, p. 1131). Given the nature of the outputs, different methods, such as bibliometrics and citations, are used to determine research productivity (Abramo et al., 2012; Caminiti et al., 2015; Heng et al., 2020). Abramo et al. (2012) noted that both methods have strengths and weaknesses.

The literature review revealed that several studies have been published on research productivity. Some studies on lecturers' research activities and outputs focused on developing models for predicting faculty research productivity (Bland et al., 2005; Cali & Gerdoci, 2023; Kern, 2011), some focused on establishing research groups/teams (Brower et al., 2021), and others examined faculty conceptions of research (Brew et al., 2016) and the relationship between research productivity, and their determinants (Abramo et al., 2017; Cali & Gerdoci, 2023). Some of these sources and others are discussed later under the literature review section.

BACKGROUND OF THE STUDY

The institution used for the study began as a college in the 1950s; however, it became a university in 1995. It offers undergraduate and postgraduate programs to over 13,000 students. These programs are offered through three colleges and five faculties. The School of Graduate Studies, Research and Entrepreneurship is responsible for developing and delivering graduate courses and implementing the research mandate for the university. The School is responsible for the university journal and the press and offers seed grants for research activities (University of Technology [UTech], Jamaica – Student Handbook, 2019).

Staff members and students are encouraged to research and publish through the university press and journal. Furthermore, the School tracks the research activities of staff members, such as published articles, books and book chapters, presentations at local and international conferences, postgraduate students' supervision, local and international research grants, editorial duties, and patents and licenses.

STATEMENT OF THE PROBLEM

Although the school documents and reports staff members' research activities, no study has been done to ascertain lecturers' perceptions of their research productivity, their level of satisfaction, and the factors contributing to their research outputs.

Two studies on lecturers' research activities were found in the existing literature. The first was by Onyefulu and Johnson (2009), which examined lecturers' views on establishing research groups in a faculty at a university in Jamaica. The essence was to find out how lecturers felt about using research groups to improve research outputs. A more recent cross-sectional study by Usman (2024) examined lecturers' research output and knowledge at the same university and also focused on lecturers in a college. Hence, the current study was designed to address the gap in the existing literature on lecturers' perceptions of their research productivity, their satisfaction with research infrastructure, and the factors influencing their research outputs.

PURPOSE OF THE STUDY

The purpose of the study is threefold: First, to assess lecturers' perceptions of conducting research and publishing. Second, to determine lecturers' satisfaction with the infrastructure provided at the university for research work. Third, to ascertain the factors impacting their research productivity and their willingness to improve their research output and competencies through teamwork, mentorship, and collaboration.

RESEARCH QUESTIONS

The following research questions guided the study:

1. What is the rate of research productivity among lecturers?
2. What factors determine academic research productivity?
3. What are lecturers' perceptions of conducting research and publishing?
4. To what extent are lecturers satisfied with research and publication infrastructure, facilities and opportunities?
5. To what extent can research teamwork, mentoring and collaborative efforts improve research productivity among lecturers?

DELIMITATIONS OF THE STUDY

The study focused only on lecturers' perceptions of research and publication and excluded the views of the university's non-academic staff that do research. This was done to eliminate differences in the roles and expectations of lecturers and non-academic staff regarding research.

SIGNIFICANCE OF THE STUDY

The results of this study will be beneficial in several ways. First, it will contribute to the existing knowledge on research productivity in Jamaica. Second, university administrators can use the results to inform decisions and formulate guidelines to promote and improve research and publication among lecturers. Third, although the study was done at one university, the results can be useful to other institutions in Jamaica trying to improve lecturers' research outputs, especially in emerging institutions of higher learning where there is a lack of research culture. Finally, the study results can pave the way for further exploration of research productivity.

ORGANIZATION OF THE REST OF THE CHAPTER

The rest of the chapter is organized under the following main sections: literature review, methodology and methods, results, conclusion, implications, and suggestions for further studies.

LITERATURE REVIEW

The literature review was conducted using Google Scholar and databases like EBSCO Host, ERIC and ProQuest. The keywords used for the search were research activities, motivation to publish, research productivity, teamwork research, and research mentorship and collaboration. The literature is organized according to themes: Lecturers' Perceptions of Research and Publications, Factors Impacting the Research Productivity among University Lecturers, Research and Publication Infrastructure, Facilities and Opportunities, and Using Teamwork, Mentoring and Collaboration to Improve Research Productivity.

Lecturers' Perceptions of Research and Publications

In the literature, there is a wide variety of studies on lecturers' perceptions of research. For instance, Jordan (2022) investigated academics' perceptions of 107 academics on the research impact and engagement and their interactions on social media platforms using a qualitative approach. Another study by Brinn et al. (1998) examined the acceptability of research practices in publishing in accounting journals among UK academic accountants. Their study uncovered acceptable and unacceptable practices, which had publishing implications.

Regarding lecturers' views on publishing, the notion is that they feel the pressure to publish. According to Aprile et al. (2020), the phrase "publish or perish adage is alive and well" (p. 1131), and not just to publish but to publish in peer-reviewed, which in turn influences their research outputs in both developing and developed countries (Aprile et al., 2020; Heng et al., 2020; Johnann et al., 2024). Their study was conducted in an Australian regional university; they distinguished between intrinsic and extrinsic motivation to publish by stating that intrinsically motivated lecturers will not be pressured, while extrinsically motivated will be pressured to publish. This is partially to establish themselves and meet their institutions' expectations. Heng et al. (2020) noted that lecturers who were extrinsically and intrinsically motivated and had high levels of self-efficacy were more research-active and productive.

In summary, the studies reviewed showed that lecturers feel external pressure to publish, which positively or negatively influences their research outputs. The review also showed that motivated lecturers had better research outputs than those who lacked motivation.

Factors Impacting the Research Productivity Among University Lecturers

Studies published are accepted and published based on quality. The quality of research is a vital indicator of university academic performance and forms the basis for ranking such universities (Sayyed, 2024). Sayyed noted that the publication patterns and preferences among lecturers differ by discipline. According to Sayyed, disciplines are classified into hard and soft. Researchers in "hard disciplines," such as natural sciences, computer science, mathematics, biology, chemistry, biochemistry, physics, nutrition and food sciences, environmental toxicology, and bioinformatics, tend to publish in "prestigious journals" and do collaborative work and publish as co-authors. In contrast, lecturers in "soft disciplines," such as social sciences and education, communication arts, and languages, prefer publishing books but also do collaborative work and co-authorship. However, research productivity is not only affected by the researcher's discipline but also by factors or barriers that may impact the quality and quantity of the research outputs. Several authors have examined factors or barriers that impact research production. These include studies by Almansour (2016), Abouchedid and Abdelnour (2015), Åkerlind (2008), Çali and Gërdoçi (2023), Mantikayan and Abdulgani (2018), Muia and Oringo (2016), and Usman (2024), to list a few. The findings of these studies are discussed below.

Farzaneh et al. (2016) investigated the perceptions of 50 professors and 200 students of Ardabil University of Medical Sciences in Iran by conducting a descriptive cross-sectional study from different academic disciplines in medical sciences. Their study showed some barriers expressed by professors, such as a lack of facilities and equipment for doing research, lack of motivation from the authorities and professors, lack of incentives, a lack of time, inadequate knowledge of research methodology and statistical principles, insufficient skills, and not being important to research. Sayyed (2024), investigating research productivity among academics in Lebanon, examined how individual factors such as age, gender, academic rank, and self-efficacy, institutional factors such as reward systems, academic promotion, research funds and resources, post-graduate training, teaching load and relief, and opportunities for research collaboration, and occasional factors such as the pandemic and economic crisis impacted research productivity in hard and soft disciplines. The findings revealed that the number of productions for "hard disciplines" was higher than for the "soft disciplines." Most of the publications in both disciplines were journal articles. Apart from journal articles, the findings showed other publication patterns, such as books and conference proceedings. Regarding the factors that impact research productivity, Sayyed (2024) found that academics in "hard disciplines" were more productive and had more international collaborations than those in "soft disciplines." Other factors that impacted research productivity were teaching load, research funding, and equipment, which were consistent with the views of Abouchedid and Abdelnour (2015) and Almansour (2016). For instance, the study by Abouchedid and Abdelnour (2015), which examined faculty research productivity and budgetary allocation for research activities in 310 higher educational institutions in six Arab countries, found a low research productivity rate among academics in the region. The study by Almansour (2016) also found a lack of research infrastructure and funding for research in some universities in the Arab region. Usman's (2024) cross-sectional study of lecturers in health-related fields found that institutional and individual factors, such as lack of time, lack of research policy decisions, knowledge translation, motivation, and workload, among others, impacted research productivity. Similar findings were noted by Muia and Oringo (2016), who investigated the constraints that influence research productivity at the University of Nairobi, Kenya. Their study identified the following barriers: resource, institutional, and cultural constraints, including the "lack of funds, poor management, lack of dissemination and implementation of research findings, inadequate materials and equipment, lack of incentives and rewards to researchers and sophisticated procurement procedures" (p. 1786). The common factor in the results of Usman's

(2024) and Muia and Oringo's (2016) studies is that the countries are developing in Africa, where the institutions typically face several constraints.

Furthermore, Åkerlind (2008), in a phenomenographic research study conducted with 28 academics at a research-intensive university in Australia, noted four factors affected research productivity: (a) those with terminal degrees such as PhD, (b) academic positions held (c) personal understanding of research, and (d) societal benefit. From a developing country's perspective, Heng et al. (2020) found that age, gender, academic degrees, discipline, ranks, and time spent influenced academics' research productivity in developing countries.

In a study by Obliopas (2018), a correlational design was used to determine the relationship between research skills and productivity of 138 faculty members at Eastern Samar State University in the Philippines. Obliopas (2018) found a positive relationship between academic rank, educational attainment, and research skills. The result found a moderate positive relationship between the number of completed and presented research papers and a positive relationship between publication skills and the number of published papers. Obliopas concluded that research skills correlated to productivity and recommended the need for research skills training and workshops to promote research productivity among faculty members in the university. In a systematic review of the literature by Mantikayan and Abdulgani (2018), three factors influencing research productivity were noted. These were (a) *individual factors,* such as motivation, and commitment, (b) *institutional factors,* such as staff support, mentoring, resources, and rewards; and (c) *leadership factors,* such as providing leadership and management. The studies by Åkerlind (2008) and Obliopas (2018) addressed the individual factors of research productivity, such as the lecturer qualifications, ranks and research skills as barriers to research activities and outputs, while the study by Mantikayan and Abdulgani (2018) addressed not only the individual factor but also the institutional and leadership aspects. Studies have shown that all three barriers are essential to research and publishing.

In other studies, authors developed models to examine factors or barriers that affect research output. For instance, Cali and Gerdoci (2023) assessed the effect of access to research funds, teaching load, personal capabilities for carrying out research, personal interest in research, and access to scientific articles databases on research productivity using the regression model. From the views of 403 lecturers in higher education institutions in Albania, their results, among other things, showed that access to research funds, access to scientific databases, and the lack of research methodology capability were barriers that affected research and publication. The study by Cali and Gerdoci (2023) is consistent with findings by other authors about the effect of individual and institutional variables on research.

To better determine the quality and quantity of research outputs, Kern (2011) provided a 6-factor model for assessing research productivity: (1) funding, (2) investigator quality, (3) institutional efficiency, (4) the research mix of novelty, incremental advancement, and confirmatory studies, (5) analytic accuracy, and (6) passion. According to Kern (2011), the interactions between these factors affect research productivity.

In summary, the review showed that individual/personal factors (e.g., research skills, desire, & workload) and institutional/environmental factors (e.g., budgetary allocation, leadership, & research infrastructure) influence research productivity.

Research and Publication Infrastructure, Facilities and Opportunities

Infrastructure and support are needed for lecturers to conduct research. Lutz (2021) defined research infrastructures as resources and services available to researchers for conducting research and fostering innovation. According to French and Poznanski (2009), research can be supported by (a) establishing effective leadership that will provide direction, (b) putting in place regulatory requirements to ensure compliance, (c) putting in place someone for patient management for studies involving clinical trials, (d) getting a data coordinator or manager for data management, (e) getting someone for financial and accounting management, (f) providing support for grant applications, (g) getting someone with legal knowledge to be in charge of the contract management, and (h) providing research assistance to lecturers.

A few studies have examined lecturers' level of satisfaction with research infrastructure. A few studies focused on specific infrastructures, such as libraries and technology. For instance, a study by Marjaei et al. (2002) explored the views of 318 lecturers' satisfaction with Internet access and access to online databases in three universities in India and found that most lecturers were satisfied with Internet access, database access, and library facilities. Another study on library resources, services and facilities was done by Osaze Patrick et al. (2015). They examined users' (381) satisfaction with library services, resources, and facilities in a university in Nigeria. Their findings showed that the students were highly satisfied with the library services and other infrastructure.

Similarly, a study by Hussain and Abalkhail (2013) that examined library use among engineering students at King Saud University in Riyadh, Saudi Arabia, found that most of the users were satisfied with the overall functions and services of the library. They concluded that it was important for users to be satisfied with the services provided by the library. The same view was noted by Adesanya and Oluwafemi (2021), who noted the essential services of the library in academic institutions globally. Another study by Kassim (2009) evaluated final-year students' satisfaction with infrastructure, including the library in an academic library at a university in Malaysia. It revealed that, on average, the students were satisfied with the infrastructure, including the library. Although these studies focused on students and not lecturers, the findings were still relevant because students are one of the stakeholder groups at the higher education level. However, not all studies showed positive findings on resources in institutions of higher learning. For instance, studies by Ezeala and Yusuf (2011) and Ikolo (2015), both in Nigeria, and Saika and Gohan (2013) in India, showed that respondents were dissatisfied with library resources and services. These latter findings could be attributed to Nigeria and India's population size and limited infrastructure.

McGill and Settle (2012) conducted a cross-sectional survey study at the Forsythe institutions in the United States and Canada by investigating the levels of institutional research support provided to 343 computing academics. In general, their study showed that they were satisfied with the resources and support provided by their institutions.

Another aspect of research infrastructure is academic publication outlets, which include academic journals and presses. An academic journal may or may not be operated by a university press. These journals may be discipline-specific or multidisciplinary (Solomon et al., 2016; Wang, 2020). A university press is owned and operated by a university (Franzén, 2008). Wang (2020) described university academic journals as vessels for exchanging scientific research ideas and disseminating disciplinary knowledge. Institutions of higher learning, such as a university, may own a press and/or have academic journals for publishing scholarly articles.

In summary, the library offers services needed by students, staff, and, by extension, the university community as one aspect of research infrastructure. The studies reviewed under this theme showed mixed results regarding users' satisfaction with library resources and services. Publishing options include journals, which could be discipline-specific or multidisciplinary; another option is to use that may be presses owned by institutions and privately owned.

Using Teamwork, Mentoring and Collaboration to Improve Research Productivity

The literature on using high-performance teamwork in organizations continues to gain attention, with several authors writing about how it can be effective if done correctly (Bell et al., 2018; ONeill & Salas, 2018; Shuffler et al., 2018). Teamwork is used in different fields and for different purposes. In the current study, it was used in the context of collaborative efforts by researchers. In examining the effectiveness of team science, the National Research Council (2015) stated that the following should be considered when setting up research teams (a) the diversity of the membership,

(b) knowledge integration, (c) size, (d) goal alignment, (e) geographic dispersion, (f) and interdependence among members.

Usman's (2024) study at a university in Jamaica found that the respondents were willing to join a team. Paek's (2004) review of mentoring analysed several studies that showed that the mentor's and mentees' characteristics (gender, age, position, and level of experience) affected mentorship. Bell et al. (2018), ONeill and Salas (2018), and Shuffler et al. (2018) are just a few of the authors who have written on mentoring. The team can function effectively if there is shared cognition, information sharing, performance and innovation (Bell et al., 2018), and O'Neill and Salas (2018) added that having effective teamwork is linked to innovation, safety, fewer errors and saving lives, depending on the field of knowledge it is being used. Therefore, selection into the team is essential and should be carefully done. According to Bell et al. (2018), team composition or configuration can affect effectiveness and performance. Although team membership is intact and bounded, citing other sources, Bell et al. stated that the team composition is becoming dynamic as membership is fluid and less bounded. This fluidity could allow for team membership to change if needed.

Regarding collaborative research, some academics use collaboration or co-authorship to cope with the pressure to publish. This concept was explored by Cakir et al. (2024), who commented that academics with the highest publications co-authored or collaborated with other international academics. Abramo et al. (2014) noted in their study of lecturers in Italy the use of "intramural collaboration and extramural collaboration at the international level" (p. 17) according to the lecturers' ranks, such as associate and full professors and national collaboration for lower ranks. They also recommended analyzing the composition of the collaborations for better results. Heng et al. (2020), on the other hand, addressed international collaboration from the angle of languages and the difficulties that may arise, especially among researchers in non-English speaking countries. Therefore, it is essential to consider the different variables noted by Abramo et al. (2014) and Heng et al. (2020) if collaborative research is to be done.

In summary, studies have shown that effective research teams or groups can boost research productivity. Efforts should be made to set up the teams so that they work effectively. The review also showed that mentorship and collaboration could improve research activities.

METHODOLOGY AND METHODS

RESEARCH DESIGN AND SAMPLING

A cross-sectional survey design was used. The study was conducted at a university in Jamaica with participants who held different ranks, from lecturers to professors. These lecturers are all required to teach, conduct and publish. Seventy lecturers across the different colleges and faculties were purposefully selected based on their research productivity activities. For instance, 35 were selected based on their publications and conference presentations, while another 35 were selected because of their low research involvement. This was done to get a range of perceptions on research productivity.

Of the 70 selected lecturers, 31 (44.3%) responded. Although this number is small, it is consistent with a meta-analysis study conducted by Wu et al. (2022), who found the mean response rate for online surveys to be 44.1%.

DATA COLLECTION

Two data collection methods were used. First, an online questionnaire was created using Google Forms and document review. The questionnaire had 61 close-ended items, including Likert-type items in four of the five sections, namely, Section A with four demographic items; Section B with 22 items on perceptions of research productivity; and Section C with eight Likert-type items on level of satisfaction with infrastructures, facilities, and opportunities. Section D contained 20 Likert-type items on factors impacting research productivity. Section E had seven items on teamwork, mentoring, and collaboration, with yes/no items and reasons. The questionnaire items were generated by reviewing the literature on research productivity. Second, the university's annual research productivity reports (n.d.) were reviewed to determine the rate of research publications. As mentioned, the School of Graduate Studies, Research and Entrepreneurship tracks lecturers' research activities.

The researcher explained the study's aim and the participants' roles in an email to the participants and on the consent form. The participants gave their consent before data were collected. All information that may disclose the participants' identities was removed, and each participant was assigned a number during the data collection and analysis stages. Furthermore, all electronic data collected were stored on the university computers, which were password-protected, and only the researcher had access to the data sets. This was done to maintain the principles of the Data

Protection Act of 2020, which governs research activities in Jamaica. Furthermore, no sensitive or personal data were collected from the participants during the study (Amdur & Bankert, 2011; Data Protection Act, 2020; Stadnick et al., 2021).

RELIABILITY AND VALIDITY

The reliability of the online questionnaire was ascertained using Cronbach's alpha method for the 54 Likert-type items. The overall reliability of the questionnaire was 0.860. The acceptable reliability coefficient for questionnaire data to be considered reliable is 0.7 or higher (Bujang et al., 2018). See Table 1 for the results of the three sub-scales that were measured.

Table 1. Reliability coefficients for the online questionnaire

Section	Number of Items	Coefficient (r)
B: Perceptions of Research Productivity	22	0.763
C: Level of Satisfaction	8	0.895
D: Factors Impacting Research Productivity	20	0.915

Content validity and expert review methods were used to ensure that the questionnaire and the university's annual research productivity reports reflected the content studied. According to Taherdoost (2017), content validity is recommended for newly created instruments such as questionnaires. This was done using the specifications table to ensure the research questions were answered with the data collected (DePoy & Gitlin, 2016). Furthermore, two experts in the subject matter were asked to evaluate the questionnaire items and the document review log against the research questions (Creswell & Plano Clark, 2018; Taherdoost, 2017).

DATA ANALYSIS

The online questionnaire data was imported from the Excel sheet on Google Forms, downloaded into the SPSS program (version 26), and coded. Descriptive statistics were then used to analyze research questions 2 to 5. Conceptual content analysis was used with the university's annual research productivity reports because they were primarily text-based. Pre-determined codes and the frequencies of the codes (articles, books & book chapters, presentations at conferences, postgraduate students' supervision, research grants, editorial duties, & patents & licenses). The codes were broken up into three conceptual chunks or categories as recommended by Wilson (2011), namely, (1) BBC for books and book Chapters, (2) PRJP for peer-reviewed journal articles, and (3) CAAP for conference presentations and proceedings. Frequency counts of each code under the three categories were recorded and reported.

RESULTS

Respondents' Characteristics

Of the 31 respondents, 10 (32.3%) were males and 21 (67.7%) were females. Nine, or 29%, were under 40 years old, and 22 (71%) were over 40. Eight, or 25.8%, had a master's degree, 15 (48.4%) had a doctoral degree, and eight (25.8%) were awaiting their doctoral degrees. In terms of rank, 13 (41.9%) were lecturers, nine (29.0%) were senior lecturers, seven (22.6%) were at the associate lecturer rank, and two (6.5%) were full professors. The results of the research questions that guided the study are reported below.

The Rate of Research Productivity

Research Question 1: What is the rate of research productivity among lecturers?

To answer this research question, a document review of the university's annual research productivity reports from 2007 to 2023 was conducted to determine the rate of research publications. The University's Annual Research Productivity Reports (n.d.) contained three main categories of research-related activities: Books and book chapters (BBC), peer-reviewed journal papers (PRJP), and conference abstracts, presentations, and proceedings (CAPP). Furthermore, the reports reviewed covered 17 years of content (from 2007 to 2023). The analysis showed that, across the 17 years, conference abstracts, presentations, and proceedings were the highest among the academic staff, with 739 entries. This was followed by 580 peer-reviewed journal papers. Books and book chapters were the least across the years, with 124. The grouping of these research activities into three groups is consistent with Heng et al. (2020), who mentioned that the number of books, book chapters, journal articles, papers in conference proceedings, awarded research grants, and patents can measure research productivity.

Furthermore, the results showed modest growth in research activities over the years. This may be attributed to increased funding opportunities for staff; and the establishment of a university press. This finding was consistent with a study by Weber-Main et al. (2013) that noted increased research activities during a 10-year period (from 1997 to 2007) at the University of Minnesota in the Department of

Family Medicine and Community Health. They attributed the increase to changes in research culture, leadership, financial support, and others.

Factors Determining Academic Research Productivity

Research Question 2: What factors determine academic research productivity?

Two main factors were identified, namely, institutional and individual. As shown in Table 2, more than 70% of those who responded identified the following top institutional factors: (1) a lack of resources/facilities ($M = 3.44$, SD = 0.65), (2) a lack of research culture ($M = 3.20$, $SD = 0.76$), (3) a lack of role models/mentors ($M = 3.16$, $SD = 0.75$), (4) a lack of research assistance ($M = 3.16$, $SD = 0.80$), (5) a lack of leadership/mentorship ($M = 3.08$, $SD = 0.86$), and (6) a lack of clear policies on research productivity ($M = 3.00$, $SD = 0.71$). The reported mean values showed that many respondents agreed with the statements that reflected institutional factors, and their perceptions did not show too many variations in how they responded.

Table 2. Institutional factors

		Mean	SD
1.	Lack of research funding	2.96	0.79
2.	Lack of training opportunities	2.96	0.79
3.	Lack of research culture	3.20	0.76
4.	Lack of role models/mentors	3.16	0.75
5.	Lack of resources/facilities	3.44	0.65
6.	Lack of research assistance	3.16	0.80
7.	Lack of clear policies on research productivity	3.00	0.71
8.	Lack of encouragement to conduct research	2.92	0.76
9.	Not enough publication outlets within the university	2.88	0.78
10.	Lack of incentives	2.84	0.80
11.	Lack of leadership/mentorship	3.08	0.86

The institutional factors were consistent with the observations of Weber-Main et al. (2013), who indicated that research agenda, leadership, resources, mentoring, research culture, training, and assistance in research design and analysis were needed to improve research productivity. The results were also consistent with the studies by Usman (2024) and Muia and Oringo (2016), which found that institutional efficiency can impact research productivity.

More than 70% of those who responded identified the following top individual factors, as shown in Table 3: (1) workload ($M = 3.28$, $SD = 0.93$) and (2) stress ($M = 3.04$, $SD = 0.89$). Age ($M = 1.96$, $SD = 1.09$) was not a significant factor in determining academic research productivity. These mean values showed that many respondents also agreed with the statements that reflected individual factors, and their perceptions showed a little more variation compared to how they responded to the institutional factors. The results were similar to Usman's (2024) study that found barriers to research output by lecturers in the health and nursing fields.

Table 3. Individual factors

		Mean	SD
12.	**Lack of experience**	2.88	1.01
13.	Pressure to publish	2.92	0.91
14.	Stress	3.04	0.89
15.	Lack of motivation	2.84	0.94
16.	Workload	3.28	0.93
17.	Level of qualification	2.28	1.10
18.	Type of post-graduate degree obtained	2.36	1.08
19.	My age	1.96	1.09
20.	Not interested	2.28	1.31

The individual factors identified in the current study align with the results of the studies by Usman (2024) and Muia and Oringo (2016), which found experience, motivation, time, and the type of qualification as barriers to research productivity. According to Kern (2011), research productivity can be impacted by the investigator's quality (training, experience, etc.), passion, and others. Albert et al. (2016) noted that workload is a barrier because those who devote less time to teaching are more productive in research and publication.

Perceptions of Lecturers on Research and Publication

Research Question 3: What are lecturers' perceptions of conducting research and publishing?

The lecturers were asked about their views on conducting research and publication using the 22 Likert-type items in the online questionnaire. The responses are reported in three sub-headings: (a) motivation, (b) assistance, (c) and mandatory.

Motivation. Table 4 shows that the respondents' reasons for research and publication were externally driven (see the first 5 items). The mean values ranged from 3.20 to 3.56, indicating that a majority (over 70%) of the respondents agreed or strongly agreed in their responses. This also showed positive perceptions of research and publication. The standard deviation (SD) values showed fewer variations in the responses.

Table 4. Extrinsic motivation for research and publication

Extrinsic Motivation		Mean	SD
13.	I am interested in doing research to get promotion and tenure	3.32	0.852
17.	Publishing will enable me to find a better job at another university	3.44	0.507
18.	Publishing will help me achieve peer recognition	3.36	0.490
19.	Peer recognition of my work inspires me to do more research	3.56	0.507
22.	I conduct research as a part of my routine as an academic staff	3.20	0.645

As shown in Table 5, the respondents indicated they were motivated internally and altruistically. The mean values for intrinsic motivation ranged from 3.40 to 3.52, indicating that a majority (over 70%) of the respondents agreed or strongly agreed in their responses. This also showed that their perceptions of research and publication were positive. The standard deviation (SD) values showed fewer variations in their responses to these items. This indicated that the SD values were closer to the mean values.

The mean values for altruistic motivation ranged from 2.60 to 3.40, indicating that a few respondents disagreed and agreed with the item: *By publishing, I satisfy my need to contribute to my field*. This item's standard deviation (SD) value showed more variations in the lecturers' responses. Most (over 70%) of the respondents agreed or strongly agreed with their responses to the item: *I research to help solve problems within my field*, which also showed that their perceptions of this item were more positive. The standard deviation (SD) value for this item showed fewer variations in their responses, which indicated that the SD values were closer to the mean values. The findings reinforced altruistic motivation and personal satisfaction, as Albert et al. (2015) noted among researchers in Spain.

Table 5. Intrinsic and altruistic motivation for research and publication

Intrinsic Motivation		Mean	SD
1.	I like doing research	3.48	0.653
2.	Getting my papers published makes me happy	3.52	0.653
6.	I am motivated to do research	3.40	0.764
7.	I am motivated to publish my research papers	3.44	0.768
Altruistic Motivation			
14	I research to help solve problems within my field	3.40	0.764
15.	By publishing, I satisfy my need to contribute to my field	2.60	1.000

This indicated that the SD values were closer to the mean values. Motivation is a driving force affecting people's behaviour, such as lecturers' research involvement, productivity, and the expectancy to succeed (Dornyei, 2001; Zhao, 2021). Other variables that could impact motivation are individual factors (self-confidence & self-efficacy) and institutional factors (expectancy of the university for lecturers to publish or perish (Dornyei, 2001; Zhao, 2021).

Mandatory. Table 6 shows the responses to the two items that measured whether research and publication should be mandatory. The mean values (2.04 & 3.00) of the respondents' perceptions showed that a majority (over 70%) agreed. Although more respondents agreed about making research and publication mandatory, policy changes and more consultations with lecturers are needed for this to be considered and supported. The standard deviation (SD) values showed fewer variations in the responses. This indicates that the lecturers' responses were more unified, especially for research than publication. However, mandating research and not publication does not make sense since both go together if new knowledge is to be produced and disseminated.

Table 6. Making research and publication mandatory

	Item	Mean	SD
10.	All lecturers should be required to do research	3.04	0.790
11.	All lecturers should be required to publish	3.00	0.913

Assistance. Table 7 shows the respondents' perceptions of items that measured seeking assistance for research and publication. The mean values ranged from 2.60 to 3.52, indicating that a majority (over 70%) of the respondents agreed, except for the item, *By publishing, I satisfy my need to contribute to my field*, which had a slightly lower mean value. This showed that more of the respondents were not satisfied with the contributions of their studies to their field. The standard deviation (SD) values showed fewer variations in the responses, indicating that their responses were more similar. *Table 7. Assistance in improving research and publication*

	Item	Mean	SD
9.	I lack the confidence needed to do research	2.16	1.07
8.	I am interested in acquiring more research knowledge	3.60	0.50
3.	I need help with doing research	3.12	0.88
4.	I need help in getting published	3.04	0.98
5.	I would like to have a research mentor/mentee	2.96	1.06
20.	I feel that attending conferences really helps in increasing knowledge	2.04	0.98
22.	Attending conferences has had a positive impact on my research work	3.20	0.65

Two items could not be captured under the sub-headings presented above. These are: (a) *Doing research is a burden to me* (M = 2.04, SD = 0.98). The responses showed that most lecturers disagreed with this item, meaning that research was not considered a burden, which is encouraging. The standard deviation showed a little more variations in their responses. (b) *My college/faculty supports my research activities* (M = 2.60, SD = 1.00). The lecturers' responses were mixed because some disagreed while others agreed. This is supported by the standard deviation value that showed variations in their responses.

Level of Satisfaction with Research and Publication Facilities and Opportunities

Research Question 4: To what extent are lecturers satisfied with research and publication infrastructure, facilities and opportunities?

The lecturers were asked about their views on conducting research and publishing using the eight Likert-type items in Section C of the online questionnaire. As shown in Table 8, the mean values ranged from 1.56 to 2.40, indicating that most respondents disagreed with these items that measured their level of satisfaction. The results showed that the lecturers were particularly dissatisfied with the funding, time, and compensation amount given for research. The standard deviation values ranged from 0.81 to 0.97, indicating fewer variations in their responses. The results were similar to studies that found some lecturers to be satisfied with infrastructure while some were not satisfied (Ezeala & Yusuf, 2011; Ikolo, 2015; Hussain & Abalkhail, 2013; Marjaei et al., 2002; Osaze Patrick et al., 2015; Saika & Gohan, 2013).

Table 8. Lecturers' level of satisfaction with research and publication facilities and opportunities

	I am satisfied with the:	Mean	SD
1.	electronic library facilities at my university	2.36	0.81
2.	number of conference opportunities available to me	2.40	0.87
3.	amount of funding available for research at my university	1.92	0.86
4.	assistance in gathering and compilation of data	2.00	0.82
5.	time available to me for research apart from teaching	1.56	0.87
6.	research training given at my university	2.16	0.89
7.	compensation amount given for research	1.88	0.93
8.	my annual research output	2.24	0.97

Improving Research Productivity through Teamwork and Collaborative Efforts

Research Question 5: To what extent can research teamwork, mentoring and collaborative efforts improve research productivity among lecturers?

The responses are grouped under three themes: publication, mentoring programme, and collaborative research.

Publication. The lecturers were asked if they had published a journal article, book, or book chapter. Seventeen (54%) said yes, and 14 (45.2%) said no. Of the 14 who said no, 8 (57.1%) indicated they would be willing to join a team/group to improve their research productivity rate, and 6 (42.9%) said no. Their reasons included (a) group dynamics, (b) team effectiveness, (c) group interaction, (d) leadership, and (e) team maintenance. Research has shown that specific qualities should be observed when selecting a team to function effectively (Bell et al., 2018; O'Neill & Salas, 2018; Shuffler et al., 2018). This will undoubtedly address the lecturers' concerns that indicated no in their responses.

Mentoring Program. Additionally, the respondents were asked if they would be willing to participate in a research mentoring program. Eleven (35.5%) said yes, 13 (41.9%) said no, and 7 (22.6%) said maybe. The reasons given by those who said no gave the following reasons, (a) I do not need mentorship in research, (b) I do not have the time to be in a mentorship program, (c) I am not inspired to join, and (d) I have to know more about the program before joining. This result was encouraging since more lecturers were interested in having a mentor. However, as Paek (2004) suggested, mentors' and mentees' dynamics must be considered for this to work well. Similarly, Usman (2024) also found that lecturers were willing to be guided.

Collaborative Research. The respondents were also asked if they would be willing to do collaborative research, that is, a partnership between two or more researchers. Ten (32.3%) indicated their willingness, 14 (45.2%) said no, and 7 (22.5%) said maybe. The following were their reasons (1) I do not need to collaborate to do research, (b) I do not have the time to collaborate, (c) I am not motivated to collaborate, and (d) I have to know more about the partners before making a decision. Interestingly, some lecturers in the current study were willing to collaborate with colleagues to conduct and publish research. Abramo et al. (2014) and Heng et al. (2020) supported collaboration to improve research productivity. Additionally, Abramo et al. (2014) suggested that collaboration could be done according to the ranks of the lecturers, such as full and associate professors.

Some limitations of the study were noted. First, there was a time constraint, which resulted in the study being conducted at one university in Jamaica. Second, the sample size was small ($n = 31$) due to the low response rate. As a result, the findings cannot be generalized. Finally, there was limited literature on Jamaica and the Caribbean. However, despite these limitations, the study results are very useful in understanding lecturers' perceptions of research productivity and factors impacting it in higher education in Jamaica, as well as possible ways to address it through teamwork, mentorship, and collaboration.

CONCLUSION

This study investigated lecturers' perceptions of research productivity, factors impacting research productivity, and how to develop lecturers' competencies through teamwork, mentorship, and collaboration to improve research productivity. Five research questions guided the study and were answered using an online questionnaire and document review. The sample size was 31 lecturers from a single university in Jamaica. The results revealed that the rate of research productivity among lecturers has been increasing over the years. The results showed that across the 17 years examined, conference abstracts, presentations, and proceedings were the highest. Peer-reviewed journal papers follow this, with books and book chapters being the least. The lecturers' reasons for research and publication were mainly externally driven. Others were internally and altruistically motivated. The results showed that individual factors, such as stress, workload, pressure to publish, lack of motivation, and lack of experience, institutional factors, such as funding, lack of research culture, lack of mentors, lack of resources, lack of policies, and lack of mentorship, influenced research productivity. Some lecturers agreed that research and publication should be mandatory, and most agreed that they needed assistance improving their research outputs. Although more lecturers have published, they were still willing to join a team/group, be mentored, and collaborate with colleagues to improve their research productivity rate.

The results have implications for university leaders in managing research and publication expectations for better results. Some lecturers believed there was a lack of clear research productivity policies. This has implications for research and publication. Without clear policies, the university's research agenda cannot be fully realized.

Based on the study's limitations, it is recommended that future studies be conducted with a larger sample size to make the results more generalizable. The mixed-methods approach could be used to gain deeper insights into lecturers' views of research productivity.

REFERENCES

Abouchedid, K., & Abdelnour, G. (2015). Faculty research productivity in six Arab countries. *International Review of Education*, 61, 673–690.

Abramo, G., Cicero, T., & D'Angelo, C. A. (2012). A sensitivity analysis of researchers' productivity rankings to the time of citation observation. *Journal of Informetrics*, 6(2), 192–201.

Abramo, G., D'Angelo, A. C., & Murgia, G. (2017). The relationship among research productivity research collaboration, and their determinants. *Journal of Informetrics*, 11(4), 1016–1030. DOI: 10.1016/j.joi.2017.09.007

Abramo, G., & D'Angelo, C. A. (2014). How do you define and measure research productivity? *Scientometrics*, 101, 1129–1144. DOI: 10.1007/s11192-014-1269-8

Abramo, G., D'Angelo, C. A., & Murgia, G. (2014). Variation in research collaboration patterns across academic ranks. *Scientometrics*, 98(3), 2275–2294. DOI: 10.1007/s11192-013-1185-3

Adesanya, O. O., & Oluwafemi, V. S. (2021). Users' satisfaction on library resources and service in universities affiliated programmes in federal colleges of education in South-west, Nigeria. *Library Philosophy and Practice (e-journal)*, 5505. https://digitalcommons.unl.edu/libphilprac/5505

Åkerlind, G. (2008). An academic perspective on research and being a researcher: An integration of the literature. *Studies in Higher Education*, 33, 17–31. DOI: 10.1080/03075070701794775

Albert, N. M., Rice, K. L., Waldo, M. J., Bena, J. F., Mayo, A. M., Morrison, S. L., Westlake, C., Ellstrom, K., Powers, J., & Foster, J. (2016). Clinical Nurse specialist roles in conducting research: Changes over 3 years. *Clinical Nurse Specialist CNS*, 30(5), 292–301. DOI: 10.1097/NUR.0000000000000236

Almansour, S. (2016). The crisis of research and global recognition in Arab universities. *Near and Middle Eastern Journal of Research in Education*, 1. http://dx.doi.org/.DOI: 10.5339/nmejre.2016.1

Amdur, R., & Bankert, A. E. (2011). *Institutional review board: Member handbook* (3rd). Jones & Barlett Publishers.

Aprile, K. T., Ellem, P., & Lole, L. (2020). Publish, perish, or pursue? Early career academics' perspectives on demands for research productivity in regional universities. *Higher Education Research & Development*, 40(6), 1131–1145. DOI: 10.1080/07294360.2020.1804334

Bell, S. T., Brown, S. G., & Weiss, J. A. (2018). A conceptual framework for leveraging team composition decisions to build human capital. *Human Resource Management Review*, 28(4), 450–463. DOI: 10.1016/j.hrmr.2017.06.003

Bland, C., Center, B. A., Finstad, D. A., Risbey, K. R., & Staples, J. G. (2005). A theoretical, practical, predictive model of faculty and department research productivity. *Academic Medicine*, 80(3), 25–237.

Brew, A., Boud, D., Namgung, S. U., Lucas, L., & Crawford, K. (2016). Research productivity and academics' conceptions of research. *Higher Education*, 71, 681–697. DOI: 10.1007/s10734-015-9930-6

Brinn, T., Jones, J. M., & Pendlebury, M. (1998). UK academic accountants: Perceptions of research and publication practices. *The British Accounting Review*, 30(4). Advance online publication. DOI: 10.1006/bare.1998.0074

Brower, H. H., Nicklas, B. J., Nader, M. A., Trost, L. M., & Miller, D. P. (2021). Creating effective academic research teams: Two tools borrowed from business practice. *Journal of Clinical and Translational Science*, 5(1), e74. DOI: 10.1017/cts.2020.553

Bujang, M. A., Omar, E. D., & Baharum, N. A. (2018). A review on sample size d for Cronbach's Alpha test: A simple guide for researchers. *The Malaysian Journal of Medical Sciences : MJMS*, 25(6), 85–99. DOI: 10.21315/mjms2018.25.6.9

Cakir, A., Kuyurtar, D., & Balyer, A. (2024). The effects of the publish or perish culture on publications in the field of educational administration in Türkiye. *Social Sciences & Humanities Open*, 9, 100817. https://doi.org/10.1016/j.ssaho.2024.100817

Çali, M., & Gërdoçi, B. (2023). *Research barriers and academic productivity.* The IAFOR International Conference on Education in Hawaii 2023 Official Conference Proceedings. doi:10.22492/issn.2189-1036.2023.33

Caminiti, C., Iezzi, E., Ghetti, C., De'Angelis, G., & Ferrari, C. (2015). A method for measuring individual research productivity in hospitals: Development and feasibility. *BMC Health Services Research*, 15, 468. DOI: 10.1186/s12913-015-1130-7

Conklin, M. H., & Desselle, S. P. (2006). *Development and construct validation of a scale to measure a   pharmacy academician's job satisfaction*. Paper presented at the American Association of Colleges of Pharmacy Annual Conference, San Diego, Calif.

Creswell, J. W., & Plano Clark, V. L. (2018). *Designing and conducting mixed methods research* (3rd ed.). Sage.

Data Protection Act. (2020). *Jamaica Data Protection Act of Jamaica.* https://www.privacylaws.com/media/4524/jamaica-data-protection-act-2020.pdf

DePoy, E., & Gitlin, L. N. (Eds.). (2016). *Collecting data through measurement in experimental-type research. Introduction to Research* (5th ed., pp. 227–247). Mosby., DOI: 10.1016/B978-0-323-26171-5.00017-3

Dornyei, Z. (2001). *Teaching and researching motivation.* Pearson Education.

Ezeala, L. O., & Yusuff, E. O. (2011). User satisfaction with library resources and services in Nigerian agricultural research institutes. *Library Philosophy and Practice (e-journal).* 564. http://unllib.unl.edu/LPP

Farzaneh, E., Amani, F., Taleghani, Y. M., Fathi, A., Kahnamouei-aghdam, F., & Fatthzadeh-Ardalani, G. (2016). Research barriers from the viewpoint of faculty members and students of Ardabil University of Medical Sciences, Iran, 2014. *International Journal of Research in Medical Sciences*, 4(6), 1926–1932.

Franzén, E. (2008). The benefits of using print-on-demand or POD. In Zemliansky, P., & St. Amant, K. (Eds.), *Handbook of research on virtual workplaces and the new nature of business practices* (pp. 668–680). IGI Global Publishing., DOI: 10.4018/978-1-59904-893-2

French, J., & Poznanski, D. (2009). Managing research—A guide to research infrastructure. *Journal of Medical Imaging and Radiation Sciences*, 40(4), 165–169. DOI: 10.1016/j.jmir.2009.09.002

Heng, K., Hamid, M. O., & Khan, A. (2020). Factors influencing academics' research engagement and productivity: A developing countries perspective. *Issues in Educational Research*, 30(3), 965–987.

Hiebert, J., Cai, J., Hwang, S., Morris, A., & Hohensee, C. (2022). What Is research, and why do people do it? In *Doing research: A new researcher's guide. Research in mathematics education* (pp. 1–15). Springer., DOI: 10.1007/978-3-031-19078-0_1

Hipni, A., Ramli, N. L., & Wan Ghopa, W. A. (2011). Motivation for research and publication: Experience as a researcher and an academic. *Procedia: Social and Behavioral Sciences*, 18, 213–219. DOI: 10.1016/j.sbspro.2011.05.030

Hussain, A., & Abalkhail, A. M. (2013). Determinants of library use, collections and services among the students of engineering: A case study of King Saud University. *Collection Building & Management*, 32(3), 100–110. DOI: 10.1108/CB-07-2012-0033

Ikolo, V. E. (2015). User satisfaction with library services: A case study of Delta State University library. *International Journal of Information and Communication Technology Education*, 11(2), 80–89.

Iqbal, M. Z., & Mahmood, A. (2011). Factors related to low research productivity at higher education level. *Asian Social Science*, 7(2), 188–193. DOI: 10.21522/TIJAR.2014.11.01.Art013

Johann, D., Neufeld, J., Thomas, K., Rathmann, J., & Rauhut, H. (2024). The impact of researchers' perceived pressure on their publication strategies. *Research Evaluation*, 00, 1–16. DOI: 10.1093/reseval/rvae011

Jordan, K. (2022). Academics' perceptions of research impact and engagement through interactions on social media platforms. *Learning, Media and Technology*, 48(3), 415–428. https://doi.org/10.1080/17439884.2022.2065298

Kassim, N. (2009). Evaluating users' satisfaction on academic library performance. *Malaysian Journal of Library and Information Science*, 14(2), 101–115. https://ejournal.um.edu.my/index.php/MJLIS/article/view/6960

Kern, S. (2011). Analytic model for academic research productivity having factors, interactions and implications. *Cancer Biology & Therapy*, 12(11), 949–956. DOI: 10.4161/cbt.12.11.18368

Lutz, G. (2021, May 4). *The world of research infrastructure.* https://forscenter.ch/wp-content/uploads/2021/05/presentation-research-infrastructures-4.5.2021_compressed.pdf

Mantikayan, J. M., & Abdulgani, M. A. (2018). Factors affecting faculty research productivity: Conclusions from a critical review of the literature. *JPAIR Multidisciplinary Research*, 31, 1–21. DOI: 10.7719/jpair.v31i1.56

Marjaei, S., Ahmadianyazdi, F., & Chandrashekara, M. (2002). Awareness and satisfaction of research scholars using library resources and services in academic libraries. *Library Philosophy and Practice* (e-journal). 6898. https://digitalcommons.unl.edu/libphilprac/6898

McGill, M. M., & Settle, A. (2012). Institutional support for computing faculty research productivity: Does gender matter? *Proceedings of the Annual Southeast Conference*. doi:DOI: 10.1145/2184512.2184522

Mehta, V., Chugh, C., & Perwez, A. (2017). Why should you do Research? *Journal of Medical Research and Innovation*, 1(1), 17.

Mohrman, K., Ma, W., & Baker, D. (2008). The research university in transition: The emerging global model. *Higher Education Policy*, 21, 5–27. DOI: 10.1057/palgrave.hep.8300175

Muia, A. M., & Oringo, J. O. (2026). Constraints on research productivity in Kenyan universities: Case study of University of Nairobi, Kenya. *International Journal of Recent Advances in Multidisciplinary Research, 03*(08), 1785-1794.

National Research Council. (2015). Overview of the research on team effectiveness. In Cooke, N. J., & Hilton, M. L. (Eds.), *Enhancing the effectiveness of team science*. National Academies Press., https://www.ncbi.nlm.nih.gov/books/NBK310384/

Niles, M. T., Schimanski, L. A., McKiernan, E. C., & Alperin, J. P. (2020). Why we publish where we do: Faculty publishing values and their relationship to review, promotion and tenure expectations. *PLoS One*, 15(3), e0228914. DOI: 10.1371/journal.pone.0228914

O'Neill, T. A., & Salas, E. (2018). Creating high performance teamwork in organizations. *Human Resource Management Review*, 28(4), 325–331. DOI: 10.1016/j.hrmr.2017.09.001

O'Neill, T. A., & Salas, E. (2018). Creating high performance teamwork in organizations. *Human Resource Management Review*, 28(4), 325–331. DOI: 10.1016/j.hrmr.2017.09.001

Onyefulu, C., & Johnson, H. (2009). A survey of lecturers' views on establishing research groups in a faculty in the University of Technology, Jamaica. In Ezenne, A. (Ed.), *Higher Education in the Caribbean: Research, Challenges and Prospects* (pp. 231–264). C & A Publishers Ltd.

Osaze Patrick, I., Aghojare, B., & Ferdinand, O. A. (2015). Assess users' satisfaction on academic library performance: A study. *International Journal of Academic Research and Reflection*, 3(5), 67–77.

Paek, J. (2004). A systems approach to mentoring: A review of literature. Paper presented at the *Academy of Human Resource Development International Conference* (AHRD), Austin, TX, 367- 374.

Probert, B., & Sachs, J. (2015). The Rise of Teaching Focused Academics in Universities. *International Journal of Chinese Education*, 4(1), 48–67. DOI: 10.1163/22125868-12340044

Saika, M., & Gohain, A. (2013). Use and user's satisfaction in library resources and services: A study in Tezpur University (India). *International Journal of Library and Information Science*, 5(6), 167–175.

Sayyed, K. (2024). Assessing research productivity and quality across disciplines in the School of Arts and Sciences at the Lebanese American University. *SAGE Open*, •••, 1–21. DOI: 10.1177/21582440241237050

Shuffler, M. L., Kramer, W. S., Carter, D. R., Thayer, A. L., & Rosen, M. A. (2018). Leveraging a team-centric approach to diagnosing multiteam system functioning: The role of intrateam state profiles. *Human Resource Management Review, 28* (4), 361-377.FRENCH https://doi.org/DOI: 10.1016/j.hrmr.2017.08.003

Solomon, G. E., Carley, S., & Porter, A. L. (2016). How multidisciplinary are the multidisciplinary journals science and nature? *PLoS One*, 11(4), e0152637. DOI: 10.1371/journal.pone.0152637

Sotodeh Asl, N., Ghorbani, R., & Rashidy-Pour, A. (2014). Viewpoints of faculty members of Semnan University of Medical Sciences about research barriers. *Koomesh*, •••, 1–7. http://eprints.semums.ac.ir/346/

Stadnick, N. A., Poth, C. N., Guetterman, T. C., & Gallo, J. J. (2021). Advancing discussion of ethics in mixed methods health services research. *BMC Health Services Research*, 21(577). Advance online publication. DOI: 10.1186/s12913-021-06583-1

Taherdoost, H. (2017). Validity and reliability of the research instrument: How to test the validation of a questionnaire/survey in a research. *International Journal of Academic Research in Management, 5*(3), 28-36. United Nations Educational, Scientific and Cultural Organization. (2024). *What you need to know about higher* educationhttps://www.unesco.org/en/higher-education/need-know

University of Technology. Jamaica. (2019). *Student Handbook for graduate and undergraduate students: 2019-2020.* PeartreeXpress. University of Technology, Jamaica. (n.d.). *University's annual research productivity reports.* SGRE.

Usman, A. G. (2024). Research output and knowledge translation among faculty members of University of Technology, Jamaica. *Texila International Journal of Academic Research*, 11(1), 134–154. DOI: 10.21522/TIJAR.2014.11.01.Art013

Wang, S. (2020). The role and path of university academic journals in research integrity building. *Advances in Social Science, Education and Humanities Research*, 505, 401–407.

Weber-Main, A. M., Finstad, D. A., Center, B. A., & Bland, C. J. (2013). An adaptive approach to facilitating research productivity in a primary care clinical department. *Academic Medicine*, 88(7), 929–938. DOI: 10.1097/ACM.0b013e318295005f

Weerasinghe, I. M. S., Lalitha, R., & Fernando, S. (2017). Students' satisfaction in higher education literature review. *American Journal of Educational Research*, 5(5), 533–539. DOI: 10.12691/education-5-5-9

Wilson, V. (2011). Research methods: Content analysis. *Evidence Based Library and Information Practice*, 6(4), 177–179. DOI: 10.18438/B8CG9D

Wu, M.-J., Zhao, K., & Fils-Aime, F. (2022). Response rates of online surveys in published research: A meta-analysis. [Zain, S. M., Ab-Rahman, M. S., Mohd Ihsan, A. K. A., Zahrim, A., Mohd Nor, M. J., Mohd Zain, M. F.]. *Computers in Human Behavior Reports*, 7, 100206. DOI: 10.1016/j.chbr.2022.100206

Zhao, L. (2012). Investigation into motivation types and influences on motivation: The case of Chinese non-English majors. *English Language Teaching*, 5(3), 100–122.

Chapter 13
Fusion Femme:
Exploring Virtual Collaboration Among Women in Academic Spaces

Eraldine S. Williams-Shakespeare
https://orcid.org/0009-0001-7169-579X
University of Technology, Jamaica

Joyce Esi Tawiah-Mensah
https://orcid.org/0009-0003-8583-1902
University of Cape Coast, Ghana

Sharlene M. Smith
Georgian Court University, USA

Natasha G. Swann
University of Bahamas, Bahamas

Taneisha Wright-Cameron
https://orcid.org/0009-0009-3392-3665
University of Technology, Jamaica

Adhwaa Alahmari
https://orcid.org/0000-0001-6180-7201
King Khalid University, Saudi Arabia

ABSTRACT

This intrinsic case study explored six women of colour in varying stages of their academic careers across five universities in the Caribbean, North America, Africa and Asia, reflecting on their experiences with virtual teamwork and its influence on research, teaching innovation and leadership. The chapter presents challenges experienced by early to mid-career academics and outlines opportunities that virtual collaborative engagement efforts may yield. The research question guiding this study was "how can women of colour in academia support each other virtually in areas of research, teaching excellence and leadership?" Data collected via a focus group discussion revealed several challenges related to each key area of interest and ranged from discrimination to lack of mentorship on the job. The findings highlight several factors that affect research (funding and time affordance), teaching (mentorship

DOI: 10.4018/979-8-3693-3852-0.ch013

Copyright © 2025, IGI Global. Copying or distributing in print or electronic forms without written permission of IGI Global is prohibited.

and support) and leadership (mindset of long-service over merit and gender and personal biases) progress for women of colour. The ability to collaborate virtually offered these women an avenue through which they can support each other while increasing research output, improving teaching skills and positioning themselves to excel in leadership.

INTRODUCTION

Academic life, though rewarding, is challenging for many faculty members, even more so for early to mid-career women who are trying to establish themselves as researchers on a path to tenure. Brukinshaw and White (2017) in their examination of how new managerialism impacts the careers of women in academia found women are disproportionately affected by the emphasis on research as they are often less likely to experience the success of men in attracting research funding. With research in most institutions carrying the highest value in terms of importance, the challenge is even greater for women. Furthermore, Greska (2023) states that women hold a minority of professorships across academic disciplines "even in those disciplines where the majority of college students are female" (p. 102). While some women in academia are performing extremely well all-round and have excelled in research to be promoted to the highest rank in their field, there is evidence of many who are struggling to get past the one publication marker, and some have encountered difficulty in terms of the time available for research, given their teaching load (Greska, 2023).

This shines the spotlight on the fact that the academic journey, at least for women, may seem or is more challenging when meeting these various demands individually. The academic journey is not an individualistic one, rather one that requires collaboration, networking and a willingness to mentor and be mentored (Morton & Gil, 2019). The absence of a culture of collaboration that supports mentorship of young (new) faculty in research makes the experience more difficult, especially in environments where the research culture is not strong. Beyond research there is the need for support in teaching innovation and preparation for leadership as the three areas are critical for success.

OVERVIEW

The challenge of balancing all that is needed to be considered for advancement in academia often cripples early to mid-career academics, this against a backdrop of the competitive nature of the space. Teamwork offers an opportunity to explore possibilities for strengthening individual and collective capacities in research, teaching excellence and leadership. Dinh and Salas (2017) cite the expanding science of teams and their importance in practice within academic spaces. In fact, Dusdal and Powell (2021) view cross-cultural and organizational collaboration as valuable in the field of research because of the possibilities for increased discovery. They contend that "international collaborative research projects often provide findings beyond what one team could achieve alone" (p. 235).

Teaching mentorship and support often provided through in-house centres of excellence enables some cushion but is not usually discipline specific. Thus, opportunities for sharing of ideas, teaching success or resources may be unavailable at times. Required teaching time varies across institutions and is based on the unique nuances of individual institutions. So, faculty with heavy teaching loads are challenged to research in a way that helps to grow their research portfolio. Teaching and research are major determinants for academic advancement, with service being the third link. In many instances, this service is reflected in academic leadership roles. These academic leadership positions are rotational in many contexts but not readily available. Additionally, opportunities to gain experience in leadership roles and secure time off to allow for research are often not within reach.

Studies have shown that virtual collaboration promotes leadership opportunities (Abdelrahman et al., 2021; Gilsen & Maynard, 2015; Hill & Bartol, 2016; Larson & DeChurch, 2020) and could have a positive impact on empowering leadership skills via mentor-mentee relationships between persons who may be in different parts of the world through virtual activities (Hill & Bartol, 2016; Larson & DeChurch, 2020). Thus, women of colour could be virtually mentored in the acquisition of leadership skills. The acquisition of virtual leadership could be intentional and/or unintentional. It is intentional when members of the collaborative team with leadership experience and skills purpose to coach and mentor the early career members (Mysirlaki & Paraskeva, 2012) as part of the virtual collaboration. On the other hand, virtual collaborative activities provide opportunities for members to learn good leadership practices in terms of knowledge and attitudes towards work from other members indirectly, which tends to boost leadership skills.

Virtual collaborative platforms enable groups, including women of colour, with different functional expertise, to work together on projects with common goals. Such opportunities open new lines of communication and collaboration that produce fresh ideas and solutions. These opportunities unearth a variety of talents and creativity and bring voices together to boost knowledge and skills. These examples link with Gilsen and Maynard's (2015) assertion that virtual collaboration can encourage globalization that promotes diversity of thought, as well as present opportunities for individuals to develop and emerge as leaders.

Likewise, access to groups that provide support through mentorship and collaborative team effort can be a catalyst to boost faculty research output and teaching quality and prepare women in academia for positions of leadership. The varying roles that may be established within research groups allow for persons to highlight their strengths and learn from others to improve their weaknesses. Additionally, faculty can benefit from interdisciplinary research, culturally diverse interactions about teaching, research practices and innovations.

Further, collaboration among academics in different countries is said to contribute to research that is considered more influential and often cited (Dusdal & Powell, 2021). Benefits cited by the authors are learning from and helping each other, sharing workload, the development of theoretical approaches and methods resulting from multidisciplinary advances, and career advancement. Friendship among team members is also cited by the authors as a benefit of engaging a teamwork approach to research. Interestingly, collaboration among academics who have different cultural norms and expectations along with differences in their organisational realities may incur some challenges. Participants may also encounter variations in the needs of individual members of the team.

FOCUS AND SIGNIFICANCE OF THE STUDY

This intrinsic case study reflects the voices of six women of colour in varying stages of their academic careers across five universities in the Caribbean, North America, Africa, and Asia. The researchers explored the influence of virtually facilitated teamwork on research. Teaching excellence and leadership experiences are also described with a view to understanding the challenges involved in their execution and attainment, respectively, as well as the opportunities that collaborative research efforts may yield. The research question that guided this study was, "How can women of colour in academia support each other virtually in areas of research, teaching excellence, and leadership?" The goal of the study was to ascertain the possibilities for strengthening research quality and output through a collaborative approach that will allow for the exchange of ideas, and research that may foster teaching success, as well as boost morale and provide mentorship for leadership posts as they become available for women of colour in academia.

This study's significance from a practical standpoint lies in its potential benefit to women of colour who continue to navigate the often-times challenging academic landscape, providing an avenue through which the shared responsibilities and efforts could lead to improved output. Theoretically, the study's results add to the body of knowledge on early to mid-career women of colour engaging in collaborative virtual teams as a catalyst to boost research output, improve teaching excellence, and help prepare each other for leadership positions in academia.

CONCEPTUAL FRAMEWORK

In conceptualizing a framework for understanding the challenges and opportunities of virtual collaboration and more precisely, exploring collaboration among women of colour in academic spaces across different geographical locations and specialisations, two theoretical concepts were found adequate to describe and comprehend their encounters. The Intersectionality Theory and Collaboration within the E-Research Environment Concept are theoretical lenses through which the experiences of women of colour in higher education institutions can be comprehended in relation to their overlapping identities (Johnson, 2023), collaborating within virtual spaces.

INTERSECTIONALITY – WOMEN OF COLOUR IN HIGHER EDUCATION

According to Johnson (2023), the Intersectionality Theory explains how the needs of women of colour in higher education can successfully be met, thereby encouraging their advancement and providing a platform that is open to the diverse perspectives that female leaders in education bring to their institutions. Intersectionality is not a new term or phenomenon. It has been in use for more than 30 years. The term was coined by a black feminist and critical race scholar, Kimberle' Crenshaw. The term has become more nuanced in various public arenas or discourses (Runyan, 2018). Intersectionality refers to oppressions relative to race, gender, class, sexuality, disability, nationality, or other social categories (Runyan, 2018). Intersectional analysis helps to understand any concerns or issues, such as the status of black women faculty in rank and tenure, pay equity, or women in leadership in higher education. Race, class, citizenship status and sexuality significantly determine who is most at risk, how they are treated, and support given and remedies available to address those concerns (Runyun, 2018).

Wendy's (2016) study explored the experiences of women of colour in higher education through the lens of intersectionality. She used three major lessons of intersectionality research to support the experiences of women of colour in the academy, and particularly the importance of identity for women of colour's experiences in an area of smaller numbers. Her study identified supports, and intervention strategies that can help women of colour survive to tenure and build sustainable careers. The strategies and interventions identified included allies such as department heads, deans and other senior university leaders who can support the career-sustaining decisions made by women of colour (Wendy, 2016). This concept is useful in helping to frame a perspective on research, teaching, and leadership advancements for women of colour in academia.

COLLABORATION WITH THE E-RESEARCH ENVIRONMENT CONCEPT

With consideration of the previous understanding of the nature, history, and situations of women of colour, online collaboration tool sets provide an opportunity to overcome some of these inherent barriers that seem to affect women of colour in conducting research and thereby meeting publication requirements within their respective institutions. These toolsets are vested in the Collaboration within the E-Research Environment Concept. In this context collaboration is seen to be more than just cooperation and coordination (Anandarajan, 2010). Mattessich et al (2001) stated collaboration involves people who are committed to mutual goals and relationships, accountability and authority for success, shared responsibility and jointly developed structure, as well as sharing of resources and rewards. Anandarajan (2010) further outlines there are seven crucial elements if collaboration is to be successful in the electronic environment. These elements are communication, trust and respect, equality and power, strategic alliances, incentives, negotiation, and organisational knowledge sharing. George et al. (2020) shared similar sentiments that a culture of trust and collective leadership along with academic and non-academic variables play important roles in supporting virtual collaboration in academia.

These theories provide an underpinning for describing and understanding the unique nature and challenges of Black women/women of colour in higher education who seek to use electronic research collaboration, teamwork, and teaching mentorship as tools to overcome the inherent challenges faced in meeting predetermined research publication expectations that are necessary for tenure and success in academia in their respective institutions. The potential exists also for advancement of teaching capacity through mentorship and action research output.

LITERATURE REVIEW

In this review, we examined literature on research, teaching, and leadership among women of colour. We also assessed technology as a catalyst for sustaining collaboration among women of colour in academia. Therefore, the themes under which the literature is discussed are: a perspective on teaching realities for women of colour in academia; research experiences of women of colour; the role of collaboration in enhancing research productivity and impact on women of colour; unique challenges faced by women of colour in academic leadership positions: collaboration a possible intervention; teamwork and technology as vehicles of support for change in higher education; and benefits of virtual collaboration as women of colour.

A Perspective on Teaching Realities for Women of Colour in Academia

Studies indicate that the progression of women in higher education has outpaced that of men (NCES, 2019). That is, statistics show that women are enrolling and graduating at higher rates in higher education institutions. There is also research evidence that women, especially women of colour, in higher education demonstrate a higher level of resilience (Kim & O'Brien, 2018; Vaccaro, 2017). However, when it comes to teaching regarding faculty, this hardly reflects (De Welde, 2017; Mkhize, 2024; Whitaker & Denise, 2018). This expression of inequality in academia may be attributed to race, gender, colour, ethnicity, and cultural beliefs (Aiston & Jung, 2016; Mkhize, 2024). While women of colour experience racism and colour discrimination in mostly white/male dominated institutions, black women in the Caribbean, Africa and Asia tend to experience cultural and gender discrimination which conspicuously affects women in their teaching and research in the spaces of higher education institutions. Extant research shows that black women, and for that matter women of colour within academia face many challenges based on their identities (Marbley et al., 2011).

A study conducted by Mkhize (2024) on young black women's teaching experiences in universities revealed that women of colour face varied challenges including race, gender, age, and class. Viewed through the lens of intersectionality, her qualitative study explored nine Black Millennial women's teaching experiences in universities in South Africa. The findings showed that the young Black Millennial women faculty who participated in the study faced racism, sexism, and agism in their working space. It was revealed that the participants' experiences were varied based on the nature of the university in which they were teaching. The findings indicated that those in white dominated universities experienced more hostility from both faculty and students than their counterparts in Black dominated institutions. The relevance of this study to the current study goes beyond highlighting the challenges women of colour face regarding teaching at the universities, but to include the suitability of the intersectionality framework used to frame this study.

Lin and Kennette (2022) also looked at challenges faced by women of colour in academia. The study emphasised the additional burdens women of colour face because of societal expectations, biases, and systemic inequities. It highlights the impact of these challenges on their professional responsibilities, including the need to provide social support to students and navigate educational responsibilities, in addition to addressing their own children's education. The paper also discussed the disparities in research activity and productivity between white male faculty and women of colour faculty, particularly during the pandemic. The paper advocated for committees and campus leaders that oversee tenure processes to be mindful of these extraneous variables when evaluating tenure portfolios for women of colour faculty. Additionally, it stresses the importance of reducing the burden on marginalised faculty members, especially women of colour, and advocates for institutional changes to promote equity and support the success of individuals from marginalised identities in academia.

Furthermore, Fox Tree and Vaid (2022) in their quest to find the challenges faced by women faculty of colour in academia reviewed and analysed existing findings from various sources of reports and scholarly articles. Their intent was to provide insights into the disparities and biases experienced by women of colour in research, teaching, and service assessment in academic settings. Their findings indicated that women of colour are disproportionately underrepresented in academia, especially at senior ranks in research-intensive universities. It also came out that the disparities that exist in the assessment of research, teaching, and service in academia impact negatively on the professional visibility of women faculty of colour. The findings showed that women often face challenges of being recognized for their research contributions and may experience biases in the publication process. These findings underscore the importance of addressing systemic biases and encourage avenues that support the professional development of women of colour in academia. This in turn could promote diversity and inclusion in higher education institutions. Therefore, encouraging, and empowering women of colour through collaboration could be one of the powerful avenues in addressing the systemic biases in academia, hence this study.

Research Experiences of Women of Colour

Research is a critical element in the professional lives of academicians. It has implications for improved practice, professional development and by extension nation building. Various factors challenge research output (quality and volume) to include availability of time, funding, and support. As established earlier in this chapter, the difficulties are even more profound for women. Collaboration is one way that is being engaged globally to boost research output, generally. The literature examined here focuses on the role of collaboration in enhancing research output for women of colour.

One of the key challenges in improving the representation of women of colour in academia is assessing the quality of research. Bias influences various aspects of research evaluation. A study by Hofstra et al. (2020) that analysed more than a million dissertations showed that women and individuals from different backgrounds often establish innovative connections in their research. However, they are less likely to receive recognition for their creativity through opportunities for research careers.

In research publications, the contributions of women and people of colour are often undervalued. Women are typically underrepresented in key authorship positions, including first, as well as in single-authored papers (West et al., 2013). Additionally, female scholars across various disciplines in both natural and social sciences receive fewer citations (Caplar et al., 2017; Dion et al., 2018; Fox & Paine, 2019).

The Role and Impact of Collaboration: Enhancing Research Productivity on Women Of Colour

Research in academia is the yardstick for progression or opportunity for upward mobility. It is in this vein that Morley (2014) asserted that "research performance is implicitly associated with the prestige economy in higher education and is a pathway to academic seniority and indicator for promotion" (p. 116). As hinted in the preceding paragraph, research output is another area of challenge for women of colour in academia. That is, women academics, especially women of colour, publish less on average than their male colleagues and this in turn has a negative effect on their upward mobility (Brukinshaw & White, 2017).

Extant research findings indicate there is a gender gap regarding research output in the world of academia. Aiston and Jung (2015) explored the issue of gender and research productivity from an international perspective. They used Changing Academic Profession (CAP) survey data to analyze research publications in five countries Japan, Hong Kong, Germany, the USA, and Finland. Their findings confirmed males publish more than their female counterparts. That is, women in academia publish fewer journal articles and book chapters. However, their study revealed that familial responsibilities do not generally adversely affect the outcome of women's research output, and this finding contradicts many existing research findings (Sax et al. 2002). Even though this study did not focus only on women of colour in academia, its findings are relevant to the current study as they link with our present focus. Also, the latter finding is interesting as it could be an area of interest to the present study because it involves women of colour in academia with families. The findings of this research call for women in academia, especially women of colour, to sit up and encourage one another or collaborate in research to enhance their research visibility, as well as their upward mobility in higher education.

The role of collaboration in enhancing research productivity and its impact on women of colour scholars cannot be overemphasised. Collaboration of scholars creates the opportunity for each to be mentored and to mentor. This not only enhances career advancement but also leads to the establishment of a strong research portfolio in that collaborative work with colleagues from diverse backgrounds exposes team members to new research methodologies and enhances the impact of their research within the academic community (Misra et al., 2017).

Collaborative research, therefore, leads to innovative research ideas and approaches that can have a broader impact on their respective fields. This in turn could result in increased research output, co-authored publications, and citations, which contribute to the visibility and impact of women of colour scholars' research outcomes (Morley, 2014). Furthermore, research collaboration creates an enabling and supportive environment as well as networking opportunities that can lead to new research partnerships, funding opportunities, and access to resources that enhance research productivity (Johnston et al., 2020; Pardee, Fothergill, Weber & Peek, 2017). Enhanced research productivity could possibly serve as a catalyst for access to leadership opportunities in academia.

Unique Challenges Faced by Women of Colour in Academic Leadership Positions: Collaboration a Possible Intervention

Extensive research has been carried out on women's leadership in higher education over the years (Alotaibi, 2020; Madsen, 2012; Maheshwari & Nayak, 2022). Conversely, there is a dearth of research addressing minorities in higher education leadership (Davis & Maldonado, 2015). Furthermore, the challenges experienced by black women in leadership roles within colleges and universities have not received much attention in studies (Chance, 2022).

Despite efforts to promote gender equality and improvements in women's education, women continue to be noticeably underrepresented in senior leadership roles and important positions along the academic journey (American Council on Education, 2007). Nations and regions may differ in cultural norms, achievements, and levels of development, however, the barriers hindering women's representation in academia exhibit striking similarities across many regions (Yousaf & Schmiede, 2017). Though this is changing, it is apparent that women grapple with biases in hiring practices, uneven distribution of workloads, pay disparities, and limited opportunities for career growth (Deanet al., 2023).

Women of colour, unlike white women, experience a dual challenge of gender and racial biases, ingrained both systemically and institutionally (Gause, 2021). These constraints limit their avenues for career advancement and impede their ability to succeed within organisations, thus, highlighting their underrepresentation and the adversity they encounter in pursuing or achieving senior leadership positions in higher education (Chance, 2022).

Apart from disparities in authorship outlined in previous paragraphs, women and people of colour experience limited professional visibility in other spheres of the workforce. For example, they are frequently excluded from invitations to give talks. A study examining talks at a geophysical conference between 2014 and 2016 showed that Black/African American, Latina and Native American scholars received fewer invitations compared to White and Asian American scholars, with underrepresented women experiencing the most significant disparity (Ford et al., 2019). Research and other avenues for professional visibility are directly and indirectly catalysts to leadership opportunities. Other inequalities such as disparities in research funding, student evaluations of teaching, biases towards marginalised faculty among students, and unequal distribution of service responsibilities all contribute to impeding the upward mobility of women of colour within the academic hierarchy (Fox Tree & Vaid, 2022).

Institutions and organisations barely recognize the enormous advantages women can bring when they are actively engaged on boards and leadership teams. Madsen and Longman (2020) found that women's involvement in leadership improved financial outcomes, created a more favourable environment, enhanced corporate social responsibility and reputation, ensured effective utilisation of talent, and increased innovation and collective intelligence.

Teamwork and Virtual Technology as Vehicles of Support for Change in Higher Education

When one feels a sense of belonging, (Aelteman et al. 2007) active, and engaged as a member of a team, goals can be accomplished. Sacrifices are made when one feels supported (Somech, 2005). According to Kiral (2021), teamwork is carried out to increase solidarity and even strengthen the goal of the team despite individual differences in backgrounds and settings. In truth, the individuality and diversity of people within a given team can be used as a benefit to support the common goal of the team. Across industries the engagement of virtual teams and global virtual teams (Jimenez et al., 2017; Morrison-Smith & Ruiz, 2020; Richter et al., 2021) is now a norm. It is not surprising that this is quickly becoming a reality in education. As early to mid-career professionals grapple with challenges related to academic life, teamwork in technology enabled virtual spaces is becoming more and more attractive. In the case of this study, it provided an avenue through which geographically dispersed women of colour, who are experiencing similar challenges, explored avenues for improving their research profiles, and teaching quality.

According to George et al. (2020), high expectations, shared goals, professionalism, and peer accountability are drivers of successful collaboration in groups. The authors further posit that there are competing factors that challenge team success to include, academic and non-academic issues and the matter of trust development and collective leadership. To accomplish many things in an expedient amount of time, teamwork is essential in many capacities. Teamwork is defined as "organisational structures in which individuals from different backgrounds, different strengths and different perspectives come together to achieve common goals in corporation as a whole and in the most effective ways (Gidis & Kiral, 2023, p, 467). Additionally, teamwork is seen as the structured engagement of individuals with similar interests who have formed alliances to reach a particular goal (Forsyth, 2014).

Scholars from three separate and distinct universities in North America, Africa and Eurasia collaborated to pair their undergraduate students with diverse backgrounds and competencies to decipher the advancing of transversal and intercultural skills through a virtual teamwork experience. These scholars, Howard et al. (2023) found that with a shared vision in creating realistic projects for their students, despite the challenges of cultural differences, infrastructure for technology platforms, time zones, languages, and others, their students were successful in these virtual class spaces. To accomplish any feat, teamwork has been integrated with institutions, across spaces, time, and cultures. Once there is a shared vision and an effective alliance, teamwork can work as a vehicle of change.

On the other hand, Johari et al. (2021) examined the relationship between teamwork, principal support, humour and innovative work behaviour. They admonished teamwork as "collaboration of individuals in a cooperative environment with effective and mutual relationship to achieve common team goals" (p. 74). In their findings they learned that there is a strong correlation between effective teamwork and teachers producing work that is innovative and creative in their classes.

Technology greatly influences this collaborative teamwork process whether within teams locally or across geographical boundaries. It has enabled increased opportunities for academics to form virtual teams to boost research output. Virtual working environments offer myriad opportunities for interaction and connection (Greimel et al, 2023). George et al. (2020) states that virtual collaboration has the potential to be an effective strategy to enhance research output which is a common practice in academia. Furthermore, there are equal opportunities that technology presents to research teams to include access to tools that can support data collection and analysis in innovative ways allowing groups to work together synchronously and asynchronously to complete research. However, Morrison-Smith and Ruiz (2020) posit that geographical factors challenge the success of virtual teams. These factors include social and emotional factors such as trust, motivation, and conflicts.

Johnston et al. (2020) explored the role of technology in supporting collaborative research teams in higher education. The focus of the study was to explore how technology-powered connectivity approaches are used to support collaborative research in higher education and to identify successful attributes and frameworks of collaborative research teams. Their study indicated that technology is a catalyst for change in research practices as it enables diverse groups of researchers to connect, share resources, and discuss emerging trends. It underscored the importance of collaboration in enhancing the research productivity and impact of women of colour scholars and that collaborative research allows isolated individuals to create and manage research effectively.

The study further emphasised the importance of interdisciplinary collaboration and the use of technology to enhance research networks and professional development in academia. This paper highlights the relevance of the current study as it explains how virtual collaborative research plays a vital role in enhancing the research productivity and impact of women of colour scholars by providing a platform for knowledge sharing and professional development within academia. Collaborative research is a viable practice for women, especially women of colour, to leverage their unique perspectives and expertise to contribute meaningfully to research projects and advance their academic careers. This shows that the current research study is in the right direction as it is a virtual collaboration of women of colour from different parts of the world teaching and researching in higher education.

Benefits of Virtual Collaboration as Women of Colour

The benefits of virtual collaboration in the contemporary world cannot be overemphasised. Virtual collaboration offers flexibility regarding the time and place of working. It also contributes to narrowing the gender gap (especially of women of colour) and accommodating diverse backgrounds and roles (Howard, et al., 2023; Zakaria, 2017). Virtual collaboration affords women of colour the opportunity to work on research projects at any time of the day, irrespective of the location, an opportunity rare in in-person collaboration. In other words, virtual collaboration can mitigate physical barriers that present themselves as challenges in in-person research environments (Altebarmakian & Alterman, 2019; McLoughlin et al., 2018). These challenges are easily resolved when virtual collaborations and activities are designed to be culturally responsive for members (Kumi-Yeboah et al., 2017; McLoughlin et al., 2018;)

Another benefit of virtual collaboration for women of colour is the availability of tools that simplify teamwork in real time for research activities. This is particularly for those who seldom get the opportunity to have more women of colour in leadership positions or workplaces, which is a platform to engage in research activities. Virtual collaboration tools have become an empowering facility not only for students to enhance learning experiences, communication, and interaction which leads to the achievement of common goals (Altebarkmakian & Alterman, 2019) but also for women of colour to assist each other to advance their research skills (Howard et al., 2023). These virtual communities can exist in academic environments (Kumi-Yeboah et al., 2017) as well as professional environments (Olaisen & Revang, 2017; Zakaria, 2017). For example, Olaisen and Revang (2017) assert that participation in virtual collaboration can promote collective work and knowledge sharing that yield innovation and building of trust among members. Zakaria (2017), in support of this assertion, contends that virtual collaboration builds relationships and provides opportunities for cross-cultural communication.

In addition, virtual collaboration is more task-focused and creates an environment where cultural differences are less likely to impede the completion of tasks or goals as compared with in-person environments. Studies demonstrated that virtual collaboration benefits organisations by reducing costs, creating more opportunities for ideation, and increasing productivity and work output (Gilsen & Maynard, 2015; Olaisen & Revang, 2017; Zakaria, 2017). Inferences from these studies show that virtual research collaboration is less expensive as collaborators can sit in the comfort of their homes and work without transportation issues. This, in effect, saves time as well. For example, the researchers in the current study are in different continents on the globe. However, by virtue of virtual platforms, we can connect and work effectively at our convenient time, thereby saving cost and time. This example aligns with Olaisen and Revang's (2017) assertion that the ability to collaborate in an online environment can increase the pace at which work is completed and offer opportunities for individuals to grow and develop in their job roles. As women of colour in higher education located in different parts of the world, the use of virtual collaboration has enabled us to collaborate and embark on this research, which is not only enhancing our research skills, but this opportunity is equally promoting our visibility at the research space as well.

METHODOLOGY

This qualitative study engaged an intrinsic case study research design that explored the lived experiences of six women (n=6) of colour working in academic spaces across three broad areas: teaching, research, and leadership. Intrinsic case study as a methodology helps us to explore in-depth real-life experiences of multiple cases and, more precisely, understand the unusual nature of each case. In this study, this is reflected in the researchers' participation in several universities and geographical locations and their collaboration virtually (Creswell & Gutterman, 2019). The researchers involved also span the entry to mid-career spectrum. Most participants are at least six years into the academic journey having completed doctoral studies, with one occasionally, working as an adjunct while advancing preparations to start a doctoral degree. All participants have a background in curriculum education with varying specialties, adult education and autism, special education, literacy, early childhood education, assessment, restorative justice, instructional technology, educational assessment, and evaluation. The research question guiding this study was "how can women of colour in academia support each other virtually in areas of research, teaching excellence, and leadership?"

The primary method of data collection were virtual focus group discussions. According to Pearson et al. (2015) a benefit of case study methodology "is the flexibility offered in terms of data collection methods", (p. 3). This method of gathering data allowed for all six participants who are women of colour in higher education with shared understanding to interact among themselves about their experiences (Creswell & Guetterman, 2019). The focus group discussion was conducted via Zoom web conferencing, recorded, and transcribed using Zoom-enabled AI transcription. Additionally, data was collected over a sustained period (six meetings), which is reflective of a qualitative case study design (Creswell, 2014). Meeting notes were maintained for all sessions. Transcriptions and notes were member checked and analysed thematically. The goal of the analysis was to identify participants' experiences and identify ways in which the team engagement can support research, teaching, and leadership preparation. Ethical clearance was obtained from the primary researcher's university's Ethics Committee.

DISCOVERIES

The findings are presented according to key themes that emerged from the study. These include essential elements of effective teamwork, challenges faced by women of colour in academia, the importance of leadership as a support structure, and the role of mentorship in career advancement.

Essential Elements of Effective Teamwork

The characteristics participants considered important to the success of teamwork and among women of colour in academia were trust, open and effective communication, the ability to leverage individual strengths on diverse skill sets, shared vision, resilience and determination, supportive leadership, team dynamics, and collaboration.

Trust and Open Communication: Essential Element in Teamwork

The findings indicated that in building effective teams, open communication and trust are crucial and foundational for success because they create a safe and supportive environment that fosters trust among team members. Participants in the focus group expressed the need to be able to share personal experiences within a group without judgement and having moments within the experience that allow for unwinding and relaxation. Creating safe and trusting work environments addresses the nature of a work environment that supports success for women of colour. This involved being able to trust colleagues which would ensure growth and development in the areas of research, teaching, and leadership. Participant OP expressed *"I feel trust is the first thing, then the ethics. So, then I can collaborate ... we work together and share resources regarding teaching [and] research."* Participant CC also shared, *"I think trust, finding that camaraderie, or that sisterhood, ... where you can share similar goals, have that open communication, can help support one another. I think that is very important from my experience."* Furthermore, Participant AJ in relaying an experience she had, expressed the importance of psychological safety. *"The idea of being in a psychological safe space is critical. I am free to let my hair down...and I don't have the sense that I'm gonna be judged"*. Safe spaces as support structures were deemed essential. Participant CC concurred "women want to have a safe space where we can talk about experiences and encourage one another". Similarly, Participant AJ stated: *"I believe I'm gonna be in agreement with the group that the idea of being in a psychological safe space is critical."* The additional layer of trust in colleagues, especially in collaborative research contexts was considered integral for success.

Humility, Vulnerability, and Individual Strengths: A Necessary Triad

Other factors reported in relation to team success were leveraging individual strengths, humility, and the willingness to be vulnerable. In fact, vulnerability was cited as an essential element for personal and professional growth because it allows for team members to accept feedback and learn from their experiences, *"that ability to be vulnerable, that ability to let somebody else handle...you know shines bright* (Participant HI)." On the matter of leveraging individual strengths Participant AJ shared, *"for us as women of colour [we have] to be able to recognize and appreciate the different strengths that we bring to the table and collaborate in unifying our strengths to make something beautiful."* This requires humility, which for Participant AB is *"one of the key characteristics for success"*. Together these factors serve to facilitate an effective team dynamic.

The study found when team members have shared visions or goals, they leverage individual members' strengths to enhance the team's effectiveness to produce quality outcomes. Participant RS shared *"one of the things I always consider is ensuring that women have a shared vision. Whatever the responsibility or the role, there must be a shared vision, a clear understanding of what that vision is. There must be a buy-in to that vision."* A shared vision was also considered important in fostering collaboration and team dynamics.

Team Dynamics and Collaboration

Team dynamics are enriched when diversity is recognized and appreciated in groups. Participants shared the value they are gaining from engaging with and interacting with each other in the group. *"Who has what strength? Let us partner and engage and build on each other's strengths, because in our individual spaces we'd be struggling through all of this...So we're bringing all our expertise and our knowledge* [together] (Participant AJ)." Participant HI in support shared: *"AJ just mentioned each person's strength, and coming with different perspectives, that will bring about support and is also an effective way for us...to share our teaching resources."* Each participant brought to the space varying skills, knowledge and attitudes that allowed for the interweaving of multiple perspectives around a wide range of education related issues.

Resilience and Determination in Overcoming Barriers

Resilience was evident in the experiences of all the women involved in the study. All six had similarities to include persistence in the achievement of their goals and overcoming various challenges faced throughout their academic lives. Interestingly, it was determined that a key factor contributing to our resilience is humility - a willingness to learn from each other and acknowledging our individual strengths and weaknesses. Participant AB stated that *"resilience is one of the key categories that can make us. Because when you are resilient the 'pull her down kind of thing' will not deter you from getting to the goal that you have set for yourself"*. She further stated, *"if you are resilient, challenges will be seen as steppingstones because you will not let the little things bring you down, but they would rather urge you to move ahead."*

Challenges Faced by Women of Colour in Academia

As participants shared lived experiences working in academic spaces, several challenges were discovered. Some were common to all participants while others were specific to individuals based on cultural and geographic realities. The challenges highlighted were classified into the four broad areas of focus and are presented below:

Teaching Related Challenges

Teaching related challenges were related to incidents of microaggression, language related difficulties, lack of onboarding and mentorship for new faculty. Microaggression was experienced by two participants who shared student related experiences with language barriers and accents. They shared that students were disrespectful in their approach to expressing difficulty understanding their accents. These challenges were viewed as forms of microaggressions, and biases experienced as a result of their teaching which were directly tied to race. Participant RS shared *"there were bouts of subtle racial microaggression"* and Participant AB agreed, *"the microaggression for my first year. It wasn't easy."* Both experiences were recorded while the participants were studying and teaching abroad.

Another language related issue experienced by a participant, who is a non-native English speaker, was not having access to sufficient resources in her native language in her field of specialization. *"My masters and PhD are from the USA. All my resources are based in English language... so when I teach them [students] they don't know any English. And sometimes I use articles when I teach, but it's not enough, or my expectation is not met. Sometimes they try to translate some articles to English, but it's not helpful!"* (Participant OP). This collaborative experience of working with native speakers of English and engaging technology tools helps to bridge the gap.

Another teaching related challenge was the feeling that more is expected when one is a person of colour, and this was evident in the experiences shared. According to participant CC, the feeling is *"you almost have to be twice as good as your counterpart"* to be recognized for your efforts. For other participants, there was a noted absence of onboarding support for teaching. The typical experience is to be handed a syllabus and left to find your own way. One Participant shared "in *the Caribbean environment there seems to be competition"* versus collaboration. The tendency also of some seasoned colleagues not wanting to share resources or provide support was a reality for at least four other participants. In the teaching arena, participants recognized the absence of mentorship to include guidance from some unit heads. The mindset of some seasoned faculty is that early to mid-career faculty were not ready for teaching advanced courses. Four participants reported this experience which was reflected more in the Caribbean context. Colonial legacy was cited by Participant CC as a possible contributor to this reality. Consistent with this colonial legacy were the long teaching hours which were reported as a hindrance not just to productivity but also to research output.

Research Related Challenges

Compounding factors challenging research output included time management, and accessibility of resources to include funding. Time off to engage in research was not readily available to all participants. Those in the group (four) whose job functions included both teaching and administrative roles often struggled to find time to research. This was identified as one of the reasons why collaboration was perceived as an avenue to counter this difficulty.

Funding was cited as a major research challenge for participants. Research for all, but one participant, is primarily self-funded, and this is difficult especially in contexts where salaries are low. Participant OP shared *"so this is one of the challenges, because I want good funding"*. For the participant who is self-funded, virtual collaborative projects are viewed as ideal to counter the difficulties encountered. *"A person like me, to conduct research and publish papers, you find that the opportunity comes along with being included as a part of a team such as this one"* (Participant HI). The matter of high competition for the limited pool of research funding in other contexts was also mentioned. The process of applying for funding was identified as worrisome and disheartening. According to Participant AJ *"it* [funding application process] *is intimidating, because when you apply for funding, somebody is going to sit, and it usually is somebody outside of your discipline, and they are gonna make a judgement call on your proposal and they are gonna decide, that, yeah you are not getting funding for this"*. Compounding this is the perceived yet real, public, and institutional, pressure to 'publish or perish' to ensure continued relevance and career advancement which remains a millstone around the necks of many academics. This was particularly significant for the women in this study.

The matter of language as a hindrance to research output was shared by Participant OP, who is not a native speaker of English. She states, *"I do several articles in English, but you need someone who is native, or at least graduate from native countries to help or collaborate with research"*. Journals in her discipline are primarily published in English. The challenge to publish arises because of this limitation and she expressed the value added in having a native speaker within research groups to address this issue.

Participants expressed an understanding of the role institutional barriers play in limiting research. For five of the six participants there were noted institutional based factors that challenge their research journey. According to Participants AB, CC, RS, AJ, and SA these included the staffing designs that reflect long teaching hours, systems that mandate supervisor approvals for research direction, the absence of time off mechanisms for research despite a research requirement for advancement, lack of funding for research projects, conferences, etc and other constraining factors. According to Participant OP *"you don't get a good amount of funding, so I ignored the funding process and did the research"*. Participant AB shared that *"institutional bureaucracy also challenges my ability to research"*.

Leadership Related Challenges

Additionally, the participants in the study cited several challenges related to leadership and opportunities for advancement, to include, unseen barriers, bureaucracies, undermining behaviours of colleagues and time-based limitations. These challenges do not allow for persons to be adequately onboarded or given enough time to achieve target goals. In most contexts responsibilities were rotational and some time periods were considered challenging. Participants also expressed challenges in the form of racial bias and discrimination with at least two having to provide proof of competence beyond that which is typically required elsewhere or of other staff. There was a consensus among focus group participants that women of colour face perception biases which make navigating the leadership roles more difficult thus requiring resilience and support from others. The lack of opportunities for leadership for some participants was cited as a challenge along with weak or no succession planning which creates further disconnect in the absence of shared vision.

Lack of support and bias in treatment were listed among the support and collaboration challenges participants encountered in relation to leadership. Qualification and gender-based discrimination were linked to research and leadership. The notion of waiting for one's time - long-service vs merit - outlined by Participant HI under teaching challenges was also a concern for leadership opportunities. According to Participant AJ *"when I think about opportunities to pursue leadership roles or to advance, it is that white elephant in the room, that unseen hand that says, not your time stay suppressed"* that acts as a barrier.

Generally, the women in this intrinsic case study shared that it was challenging to navigate leadership roles. Participant OP shared this experience where her efforts at leadership were compromised, *"...last summer I was promoted to associate professor. I made a decision because I really couldn't do the research with the amount of leadership work and teaching. So, I neglected the leadership, I just did my research"*. Then there was the added layer of having to overcome stereotypes and perception biases. In some contexts, the gender bias as it relates to leadership was stronger than others, this led to delayed promotions and assignments to higher offices for some members of the team. Participants RS and AB were affected by this issue. Reported also was the expectation that the woman's role should be out of professional life and in the home. Participant AB shared her experience of getting negative feedback from male colleagues who had difficulty accepting women in positions of leadership and even as colleagues. The patriarchal way of thinking was evident in the discourse shared. *"You are a woman. Go home and serve your husband and children and leave us to lead that thing"* (Participant AB). Additionally, gender factored in some participants being denied leadership roles.

Improper succession planning was identified as an area of concern which directly affected opportunities to assume leadership roles. Participants shared that where there was a trust deficit it complicated experiences for persons in positions of leadership. Some colleagues were not keen on sharing skills learned and this influenced the perceived support team members received when they assumed responsibility positions. *"Sometimes we're in a space, and we have certain skill sets, but we don't share it because we're threatened. Insecurities come into play"* (Participants AJ). The absence of opportunities for training and mentorship also factored negatively on participants' experiences and created a gap that they felt they could and should be filled. Participant HI proffered that when given the opportunity women of colour should be each other's keepers. *"We as women of colour, especially those who are in spaces like CC, ... you're in the minority, and there are certain biases or certain challenges to overcome. Then, as women of colour, you know you willingly provide support ..., especially to younger colleagues that may come in."*

Personal and Professional Challenges

Gender and societal expectations, work-life balance struggles and time management were the key personal challenges cited in this study. Professional challenges included workload management, career advancement pressures, collaborating and networking, professional development, and career advancement. These factors impacted the experiences of research participants across all three areas of the research focus.

Gender roles and expectations as a sub-theme of challenges experienced by women of colour in academia involved navigating multiple roles as women - that of mother, wife, professional, etc. Participant RS in recounting her reality shared *"... navigating children, and I came home like, Oh, my gosh! I have a meeting. Oh, my gosh! I have to cook!"* There are also societal pressures to fulfil traditional gender roles, such as managing the household responsibilities, getting married/pregnant within a certain timeframe. All the women in the study expressed issues related to work-life balance and the struggle to balance family and work responsibilities. For Participant AB *"being a mother, a wife, and others is not easy. Actually, if AJ had not called me today, I wouldn't have joined this meeting. I told them* [family], *I have a meeting at this time. I'm just sitting where I was sitting. I don't know. I slept off just because I have so many things doing today."*

Similarly, Participant OP shared *"you know, it's stressful work, plus mother who works, when I come home, I didn't do anything. I just rest and give my kids time."* The result is often a negative impact on their personal well-being. Difficulties stemming from time management related issues were also cited especially against the backdrop of other commitments thus creating the need for efficient time management strategies. Participant OP's decision to focus on research and ignore some assigned responsibilities when she faced a time crisis is one such example. Participants shared some ways they manage roles and responsibilities citing this collaborative project as one avenue as the participants can share the responsibilities of the research project.

The professional challenges listed by participants included heavy workloads, particularly in instances where the participant held administrative responsibility which impacted workload management. This factor is considered a deterrent to professional development and career advancement. Finally, the focus group discussion revealed that early and mid-career women of colour sometimes had trouble finding collaborators. Participants AJ, RS and AB noted this challenge.

Support Structures for Early to Mid-Career Women of Colour

Emanating from this intrinsic case study was the importance of structures or systems to support early to mid-career women of colour in academia. Supportive leadership and collaboration were highlighted by participants as elements of importance in ensuring success. Beyond team dynamics (trust and having a diversified skill set resident within the team) the success of collaborative engagement in academic spaces was found to be dependent on the quality and nature of support structures available. According to Participant CC, *"black women or women of colour in higher education to be successful it requires having a Dean and Vice President in leadership who may not be of colour but are very supportive of them to help them"*. This leadership is one within which there is a shared vision.

All participants agreed that the institution and faculty visions should be in alignment. Participant RS shared *"whatever the task might be or whatever the responsibility or the role, there must be a shared vision, a clear understanding of what that vision is."* Thus, institutional leadership was considered an important support structure for women of colour in academic spaces. Overall, leadership (institutional) and community (family, peers, etc) support, trust in colleagues and working within a safe space where recognition is given for varying competencies were also considered to be important support structures. Mentorship and a system that supports early to mid-career faculty were factors that were also considered important for career advancement.

Role of Mentorship in Advancing Women of Colour

Mentorship was identified as being particularly important for each of the participants. Mentorship through varying initiatives, relationships, and mentorship benefits were explored. Participants shared the role of having a mentor and mentorship plays in their professional growth and development. Participant HI shared how having a mentor was significant for her. *"I remember my lecturer ... she was the one who saw in me this strong research ability...she was the one who approached the head of the department and invited me to be a graduate teaching assistant with her."*

Participant CC shared her experience of being mentored by a faculty member who invited her to a team of researchers. *"One of my professors in the special Ed program invited me to be a part of a research team. She was just mentoring me and this other student."* She shared that this experience was beneficial to her. Mentorship is felt to play a crucial role in the success of women of colour in academic spaces because it allows for participants to engage in meaningful, authentic experiences. Participants reported benefitting from the provision of guidance, support, and opportunities for growth. Participants who received mentorship across the three areas of focus (teaching, research, and leadership) described the experience as profound. Academic and emotional support was provided as part of this process, and this served as a catalyst for the overall growth and development of the participants who benefitted from this.

DISCUSSION

This study has revealed a need for purposeful and intentional networking among women of colour in academia to boost their professional development and research output. Arguably, the greatest potential lies in the opportunity working as a virtual team can bring to the business of research in academia for this group of women (Dusdal & Powell, 2021) who have a shared vision of maintaining a successful virtual team.

With a common base in education and a diverse spread in terms of the areas of specialization, this group is poised to work intra-discipline and across specializations to increase research output and to find avenues through which to collaborate and possibly identify and seek grant funding to support research. As a collective there is every possibility for us to harness the full potential of virtual teamwork to respond to research calls, present at conferences and publish various forms of scholarly work (Dinh & Salas, 2017; Dusdal & Powell, 2021).

As we discuss the major findings, we note the influence of gender and perception biases on the experiences of the women in the study. This is consistent with Mkhize's (2024) study where women of colour faced varied challenges to include race, gender, and age. Subtle discriminatory behaviours and cultural attitudes also affected recognition and treatment. This was consistent with the experiences of some of the participants in this study. Of concern is the impact these biases continue to have on teaching, research, and leadership for women of colour.

Essentially, intersectional feminist approaches are needed to address the unique challenges faced by women of colour in academia, thus, there is a need for advocacy for policy changes to promote inclusivity and equity in academia. Hence, Intersectionality must be recognized and addressed to create inclusive environments that support the advancement of women of colour. In this study, the engagement of intersectionality theory helped us to situate our realities within a larger framework and identify solutions that could be engaged to counter the problems experienced. Effective support systems become important elements in addressing this and other challenges.

To this end, supportive leadership is encouraged. The value of supportive leadership in strengthening teaching quality cannot be underemphasized. There must be a period of onboarding allowing early career educators to learn while on the job and not feel fearful or experience imposter syndrome. This type of leadership, especially from individuals in positions of power, is crucial for women of colour in academia. The teaching experiences of women of colour are influenced by the intersection of gender, race, socioeconomic status, and academic rank (Runyun, 2018). Though this can be problematic at times, there has to be a willingness to be vulnerable in the team space, share experiences, and then benefit from the perspectives, feedback and mentorship of each other without the fear of intersectionality related issues. Furthermore, the stories shared by the women in this study highlight, where trust and communication are the foundation principles, research will thrive. In this space, an advantage can be made of the diversity of perspectives and skills which could enhance collaboration and innovation, allowing each member to feel engaged and a part of the process.

Furthermore, the findings of the study highlighted the challenges experienced when leadership related issues negatively impacted the progress and success of women of colour. The limited opportunities and inadequate preparation for positions of leadership coupled with gender related discrimination created frustration for participants in the study. The development of a team such as this offers some respite through the encouragement and motivation that members have received from each other. Wendy's (2016) study supports the value added of having supportive leadership to include deans and heads of departments, this was also found in the study.

Anandarajan's (2010) Collaboration within the E-Research Environment Concept helped us to appreciate the value added that technology affords in enabling us to engage in a supportive space that promises each member the opportunity for increased research output and allows for the sharing of best practices. There is the additional layer of emotional support around hard decisions and motivation when opportunities arise. The technology enabled affordances that support virtual meetings, recordings, and transcriptions greatly enhance our experiences against the backdrop of time limitations and geographical boundaries.

Johnston et al (2020) noted the valuable role technology plays in advancing research within diverse groups and the ability researchers have to connect, share resources and discuss trends. We found this to be our reality as we are collaborating virtually to produce publications from our shared experiences. In doing so it confirms that research output can be increased and within a shorter period working in virtual spaces (George et al, 2020). Altebarkmakian & Alterman (2019) in support shared how virtual collaboration tools empower faculty, this was also our experience. The virtual space allowed for cross continent engagement among participant researchers and served as a catalyst for us to advance further projects (Zakaria, 2017). The theories further allowed us to explore our experiences as women of colour in higher education institutions and we were able to understand our realities in relation to our overlapping identities collaborating within a virtual space consistent with Johnson (2023) and Anandarajan, (2010).

Building community support networks and safe spaces is essential for overcoming challenges and fostering success. Of great importance within these communities is psychological safety, which is crucial for effective teamwork, especially for women of colour, as it allows us to be ourselves without fear of judgement. Furthermore, vulnerability is essential for personal and professional growth, as it enables individuals to accept feedback and learn from experiences. Humility and resilience are key personal attributes that contribute to individual and team success. This resilience enables us to overcome challenges in our pursuit of success. While Kim & O'Brien, (2018) shared that women of colour demonstrate higher levels of resilience, De Welde, (2017); Mkhize, 2024; and Whitaker and Denise, (2018) found that this was not the case in teaching contexts. This study however, revealed that despite the challenges encountered we remain resilient and continue to push and redefine boundaries in managing work and life responsibilities.

Within the context of Johnson's (2023) Intersectionality Theory we also recognized that even where there is a strong collective of women there remains a deficit of purposeful support to help mentor and guide early to mid-career academics. Mentorship (Mysirlaki & Paraskeva, 2012) plays a crucial role in the success of women of colour in academia, providing guidance, support, and opportunities for growth. The experience thus far, and expectation going forward is that mentorship will be an essential part of the team's engagement. Furthermore, diversity in mentorship offerings is important to address the needs of women of colour in academia. Hill and Bartol (2016) and Larson and DeChurch (2020) shared that mentor-mentee relationships between persons in different parts of the world through virtual activities can have a positive impact on leadership skills. We have also found this to be true for teaching and research. Mentorship is an excellent tool to break down barriers. Absence of formal mentorship programmes contributes to the mentorship gap for women of colour, and from experiences shared in this study, informal mentorship arrangements are insufficient to address systemic inequalities. The importance of breaking down barriers to collaboration and communication in fostering a supportive academic environment cannot be over emphasized. The study, therefore, revealed the need for institutionally driven mentorship support for faculty during their early to mid-career period. Overall, the study highlights the significance of mentorship, collaboration, effective communication, and addressing challenges faced by women of colour in academic research.

IMPLICATIONS

Women of colour in academia face unique challenges in navigating multiple roles as professionals, mothers, caregivers and wives. To counter these challenges, we need to ensure work-life balance as it is crucial for personal well-being and professional productivity. Researchers working in teams can function as accountability partners helping each other to strategically manage their time to meet the demands of life in academic and personal spaces. Another important consideration is that collaboration and networking are critical for research productivity, especially in overcoming language barriers and accessing diverse expertise. Finally, institutional support and funding are necessary for promoting research excellence and career advancement for women of colour in academia.

Professional development is an avenue through which women can support each other. As part of a research group, continuous improvement can be gained through documentation, sharing, and learning from colleagues' experiences. This process of documenting and sharing in team spaces can encourage collective improvement in teaching effectiveness. Additionally, in relation to teaching, women can strive to demonstrate cultural competence by adapting teaching approaches to accommodate diverse student populations and addressing biases and microaggressions. Furthermore, women can explore and implement innovative teaching methods and approaches to ensure students are engaging effectively. Additionally, virtual peer learning and observation are strategies that can be engaged. Through the virtual observation of colleagues' teaching methods and the sharing of experiences, teams and in particular, women of colour, can foster a culture of continuous learning and improvement among faculty members.

Women of colour face systemic barriers in career advancement due to racism and microaggression. And colonial legacies contribute to economic status biases in leadership opportunities. Proper networking and trust can open doors to leadership roles. When engaged, succession planning and skill sharing are essential elements for fostering leadership development. As women of colour in academia strive to develop professionally, advocacy and support is needed from peers as well as from supervisors. When faculty are empowered through mentorship and training, a culture of collaboration and advancement develops. Finally, institutional support and proactive measures such as succession planning can help to reduce or eliminate bias and provide diversity in leadership. Thus, advocacy and empowerment are critical to supporting women of colour in leadership. Effective leadership development programmes and opportunities for women of colour are essential for addressing the underrepresentation of diverse leaders in academia.

As the team continues this journey, there is much reliance on maximizing output and opportunities for personal and professional growth through shared experiences. Commitment to being accountability partners for each member and identifying other women of colour who we can mentor, and support signals the way forward for Femme Fusion to serve as a catalyst for change in and among women of colour in academia.

REFERENCES

Aelterman, A., Engels, N., Van Petegem, K., & Verhaeghe, J. P. (2007). The well-being of teachers in Flanders: The importance of a supportive school culture. *Educational Studies*, 33(3), 285–297. DOI: 10.1080/03055690701423085

Aiston, S. J., & Jung, J. (2015). Women academics and research productivity: An international comparison. *Gender and Education*, 27(3), 205–220. DOI: 10.1080/09540253.2015.1024617

Alotaibi, F. T. (2020). Saudi women and leadership: Empowering women as leaders in higher education institutions. *Open J Leadersh*, 9(3), 156–177. DOI: 10.4236/ojl.2020.93010

Altebarmakian, M., & Alterman, R. (2019). Cohesion in online environments. *International Journal of Computer-Supported Collaborative Learning*, 14(4), 443–465. DOI: 10.1007/s11412-019-09309-y

Anandarajan, M. (2010). (Ed.). *E-Research collaboration: Theory, techniques and challenges* (1. Aufl.). Springer-Verlag. https://doi.org/DOI: 10.1007/978-3-642-12257-6

Burkinshaw, P., & White, K. (2017). Fixing the women or fixing universities: Women in HE leadership. *Administrative Sciences*, 7(3), 30. DOI: 10.3390/admsci7030030

Caplar, N., Tacchella, S., & Birrer, S. (2017). Quantitative Evaluation of Gender Bias in Astronomical Publications from Citation Counts. *Nature Astronomy*, 1(6), 1–5. DOI: 10.1038/s41550-017-0141

Chance, N. L. (2022). Resilient leadership: A phenomenological exploration into how Black women in higher education leadership navigate cultural adversity. *Journal of Humanistic Psychology*, 62(1), 44–78. DOI: 10.1177/00221678211003000

Collins's Black Feminist Thought. (2015). Patricia Hill Collins's *Black Feminist Thought: Knowledge, Consciousness and the Politics of Empowerment*. Ethnic and Racial Studies, 38(13), 2314–2314. https://doi.org/. DOI: 10.1080/01419870.2015.1058515

Creswell, J. W., & Guetterman, T. C. (2019). *Educational research: Planning, conducting, and evaluating quantitative and qualitative research*. Pearson.

Davis, D. R., & Maldonado, C. (2015). Shattering the glass ceiling: The leadership development of African American women in higher education. *Advancing Women in Leadership Journal*, 35, 48–64. DOI: 10.21423/awlj-v35.a125

Davis, S. M., & Afifi, T. D. (2019). The Strong Black Woman Collective Theory: Determining the prosocial functions of strength regulation in groups of black women friends†. *Journal of Communication*, 69(1), 1–25. DOI: 10.1093/joc/jqy065

Dean, D. R., Bracken, S. J., Allen, J. K., & Van Ummersen, C. (2023). *Women in Academic Leadership*. Routledge., DOI: 10.4324/9781003448785

Dinh, J. V., & Salas, E. (2017). Factors that influence teamwork. *The Wiley Blackwell handbook of the psychology of team working and collaborative processes*, 13-41. https://doi.org/DOI: 10.1002/9781118909997.ch2

Dion, M. L., Sumner, J. L., & Mitchell, S. M. (2018). Gendered Citation Patterns across Political Science and Social Science Methodology fields. *Political Analysis*, 26(3), 312–327. DOI: 10.1017/pan.2018.12

Dusdal, J., & Powell, J. J. (2021). Benefits, motivations, and challenges of international collaborative research: A sociology of science case study. *Science & Public Policy*, 48(2), 235–245. DOI: 10.1093/scipol/scab010

Ford, H. L., Brick, C., Azmitia, M., Blaufuss, K., & Dekens, P. (2019). Women from Some Under-represented Minorities Are Given Too Few Talks at World's Largest Earth-Science Conference. *Nature*, 576(7785), 32–35. DOI: 10.1038/d41586-019-03688-w PMID: 31797914

Forsyth, D. R. (2014). *Group dynamics*. Wadsworth Cengage Learning.

Fox, C. W., & Paine, C. E. T. (2019). Gender differences in peer review outcomes and manuscript impact at six journals of ecology and evolution. *Ecology and Evolution*, 9(6), 3599–3619. DOI: 10.1002/ece3.4993 PMID: 30962913

Fox Tree, J. E., & Vaid, J. (2022). Why so few, still? Challenges to attracting, advancing, and keeping women faculty of color in academia. *Frontiers in Sociology*, 6, 792198. DOI: 10.3389/fsoc.2021.792198 PMID: 35118155

Gause, S. A. (2021). White privilege, Black resilience: Women of color leading the academy. *Leadership*, 17(1), 74–80. DOI: 10.1177/1742715020977370

George, T. P., DeCristofaro, C., & Rosser-Majors, M. (2020). Virtual Collaboration in Academia. *Creative Nursing*, 26(3), 205–209. DOI: 10.1891/CRNR-D-19-00023 PMID: 32883822

Gidis, Y., & Kiral, B. (2023). The mediating role of teamwork in the correlation between administrative support and school belonging. *Educational Policy Analysis and Strategic Research*, 18(3), 465–482. DOI: 10.29329/epasr.2023.600.22

Gilson, L. L., Maynard, M. T., Jones Young, N. C., Vartiainen, M., & Hakonen, M. (2015). Virtual teams research: 10 years, 10 themes, and 10 opportunities. *Journal of Management*, 41(5), 1313–1337. DOI: 10.1177/0149206314559946

Greimel, N. S., Kanbach, D. K., & Chelaru, M. (2023). Virtual teams and transformational leadership: An integrative literature review and avenues for further research. *Journal of Innovation & Knowledge*, 8(2), 100351. DOI: 10.1016/j.jik.2023.100351

Greska, L., McCormick, D., & Cascino, J. (2023). Women in academia: Why and where does the pipeline leak, and how can we fix it? *Parity*, 40, 102–109. DOI: 10.38105/spr.xmvdiojee1

Hajibabaei, A., Schiffauerova, A., & Ebadi, A. (2023). Women and key positions in scientific collaboration networks: Analyzing central scientists' profiles in the artificial intelligence ecosystem through a gender lens. *Scientometrics*, 128(2), 1219–1240. DOI: 10.1007/s11192-022-04601-5

Haynes, C., Joseph, N. M., Patton, L. D., Stewart, S., & Allen, E. L. (2020). Toward an understanding of intersectionality methodology: A 30-year literature synthesis of black women's experiences in higher education. *Review of Educational Research*, 90(6), 751–787. DOI: 10.3102/0034654320946822

Hill, N. S., & Bartol, K. M. (2016). Empowering leadership and effective collaboration in geographically dispersed teams. *Personnel Psychology*, 69(1), 159–198. DOI: 10.1111/peps.12108

Howard, B., Ilyashenko, N., & Jacobs, L. (2023). Cross-cultural collaboration through virtual learning in higher education. *Perspectives in Education*, 41(1), 74–87. DOI: 10.38140/pie.v41i1.6319

Jimenez, A., Boehe, D. M., Taras, V., & Caprar, D. V. (2017). Working across boundaries: Current and future perspectives on global virtual teams. *Journal of International Management*, 23(4), 341–349. DOI: 10.1016/j.intman.2017.05.001

Johari, A. B., Wahat, N., & Zaremohzzabieh, Z. (2021). Innovative work behavior among teachers in Malaysia: The effects of teamwork, principal support and humor. *Asian Journal of University Education*, 17(2), 72–84. DOI: 10.24191/ajue.v17i2.13387

Johnson, L. (2023). Black women and theoretical frameworks. *The Scholarship Without Borders Journal*, 1(2). Advance online publication. DOI: 10.57229/2834-2267.1018

Johnston, E., Burleigh, C., & Wilson, A. (2020). Interdisciplinary collaborative research for professional academic development in higher education. *Higher Learning Research Communications*, 10(1), 62–77. DOI: 10.18870/hlrc.v10i1.1175

Kıral, E., & Durdu, İ. (2021). The relationship between tendency to gossip and organizational commitment. *International Online Journal of Education & Teaching*, 8(3), 1833–1856.

Kumi-Yeboah, A., Yuan, G., & Dogbey, J. (2017). Online collaborative learning activities: The perceptions of culturally diverse graduate students. *Online Learning : the Official Journal of the Online Learning Consortium*, 21(4), 5–28. DOI: 10.24059/olj.v21i4.1277

Larson, L., & DeChurch, L. A. (2020). Leading teams in the digital age: Four perspectives on technology and what they mean for leading teams. *The Leadership Quarterly*, 31(1), 101377. DOI: 10.1016/j.leaqua.2019.101377 PMID: 32863679

Lin, P. S., & Kennette, L. N. (2022). Creating an inclusive community for BIPOC faculty: Women of colour in academia. *SN Social Sciences*, 2(11), 246. DOI: 10.1007/s43545-022-00555-w PMID: 36339527

Madsen, S. R. (2012). Women and leadership in higher education: Learning and advancement in leadership programs. *Advances in Developing Human Resources*, 14(1), 3–10. DOI: 10.1177/1523422311429668

Madsen, S. R., & Longman, K. A. (2020). Women's leadership in higher education: Status, barriers, and motivators. *Journal of Higher Education Management*, 35(1), 13–24.

Maheshwari, G., & Nayak, R. (2022). Women leadership in Vietnamese higher education institutions: An exploratory study on barriers and enablers for career enhancement. *Educational Management Administration & Leadership*, 50(5), 758–775. DOI: 10.1177/1741143220945700

Marbley, A. F., Wong, A., Santos-Hatchett, S. L., Pratt, C., & Jaddo, L. (2011). Women faculty of colour: Voices, gender, and the expression of our multiple identities within academia. *Advancing Women in Leadership*, 31(1), 166–174.

Mattessich, P. W., & Johnson, K. M. (2018). *Collaboration: What makes it work* (3rd ed.). Fieldstone Alliance.

McLoughlin, C., Patel, K. D., O'Callaghan, T., & Reeves, S. (2018). The use of virtual communities of practice to improve interprofessional collaboration and education: Findings from an integrated review. *Journal of Interprofessional Care*, 32(2), 136–142. DOI: 10.1080/13561820.2017.1377692 PMID: 29161155

Misra, J., Smith-Doerr, L., Dasgupta, N., Weaver, G., & Normanly, J. (2017). Collaboration and gender equity among academic scientists. *Social Sciences (Basel, Switzerland)*, 6(1), 1–22. DOI: 10.3390/socsci6010025

Mkhize, Z. V. (2024). Teaching while black: Black women millennials' experiences of teaching in South African universities. *Journal of Women and Gender in Higher Education*, 1-18. https://doi.org/DOI: 10.1080/26379112.2023.2286990

Morrison-Smith, S., & Ruiz, J. (2020). Challenges and barriers in virtual teams: A literature review. *SN Applied Sciences*, 2(6), 1–33. DOI: 10.1007/s42452-020-2801-5

Morton, B. C., & Gil, E. (2019). Not a solo ride: Co-constructed peer mentoring for early-career educational leadership faculty. *International Journal of Mentoring and Coaching in Education*, 8(4), 361–377. DOI: 10.1108/IJMCE-02-2019-0026

Olaisen, J., & Revang, O. (2017). Working smarter and greener: Collaborative knowledge sharing in virtual global project teams. *International Journal of Information Management*, 37(1), 1441–1448. DOI: 10.1016/j.ijinfomgt.2016.10.002

Pardee, J. W., Fothergill, A., Weber, L., & Peek, L. (2017). The collective method: Collaborative social science research and scholarly accountability. *Qualitative Research*, 18(6), 671–688. DOI: 10.1177/1468794117743461

Pearson, M. L., Albon, S. P., & Hubball, H. (2015). Case study methodology: Flexibility, rigour, and ethical considerations for the scholarship of teaching and learning. *The Canadian Journal for the Scholarship of Teaching and Learning*, 6(3), 12. DOI: 10.5206/cjsotl-rcacea.2015.3.12

Richter, N. F., Martin, J., Hansen, S. V., Taras, V., & Alon, I. (2021). Motivational configurations of cultural intelligence, social integration, and performance in global virtual teams. *Journal of Business Research*, 129, 351–367. DOI: 10.1016/j.jbusres.2021.03.012

Runyan, A. S. (2018). What is intersectionality and why it is important. *American Association of University Professors*, 104(6), 10–14.

Sax, L. J., Hagedorn, L. S., Arredondo, M., & Dicrisi, F. A.III. (2002). Faculty research productivity: Exploring the role of gender and family-related factors. *Research in Higher Education*, 43(4), 423–446. DOI: 10.1023/A:1015575616285

Smooth, W. G. (2016). Intersectionality and women's advancement in the discipline and across the academy. *Politics, Groups & Identities*, 4(3), 513–528. Advance online publication. DOI: 10.1080/21565503.2016.1170706

Somech, A. (2005). Teachers' personal and team empowerment and their relations to organizational outcomes: Contradictory or compatible constructs? *Educational Administration Quarterly*, 41(2), 237–266. DOI: 10.1177/0013161X04269592

West, J. D., Jacquet, J., King, M. M., Correll, S. J., & Bergstrom, C. T. (2013). The Role of Gender in Scholarly Authorship. *PLoS One*, 8(7), e66212. DOI: 10.1371/journal.pone.0066212 PMID: 23894278

Whitaker, M., & Denise, E. J. (Eds.). (2018). *Counternarratives from women of colour academics: Bravery, vulnerability, and resistance*. Routledge. DOI: 10.4324/9780429465505

Yousaf, R., & Schmiede, R. (2017). Barriers to women's representation in academic excellence and positions of power. *Asian Journal of German and European Studies*, 2(1), 1–13. DOI: 10.1186/s40856-017-0013-6

Zakaria, N. (2017). Emergent patterns of switching behaviors and intercultural communication styles of global virtual teams during distributed decision making. *Journal of International Management*, 23(4), 350–366. DOI: 10.1016/j.intman.2016.09.002

Chapter 14
Interrogating the Third Space in Collaborative Research:
A Critical Narrative Discourse

Hope Mayne
University of Technology, Jamaica

Shermaine Barrett
https://orcid.org/0000-0001-5957-0487
University of Technology, Jamaica

Dwaine Hibbert
University of Technology, Jamaica

ABSTRACT

In this research project, three researchers from three different research backgrounds and academic disciplines drew on Bhabha's third space theory to reflect on their experience conducting collaborative research. The collaborative research process created a third space where the researchers were able to share their perspectives and challenge ideas to achieve consensus. Utilising a critical narrative inquiry approach, the researchers shared their experiences of working with each other in a collaborative research project. They sought to explore: 1) How do three different perspectives of research contribute to the research process? 2) What does the collaborative research practice look like? 3) How can this process contribute to new positions in qualitative research? Narratives were analysed using a cross-case thematic analysis. The findings revealed that the research process was not linear and prescriptive but more so a descriptive process, which created a space for new understandings about collaborative research to emerge.

DOI: 10.4018/979-8-3693-3852-0.ch014

INTRODUCTION

This chapter focuses on an interdisciplinary qualitative research collaboration. It highlights the emergence of a "third space (Bhabha, 1994) arising within the process of a research collaboration. Through a narrative inquiry approach, the researchers went beyond the boundaries of the original research to reflect on their experiences working together as researchers. They engaged in a contest and interrogation of their epistemological and ontological understandings of research. This results in the emergence of a "third space," creating new opportunities and a negotiated space that stimulates innovative thinking and serves as a lens for reaching a final consensus. The chapter highlights some lessons learned about collaborative teams and how it opens new understandings of self and the collaborative space.

The collaborative space reflects shared experiences and engagement in the collaborative research process. Against this background, we questioned: 1) How do three different perspectives of research contribute to the research process? (2) What does the collaborative research practice look like? 3) How can this process contribute to new positions in qualitative research?

BACKGROUND

Our critical collaborative research dialogue focused on what we observed about ourselves while conducting research on promoting Science, Technology, Engineering and Mathematics (STEM) education through the implementation of Computer Numerical Machine (CNC) technology in secondary high schools.

This was not the initial intention, but as the research process unfolded, we recognized that the differences and similarities in our thought processes and ontological and epistemological understandings informed the lens through which we interpreted the data and our experience in the field. Our journey began when a colleague from the Faculty of Engineering and Computing, who is an engineer with research interests in industrial automation, robotics, and STEM education reached out to two colleagues from the Faculty of Education and Liberal Studies (FELS) to collaborate on a research project. He was working on building a CNC machine for some time with the intention of giving it to schools as a way to promote STEM education, and increase interest. He approached his head of department and other stakeholders with the idea. One stakeholder recommended that rather than simply donating the CNC machine to schools, he should see it as a research project to promote STEM. He was then encouraged to work with two colleagues in education who had expertise in conducting research in STEM. He was already familiar with one of the two colleagues through a student-teacher relationship and had much respect for her. The two colleagues from FELS operated within the qualitative research genre and had previously collaborated on a number of other scholarly works. Due to the nature of the phenomenon that was being explored, that is to study the factors that foster or inhibit the successful integration of the CNC technology in the grades 7 – 9 STEM classroom, the qualitative research genre was selected as the design. Although the Engineer did not know much about qualitative research, he was willing to learn for the sake of the study.

As the research lead, the Engineer brought his expertise in the CNC machine application, while the two collaborating researchers focused on the methodology. This collaboration began the journey towards an interdisciplinary approach to collaboration. Little did we know that this interdisciplinary collaboration would create an intersection of three minds that would view data collection and analysis through different lenses. This established interdisciplinary collaboration provided insights into how a collaborative research process contributes to new positions and understandings in research. Through the journey of intellectual exchange, what has been called a "third space" emerged (Bhabha, 1994). In this space, the researchers were awakened to the consciousness of self, that is how our lens have been shaped by our individual disciplines and experiences which in turn shaped and reshaped our positionality in the research process. This chapter represents the researchers' reflection on their experiences as collaborating researchers and seeks to shed light on some of the challenges and possibilities of interdisciplinary collaborative research arising from this third space experience.

LITERATURE REVIEW

Collaboration

Keyton (2017, 165) describes collaboration as "a type interaction in which individuals, or team or organizational members, work together to reach a common shared goal, activity, or production". Collaborations are usually seen as temporary negotiated sites of interactions in which there are at least two parties that interact, shared goals or activities, some degree of interdependence among the parties, and interaction over some time interval (Keyton, 2017). Lewis (2006) identified what is described as the emergent, informal, and volitional nature of collaborations. From this perspective, collaborations are not forced; rather, they are arrangements into which people enter freely and without coercion.

Keyton, et.al (2008, 2012) highlight the fact that despite the perceived benefits of collaborations, the relationship does pose some challenges, which resonate with the collaboration being shared in this chapter. A key challenge identified by Keyton et al. (2012) is that of identity. This speaks to the question of who belongs. Collaborating members bring an identity that is personal and creates the lens through which members communicate during the collaboration. Another challenge identified in the literature (Source) is "equality versus power." In collaborations, power acknowledges that there is seldom neutrality in power relations between members. Power in collaboration may emerge from who initiates the collaboration, from the roles assigned to individuals, or from how members communicate with each other and what they say. Collaboration can take place between experts within a particular discipline or among disciplines, the latter giving rise to what is termed interdisciplinary collaboration.

Interdisciplinary Collaboration

According to Anderson (2023) interdisciplinary collaboration is a process of bringing researchers from different disciplines together to implement projects outside of their academic space. It enables the development of a research framework that moves beyond the boundaries of individual disciplines. It moves people away from working in isolation towards a collaborative process from inception to completion. Each team member brings their own unique, epistemological perspectives, methods, and ideas to the project.

This type of collaboration is being valued more and more as academics seek to address complex problems, which often requires interdisciplinary collaborations between experts from distinct disciplines (Baalen & Boon, 2024). Effective collaboration in interdisciplinary research is influenced by several factors. According to Klein (2008), clear communication, mutual respect, and shared goals are essential for fostering successful interdisciplinary teams. Additionally, the literature outlines some best practices in relation to collaborative research (Bammer, 2008; Stokols et al., 2008; Wuchty et al., 2007). Among these are:

- **Establishing Clear Goals and Roles**: Clearly defining research goals, roles, and responsibilities helps maintain focus and accountability within the team
  Building Trust and Communication: Fostering trust and open communication among collaborators promotes collaboration and reduces conflicts
- **Developing Collaborative Skills**: Training and support for researchers in collaborative skills, such as negotiation and teamwork, enhance the effectiveness of collaborative efforts
- **Leveraging Technology**: Utilizing collaborative tools and technologies facilitates communication, data sharing, and project management across distributed teams

Collaborative interdisciplinary research is the integration of insights, methods, and theories from different disciplines to alleviate multifaceted problems. According to a meta-analysis by Hall et al. (2018), the benefits of collaborative research are many and include enhanced creativity, increased citation impact, and the ability to address complex problems more comprehensively than single-discipline approaches.

However, it has its challenges, Roy et al. (2013) and Yegros-Yegros et al. (2015) make the point that getting disciplines to work together substantively on problems has proven difficult. These difficulties may be institutional or administrative or barriers at the individual level arising from cognitive difficulties that pervade, constrain and even block collaborative interdisciplinary work (MacLeod, 2016). which include difficulties in communication and language barriers between disciplines (Hadorn et al., 2010).

Turner et al (2015) refer to these challenges as essential tensions that have the potential to inform the groups direction and fate based on the choices they make to address the tensions. This arises from the fact that the way experts use and produce knowledge is largely guided by their disciplinary lenses. Consequently, each researcher is guided by his/her own disciplinary perspectives thereby posing challenges for individual and collective sense making among the researchers (Baalen & Boon, 2024). he tensions also include issues related to power dynamics and leadership in collaborative teams (Wagner et al., 2011), and the potential for conflicts arising from differing epistemological and methodological approaches (Jantsch, 1970). Here is where Bhabha third space served as a critical theoretical framework to reflect on our interactions as a research team and to address the tensions to enable the collective sense making.

Theoretical Framework

Bhabha's (1994) notion of the third space formed the theoretical framework which provided the lens through which the interdisciplinary collaboration discussed in this chapter was interrogated. This framework helped the collaborating researchers to unpack our experience within the collaboration and to arrive at new understandings of ourselves in the collaboration and to better understand the collaborative experience itself.

According to Bhabha (1994) the "third space" provides an effective framework for examining collaborative environments. According to this theoretical framework, an entirely new hybrid space that is a unique synthesis of the distinct cultures or identities that interact arises. Its capacity to undermine binary oppositions, subvert prevailing narratives, and generate novel forms of creativity and knowledge are what define this Third Space. When it comes to collaborative spaces, the Third Space can be thought of as a vibrant area where people from different backgrounds congregate to work on common projects. This space, where many viewpoints, values, and experiences converge, is both a real and conceptual place.

Bhabha's concept of the "Third Space" suggests that when two distinct cultures or identities interact, a unique synthesis emerges. This concept is particularly relevant in collaborative spaces, where researchers from diverse backgrounds, values, and experiences come together to construct knowledge. The third space is characterized by its ability to destabilize binary oppositions, challenge dominant narratives, and produce innovative knowledge and creativity.

Key characteristics of the third space include hybridity (separate positionalities and perspectives combine to form new understandings), negotiation, creativity, and power dynamics. To foster a productive Third Space, it is essential to create a safe, inclusive environment, encourage dialogue, challenge dominant narratives, and recognize and address power imbalances. By understanding and embracing the Third Space, collaborative spaces can become catalysts for innovation, creativity, and transformation (Bhabha, 1994).

Bhabha contends that a third space is an ambivalent space where cultural meaning and representation have no "unity or fixity." It is an "interruptive, interrogative, and enunciative" (Bhabha, 1994, p. 117) space for new forms of meaning and identity, articulating a productive and reflective space that opens up new possibilities. In this third space subject-positions and hegemonic constructions are denounced. The third space is also an intervening and hybrid space. In this space, cultures, identities, and ideas intersect and interact, which frames new understandings. In applying Bhabha's third space to interdisciplinary collaborative research, there can be several implications, such as the negotiation of identities and power dynamics, critical reflexivity, and conflicts arising from epistemological and ontological perspectives.

The seminal work of Vygotsky (1962) provides some help in conceptualizing how Bhabba's third space is useful for learning within an interdisciplinary collaborative space. He states that we learn through our interactions with each other, and our social environment influences the learning process. His work underscores the belief that learning and cognitive development are socially mediated processes deeply embedded in cultural contexts. Consequently, the interaction in the third space leads to new discoveries about oneself and others, as well as the subject matter being interrogated.

METHODOLOGY

Connelly and Clandinin (1990) have made significant contributions to the field of narrative inquiry. In their recent work Connelly and Clandinin (2013) provided a theoretical framework and practical guidance for the use of narrative inquiry. There work underscores the importance of understanding narrative as a way of knowing and sense making of the world. The role of the researcher is to shape the narrative inquiry process through reflexivity.

A narrative inquiry approach was used to capture the experiences of the three researchers in an interdisciplinary collaborative research space. Narrative Inquiry is conceptualized by Connelly and Clandinin (1990). They posit that Narrative Inquiry interprets experiences through stories of practice. They categorize narrative inquiry through three dimensions, spatiality, temporality, and sociality. Spatiality explores physical and psychological spaces, temporality explores how individuals experience sequence and time of events, while sociality examines relationships, cultural context and agency.

In our narrative inquiry we employed three phases that framed the narratives of the researchers' experiences. Phase one focused on reflecting on our environment (spatiality). We engaged in weekly meetings and discussions on the methodological procedures. A clear understanding of the protocol and procedures was needed to frame weekly meetings. In the first phase of our weekly meetings, we discussed the qualitative methodology to be used in the research, divided the tasks, designed instruments for data collection, and scheduled school visits. This was established as the platform phase. In the platform phase, it was the beginning of a friendship rather than just collaborating in the academic space. We communicated outside of group meetings through *WhatsApp* and *phone calls*. We checked in with each other to see if we had arrived at the data collection site and shared humor about the experiences we had during data collection. This was the beginning of establishing a *nesting (comfort)* space while working with each other.

Second, a reflection on the collaborative research process frames phase two. In this phase, researchers engaged in critical dialogue on critical moments, contributing to the temporality and sociality dimensions of our inquiry. We reflected on what stood out in the collaborative research dialogue. Critical moments included how we interacted with each other, what we learned about the research process, how we situated our experience in relation to the research practice and how the collaborative research process empowered us. Essentially, Phase two focused on validating the researchers' shared experiences and interpretations.

Third phase, emanated from the reflection and the discussion in the first two phases, three themes emerged from our narratives. These included: 1) ontological and epistemological contestations; 2) divesting personal positions for the interest of the research project; and 3) personal discomfort. These themes in our narratives provided answers to the questions: 1) What does a collaborative research practice look like? 2) How do three different perspectives on research contribute to the research process? 3) How does the collaborative research process contribute to new positions in qualitative research?

RESULTS

Research Question 1: What Does the Collaborative Research Space Look Like?

Ontological and Epistemological Contesting

Our stories revealed our ontological and epistemological contestations in the group. The engineer, referred to as "Positivist," shared concerns about the qualitative research protocol and questioned the need for a reflection to be carried out while conducting the research. Since he did not have a background in qualitative research, he wanted to contest his understanding of research within the group. He noted:

I have come to appreciate why every interaction with the research participants can be an opportunity to collect critical data. On one such occasion, I remember when we went to speak with a group of participants regarding delays in their submission of a set of data. It was through casual dialogue with the group that it was discovered that critical information about an aspect of the study needed to be collected. One of my research colleagues, in particular, would regularly emphasise the need for reflections to be written after all our field visits. The significance of the reflections I do recognise as important, but I experienced an unintentional reluctance to complete them. I believe that, to a great extent, this was due to the fact that the writing of reflections was not a practice for me as a quantitative researcher.

Reflecting and deliberating about the process, the Case Study Researcher shared her dilemma:

I was particularly struck by how differently my colleague and I, both qualitative researchers, approached both the collection of data through observation and interviews and the analysis of data. I struggled with thoughts about how two people can work from within the qualitative paradigm and be so different in their approach. Epistemologically, we shared similar views about ways of knowing (the voice of the participant is important), but it was evident that there were differences in our understanding about how much data, for example, was necessary for effective analysis to take place and to remain true to the voice of the respondent being heard. "One of us must be doing things wrong," I thought. I struggled as I tried to find harmony between our ways of doing things and ease my discomfort. But the more we deliberated and discussed various points of disagreement and just clarified points, it became so clear to me that the differences between us rested in the protocol of the different genres that we represented.

Research Question 2: How Do Three Different Perspectives on Research Contribute to the Collaborative Research Process?

Divesting Personal Positions for the Interest of the Research Project

The Qualitative Researcher referred to as "Miss Phenomenologist" stated:

I recognise that within my subconscious state of mind, I came to the research platform as a knower (dominant and powerful) and unintentionally exercised that position or disposition throughout the collaborative research process. I recognise that because of my qualitative research background, I had limited patience when communicating with Mr. Positivist, whom I viewed as the "Other" or "Outsider". I thought of him in that way because he was outside of the realm of the qualitative paradigm and more of the crunching numbers guru (quantitative expert). Thus, I felt power from an epistemological and feminist stance, given my co-researcher, who was female and also an avid qualitative researcher.

Research Question 3: How Does the Collaborative Research Process Contribute to New Positions in the Collaborative Research?

Tackling Personal Discomfort

Miss Phenomenologist noted that at times when her co-researcher (numbers guru) questioned her data reporting, she felt that this was just not necessary. Often times, saying *'OMG' Do I have to go through this? Is it that he does not understand me? Is he questioning my methodology? Why is he looking at me with a microscopic lens?*

The outsider (numbers guru), Miss Phenomenologist, feels comfortable yet uncomfortable. The other/outsider became the microscope and offered a level of scrutiny. His questions were relevant and pushed her to reflect on the data again.

Miss Phenomenologist reflected on an instance when they were preparing to report the findings of the research at the University's Research Day. "The team decided on the themes, and the decision was made to just present those themes. I deviated from the task and went ahead and presented on themes that should not be included. The 'numbers guru' was quick to interrogate me, but I was adamant that what I did was correct. In the end, it turned out the numbers guru got it right." In a three-person collaborative dialogue, Miss Phenomenologist realized the importance of creating a space for listening. She questioned the notion of trust in the research process.

Mr. Positivist reflected and shared his initial vision for the collaboration research process. This vision was shared and agreed upon by all of us:

In this research, all three researchers would actively participate in all aspects of the research process, from the development of the proposal through the compilation of a journal paper….report. I believe this demanded a higher-than-normal level of collaborative effort than would have been required if the researchers were to give attention to the areas that pertained to their expertise. In all my past collaborative work, I have focused only on the areas of my expertise. *Therefore, while working on qualitative data collection and analysis, an area new to me, I experienced much discomfort as I felt that I needed to make a greater contribution.*

DISCUSSION

As noted earlier in the chapter Bhabha's (1994) third space provides a framework for understanding collaborative research. It is an intermediary space where different ideological positions intersect and create new understandings about the phenomenon being explored. It fosters critical reflexivity, which allows the researcher to examine how their own understandings can contribute to new knowledge. In the third space, there is also interconnectedness in the collaborative space, which strengthens the collaboration.

We contend that the evolution of the third space in collaborative practice engenders a process of reflection, the challenging of ideas, contesting ontological and epistemological perspectives, and negotiations. This is because often collaborations represent the coming together of individuals with conflicting epistemic values, and sometimes large conceptual and methodological divides (Macleod, 2016).

In our collaboration, the experience within the space brought personal discomfort, demanded the divesting of personal positions, a willingness to be challenged and have one's ideas contested, and the need for trust among collaborating members and honoring each other. This experience harks back to what Turner et al, (2015) describes as the "pull between individual intellectual independence and the epistemic dependence of the group as well as between organized skepticism that ensures academic rigor and the need for intellectual trust among group members with differing expertise (p 6).

The three different minds in our collaboration required the convergence of ideas, perspectives, and ways of thinking. We found that the convergence of ideas created tensions arising from the differences and similarities of thought among the members (Turner et.al, 2015). In this collaborative space, we managed the convergence of mindsets by being respectful to each other. Although there were times when there was an outburst of the inner tensions, there was a level of control because of respect in the academic space.

The literature speaks about the need for a structured environment with clear roles (Bammer, 2008; MacLeod, 2016). In our experience the leader of the group was established based on the fact that he was the initiator of the research project. The collaborators who were well-established qualitative researchers - phenomenologists and case study researcher - were respected because of their understanding of the research genre. Essentially, the collaboration worked because of the respect for positions.

Critical to this interdisciplinary process was the emergence of self-identity. Self-identity brought us to consciousness in the 'third space'. We knew who we were as researchers through each other. Working on research alone does not give you the opportunity to see yourself. In a group, it opens you up to much criticism of self.

According to Bhabha (1994), a third space is a negotiated space that provokes new thinking and engenders new possibilities. It was within that space that our perspectives were contested and interrogated. Critical to what was learned from this third space is transformational practice. Within the collaborative space, we observed how we transformed in our relationship with each other and also in our thought process about research. We also understood what it meant to triangulate data through three researcher's lenses. This provided much credibility to our narratives which accords with Lincoln and Guba (1985), idea that triangulation is used as a method for corroborating findings and as a test for validity.

We contend that the evolution of the third space in collaborative practice engenders a process of reflection, the challenging of ideas, contesting ontological and epistemological perspectives, and negotiations. This is because often collaborations represent the coming together of individuals with conflicting epistemic values, and sometimes large conceptual and methodological divides (Macleod, 2016).

In our collaboration, the experience within the space brought personal discomfort, demanded the divesting of personal positions, a willingness to be challenged and have one's ideas contested, and the need for trust among collaborating members and honoring each other. This experience harks back to what Turner et al, (2015) describes as the "pull between individual intellectual independence and the epistemic dependence of the group as well as between organized skepticism that ensures academic rigor and the need for intellectual trust among group members with differing expertise (p 6).

We also acknowledge that it is difficult to know how a collaborative research project will develop because a collaboration brings together individuals with different backgrounds, experiences, and viewpoints. While this diversity can lead to innovative solutions, it also increases the likelihood of disagreements. In collaborative contexts, social-emotional interactions can affect the researchers' cognitive processes, collaboration satisfaction, and learning outcomes (Haung & Lajoie, 2023). Collaborative processes involve complex interactions among team members. Differing roles, goals, and communication styles can lead to misunderstandings and tensions as was the case between Mr. Positivist and Miss Phenomenologist in the current collaboration.

Differences in professional training and work demands can create collaborative tensions (Drotar, 1993, 1995). Acknowledging positionality, ontological, and epistemological perspectives, however, frames a successful collaboration. We therefore argue that there is a need to anticipate and manage disagreements and tensions in the collaborative process. (Armstrong, 2009; Bennett & Gadlin, 2012; Gray, 2008).

Communication, interest in learning from collaborators, and the willingness to be challenged and contested are important skills and attitudes in the collaborative space. Our research collaboration triangulates findings and strengthens the credibility of the findings. The collaboration encourages deeper, more critical thinking among the team members. Working together exposes the team to a variety of perspectives, promoting analytical thinking and problem-solving abilities. Through discussion and debate, the researchers were able to evaluate different viewpoints, develop reasoned arguments, and arrive at well-thought-out conclusions.

CONCLUSION

What dominated the collaborative research process was our compromise and how we negotiated and contested to arrive at a "third space." This third space has shaped and reshaped us as researchers. Bhabha (1994) contends that there is an intermediate space in between subject positions that displaces hegemonic practices. He notes that this is a "third space," which is productive, reflective, and engenders new possibilities. Critical consciousness is brought about not through an intellectual effort alone but through praxis, and the authentic union of action and reflection. Such reflective action cannot be denied to the people (Freire, 1972, p. 78).

REFERENCES

Anderson, B. (November 22, 2023). Strategies for successful interdisciplinary collaborations. *Effective Team Dynamics Initiative.*https://etd.gatech.edu/2023/11/22/strategies-for-successful-interdisciplinary-collaborations/

Armstrong, M. (2009). *Armstrong's Handbook of Human Resource Management Practice* (11th ed.). Kogan Page Limited.

Baalen, S. V., & Boon, M. (2024). Understanding disciplinary perspectives: A framework to develop skills for interdisciplinary research collaborations of medical experts and engineers. *BMC Medical Education*, 24(1), 1000. Advance online publication. DOI: 10.1186/s12909-024-05913-1 PMID: 39272191

Bammer, G. (2008). Enhancing research collaborations: Three key challenges. *Research Policy*, 37(5), 875–887. DOI: 10.1016/j.respol.2008.03.004

Bennett, L. M., & Gadlin, H. (2012). Collaboration and team science: From theory to practice. *Journal of Investigative Medicine*, 60(5), 768–775. DOI: 10.2310/JIM.0b013e318250871d PMID: 22525233

Bhabha, H. K. (1994). *The location of culture*. Routledge.

Connelly, F. M., & Clandinin, D. J. (1990). Stories of experience and narrative inquiry. *Educational Researcher*, 19(5), 2–14. DOI: 10.3102/0013189X019005002

Connelly, F. M., & Clandinin, D. J. (2013). *Narrative inquiry: Research for understanding*. Teachers College Press.

Cummings, J. N., & Kiesler, S. (2005). Collaborative research across disciplinary and organizational boundaries. *Social Studies of Science*, 35(5), 703–722. DOI: 10.1177/0306312705055535

Drotar, D. (1989). Psychological research in pediatric settings: Lessons from the field. *Journal of Pediatric Psychology*, 14(1), 63–74. DOI: 10.1093/jpepsy/14.1.63 PMID: 2656968

Drotar, D. (1993). Influences on collaborative activities among psychologists and pediatricians: Implications for practice, training, and research. *Journal of Pediatric Psychology*, 18(2), 159–172. DOI: 10.1093/jpepsy/18.2.159 PMID: 8492270

Freire, P. (1972). *Cultural action for freedom*. Penguin Books.

Gray, B. (2008). Enhancing transdisciplinary research through collaborative leadership. *American Journal of Preventive Medicine*, 35(2), S124–S132. DOI: 10.1016/j.amepre.2008.03.037 PMID: 18619392

Hadorn, G., Pohl, C., & Bammer, G. (2010). Solving problems through transdisciplinary research. *The Oxford Handbook of Interdisciplinarity*. 431-452

Hall, K. L., Feng, A. X., Moser, R. P., Stokols, D., & Taylor, B. K. (2018). Moving the science of team science forward: Collaboration and creativity. *American Journal of Preventive Medicine*, 54(6), S230–S239. PMID: 18619406

Huang, X., & Lajoie, S. P. (2023). Social emotional interaction in collaborative learning: Why it matters and how can we measure it? *Social Sciences & Humanities Open*, 7(1), 100447. DOI: 10.1016/j.ssaho.2023.100447

Jantsch, E. (1970). Inter- and transdisciplinary university: A systems approach to education and innovation. *Policy Sciences*, 1(1), 403–428. DOI: 10.1007/BF00145222

Keyton, J. (2017). Communication in organizations. *Annual Review of Organizational Psychology and Organizational Behavior*, 4(1), 501–526. DOI: 10.1146/annurev-orgpsych-032516-113341

Keyton, J., Ford, D. J., & Smith, F. L. (2008). A Mesolevel Communicative Model of Collaboration. *Communication Theory*, 18(3), 376–406. DOI: 10.1111/j.1468-2885.2008.00327.x

Keyton, J., Ford, D. J., & Smith, F. L. (2012). Communication, collaboration, and identification as facilitators and constraints of multiteam systems. In S. J. Zaccaro, M. A. Marks, & L. A. DeChurch (Eds.), *Multiteam systems: An organization form for dynamic and complex environments* (pp. 173–190). Routledge/Taylor & Francis Group.

Klein, J. T. (2008). Evaluation of interdisciplinary and transdisciplinary research. *American Journal of Preventive Medicine*, 35(2), S116–S123. DOI: 10.1016/j.amepre.2008.05.010 PMID: 18619391

Klein, J. T. (2010). *Creating interdisciplinary campus cultures*. John Wiley & Sons.

Klein, J. T., Häberli, R., Scholz, R. W., Grossenbacher-Mansuy, W., Bill, A., & Welti, M. (2001). Transdisciplinarity: Joint problem solving among science, technology, and society. In *Birkhäuser Basel eBooks*.

Lewis, T. (2006). Creativity: A framework for the design/problem solving discourse in technology education. *Journal of Technology Education*, 17, 36–53.

Lincoln, Y. S., & Guba, E. G. (1985). *Naturalistic Inquiry*. SAGE. DOI: 10.1016/0147-1767(85)90062-8

MacLeod, M. (2016). What makes iterdisciplinarity difficult? Some consequences of domain specificity in interdisciplinary practice. https://link.springer.com/article/10.1007/s11229-016-1236-4

Roy, E. D., Morzillo, A. T., Seijo, F., Reddy, S. M., Rhemtulla, J. M., Milder, J. C., Kuemmerle, T., & Martin, S. L. (2013). The elusive pursuit of interdisciplinarity at the human-environment interface. *Bioscience*, 63(9), 745–753. DOI: 10.1093/bioscience/63.9.745

Stokols, D., Hall, K. L., Taylor, B. K., & Moser, R. P. (2008). The science of team science: Overview of the field and introduction to the supplement. *American Journal of Preventive Medicine*, 35(2), S77–S89. DOI: 10.1016/j.amepre.2008.05.002 PMID: 18619407

Vygotsky, L. (1962). Thought and language. In *MIT Press eBooks*. DOI: 10.1037/11193-000

Wagner, C., Garner, M., & Kawulich, B. (2011). The state of the art of teaching research methods in the social sciences: Towards a pedagogical culture. *Studies in Higher Education*, 36(1), 75–88. DOI: 10.1080/03075070903452594

Wuchty, S., Jones, B. F., & Uzzi, B. (2007). The increasing dominance of teams in production of knowledge. *Science*, 316(5827), 1036–1039. DOI: 10.1126/science.1136099 PMID: 17431139

Yegros-Yegros, A., Rafols, I., & D'Este, P. (2015). Does interdisciplinary research lead to higher citation impact? The different effect of proximal and distal interdisciplinarity. *PLoS One*, 10(8), e0135095. DOI: 10.1371/journal.pone.0135095 PMID: 26266805

Cracking the Code of
Your Very Own Genes

Section 5
Cracking the Code of Team Dynamics Success

Chapter 15
The Teamwork Equation:
Why 1 + 1 = Much More Than 2 in Academic Union Success

Eraldine S. Williams-Shakespeare
https://orcid.org/0009-0001-7169-579X
University of Technology, Jamaica

Tashieka S. Burris-Melville
https://orcid.org/0000-0002-5321-8877
University of Technology, Jamaica

Clavery O. Allen
https://orcid.org/0009-0003-0321-3001
University of Technology, Jamaica

Nadine A. Barrett-Maitland
University of Technology, Jamaica

Denise Allen
https://orcid.org/0009-0003-5551-9889
University of Technology, Jamaica

Atherine Anneth Marie Salmon
https://orcid.org/0000-0003-4489-3720
University of Technology, Jamaica

Joan L. Lawla
https://orcid.org/0009-0000-4007-8361
University of Technology, Jamaica

Robert A. Johnson
https://orcid.org/0009-0001-2629-5674
University of Technology, Jamaica

Meredith Williams
University of Technology, Jamaica

ABSTRACT

This study examined the critical link between team dynamics and effectiveness within an academic staff union. The research underscores the importance of teamwork in achieving union success, particularly in an environment where workers' rights can be overshadowed. The investigation explored how strong team dynamics, characterized by dedication, collaboration, and strategic maneuvering, empower academic

DOI: 10.4018/979-8-3693-3852-0.ch015

Copyright © 2025, IGI Global. Copying or distributing in print or electronic forms without written permission of IGI Global is prohibited.

staff unions to secure and uphold faculty well-being. A convergent parallel mixed-methods approach was employed. The study's findings highlight the importance of team dynamics and collaboration within academic staff unions.

INTRODUCTION

Thomas Reid's (1786) quote, "You are only as strong as your weakest link," should perhaps be a key reminder for any union that understands the importance of the power of oneness. Unions play a critical role in ensuring the well-being of their members and providing balance in a world where workers' rights are not always the priority of employers. Success in this endeavour requires teamwork, dedication, and a tremendous amount of mental torque to ensure that the union delivers the services required to support members' rights. This will allow members to meet their basic needs and, by extension, reach their full potential. Most working environments with unions are either externally facilitated or internally formed and run by elected members of the larger working group. Early 20th-century social, political, and economic changes in Jamaica that plagued the country's economy—which saw harsh working conditions and rising unemployment for the working class—were the driving forces behind the establishment of the trade union movement (Hart, 1999). The lack of legal recognition for trade unions during this period hindered their growth and development into contemporary union models (Hart, 1999). Hence, many unions formed in Jamaica up to 1919 were illegal. The passage of the Trade Union Law in 1919 provided the first legal basis for trade union activity in Jamaica. Since the birth of trade unionism, Jamaica has instituted additional laws in furtherance of the trade union movement and the advocacy of workers' rights, such as the Industrial Relations and Disputes Act that gives the right to every worker to choose to be a part of a union and participate in union activities (IDTA, Section 4(1)).

Collective bargaining on behalf of staff, therefore, transcends the working class of artisans to the academic prestige of universities, with the formation of the first academic staff association in Canada, the Carleton University Academic Staff Association (CUASA), in the mid-70s (Bufton, 2013). The University of Technology Academic Staff Union (UTASU), formed in the 1970s as the College of Arts, Science, and Technology Academic Staff Union (CASU), is one such body that seeks to ensure the well-being of staff. UTASU is a registered in-house union and operates under the Trade Union Act. The Union is governed internally by its constitution. UTASU is currently led by a team of nine members: seven duly elected, one appointed, and the immediate past president (UTASU. Const. art IX, § 1). The leadership team is two-tiered, with a supporting group of 20 school representatives, one per school, who act as the liaison between the general membership and the core executive.

The current union executive committee comprises nine academic staff members representing their colleagues across five faculties and three colleges.

The role of the union in any institution cannot be overemphasized. One such role was acknowledged by the American Association of University Professors (AAUP, n.d.), which intimated that "unions reinforce the collegiality necessary to preserve the vitality of academic life under such threats as deprofessionalization and fractionalisation of the faculty, privatization of public services, and the expanding claims of managerial primacy in governance" (para 4). Thus, unions play a significant role in helping improve the working lives of employees. The key variable for success is how well union executives work as a unit. Teamwork is a critical component for the success of any union, and academia is no different. The nature of the academic domain does not always foster teamwork. However, the success of unions in this domain is dependent on teamwork.

UTASU's current leadership team is presently in its first year of leadership. Thus, it is an apt time to conduct this study as a baseline for reviewing the team's effectiveness after the group's term has expired. The term is for two years, with the opportunity for re-election for serving members. There is a need to assess the teams' effectiveness and the perceptions of the general membership in relation to the perceived effectiveness of the team and their overall satisfaction with performance. In the context surrounding this case, three unions are in action. Individually and collectively, the groups have, over the years, been engaged in numerous negotiations, lobbying sessions, and where and as needed in activities to register members' protests.

PURPOSE OF THE STUDY

This convergent parallel mixed-methods study examined how a strong core executive team, characterized by trust, shared vision, and clear roles, can foster a more collaborative and effective executive group. It sought to investigate how their dynamics influence team functioning and the satisfaction of the broader membership.

RESEARCH QUESTIONS

The following research questions guided the study:

1. To what extent does the core team demonstrate characteristics of psychological safety, shared goals, and clear roles?

2. How does the result of the TEQ for school representatives compare with those of core executive members?
3. What strategies can the core executive team implement to strengthen the collaboration and synergy of the larger executive group?

SIGNIFICANCE OF THE STUDY

This study has theoretical and practical significance. Theoretically, it adds to the limited body of knowledge about the power of collaboration and teaming within unions and the far-reaching implications of teamwork. Additionally, the study adds value within academia, given the paucity of information on team effectiveness in regional unions. From a practical standpoint, this research can support the development of policies to support relations within the union's leadership and, by extension, influence the relationship with and quality of service to members.

HISTORY AND DEVELOPMENT OF ACADEMIC UNIONS IN JAMAICA

Trade unions have acted as the virtual voice of the masses in the public domain since their development. However, there is an evident diminishing effect of the weight and power of the unions. This can be attributed to various factors, including globalization, individualization of work, and technological enhancements. According to a study by Eaton (1962), the development of unions in Jamaica and other developing countries was born not from industrial capitalism but from a protest against poverty, which hampered industrial development. Eaton (1962) further opined that the labor discontent that existed then was the kernel and springboard for developing trade unions, which drove the pathways for independence movements. After the seminal Emancipation Act of 1834 and, with it, the end of slavery, the ensuing period of apprenticeship introduced the choice of employment and employer for the people with labor to sell. The period following the end of apprenticeship on August 1, 1838, was plagued with strikes where wages were poor, employment when available was irregular, and appeals, as allowed then to the Secretary of State for Colonies or even to the Queen, did not give satisfactory results. Hardship was the order of the day for workers in Jamaica, resulting in the Morant Bay rebellion of 1865. Out of this state of affairs, a trade union was formed in Jamaica.

In 1894, the first trade union was formed, notably without any legal framework for protection) and, not surprisingly, was formed by academics. The trade union was called the Jamaica Union of Teachers, now known as The Jamaica Teachers Association, and it was followed by the formation of the Artisan's Union, referred to as the Carpenters, Bricklayers, and Painters Union, in 1898. These were quickly followed by the Printer's Union (1907), Longshoremen's Union No. 1 (1918), and the Civil Service Association (1919). The Trade Union Ordinance was passed in 1919 to implement the first legal framework and was now protected from criminal sanctions for organizing union activities. Though criticized for not being thorough enough, it was not until the high levels of activism and the Moyne Commission that the Trade Union Act was amended in 1938 to provide some protection for unions and their members.

The Growth of Academic Unions

Cumulatively, academic union membership represents a large proportion of union membership in Jamaica, and this is led by the membership size of the Jamaica Teachers Association (JTA) (Palamidessi & Legarralde, 2006). In every public university, over 80% of academic staff are union members. This state is not an accident, as universities were originally closed shops, and management has taken steps to dramatically reduce the power of unions by making systematic changes to employment contracts to the detriment of the unions (Kochan & Kimball, 2019; Lafer, 2003).

Miller (2018) suggested that the early associations had as their mission to improve the quality of education being offered and focused on seminars to develop pedagogical content. As the associations teamed up to form unions, the mission changed to defending the rights of teachers. This was also the case for lecturers at tertiary institutions who formed unions. The body representing teachers called itself an "association" but operates like a union, though it is not a registered union.

The Jamaica Teachers Association (JTA). JTA came into being on April 2, 1964, when the instruments governing the membership and procedures of the body were examined and ratified at the inaugural conference held on that date (Jamaica Teachers Association [JTA], 2024). The association's resolutions were passed at a special Excelsior High School auditorium conference on December 14, 1963. The Association was formed from the merger of five teachers' associations. Consequently, the executives of the five groups formed the Joint Executives of Teachers' Associations (JETA) in 1957 (JTA, 2024). It was mandated to make representation on matters related to education and teachers. In pursuance of this mandate, the groups eventually decided to unify into a single teacher's organization, the Jamaica Teachers' Association (JTA, 2024). It should be noted that the associations shaping their future changed their focus from individualism to teamwork largely because of the power of teamwork.

The National Union of Democratic Teachers (NUDT). The NUDT was formed in the 1970s and battled with the JTA for rights to represent teachers as a union for a short time (Miller, 2018). This failed, so the JTA consolidated its position as the teacher's union. The formation and subsequent failure of the NUDT could be attributed to the failure of members to hone the necessary elements of teamwork. Tension and differences were created, and the rest is history. NUDT no longer exists.

West Indies Group of University Teachers (WIGUT). Propelled by the success of The Jamaica Teachers Association, the first attempt of university academic staff to form an association was in 1958 as an adjunct of the British Association of University Teachers (British AUT) (West Indies Group of University Teachers [WIGUT], 2024). This effort failed as the branches were not permitted. This led to forming an independent organization, the West Indies Group of University Teachers (WIGUT), after formally severing ties with AUT. Officially registered in 1972, WIGUT now represents its members for bargaining rights and has two other WIGUT branches. WIGUT seeks to conduct negotiations and participate fully in decision-making at the highest level of the university.

The University of Technology, Jamaica Academic Staff Union (UTASU). The University of Technology, Jamaica Academic Staff Union (UTASU) was formed in the 1970s under the name College of Arts, Science and Technology Academic Staff Union (CASU). In May 1997, the name of the union was changed to the University of Technology Academic Staff Union (UTASU), consequent on the name change of the University. UTASU is a registered in-house union and operates under the Trade Union Act, 1919 (amended 1938). The union is governed internally by its own constitution. The mission of the UTASU is to maintain a professional and vibrant organization that serves and protects the interests of its members at all UTech, Ja. Campuses and serves the interests of the University in an environment that reflects integrity, fairness, and transparency.

The Role of Academic Unions

Academic staff unions aim to improve working conditions for their members. Academic unions negotiate salaries and benefits, advocate for the rights of their members, contribute to the formation and shaping of employment policies, and assist in developing human resource policies. Additionally, they lead collective bargaining initiatives, advocate for fair working conditions, and protect their members from using the unchecked power of administrators to assign or punish them in what may be deemed oppressive supervision. The general goal is reflected in the writings of Professor Timothy Cain, who contends that academic unions can drive positive change within higher education institutions and counteract the pervasive assaults on workers' rights and the broader higher education sector (Cain, 2023).

The recent evolution of the academic landscape reveals a significant trend toward the marginalization of faculty, as documented by scholars such as (Alibašić et al. 2024; Aronowitz, 2008; Staley & Trinkle, 2011). This trend is evident in several key developments: the introduction of online degree programs in both public and private higher education institutions (Aronowitz, 2008; Cheslock & Jaquette, 2022), the modification of curricula to align with corporate demands (Aronowitz, 2008; Nevenglosky et al., 2019), the deliberate underfunding of liberal and fine arts disciplines in favour of expanding technical and business programs (Aronowitz, 2008; Baker & Powell, 2019; Vision 2030 Jamaica), and the prioritization of STEM fields for competitive advantage (Aronowitz, 2008; Mudaly & Chirikure, 2023; Singh-Wilmot, 2024). Additionally, the increasing emphasis on competitive sports has contributed to this transformation, impacting institutions like the University of Technology, Jamaica, and potentially diminishing faculty roles (Aronowitz, 2008; Lewin, 2014). Compounding these issues are the widespread comparisons between college presidents and corporate CEOs and the unabashed justification for awarding academic presidents high six-figure salaries (Aronowitz, 2008; Cornell, 2004).

The role of the academic union has taken on additional significance as there is a deepening of the chasm between administrators and faculty. Aronowitz, 2008 argued that 'academic administrators have become a part of the professional/managerial class' (p. 25). The deepening chasm relegates faculty empowerment and shared governance in this context, which is simply a matter of lip service. This may explain why academics, after completing their terms in administration, are unwilling to return to academia as the conditions are no longer attractive and deserving of their efforts (Aronowitz, 2008). The result is a departure from the academic profession. Compounding this is the disincentive buried in the practice of tenure appointment systems and their subsequent review. This matter, though receiving active consideration in discussions between management and faculty at universities, including UTech, Ja. is an obvious threat to unionism and should not be overlooked.

Benefits of Teamwork in Achieving Union Goals

While teamwork plays an undeniable role in the success of academic unions and the broader unionization efforts, the literature on the effectiveness of teamwork within these unions remains relatively sparse. Much of the existing research focuses on the challenges faced by members of academic unions rather than on the successes achieved through collaborative efforts. This gap in the literature suggests that while teamwork is recognized as important, there is a need for more comprehensive studies that explore how and why teamwork contributes to union success. Recent discussions have highlighted the growing unionization among contingent faculty and graduate workers, underscoring the importance of collective action. However, most of the literature primarily addresses the difficulties these groups encounter, such as precarious employment conditions, limited bargaining power, and the complexities of organizing across diverse academic environments (Quinn, 2024; Wicken, 2008). The challenges of fostering effective teamwork in such contexts are significant, often stemming from a lack of trust, unclear communication, and entrenched academic hierarchies, which can impede collective efforts (Gautam & Gautam, 2023).

Establishing teams and adopting teamwork are essential to contemporary business (Levi & Askay, 2020; Miller, 2003); therefore, achieving organizational goals depends on teamwork's effectiveness. Encouraging team members to focus on team goals instead of individual goals can result in increased output (Gardner et al., 2017). Research suggests that focus may seem insignificant but is powerful (Gardner et al., 2017). Establishing team goals can increase performance because it provides a guide for team members and can create a collaborative feeling within the group since individuals behave differently in groups than when acting alone (Burris-Melville et al., 2024; Gardner et al., 2017; Gençer, 2019;). Teams that work collaboratively on a mutual goal aiming at problem-solving can lead to healthy organizational behavior and positive interdependent relationships (Burris-Melville et al., 2024). According to Levi and Askay (2020), successful teams require clear goals, appropriate leadership, organizational support, suitable tasks, and accountability. There is value in both large and small teams. However, small teams mirror societal norms, individual norms, and personalities, and effectiveness is more obvious (Gençer, 2019). Focusing on maximizing individual goals can negatively impact teamwork and achieving team goals (Gardner et al., 2017). Teams are potent and dominant organisms that can influence individuals and communities (Gençer, 2019).

STAGES OF GROUP/TEAM DEVELOPMENT

The concept of team development is delineated into five distinct stages: forming, storming, norming, performing, and adjourning, as originally proposed by Tuckman and Jensen (1977) and illustrated in Figure 1.

Figure 1. Tuckman's stages of team development (Burris-Melville et al., 2024)

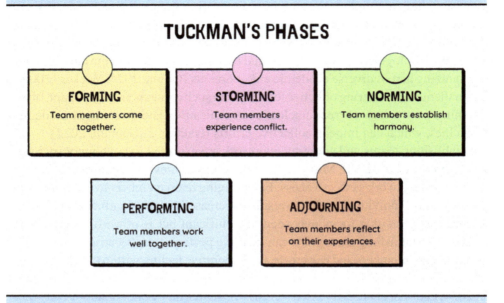

The initial stage, known as forming, involves team members becoming acquainted with one another and understanding the objectives and purposes of the team. This is followed by the storming phase, during which individuals within the team reveal their personal dispositions, and the team develops mechanisms to manage and resolve conflicts as they arise. The third stage, norming, is characterized by establishing defined roles and standards, fostering cohesion, and enhancing collaboration among team members. The performing stage represents a phase of high productivity, where the team effectively solves problems and achieves its goals. The final stage, adjourning, occurs when the team's tasks are completed or are restructured to address new objectives. This model provides a comprehensive framework for understanding the dynamic processes of team development and the evolution of team functionality over time. Researchers suggest that relationships among team members are normalized throughout the development stages, and the more educated the team members become (Fulk et al., 2011).

Team Effectiveness Models

Understanding effective teamwork dynamics within academic unions is crucial for fostering collaborative success in educational environments. This section introduces team effectiveness models that identify the critical components necessary for successful collaboration and collective action.

The STEAM Teamwork Model. Tambe's 1997 STEAM Teamwork Model developed a set of universal guidelines outlining how teams should collaborate effectively. (Schurr et al., 2005). It is essential for academic environments in which interdisciplinary teamwork is frequent. Setting a structured set of rules, this model ensures robust team performance even in the more unpredictable and complex environments of academic unions, where several varying academic disciplines and perspectives need to align toward common goals (Schurr et al., 2005).

The Teamwork Quality (TWQ). The TWQ model postulated by Hoegl and Gemuenden (2001) underscored that teamwork quality comprises communication, coordination, support, and cohesion. Such aspects are needed for the effective management of academic unions and to drive joint projects and research initiatives in various innovative educational practices. The demonstrated relationship of the TWQ model to project success in innovative settings points to its application to academic unions, indicating how structured interactions can increase outcomes.

Shared Mental Models in Teamwork. Druskat and Pescosolido (2002) emphasized shared mental models in teamwork, specifically for self-managing work teams (SMWTs) such as academic unions. The two developed a framework that urges psychological ownership and continuous learning—elements necessary for intellectual development and administrative effectiveness among academic staff. According to this model, it is proposed that supportive organizational structures are required for nurturing these mental models of teamwork to ensure that they adapt and thrive within relevant contexts (Druskat & Pescosolido, 2002). According to Schmidtke and Cummings (2017), teamwork is a pervasive process that combines shared mental models and converts these inputs to the desired output.

The Lembke and Wilson Model. Lembke and Wilson (1998) incorporated social identity and self-categorization theories into their teamwork analysis. This is particularly relevant in academic unions where individual identity and group affiliation are prominent. Their approach addressed how academic staff perceive their teams and their position in the team towards enhancing efficacy and motivation in such collaborative endeavors (Lembke & Wilson, 1998).

The Burris-Melville, Burris, and Bledsoe Model. The Burris-Melville et al. (2024) model offers a metaphorical and imaginative approach to viewing team effectiveness as if somebody were following a recipe. The metaphor could be useful for academic unions, with its own interpretation that indicates a methodic way to mix different academic talents and objectives into one composite team. This model metaphorically "bakes" the ingredients together, giving equal weight to developing trust, accountability, and systematic evaluation to develop a mutually productive and harmonious academic community. This model combines to give an all-encompassing view of the key factors that form part of successful teamwork within academic unions. When academic leaders apply an integration of these theories, it becomes possible for them to understand and develop strategies for improvement in cooperation within the collaborative environment and hence success.

Benefits of Psychological Safety for Team Performance and Innovation

According to Edmondson (1999), psychological safety revolves around a shared belief among members within a group or team that the team represents a safe space for interpersonal risk-taking, knowing the consequences. The team feels secure in an environment that presents itself as a safe space for voicing opinions, admitting mistakes when made, and asking questions without fear of repercussion or being negatively judged. According to Edmondson (1999), such an environment can make a difference between success and failure, as team members have no reservations about being honest and open during team discussions.

Edmondson (1999) further emphasized that a psychologically safe environment enables teams to engage in innovative thinking without the constraints of negativity from the team. This feeds into organizational growth and effectiveness emanating from a culture of open communication and continuous learning. Edmondson's (1999) research is supported by Patil et al. (2023), who intimated that individuals are more willing to ask daring questions, voice concerns, and seek assistance when psychological safety is present in the workplace. This leads to higher team output and fewer conflicts. Scholars have also argued that psychological safety is significantly connected to leadership styles (Carmeli et al., 2010; Edmondson, 1999; Rabiul et al., 2023).

How Leadership Styles Within Teams Foster Psychological Safety

Studies have examined the relationship between leadership styles and organizational psychological safety. In a study by Kumako and Asumeng (2013), an exploration was done on the dynamics of psychological safety and learning behaviors in teams and the role of transformational leadership in the relationship. The findings revealed a positive relationship between learning behavior and leadership style in situations where the transformational team leader moderates the relationship. Kumako and Asumeng (2013) also suggested how leaders can engage with their teams, thus encouraging psychological safety, enhancing learning behaviours, and making team members more adaptive and innovative.

Researchers have also posited through observational studies that a servant leadership style generates positive employee outcomes and affects the perception of employees' psychological safety (McKinney, 2020; Rabiul et al., 2023). Servant leaders strive to create organizational opportunities that allow followers to become self-actualized by giving them the autonomy to use their strengths to improve the whole enterprise (Luthans & Avolio, 2003). Servant leadership styles also engender positive self-concept, enhancing psychological safety by focusing on employees' needs and wants (Eva et al., 2019; Hoch et al., 2018; Rabiul et al., 2023).

In McKinney's study, the participants were subjected to abusive supervisor behaviors, resulting in a toxic work environment, as depicted by the undermining pathway in the model shown in Figure 2. Eventually, the authoritarian supervisor was replaced by a supportive leader who demonstrated servant leadership behaviors. This change positively affected the work environment and psychological safety, as represented by the enhancing pathway in the model.

Figure 2. Perceptions affection psychological safety source (Adapted from Mckinney, 2020)

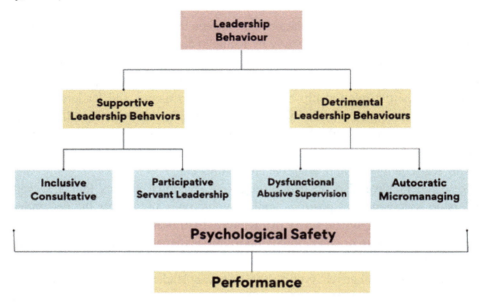

METHODOLOGY

This study utilized a convergent parallel mixed-methods design. Creswell and Plano Clark (2018) described the convergent parallel design as a process where both the quantitative and qualitative strands of the study are managed at the same time, which gives equal weight to each method, allowing for the analysis of the data separately, followed by the combining of the results. Figure 3 outlines this process.

Figure 3. Convergent parallel mixed-methods design (Adapted from Demir and Pismek, 2018)

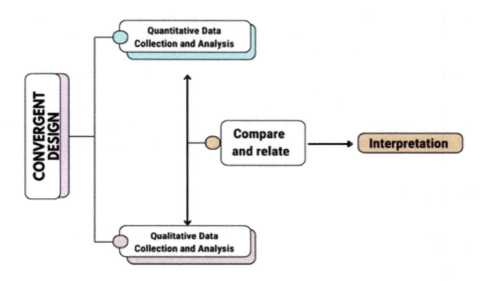

A comparison of the quantitative statistical data with the qualitative findings allows for triangulation of the data.

Population and Sample. The target population for the study was 29 members of the Academic Staff Union Executive. All 29 members were invited to participate in the study, and no sampling was done. Therefore, the sample size is (n = 29) with a 72% response rate. See Table 1 for the distribution of the membership.

Table 1. Population and sample of executive union membership

Participants	Number in Population	Number of Respondents
Union Executive Leadership Team	9	8
School Representatives	20	13
Total	29	21

Data Collection. The Team Development Measure (TDM) developed by Stock et al. (2013) and the Team Effectiveness Questionnaire (TEQ) (an adaptation of the Team Effectiveness Diagnostic developed by the London Leadership Academy, National Health Service) were to capture the core executive members' perceptions of their teaming experience. The TDM seeks to measure four key areas: cohesion, communication, roles and goals, and team primacy. The TEQ measures team effectiveness from eight dimensions – purpose and goals, roles, team processes, team relationships, intergroup relations, problem-solving, passion and commitment, and skills and learning. The school representatives (leadership tier 2) also completed the TEQ. School Representatives were also engaged in a focus group discussion to ascertain their perceptions of the team function and the effectiveness of the systems in place to support the Union's operations.

Data Analysis. Quantitative data was analyzed using SPSS for descriptive and inferential statistics, while qualitative data was coded and analyzed thematically.

Ethical Consideration. Participation in the study was voluntary, and consent forms were issued and signed before data collection for all aspects of the study. Ethical clearance was received from the Ethics Committee of the University.

FINDINGS

In an academic union, the development and effectiveness of teams are crucial for promoting collaboration, achieving shared goals, and driving overall success. Moreover, team effectiveness directly influences the union's ability to implement strategies, improve member engagement, and enhance organizational performance. The Team Development Measure and the Team Effectiveness Survey were used to collect data to assess these critical aspects. The following section presents the findings from these instruments, providing insights into the current state of team dynamics and performance within the union and identifying areas for potential growth and improvement.

Demographics

The participants in the quantitative phase of the study were members of the Union's executive team. This is a two-tiered leadership model, with 9 people in the core executive and 20 in the school representatives' group. There were 21 respondents representing 15 females (71.4%) and seven males (33.3%). The study's response rate was 21 of 29 or 72.4%. For the qualitative component five school representatives, (two males and three females) were selected and engaged in the focus group discussion.

QUANTITATIVE FINDINGS

The Team Development Measure (TDM) completed by the core executive, assesses various critical aspects of team dynamics, including cohesiveness, participation, support among members, clarity on roles and goals, and the team's effectiveness in conflict management and leadership flexibility. The results revealed that the team is very strong in communication, support, and clarity of roles (See Figure 4).

Figure 4. Strengths of the team

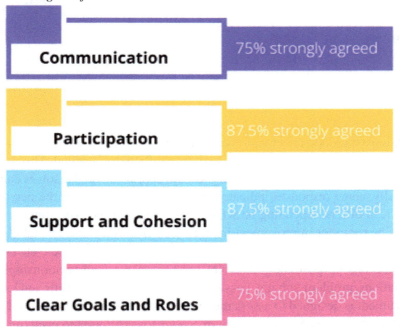

Most team members strongly agreed that communication is direct, truthful, and respectful. They also felt comfortable sharing their ideas and participating in decision-making processes. This indicates a high level of openness and inclusiveness in team interactions. Most respondents strongly agreed that team members support, nurture, and care for each other, and there is a strong sense of unity, with more of a "WE" feeling than a "ME" feeling. This suggests the team has developed a strong sense of belonging and mutual respect. Further, most respondents agreed that the team's goals are clearly understood, and the roles and responsibilities of individual team members are well-defined. This clarity likely contributes to the overall effectiveness of the team's work.

The results also highlighted opportunities for growth in conflict management and leadership adaptability. See Figure 5.

Figure 5. Areas for improvement

CONFLICT MANAGEMENT	
Strongly Agree	50%
Agree	37.5%
Disagree	12.5%
Strongly Disagree	12.5%

LEADERSHIP FLEXIBILITY	
Strongly Agree	62.5%
Agree	25%
Disagree	12.5%
Strongly Disagree	12.5%

While most respondents expressed satisfaction with the team's overall functioning, there were some disagreements regarding how conflicts are handled. This indicates a potential area for improvement in how the team approaches and resolves conflicts. Additionally, some responses indicated disagreement on whether the person who takes the lead differs depending on who is best suited for the task, suggesting that there may be room for improvement in leadership flexibility and adaptability.

The Teamwork Effectiveness Questionnaire measured team effectiveness across eight dimensions: purpose and goals, roles, team processes, team relationships, intergroup relations, problem-solving, passion and commitment, and skills and learning. The instrument is designed to assess the union's effectiveness and to identify areas that need to be improved. A maximum of 5 points was allotted to each dimension of the TEQ. The findings from the TEQ scores, as presented in Table 2, provide a comparative analysis of the perceived team effectiveness between the core executive group and the school representatives' group across the eight key dimensions.

Table 2. Comparison of scores between core and school representative groups

TEQ Dimensions	Core Group Average	School Representative Group Average
Purpose and Goals	4.5	3.5
Roles	4	3.0
Team Processes	4.2	3.3

continued on following page

Table 2. Continued

TEQ Dimensions	Core Group Average	School Representative Group Average
Team Relationships	4.4	4.0
Intergroup Relations	4.1	3.8
Problem Solving	4.1	3.8
Passion and Commitment	4.4	3.8
Skills and Learning	4.2	3.5
Total	33.9/40	29.2/40

The core executive group rated themselves highly in the dimension of purpose and goals, with an average score of 4.5. However, the school representatives provided a lower score of 3.5, indicating a perception gap regarding the clarity and alignment of purpose and goals within the core group. Similarly, in roles, the core group gave themselves a score of 4.0. At the same time, the school representatives rated them lower at 3.0, suggesting that they perceive less clarity in the roles within the core group. For team processes, the core group rated themselves at 4.2, but the school representatives rated them at 3.3, reflecting a significant difference in how effectively team processes are viewed.

Both groups rated the core executive group positively regarding team relationships, though the core group rated themselves slightly higher at 4.4 compared to the school representatives' 4.0. In the dimensions of intergroup relations and problem-solving, the core group rated themselves at 4.1, while the school representatives gave a lower rating of 3.8 for both dimensions, indicating that they perceived some room for improvement in these areas.

The core group also rated their passion and commitment highly at 4.4, whereas the school representatives rated them at 3.8, indicating a perception of lower passion and commitment from the school representatives' perspective. Finally, in the area of skills and learning, the core group rated themselves at 4.2, but the school representatives rated them at 3.5, again reflecting a perception gap.

Overall, the total scores reveal that the core executive group rated their own effectiveness at 33.9 out of 40, while the school representatives rated them at 29.2 out of 40. This comparison highlights significant perception differences between the core group's self-assessment and how they are viewed by the school representatives, particularly in areas such as roles, team processes, and skills and learning. These findings suggest that while the core group views itself as highly effective, the school representatives see opportunities for improvement in several key areas.

QUALITATIVE FINDINGS

The thematic analysis of the focus group discussions revealed key insights into the participants' experiences and perceptions of their roles, communication practices, and the overall effectiveness of teamwork within the organization. The identified themes highlight the need for clearer communication of roles, improved documentation and resources, effective use of communication channels, and ongoing support and training for members.

Role Clarity and Communication

One of the primary themes identified was the understanding of roles. Participants expressed varied levels of clarity regarding their roles, with some feeling uncertain about their responsibilities. This ambiguity highlighted the need for better communication and documentation of role expectations. For instance, one participant mentioned, *I'm not 100% sure that I fully understand what's required of me. But as I go along, I adjust.* This sentiment was echoed by others who felt that a lack of clear guidelines often led to confusion and inefficiencies.

Communication Channels and Information Sharing

The effectiveness of communication channels was another prominent theme. Participants generally found WhatsApp and email to be the primary modes of communication, but they also highlighted areas for improvement. Some suggested pinning important messages on WhatsApp to ensure visibility, while others recommended following up with phone calls for urgent matters. One participant stated, *Sometimes I get a little bit confused as to what to share, what is for us as the executive, and what is to be sent out.*

Structured Support and Training

Participants emphasized the need for structured support systems, particularly in onboarding and continuous training. New members felt overwhelmed due to a lack of proper orientation and clear guidelines. The suggestion for workshops and comprehensive onboarding programs was a recurring recommendation. One participant mentioned, *it may be good for some kind of mini-workshop so we better understand our roles.* Additionally, there was a call for accessible resources, such as a repository of information that members could refer to as needed. This continuous support was seen as vital for maintaining performance and job satisfaction.

Perceived Effectiveness of Leadership

Despite the overall satisfaction with leadership, participants identified areas for improvement, particularly in balancing strategic planning with day-to-day tasks. While some participants felt that the core team effectively communicated and supported their roles, others believed more focus was needed on strategic issues. One participant commented, *I think communication is adequate, but we could PIN important messages on WhatsApp to ensure everyone sees them.*

SUGGESTIONS FOR IMPROVEMENT

Several suggestions for improvement emerged from the discussions, focusing on documentation, communication, and engagement. Participants recommended creating comprehensive manuals or repositories that provide clear and accessible information on roles, responsibilities, and other essential aspects. The need for better documentation was emphasized, as one participant noted, *we should look into creating a website that functions as a repository for all important documents and information.* Enhanced communication was another critical area for improvement. Participants suggested optimizing the use of existing channels and introducing new methods for disseminating information.

DISCUSSION

The findings from the TDM, TEQ, and focus group discussion provide a comprehensive view of the current state of team dynamics and effectiveness within the academic staff union. These insights reveal strengths and improvement areas across various dimensions of team functioning. The results of the TEQ indicate that the core executive group perceives itself as highly effective in areas such as purpose and goals, team relationships, and passion and commitment. These perceptions align with the TDM findings, where strong communication, support, and clarity of roles were highlighted. The core group's high self-ratings in these areas suggest that the team members feel a strong sense of direction and cohesion, which are essential for effective leadership and collaboration. This is supported by existing literature, which emphasizes the importance of clear goals, strong interpersonal relationships, and mutual support in fostering effective teams (Driskell et al., 2018; Levi & Askay, 2020).

However, a significant perception gap emerged when comparing the core group's self-assessment with the views of the school representatives. The school representatives rated the core group lower across several key dimensions, including roles, team processes, and skills and learning. This discrepancy suggests that while the core group feels confident in its performance, the broader leadership team perceives areas where improvement is needed, particularly in clarifying roles and responsibilities, enhancing team processes, and developing skills. These findings are consistent with the work of Hogg et al. (2004), who found that discrepancies between internal and external perceptions can lead to challenges in achieving team cohesion and effectiveness.

It is also likely that the perception gap exists because the core leadership works intimately and engages with each other daily more than they interact with the school representatives. This closer interaction within the core group may contribute to stronger relationships and a better understanding of internal processes, which are not as visible or accessible to the school representatives. This is supported by the teamwork literature that suggests that frequent interaction and communication among team members can enhance mutual understanding, trust, and cohesion. This is particularly true in smaller, tightly knit teams where members have more opportunities to engage with one another regularly, leading to a deeper understanding of the team's processes and goals. (Kozlowski & Ilgen, 2006; Salas et al., 2005).

The TDM results further identified areas for growth, particularly in conflict management and leadership flexibility. Although the team is strong in communication and support, the findings suggest that there is room for improvement in how the team manages conflicts and adapts leadership roles to suit specific situations. The qualitative data echoed these concerns, with participants expressing uncertainty about their roles and highlighting the need for clearer communication, better documentation, and more structured support and training. These concerns align with the literature on psychological safety, which underscores the importance of effective conflict management and flexible leadership in maintaining a productive and cohesive team (Edmondson, 1999; Fulk et al., 2011).

While the UTASU core executive group demonstrates strong cohesion, communication, and role clarity within their self-assessments, there are clear areas for improvement as perceived by the broader leadership team. Addressing these discrepancies through enhanced role clarity, improved communication, and targeted skills development will be essential for aligning perceptions and strengthening the overall effectiveness of the union's leadership. The integrated findings from the TEQ, TDM, and qualitative data provide a comprehensive roadmap for these improvements, ensuring that the UTASU leadership can continue to develop and maintain a high-performing team that effectively serves its members.

There is a clear connection with the experiences of the UTASU team and the characteristics outlined in the various team effectiveness models outlined in the literature review (Burris-Melville et al., 2024; Druskat & Pescosolido, 2002; Hoegl & Gemuenden, 2001; Lembke & Wilson, 1998; Schurr et al., 2005). Druskat and Pescosolido (2002) recommendation for psychological ownership and continuous learning were evidenced in the results of the focus group where participants indicated a need to be further engaged and to be brought into the know on strategic matters.

RECOMMENDATIONS

We, therefore, recommend a three-pronged approach outlined in Figure 6 to improve the team effectiveness of the academic union leadership team, focusing on foundational building, skill development and team strengthening, and continuous engagement and improvement.

Figure 6. Roadmap for improving team effectiveness in academic union

The initial phase, foundation building, involves conducting a comprehensive needs assessment to identify key areas for improvement, setting clear objectives, and developing a detailed plan. A critical aspect of this phase is enhancing the onboarding process by creating a structured program for new members, which includes orientation sessions, mentorship, and the development of a leadership handbook.

This handbook will outline roles, responsibilities, and internal communication protocols, ensuring that all team members have a clear understanding of their duties and the union's mission. Additionally, workshops focused on role clarification will be organized to foster a shared understanding of each member's contributions to the team's goals.

The second phase, skill development and team strengthening, emphasizes the importance of building core competencies and reinforcing team cohesion. This phase includes targeted training sessions on essential skills such as communication, conflict resolution, and strategic planning. Peer learning initiatives will be introduced to facilitate knowledge sharing and the exchange of best practices among team members. To address challenges in conflict management and leadership flexibility, the union will conduct workshops focused on effective conflict resolution strategies and adaptive leadership practices. Furthermore, team-building activities such as retreats and regular meetings will be organized to strengthen interpersonal relationships and build trust within the team, ensuring a unified approach to achieving the union's objectives.

The final phase, engagement and continuous improvement, focuses on increasing the participation of school representatives and sustaining the progress made in the previous phases. This phase involves developing strategies to enhance the engagement of school representatives in decision-making processes, such as creating joint committees or task forces that include both core leaders and school representatives. Regular feedback loops will be established to ensure ongoing communication and alignment between the leadership team and the school representatives. Additionally, continuous professional development opportunities will be offered, including advanced workshops and quarterly skill refreshers, to maintain and further enhance the team's effectiveness. An annual review will be conducted to assess the team's progress, with adjustments made to the roadmap as needed to address new challenges and ensure ongoing success.

This roadmap recommendation provides a structured approach to enhancing the effectiveness of the academic union's leadership team by focusing on onboarding, skills development, role clarity, conflict management, and engagement. By following this plan, the union can build a more cohesive, adaptable, and high-performing leadership team that is well-equipped to serve its members effectively.

CONCLUSION

The study underscores the critical role of team dynamics and effectiveness within academic staff unions in promoting collaboration, achieving shared goals, and enhancing organizational performance. The findings revealed both strengths and areas for improvement, particularly highlighting the perception gaps between the core executive group and the school representatives regarding team effectiveness. The quantitative data supported by qualitative insights provided a comprehensive view of the current state of the union's leadership dynamics. The results suggest that while the core executive group demonstrates strong internal cohesion, communication, and role clarity, there is a need to address discrepancies in role perception, team processes, and leadership flexibility as seen by the broader leadership team. By implementing the recommended strategies—focused on enhanced onboarding, structured training, improved communication, and increased engagement—the academic union can align perceptions and further strengthen the effectiveness of its leadership, ensuring continued success in its mission to serve and protect the interests of its members.

REFERENCES

Alibašić, H. L., Atkinson, C., & Pelcher, J. (2024). The liminal state of academic freedom: Navigating corporatization in higher education. *Discover Education*, 3(1). Advance online publication. https://doi.org/10.1007/s44217-024-00086-x

American Association of University Professors. (n.d.). AAUP unionism. https://www.aaup.org/chapter-organizing/aaup-unionism

Aronowitz, S. (2008). *Against schooling: For an education that matters*. Routledge., https://doi.org/10.4324/9781315636139-9

Baker, T., & Powell, E. E. (2019). Entrepreneurship as a new liberal art. *Small Business Economics*, 52(2), 405–418. https://doi.org/10.1007/s11187-018-0099-0

Bufton, M. A. (2013). Solidarity by association: *The unionization of faculty, academic librarians and support staff at Carleton University (1973–1976)* [Unpublished master's thesis]. Carleton University.

Burris-Melville, T. S., Burris, S. T., & Bledsoe, K. (2024). *Empowering teams in higher education: Strategies for success*. IGI Global., https://doi.org/10.4018/979-8-3693-1520-0

Cain, T. R. (2023). Academic union voice and the transformations in/of higher education. In Leišytė, L., Dee, J. R., & van der Meulen, B. J. R. (Eds.), *Research handbook on the transformation of higher education* (pp. 112–126). Edward Elgar Publishing Limited., https://doi.org/10.4337/9781800378216.00015

Carmeli, A., Reiter-Palmon, R., & Ziv, E. (2010). Inclusive leadership and employee involvement in creative tasks in the workplace: The mediating role of psychological safety. *Creativity Research Journal*, 22(3), 250–260. https://doi.org/10.1080/10400419.2010.504654

Cheslock, J. J., & Jaquette, O. (2021). Concentrated or fragmented? The U.S. market for online higher education. *Research in Higher Education*, 63(1), 33–59. https://doi.org/10.1007/s11162-021-09639-7

Cornell, B. (2004). Compensation and recruiting: Private universities versus private corporations. *Journal of Corporate Finance*, 10(1), 37–52. https://doi.org/10.1016/S0929-1199(02)00025-1

Creswell, J. W., & Plano Clark, V. L. (2018). *Designing and conducting mixed methods research*. Sage Publications.

Demir, S. B., & Pismek, N. (2018). A convergent parallel mixed-methods study of controversial issues in Social Studies classes: A clash of ideologies. *Educational Sciences: Theory & Practice*, 18(1), 119–149.

Driskell, J. E., Salas, E., & Driskell, T. (2018). Foundations of teamwork and collaboration. *The American Psychologist*, 73(4), 334–348. https://doi.org/10.1037/amp0000241

Druskat, V. U., & Pescosolido, A. T. (2002). The content of effective teamwork mental models in self-managing teams: Ownership, learning and heedful interrelating. *Human Relations*, 55(3), 283–314. https://doi.org/10.1177/0018726702553001

Dutton, & R. E. Quinn (Eds.), *Positive organizational scholarship: Foundations of a new discipline* (pp. 241–258). Berrett-Koehler Publishers.

Eaton, G. (1962). Trade union development in Jamaica. *Caribbean Quarterly*, 8(1), 43–53. https://doi.org/10.1080/00086495.1962.11829842

Edmondson, A. (1999). Psychological safety and learning behavior in work teams. *Administrative Science Quarterly*, 44(2), 350–383.

Eva, N., Robin, M., Sendjaya, S., van Dierendonck, D., & Liden, R. C. (2019). Servant leadership: A systematic review and call for future research. *The Leadership Quarterly*, 30(1), 111–132. https://doi.org/10.1016/j.leaqua.2018.07.004

Fulk, H. K., Bell, R. L., & Bodie, N. (2011). Team management by objectives: Enhancing developing teams' performance. *Journal of Management Policy and Practice*, 12(3), 17–26.

Gardner, A. K., Kosemund, M., Hogg, D., Heymann, A., & Martinez, J. (2017). Setting goals, not just roles: Improving teamwork through goal-focused debriefing. *American Journal of Surgery*, 213(2), 249–252. https://doi.org/10.1016/j.amjsurg.2016.09.040

Gautam, P. K., & Gautam, R. R. (2023). Organizational culture orientation and union influence. *Management Dynamics*, 26(1), 43–55. https://doi.org/10.3126/md.v26i1.59150

Gençer, H. (2019). Group dynamics and behaviour. *Universal Journal of Educational Research*, 7(1), 223–229. https://doi.org/10.13189/ujer.2019.070128

Hart, R. (1999). The birth of the trade union movement in the English-speaking Caribbean area. *Social and Economic Studies*, 48(3), 173–196.

Hoch, J. E., Bommer, W. H., Dulebohn, J. H., & Wu, D. (2016). Do ethical, authentic, and servant leadership explain variance above and beyond transformational leadership? A meta-analysis. *Journal of Management*, 44(2), 501–529. https://doi.org/10.1177/0149206316665461

Hoegl, M., & Gemuenden, H. G. (2001). Teamwork quality and the success of innovative projects: A theoretical concept and empirical evidence. *Organization Science*, 12(4), 435–449. https://doi.org/10.1287/orsc.12.4.435.10635

Hogg, M. A., Abrams, D., Otten, S., & Hinkle, S. (2004). The social identity perspective: Intergroup relations, self-conception, and small groups. *Small Group Research*, 35(3), 246–276. https://doi.org/10.1177/1046496404263424

Jamaica Teachers Association. (2024). History of the JTA. https://www.jta.org.jm/pages/history-jta Lafer, G. (2003). Graduate student unions: Organizing in a changed academic economy. *Labor Studies Journal, 28*(2), 25–43. https://doi.org/10.1353/lab.2003.0039

Kochan, & Kimball. (2019). Unions, worker voice, and management practices: Implications for a high-productivity, high-wage economy. *RSF: The Russell Sage Foundation Journal of the Social Sciences, 5*(5), 88–108. https://doi.org/10.7758/rsf.2019.5.5.05

Kozlowski, S. W. J., & Ilgen, D. R. (2006). Enhancing the effectiveness of work groups and teams. *Psychological Science in the Public Interest*, 7(3), 77–124. https://doi.org/10.1111/j.1529-1006.2006.00030.x

Kumako, S. K., & Asumeng, M. A. (2013). Transformational leadership as a moderator of the relationship between psychological safety and learning behaviour in work teams in Ghana. *SA Journal of Industrial Psychology*, 39(1). Advance online publication. https://doi.org/10.4102/sajip.v39i1.1036

Labour Relations and Industrial Disputes Act. (1975). https://www.mlss.gov.jm/wp-content/uploads/2018/02/Laboour-Relations-and-Industrial-Disputes-Act5b15d.pdf

Lembke, S., & Wilson, M. G. (1998). Putting the "team" into teamwork: Alternative theoretical contributions for contemporary management practice. *Human Relations*, 51(7), 927–944. https://doi.org/10.1177/001872679805100704

Levi, D., & Askay, D. (2020). *Group dynamics for teams* (6th ed.). SAGE Publications.

Lewin, T. (2014, April 17). *Colleges increasing spending on sports faster than on academics, report finds*. The New York Times. https://www.nytimes.com/2014/04/07/education/colleges-increasing-spending-on-sports-faster-than-on-academics-report-finds.html

Luthans, F., & Avolio, B. J. (2003). Authentic leadership development. In Cameron, K. S. (Ed.), *J. E.*

McKinney, T. (2020). *Fostering psychological safety: What is a leader to do?* (Publication No. 2446975937). [doctoral dissertation, Benedictine University]. ProQuest Dissertations and Theses Global.

Miller, J. (2018, October 6). *Are the traditional roles of teachers' unions changing?* https://errolmiller.com/traditional-roles-of-teachers-unions-changing/#google_vignette

Mudaly, R., & Chirikure, T. (2023). STEM education in the Global North and Global South: Competition, conformity, and convenient collaborations. *Frontiers in Education*, 8. Advance online publication. https://doi.org/10.3389/feduc.2023.1144399

Nevenglosky, E. A., Cale, C., & Panesar Aguilar, S. (2019). Barriers to effective curriculum implementation. *Research in Higher Education*, 36, •••. https://files.eric.ed.gov/fulltext/EJ1203958.pdf

Palamidessi, M., & Legarralde, M. (2006). *Teachers' unions, governments and educational reforms in Latin America and the Caribbean: Conditions for dialogue.* Inter-American Bank Regional Policy Dialogue.

Patil, R., Raheja, D. K., Nair, L., Deshpande, A., & Mittal, A. (2023). The power of psychological safety: Investigating its impact on team learning, team efficacy, and team productivity. *The Open Psychology Journal*, 16(1).

Phelps, O. W. (1960). Rise of the labour movement in Jamaica. *Social and Economic Studies*, 9(4), 417–468.

Quinn, R. (2023, August 29). Higher Ed unionization has surged since 2012, bucking U.S. labor trends. Insider Higher Ed. https://www.insidehighered.com/news/faculty-issues/labor-unionization/2024/08/29/higher-ed-unionization-bucks-labor-trends-surged

Rabiul, M. K., Karatepe, O. M., Karim, R. A., & Panha, I. (2023). An investigation of the interrelationships of leadership styles, psychological safety, thriving at work, and work engagement in the hotel industry: A sequential mediation model. *International Journal of Hospitality Management*, 113, 103508. https://doi.org/10.1016/j.ijhm.2023.103508

Salas, E., Sims, D. E., & Burke, C. S. (2005). Is there a "big five" in teamwork? *Small Group Research*, 36(5), 555–599. https://doi.org/10.1177/1046496405277134

Schmidtke, J. M., & Cummings, A. (2017). The effects of virtualness on teamwork behavioral components: The role of shared mental models. *Human Resource Management Review*, 27(4), 660–677. https://doi.org/10.1016/j.hrmr.2016.12.011

Schurr, N., Okamoto, S., Maheswaran, R. T., Scerri, P., & Tambe, M. (2005). Evolution of a teamwork model. In Sun, R. (Ed.), *Cognition and multi-agent interaction: From cognitive modeling to social simulation* (pp. 307–327). Cambridge University Press., https://doi.org/10.1017/cbo9780511610721.013

Singh-Wilmot, M. (2024, May 13). *Jamaica the 'STEM Island' – A dream that can come true*. The Gleaner. https://jamaica-gleaner.com/article/news/20240513/dr-marvadeen-singh-wilmot-jamaica-stem-island-dream-can-come-true

Staley, D., & Trinkle, D. (2011, February 11). *The changing landscape of higher education*. EDUCASE Review. https://er.educause.edu/articles/2011/2/the-changing-landscape-of-higher-education

Stock, R., Mahoney, E., & Carney, P. A. (2013). Measuring team development in clinical care settings. *Family Medicine*, 45(10), 691–700.

Trade Union Act. (1919). https://laws.moj.gov.jm/library/statute/the-trade-union-act

West Indies Group of University Teachers. (2024). The origin. http://wigut.uwimona.edu.jm/content/about

Wickens, C. M. (2008). The organizational impact of university labor unions. *Higher Education*, 56(5), 545–564. https://doi.org/10.1007/s10734-008-9110-z

Chapter 16
Sculpting Educational Excellence
Brand Building Approaches for Higher Education Institutions

Remi John Thomas
https://orcid.org/0000-0002-4003-9941
Vishwakarma University, India

Madhuri Sawant
Dr. Babasaheb Ambedkar Marathwada University, India

ABSTRACT

This paper presents a comprehensive seven-stage conceptual framework for branding in higher education institutions, based on a study conducted in Maharashtra, India. It addresses research gaps in understanding the challenges faced by institutions in this diverse and dynamic setting. Drawing on personal experience, literature review, and marketing theories, the framework guides institutions in brand development and sustainability. The study emphasizes stages such as defining vision and purpose, creating a distinct brand identity, positioning the brand, enhancing awareness and performance, conducting brand audits, and sustaining brand equity. It offers valuable insights for institutions aiming to strengthen their brand presence in the competitive academic landscape.

1. INTRODUCTION

A brand is a name, term, slogan, symbol, illustration, or a combination thereof, intended to differentiate the products and services of one seller or group of sellers and to distinguish between the goods and services of one seller or group of sellers," according to the American Marketing Association (AMA). The traditional meaning of a brand was as follows: "the mark that is associated with one or more products in a product line and is used to determine the item's origin (s). Kapferer (1997) and Solomon et al. (2020) explained that the mark is an exterior symbol whose purpose is to expose the secret features of the product that are inaccessible to touch. "Creating an impactful and distinctive logo is the problem today." Concerning the method of brand management as applied to a brand's use as an identifier. Chiaravalle and Schenck (2007) suggested that a brand can encompass a variety of entities, including a product, service, organization, nation, location, or people. Because of their peculiarity and inclusion in intangible brands, branding educational services is more difficult than branding products (Grljević et al., 2019). Other features of this service, like its indivisibility (requiring the presence of both the provider and the recipient), its diversity (no two services are the same), and its impossibility of preservation, all support the thesis regarding the difficulty of branding intangible brands (Domazet & Neogradi, 2018).

Elken (2020) explained that a strong and cohesive brand in higher education attracts prospective students, fosters alumni loyalty, engages faculty and staff, and enhances the institution's overall reputation. However, creating and maintaining a compelling brand identity cannot be achieved in isolation. It requires the collaborative efforts of a diverse array of stakeholders, including faculty, staff, administrators, and students. Judson, Gorchels et.al. (2006). Collaboration among teammates is an essential condition for collaborative success in companies and impacts team members' views toward the company (Al-Rawi, 2008). Bravo et al. (2019) concluded that individual characteristics (cooperativeness and collaborative behaviour) have a favourable impact on team cohesion, but task elements (workload and job complexity) have a negative effect. Educating students on how to work in groups is important in higher education, particularly in business courses. Despite the importance of team cohesion in cooperation, there have been few empirical investigations on its antecedents and implications (Müceldili & Erdil, 2015).

Oliver (2001) explained that teamwork might be described "as a cooperative process that enables common people to achieve extraordinary results." Teams allow individuals to leverage their strengths to achieve a common objective. Effective teams foster shared learning, social sensitization, a sense of belonging, and camaraderie. Successful teams prioritize synergy to foster enthusiasm, efficacy, and win-win circumstances. Team members must adapt to cooperative situations, prioritizing cooperation and social interdependence over individual, competing aims.

Culture and Values as a Brand Builder

An institution of higher learning's organizational culture is crucial to its brand development. The reputation and efficacy of the organization may be improved by creating an environment that values cooperation, diversity, and creativity.

Characteristics of a Positive Culture

1. **Engagement**: Increased levels of engagement result from a culture that promotes everyone's active involvement. Faculty and students are more inclined to constructively contribute to the objectives of the institution when they feel heard and respected.
2. **Transparency**: Open dialogue among interested parties promotes trust. Strong ties between institutions and the community are more probable to develop when they uphold transparency on their accomplishments, difficulties, and methods of operation.
3. **Recognition**: Honouring accomplishments, no matter how modest, promotes an attitude of gratitude. Acknowledging the work of educators and learners not only improves morale but also fortifies their dedication to the mission of the school.
4. **Collaboration**: Fostering cross-departmental collaboration can result in creative ideas and improved learning opportunities. Multidisciplinary programs, cooperative projects, and team-building exercises can all help to foster this collaborative attitude.

The role of values is important in decision-making and conflict resolution, regardless of how they are defined-broadly, as preferred forms of behaviour or narrowly, as thoughts about what is desirable.

Values have an impact on how an individual's morals are shaped and help to stabilize their behaviour. According to Kiros (1998), value also denotes things that are deserving of respect from others, as well as values and norms that society holds dear and inherently desirable.

Any field that deals with adult education, adult education policy, or the idea of lifelong learning is affected by the branding process in higher education, both practically and scientifically. Students have a clear opinion on the role of instrumental values in the construction of the ideal brand of the faculty and, in turn, of the higher education institution.

A leader's presence not only symbolizes an organization's existence but also positively influences its development. Leadership is a crucial component of an organisation, acting as a driving force through managing and handling change (Sarmila et al., 2023).

The managerial ability of leaders who consistently cooperate with positive plans to collaborate by including stakeholders and sustaining and promoting ongoing contacts is known as collaborative leadership. Collaborative leaders operate in coalitions, partnerships, and alliances, reaching choices collectively as opposed to acting alone. (Siagian, 2015)

Figure 1. Leaderships role in shaping culture (www.fastercapital.com)

Figure 2. Sustaining a strong brand culture (www.fastercapital.com)

In organisational life, it is widely acknowledged that organisational leaders have an impact on how organisational culture develops and is maintained. The conception of organisational culture affects the responsibilities and difficulties faced by leaders within an organisation.

Device et al. (2015) concluded that effective communication is essential for teamwork success and that a more comprehensive approach to teamwork skills development is needed. They also highlighted the importance of experiential learning and formative assessment in facilitating sustainable learning.

The success of higher education branding initiatives hinges on the ability to harness the collective talents and insights of the entire institution. By fostering a culture of collaboration and teamwork, higher education institutions can create a cohesive and compelling brand identity that stands out in a crowded marketplace and resonates deeply with all stakeholders (Smith, 2024). In this collaborative environment, every member of the institution becomes an ambassador for the brand, contributing to its growth, evolution, and enduring success.

As per, Ruoslahti, (2018) ssuccessful branding is basically a collaborative endeavour that relies on cooperation and the active participation of all stakeholders. Alford & Duan (2018) concluded that institutional branding includes not just internal teams, but also external stakeholders like consumers, partners, and suppliers in the branding process. Their observations can give crucial input, shaping the brand's path.

Hamdan, Andersen, & De Boer, (2021) explained that ccollaboration among all stakeholders, clear communication, establishing confidence, and common goals are key to successful branding. Organisations may build a strong brand image that connects with their intended consumers and stands out in fiercely competitive markets by cultivating a team-oriented atmosphere.

By focussing on these methods, businesses can successfully cooperate with stakeholders to develop a cohesive branding approach that improves exposure, generates engagement, and, ultimately, leads to higher market success.

2. ROLE OF MARKETING MIX IN BRANDING

The marketing mix concept is one example of supply-side marketing analysis that has emerged in higher education marketing. Kotler and Fox (1995) modified and extended the 4P's marketing blend that educational institutions in a product specifically use marketing into a model. Advertisers largely agreed in the late 1970s that the marketing mix should be changed. This, in turn, led to Booms & Bitner's development of the Expanded Marketing Mix in 1981, which incorporated three additional components to the 4P Concept. This has now resulted in having items that are services rather than just actual objects in the expanded Marketing Mix. Any of the elements of the marketing mix of the 7Ps illustrates an area of importance to be tackled by the marketing campaign of an educational institution.

1. The programs (**Product**) available is part of the learning opportunity (Kotler & Fox, 1995).
2. **Place** applies to the forms of distribution (Kotler & Fox, 1994), which may be actual or simulated sites.
3. **Price** applies to tuition, fees, loans, loan services, fundraising, and non-monetary expenses (Hanson & Henry, 1992).
4. After pricing, this is the promotional part. Despite having most of our marketing mix right, we might need to do more marketing to help our customers better appreciate our product and its functionality and quality. **Promotion** is the means an institution uses to engage with its many markets, be the future students, alums, and supporters. (Harrison-Walker, 2009).
5. Its employees. Those people who are interested in marketing, designing, leading staff, serving clients, etc., the list is moving on. The '**people**' aspect of the 7Ps includes everyone personally or ramblingly engrossed in the company's commercial side.

6. The **process** is the way things happen. Citizens apply to those who administer the agency's services (Kotler & Fox, 1994). The systemic process that transforms a person or a state into another is how things happen (Kotler & Armstrong, 2010).
7. **Physical evidence** is the tangible things available to customers (Hanson et al. 1992), which include classrooms, books, chairs, dorm rooms, etc., in the case of an institution. Some experts say 8P is in the Marketing Mix- viz. **Productivity** & Quality Productivity. This **P** is about consistent product quality and performance enhancement to improve customer satisfaction.

Joachimsthaler and Aaker (2009) discussed the traditional branding model, where a brand management team was responsible for creating and coordinating the brand's management program. Kamath (2018) noted that many scholars have identified multiple models, but it is found that there is still a difference between the understanding of brand builders and the perceptions of students about a brand.

3. LITERATURE REVIEW & CONCEPTUAL FRAMEWORK

According to previous studies, cost, location, popularity, marketing, facilities, campus lifestyle type, infrastructure, and other factors are used as components of brand growth. They often serve as a deciding factor for students when selecting a course. Under the 7P's of services marketing, these variables are grouped as a program, price, ads, physical evidence, people, and process. Below are a few notable brand-building literature reviews. When it comes to brand construction, there are two sides: supply and demand (Stachowski, 2011). Marketing strategy and incentives, strategic marketing strategies, the customer as the user, marketing procedure, relational versus relational marketing methods, and marketing structures are all part of the supply side. The demand side of branding includes student desires, behaviors, and student retention at higher education institutions (Hemsley-Brown, & Oplatka, 2006). Higher education institutions' branding research incorporates both aspects but concentrates on the supply side, so a brand is concerned with perceptions. However, the literature on branding for higher education needs to be more extensive and needs additional development (Steen, 2020). The literature has proposed multiple styles of brand branding.

So many inner and outside limitations make logo construction difficult for any enterprise (Chen, 2016), and most of those issues are beneath the enterprise's control. The assignment of logo construction cannot be regarded as insuperable, as Hogan et al. (2005) have noted, and numerous logo leaders have verified that an asset that can have an actual long-time fee may be advanced and sustained.

As per (Aaker & Joachimsthaler, 2000), three primary logo-constructing spots can be set via way of means of (i) setting up awareness (which includes acknowledgment, unaided recall, and so-called 'top-of-mind' status); (ii) forming clean connections (to differentiate the logo); and (iii) cultivating deep consumer relationships (such that the logo will become a first-rate a portion of the existence and self/ idea of every consumer). Aaker (2012) created a version for logo identification guidance including three most important phases: (i) strategic logo research (which means that the logo method is centered on purchaser analysis, competitor analysis, and self-analysis); (ii) logo identification framework (which includes setting up logo identification, fee proposition, reputation, and partnership among logo and consumer); and (iii) logo identification execution.

Five levels of company branding have been defined via way of means of Hatch and Schultz (2002) (i) stating (expressing the existing identification of the enterprise and what it wishes to turn out to be in phrases of its strategic goal); (ii) coordinating (helping the logo's described imaginative and prescient and identification via way of means or reshaping organizational frameworks and processes) ; (iii) involving (attracting all associated stakeholders in the realization of the company logo) (iv) merging (lowering variations that might arise among the identity of the logo and the representations of the imaginative and prescient. society. and stakeholder); and (v) tricking (measuring the logo's fulfilment approximately all logo additives and their relationships). Ghodeswar (2008) gave a conceptual version for growing manufacturers within side the Indian context and turned them into an advanced way of company branding via new forms of logo designing. The performance includes 4 phases: (i) logo positioning (defining the traits, seen and intangible traits, product features, and logo benefits); (ii) logo message coordination (selecting promotional strategies, trends, personalities, sports, shows, and customers); (iii) logo overall performance distribution (making sure the overall performance of merchandise and services. consumer support, consumer loyalty, and consumer delight); and (iv) logo fairness leveraging (defining line and logo extensions, co-branding, component branding, logo partnerships, and social integration). Three dominant issues have been set up via way of Merrilees and Miller (2008) who focused on company rebounding in place of the release of a newly formulated company logo: (i) the want to revise the logo primarily based totally on a stable consumer understanding; (ii) the usage of internal marketing (or 'inner branding') to make sure the engagement of the applicable stakeholders; and (iii) the position of publicizing.

METHODOLOGY FOR CONCEPTUAL FRAMEWORK

Ravitch and Reegan (2017) provided an in-depth grasp of the conceptual framework. They found that a conceptual framework is a rationale for the study, in which the rationale indicates the coherence of the research questions, data collection and analysis, and application of rigorous techniques to perform the investigation. According to Miles et. al. (2014), the process of developing a visual representation of the conceptual framework provides an expanded look at how variables in research are associated, described, and how data instruments are chosen. Maxwell (2013) stated that the investigator must establish or construct an integrated representation of the topic using personal experience, preceding research, and published theory. Inspired by these prime and important works in defining conceptual framework, the researcher has followed the points highlighted by Miles et.al. (2014) and Maxwell (2013) and constructed the conceptual framework for branding of higher education institutions in Maharashtra, India.

The researcher has worked closely with educational institutions/universities and has shared his valuable insights into the unique challenges they face in a competitive landscape. His collaborations with universities and colleges in his previous work experiences have allowed him to witness firsthand the implementation of branding strategies, including the development of marketing materials, campaigns, and outreach programs. During his tenure, he has gained invaluable insights through engagement with academic administrators, faculty, and students, The work experience and working as a business development and a marketing professional for a universities and institutions and also gathering responses from other marketing professionals has nuanced his understanding of how brand perception influences various stakeholders in higher education. This personal experience instigated the research idea to develop a framework. The researcher suggested a conceptual brand-building model for Higher Education Institutes in Maharashtra, India after examining numerous models or brand-building strategies by prominent authors. The conceptual model developed by the investigator is based on the Brand Model. In Summary, for the proposed Brand Building Strategy Model at Higher Education Institutes, the conceptual structure for the creation of possible products has seven main stages in which it is possible to frame how every management institute can develop the brand. The researcher has also shown in their graphical representation the inter linkages of these seven stages and their variables. The below given are the steps and explanation of the model which the researchers have developed using personal experience, preceding research, and published theory.

Stage 1 - Organizational Commitments

Lately, as a wellspring of the economic upper hand, labeling has steadily become important. Educational organizations strive to take adequate responsibility for the viable enhancement of the brand picture. Marking is increasingly relevant in communication, and a path for every educational institution is to try to recount its story. The brand message is critical because it promises to fulfill the consumer's needs. This promise empowers companies to make their offering or administration unique to the opposition. In this development, we see how once Organizational Purpose, recognizing Vision, and once found goal characterize how its way of life influences brand improvement and incentives between partners.

a) **Organizational Purpose**: Any Management Institute's rationale no longer concerns the question, "What do you do?" The answer is typically made up of a specialty of goods, offerings, and clients, however as a substitute, the solution to the question, "Why is it vital to do the task you do!" which means in the back of the intention, what are the motivating and motivational variables, which needs to be sought through control. It is the motive that determines, through paintings, their dedication to society. To make a profit, organizations exist; however, they nonetheless exist to make a distinction. Individuals could make a distinction through paintings and be a part of a significant legacy (Herbert, 2001). An assertion of rationale must be quick and broad. Please keep it brief and sufficient so people can remember and use it to direct their regular acts. The aim must be comprehensive to permit the business enterprise to alternate through the years to an evolving environment, even though its middle emphasis stays unchanged. Products and offerings may also shift; however, the corporation needs to survive. Living entities which are these organizations are automobiles for enhancing existence and the arena we stay in. (Sosna et.al. 2010).

b) **Identifying Vision:** Brand imagination and prescience are essential to constructing accountable manufacturers as they offer reasonable and steer the corporation's efforts. An appropriate emblem, imaginative and prescient, satisfies the company emblem's present middle values even as making sure that the brand logo is vital to modem instances at an identical time (Wreden, 2007). Higher Education Institutes need to contain the complete business enterprise, now no longer simply senior control, within the formation of the business enterprise to ensure that each person is devoted to its implementation.

A successful emblem, imaginative and prescient, in keeping with (De Chernatony, 2003), includes three components: (i) an appropriate destiny environment; (ii) the objective; and (iii) the principles. These factors are interlinked and self-sustaining.

Concerning the primary of these, the business enterprise must have a view of the destiny global ten years from now, which includes possible discontinuities so that it will bring about upgrades to the arena.

c) **Organizational Objectives:** Once a vision is installed, corporate desires will make their manner through the fulfillment of a control organization so that it will act as quick-time and medium-time period desires. (Witting, 2006). The wishes of a business enterprise will play a chief position in growing organizational rules and figuring out generous resource allocation. Achieving object, a corporation could accomplish the general strategic goals, which can be alleged to be performed at described intervals, and sports must be centered on the more extended period, in preference to truly being a 'spur-of-the-moment' operation centered at making a quick profit. To ensure everyone's range of the business enterprise is devoted to them, particular long-term goals must be installed and revisited throughout the emblem improvement process. (Lee et al., 2015).

d) **Organizational Values** – Corporate values direct how we affect, interact with one another, and cooperate to achieve results. Organizational values are the unseen drivers of our activities, based on our deeply held beliefs that direct decision-making. They are not exempting from the job we do or the tools we use to accomplish our mission; they are the invisible drivers of our actions based on our deeply held convictions that guide decision-making. According to Christer Eldh (2016), the study has revealed three distinct interpretations of the function of core values:
   1. To 'build meaning' (increase or optimize an organization's strategic value to society outside money)
   2. To signal the ethical values that represent an organization
   3. To signal the moral will characterize an organization

   The values guide both the organization's perspective and its actions.

e) **Organizational Culture** – Organizational culture is described as an organization's goals, experiences, ideology, and ideals that bind it together. It is embodied in the organization's self-image, inner workings, relationships with the outside world, and future aspirations. According to Bogdan et al. (2016), the organizational culture of today's higher education institutions is dependent on the ongoing involvement of teachers; and students who want to participate not only to understand their personal and technical skills when progressing in their careers and to harmonize internal and intragroup relationships to strengthen the psychological environment.

Stage 2 - Creating Brand Identity

Brand identification is gathering all factors a control organization utilizes to create and paint its consumer with the right image. Even though those phrases are now and again handled interchangeably, brand identification is one of a kind from "emblem image" and "branding." The first step towards developing effective manufacturers is establishing and upkeep an emblem name (Aaker & Keller, 1990). The emblem identification displays how companies aspire to be regarded, and the reason for emblem identification is to create a consumer-emblem partnership (Sääksjärvi, & Samiee, 2011) Two factors encompass emblem identification: (i) valuable identification; and (ii) increased identification. The first of those, the character of the emblem, is the valuable branding, which incorporates the connections which might be meant to stay unchanged because the logo expands into new markets which goods. The standards and valuable identification of the employer must be in close correspondence. The increased branding offers the 'texture' arid specifics that entire the emblem and serve to demonstrate what it stands for (Aaker, 2002).

The promoting combo will decide their show-off phase, and every component of that mix will assist in outlining the character of their image. We have used feasible 7P's (Program, Product, Price, Location, Promotion, People, Process, and Physical Evidence) to construct and sell Brand Identity. Each Management Institute trying out a combo may be completely customized, and none are identical; however, they may shape them right into a triumphant equation with the aid of using ultimate dependability with emblem estimates and character. (Mallik & Achar, 2020).

Stage 3- Establishing Brand Positioning

The positioning argument can be conveyed as positioning after the brand picture has offered the consumers a fresh opportunity focused on primary rivals. The informative and all-encompassing declaration is an incredible asset for adding core and clarity, presenting tactics, publicizing efforts, and time-limited methods. When used correctly, this announcement will help you settle for clear choices to help differentiate your image, bring in your objective customers, and win a part of the business from your opposition. To put your picture in the psyche of your undergraduate studies, the Higher Education Institutes must, starting from within, hover over their effect, which is the perfect articulation of your status. (Williams, 2013). Furthermore, as everybody is in touch with the customer here and there, everybody should be the best articulation of the role. Brand placement is the way to put your image in the brain of your customers. More than a slogan or an extravagant logo, brand situating is the system used to separate your business from the rest.

To create realistic Brand Positioning, we need a better understanding of the below mentioned, and they are:

a) Target Audience

It is a descriptive overview of the attitudinal and demographic definition of the potential consumer population (students as customers) that aims to cater to and attract the brand we are targeting and expect to be admitted.

b) Competitor Analysis

In what segment does the brand engage once, and in what way does the management institute have a brand that is important to your clients? When you have decided who your rivals are, it is time for an in-depth market study. Business institutes need to examine how competition places their brand to compete. Your analysis can, at its simplest, include the following:

What type of Programs or services do our competitors offer?

1. What are their strengths and weaknesses?
2. What marketing strategies are they using successfully?
3. What is their position in the current market?
   c) Brand Promise

As of late, educational organizations are facing an undeniably serious situation whereby they can discover ways to distinguish their company and cannot recount their narrative. What is the most apparent advantage to your understudies (passionate/sane) that the brand should have & a competitive advantage over your opposition? Building a brand promise depending on intellectual contributions, comprehension of the understudy, or the differentiation of a foundation makes a straightforward idea feasible. Understanding understudy, or the differentiation of a base, renders a genuine viable. The board of directors must understand the need to develop gratitude for what makes them one of a kind. (Judson et.al., 2008).

Nevertheless, while a few colleges can be seen as "extraordinary" brands, most are not. It could also be a direct outcome of how advanced education approaches marking. Marking derives from the inside. So that you know, all individuals from your locale need to put stock in and maintain it. Great brands are those whose key needs to be a part of the fact that they are the network's wishes. It goes from guarantee to the real world when a brand is network-driven.

d) Reason to Believe

A brand is a confirmation of the tremendous feeling and the expectations that prevail in the psyche of any understudy regarding the construction of various administration programs. Marking is associated with creating an enthusiastic alliance. What is the most compelling evidence that the image offers for its image warranty?

After carefully responding to these four questions, it would be before you have your situational interpretation.

Stage 4 – Brand Awareness

Brand knowledge is the possibility of learners getting acquainted with the life and availability of different programs delivered by every higher educational institute. That is the degree to which students equate the bond with a specific service. It is calculated as a niche consumer percentage that has previous brand recognition. Knowledge of the brand requires both brand recognition and brand recall. Brand recognition is increased to the degree to which brand names are chosen, which is easy. Furthermore, easy to pronounce or spell, known as arid expressive, unique, and distinct. (Ullal et al., 2021). A good brand explains to students and other customers what every educational institute does and how it does it, and at the same time, creates trust and reputation. Communicating and building brand awareness can become an automatic identification, and a brand affiliation and a sense of perceived quality among stakeholders will be generated with the right brand contact. We have categorically clarified Brand Awareness, which is a primary factor in recognizing the role of the brand in two pieces, i.e., a mixture of traditional and futuristic methods of creating Brand Awareness through an efficient communication channel.

1. IMC Tools
2. PESO Model

1. Integrated Marketing Communication Tools

Integrated marketing engagement devices allude to the coordination of numerous display resources, such as ads, web-based ads, open link exercises, direct advertising, and crusades to advance products, intending to contact a broader audience with a comparable message. The incorporation of numerous specialist machinery of the brand progresses items and administrations. (Fitri & Herdiansyah, 2021). The associations must negotiate appropriately with the customers to conduct integrated showcase correspondence. We must consider how our end-customers will benefit from our goods or administrations. The more we advance our image correctly, the more interest it will have in the business. Distinguish our expected community of interests. Bear in mind that only some entities would need our commodity (Kushwaha et al., 2020). Unless we have something exceptional and intriguing to give, do we understand why a person would put resources into our image? The advantages of the brand should be imparted viably. A significant type of brand correspondence is:

i. Word-of-Mouth

As Wirtz and Chew (2002) indicated, several investigations have verified a fantastic connection between fulfilled understudies and WOM. At the same time, a few have verified a poor relationship. Per them, this could be clarified through a topsy-turvy U-form connection between customer loyalty and WOM. This well-known shows us that WOM more and more visits while the patron is fulfilled or disappointed. Both Berry (2000) and Wirtz and Chew (2002) declared that due to the fact administrations are greater extreme than merchandise to check earlier than the very last order, the customer is sure to consciousness on a couple of customers' experiences -primarily based totally results.

Grönroos (1995) indicated that a Frame of Reference man or woman who has met the management seems like a more and more targeted statistics wellspring for a likely customer. Therefore, if there is a war between a promotional commercial and WOM, it will forfeit the promotion. WOM's motivating effect is more significant than the correspondence structure. The opportunity that WOM is created through satisfied customers is broadly known (Gremier et al., 2001; Gronroos, 2004).

ii. Publicity

Publicity is relevant when; "A superior organization is seen as a superior organization and its recognition is related to being well established" (Marconi, 2014). When a superior organization is understood as superior, a common misunderstanding is that ads (PR) are equal to exposure. Instead. Publicity is PR alongside advances, network connections, public relations, etc. (Marconi, 2014). Exposure is correlated with data tracking intended for at least one crowd to affect their perceptions or decisions (Marconi, 1999). Mostly, the term exposure is associated with favorable consideration. In any event, (Marconi, 1999) emphasized that it is important to remember that there is indeed such a mind-bending term as terrible exposure. Even though Berry (2000) noted that exposure is largely unregulated, it is influenced and attempted to supervise by approaches (Marconi. 1999; 2014). Exposure is usually modest in contrast to advertising (Marconi. 1999). Exposure is regularly a part of a broader advertising campaign, and it is imperative to coordinate exposure as a segment under certain circumstances. Marconi (1999) claimed that exposure is mostly dealt with in a distinct division from ads, which often carry contradictory signals to the consumer. The showcase and exposure offices must work together and exchange data to keep a strategic distance from this. Marconi (1999) emphasized that it has more legitimacy, and publicity should be regulated as a promotion.

iii. Advertisement and Promotion

Promoting division of curriculum is famously testing. Important hurdles include spending restrictions and appealing to a different audience every year. With the emergence of computerized media platforms, it is becoming even more serious and complicated to show that your educational institution is viable. (Morris & Ogan, 2018). Understudies (and their folks) currently expect online segment systems and proximity from web-based networking media, and candidate enlistment is an all-year action. As advanced networks evolve, their advertisement framework should be re-examined annually by settled instructive providers. Colleges and schools consistently dream about energizing, innovative classes in the world with many informed understudies. For certain qualifications and degrees, the advanced education room is being reclassified by the growth of strategy, conveyance, and employability. That is why advanced education institutions invite creative correspondence and promotional professionals on board to keep their foundations and initiatives transparent and appealing. Interesting promotion methodologies help to bring problems to the light of courses and initiatives when acquiring fresh understudies and materials required to promote online initiatives (Eckel & Kezar, 2003).

Establishments are going beyond the normal flyers, magazines, and boards; and are now pushing assets to talk to the specialized promotional scene that is increasingly evolving. There is an increasingly expanding perceptibility of their software, and they could have more broad scope and prominent ability. The following are five main areas explored by many advanced education foundations to market their ventures innovatively and arrive at a more detailed exhibit of future understudies and other entertainers of advanced education.

2. PESO Model (Futuristic, Influencer, Communication, Strategy)

Gini Dietrich gave the PESO model which means "paying, earned, shared, owned" and fills in to split much of the advancing networks into separate meetings at a brand's trade. Via either of these four core focuses, it helps us to take a gander at our attempts to validate whether there are openings to enter external networks in our current or established operations. (Macnamara et.al., 2016). The model helps one to comprehend and construct the coordinates we are referring to. What the individual channels mean: we should separate:

1. Pay: money exchange for distribution, be it in ad or material
2. Earned: Trading of useful content for a public audience of an existing authority

3. Shared: Enhance the audience's content
4. Owned: To group a crowd that looks for content and then deliver your content to the public.

The certifiable achievement of the PESO model lies in joining the four spread-out channels. We, as a whole, remain to pick up benefits from the PESO model by taking a significant step back and offering the friendly exchange: "How might I achieve my goals utilizing different parts of the PESO model?" For years, the PESO model paradigm has divided paid, earned, shared, and owned media. Some PR and marketing experts are implementing the contact structure to coordinate their attempts to target consumers. In the decision-making process, the PESO Venn diagram gives a holistic view of the multiple networks that impact the buyer behaviors of audiences (Smith, 2020).

Stage 5 – Brand Performance

Brand success refers to a brand's ability to fulfill stakeholder needs. When the aspirations created by promotional practices are incongruent with the constituent truth, the institution's reputation is tarnished, morale is undermined, and the student's frustration can rise, which may contribute to the brand's illusion. Brand success is accomplished in higher education only by delivering the brand's promise (De Vries & Carlson, 2014). Congruence can decide the amount of happiness of the students with what an institution appears to be and what the students currently encounter on campus. Various steps in the success of the brand are (i) quality performance, (ii) performance-related support, (iii) customer care, and (iv) customer delight.

From the viewpoint of the higher education college, with its satisfaction index and organization success dependent on characteristics, brand performance can impact student preference by achieving high standards from stakeholders, which will, in turn, decide the academic institution's performance. Positive brand success increases an educational institution's performance in the following ways:

1. Satisfied learners will implicitly drive entry by word of mouth to spread the institution's prestige.
2. The prestige of universities would increase the involvement of quality students and faculty members.
3. The involvement of professors and high-quality students would increase the institution's academic performance.
4. Good academic success improves the potential for a good selection, allowing quality students to be accepted.

Brand performance may positively or negatively impact the student choice factor and student satisfaction index. In university, Brand performance is measured as student feedback while leaving the course (Singh & Sonnenburg, 2012).

Stage 6 - Brand Audit

A brand audit is a complete evaluation of the general marketplace role of an emblem relative to its opponents and an evaluation of its efficacy. Along with its thaws or contradictions and capacity for alternatives and innovations, this allows you to investigate the energy of your emblem. Brand audit lets the enterprise and the emblem rely upon all modem and capacity purchasers and fulfill their wishes and standards. It facilitates explaining whether or not or now no longer the consumer is unswerving to the company, what the motives function a pulling pressure to make the brand-new clients attain the company, and what moves want to be taken to set up an approach or method to maintain the clients unswerving to the logo withinside the face of hard marketplace rivalry (Keller & Swaminathan, 2019).

Keller (1998) refers back to the logo audit as a "complete evaluation of the fitness of a logo in phrases of its logo fairness shops from the point of view of the enterprise five and the consumer," while Ambler et al. (2002) cope with the want to evaluate the significance of the logo and its members of the family approximately the site withinside the thoughts of the consumer and vulnerability to aggressive attacks. Brand lifestyles cycle literature defines a cycle from the beginning of the logo thru the growth, maturity, decline, and subsequent death or elimination of the logo, with the decline of the logo emblems the shortage of logo salience (Barwise & Meehan, 2004; Lehu, 2006; Jevons et al., 2007).

Keller, (1998) factors out that the 'breadth' of logo popularity consists of difficulty for a deteriorating logo, which means that the logo is regarded in a slender manner and repositioning is probably in order. A brand audit aims to decide how your organization performs in the eyes of your clients. It gives you the following advantages:

1) It lets you assess the existing Higher Education Institute's positioning and prepare corrective strategies
2) It allows you to explore the strengths and shortcomings of the institutions of education
3) Directs you to match your deals more closely with consumer preferences.
4) Helps you to get up to date on your company's expectations (positive or negative)

In certain conditions, a company must review stage 2 (Creating Brand Identity), look introspectively at missed ties and improve if the brand audit appears adverse.

Stage 7 – Developing Brand Equity

Those diagnosed with the aid of Aaker (1991) are the maximum noted dimensions of logo fairness: brand loyalty, brand reputation, perceived consistency, brand associations, and different logo assets (Bravo et al., 2007). In branding literature, that is constantly associated with the maybe is typically regarded component of logo fairness. More regularly than not, logo loyalty is made from an excessive diploma of logo fairness. As loyalty additionally transforms the income stream, a successful manner to address logo price is regularly relied upon (Aaker, 1992). Brand reputation is likewise crucial and may be described because of the diploma to which customers bear in mind the logo at some point in the decision-making system in their purchase. It is extra or much less the consumer's acquaintance with the company. The development in mindset depth for a product and the use of the commodity (Farquhar, 1990) represents logo fairness from the perspective of a real customer (Su & Tong, 2015).

Ivy (2008) had deduced that strong brand value can help create a special place in customers' minds. To convey the generated brand identity to the stakeholders, the conceptual model built by the researcher is centered on the 7Ps of the service marketing mix that helps to construct brand identity (Gajić, 2012). In the eyes of consumers (students, parents, businesses, and society), brand promise and engagement can produce a brand profile. The congruence unity brand pledge and the student's experience would improve the student satisfaction index, which applies to the audited brand that has the potential to increase the academic and placement success of the educational institution. This institution's success will become the solid basis for brand engagement that can be applied to the marketing mix as the 8th phase (Brahmbhatt & Shah, 2017).

Universities must consciously monitor the mechanisms associated with creating their knowledge assets in a broader global higher education context. They recognized the relevance of their intellectual capital in their branding strategies. Other brand trust-building strategies must be considered, such as focusing on the brand promise and growing the brand's perception. Collegiate rating methodologies that make the value propositions of organizations transparent but need to be more precise intensify the challenge of creating an educational brand (Mourad et al., 2011). While academic quality is highly important as organizations seek to create a public identity or picture, quality interpretations may vary.

In conclusion, higher education institutions now need to highlight the importance of their brand in attracting eligible faculty and students at national and international levels, thus improving the country's overall economy. Therefore, higher education has become wider and more central to society and individuals; a framework for measuring and analyzing brand performance indicators must be developed.

Figure 3. Brand building strategy in higher education institutes – proposed framework in building responsible brands

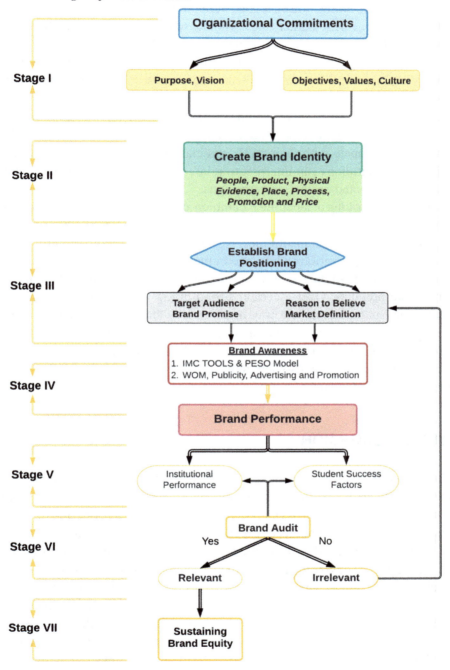

7. CONCLUSION AND FUTURE DISCUSSION

A stable brand's foundation cannot be built on fundamental instinct, shifting inclinations of the business market, and corporate self-advancement. The framework of a trustworthy brand requires efficient arrangement and facilitated operations, not basic advertising, to be successful. In building a known brand, a company may make any character it wants for all intents and purposes and impart the brand in any way it prefers; in any case, this is hasty in building a conscious brand. For the educational brand strategy, there should be a large reach. The study aims to lead to a deeper understanding of branded educational institutions' metrics that help allow institutions to compete with their rivals and clarify the importance of marketing practices that institutions can interpret to reinforce them. It should not be limited only to advertising and promotion campaigns.

Even though marking or labelling is common and exceedingly widespread among higher education institutions, in India, marking criteria is comparatively new in the design of higher education institutions. Nevertheless, the institution must get into marking to build up a serious advantage in the market and make a lasting benefit to the institution due to the rise in competitiveness and loss of freedom in making differentiable products. Over a certain period, a few models have been built by neutral scientists to explain the way organizations should create brands. Nevertheless, these models must explain the influence of labeling on the association in presentation. The different phases of brand-building activities not only form the brand value foundation but also help to upgrade the all-out seat symbol of India's Higher Education standard.

FUTURE DISCUSSION

Simple instincts, shifting consumer tastes, and corporate self-promotion should not be the cornerstone of creating a trustworthy brand. To be effective, it takes strategic preparation and organized behavior, not mere ads, to create a trustworthy brand. A business can establish essentially any branding to create a known brand and express it as it makes, but this needs to be revised to create a trustworthy brand. As Henderson et al. (2003) has observed, advertisements generate a kind of 'fantasy meaning' that outstrips the truth of what they endorse. This is risky in the case of trustworthy brands, but if they want to stay trustworthy, those brands need to be founded on fact. Responsible brands will likely draw more cynical detractors than other brands. Therefore, the internal and external views must be coherent. The brand's reputation would be destroyed if promises were broken, and once destroyed, it is impossible to restore. The implications of betraying customers' trust are equally detrimental in the construction of general products, but not to the same degree as when a company is ostensibly committed to being trustworthy. Building trustworthy brands are also difficult; if it is done well, many advantages can be achieved.

Finally, for business education leaders, higher education institutions' branding has become a significant concern as it communicates about the quality of their transactions, colleges, students, placements, financial resources, and so on. Higher education institutions now face cut-throat competition within and across distinct styles or business education providers. The proper positioning and production of correct branding strategies for Higher education institutions is a must in such a scenario. The right branding strategy could be developed for Higher education institutions by understanding the expectations of its stakeholders.

REFERENCES

Aaker, D. A. (1996). Measuring brand equity across products and markets. *California Management Review*, 38(3), 102–120. DOI: 10.2307/41165845

Aaker, D. A. (2009). *Managing brand equity*. Simon and Schuster.

Aaker, D. A. (2012). *Building strong brands*. Simon and Schuster.

Aaker, D. A., & Joachimsthaler, E. (2000). The brand relationship spectrum: The key to the brand architecture challenge. *California Management Review*, 42(4), 8–23. DOI: 10.1177/000812560004200401

Aaker, D. A., & Keller, K. L. (1990). Consumer evaluations of brand extensions. *Journal of Marketing*, 54(1), 27–41. DOI: 10.1177/002224299005400102

Alford, P., & Duan, Y. (2018). Understanding collaborative innovation from a dynamic capabilities' perspective. *International Journal of Contemporary Hospitality Management*, 30(6), 2396–2416. DOI: 10.1108/IJCHM-08-2016-0426

Ambler, T. (2008). Marketing and the bottom line: assessing marketing performance. In *Performance management* (pp. 137–148). Palgrave Macmillan. DOI: 10.1057/9780230288942_10

Berry, L. L. (2000). Cultivating service brand equity. *Journal of the Academy of Marketing Science*, 28(1), 128–137. DOI: 10.1177/0092070300281012

Brahmbhatt, D., & Shah, J. (2017). Determinants of brand equity from the consumer's perspective: A literature review. *IUP Journal of Brand Management*, 14(4), 33–46.

Bravo, R., Catalán, S., & Pina, J. M. (2019). Analysing teamwork in higher education: An empirical study on the antecedents and consequences of team cohesiveness. *Studies in Higher Education*, 44(7), 1153–1165. DOI: 10.1080/03075079.2017.1420049

Bravo, R., Fraj, E., & Martínez, E. (2007). Intergenerational influences on the dimensions of young customer-based brand equity. *Young Consumers*, 8(1), 58–64. DOI: 10.1108/17473610710733794

Chen, C. T. (2016). The Investigation on Brand Image of University Education and Students' Word-of-Mouth Behavior. *Higher Education Studies*, 6(4), 23–33. DOI: 10.5539/hes.v6n4p23

De Chernatony, L. (2010). *From brand vision to brand evaluation*. Routledge. DOI: 10.4324/9780080966649

De Vries, N. J., & Carlson, J. (2014). Examining the drivers and brand performance implications of customer engagement with brands in the social media environment. *Journal of Brand Management*, 21(6), 495–515. DOI: 10.1057/bm.2014.18

Devece, C., Peris-Ortiz, M., Merigó, J. M., & Fuster, V. (2015). Linking the development of teamwork and communication skills in higher education. *Sustainable Learning in Higher Education: Developing Competencies for the Global Marketplace*, 63-73.

Eckel, P. D., & Kezar, A. J. (2003). *Taking the reins: Institutional transformation in higher education*. Greenwood Publishing Group. DOI: 10.5040/9798216192480

Eldh, C., Rejmer, A., Carlsson, B., & Ryderheim, B. (2016). Core values work in academia, with experiences from Lund University.

Elken, M. (2020). Marketing in higher education. In *The International Encyclopedia of Higher Education Systems and Institutions* (pp. 2032–2037). Springer Netherlands. DOI: 10.1007/978-94-017-8905-9_569

Fitri, U. D., & Herdiansyah, H. (2021). The Influence of IMC Implementation on the Brand Awareness of BLANJA. com. *Jurnal Komunikasi Global*, 10(1), 120–136. DOI: 10.24815/jkg.v10i1.20156

Gajić, J. (2012). Importance of marketing mix in higher education institutions. *The European Journal of Applied Economics*, 9(1), 29–41.

Ghodeswar, B. M. (2008). Building brand identity in competitive markets: A conceptual model. *Journal of Product and Brand Management*, 17(1), 4–12. DOI: 10.1108/10610420810856468

Grönroos, C. (1995). Relationship marketing: The strategy continuum. *Journal of the Academy of Marketing Science*, 23(4), 252–254. DOI: 10.1007/BF02893863

Hamdan, H. A., Andersen, P. H., & De Boer, L. (2021). Stakeholder collaboration in sustainable neighborhood projects—A review and research agenda. *Sustainable Cities and Society*, 68, 102776. DOI: 10.1016/j.scs.2021.102776

Hanson, E. M., & Henry, W. (1992). Strategic marketing for educational systems. *School Organization*, 12(3), 255–267. DOI: 10.1080/0260136920120302

Hanson, E. M., & Henry, W. (1992). Strategic marketing for educational systems. *School Organization*, 12(3), 255–267. DOI: 10.1080/0260136920120302

Harrison-Walker, L. J. (2009). Strategic positioning in higher education. *Academy of Educational Leadership Journal*, 13(1), 103.

Hatch, M. J., & Schultz, M. (2002). The dynamics of organizational identity. *Human Relations*, 55(8), 989–1018. DOI: 10.1177/0018726702055008181

Hemsley-Brown, J., & Oplatka, I. (2006). Universities in a competitive global marketplace: A systematic review of the literature on higher education marketing. *International Journal of Public Sector Management*, 19(4), 316–338. DOI: 10.1108/09513550610669176

Henderson, P. W., Cote, J. A., Leong, S. M., & Schmitt, B. (2003). Building strong brands in Asia: Selecting the visual components of image to maximize brand strength. *International Journal of Research in Marketing*, 20(4), 297–313. DOI: 10.1016/j.ijresmar.2003.03.001

Herbert, D. (2001). Literary places, tourism and the heritage experience. *Annals of Tourism Research*, 28(2), 312–333. DOI: 10.1016/S0160-7383(00)00048-7

Hogan, S., Almquist, E., & Glynn, S. E. (2005). Brand-building: Finding the touchpoints that count. *The Journal of Business Strategy*, 26(2), 11–18. DOI: 10.1108/02756660510586292

Ivy, J. (2008). A new higher education marketing mix: The 7Ps for MBA marketing. *International Journal of Educational Management*, 22(4), 288–299. DOI: 10.1108/09513540810875635

Jevons, C. (2006). Universities: A prime example of branding going wrong. *Journal of Product and Brand Management*, 15(7), 466–467. DOI: 10.1108/10610420610712856

Joachimsthaler, E., & Aaker, D. A. (2009). *Brand leadership: Building assets in an information economy*. Simon and Schuster.

Judson, K. M., Aurand, T. W., Gorchels, L., & Gordon, G. L. (2008). Building a university brand from within: University administrators' perspectives of internal branding. *Services Marketing Quarterly*, 30(1), 54–68. DOI: 10.1080/15332960802467722

Judson, K. M., Gorchels, L., & Aurand, T. W. (2006). Building a university brand from within: A comparison of coaches' perspectives of internal branding. *Journal of Marketing for Higher Education*, 16(1), 97–114. DOI: 10.1300/J050v16n01_05

Kamath, B. (2018). An Empirical Study of the Brand Building of Engineering Institutions in Karnataka: A Strategic Framework (Doctoral dissertation, National Institute of Technology Karnataka, Surathkal).

Kapferer, J. N. (1997). *Strategic brand management: Creating and sustaining brand equity long term*. Kogan Page Publishers.

Keller, K. L. (2013). *Building*. Measuring, and Managing Brand Equity.

Keller, K. L., & Swaminathan, V. (2019). *Strategic brand management: Building, measuring, and managing brand equity*. Pearson.

Keller, K. L., & Swaminathan, V. (2019). *Strategic brand management: Building, measuring, and managing brand equity*. Pearson.

Kotler, P. (2009). *Marketing management: A south Asian perspective*. Pearson Education India.

Kotler, P., & Armstrong, G. (2010). *Principles of marketing*. Pearson education.

Kotler, P., & Fox, K. F. (1995). *Strategic marketing for educational institutions*. Prentice Hall.

Kushwaha, B. P., Singh, R. K., Varghese, N., & Singh, V. N. (2020). Integrating social media and digital media as new elements of integrated marketing communication for creating brand equity. Journal of Content. *Community & Communication*, 11(6), 52–64.

Lee, J. Y., Kozlenkova, I. V., & Palmatier, R. W. (2015). Structural marketing: Using organizational structure to achieve marketing objectives. *Journal of the Academy of Marketing Science*, 43(1), 73–99. DOI: 10.1007/s11747-014-0402-9

Macnamara, J., Lwin, M., Adi, A., & Zerfass, A. (2016). 'PESO' media strategy shifts to 'SOEP': Opportunities and ethical dilemmas. *Public Relations Review*, 42(3), 377–385. DOI: 10.1016/j.pubrev.2016.03.001

Mallik, D. M. A., & Achar, A. (2020). Comparative analysis of 7P's marketing mix in brand building among management institutes-An empirical. *International Journal of Scientific and Technology Research*, 9(3), 6691–6699.

Marconi, J. (1999). *The complete guide to publicity: Maximize visibility for your product, service, or organization*. Contemporary Books.

Marconi, J. (2004). *Public relations: The complete guide*. South-Western Pub.

Marjanović, J., Domazet, I., & Miljković, J. (2023). Higher Education Branding through Instrumental Values. *JWEE*, (3/4), 75–94.

Maxwell, J. A. (2012). *Qualitative research design: An interactive approach*. Sage publications.

Merrilees, B., & Miller, D. (2008). Principles of corporate rebranding. *European Journal of Marketing*, 42(5/6), 537–552. DOI: 10.1108/03090560810862499

Miles, Huberman & Saldaña (2014). Qualitative Data Analysis: A Methods Sourcebook and The Coding Manual for Qualitative Researchers, Thousand Oaks, CA: SAGE, 303 pp.

Moore, J. Ind, N. (Ed.). (2003). Beyond branding. Kogan Page Publishers. pp 104-121

Morris, M., & Ogan, C. (2018). The Internet as mass medium. In The Media, Journalism and Democracy (pp. 389-400). Routledge. DOI: 10.4324/9781315189772-25

Mourad, M., Ennew, C., & Kortam, W. (2011). Brand equity in higher education. *Marketing Intelligence & Planning*, 29(4), 403–420. DOI: 10.1108/02634501111138563

Oliver, R. (2001). Developing e-learning environments that support knowledge construction in higher education. Presented at the *2nd International We-B Conference*, p. 407 – 416. Perth, Western Australia.

Ravitch, S. M., & Riggan, M. (2017). Reason & rigor: How theoretical frameworks guide. *The Qualitative Report*, 21(9), 1708.

Ruoslahti, H. (2018). Co-creation of knowledge for innovation requires multi-stakeholder public relations. In *Public relations and the power of creativity: Strategic opportunities, innovation and critical challenges* (pp. 115–133). Emerald Publishing Limited. DOI: 10.1108/S2398-391420180000003007

Sääksjärvi, M., & Samiee, S. (2011). Relationships among brand identity, brand image and brand preference: Differences between cyber and extension retail brands over time. *Journal of Interactive Marketing*, 25(3), 169–177. DOI: 10.1016/j.intmar.2011.04.002

Schultz, M., & De Chernatony, L. (2002). Introduction: The challenges of corporate branding. *Corporate Reputation Review*, 5(2-3), 105–105. DOI: 10.1057/palgrave.crr.1540168

Singh, S., & Sonnenburg, S. (2012). Brand performances in social media. *Journal of Interactive Marketing*, 26(4), 189–197. DOI: 10.1016/j.intmar.2012.04.001

Smith, D. G. (2024). *Diversity's promise for higher education: Making it work*. JHU Press. DOI: 10.56021/9781421449241

Smith, R. D. (2020). *Strategic planning for public relations*. Routledge. DOI: 10.4324/9781003024071

Solomon, C., Harvey, B., Kahn, K., Lieberman, H., Miller, M. L., Minsky, M., . . . Silverman, B. (2020). History of logo. Proceedings of the ACM on Programming Languages, 4(HOPL), 1-66. DOI: 10.1145/3386329

Sosna, M., Trevinyo-Rodríguez, R. N., & Velamuri, S. R. (2010). Business model innovation through trial-and-error learning: The Naturhouse case. *Long Range Planning*, 43(2-3), 383–407. DOI: 10.1016/j.lrp.2010.02.003

Stachowski, C. A. (2011). Educational marketing: A review and implications for supporting practice in tertiary education. *Educational Management Administration & Leadership*, 39(2), 186–204. DOI: 10.1177/1741143210390056

Steen, J. L. (2020). Branding in Higher Education: How Meaning-Making Efforts Lead to Successful Branding Outcomes that Positively Influence Reputation and a Strong Institutional Culture (Doctoral dissertation, Azusa Pacific University).

Su, J., & Tong, X. (2015). Brand personality and brand equity: Evidence from the sportswear industry. *Journal of Product and Brand Management*, 24(2), 124–133. DOI: 10.1108/JPBM-01-2014-0482

Ullal, M. S., Hawaldar, I. T., Samartha, V., Suhan, M., Padmanabha Achar, A., & Srivastava, D. (2021). How to build a brand: Inside an Indian customers' mind? *Academy of Strategic Management Journal*, ●●●, 20.

Urde, M. (2003). Core value-based corporate brand building. *European Journal of Marketing*, 37(7/8), 1017–1040. DOI: 10.1108/03090560310477645

Wheeler, A. (2017). *Designing brand identity: an essential guide for the whole branding team*. John Wiley & Sons.

Williams, D. A. (2013). *Strategic diversity leadership: Activating change and transformation in higher education*. Stylus Publishing, LLC.

Wirtz, J., & Chew, P. (2002). The effects of incentives, deal proneness, satisfaction and tie strength on word-of-mouth behaviour. *International Journal of Service Industry Management*, 13(2), 141–162. DOI: 10.1108/09564230210425340

Witting, M. (2006). Relations between organizational identity, identification and organizational objectives: An empirical study in municipalities (Master's thesis, University of Twente).

Wreden, N. (2007). *Profit Brand: How to Increase the Profitability Accountability and Sustainability of Brands*. Kogan Page Publishers.

# Section 6
The Ongoing Journey Towards Diversity and Inclusion

Chapter 17
Leveraging Diversity and Inclusion for Enhanced Team Outcomes in Higher Education

Muhammad Usman Tariq
https://orcid.org/0000-0002-7605-3040
Abu Dhabi University, UAE & University College Cork, Ireland

ABSTRACT

This chapter examines the central role of diversity and inclusion in improving team outcomes in higher education. By leveraging the diverse perspectives, experiences, and talents of team members, colleges can foster innovation, promote collaboration, and promote academic excellence. The discussion will address key principles, strategies and practices for realizing the potential of diverse and inclusive teams, including communication, diverse leadership, intercultural competence and equity-focused initiatives. Through an analysis of case studies, best practices, and future trends, the chapter highlights the transformative impact of diverse and inclusive teams on research, teaching, and institutional culture. In addition, it explores the challenges and opportunities associated with building and maintaining diverse teams and the continued importance of diversity and inclusion as drivers of academic excellence in a rapidly changing global environment.

INTRODUCTION

Diversity and incorporation within the setting of cooperation allude to the acknowledgement, appreciation, and compelling utilization of the different characteristics that distinguish people from one another. These characteristics include a wide range of traits, counting but not constrained to race, ethnicity, sex, age, sexual introduction, incapacity status, social foundation, instructive foundation, and individual encounters. Incorporation goes past insignificant representation, centering on making an environment where all group individuals feel esteemed, regarded, and able to contribute completely to the team's victory.

In modern organizational settings, differences and considerations are progressively recognized as basic drivers of advancement, inventiveness, and general execution. Assorted groups bring a huge number of viewpoints, which can lead to stronger problem-solving and decision-making forms. Consideration guarantees that the benefits of differing qualities are realized by cultivating a culture where all members are empowered to share their interesting bits of knowledge and concepts. This comprehensive culture is pivotal for leveraging the complete potential of a differing group because it advances collaboration, decreases the probability of group thinking, and improves group cohesion (Shore et al., 2011).

BACKGROUND

Examination of Important Speculations and Models

A few hypothetical systems and models support the esteem of diversity in group elements, giving experiences into how different teams function and why they frequently beat more homogeneous bunches. These speculations highlight the components through which differences impacts group forms and results.

Social Character Hypothesis and Self-Categorization Hypothesis

Social Personality Hypothesis, created by Tajfel and Turner (1979), states that people determine a critical portion of their personality from the bunches to which they have a place. This hypothesis is closely connected with the Self-Categorization Hypothesis (Turner et al., 1987), which clarifies how people categorize themselves and others into different social bunches. Within the setting of group elements, these hypotheses recommend that group members' discernments and behaviors are affected by their gathered enrollments.

When connected to different groups, the Social Personality Hypothesis highlights the potential for in-group/out-group refinements, where people may favor individuals of their claim social gather and separate against those from different groups. Be that as it may, when overseen successfully, these qualifications can be mitigated through the improvement of a superordinate team personality that includes all individuals, in any case of their personal contrasts. This may cultivate solidarity and collaboration inside the group (Van Knippenberg, De Dreu, & Homan, 2004).

Information/Decision-Making Hypothesis

The Information/Decision-Making Hypothesis emphasizes the cognitive benefits of differing qualities, centering on the assortment of information, perspectives, and abilities that assorted group individuals bring to the table. According to this hypothesis, different groups are more likely to lock in comprehensive data preparation and basic assessment of thoughts, driving more inventive arrangements and higher-quality choices (Williams & O'Reilly, 1998).

For illustration, a group composed of individuals with assorted proficient foundations, such as designing, showcasing, and back, can draw on a broader run of information and encounters when handling complex issues. These differences of thought can lead to more inventive and successful problem-solving techniques as group individuals challenge each other's presumptions and contribute special experiences.

Social Measurements Hypothesis

Geert Hofstede's Social Measurements Hypothesis provides a system for understanding how social contrasts impact group flow. Hofstede distinguished a few measurements of culture, counting independence versus collectivism, control removal, vulnerability evasion, manliness versus femininity, and long-term versus short-term introduction (Hofstede, 1980). These cultural measurements affect communication styles, decision-making processes, and struggle-determination approaches inside groups.

For occurrence, in a multicultural group, individuals from individualistic societies may prioritize individual accomplishments and coordinate communication, whereas those from collectivist societies may emphasize bunch harmony and backhanded communication. Understanding and regarding these social differences can upgrade group cohesion and collaboration as group individuals learn to explore and coordinate different social viewpoints (Taras et al., 2012).

Differing Qualities Climate Demonstrate

The Differing qualities Climate Demonstrate, proposed by Gonzalez and Denisi (2009), centers on the organizational setting and its effect on the adequacy of differing qualities activities. Concurring to this demonstration, the differing qualities climate inside an organization—defined as employees' shared discernments of the organization's diversity-related approaches, hones, and behaviors—plays a vital part in deciding the outcomes of differing qualities endeavors.

A positive differences climate, characterized by an honest-to-goodness commitment to differing qualities and consideration, can improve group execution by creating an environment where all individuals feel esteemed and bolstered. For case, organizations that execute differences preparing programs, build up difference's committees, and advance comprehensive administration are likely to cultivate a more positive differing qualities climate, which in turn can lead to higher levels of team engagement and execution (Gonzalez & Denisi, 2009).

The Categorization-Elaboration Demonstrate (CEM)

The Categorization-Elaboration Demonstrate (CEM), created by Van Knippenberg, De Dreu, and Homan (2004), coordinates viewpoints of social personality and information/decision-making hypotheses to clarify the double effects of differing qualities on group execution. Concurring with the CEM, diversity can lead to both positive and negative results, depending on how it impacts group forms, such as data elaboration and social categorization.

On the one hand, differences can improve data elaboration, as a group of individuals with diverse foundations and points of view lock in intensive talks and basic assessments of thoughts. On the other hand, differing qualities can moreover trigger social categorization forms, driving potential clashes and communication boundaries. The CEM recommends that the key to maximizing the benefits of differing qualities lies in fostering a group environment that empowers open communication, common regard, and collaborative problem-solving (Van Knippenberg et al., 2004).

Viable Suggestions and Illustrations

Understanding these hypothetical establishments has common suggestions for overseeing differences in group settings. By applying these speculations, organizations can create methodologies to upgrade the adequacy of differing groups and relieve potential challenges.

Cultivating a Comprehensive Culture

Creating a comprehensive culture is fundamental for leveraging the benefits of differing qualities. This includes executing policies and hones that advance balance, regard, and collaboration among all group individuals. For this case, Google has built up a comprehensive differing qualities and consideration technique incorporating initiatives such as oblivious inclination preparing, worker asset bunches, and inclusive enlisting hones. These endeavors have contributed to a more comprehensive work environment, where differing points of view are esteemed and coordinated into decision-making forms (Google Differences Yearly Report, 2020).

Advancing Cross-Cultural Understanding

To address social contrasts inside groups, organizations can offer cross-cultural training programs that upgrade employees' social mindfulness and competence. For occasion, IBM offers intercultural competence advancement programs for its worldwide workforce, making a difference in representatives exploring social contrasts and working viably in multicultural groups. Such programs can make strides in communication, reduce misunderstandings, and cultivate a more cohesive and energetic group (IBM et al., 2019; Tariq, 2024).

Empowering Open Communication

Open communication is vital for relieving the negative impacts of social categorization and cultivating data elaboration in assorted groups. Pioneers can advance open communication by making secure spaces for discourse, empowering dynamic tuning in, and valuing diverse perspectives. For illustration, Pixar Movement Studios cultivates a culture of ingenuous input through its "Braintrust" meetings, where group individuals transparently share their ideas and evaluate without fear of judgment. This approach has been instrumental in driving imagination and development inside the company (Catmull, 2014).

Actualizing Comprehensive Authority Practices

Comprehensive administration is key to saddling the potential of assorted groups. Comprehensive pioneers illustrate behaviors such as sympathy, decency, and openness to assorted points of view. They effectively look for out and consider input from all group individuals, creating an environment where everybody feels listened to and esteemed. For case, Microsoft CEO Satya Nadella has emphasized the significance of compassion and consideration in authority, advancing a culture where differing thoughts are empowered and regarded. This comprehensive administration approach has been credited with driving Microsoft's change and victory in later a long time (Nadella, 2017; Tariq, 2024).

Leveraging Assorted Groups for Advancement

Organizations can use differing groups to drive advancement by empowering cross-functional collaboration and different points of view in problem-solving forms. For occasion, Procter & Bet (P&G) encompasses a long history of shaping assorted advancement groups that bring together representatives from diverse capacities, foundations, and regions to handle complex challenges. This approach has led to various breakthrough advancements and item successes as different groups create a more extensive run of ideas and arrangements (Lafley & Charan, 2008).

The hypothetical establishments of differing qualities in group flow highlight the multifaceted benefits and challenges related to different groups. By understanding and applying theories such as the Social Character Hypothesis, Information/Decision-Making Hypothesis, Social Dimensions Theory, the Differences Climate Show, and the Categorization-Elaboration Demonstrate, organizations can create successful procedures to control differences. Cultivating a comprehensive culture, advancing cross-cultural understanding, empowering open communication, actualizing comprehensive authority hones, and leveraging differing groups for development are basic steps towards maximizing the potential of assorted groups. As organizations proceed to grasp differing qualities and considerations, they will be way better situated to explore the complexities of the present-day worldwide commercial center and accomplish maintained victory.

2-BENEFITS OF DIVERSE TEAMS IN HIGHER EDUCATION

Improving Inventiveness, Advancement, and Problem-Solving in Scholastic Groups

Differences in scholastic groups allude to the consideration of people from different foundations, counting diverse races, ethnicities, sexual orientations, ages, social foundations, and scholarly disciplines. This difference brings a riches of viewpoints and encounters to the table, which can essentially improve imagination, development, and problem-solving inside scholarly settings (Tariq, 2024).

One of the essential ways differing qualities improve inventiveness is through the presentation of shifted perspectives. When group individuals come from distinctive foundations, they are likely to approach issues and errands from interesting points. These differing qualities of thought cultivate an environment where inventive arrangements can arise. For this case, a study by Page (2007) found that bunches with assorted individuals beat homogeneous bunches in tackling complex issues since they bring distinctive heuristics and viewpoints to the table. In higher instruction, this may be interpreted as inventive investigative thoughts and educating strategies that might not surface in more homogeneous groups (Tariq, 2024).

Advancement is another range where different scholastic groups exceed expectations. Assorted groups are more likely to challenge the status quo and think outside the box. Usually vital in scholarly settings where pushing the boundaries of information may be a key objective. Concurring to Hong and Page (2004), differing qualities in problem-solving approaches can lead to way better results than homogeneity among high-ability issue solvers. This rule is especially pertinent in intrigue inquiries about groups, where combining mastery from distinctive areas can lead to groundbreaking revelations. For occasion, a group comprising scholars, engineers, and computer researchers can collaborate to create progressed therapeutic innovations that coordinate information from each of their areas (Tariq, 2024).

Problem-solving benefits from differing qualities through the pooling of a wide range of abilities and information bases. Assorted groups can approach issues with a comprehensive toolkit of methodologies and methods, which improves their capacity to discover successful arrangements. An assorted group is additionally way better prepared to anticipate potential issues and address them proactively, much obliged to the changed encounters and experiences of its individuals (Williams & O'Reilly, 1998). In higher instruction, this implies that assorted scholarly groups can handle inquiries about questions more vigorously and create more all-encompassing and viable educational modules (Tariq, 2024).

Effect on Investigate Yield and Instructing Quality

Assorted scholarly groups also have a positive effect on inquiring about output and instructing quality. The collaboration of group individuals with distinctive foundations and expertise can lead to more comprehensive and impactful inquiries. It has appeared that differences in investigative groups lead to higher quotation rates and more prominent acknowledgement in scholastic distributions (Freeman & Huang, 2015). Typically, likely since differing groups can draw on a broader extent of information and techniques, coming about in more careful and imaginative inquiries about discoveries.

For illustration, a study by Freeman and Huang (2015) analyzed over 2.5 million logical papers and found that papers composed by ethnically different groups were more likely to be cited than those composed by homogenous groups. This proposes that the consideration of different points of view not only improves the investigative preparation but also enhances the validity and impact of the inquiry about results.

In areas like social sciences and humanities, where understanding human behavior and societal patterns is vital, differing groups can offer deeper bits of knowledge and more nuanced investigations.

In terms of instructing quality, different scholastic groups contribute to a wealthier learning environment. Understudies have an advantage from introduction to an assortment of perspectives and educating styles, which can improve their basic considering and flexibility. A diverse faculty can moreover serve as part models for understudies from underrepresented backgrounds, promoting greater inclusivity and engagement inside the understudy body. According to Milem (2003), staff differences are related to positive instructive results for understudies; counting made strides in cognitive abilities and more prominent fulfilment with their instructive involvement (Tariq, 2024).

Moreover, assorted education groups can plan and actualize educational programs that are more comprehensive and intelligent in a globalized world. For this case, a history division with workforce individuals from diverse social foundations can offer a more comprehensive and adjusted see of world history, joining points of view that can be neglected in a less different setting. This not only improves students' learning encounters but also plans them to flourish in assorted and multicultural situations (Tariq, 2024).

Assorted scholastic teams also cultivate a more comprehensive scholastic culture, which is basic for pulling in and holding ability. When colleges effectively advance differences and consideration, they end up more alluring to a broader pool of gifted scholastics and understudies. This can improve the institution's notoriety and competitiveness on a worldwide scale. For occasion, the College of California, Berkeley, has executed different activities that have contributed to its notoriety as a driving worldwide inquiries about college. These initiatives include programs aimed at expanding staff differing qualities and back for underrepresented minority students, which have collectively upgraded the institution's scholarly brilliance and advancement capacity (College of California, Berkeley, 2020).

In outline, different scholarly groups offer significant benefits in terms of imagination, advancement, and problem-solving. The varied viewpoints and encounters of group individuals contribute to more comprehensive and inventive investigative results and improve the quality of instruction. Assorted groups are better prepared to handle complex issues and create comprehensive educational programs that reflect a globalized world. Also, advancing differences and consideration inside academic institutions can pull in a broader pool of ability and cultivate a more comprehensive scholarly culture. By grasping differing qualities, higher education can improve their inquiry about yield, quality, and generally scholarly fabulousness.

3-CHALLENGES AND BARRIERS TO INCLUSIVE TEAMWORK

Common Obstacles to Forming and Maintaining Diverse Teams in Academic

In spite of the well-documented benefits of differences in scholastic groups, various challenges and obstructions can block the arrangement and upkeep of comprehensive groups in the scholarly community. These impediments can show in different shapes, counting inclinations, communication obstructions, and social mistaken assumptions.

One noteworthy challenge is the predominance of certain predispositions, which are oblivious states of mind or generalizations that influence understanding, activities, and choices. Verifiable inclinations can impact contracting and advancement hones, regularly driving homogeneity inside scholarly groups. In this case, it has appeared that staff individuals are more likely to favor candidates who share comparable statistical characteristics or scholarly foundations (Tariq, 2024). This will result in a need for differing qualities inside divisions and investigate groups, sustaining existing imbalances.

Another deterrent is the nearness of auxiliary boundaries inside scholarly teaching. These obstructions incorporate biased getting to assets, mentorship, and organizing openings for underrepresented bunches. For occasion, female scholastics and researchers from minority foundations regularly confront more prominent challenges in securing inquiries about subsidizing and distributing their work in prestigious diaries (Ginther et al., 2011). These incongruities can prevent the proficient headway of differing workforce individuals, restricting their representation in senior positions and powerful investigative groups.

Communication boundaries, moreover, pose noteworthy challenges to comprehensive cooperation. Assorted groups frequently include individuals with distinctive communication styles molded by their social foundations and individual encounters. These contrasts can lead to mistaken assumptions, misinterpretations, and clashes. For illustration, coordinate communication, which is esteemed in a few societies, could be seen as angry by people from societies that are inclined toward circuitous communication. Such inconsistencies can make contact and ruin compelling collaboration (Gudykunst, 2003).

Social errors encourage and complicate the flow of assorted scholastic groups. When group individuals come from distinctive social foundations, they may have to change desires with respect to hierarchy, decision-making forms, and strife determination. For example, in a few societies, choices are made collectively, whereas in others, they are ordinarily made by people specialists. Misalignment of these desires can lead to disappointment and wasteful aspects inside the group (Hofstede, 1980).

Techniques to Overcome Predispositions, Communication Obstructions, and Social Errors

To address these challenges and cultivate comprehensive cooperation in the scholarly community, educate and group pioneers can execute a few procedures. These techniques point to relieve inclinations, improve communication, and bridge social contrasts, in this manner making a steadier and more collaborative environment for different groups.

Mindfulness and Preparing Programs

One compelling approach to overcoming understood predispositions is through mindfulness and preparing programs. These programs can offer assistance and help the workforce and staff recognize their claim inclinations and understand how these predispositions affect their choices and intelligence. For illustration, oblivious inclination preparation can raise mindfulness in the inconspicuous ways in which predispositions show and give techniques to check them (Devine et al., 2012). Colleges like Harvard and Stanford have executed such preparation programs to advance inclusivity and value in their contracting and advancement hones.

Tending to auxiliary obstructions requires guaranteeing evenhanded access to assets and openings for all staff individuals. This can be accomplished by executing arrangements that advance straightforwardness and reasonableness in asset allotment. For instance, colleges can set up programs particularly aimed at supporting inquiries by underrepresented researchers. Furthermore, giving mentorship and sponsorship programs can offer assistance to bridge the crevice for those who may need to get to compelling systems. The College of Michigan's Development program, which centers on expanding the representation and victory of ladies and underrepresented minorities in STEM areas, is an illustration of such an activity (College of Michigan Development, 2020).

Comprehensive Communication Hones

To address communication obstructions, groups can embrace comprehensive communication hones that suit assorted styles. This incorporates cultivating an environment where all group individuals feel comfortable communicating their thoughts and concerns. Procedures such as dynamic tuning in, where group individuals mindfully tune in and reflect on what others are saying, can offer assistance to guarantee that everyone's voice is listened to. Moreover, utilizing clear and clear dialects can minimize errors. Providing training on intercultural communication can also prepare group individuals with the aptitudes required to explore and consider distinctive communication styles (Ting-Toomey, 1999).

Social Competence Advancement

Creating social competence is fundamental for overseeing social errors inside differing groups. Social competence includes understanding and appreciating social contrasts and being able to connect viably with individuals from different social foundations. Teachers can offer workshops and courses on social competence to assist the workforce and understudies in creating these abilities. For illustration, the College of California, San Francisco, offers a social competence instruction program that incorporates workshops on understanding social contrasts and cultivating comprehensive situations (UCSF Office of Differences and Outreach, 2021).

Comprehensive Administration

Comprehensive authority is vital for making and keeping up assorted scholastic groups. Comprehensive pioneers effectively look for out and esteem assorted viewpoints, guaranteeing that all group individuals feel regarded and included. They make a secure environment where contrasts are celebrated, and clashes are overseen helpfully. Pioneers can cultivate inclusivity by setting clear desires for aware behavior, empowering collaboration, and being open to criticism. For case, Microsoft CEO Satya Nadella has emphasized the importance of sympathy and inclusivity in authority, which has been instrumental in changing Microsoft's corporate culture (Nadella, 2017).

Organized Decision-Making Forms

Executing organized decision-making forms can offer assistance in relieving the effect of predispositions and social errors. For occurrence, utilizing standardized criteria for assessing candidates amid enlisting or advancement forms can decrease the impact of verifiable inclinations. Similarly, adopting collaborative decision-making systems that include input from all groups of individuals can guarantee that differing viewpoints are considered. Strategies such as consensus-building and voting can facilitate more equitable and comprehensive decision-making (Page, 2007).

In conclusion, whereas different scholastic groups confront a few challenges, counting predispositions, communication boundaries, and social errors, these impediments can be overcome through ponder and vital activities. Mindfulness and preparing programs, impartial get-to-assets, comprehensive communication hones, social competence advancement, comprehensive authority, and organized decision-making forms are viable methodologies for cultivating comprehensive cooperation. By actualizing these methodologies, scholarly education can create situations where assorted groups flourish, eventually upgrading inventiveness, advancement, and scholastic fabulousness.

4-BEST PRACTICES FOR CULTIVATING INCLUSIVE TEAMS

Guidelines for Creating an Inclusive Team Environment

Making a comprehensive group environment that regards and values personal contrasts is basic for cultivating collaboration, advancement, and efficiency. To attain this, groups can follow a few rules:

> **Build up Clear Desires:** Begin by setting clear desires for conscious behavior and inclusivity inside the group. Clearly communicate the team's values and commitment to differences and consideration. For example, ground rules for gatherings should be built that advance dynamic tuning in, shared regard, and appreciation for differing points of view (McIntosh, 1989).
>
> **Advance Mental Security:** Make a secure space where all group individuals feel comfortable communicating their thoughts, suppositions, and concerns without fear of judgment or retaliation. Energize open discourse and useful input. For occasion, Google's Venture Aristotle found that mental safety—where team individuals feel secure to require dangers and be vulnerable—was the foremost basic calculate in deciding group viability (Duhigg, 2016).
>
> **Grasp Differing qualities:** Celebrate and grasp the differences of your group members' foundations, encounters, and viewpoints. Recognize the esteem that each person brings to the group. Energize group individuals to share their interesting bits of knowledge and abilities. For illustration, Airbnb advances differences and having a place through its Worker Asset Bunches (ERGs), which give gatherings for workers to put back and celebrate their different identities and interfaces (Airbnb, n.d.).
>
> **Guarantee Evenhanded Cooperation:** Effectively include all group individuals in decision-making forms and project assignments. Maintain a strategic distance from favoritism or exclusionary hones that will marginalize certain people or bunches. Endeavour for evenhanded dissemination of opportunities and duties. For illustration, turn authority parts and venture assignments to supply everybody with a chance to contribute and develop (Smith et al., 2018).

Cultivate Collaboration: Empower collaboration by making openings for group individuals to work together towards common objectives. Cultivate a culture of participation and shared back. For instance, cross-functional teams or working groups can be built to bring together individuals with differing abilities and viewpoints to handle complex issues (Katzenbach & Smith, 2015).

Give Assets and Support: Guarantee that all group individuals have get to the assets and back they ought to succeed. This may incorporate preparation, mentorship, proficient advancement openings, and housing for person needs. Recognize and address systemic obstructions that will prevent the progression of certain bunches. For case, offer adaptable work courses of action to suit caregivers or people with inabilities (Catalyst, n.d.).

Tips for Comprehensive Leadership Practices

Comprehensive authority hones play a pivotal part in advancing cooperation and value among team individuals. Here are a few tips for comprehensive administration:

Lead by Case: Show comprehensive behavior and attitudes in your intelligence with group individuals. Illustrate sympathy, regard, and openness to assorted points of view. Appear appreciation for commitments from all group members. For occasion, effectively tune in to what others have to be say, approve their encounters, and recognize their endeavors (Goleman, 2000).

Make a Shared Vision: Lock in group individuals within the advancement of a shared vision and objectives that reflect the team's values and goals. Energize input from all group individuals and guarantee that everyone feels proprietorship over the vision. This cultivates a sense of having a place and commitment to common destinations. For example, collaborative visioning sessions can be held where individuals can brainstorm thoughts and express their aspirations for the group (Sinek, 2009).

Provide Back and Advancement: Contribute to the proficient advancement and development of all group individuals, notwithstanding their foundation or position. Offer coaching, mentorship, and learning openings custom fitted to person needs and yearnings. Cultivate a culture of nonstop learning and improvement. For illustration, give get to authority advancement programs, skill-building workshops, and organizing events (Llopis, 2013).

Enable and Designate: Enable group individuals by designating specialist and decision-making duties. Energize independence and initiative. Believe group individuals to require proprietorship of their work and make important commitments. Give direction and bolster as needed, but dodge micromanaging or undermining certainty. For example, delegating errands based on individuals' qualities and interface allows them to exceed expectations in ranges where they have mastery (Pink, 2009).

Address Predisposition and Imbalance: Be watchful approximately recognizing and tending to predisposition and imbalance inside the group. Challenge assumptions and generalizations which will contribute to avoidance or discrimination. Take proactive steps to mitigate the effect of inclination on decision-making forms and group elements. For illustration, execute dazzle enrollment hones to decrease unconscious bias in enlisting or advancement choices (Ely & Meyerson, 2000).

Advance Accountability and Criticism: Hold group individuals accountable for their activities and behaviors, counting adherence to comprehensive standards and values. Give standard criticism on execution and conduct, centering on regions for advancement and development. Make a culture of responsibility where everybody feels capable of upholding inclusivity and tending to any occurrences of separation or inclination. For case, set up instruments for reporting and tending to concern around segregation or badgering in a secure and private way (Deloitte, n.d.).

By taking after these best practices for developing comprehensive groups and embracing comprehensive authority hones, organizations can make situations where all group individuals feel respected, esteemed, and engaged to contribute their best work. Embracing differences and cultivating inclusivity not as it were upgrades group execution and development but moreover advances value and social equity within the work environment.

5-CASE STUDIES: SUCCESSFUL DIVERSE TEAMS IN HIGHER EDUCATION

In higher instruction, assorted groups have ended up progressively recognized for their capacity to create imaginative thoughts, cultivate collaboration, and improve results over different spaces. Real-world illustrations of scholarly groups that have successfully utilized differences offer profitable bits of knowledge into the benefits and challenges of differing qualities in the scholarly community. This talk will investigate two cases of fruitful different groups in higher instruction, in conjunction with the lessons learned and key takeaways from each.

Case Consider 1

MIT Media Lab

The Massachusetts Founded of Innovation (MIT) Media Lab is famous for its intriguing investigative approach, bringing together researchers, researchers, engineers, originators, and specialists from differing foundations to investigate rising innovations and their societal impacts (MIT Media Lab, n.d.). The lab's differing group composition has been instrumental in driving inventiveness, development, and groundbreaking disclosures in areas such as fake insights, computerized media, and biotechnology.

> Key Takeaways:
> Intrigue Collaboration:
> The MIT Media Lab represents the control of intrigue collaboration in driving advancement. By joining experiences from different disciplines, counting computer science, brain research, and plan, the lab has spearheaded groundbreaking innovations and applications that have changed different businesses.
> Social Differences:
> The lab's commitment to social differing qualities and incorporation has enhanced its inquiry about endeavors. By grasping people from different social foundations, the lab cultivates a dynamic mental environment where diverse points of view and concepts are esteemed and regarded.
> Development Biological system:
> The MIT Media Lab serves as an advanced biological system that sustains inventiveness and experimentation. Through its collaborative ventures, workshops, and occasions, the lab energizes group individuals to investigate offbeat thoughts, take dangers, and push the boundaries of information.

Case Consider 2

Stanford Virtual Human Interaction Lab

The Stanford Virtual Human Interaction Lab (VHIL) is at the bleeding edge of investigating virtual reality (VR) and its applications in brain research, instruction, and natural preservation (Stanford VHIL, n.d.). Driven by differing staff individuals with skills in brain research, computer science, and communication, the lab leverages intriguing collaboration to examine the mental and behavioral impacts of immersive virtual encounters.

Key Takeaways:
Cross-Disciplinary Inquire about:
The VHIL illustrates the esteem of cross-disciplinary investigation in progressing information and advancement. By coordination experiences from brain research, computer science, and communication, the lab has spearheaded groundbreaking inquiries about the mental and social impacts of virtual reality.
Instructive Affect:
The lab's investigation has critical suggestions for instruction and learning. By creating immersive VR encounters, the VHIL has investigated inventive approaches to educating and preparing in areas such as healthcare, natural science, and social equity.
Worldwide Engagement:
The VHIL effectively locks in with differing communities to promote global understanding and collaboration. Through its outreach activities and organizations with worldwide organizations, the lab looks for to democratize get to VR innovation and cultivate comprehensive investigate hones.

Lessons Learned

This case ponders, a few key lessons develop with respect to the victory components for assorted groups in higher instruction:

Intrigue Collaboration:
Intrigue collaboration is fundamental for tending to complex challenges and driving development in higher instruction. By bringing together people with assorted abilities and points of view, groups can create novel experiences and arrangements that rise above disciplinary boundaries.
Social Differences:
Social differing qualities enhance the mental environment of scholastic education and cultivate a culture of consideration and regard. Grasping people from assorted social foundations improves inventiveness, basic consideration, and worldwide engagement.
Advancement Biological system:
Making an advanced biological system that supports inventiveness and experimentation is fundamental for cultivating breakthrough disclosures in higher instruction. Scholarly teaching ought to give back for collaborative inquiry about ventures, intrigue activities, and entrepreneurial ventures.

The case considers the MIT Media Lab and Stanford Virtual Human Interaction Lab to outline the transformative effect of differing groups in higher education. By grasping differences, cultivating intrigue and collaboration, and developing biological systems, these groups have accomplished exceptional results in inquiry about instruction and worldwide engagement. The lessons learned from this case give profitable experiences for scholastic educators looking to tackle the control of differences to drive greatness and advancement in higher instruction.

6-LEVERAGING TECHNOLOGY AND DIGITAL TOOLS FOR DIVERSE AND VIRTUAL TEAM COLLABORATION

In today's interconnected world, innovation plays an essential part in empowering collaboration among different groups in any case of topographical or social obstructions. Computerized stages and devices offer openings for consistent communication, information sharing, and extended administration, in this manner upgrading the efficiency and viability of virtual groups. This investigation will dig into the advanced stages and devices that back different virtual group collaborations, as well as the innovation in bridging topographical and social holes among group individuals.

Computerized Stages and Instruments for Group Collaboration

Video Conferencing Stages

Video conferencing stages like Zoom, Microsoft Groups, and Google Meet have become crucial devices for virtual group collaboration. These stages encourage face-to-face communication, permitting group individuals to hold gatherings, introductions, and conceptualizing sessions in genuine time. Highlights such as screen sharing, chat, and breakout rooms improve collaboration and engagement among group individuals (Holladay, 2020).

Collaboration Suites

Collaboration suites like Microsoft Office 365, Google Workspace (once G Suite), and Slack give a centralized stage for communication, record sharing, and venture administration. These suites offer an extent of apparatuses, counting e-mail, moment informing, report collaboration, and errand following, empowering consistent coordination and collaboration among group individuals (Kane, 2021).

Extend Administration Instruments

Extend administration apparatuses such as Trello, Asana, and Jira offer assistance to virtual groups to organize errands, track advance, and oversee due dates viably. These apparatuses offer highlights such as errand sheets, kanban sheets, and Gantt charts, permitting group individuals to imagine extended workflows and designate assets productively. Integration with collaboration suites and communication stages assists in streamlining coordination and communication (Ramesh, 2021).

Virtual Whiteboarding Devices

Virtual whiteboarding devices like Miro, Wall painting, and Lucid spark empower groups to ideate, brainstorm, and visualize thoughts collaboratively. These instruments reproduce the involvement of conventional whiteboards in an advanced environment, permitting group individuals to outline graphs, make intellect maps, and explain reports in genuine time. Virtual whiteboarding cultivates imagination, development, and problem-solving among dispersed groups (Nguyen, 2021).

The Part of Innovation in Bridging Geological and Social Holes

Encouraging Communication

Innovation serves as a bridge for communication among geologically scattered groups of individuals. Video conferencing, moment informing, and mail empower real-time communication, decreasing the obstructions forced by separate time zones. By cultivating customary and straightforward communication, innovation makes a difference in constructing beliefs and compatibility among group individuals in any case of their area (Shockley-Zalabak et al., 2000).

Improving Collaboration

Innovation upgrades collaboration by giving virtual spaces where group individuals can collaborate on ventures, share thoughts, and give criticism. Collaboration suites, extend administration instruments, and virtual whiteboarding stages encourage synchronous and nonconcurrent collaboration, empowering groups to work together consistently over distinctive time zones and social settings (Petersen & Wohlin, 2009).

Advancing Inclusivity

Innovation advances inclusivity by giving a break even with getting to data and assets for all group individuals, in any case of their geological or social foundation. Computerized stages and devices guarantee that everybody incorporates a voice and can take an interest in talks and decision-making forms. By levelling the playing field, innovation cultivates a sense of having a place and strengthening among assorted group individuals (Bolinger & Olivas-Luján, 2017).

Thus, innovation plays a vital part in supporting assorted and virtual group collaboration by giving computerized stages and apparatuses for communication, coordination, and extend administration. Video conferencing stages, collaboration suites, venture administration devices, and virtual whiteboarding stages empower groups to overcome geological and social boundaries and work together successfully in virtual situations. By leveraging innovation, organizations can tackle the collective ability and inventiveness of differing groups, driving more noteworthy advancement, efficiency, and victory in today's globalized world.

7-MEASURING SUCCESS AND IMPACT OF DIVERSE TEAMS

Surveying the adequacy and effect of differing scholarly groups is basic for understanding their commitments to inquire about, educating, and regulating objectives. By recognizing important measurements and markers, education can gauge the execution of different groups and track advances towards differences and consideration destinations. This discourse investigates different measurements and approaches for measuring the victory and effect of different groups in the scholarly world, as well as methodologies for nonstop advancement and supportability of differing qualities and consideration endeavors.

Measurements and Markers for Evaluating Viability

Representation and Socioeconomics

One key metric for evaluating the viability of assorted groups is representation and socioeconomics. This incorporates the following statistical composition of groups in terms of sexual orientation, race, ethnicity, nationality, and other measurements of differing qualities. By comparing the composition of groups to the broader regulation populace or pertinent benchmarks, teachers can distinguish ranges for advancement and guarantee evenhanded representation (Page, 2007).

Maintenance and Whittling Down Rates

Maintenance and steady loss rates give experiences into the inclusivity and fulfillment of assorted group individuals. Tall maintenance rates recommend that the group environment is steady and conducive to career progression for all individuals. Alternately, tall whittling down rates, especially among underrepresented bunches, may demonstrate fundamental issues related to predisposition, separation, or need of bolster (Hewlett et al., 2013).

Inquire about Yield and Effect

Inquiry about yield and effect are imperative pointers of the viability of assorted scholarly groups. Measurements such as distributions, citations, financing, and grants can illustrate the commitments of different groups to the information era and its spread. Educators can track the efficiency and effect of different groups over time and benchmark their execution against inner and outside benchmarks (Ginther et al., 2011).

Instructing and Mentorship Viability

For scholastic groups included in educating and mentorship, adequacy can be measured through understudy results, assessments, and criticism. Tall understudy fulfilment, maintenance, and scholarly execution show the quality of instruction and mentorship given by different groups. Also, following the representation of differing workforce individuals in administration and mentorship parts can evaluate their effect on understudy victory and proficient advancement (Felder & Brent, 2016).

Approaches to Nonstop Enhancement

Data-Informed Choice Making

Nonstop change endeavors ought to be educated by information and proof. Educators can collect and analyze quantitative and subjective information on differing qualities, values, and considerations to distinguish patterns, designs, and regions for change. Normal overviews, center bunches, and climate evaluations can give profitable bits of knowledge into the encounters and recognitions of different groups of individuals (Whirlpool et al., 2014).

Preparing and Proficient Advancement

Giving preparing and proficient advancement openings for workforce, staff, and understudies is fundamental for cultivating a culture of differences and incorporation. Educate can offer workshops, classes, and assets on themes such as oblivious predisposition, intercultural competence, and comprehensive instructional methods. These activities enable people to recognize and address predispositions, advance social competence, and make comprehensive learning and work situations (Devine et al., 2012).

Authority and Responsibility

Compelling authority and responsibility are basic for driving differences and consideration endeavors forward. Regulation pioneers ought to verbalize a clear vision and commitment to differences, values, and considerations and hold themselves and others responsible for advancing towards objectives. Building up differing qualities and incorporating measurements as a portion of execution assessments and key arranging forms fortifies the significance of these endeavors and guarantees responsibility at all levels of the institution (Thomas & Ely, 1996).

Collaboration and Associations

Collaboration and associations with inner and outside partners can open up the effect of differences and consideration activities. By working with the workforce, staff, understudies, graduated classes, community organizations, and industry accomplices, teachers can use collective mastery, assets, and systems to develop differences and consideration objectives. Collaborative activities such as differences in assignment strengths, liking bunches, and community engagement ventures cultivate a sense of shared duty and possession for making comprehensive situations (Page, 2007).

Supportability of Differing Qualities and Incorporation Endeavors

Regulation Commitment

Maintaining differences and incorporation endeavors requires a commitment to long-term regulation. Teachers' ought to implant differences, values, and consideration standards into their mission, vision, values, and key needs. Administration turnover, budget imperatives, and competing needs can pose challenges to maintainability, underscoring the significance of institutionalizing differences and consideration as central regulation values (Milem, 2003).

Social Alter and Organizational Improvement

Feasible alteration requires social change and organizational improvement. Educate ought to cultivate a culture of differing qualities, values, and incorporation that penetrates all viewpoints of the organization, from approaches and hones to standards and behaviors. This includes challenging and changing institutionalized frameworks of inclination, segregation, and prohibition and advancing a culture of having a place, regard, and value for all individuals in the community (Chrobot-Mason & Abramovich, 2013).

Ceaseless Checking and Assessment

Maintainability endeavors ought to be persistently checked, assessed, and balanced based on criticism and results. Teach ought to set up instruments for following advance, evaluating effect, and recognizing regions for enhancement. Standard climate evaluations, value reviews, and differing qualities scorecards can give profitable information and experiences to educate continuous endeavors and guarantee responsibility (Hurtado & Carter, 1997).

Community Engagement and Associations

Locks in the broader community and building organizations with outside partners are fundamental for supporting differences and consideration endeavors. Educate ought to collaborate with the graduated class, benefactors, policymakers, managers, and community organizations to earn bolster, share best hones, and advocate for alter. By mobilizing collective activity and assets, education can make enduring effects and advance differing qualities, values, and considerations past campus borders (Bowen et al., 2009). Measuring the victory and effect of differing groups in the scholarly community requires cautious thought of significant measurements, pointers, and approaches. By surveying representation and maintenance, inquiring about yield, instructing viability, and other components, education can assess the adequacy of different groups and track advances towards differences and incorporation objectives. Nonstop enhancement endeavors, educated by information, preparation, administration, collaboration, and community.

8-FUTURE DIRECTIONS AND EMERGING TRENDS IN DIVERSITY AND INCLUSION WITHIN HIGHER EDUCATION TEAMWORK

As higher instruction proceeds to advance in reaction to worldwide patterns and statistic shifts, the scene of differences and incorporation inside scholastic cooperation is additionally experiencing change. Expected advancements and developing patterns in this region carry critical suggestions for group composition, collaboration, and regulation hones. This talk investigates future bearings and developing patterns in differing qualities and incorporation inside higher instruction cooperation, as well as the suggestions of worldwide patterns and statistic shifts.

Expected Advancements in Differences and Consideration

Intersectionality and Comprehensive Fabulousness

Future endeavors in differing qualities and incorporation inside higher instruction collaboration are likely to center on intersectionality and comprehensive brilliance. Intersectionality recognizes the interconnected nature of social personalities and encounters, such as race, sex, course, sexuality, and incapacity. Teachers will progressively embrace intersectional approaches to address the one-of-a-kind needs and encounters of people with crossing marginalized personalities. Comprehensive brilliance systems will emphasize the integration of differences, values, and incorporation into all viewpoints of organizational culture, arrangements, and hones (Chang et al., 2006).

Differing Authority and Representation

There will be a developing accentuation on advancing differing authority and representation inside scholastic groups and teachers. Educate will prioritize enlisting, holding, and progressing assorted workforce, staff, and chairmen, especially from verifiably underrepresented bunches. Assorted administration upgrades organizational adequacy, advancement, and versatility by bringing differing perspectives, experiences, and abilities to decision-making forms (Smith & Turner, 2015).

Globalization and Intercultural Competence

With expanding globalization and interconnecting, there will be a more noteworthy acknowledgement of the significance of intercultural competence in higher instruction cooperation. Teach will prioritize cultivating intercultural competence among the workforce, staff, and understudies to explore differing social settings, collaborate viably over borders, and address worldwide challenges. Intercultural competence includes abilities such as social mindfulness, communication, sympathy, and versatility, which are fundamental for building comprehensive and collaborative groups in a globalized world (Deardorff, 2006).

Suggestions of Worldwide Patterns and Statistic Shifts

Statistic Differing Qualities and Multiculturalism

Statistical shifts, counting expanding ethnic, racial, and social differences, will essentially affect group composition and collaboration inside higher instruction. Teachers will have to adjust to the changing socioeconomics of understudy populaces, workforce socioeconomics, and workforce socioeconomics by cultivating Multiculturalism and grasping differences as a source of quality and development. Socially responsive instructional methods, comprehensive educational programs, and assorted representation in administration and decision-making parts will end up progressively vital for making comprehensive learning and work situations (Hurtado et al., 2008).

Mechanical Progressions and Virtual Collaboration

Innovative progressions and the multiplication of computerized platforms will shape the long run of collaboration inside higher instruction collaboration. Virtual collaboration instruments, increased reality, counterfeit insights, and immersive innovations will empower groups to collaborate across geological and social boundaries, encouraging worldwide organizations and information trade. Educate will ought to contribute to the framework, preparing and bolstering virtual collaboration to guarantee evenhanded get to and support for all group individuals (Tariq, 2025)

Value and Social Equity

The interest in value and social equity will be central to future endeavors in differing qualities and incorporation inside higher instruction cooperation. Educate will prioritize tending to systemic obstructions, predispositions, and imbalances that perpetuate avoidance and segregation. This incorporates executing evenhanded approaches and hones, advancing anti-racist instructional methods, and progressing social justice-oriented investigation and promotion. By cultivating a culture of value and social equity, teachers can create situations where all group individuals feel esteemed, regarded, and enabled to succeed (Tariq, 2024)

Future headings and rising patterns in differing qualities and incorporation inside higher instruction collaboration reflect broader societal shifts and objectives for alteration. Intersectionality, different administration, intercultural competence, statistics differing qualities, innovative headways, and social equity will shape long-standing time scenes of differing qualities and consideration inside scholastic groups and education. By grasping these patterns and proactively tending to challenges, teachers can cultivate comprehensive, impartial, and imaginative situations where different groups thrive and contribute to the headway of information and society (Tariq, 2024).

CONCLUSION

In summary, the use and inclusion of the diversity of academic groups are necessary to promote academic excellence, innovation, and social development. During this discussion, we explored key principles, strategies, and practices for harnessing the potential of diverse and inclusive teams in higher education.

SUMMARY OF KEY PRINCIPLES AND STRATEGIES INTERSECTIONALITY AND INCLUSIVE EXCELLENCE

Embrace intersectionality and implement comprehensive excellence frameworks that prioritize diversity, equity, and inclusion in all aspects of institutional culture and practices.

Diverse Leadership and Representation: Promote diverse leadership and representation in academic groups by recruiting, retaining, and promoting individuals from historically underrepresented groups.

Globalization and Intercultural Competence: To promote the intercultural competence of faculty, staff, and students in navigating different cultural contexts, collaborating effectively across borders, and responding to global challenges.

Equity and Social Justice: Seek equity and social justice by addressing the systemic barriers, biases, and inequities that perpetuate marginalization and discrimination in higher education.

Data-driven decision-making: Apply data and evidence to decision-making processes, evaluate the effectiveness of diversity and inclusion initiatives, and track progress toward diversity goals.

Training and Professional Development: Provide training and professional development opportunities on topics such as unconscious bias, intercultural competence and inclusive pedagogy to enable people to create inclusive learning and work environments. Collaborations and Partnerships: Foster collaborations and partnerships with internal and external stakeholders to enhance the impact of diversity and inclusion efforts and advance joint action toward common goals.

FINAL THOUGHTS

Diverse and inclusive teams are essential not only to solving complex challenges and promoting innovation in higher education but also to reflect the values of equity, fairness, and social justice that underpin our mission. Academic institutions. By embracing diversity and inclusion, institutions can create environments where all people feel valued and appreciated and can contribute their unique perspectives, talents and experiences to the advancement of knowledge and society. In an increasingly compact and diverse world, the importance of diverse and inclusive teams in promoting academic excellence cannot be overstated. As we anticipate the opportunities and challenges of the future, let us continue to uphold diversity, equity and inclusion as foundational principles that enrich our educational institutions, enhance our research and enable our communities to thrive. Together, we can build a more inclusive, fair and sustainable future for higher education and society.

REFERENCES

Airbnb. (n.d.). *Diversity & Belonging*. Retrieved from https://www.airbnb.com/diversity

Bowen, W. G., Chingos, M. M., & McPherson, M. S. (2009). *Crossing the finish line: Completing college at America's public universities*. Princeton University Press. DOI: 10.1515/9781400831463

Catalyst. (n.d.). *Work-Life Effectiveness*. Retrieved from https://www.catalyst.org/topics/work-life-effectiveness

Catmull, E., & Wallace, A. (2014). *Creativity, Inc.: Overcoming the unseen forces that stand in the way of true inspiration*. Random House.

Chang, M. J., Denson, N., Sáenz, V., & Misa, K. (2006). The educational benefits of sustaining cross-racial interaction among undergraduates. *The Journal of Higher Education*, 77(3), 430–455. DOI: 10.1080/00221546.2006.11778933

Deardorff, D. K. (2006). Identification and assessment of intercultural competence as a student outcome of internationalization. *Journal of Studies in International Education*, 10(3), 241–266. DOI: 10.1177/1028315306287002

Devine, P. G., Forscher, P. S., Austin, A. J., & Cox, W. T. (2012). Long-term reduction in implicit race bias: A prejudice habit-breaking intervention. *Journal of Experimental Social Psychology*, 48(6), 1267–1278. DOI: 10.1016/j.jesp.2012.06.003 PMID: 23524616

Duhigg, C. (2016). What Google learned from its quest to build the perfect team. *The New York Times Magazine*. Retrieved from https://www.nytimes.com/2016/02/28/magazine/what-google-learned-from-its-quest-to-build-the-perfect-team.html

Ely, R. J., & Meyerson, D. E. (2000). Theories of gender in organizations: A new approach to organizational analysis and change. *Research in Organizational Behavior*, 22, 103–151. DOI: 10.1016/S0191-3085(00)22004-2

Felder, R. M., & Brent, R. (2016). *Teaching and learning STEM: A practical guide*. John Wiley & Sons.

Freeman, R. B., & Huang, W. (2015). Collaborating with people like me: Ethnic co-authorship within the US. *Journal of Labor Economics*, 33(S1), S289–S318. DOI: 10.1086/678973

Ginther, D. K., Schaffer, W. T., Schnell, J., Masimore, B., Liu, F., Haak, L. L., & Kington, R. (2011). Race, ethnicity, and NIH research awards. *Science*, 333(6045), 1015–1019. DOI: 10.1126/science.1196783 PMID: 21852498

Goleman, D. (2000). Leadership that gets results. *Harvard Business Review*, 78(2), 78–90.

Gonzalez, J. A., & Denisi, A. S. (2009). Cross-level effects of demography and diversity climate on organizational attachment and firm effectiveness. *Journal of Organizational Behavior*, 30(1), 21–40. DOI: 10.1002/job.498

Google. (2020). *Google Diversity Annual Report*. Retrieved from https://diversity.google/annual-report/

Gudykunst, W. B. (2003). *Cross-cultural and intercultural communication*. Sage Publications.

Hofstede, G. (1980). *Culture's consequences: International differences in work-related values*. Sage Publications.

Hong, L., & Page, S. E. (2004). Groups of diverse problem solvers can outperform groups of high-ability problem solvers. *Proceedings of the National Academy of Sciences of the United States of America*, 101(46), 16385–16389. DOI: 10.1073/pnas.0403723101 PMID: 15534225

Hurtado, S., & Carter, D. F. (1997). Effects of college transition and perceptions of the campus racial climate on Latino college students' sense of belonging. *Sociology of Education*, 70(4), 324–345. DOI: 10.2307/2673270

IBM. (2019). *IBM Diversity & Inclusion Report*. Retrieved from https://www.ibm.com/annualreport/assets/downloads/IBM_2019_Annual_Report.pdf

Katzenbach, J. R., & Smith, D. K. (2015). *The wisdom of teams: Creating the high-performance organization*. Harvard Business Review Press.

Lafley, A. G., & Charan, R. (2008). *The game-changer: How you can drive revenue and profit growth with innovation*. Crown Business.

Llopis, G. (2013). *The innovation mentality: Six strategies to disrupt the status quo and reinvent the way we work*. Entrepreneur Press.

Milem, J. F. (2003). The educational benefits of diversity: Evidence from multiple sectors. In *Compelling interest: Examining the evidence on racial dynamics in higher education* (pp. 126–169). Stanford University Press. DOI: 10.1515/9780804764537-009

MIT Media Lab. (n.d.). *About the Media Lab*. Retrieved from https://www.media.mit.edu/about/

Nadella, S. (2017). *Hit refresh: The quest to rediscover Microsoft's soul and imagine a better future for everyone*. Harper Business.

Page, S. E. (2007). *The Difference: How the Power of Diversity Creates Better Groups, Firms, Schools, and Societies*. Princeton University Press.

Pink, D. H. (2009). *Drive: The Surprising Truth About What Motivates Us*. Riverhead Books.

Shore, L. M., Randel, A. E., Chung, B. G., Dean, M. A., Ehrhart, K. H., & Singh, G. (2011). Inclusion and diversity in work groups: A review and model for future research. *Journal of Management*, 37(4), 1262–1289. DOI: 10.1177/0149206310385943

Sinek, S. (2009). *Start with Why: How Great Leaders Inspire Everyone to Take Action*. Portfolio.

Smith, D. G., & Turner, C. S. V. (2015). *The Radical Transformation of Diversity and Inclusion: The Millennial Influence*. Deloitte University Leadership Center for Inclusion.

Stanford Virtual Human Interaction Lab. (n.d.). Retrieved from https://vhil.stanford.edu/

Taras, V., Kirkman, B. L., & Steel, P. (2010). Examining the impact of culture's consequences: A three-decade, multilevel, meta-analytic review of Hofstede's cultural value dimensions. *The Journal of Applied Psychology*, 95(3), 405–439. DOI: 10.1037/a0018938 PMID: 20476824

Tariq, M. U. (2024). Generative AI in Curriculum Development in Higher Education. In Fields, Z. (Ed.), *Impacts of Generative AI on Creativity in Higher Education* (pp. 227–258). IGI Global., DOI: 10.4018/979-8-3693-2418-9.ch009

Tariq, M. U. (2024). Integrating ESG Principles Into Corporate Governance for Sustainable Ecosystem Services. In Castanho, R. (Ed.), *ESG and Ecosystem Services for Sustainability* (pp. 89–118). IGI Global., DOI: 10.4018/979-8-3693-3771-4.ch004

Tariq, M. U. (2024). Streamlining Operations Insights and Innovations From the Gulf Cooperation Council (GCC). In Ayed, T., Ali, I., Abdelhamid, H., & Mohamed, A. (Eds.), *Utilizing Case Studies in Business Education* (pp. 188–216). IGI Global., DOI: 10.4018/979-8-3693-3779-0.ch010

Tariq, M. U. (2024). Harnessing Persuasive Technologies for Enhanced Learner Engagement and Motivation. In M. Sanmugam, D. Lim, N. Mohd Barkhaya, W. Wan Yahaya, & Z. Khlaif (Eds.), *Power of Persuasive Educational Technologies in Enhancing Learning* (pp. 30-62). IGI Global. https://doi.org/DOI: 10.4018/979-8-3693-6397-3.ch002

Tariq, M. U. (2024). Smart Transportation Systems: Paving the Way for Sustainable Urban Mobility. In Munuhwa, S. (Ed.), *Contemporary Solutions for Sustainable Transportation Practices* (pp. 254–283). IGI Global., DOI: 10.4018/979-8-3693-3755-4.ch010

Tariq, M. U. (2024). Integration of IoMT for Enhanced Healthcare: Sleep Monitoring, Body Movement Detection, and Rehabilitation Evaluation. In Liu, H., Tripathy, R., & Bhattacharya, P. (Eds.), *Clinical Practice and Unmet Challenges in AI-Enhanced Healthcare Systems* (pp. 70–95). IGI Global., DOI: 10.4018/979-8-3693-2703-6.ch004

Tariq, M. U. (2024). Cybersecurity Risk Assessment Models and Theories in the Travel and Tourism Industry. In Thealla, P., Nadda, V., Dadwal, S., Oztosun, L., & Cantafio, G. (Eds.), *Corporate Cybersecurity in the Aviation, Tourism, and Hospitality Sector* (pp. 1–17). IGI Global., DOI: 10.4018/979-8-3693-2715-9.ch001

Tariq, M. U. (2024). Data Breach Incidents and Prevention in the Hospitality Industry. In Thealla, P., Nadda, V., Dadwal, S., Oztosun, L., & Cantafio, G. (Eds.), *Corporate Cybersecurity in the Aviation, Tourism, and Hospitality Sector* (pp. 181–199). IGI Global., DOI: 10.4018/979-8-3693-2715-9.ch010

Tariq, M. U. (2024). Navigating the Personalization Pathway: Implementing Adaptive Learning Technologies in Higher Education. In Minh Tung, T. (Ed.), *Adaptive Learning Technologies for Higher Education* (pp. 265–291). IGI Global., DOI: 10.4018/979-8-3693-3641-0.ch012

Tariq, M. U. (2024). Enhancing Students and Learning Achievement as 21st-Century Skills Through Transdisciplinary Approaches. In Kumar, R., Ong, E., Anggoro, S., & Toh, T. (Eds.), *Transdisciplinary Approaches to Learning Outcomes in Higher Education* (pp. 220–257). IGI Global., DOI: 10.4018/979-8-3693-3699-1.ch007

Tariq, M. U. (2024). The role of AI in skilling, upskilling, and reskilling the workforce. In Doshi, R., Dadhich, M., Poddar, S., & Hiran, K. (Eds.), *Integrating generative AI in education to achieve sustainable development goals* (pp. 421–433). IGI Global., DOI: 10.4018/979-8-3693-2440-0.ch023

Tariq, M. U. (2024). AI-powered language translation for multilingual classrooms. In Doshi, R., Dadhich, M., Poddar, S., & Hiran, K. (Eds.), *Integrating generative AI in education to achieve sustainable development goals* (pp. 29–46). IGI Global., DOI: 10.4018/979-8-3693-2440-0.ch002

Tariq, M. U. (2024). AI and the future of talent management: Transforming recruitment and retention with machine learning. In Christiansen, B., Aziz, M., & O'Keeffe, E. (Eds.), *Global practices on effective talent acquisition and retention* (pp. 1–16). IGI Global., DOI: 10.4018/979-8-3693-1938-3.ch001

Tariq, M. U. (2024). Application of blockchain and Internet of Things (IoT) in modern business. In Sinha, M., Bhandari, A., Priya, S., & Kabiraj, S. (Eds.), *Future of customer engagement through marketing intelligence* (pp. 66–94). IGI Global., DOI: 10.4018/979-8-3693-2367-0.ch004

Tariq, M. U. (2024). The role of AI ethics in cost and complexity reduction. In Tennin, K., Ray, S., & Sorg, J. (Eds.), *Cases on AI ethics in business* (pp. 59–78). IGI Global., DOI: 10.4018/979-8-3693-2643-5.ch004

Tariq, M. U. (2024). Challenges of a metaverse shaping the future of entrepreneurship. In Inder, S., Dawra, S., Tennin, K., & Sharma, S. (Eds.), *New business frontiers in the metaverse* (pp. 155–173). IGI Global., DOI: 10.4018/979-8-3693-2422-6.ch011

Tariq, M. U. (2024). Neurodiversity inclusion and belonging strategies in the workplace. In J. Vázquez de Príncipe (Ed.), *Resilience of multicultural and multigenerational leadership and workplace experience* (pp. 182-201). IGI Global. https://doi.org/DOI: 10.4018/979-8-3693-1802-7.ch009

Tariq, M. U. (2024). AI and IoT in flood forecasting and mitigation: A comprehensive approach. In Ouaissa, M., Ouaissa, M., Boulouard, Z., Iwendi, C., & Krichen, M. (Eds.), *AI and IoT for proactive disaster management* (pp. 26–60). IGI Global., DOI: 10.4018/979-8-3693-3896-4.ch003

Tariq, M. U. (2024). Empowering student entrepreneurs: From idea to execution. In Cantafio, G., & Munna, A. (Eds.), *Empowering students and elevating universities with innovation centers* (pp. 83–111). IGI Global., DOI: 10.4018/979-8-3693-1467-8.ch005

Tariq, M. U. (2024). The transformation of healthcare through AI-driven diagnostics. In Sharma, A., Chanderwal, N., Tyagi, S., Upadhyay, P., & Tyagi, A. (Eds.), *Enhancing medical imaging with emerging technologies* (pp. 250–264). IGI Global., DOI: 10.4018/979-8-3693-5261-8.ch015

Tariq, M. U. (2024). The role of emerging technologies in shaping the global digital government landscape. In Guo, Y. (Ed.), *Emerging developments and technologies in digital government* (pp. 160–180). IGI Global., DOI: 10.4018/979-8-3693-2363-2.ch009

Tariq, M. U. (2024). Equity and inclusion in learning ecosystems. In Al Husseiny, F., & Munna, A. (Eds.), *Preparing students for the future educational paradigm* (pp. 155–176). IGI Global., DOI: 10.4018/979-8-3693-1536-1.ch007

Tariq, M. U. (2024). Empowering educators in the learning ecosystem. In Al Husseiny, F., & Munna, A. (Eds.), *Preparing students for the future educational paradigm* (pp. 232–255). IGI Global., DOI: 10.4018/979-8-3693-1536-1.ch010

Tariq, M. U. (2024). Revolutionizing health data management with blockchain technology: Enhancing security and efficiency in a digital era. In Garcia, M., & de Almeida, R. (Eds.), *Emerging technologies for health literacy and medical practice* (pp. 153–175). IGI Global., DOI: 10.4018/979-8-3693-1214-8.ch008

Tariq, M. U. (2024). Emerging trends and innovations in blockchain-digital twin integration for green investments: A case study perspective. In Jafar, S., Rodriguez, R., Kannan, H., Akhtar, S., & Plugmann, P. (Eds.), *Harnessing blockchain-digital twin fusion for sustainable investments* (pp. 148–175). IGI Global., DOI: 10.4018/979-8-3693-1878-2.ch007

Tariq, M. U. (2024). Emotional intelligence in understanding and influencing consumer behavior. In Musiolik, T., Rodriguez, R., & Kannan, H. (Eds.), *AI impacts in digital consumer behavior* (pp. 56–81). IGI Global., DOI: 10.4018/979-8-3693-1918-5.ch003

Tariq, M. U. (2024). Fintech startups and cryptocurrency in business: Revolutionizing entrepreneurship. In Kankaew, K., Nakpathom, P., Chnitphattana, A., Pitchayadejanant, K., & Kunnapapdeelert, S. (Eds.), *Applying business intelligence and innovation to entrepreneurship* (pp. 106–124). IGI Global., DOI: 10.4018/979-8-3693-1846-1.ch006

Tariq, M. U. (2024). Multidisciplinary service learning in higher education: Concepts, implementation, and impact. In S. Watson (Ed.), *Applications of service learning in higher education* (pp. 1-19). IGI Global. https://doi.org/DOI: 10.4018/979-8-3693-2133-1.ch001

Tariq, M. U. (2024). Enhancing cybersecurity protocols in modern healthcare systems: Strategies and best practices. In Garcia, M., & de Almeida, R. (Eds.), *Transformative approaches to patient literacy and healthcare innovation* (pp. 223–241). IGI Global., DOI: 10.4018/979-8-3693-3661-8.ch011

Tariq, M. U. (2024). Advanced wearable medical devices and their role in transformative remote health monitoring. In Garcia, M., & de Almeida, R. (Eds.), *Transformative approaches to patient literacy and healthcare innovation* (pp. 308–326). IGI Global., DOI: 10.4018/979-8-3693-3661-8.ch015

Tariq, M. U. (2024). Leveraging artificial intelligence for a sustainable and climate-neutral economy in Asia. In Ordóñez de Pablos, P., Almunawar, M., & Anshari, M. (Eds.), *Strengthening sustainable digitalization of Asian economy and society* (pp. 1–21). IGI Global., DOI: 10.4018/979-8-3693-1942-0.ch001

Tariq, M. U. (2024). Metaverse in business and commerce. In Kumar, J., Arora, M., & Erkol Bayram, G. (Eds.), *Exploring the use of metaverse in business and education* (pp. 47–72). IGI Global., DOI: 10.4018/979-8-3693-5868-9.ch004

Tariq, M. U. (2025). Cultivating Cultural Intelligence for the Global Workforce. In Huzooree, G., & Chandan, H. (Eds.), *Revitalizing Student Skills for Workforce Preparation* (pp. 297–332). IGI Global., DOI: 10.4018/979-8-3693-3856-8.ch010

Tariq, M. U. (2025). Vision and Strategy: Steering Modern Enterprises Towards Long-Term Success. In Sedky, A. (Ed.), *Resiliency Strategies for Long-Term Business Success* (pp. 51–78). IGI Global., DOI: 10.4018/979-8-3693-9168-6.ch003

Ting-Toomey, S. (1999). *Communicating Across Cultures*. The Guilford Press.

Turner, J. C., Hogg, M. A., Oakes, P. J., Reicher, S. D., & Wetherell, M. S. (1987). *Rediscovering the Social Group: A Self-Categorization Theory*. Basil Blackwell.

Van Knippenberg, D., De Dreu, C. K. W., & Homan, A. C. (2004). Work group diversity and group performance: An integrative model and research agenda. *The Journal of Applied Psychology*, 89(6), 1008–1022. DOI: 10.1037/0021-9010.89.6.1008 PMID: 15584838

Williams, K. Y., & O'Reilly, C. A. (1998). Demography and diversity in organizations: A review of 40 years of research. *Research in Organizational Behavior*, 20, 77–140.

Compilation of References

Aaker, D. A. (1996). Measuring brand equity across products and markets. *California Management Review*, 38(3), 102–120. DOI: 10.2307/41165845

Aaker, D. A. (2009). *Managing brand equity*. Simon and Schuster.

Aaker, D. A. (2012). *Building strong brands*. Simon and Schuster.

Aaker, D. A., & Joachimsthaler, E. (2000). The brand relationship spectrum: The key to the brand architecture challenge. *California Management Review*, 42(4), 8–23. DOI: 10.1177/000812560004200401

Aaker, D. A., & Keller, K. L. (1990). Consumer evaluations of brand extensions. *Journal of Marketing*, 54(1), 27–41. DOI: 10.1177/002224299005400102

Abdullah Alharbi, M., & Mohammed Hassan Al-Ahdal, A. A. (2024). Communication barriers in the EFL classroom: Is poor listening the culprit that obstructs learning? *Interactive Learning Environments*, 32(2), 772–786. DOI: 10.1080/10494820.2022.2098776

Abedini, A., Abedin, B., & Zowghi, D. (2021). Adult learning in online communities of practice: A systematic review. *British Journal of Educational Technology*, 52(4), 1663–1694. DOI: 10.1111/bjet.13120

Abouchedid, K., & Abdelnour, G. (2015). Faculty research productivity in six Arab countries. *International Review of Education*, 61, 673–690.

Abramo, G., Cicero, T., & D'Angelo, C. A. (2012). A sensitivity analysis of researchers' productivity rankings to the time of citation observation. *Journal of Informetrics*, 6(2), 192–201.

Abramo, G., D'Angelo, A. C., & Murgia, G. (2017). The relationship among research productivity research collaboration, and their determinants. *Journal of Informetrics*, 11(4), 1016–1030. DOI: 10.1016/j.joi.2017.09.007

Abramo, G., & D'Angelo, C. A. (2014). How do you define and measure research productivity? *Scientometrics*, 101, 1129–1144. DOI: 10.1007/s11192-014-1269-8

Abramo, G., D'Angelo, C. A., & Murgia, G. (2014). Variation in research collaboration patterns across academic ranks. *Scientometrics*, 98(3), 2275–2294. DOI: 10.1007/s11192-013-1185-3

Addi, M. M., Alias, N., Harun, F. C., Safri, N. M., & Ramli, N. (2013). *Impact of implementing class response system in electronics engineering courses towards students' engagement in class.* Paper presented at the INTED 2013 Proceedings, Valencia.

Addi, R., O'Brien, D., & Williams, C. (2013). The impact of internships on student learning and career development. *The Journal of Higher Education*, 84(1), 1–15. PMID: 23606758

Adesanya, O. O., & Oluwafemi, V. S. (2021). Users' satisfaction on library resources and service in universities affiliated programmes in federal colleges of education in South-west, Nigeria. *Library Philosophy and Practice (e-journal)*, 5505. https://digitalcommons.unl.edu/libphilprac/5505

Adler, R. B., & Rodman, G. R. (2009). *Understanding human communication* (10th ed.). Oxford University Press.

Adler, S. (Ed.). (2006). *Critical issues in social studies teacher education.* IAP.

Adu-Oppong, A. (2014). Communication In the Workplace: Guidelines for Improving Effectiveness. *Global Journal of Commerce & Management Perspectives.* 208-213.

Aelterman, A., Engels, N., Van Petegem, K., & Verhaeghe, J. P. (2007). The wellbeing of teachers in Flanders: The importance of a supportive school culture. *Educational Studies*, 33(3), 285–297. DOI: 10.1080/03055690701423085

Afdal, H. W., & Spernes, K. (2018). Designing and redesigning research-based teacher education. *Teaching and Teacher Education*, 74(1), 215–228. DOI: 10.1016/j.tate.2018.05.011

Airbnb. (n.d.). *Diversity & Belonging.* Retrieved from https://www.airbnb.com/diversity

Aiston, S. J., & Jung, J. (2015). Women academics and research productivity: An international comparison. *Gender and Education*, 27(3), 205–220. DOI: 10.1080/09540253.2015.1024617

Åkerlind, G. (2008). An academic perspective on research and being a researcher: An integration of the literature. *Studies in Higher Education*, 33, 17–31. DOI: 10.1080/03075070701794775

Akiba, M., Murata, A., Howard, C. C., & Wilkinson, B. (2019). Lesson study design features for supporting collaborative teacher learning. *Teaching and Teacher Education*, 77, 352–365. DOI: 10.1016/j.tate.2018.10.012

Akkilinc, F. (2018). The importance of navigating cultural differences and comprehending cross-cultural communication. *Journal of International Social Research.*, 1(59), 607–613. DOI: 10.17719/jisr.2018.2666

Akoto, M. (2021). Collaborative multimodal writing via Google Docs: Perceptions of French FL learners. *Languages (Basel, Switzerland)*, 6(3), 140. DOI: 10.3390/languages6030140

Akour, M. & Alenezi, M. (2022). Higher education future in the era of digital transformation. Education Sciences. DOI: 10.3390/educsci12110784

Al Rawashdeh, A. Z., Mohammed, E. Y., Al Arab, A. R., Alara, M., Al-Rawashdeh, B., & Al-Rawashdeh, B. (2021). Advantages and disadvantages of using e-learning in university education: Analyzing students' perspectives. *Electronic Journal of e-Learning*, 19(3), 107–117. DOI: 10.34190/ejel.19.3.2168

Alam, A., & Mohanty, A. (2022). Metaverse and Posthuman animated avatars for teaching-learning process: interperception in virtual universe for educational transformation. In *International Conference on Innovations in Intelligent Computing and Communications* (pp. 47-61). Springer, Cham. DOI: 10.1007/978-3-031-23233-6_4

Al-Balas, M., Al-Balas, H. I., Jaber, H. M., Obeidat, K., Al-Balas, H., Aborajooh, E. A., ... & Al-Balas, B. (2020). Distance learning in clinical medical education amid COVID-19 pandemic in Jordan: current situation, challenges, and perspectives. BMC medical education, 20, 1-7. DOI: 10.1186/s12909-020-02257-4

Albert, N. M., Rice, K. L., Waldo, M. J., Bena, J. F., Mayo, A. M., Morrison, S. L., Westlake, C., Ellstrom, K., Powers, J., & Foster, J. (2016). Clinical Nurse specialist roles in conducting research: Changes over 3 years. *Clinical Nurse Specialist CNS*, 30(5), 292–301. DOI: 10.1097/NUR.0000000000000236

AlDahdouh, A., Osorio, A., & Caires, S. (2015). Understanding knowledge network, learning and connectivism. *International journal of instructional technology and distance learning, 12*(10).

Alford, P., & Duan, Y. (2018). Understanding collaborative innovation from a dynamic capabilities' perspective. *International Journal of Contemporary Hospitality Management*, 30(6), 2396–2416. DOI: 10.1108/IJCHM-08-2016-0426

Ali, S., Abuhmed, T., El-Sappagh, S., Muhammad, K., Alonso-Moral, J. M., Confalonieri, R., ... & Herrera, F. (2023). Explainable Artificial Intelligence (XAI): What we know and what is left to attain Trustworthy Artificial Intelligence. Information fusion, 99, 101805. DOI: 10.1016/j.inffus.2023.101805

Ali, A. D. (2021). Using Google Docs to enhance students' collaborative translation and engagement. *Journal of Information Technology Education*, 20, 503–528. Advance online publication. DOI: 10.28945/4888

Alibašić, H. L., Atkinson, C., & Pelcher, J. (2024). The liminal state of academic freedom: Navigating corporatization in higher education. *Discover Education*, 3(1). Advance online publication. https://doi.org/10.1007/s44217-024-00086-x

Allande- Cussó, R., García, J. J., Facundo, J., Navarro, Y., Climent, J.A., Gómez, J. (2022). Salud mental y trastornos mentales en los lugares de trabajo. *Revista Española de Salud Pública*, 96, 1–11.

Alleyne, M. L. (2019). Academic writing in the Caribbean: Attitudes matter. In Milson-Whyte, V., & Oenbring, R. (Eds.), *Creole composition: Academic writing and rhetoric in the Anglophone Caribbean* (pp. 125–154). Parlor Press LLC.

Almansour, S. (2016). The crisis of research and global recognition in Arab universities. *Near and Middle Eastern Journal of Research in Education*, 1. http://dx.doi.org/.DOI: 10.5339/nmejre.2016.1

Almendros, P., Montoya, M., & Pablo-Lerchundi, I. (2021). Flipped classroom and collaborative learning in chemistry. *Educación en la Química*, 32(4), 142–153. DOI: 10.22201/fq.18708404e.2021.5.78412

Alotaibi, F. T. (2020). Saudi women and leadership: Empowering women as leaders in higher education institutions. *Open J Leadersh*, 9(3), 156–177. DOI: 10.4236/ojl.2020.93010

Alpala, L. O., Quiroga-Parra, D. J., Torres, J. C., & Peluffo-Ordóñez, D. H. (2022). Smart factory using virtual reality and online multi-user: Towards a metaverse for experimental frameworks. Applied Sciences, 12(12), 6258. DOI: 10.3390/app12126258

Alshammary, F. M., & Alhalafawy, W. S. (2022). Sustaining enhancement of learning outcomes across digital platforms during the COVID-19 pandemic: A systematic review. *Journal of Positive School Psychology*, 6(9), 2279–2301. http://mail.journalppw.com/index.php/jpsp/article/view/12650/8202

Altebarmakian, M., & Alterman, R. (2019). Cohesion in online environments. *International Journal of Computer-Supported Collaborative Learning*, 14(4), 443–465. DOI: 10.1007/s11412-019-09309-y

Álvarez-Pérez, P. R., González-Benítez, N., & López-Aguilar, D. (2023). Perspectivas y retos de una universidad inclusiva desde un enfoque psicopedagógico. *Revista Costarricense de Orientación*, 2(2), 1–15. Advance online publication. DOI: 10.54413/rco.v2i2.34

Alzahrani, N. M. (2020). Augmented reality: A systematic review of its benefits and challenges in e-learning contexts. Applied Sciences. DOI: 10.3390/app10165660

Amabile, T. M., Fisher, C. M., & Pillemer, J. (2014). IDEO's culture of helping: By making collaborative generosity the norm, the design firm has unleashed its creativity. *Harvard Business Review*.https://hbr.org/2014/01/ideos-culture-of-helping

Amador, J., & Weiland, I. (2015). What preservice teachers and knowledgeable others professionally notice during LS. *Teacher Educator*, 50(2), 1–18. DOI: 10.1080/08878730.2015.1009221

Ambler, T. (2008). Marketing and the bottom line: assessing marketing performance. In *Performance management* (pp. 137–148). Palgrave Macmillan. DOI: 10.1057/9780230288942_10

Amdur, R., & Bankert, A. E. (2011). *Institutional review board: Member handbook* (3rd). Jones & Barlett Publishers.

American Association of University Professors. (n.d.). AAUP unionism. https://www.aaup.org/chapter-organizing/aaup-unionism

Anandarajan, M. (2010). (Ed.). *E-Research collaboration: Theory, techniques and challenges* (1. Aufl.). Springer-Verlag. https://doi.org/DOI: 10.1007/978-3-642-12257-6

Anderson, B. (November 22, 2023). Strategies for successful interdisciplinary collaborations. *Effective Team Dynamics Initiative*.https://etd.gatech.edu/2023/11/22/strategies-for-successful-interdisciplinary-collaborations/

Andrade, C., & Roshay, A. (2023). Using Google Docs for collaborative writing feedback with international students. *The CATESOL Journal*, 34(1), 1–8. http://www.catesoljournal.org/wp-content/uploads/2023/06/CJ34-1_Andrade-Roshay_Formatted.pdf

Andreatta, B. (2018, November 21). Leading with emotional intelligence [Video]. *LinedIn.* https://www.linkedin.com/learning/leading-with-emotional-intelligence-3/lead-with-emotional-intelligence?resume=false&u=43761300

Anggarista, S., & Wahyudin, A. Y. (2022). a Correlational Study of Language Learning Strategies and English Proficiency of University Students At Efl Context. Journal of Arts and Education.

Aprile, K. T., Ellem, P., & Lole, L. (2020). Publish, perish, or pursue? Early career academics' perspectives on demands for research productivity in regional universities. *Higher Education Research & Development*, 40(6), 1131–1145. DOI: 10.1080/07294360.2020.1804334

Arabacı, I. B. (2010). Academic and administration personnel's perceptions of organizational climate (Sample of Educational Faculty of Fırat University). *Procedia: Social and Behavioral Sciences*, 2(2), 4445–4450. DOI: 10.1016/j.sbspro.2010.03.709

Aranzamendez, G., James, D., & Toms, R. (2015). Finding antecedents of psychological safety: A step toward quality improvement. *Nurse Forum, 50* (3), 171-178. DOI: 10.1111/nuf.12084

Arco-Tirado, J. L., Fernández-Martín, F. D., & Hervás-Torres, M. (2020). Evidence-based peer-tutoring program to improve students' performance at the university. *Studies in Higher Education*, 45(11), 2190–2202. DOI: 10.1080/03075079.2019.1597038

Ardito, C., Desolda, G., Lanzilotti, R., Malizia, A., Matera, M., Buono, P., & Piccinno, A. (2020). User-defined semantics for the design of IoT systems enabling smart interactive experiences. Personal and Ubiquitous Computing, 24, 781-796. DOI: 10.1007/s00779-020-01457-5

Arfstom, M. (2014). Flipped learning. Extension of a review of Flipped learning. *International Journal of Scientific Research*, (3), 2–18.

Arias, M. I. B. (2014). Efectos del conocimiento compartido y la seguridad psicológica en la eficacia de los equipos de trabajo. *Criterio Libre*, 12(20), 185–198. DOI: 10.18041/1900-0642/criteriolibre.2014v12n20.232

Arifuddin, A., Lita, W., Catherine, S., & Yingxiang, S. (2023). The influence of leadership style and work motivation on employee performance. *Journal Markcount Finance*, 1(3), 206–215. DOI: 10.55849/jmf.v1i3.116

Armstrong, M. (2009). *Armstrong's Handbook of Human Resource Management Practice* (11th ed.). Kogan Page Limited.

Arnold, S., & Jeglic, E. L. (2024). Stereotypes and unconscious bias in institutional child sexual abuse: Barriers to identification, reporting and prevention. *Child Abuse Review*, 33(2), e2865. Advance online publication. DOI: 10.1002/car.2865

Aronowitz, S. (2008). *Against schooling: For an education that matters*. Routledge., https://doi.org/10.4324/9781315636139-9

Aruleba, K., & Jere, N. (2022). Exploring digital transforming challenges in rural areas of South Africa through a systematic review of empirical studies. *Scientific African*, 16, e01190. Advance online publication. DOI: 10.1016/j.sciaf.2022.e01190

Asad, M. M., Naz, A., Churi, P., & Tahanzadeh, M. M. (2021). Virtual reality as pedagogical tool to enhance experiential learning: a systematic literature review. Education Research International, 2021, 1-17. DOI: 10.1155/2021/7061623

Asana, T. (2024, May 24). *Fiedler's contingency theory: Why leadership isn't uniform*. Asana. https://asana.com/resources/fiedlers-contingency-theory

Asumah, S. N., & Nagel, M. (2024). *Reframing Diversity and Inclusive Leadership: Race*. Gender, and Institutional Change.

Ayo, L., & Frazer, C. (2008). The four constructs of collegiality. *International Journal of Evidence Based Coaching and Mentoring*, 6(1), 57–65.

Aysha, S., Berhannudin, M., Zulida, K., & Sazuliana, S. (2016). The relationship between organizational communication and employees productivity with new dimensions of effective communication flow. *Journal of Business and Social Review in Emerging Economies*, 2(93), 93–100. Advance online publication. DOI: 10.26710/jbsee.v2i2.35

Azizi, T., De Araujo, L. C., Cetecioglu, Z., Clancy, A. J., Feger, M. L., Liran, O., ... & Lund, P. A. (2022). A COST Action on microbial responses to low pH: Developing links and sharing resources across the academic-industrial divide. New Biotechnology, 72, 64-70. DOI: 10.1016/j.nbt.2022.09.002

Baalen, S. V., & Boon, M. (2024). Understanding disciplinary perspectives: A framework to develop skills for interdisciplinary research collaborations of medical experts and engineers. *BMC Medical Education*, 24(1), 1000. Advance online publication. DOI: 10.1186/s12909-024-05913-1 PMID: 39272191

Babbie, E. (2020). *The practice of social research*. Cengage.

Babun, L., Denney, K., Celik, Z. B., McDaniel, P., & Uluagac, A. S. (2021). A survey on IoT platforms: Communication, security, and privacy perspectives. Computer Networks, 192, 108040. DOI: 10.1016/j.comnet.2021.108040

Badshah, S. (2012). Historical study of leadership theories. *Journal of Strategic Human Resource Management*, 1(1), 49–59.

Baker, J., DeLiema, D., Hufnagle, A. S., Carlson, S. M., Sharratt, A., & Ridge, S. W. (2022, September). Impasses in the wild: Autonomy support in naturalistic, parent-child outdoor play. In Frontiers in Education (Vol. 7, p. 885231). Frontiers. DOI: 10.3389/feduc.2022.885231

Baker, T., & Powell, E. E. (2019). Entrepreneurship as a new liberal art. *Small Business Economics*, 52(2), 405–418. https://doi.org/10.1007/s11187-018-0099-0

Ball, D. L., Sleep, L., Boerst, T. A., & Bass, H. (2009). Combining the development of practice and the practice of development in teacher education. *The Elementary School Journal*, 109(5), 458–474. DOI: 10.1086/596996

Bammer, G. (2008). Enhancing research collaborations: Three key challenges. *Research Policy*, 37(5), 875–887. DOI: 10.1016/j.respol.2008.03.004

Baque, P. G. C., Cevallos, M. A. M., Natasha, Z. B. M., & Lino, M. M. B. (2020). The contribution of connectivism in learning by competencies to improve meaningful learning. *International Research Journal of Management. IT and Social Sciences*, 7(6), 1–8.

Baran, B. E., & Woznyj, H. M. (2020). Managing VUCA: The human dynamics of agility. *Organizational Dynamics*, 100787(Aug), DOI: 10.1016/j.orgdyn.2020.100787 PMID: 32843777

Bariso, J. (2018). *EQ applied: The real-world guide to emotional intelligence: How to make emotions work for you, instead of against you*. Borough Hall.

Barkhuizen, G., & Consoli, S. (2021). *Pushing the edge in narrative inquiry* (Vol. 102). Elsevier.

Barkley, E. F., Cross, K. P., & Major, C. H. (2014). *Collaborative learning techniques: A handbook for college faculty*. Stylus Publishing, LLC.

Barnett, S. (2019). Application of Vygotsky's Social Development Theory. *Journal of Education and Practice*, 10(35), 1–4.

Barnlund, D. C. (1970). A transactional model of communication. In Sereno, K. K., & Mortenson, C. D. (Eds.), *Foundations of communication theory* (pp. 83–92). Harper and Row.

Barr, R. B., & Tagg, J. (1995). From teaching to learning - A new paradigm for undergraduate education. Change. *Change*, 27(6), 12–26. DOI: 10.1080/00091383.1995.10544672

Baskin, O., & Bruno, S. J. (1977). A Transactional Systems Model of Communication: Implications for transactional analysis. *Journal of Business Communication*, 15(1), 65–73. DOI: 10.1177/002194367701500106

Bassett-Jones, N. (2005). The paradox of diversity management, creativity and innovation. *Creativity and Innovation Management*, 14(2), 169–175. DOI: 10.1111/j.1467-8691.00337.x

Bauman, Z. (2003). *Modernidad líquida*. Fondo de Cultura Económica.

Baumgartner, D., Bay, M., Lopez-Reyna, N. A., Snowden, P. A., & Maiorano, M. J. (2015). Culturally responsive practice for teacher educators: Eight recommendations. *Multiple Voices for Ethnically Diverse Exceptional Learners*, 15(1), 44–58. DOI: 10.56829/2158-396X.15.1.44

Baviera, T., Baviera-Puig, A., & Escribá-Pérez, C. (2022). Assessing Team Member Effectiveness among higher education students using 180 perspective. *International Journal of Management Education*, 20(3), 100702. DOI: 10.1016/j.ijme.2022.100702

Beck, R., & Harter, J. (2014). Why great managers are so rare. *Gallup Business Journal, 25*.

Beck, S., Bergenholtz, C., Bogers, M., Brasseur, T. M., Conradsen, M. L., Di Marco, D., ... & Xu, S. M. (2022). The Open Innovation in Science research field: a collaborative conceptualisation approach. Industry and Innovation, 29(2), 136-185. DOI: 10.1080/13662716.2020.1792274

Belbin, M. (2013). *Roles de Equipo en el trabajo*. Belbin Spain & Latam.

Bellare, Y., Smith, A., Cochran, K., & Lopez, S. G. (2023). Motivations and barriers for adult learner achievement: Recommendations for institutions of higher education. *Adult Learning*, 34(1), 30–39. DOI: 10.1177/10451595211059574

Bell, S. T., Brown, S. G., & Weiss, J. A. (2018). A conceptual framework for leveraging team composition decisions to build human capital. *Human Resource Management Review*, 28(4), 450–463. DOI: 10.1016/j.hrmr.2017.06.003

Bennett, L. M., & Gadlin, H. (2012). Collaboration and team science: From theory to practice. *Journal of Investigative Medicine*, 60(5), 768–775. DOI: 10.2310/JIM.0b013e318250871d PMID: 22525233

Bényei, R., & Csernoch, M. (2022). PEDAGOGICAL EVALUATION PHASES – LESSON STUDY SURVEY. *Education and New Developments 2022 – Volume I*.https://doi.org/.DOI: 10.36315/2022v1end122

Bergmann, J., & Sams, A. (2012). *Flip your classroom: Reach every student in every class every day*. International society for technology in education.

Berry, L. L. (2000). Cultivating service brand equity. *Journal of the Academy of Marketing Science*, 28(1), 128–137. DOI: 10.1177/0092070300281012

Bhabha, H. K. (1994). *The location of culture*. Routledge.

Bhargava, S., & Sharma, R. (2024). Student engagement through teamwork skills: The mediating role of psychological well-being. *Higher Education, Skills and Work-based Learning*, 14(2), 271–292. DOI: 10.1108/HESWBL-06-2022-0126

Biasutti, M. (2017). A comparative analysis of forums and wikis as tools for online collaborative learning. *Computers & Education*, 111, 158–171. DOI: 10.1016/j.compedu.2017.04.006

Biggam, J. (2011). *Succeeding with your masters dissertation: A step-by-step handbook*. New Open University Press and McGraw Hill.

Bigg, J. (2018). Internships: A valuable learning experience for students. *Journal of Vocational Education and Training*, 70(1), 1–10.

Bigg, M., Brooks, I., Clayton, W., Darwen, J., Gough, G., Hyland, F., & Willmore, C. (2018). Bridging the gap: A case study of a partnership approach to skills development through student engagement in Bristol's Green Capital year. *Higher Education Pedagogies*, 3(1), 417–428. DOI: 10.1080/23752696.2018.1499419

Bjuland, R., & Helgevold, N. (2018). Dialogic processes that enable student teachers' learning about pupil learning in mentoring conversations in a LS field practice. *Teaching and Teacher Education*, 70, 246–254. DOI: 10.1016/j.tate.2017.11.026

Bjuland, R., & Mosvold, R. (2015). LS in teacher education: Learning from a challenging case. *Teaching and Teacher Education*, 52, 83–90. DOI: 10.1016/j.tate.2015.09.005

Bland, C., Center, B. A., Finstad, D. A., Risbey, K. R., & Staples, J. G. (2005). A theoretical, practical, predictive model of faculty and department research productivity. *Academic Medicine*, 80(3), 25–237.

Blau, I., Shamir-Inbal, T., & Avdiel, O. (2020). How does the pedagogical design of a technology-enhanced collaborative academic course promote digital literacies, self-regulation, and perceived learning of students? *The Internet and Higher Education*, 45, 100722. https://doi.org/https://doi.org/10.1016/j.iheduc.2019.100722. DOI: 10.1016/j.iheduc.2019.100722

Blau, P. (1964). *Exchange and power in social life*. Routledge.

Blumberg, P. (2009). *Developing learner-centered teaching: A practical guide for faculty*. Jossey- Bass.

Blumberg, P. (2016). Factors that influence faculty adoption of learning-centered approaches. *Innovative Higher Education*, 41(4), 303–315. DOI: 10.1007/s10755-015-9346-3

Bolick, C., Berson, M., Coutts, C., & Heinecke, W. (2003). Technology applications in social studies teacher education: A survey of social studies methods faculty. *Contemporary Issues in Technology & Teacher Education*, 3(3), 300–309. https://www.learntechlib.org/primary/p/19913/

Bondarchuk, O. I., Balakhtar, V. V., Ushenko, Y. O., Gorova, O. O., Osovska, I. M., Pinchuk, N. I., Yakubovskam, N. O., Balakhtar, K. S., & Moskalov, M. V. (2022). The psychological safety of the educational environment of Ukrainian higher education institutions in a pandemic: Empirical data of a comparative analysis of participants' assessments studying online. In *Proceedings of the 1st Symposium on Advances in Educational Technology*, 1, 14-31. Doi:DOI: 10.5220/0010920100003364

Bonotti, M., & Zech, S. T. (2021). *Understanding Ccvility. Recovering civility during COVID-19*. Palgrave Macmillan., DOI: 10.1007/978-981-33-6706-7

Boston Consulting Group. (17th May of 2018). It's time to Reimagine Diversity, Equity & Inclusion. https://www.bcg.com/press/1june2021-necessary-redefine-the-diversity-policies-equity-and-inclusion-in-companies

Bouchrika, I., Harrati, N., Wanick, V., & Wills, G. (2021). Exploring the impact of gamification on student engagement and involvement with e-learning systems. *Interactive Learning Environments*, 29(8), 1244–1257. DOI: 10.1080/10494820.2019.1623267

Bouckenooghe, D., Zafar, A., & Raja, U. (2015). How ethical leadership shapes employees' job performance: The mediating role of goal congruence and psychological capital. *Journal of Business Ethics*, 129(2), 251–264. DOI: 10.1007/s10551-014-2162-3

Bowen, W. G., Chingos, M. M., & McPherson, M. S. (2009). *Crossing the finish line: Completing college at America's public universities*. Princeton University Press. DOI: 10.1515/9781400831463

Bower, M., & Sturman, D. (2015). What are the educational affordances of wearable technologies? *Computers & Education*, 88, 343–353. DOI: 10.1016/j.compedu.2015.07.013

Bradley, B. H., Postlethwaite, B. E., Klotz, A. C., Hamdani, M. R., & Brown, K. G. (2012). Reaping the benefits of task conflict in teams: The critical role of team psychological safety climate. *The Journal of Applied Psychology*, 97(1), 151–158. DOI: 10.1037/a0024200 PMID: 21728397

Brahmbhatt, D., & Shah, J. (2017). Determinants of brand equity from the consumer's perspective: A literature review. *IUP Journal of Brand Management*, 14(4), 33–46.

Brainard, R., & Watson, L. (2020). Zoom in the classroom: Transforming traditional teaching to incorporate real-time distance learning in a face-to-face graduate physiology course. *The FASEB Journal*, 34(S1), 1. Advance online publication. DOI: 10.1096/fasebj.2020.34.s1.08665

Brandenburger, J., & Janneck, M. (2021). A Teamwork Tool to Support Group Work in Online-based Higher Education: Exploring User Experience and the Use of Support Mechanisms by Students. WEBIST, Brookfield, S. (1985). A critical definition of adult education. *Adult Education Quarterly*, 36(1), 44–49.

Braun, V., & Clarke, V. (2006). Using thematic analysis in psychology. *Qualitative Research in Psychology*, 3(2), 77–101. DOI: 10.1191/1478088706qp063oa

Bravo, R., Catalán, S., & Pina, J. M. (2019). Analysing teamwork in higher education: An empirical study on the antecedents and consequences of team cohesiveness. *Studies in Higher Education*, 44(7), 1153–1165. DOI: 10.1080/03075079.2017.1420049

Bravo, R., Fraj, E., & Martínez, E. (2007). Intergenerational influences on the dimensions of young customer-based brand equity. *Young Consumers*, 8(1), 58–64. DOI: 10.1108/17473610710733794

Brekke, T. S. K. (2015). Engaging publics through social Media: A study of how Netcom and Altibox communicate to create engagement on Facebook. (Publication no. 10852) [Masters dissertation, University of Oslo] University of Oslo e-Repository

Brew, A. (2017). *Research and teaching: Beyond the divide*. Bloomsbury Publishing.

Brew, A., Boud, D., Namgung, S. U., Lucas, L., & Crawford, K. (2016). Research productivity and academics' conceptions of research. *Higher Education*, 71, 681–697. DOI: 10.1007/s10734-015-9930-6

Brewer, E. W., & Holmes, G. A. (2016). Cooperative learning in technology-rich environments. *Journal of Education for Business*, 91(8), 425–431. DOI: 10.1080/08832323.2016.1256264

Bridwell, T. (2022, March 10). Leading with authentic-influence. Tony Bridwell. com. https://www.tonybridwell.com/resources/leading-with-authentic-influence

Briker, R., Walter, F., & Cole, M. S. (2020). The consequences of (not) seeing eye-to-eye about the past: The role of supervisor–team fit in past temporal focus for supervisors' leadership behavior. *Journal of Organizational Behavior*, 41(3), 244–262. DOI: 10.1002/job.2416

Brinn, T., Jones, J. M., & Pendlebury, M. (1998). UK academic accountants: Perceptions of research and publication practices. *The British Accounting Review*, 30(4). Advance online publication. DOI: 10.1006/bare.1998.0074

Brissaud, D., Sakao, T., Riel, A., & Erkoyuncu, J. A. (2022). Designing value-driven solutions: The evolution of industrial product-service systems. CIRP annals. DOI: 10.1016/j.cirp.2022.05.006

Broman, M. M., Finckenberg-Broman, P., & Bird, S. (2024). Cyberspace Outlaws–Coding the Online World. International Journal for the Semiotics of Law-Revue internationale de Sémiotique juridique, 1-31. DOI: 10.1007/s11196-023-10100-4

Brower, H. H., Nicklas, B. J., Nader, M. A., Trost, L. M., & Miller, D. P. (2021). Creating effective academic research teams: Two tools borrowed from business practice. *Journal of Clinical and Translational Science*, 5(1), e74. DOI: 10.1017/cts.2020.553

Bru-Luna, L. M., Martí-Vilar, M., Merino-Soto, C., & Cervera-Santiago, J. L. (2021, December). Emotional intelligence measures: A systematic review. In Healthcare (Vol. 9, No. 12, p. 1696). DOI: 10.3390/healthcare9121696

Bryk, A., & Schneider, B. (2002). *Trust in schools: A core resource for improvement.* Russell Sage Foundation.

Bucic, T., Robinson, L., & Ramburuth, P. (2010). Effects of leadership style on team learning. *Journal of Workplace Learning*, 22(4), 228–248. DOI: 10.1108/13665621011040680

Buerkle, A., Eaton, W., Al-Yacoub, A., Zimmer, M., Kinnell, P., Henshaw, M., ... & Lohse, N. (2023). Towards industrial robots as a service (IRaaS): Flexibility, usability, safety and business models. Robotics and Computer-Integrated Manufacturing, 81, 102484. DOI: 10.1016/j.rcim.2022.102484

Bufton, M. A. (2013). Solidarity by association: *The unionization of faculty, academic librarians and support staff at Carleton University (1973–1976)* [Unpublished master's thesis]. Carleton University.

Buhalis, D., Leung, D., & Lin, M. (2023). Metaverse as a disruptive technology revolutionising tourism management and marketing. Tourism Management. DOI: 10.1016/j.tourman.2023.104724

Bujang, M. A., Omar, E. D., & Baharum, N. A. (2018). A review on sample size d for Cronbach's Alpha test: A simple guide for researchers. *The Malaysian Journal of Medical Sciences : MJMS*, 25(6), 85–99. DOI: 10.21315/mjms2018.25.6.9

Bullock, O., Colon, A. D., Shulman, H., & Dixon, G. (2019). Jargon as a barrier to effective science communication: Evidence from metacognition. *Public Understanding of Science (Bristol, England)*, 28(7), 096366251986568. DOI: 10.1177/0963662519865687 PMID: 31354058

Burkinshaw, P., & White, K. (2017). Fixing the women or fixing universities: Women in HE leadership. *Administrative Sciences*, 7(3), 30. DOI: 10.3390/admsci7030030

Burns, M. (2011). *Distance education for teacher training: Modes, models and methods*. Education Development Center Inc. Scribbr. http://library.uog.edu.gy/eBooks/Distance_Education_for_Teacher_Training_by_Mary_B urns_EDC.pdf

Burris-Melville, T. S. (2020). An investigation into the challenges undergraduate students face in academic writing at a Jamaican University [Doctoral dissertation, Trevecca Nazarene University]. ProQuest Dissertations and Theses Global.

Burris-Melville, T. S., Burris, S. T., & Bledsoe, K. (2024). *Empowering teams in higher education: Strategies for success*. IGI Global., https://doi.org/10.4018/979-8-3693-1520-0

Butcher, J. (2020). *Unheard: The voices of part-time adult learners*. Higher Education Policy Institute.

Butler, M. G., Church, K. S., & Spencer, A. W. (2019). Do, reflect, think, apply: Experiential education in accounting. *Journal of Accounting Education*, 48, 12–21. DOI: 10.1016/j.jaccedu.2019.05.001

Butow, P. & Hoque, E. (2020). Using artificial intelligence to analyse and teach communication in healthcare. The breast. DOI: 10.1016/j.breast.2020.01.008

Buttner, E. H., & Lowe, K. B. (2017). Addressing internal stakeholders' concerns: The interactive effect of perceived pay equity and diversity climate on turnover intentions. *Journal of Business Ethics*, 143(3), 621–633. DOI: 10.1007/s10551-015-2795-x

Cabrera, H., Rodríguez Pérez, B., León González, J. L., & Medina León, A. (2021). Bases y oportunidades de la vinculación universidad-empresa. *Revista Universidad y Sociedad, 13*(1), 300-306. https://rus.ucf.edu.cu/index.php/rus/article/view/1926

Cadet, L. B. & Chainay, H. (2021). How preadolescents and adults remember and experience virtual reality: The role of avatar incarnation, emotion, and sense of presence. International Journal of Child-Computer Interaction. DOI: 10.1016/j.ijcci.2021.100299

Cain, T. R. (2023). Academic union voice and the transformations in/of higher education. In Leišytė, L., Dee, J. R., & van der Meulen, B. J. R. (Eds.), *Research handbook on the transformation of higher education* (pp. 112–126). Edward Elgar Publishing Limited., https://doi.org/10.4337/9781800378216.00015

Cakir, A., Kuyurtar, D., & Balyer, A. (2024). The effects of the publish or perish culture on publications in the field of educational administration in Türkiye. *Social Sciences & Humanities Open*, 9, 100817. https://doi.org/10.1016/j.ssaho.2024.100817

Calderon, O. & Sood, C. (2020). Evaluating learning outcomes of an asynchronous online discussion assignment: a post-priori content analysis. Interactive Learning Environments.

Çali, M., & Gërdoçi, B. (2023). *Research barriers and academic productivity.* The IAFOR International Conference on Education in Hawaii 2023 Official Conference Proceedings. doi:10.22492/issn.2189-1036.2023.33

Camas, F. (2015). La emergencia de la igualdad de género. Cambios y persistencias de las actitudes de las y los jóvenes en España (1994-2010). [Doctoral thesis, Universidad de Granada, Granada, Spain].

Cambridge University Press & Assessment. (n.d.). Inclusion. In *Cambridge Academic Content Dictionary*. Retrieved on August 9, 2024, from https://dictionary.cambridge.org/us/dictionary/english/inclusion#google_vignette

Cameron, K. S., & Quinn, R. E. (2011). *Diagnosing and changing organizational culture:Based on the competing values framework*. Jossey-Bass.

Caminiti, C., Iezzi, E., Ghetti, C., De'Angelis, G., & Ferrari, C. (2015). A method for measuring individual research productivity in hospitals: Development and feasibility. *BMC Health Services Research*, 15, 468. DOI: 10.1186/s12913-015-1130-7

Campbell, J. P., Dunnette, M. D., Lawler, E. E., & Weick, K. E. (1970). *Managerial behaviour, performance and effectiveness*. McGraw Hill., DOI: 10.2307/2521540

Canavesi, A., & Minelli, E. (2022). Servant leadership and employee engagement: A qualitative study. *Employee Responsibilities and Rights Journal*, 34(4), 413–435. DOI: 10.1007/s10672-021-09389-9

Capdeferro, N., & Romero, M. (2012). Are online learners frustrated with collaborative learning experiences? *International Review of Research in Open and Distance Learning*, 13(2), 26–44. DOI: 10.19173/irrodl.v13i2.1127

Caplar, N., Tacchella, S., & Birrer, S. (2017). Quantitative Evaluation of Gender Bias in Astronomical Publications from Citation Counts. *Nature Astronomy*, 1(6), 1–5. DOI: 10.1038/s41550-017-0141

Carless, D. (2022). From teacher transmission of information to student feedback literacy: Activating the learner role in feedback processes. *Active Learning in Higher Education*, 23(2), 143–153. DOI: 10.1177/1469787420945845

Carlisle, J. (2017). The role of internships in developing teamwork skills. *Journal of Career Development*, 44(1), 1–15.

Carlisle, S. K., Gourd, K., Rajkhan, S., & Nitta, K. (2017). Assessing the impact of community-based learning on students: The Community Based Learning Impact Scale (CBLIS). *Journal of Service-Learning in Higher Education*, 6, 1–19.

Carmeli, A., Reiter-Palmon, R., & Ziv, E. (2010). Inclusive leadership and employee involvement in creative tasks in the workplace: The mediating role of psychological safety. *Creativity Research Journal*, 22(3), 250–260. https://doi.org/10.1080/10400419.2010.504654

Carmona, C. E. (2021). *Ámbitos para el aprendizaje: una propuesta interdisciplinar*. Ediciones Octaedro.

Cashman, J., Linehan, P. C., Purcell, L., Rosser, M., Schultz, S., & Skalski, S. (2014). *Leading by convening: A blueprint for authentic engagement*. Idea Partnership. https://eric.ed.gov/?id=ED584148

Castleberry, A., & Nolen, A. C. (2018). Thematic analysis of qualitative research data: Is it as easy as it sounds? *Currents in Pharmacy Teaching & Learning*, 10(6), 807–815. DOI: 10.1016/j.cptl.2018.03.019 PMID: 30025784

Catalyst. (n.d.). *Work-Life Effectiveness*. Retrieved from https://www.catalyst.org/topics/work-life-effectiveness

Catmull, E., & Wallace, A. (2014). *Creativity, Inc.: Overcoming the unseen forces that stand in the way of true inspiration*. Random House.

Chance, N. L. (2022). Resilient leadership: A phenomenological exploration into how Black women in higher education leadership navigate cultural adversity. *Journal of Humanistic Psychology*, 62(1), 44–78. DOI: 10.1177/00221678211003000

Chang, H. (2016). *Autoethnography as Method* (Vol. 1). Routledge. DOI: 10.4324/9781315433370

Chang, M. J., Denson, N., Sáenz, V., & Misa, K. (2006). The educational benefits of sustaining cross-racial interaction among undergraduates. *The Journal of Higher Education*, 77(3), 430–455. DOI: 10.1080/00221546.2006.11778933

Chan, S. C. H., & Mak, W. (2014). The impact of servant leadership and subordinates' organisational tenure on trust in leader and attitudes. *Personnel Review*, 43(2), 272–287. DOI: 10.1108/PR-08-2011-0125

Charmaz, K., & Belgrave, L. L. (2015). Grounded theory. In Ed. (G. Ritzer), *The Blackwell encyclopedia of sociology*. Hoboken: Wiley Online Library. beosg070. pub2DOI: 10.1002/9781405165518.wbeosg070.pub2

Chaubey, A., & Bhattacharya, B. (2015). Learning management system in higher education. *International Journal of Science Technology & Engineering*, 2(3), 158–162.

Chen, C. T. (2016). The Investigation on Brand Image of University Education and Students' Word-of-Mouth Behavior. *Higher Education Studies*, 6(4), 23–33. DOI: 10.5539/hes.v6n4p23

Chen, C., Liao, J., & Wen, P. (2014). Why does formal mentoring matter? The mediating role of psychological safety and the moderating role of power distance orientation in the Chinese context. *International Journal of Human Resource Management*, 25(8), 1112–1130. DOI: 10.1080/09585192.2013.816861

Cheng, E. C. (2020). Knowledge management strategies for sustaining Lesson Study. *International Journal for Lesson and Learning Studies*, 9(2), 167–178. DOI: 10.1108/IJLLS-10-2019-0070

Chen, H., Zhang, Y., Jin, Q., & Wang, X. (2022, August). Exploring Patterns of Academic-Industrial Collaboration for Digital Transformation Research: A Bibliometric-Enhanced Topic Modeling Method. In *2022 Portland International Conference on Management of Engineering and Technology (PICMET)* (pp. 1-9). IEEE. DOI: 10.23919/PICMET53225.2022.9882847

Chen, J. C. C., & Kent, S. (2020). Task engagement, learner motivation and avatar identities of struggling English language learners in the 3D virtual world. *System*, 88, 102168. Advance online publication. DOI: 10.1016/j.system.2019.102168

Cherkowski, S., Kutsyuruba, B., Walker, K., & Crawford, M. (2021). Conceptualising leadership and emotions in higher education: Well-being as wholeness. *Journal of Educational Administration and History*, 53(2), 158–171. DOI: 10.1080/00220620.2020.1828315

Cheslock, J. J., & Jaquette, O. (2021). Concentrated or fragmented? The U.S. market for online higher education. *Research in Higher Education*, 63(1), 33–59. https://doi.org/10.1007/s11162-021-09639-7

Cheung, W. M., & Wong, W. Y. (2014). Does LS work? *International Journal for Lesson and Learning Studies.*, 3(2), 137–149. DOI: 10.1108/IJLLS-05-2013-0024

Chiang, F. K., Tang, Z., Zhu, D., & Bao, X. (2024). Gender disparity in STEM education: A survey research on girl participants in World Robot Olympiad. *International Journal of Technology and Design Education*, 34(2), 629–646. DOI: 10.1007/s10798-023-09830-0 PMID: 37359821

Chiang, J. T. J., Chen, X. P., Liu, H., Akutsu, S., & Wang, Z. (2021). We have emotions but can't show them! Authoritarian leadership, emotion suppression climate, and team performance. *Human Relations*, 74(7), 1082–1111. DOI: 10.1177/0018726720908649

Chinchilla, N., & Cruz, H. (2016). Diversidad y paradigmas de empresa: Un nuevo enfoque. *Revista Empresa y Humanismo*, 14(1), 47–79. DOI: 10.15581/015.14.4259

Chiong, R., & Jovanovic, J. (2012). Collaborative learning in online study groups: An evolutionary game theory perspective. *Journal of Information Technology Education*, 11(1), 81–101. https://www.learntechlib.org/p/111494/. DOI: 10.28945/1574

Chiu, C. Y. C., Owens, B. P., & Tesluk, P. E. (2016). Initiating and utilising shared leadership in teams: The role of leader humility, team proactive personality and team performance capability. *The Journal of Applied Psychology*, 101(12), 1705–1720. DOI: 10.1037/apl0000159 PMID: 27618409

Chong, J. S. Y., Han, S. H., Abdullah, N. A., Chong, M. S. F., Widjaja, W., & Shahrill, M. (2017). Utilizing LS in improving year 12 students' learning and performance in mathematics. *Mathematics Education Trends and Research*, 2017(1), 1–8. DOI: 10.5899/2017/metr-00095

Clark, L. (2020). Leadership imperatives for success: Cultivating trust. https://www.harvardbusiness.org/leadership-imperatives-for-success-cultivating-trust-2-of-3/

Clarke, C., Daynauth, R., Wilkinson, C., Devonish, H., & Mars, J. (2024). Guylingo: The Republic of Guyana Creole corpora. arXiv preprint arXiv:2405.03832. https://doi.org//arXiv.2405.03832 DOI: 10.18653/v1/2024.naacl-short.70

Clark, T. R. (2020). *The 4 stages of psychological safety: Defining the path to inclusion and innovation.* Berrett-Koehler Publishers, Inc.

Coco, C. M. (2011). Emotional intelligence in higher education: Strategic implications for academic leaders. *Journal of Higher Education Theory and Practice*, 11(2), 112–117.

Coenders, F., & Verhoef, N. (2019). LS: Professional development (PD) for beginning and experienced teachers. *Professional Development in Education*, 45(2), 217–230. DOI: 10.1080/19415257.2018.1430050

Cohen, L., Manion, L., & Morrison, K. (2007). *Observation. Research methods in education*. Routledge. Scribbr. https://www.researchgate.net/

Coleman, B. (2023). Hello avatar: rise of the networked generation.

Collins's Black Feminist Thought. (2015). Patricia Hill Collins's *Black Feminist Thought: Knowledge, Consciousness and the Politics of Empowerment. Ethnic and Racial Studies*, 38(13), 2314–2314. https://doi.org/. DOI: 10.1080/01419870.2015.1058515

Confucius' three keys to successful leadership. (2013, June 19). Forbes. https://www.forbes.com/2009/05/21/confucius-tips-wisdom-leadership-managing-philosophy.html

Conklin, M. H., & Desselle, S. P. (2006). *Development and construct validation of a scale to measure a pharmacy academician's job satisfaction.* Paper presented at the American Association of Colleges of Pharmacy Annual Conference, San Diego, Calif.

Connelly, F. M., & Clandinin, D. J. (1990). Stories of experience and narrative inquiry. *Educational Researcher*, 19(5), 2–14. DOI: 10.3102/0013189X019005002

Connelly, F. M., & Clandinin, D. J. (2013). *Narrative inquiry: Research for understanding*. Teachers College Press.

Connolly, B. (2008). *Adult learning in groups* (1st ed.). Open University Press.

Cook, A., Keyte, R., Sprawson, I., Matharu, A., & Mantzios, M. (2022). Mental health first aid experiences: A qualitative investigation into the emotional impact of mental health first aid responsibilities. Doi: DOI: 10.21203/rs.3.rs-1393314/v1

Cornell, B. (2004). Compensation and recruiting: Private universities versus private corporations. *Journal of Corporate Finance*, 10(1), 37–52. https://doi.org/10.1016/S0929-1199(02)00025-1

Cote, C. (28th of March, 2024). How to build a psychologically safe workplace. https://online.hbs.edu/blog/post/psychological-safety-in-the-workplace

Cox, T., Griffiths, A. J., & Rial-González, E. (2000). *Research on work-related stress*. Agencia Europea para la Seguridad y la Salud en el Trabajo. Oficina de Publicaciones Oficiales de las Comunidades Europeas. http://agency.osha.eu.int/publications/reports/stress

Creed, A. (2023). Empowering change: Psychological safety in higher education project teams. Available at https://www.linkedin.com/pulse/fostering-psychological-safety-university-learning-creed-ph-d-7zbrc/ accessed 23 March 2024

Creswell, J. W. (2013). *Research Design Qualitative, Quantitative, and Mixed Method Approaches* (4th ed.). SAGE Publications.

Creswell, J. W. (2015). *A concise introduction to mixed methods research*. Sage Publications.

Creswell, J. W., & Creswell, J. D. (2018). *Research design: Qualitative, quantitative, and mixed methods approaches* (5th ed.). Sage publications.

Creswell, J. W., & Guetterman, T. C. (2019). *Educational research: Planning, conducting, and evaluating quantitative and qualitative research*. Pearson.

Creswell, J. W., & Plano Clark, V. L. (2018). *Designing and conducting mixed methods research* (3rd ed.). Sage.

Cristóbal, E. P., & Rubio, L. A. (2022). Los hackathones como herramientas para trabajar las competencias de emprendimiento en economía azul fuera de las aulas: Experiencia de la universidad de Cádiz a través del laboratorio social Coedpa. In C. Hervás-Gómez; C. Corujo; A.M., de la Calle and L. Alcántara (Eds). *Formación del profesorado y metodologías activas en la educación del siglo XXI* (pp. 1008-1029). Dykinson.

Crocco, M., & Cramer, J. (2005). Technology use, women, and global studies in social studies teacher education. *Contemporary Issues in Technology & Teacher Education*, 5(1), 38–49. https://www.learntechlib.org/primary/p/5951/

Crosby, J., & Harden, R.M., (2000). AMEE Guide No 20: *The good teacher is more than a lecturer- the twelve*

Crowe, A. R., & Cuenca, A. (Eds.). (2016). *Rethinking social studies teacher education in the twenty-first century*. Springer International Publishing. DOI: 10.1007/978-3-319-22939-3

Crowley, R. M., & Smith, W. (2015). Whiteness and social studies teacher education: Tensions in the pedagogical task. *Teaching Education*, 26(2), 160–178. DOI: 10.1080/10476210.2014.996739

Culhane, J. (2018). The importance of networking for career success. *Journal of Career Development*, 45(1), 1–15.

Culhane, J., Niewolny, K., Clark, S., & Misyak, S. (2018). Exploring the intersections of interdisciplinary teaching, experiential learning, and community engagement: A case study of service learning in practice. *International Journal on Teaching and Learning in Higher Education*, 30(3), 412–422.

Cummings, J. N., & Kiesler, S. (2005). Collaborative research across disciplinary and organizational boundaries. *Social Studies of Science*, 35(5), 703–722. DOI: 10.1177/0306312705055535

da Cruz, M. R. P., Nunes, A. J. S., & Pinheiro, P. G. (2011). Fiedler's contingency theory: Practical application of the least preferred coworker (LPC) scale. *IUP Journal of Organizational Behavior*, 10(4), 7–26.

Dahleez, K., & Aboramadan, M. (2022). Servant leadership and job satisfaction in higher education: The mediating roles of organisational justice and organisational trust. *International Journal of Leadership in Education*, ●●●, 1–22. DOI: 10.1080/13603124.2022.2052753

Darling-Hammond, L., & Richardson, N. (2009). Research review/teacher learning: What matters. [Scribbr. https://outlier.uchicago.edu/]. *Educational Leadership*, 66(5), 46–53.

Dash, B. (2022). *Significance of nonverbal communication and paralinguistic features in communication: A critical analysis.* https://doi.org/.DOI: 10.2015/IJIRMF/202204029

Data Protection Act. (2020). *Jamaica Data Protection Act of Jamaica.* https://www.privacylaws.com/media/4524/jamaica-data-protection-act-2020.pdf

Dauenhauer, B. P. (2020). Ricoeur and the tasks of citizenship. Paul Ricoeur and contemporary moral thought.

Davis, D. R., & Maldonado, C. (2015). Shattering the glass ceiling: The leadership development of African American women in higher education. *Advancing Women in Leadership Journal*, 35, 48–64. DOI: 10.21423/awlj-v35.a125

Davis, S. M., & Afifi, T. D. (2019). The Strong Black Woman Collective Theory: Determining the prosocial functions of strength regulation in groups of black women friends†. *Journal of Communication*, 69(1), 1–25. DOI: 10.1093/joc/jqy065

De Chernatony, L. (2010). *From brand vision to brand evaluation.* Routledge. DOI: 10.4324/9780080966649

De Smet, A., Rubenstein, K., & Schrah, G. (2023). Psychological safety and the critical role of leadership development. https://www.mckinsey.com/capabilities/people-and-organisational-performance/our-insights/psychological-safety-and-the-critical-role-of-leadership-development#/

De Vries, N. J., & Carlson, J. (2014). Examining the drivers and brand performance implications of customer engagement with brands in the social media environment. *Journal of Brand Management*, 21(6), 495–515. DOI: 10.1057/bm.2014.18

Dean, D. R., Bracken, S. J., Allen, J. K., & Van Ummersen, C. (2023). *Women in Academic Leadership*. Routledge., DOI: 10.4324/9781003448785

Deardorff, D. K. (2006). Identification and assessment of intercultural competence as a student outcome of internationalization. *Journal of Studies in International Education*, 10(3), 241–266. DOI: 10.1177/1028315306287002

Dede, C. (2016). The evolution of distance education: Emerging technologies and distributed learning. *American Journal of Distance Education*, 10(2), 4–36. DOI: 10.1080/08923649609526919

Demir, S. B., & Pismek, N. (2018). A convergent parallel mixed-methods study of controversial issues in Social Studies classes: A clash of ideologies. *Educational Sciences: Theory & Practice*, 18(1), 119–149.

Dennen, V. P. (2000). *Collaborative learning: A guide to creating and sustaining effective learning communities*. Stylus Publishing, LLC.

Denzin, N. K., & Lincoln, Y. S. (Eds.). (2018). *The Sage handbook of qualitative research* (5th ed.). Sage.

DePoy, E., & Gitlin, L. N. (Eds.). (2016). *Collecting data through measurement in experimental-type research. Introduction to Research* (5th ed., pp. 227–247). Mosby., DOI: 10.1016/B978-0-323-26171-5.00017-3

Deredzai, M., Goronga, P., & Maupa, B. (2024). Mental health and well-being of students and faculty: Enhancing quality mental health and well-being of female students and faculty in colleges. In Kayyali, M. (Ed.), *Building resiliency in higher education: Globalisation, digital skills, and student wellness* (pp. 332–353). IGI Global., DOI: 10.4018/979-8-3693-5483-4.ch018

Deschênes, A. A. (2024). Digital literacy, the use of collaborative technologies, and perceived social proximity in a hybrid work environment: Technology as a social binder. Computers in Human Behavior Reports. DOI: 10.1016/j.chbr.2023.100351

Devece, C., Peris-Ortiz, M., Merigó, J. M., & Fuster, V. (2015). Linking the development of teamwork and communication skills in higher education. *Sustainable Learning in Higher Education: Developing Competencies for the Global Marketplace*, 63-73.

Devine, P. G., Forscher, P. S., Austin, A. J., & Cox, W. T. (2012). Long-term reduction in implicit race bias: A prejudice habit-breaking intervention. *Journal of Experimental Social Psychology*, 48(6), 1267–1278. DOI: 10.1016/j.jesp.2012.06.003 PMID: 23524616

Devonish, H., & Thompson, D. (2012). Guyanese Creole. In Kortmann, D., & Lunkenheimer, K. (Eds.), *The Mouton world atlas of variation in English* (pp. 265-278). de Gruyter Mouton. https://doi.org/DOI: 10.1515/9783110280128.265

Deysolong, J. (2023). Assessing the benefits of cooperative learning or group work: Fostering collaboration and enhancing learning outcomes. *International Journal of e-Collaboration*. DOI: 10.6084/m9.figshare.23009159

Dias, M., Vieira, P., Pereira, L., Quintão, H., & Lafraia, J. (2023). Leadership theories: A systematic review based on bibliometric and content analysis methods. *GPH-International Journal of Business Management,* 6(05), 01-16.

Dillenbourg, P. (1999). *What do We Mean by Collaborative Learning*. Elsevier.

Dinh, J. V., & Salas, E. (2017). Factors that influence teamwork. *The Wiley Blackwell handbook of the psychology of team working and collaborative processes*, 13-41. https://doi.org/DOI: 10.1002/9781118909997.ch2

Dinh, J. V., Reyes, D. L., Kayga, L., Lindgren, C., Feitosa, J., & Salas, E. (2021). Developing team trust: Leader insights for virtual settings. Organizational Dynamics, 50(1), 100846. DOI: 10.1016/j.orgdyn.2021.100846

Dinkelman, T., & Cuenca, A. (2020). A turn to practice: Core practices in social studies teacher education. *Theory and Research in Social Education*, 48(4), 583–610. DOI: 10.1080/00933104.2020.1757538

Dion, M. L., Sumner, J. L., & Mitchell, S. M. (2018). Gendered Citation Patterns across Political Science and Social Science Methodology fields. *Political Analysis*, 26(3), 312–327. DOI: 10.1017/pan.2018.12

Dooley, L. M., & Bamford, N. J. (2018). Peer feedback on collaborative learning activities in veterinary education. *Veterinary Sciences*, 5(4), 90. DOI: 10.3390/vetsci5040090 PMID: 30336578

Doria Dávila, D. P., & Manjarrés-Rodelo, M. M. (2020). Educación inclusiva: programa de sensibilización en una institución educativa de Sincelejo-Sucre. *RHS-Revista Humanismo Y Sociedad, 8*(1), 6–21. https://doi.org/DOI: 10.22209/rhs.v8n1a01

Dornyei, Z. (2001). *Teaching and researching motivation*. Pearson Education.

Driscoll, M. (2000). *Psychology of Learning for Instruction*. Allyn& Bacon.

Driskell, J. E., Salas, E., & Driskell, T. (2018). Foundations of teamwork and collaboration. *The American Psychologist*, 73(4), 334–348. https://doi.org/10.1037/amp0000241

Driskell, T., Driskell, J. E., Burke, C. S., & Salas, E. (2017). Team Roles: A Review and Integration. *Small Group Research*, 48(4), 482–511. DOI: 10.1177/1046496417711529

Drotar, D. (1989). Psychological research in pediatric settings: Lessons from the field. *Journal of Pediatric Psychology*, 14(1), 63–74. DOI: 10.1093/jpepsy/14.1.63 PMID: 2656968

Drotar, D. (1993). Influences on collaborative activities among psychologists and pediatricians: Implications for practice, training, and research. *Journal of Pediatric Psychology*, 18(2), 159–172. DOI: 10.1093/jpepsy/18.2.159 PMID: 8492270

Druskat, V. U., & Pescosolido, A. T. (2002). The content of effective teamwork mental models in self-managing teams: Ownership, learning and heedful interrelating. *Human Relations*, 55(3), 283–314. https://doi.org/10.1177/0018726702553001

Dudley, P. (2014). *LS: A handbook*.

Dufner, M., Gebauer, J. E., Sedikides, C., & Denissen, J. J. (2019). Self-enhancement and psychological adjustment: A meta-analytic review. *Personality and Social Psychology Review*, 23(1), 48–72. DOI: 10.1177/1088868318756467 PMID: 29534642

Dugan, J. P. (2017). *Leadership theory: Cultivating critical perspectives*. John Wiley & Sons.

Duhigg, C. (2016). What Google learned from its quest to build the perfect team. *The New York Times Magazine*. Retrieved from https://www.nytimes.com/2016/02/28/magazine/what-google-learned-from-its-quest-to-build-the-perfect-team.html

Duhigg, C. (2016, February 25). What Google learned from its quest to build the perfect team. The Work Issue. The New York Times Magazine. https://www.nytimes.com/2016/02/28/magazine/what-google-learned-from-its-quest-to-build-the-perfect-team.html

Ďuricová, L., & Šugereková, T. (2017). A Managers self-concept in the context of their leadership style within McGregors theory. *Človek a spoločnosť, 20*(1), 36-44.

Dusdal, J., & Powell, J. J. (2021). Benefits, motivations, and challenges of international collaborative research: A sociology of science case study. *Science & Public Policy*, 48(2), 235–245. DOI: 10.1093/scipol/scab010

Dutton, & R. E. Quinn (Eds.), *Positive organizational scholarship: Foundations of a new discipline* (pp. 241–258). Berrett-Koehler Publishers.

Dwivedi, Y. K., Kshetri, N., Hughes, L., Slade, E. L., Jeyaraj, A., Kar, A. K., ... & Wright, R. (2023). "So what if ChatGPT wrote it?" Multidisciplinary perspectives on opportunities, challenges and implications of generative conversational AI for research, practice and policy. International Journal of Information Management, 71, 102642. DOI: 10.1016/j.ijinfomgt.2023.102642

Dziminska, M., Fijalkowska, J., & Sulkowski, L. (2018). Trust-based quality culture conceptual model for higher education institutions. *Sustainability (Basel)*, 10(8), 1–22. DOI: 10.3390/su10082599

Eaton, G. (1962). Trade union development in Jamaica. *Caribbean Quarterly*, 8(1), 43–53. https://doi.org/10.1080/00086495.1962.11829842

Ebadi, S., & Rahimi, M. (2017). Exploring the impact of online peer-editing using Google Docs on EFL learners' academic writing skills: A mixed methods study. *Computer Assisted Language Learning*, 30(8), 787–815. DOI: 10.1080/09588221.2017.1363056

Ebaeguin, M., & Stephens, M. (2014). Cultural Challenges in Adapting Lesson Study to a Philippines Setting. *Mathematics Teacher Education and Development, 16.*

Eckel, P. D., & Kezar, A. J. (2003). *Taking the reins: Institutional transformation in higher education.* Greenwood Publishing Group. DOI: 10.5040/9798216192480

Eddy, S. L., & Hogan, K. A. (2014). Getting under the hood: How and for whom does increasing course structure work? *CBE Life Sciences Education*, 13(3), 453–468. DOI: 10.1187/cbe.14-03-0050 PMID: 25185229

Edmondson, A.C., Higgins, M., Singer, S.J., & Weiner, J. (2016). Promoting psychological safety in healthcare organisations and education organisations: A comparative perspective. Res Hum Dev, 13 (1), 65-83. Htttps://doi,org/DOI: 10.1080/15427609.2016.114128

Edmondson, A. (1999). Psychological safety and learning behavior in work teams. *Administrative Science Quarterly*, 44(2), 350–383. DOI: 10.2307/2666999

Edmondson, A. C. (2018). *The fearless organization: Creating psychological safety in the workplace for learning, innovation, and growth*. Wiley.

Edmondson, A. C. (2019). *The fearless organisation: Creating psychological safety in the workplace for learning, innovation and growth*. John Wiley and Sons.

Edmondson, A. C. (2023). *Right kind of wrong: The science of failing well*. Simon and Schuster.

Edmondson, A. C., & Lei, Z. (2014). Psychological safety: The history, renaissance, and future of an interpersonal construct. *Annual Review of Organizational Psychology and Organizational Behavior*, 1(1), 23–43. DOI: 10.1146/annurev-orgpsych-031413-091305

Eldh, C., Rejmer, A., Carlsson, B., & Ryderheim, B. (2016). Core values work in academia, with experiences from Lund University.

Elizondo Carmona, C. (2022). *Ámbitos para el aprendizaje*. Octaedro., DOI: 10.47916/9788418615221

Elken, M. (2020). Marketing in higher education. In *The International Encyclopedia of Higher Education Systems and Institutions* (pp. 2032–2037). Springer Netherlands. DOI: 10.1007/978-94-017-8905-9_569

Elliot, J. (1993). Three Perspectives on Coherence and Continuity in Teacher Education. Reconstructing Teacher Education. London: Falmer Press.

Elliott, J. (2016). The mentoring process and LS: Are they compatible? Open Online Journal for Research and Education, Special Issue 5. Scribbr. http://journal.ph-noe.ac.at

Elliott, S. N., Kratochwill, T. R., Littlefield Cook, J., & Travers, J. (2000). *Educational psychology: Effective teaching, effective learning* (3rd ed.). McGraw-Hill College.

Elo, S., Kääriäinen, M., Kanste, O., Pölkki, T., Utriainen, K., & Kyngäs, H. (2014). *Qualitative content analysis: A focus on trustworthiness*. Sage Publications. https://journals.sagepub.com/doi/pdf/10.1177/2158244014522633

Ely, R. J., & Meyerson, D. E. (2000). Theories of gender in organizations: A new approach to organizational analysis and change. *Research in Organizational Behavior*, 22, 103–151. DOI: 10.1016/S0191-3085(00)22004-2

Enest, P. (1994). Varieties of constructivism: Their metaphors, epistemologies and pedagogical implications. *Hiroshima Journal of Mathematics Education*, 2, 1–14.

Enest, Y. (1994). Towards a social constructivist view of mathematical learning. *Educational Studies in Mathematics*, 27(1), 67–86.

Enochsson, A. B., Kilbrink, N., Andersén, A., & Ådefors, A. (2022). Obstacles to progress: Swedish vocational teachers using digital technology to connect school and workplaces. International Journal of Training Research, 20(2), 111-127. DOI: 10.1080/14480220.2021.1979623

Enyedy, N., & Yoon, S. (2021). Immersive environments: Learning in augmented+ virtual reality. International handbook of computer-supported collaborative learning, 389-405. DOI: 10.1007/978-3-030-65291-3_21

Erickson-Davis, C., Luhrmann, T. M., Kurina, L. M., Weisman, K., Cornman, N., Corwin, A., & Bailenson, J. (2021). The sense of presence: Lessons from virtual reality. Religion, brain & behavior, 11(3), 335-351. DOI: 10.1080/2153599X.2021.1953573

Ertmer, P. A., & Newby, T. J. (1993). Conductismo, cognitivismo y constructivismo: Una comparación de los aspectos críticos desde la perspectiva del diseño de la instrucción. *Performance Improvement Quarterly*, 6(4), 50–72. DOI: 10.1111/j.1937-8327.1993.tb00605.x

Ertmer, P. A., & Ottenbreit-Leftwich, A. T. (2013). Removing obstacles to the pedagogical changes required by Jonassen's vision of authentic technology-enabled learning. *Computers & Education*, 64, 175–182. DOI: 10.1016/j.compedu.2012.10.008

Escorial, S. (25th-27th October 2023). *La universidad en el s.XXI: La educación inclusiva como eje estratégico*. VI Congreso Discapacidad y Universidad. Universidad de Salamanca y Fundación ONCE, Salamanca, Spain.

Eva, N., Robin, M., Sendjaya, S., van Dierendonck, D., & Liden, R. C. (2019). Servant leadership: A systematic review and call for future research. *The Leadership Quarterly*, 30(1), 111–132. https://doi.org/10.1016/j.leaqua.2018.07.004

Evans, R. W. (2004). *The social studies wars: What should we teach the children?* Teachers College Press.

Ezeala, L. O., & Yusuff, E. O. (2011). User satisfaction with library resources and services in Nigerian agricultural research institutes. *Library Philosophy and Practice (e-journal)*. 564. http://unllib.unl.edu/LPP

Faizah, N., Chotimah, C., & Mukhlis, I. (2020). The Implementation of LS in Economic Subjects to Improve Student's Learning Motivation. [CARJO]. *Classroom Action Research Journal*, 4(1), 44–52. DOI: 10.17977/um013v4i12020p048

Farzaneh, E., Amani, F., Taleghani, Y. M., Fathi, A., Kahnamouei-aghdam, F., & Fatthzadeh-Ardalani, G. (2016). Research barriers from the viewpoint of faculty members and students of Ardabil University of Medical Sciences, Iran, 2014. *International Journal of Research in Medical Sciences*, 4(6), 1926–1932.

Feilzer, M. Y. (2010). Doing mixed methods research pragmatically: Implications for the rediscovery of pragmatism as a research paradigm. *Journal of Mixed Methods Research*, 4(1), 6–16. DOI: 10.1177/1558689809349691

Felder, R. M., & Brent, R. (2007). Cooperative learning. In Mabrouk, P. (Ed.), *Active learning: Models from the Analytical Sciences, ACS Symposium Series 970* (pp. 34-53). American Chemical Society. DOI: 10.1021/bk-2007-0970.ch004

Felder, R. M., & Brent, R. (2016). *Teaching and learning STEM: A practical guide*. John Wiley & Sons.

Fernandez, C. (2002). Learning from Japanese Approaches to Professional Development: The Case of LS. *Journal of Teacher Education*, 53(5), 393–405. DOI: 10.1177/002248702237394

Ferradás, M. M., Freire, C., Regueiro, B., Piñeiro, I., Rodríguez, S., & Valle, A. (2015). Estrategias de self-handicapping en estudiantes universitarios. Diferencias entre cursos [Self-handicapping strategies in university students. Differences between courses]. *Revista de Estudios e Investigación en Psicología y Educación. Extr.*, 1, 63–66. DOI: 10.17979/reipe.2015.0.01.345

Fiaz, M., Su, Q., & Saqib, A. (2017). Leadership styles and employees' motivation: Perspective from an emerging economy. *Journal of Developing Areas*, 51(4), 143–156. https://doi-org.trevecca.idm.oclc.org/10.1353/jda.2017.0093. DOI: 10.1353/jda.2017.0093

Fidalgo, A., Sein-Echaluce, M. L., & García, J. (2017). Aprendizaje basado en Retos en una asignatura académica universitaria. *Revista Iberoamericana de Informática Educativa*, 25, 1–8.

Finley, A., & Reason, R. D. (2016). *Community-engaged signature work: How a high-impact practice may support student well-being. Education publications*. School of Education, Iowa State University.

Finley, L., & Reason, R. (2016). *Internships: A guide for students and employers*. Routledge.

Fischman, D., & Wasserman, K. (2017). Developing Assessment through LS. *Mathematics Teaching in the Middle School*, 22(6), 344–351. DOI: 10.5951/mathteacmiddscho.22.6.0344

Fitri, U. D., & Herdiansyah, H. (2021). The Influence of IMC Implementation on the Brand Awareness of BLANJA. com. *Jurnal Komunikasi Global*, 10(1), 120–136. DOI: 10.24815/jkg.v10i1.20156

Fittipaldi, D. (2020). Managing the dynamics of group projects in higher education: Best practices suggested by empirical research. *Universal Journal of Educational Research*, 8(5), 1778–1796. DOI: 10.13189/ujer.2020.080515

Flanagan, S. (2017). *Penn State Performance Management: Giving and receiving feedback*. Penn State University. https://hr.psu.edu/sites/hr/files/GivingAndReceivingFeedbackIndividualContributor.pdf

Flick, U. (2004). Triangulation in qualitative research. *A companion to qualitative research, 3*, 178-183.

Floyd, A. (2013). *Modern communication and intranets: Tools for effective internal communication*. https://doi.org/DOI: 10.101610.13140

Flyvbjerg, B. (2011). Case study. In Denzin, N. & Lincoln, Y. (Eds.), *The Sage handbook of qualitative research,* 4 (pp. 301-316). Sage.

Follmer, D., Groth, R., Bergner, J., & Weaver, S. (2023). Theory-based Evaluation of Lesson Study Professional Development: Challenges, Opportunities, and Lessons Learned. *The American Journal of Evaluation*. Advance online publication. DOI: 10.1177/10982140231184899

Ford, H. L., Brick, C., Azmitia, M., Blaufuss, K., & Dekens, P. (2019). Women from Some Under-represented Minorities Are Given Too Few Talks at World's Largest Earth-Science Conference. *Nature*, 576(7785), 32–35. DOI: 10.1038/d41586-019-03688-w PMID: 31797914

Forsyth, D. R. (2014). *Group dynamics*. Wadsworth Cengage Learning.

Fox Tree, J. E., & Vaid, J. (2022). Why so few, still? Challenges to attracting, advancing, and keeping women faculty of color in academia. *Frontiers in Sociology*, 6, 792198. DOI: 10.3389/fsoc.2021.792198 PMID: 35118155

Fox, C. W., & Paine, C. E. T. (2019). Gender differences in peer review outcomes and manuscript impact at six journals of ecology and evolution. *Ecology and Evolution*, 9(6), 3599–3619. DOI: 10.1002/ece3.4993 PMID: 30962913

Fox, R. (2001). Constructivism examined. *Oxford Review of Education*, 27(1), 23–35. DOI: 10.1080/03054980125310

Fox, R. (2001). Constructivism in education: A review of the literature. *Educational Psychology Review*, 13(1), 1–11. DOI: 10.1023/A:1009048817385

Franzén, E. (2008). The benefits of using print-on-demand or POD. In Zemliansky, P., & St. Amant, K. (Eds.), *Handbook of research on virtual workplaces and the new nature of business practices* (pp. 668–680). IGI Global Publishing., DOI: 10.4018/978-1-59904-893-2

Fraser, C., Kennedy, A., Reid, L., & Mckinney, S. (2007). Teachers' continuing professional development: Contested concepts, understandings and models. *Journal of In-service Education*, 33(2), 153–169. DOI: 10.1080/13674580701292913

Frazier, M. L., Fainshmidt, S., Klinger, R. L., Pezeshkan, A., & Vracheva, V. (2016). Psychological safety: A meta-analytic review and extension. *Personnel Psychology*, 70(1), 113–165. DOI: 10.1111/peps.12183

Freeman, R. B., & Huang, W. (2015). Collaborating with people like me: Ethnic co-authorship within the US. *Journal of Labor Economics*, 33(S1), S289–S318. DOI: 10.1086/678973

Freeman, S. (2020). Active learning narrows achievement gaps for underrepresented students in undergraduate science, technology, engineering, and math. *Proceedings of the National Academy of Sciences of the United States of America*, 117(12), 6476–6483. DOI: 10.1073/pnas.1916903117 PMID: 32152114

Freire, P. (1972). *Cultural action for freedom*. Penguin Books.

French, J., & Poznanski, D. (2009). Managing research—A guide to research infrastructure. *Journal of Medical Imaging and Radiation Sciences*, 40(4), 165–169. DOI: 10.1016/j.jmir.2009.09.002

Fuentes-Guerra, F. J. (2015). *El deporte en el marco de la Educación Física*. Wanceulen.

Fujii, T. (2016). Designing and adapting tasks in lesson planning: A critical process of Lesson Study. *ZDM Mathematics Education*, 2016(48), 411–423. DOI: 10.1007/s11858-016-0770-3

Fulk, H. K., Bell, R. L., & Bodie, N. (2011). Team management by objectives: Enhancing developing teams' performance. *Journal of Management Policy and Practice*, 12(3), 17–26.

Fundación Universia. (2017). *Universidad y discapacidad. IV Estudio sobre el grado de inclusión del sistema universitario español respecto de la realidad de la discapacidad*. Comité Español de Representantes de Personas con Discapacidad-CERMI. http://riberdis.cedid.es/handle/11181/5632

Fushino, K. (2010). Causal relationships between communication confidence, beliefs about group work, and willingness to communicate in foreign language group work. *TESOL Quarterly*, 44(4), 700–724. DOI: 10.5054/tq.2010.235993

Gachago, D., Strydom, S., Hanekom, P., Simons, S., & Walters, S. (2015). Crossing boundaries: Lectures' perspectives on the use of WhatsApp to support teaching and learning in higher education. *Progressio*, 37(1), 172–187. DOI: 10.25159/0256-8853/579

Gajić, J. (2012). Importance of marketing mix in higher education institutions. *The European Journal of Applied Economics*, 9(1), 29–41.

Gannon, D., & Boguszak, A. (2013). Douglas McGregor's theory x and theory y. *CRIS - Bulletin of the Centre for Research and Interdisciplinary Study*, 2013(2), vol. 85-93.

Gao, F., Luo, T., & Zhang, K. (2013). Tweeting for learning: A critical analysis of research on microblogging in education published in 2008–2011. *British Journal of Educational Technology*, 44(5), 783–801. DOI: 10.1111/j.1467-8535.2012.01357.x

Garcia, J. G., Gañgan, M. G. T., Tolentino, M. N., Ligas, M., Moraga, S. D., & Pasilan, A. A. (2021). Canvas adoption assessment and acceptance of the learning management system on a web-based platform. *arXiv preprint arXiv:2101.12344*.

García-Sánchez, I. M., & Mulero-Mendigorri, E. (2020). La Agenda 2030 y los Objetivos de Desarrollo Sostenible: Retos y oportunidades para las universidades españolas. *Revista Española del Tercer Sector*, 45, 175–190.

Gardner, A. K., Kosemund, M., Hogg, D., Heymann, A., & Martinez, J. (2017). Setting goals, not just roles: Improving teamwork through goal-focused debriefing. *American Journal of Surgery*, 213(2), 249–252. https://doi.org/10.1016/j.amjsurg.2016.09.040

Garet, M. S., Heppen, J. B., Walters, K., Parkinson, J., Smith, T. M., Song, M., . . . Borman, G. D. (2016). Focusing on Mathematical Knowledge: The Impact of Content-Intensive Teacher Professional Development. NCEE 2016-4010. National Center for Education Evaluation and Regional Assistance.

Garrison, D. R., Anderson, T., & Archer, W. (2001). Critical thinking, cognitive presence, and computer conferencing in distance education. *American Journal of Distance Education*, 15(1), 7–23. DOI: 10.1080/08923640109527071

Gause, S. A. (2021). White privilege, Black resilience: Women of color leading the academy. *Leadership*, 17(1), 74–80. DOI: 10.1177/1742715020977370

Gautam, P. K., & Gautam, R. R. (2023). Organizational culture orientation and union influence. *Management Dynamics*, 26(1), 43–55. https://doi.org/10.3126/md.v26i1.59150

Gay, G. (2018). *Culturally responsive teaching: Theory, research, and practice* (3rd ed.). Teachers College Press.

Gençer, H. (2019). Group dynamics and behaviour. *Universal Journal of Educational Research*, 7(1), 223–229. https://doi.org/10.13189/ujer.2019.070128

George, C. L., Wood-Kanupka, J., & Oriel, K. N. (2017). Impact of participation in community-based research among undergraduate and graduate students. *Journal of Allied Health*, 46(1), 15E–24E. PMID: 28255600

George, D. R., Dreibelbis, T. D., & Aumiller, B. (2017). How we used the humanities to integrate basic science and ethics in a case-based medical curriculum. *Medical Teacher*, 39(10), 1043–1049. DOI: 10.1080/0142159X.2017.1353070

George, T. P., DeCristofaro, C., & Rosser-Majors, M. (2020). Virtual Collaboration in Academia. *Creative Nursing*, 26(3), 205–209. DOI: 10.1891/CRNR-D-19-00023 PMID: 32883822

Geraghty, T. (2024, May 3). Psychological safety: A timeline. Psychological Safety. https://psychsafety.co.uk/psychological-safety-a-timeline/

Gerlach, R., & Gockel, C. (2017). We belong together: Belonging to the principal's in-group protect teachers from the negative effects of task conflict on psychological safety. *School Leadership & Management*. Advance online publication. 101080/13632434.2017.1407307

Gezuraga, M., & García, A. (2020). Recepciones de la pedagogía experiencial de Dewey en diversos enfoques metodológicos: El valor añadido del aprendizaje-servicio. *Educatio Siglo XXI*, 38(3), 295–316. DOI: 10.6018/educatio.452921

Ghodeswar, B. M. (2008). Building brand identity in competitive markets: A conceptual model. *Journal of Product and Brand Management*, 17(1), 4–12. DOI: 10.1108/10610420810856468

Giannakidou, E., Gioftsali, K., & Tzioras, E. (2013). The reflective action of teacher candidates when implementing an appied version of the LS model. *Hellenic Journal of Research in Education, 1*, 30-58. Scribbr. https://ejournals.epublishing.ekt.gr/index.php/hjre/article/view/8791/9012

Gidis, Y., & Kiral, B. (2023). The mediating role of teamwork in the correlation between administrative support and school belonging. *Educational Policy Analysis and Strategic Research*, 18(3), 465–482. DOI: 10.29329/epasr.2023.600.22

Gilson, L. L., Maynard, M. T., Jones Young, N. C., Vartiainen, M., & Hakonen, M. (2015). Virtual teams research: 10 years, 10 themes, and 10 opportunities. *Journal of Management*, 41(5), 1313–1337. DOI: 10.1177/0149206314559946

Ginther, D. K., Schaffer, W. T., Schnell, J., Masimore, B., Liu, F., Haak, L. L., & Kington, R. (2011). Race, ethnicity, and NIH research awards. *Science*, 333(6045), 1015–1019. DOI: 10.1126/science.1196783 PMID: 21852498

Girvan, C., Conneely, C., & Tangney, B. (2016). Extending experiential learning in teacher professional development. *Teaching and Teacher Education*, 58, 129–139. DOI: 10.1016/j.tate.2016.04.009

Gleason, M. A., & Julio, E. (2020). Implementación del aprendizaje experiencial en la universidad, sus beneficios en el alumnado y el rol docente. *Review of Education*, 44(2), 2215–2644. DOI: 10.15517/revedu.v44i2.40197

Glesne, C. (2016). *Becoming qualitative researchers: An introduction*. Pearson. One Lake Street, Upper Saddle River, New Jersey 07458.

Godfrey, D., Seleznyov, S., Anders, J., Wollaston, N., & Barrera-Pedemonte, F. (2018). A developmental evaluation approach to lesson study: Exploring the impact of lesson study in London schools. *Professional Development in Education*, 45(2), 325–340. DOI: 10.1080/19415257.2018.1474488

Goleman, D. (1995). *Emotional intelligence*. Bantam Books, Inc. https://asantelim.wordpress.com/wp-content/uploads/2018/05/daniel-goleman-emotional-intelligence.pdf

Goleman, D. (2000). Leadership that gets results. *Harvard Business Review*, 78(2), 78–90.

Gong, X., & Wang, P. (2017). A Comparative Study of Pre-Service Education for Preschool Teachers in China and the United States. *Current Issues in Comparative Education,* 19(2), 84-110. Scribbr. https://files.eric.ed.gov/fulltext/EJ1144805.pdf

Goñi, J., Cortázar, C., Alvares, D., Donoso, U., & Miranda, C. (2020). Is Teamwork Different Online Versus Face-to-Face? A Case in Engineering Education. *Sustainability (Basel)*, 12(24), 10444. https://www.mdpi.com/2071-1050/12/24/10444. DOI: 10.3390/su122410444

Gonzales, G., Despe, K. B., Iway, L. J., Genon, R., Intano, J. O., & Sanchez, J. (2023). Online collaborative learning platforms in science: Their influence on attitude, achievement, and experiences. *Journal of Educational Technology and Instruction*, 2(2), 1–16. https://ijeti-edu.org/index.php/ijeti/article/view/55. DOI: 10.70290/jeti.v2i2.55

Gonzales, L. D., Martinez, E., & Ordu, C. (2013). Exploring faculty experiences in a striving university through the lens of academic capitalism. *Studies in Higher Education*, 39(7), 1097–1115. DOI: 10.1080/03075079.2013.777401

González, B. (2018). ¿Cómo mejorar el aprendizaje? Influencia de la autoestima en el aprendizaje del estudiante universitario. *Revista Complutense De Educación*, 30(3), 781–795. DOI: 10.5209/rced.58899

Gonzalez, J. A., & Denisi, A. S. (2009). Cross-level effects of demography and diversity climate on organizational attachment and firm effectiveness. *Journal of Organizational Behavior*, 30(1), 21–40. DOI: 10.1002/job.498

González-Lloret, M. (2020). Collaborative tasks for online language teaching. *Foreign Language Annals*, 53(2), 260–269. DOI: 10.1111/flan.12466

Gonzalez-Mulé, E., & Cockburn, B. S. (2021). Worked to death: The relationships of work hours and worked outcomes with mortality. *Academy of Management Journal*, 64(1), 276–302. DOI: 10.5465/ambpp.2015.10934abstract

Google. (2020). *Google Diversity Annual Report*. Retrieved from https://diversity.google/annual-report/

Google. (2024). About Google Docs. https://www.google.com/docs/about/

Gopinathan, S. (2008). *Transforming teacher education: Redefined professionals for 21st century schools*.https://repository.nie.edu.sg/bitstream/10497/22550/1/Transforming-Teacher-Education_Report.pdf

Gore, J. M., Miller, A., Fray, L., Harris, J., & Prieto, E. (2021). Improving student achievement through professional development: Results from a randomised controlled trial of Quality Teaching Rounds. *Teaching and Teacher Education*, 101, 103297. DOI: 10.1016/j.tate.2021.103297

Gore, J., Lloyd, A., Smith, M., Bowe, J., Ellis, H., & Lubans, D. (2017). Effects of Professional development on the quality of teaching: Results from a randomised controlled trial of Quality Teaching Rounds. *Teaching and Teacher Education*, 68, 99–113. DOI: 10.1016/j.tate.2017.08.007

GORTT. (2022). *Digital Transformation Programme*. Trinidad and Tobago: Ministry of Education Retrieved from https://www.moe.gov.tt/digital-transformation-policy-2023-2027/#:~:text=The%20vision%20of%20the%20MOE's,development%20of%20globally%20competitive%20citizens."&text=To%20promote%20a%20learner%20centred,system%20and%20among%20all%20stakeholders.

Goudeau, S., Sanrey, C., Stanczak, A., Manstead, A., & Darnon, C. (2021). Why lockdown and distance learning during the COVID-19 pandemic are likely to increase the social class achievement gap. Nature human behaviour, 5(10), 1273-1281. DOI: 10.1038/s41562-021-01212-7

Gouillart, F., & Ramaswamy, V. (2012). *La co-creación de valor y experiencias*. Temas Grupo Editorial.

Gray, B. (2008). Enhancing transdisciplinary research through collaborative leadership. *American Journal of Preventive Medicine*, 35(2), S124–S132. DOI: 10.1016/j.amepre.2008.03.037 PMID: 18619392

Gray, D. E. (2011). *Doing research in the real world*. Sage Publications, Inc.

Greenwood, S. (2020, November 9). Conducting qualitative secondary data analysis: PGT projects working document. Edshare UK. https://edshare.gla.ac.uk/867/5/conductingsecondary qualitative data analysis.pdf

Greenwood, R. G. (1996). Leadership theory: A historical look at its evolution. *The Journal of Leadership Studies*, 3(1), 3–16. DOI: 10.1177/107179199600300102

Greimel, N. S., Kanbach, D. K., & Chelaru, M. (2023). Virtual teams and transformational leadership: An integrative literature review and avenues for further research. *Journal of Innovation & Knowledge*, 8(2), 100351. DOI: 10.1016/j.jik.2023.100351

Greska, L., McCormick, D., & Cascino, J. (2023). Women in academia: Why and where does the pipeline leak, and how can we fix it? *Parity*, 40, 102–109. DOI: 10.38105/spr.xmvdiojee1

Griffen, S. N. (2022). Collaborative Public Management in Two Police Departments to Address Cross-Jurisdictional Boundaries: A Descriptive Case Study.

Grönroos, C. (1995). Relationship marketing: The strategy continuum. *Journal of the Academy of Marketing Science*, 23(4), 252–254. DOI: 10.1007/BF02893863

Gudykunst, W. B. (2003). *Cross-cultural and intercultural communication*. Sage Publications.

Guenter, H., Gardner, W. L., Davis McCauley, K., Randolph-Seng, B., & Prabhu, V. P. (2017). Shared authentic leadership in research teams: Testing a multiple mediation model. *Small Group Research*, 48(6), 719–a765. DOI: 10.1177/1046496417732403 PMID: 29187779

Guest, G., Namey, E., O'Regan, A., Godwin, C., & Taylor, J. (2020). Comparing interview and focus group data collected in person and online. Patient-Centred Outcomes Research Institute (PCORI), Washington, DC. https://www.ncbi.nlm.nih.gov/books/NBK588708/

Gulam, K. (nd). Business communication: Basic concepts and skills, chapter 4: *Barriers to Communication* [PowerPoint slides] https://www.gpnngr.org.in/lms/EXS-First%20year%20ECS%20Chapter%204%20Barriers%20to%20Communication.pdf

Guofeng, M., Jianyao, J., Shan, J., & Zhijiang, W. (2020). Incentives and contract design for knowledge sharing in construction joint ventures. *Automation in Construction*, 119, 103343. Advance online publication. DOI: 10.1016/j.autcon.2020.103343

Hadfield, M., & Jopling, M. (2016). Problematizing lesson study and its impacts: Studying a highly contextualised approach to professional learning. *Teaching and Teacher Education*, 60, 203–214. DOI: 10.1016/j.tate.2016.08.001

Hadorn, G., Pohl, C., & Bammer, G. (2010). Solving problems through transdisciplinary research. *The Oxford Handbook of Interdisciplinarity*. 431-452

Haginoya, S., Ibe, T., Yamamoto, S., Yoshimoto, N., Mizushi, H., & Santtila, P. (2023). AI avatar tells you what happened: The first test of using AI-operated children in simulated interviews to train investigative interviewers. Frontiers in Psychology, 14, 1133621. DOI: 10.3389/fpsyg.2023.1133621

Haginoya, S., Yamamoto, S., Pompedda, F., Naka, M., Antfolk, J., & Santtila, P. (2020). Online simulation training of child sexual abuse interviews with feedback improves interview quality in Japanese university students. Frontiers in psychology, 11, 998. DOI: 10.3389/fpsyg.2020.00998

Hajibabaei, A., Schiffauerova, A., & Ebadi, A. (2023). Women and key positions in scientific collaboration networks: Analyzing central scientists' profiles in the artificial intelligence ecosystem through a gender lens. *Scientometrics*, 128(2), 1219–1240. DOI: 10.1007/s11192-022-04601-5

Hall, K. L., Feng, A. X., Moser, R. P., Stokols, D., & Taylor, B. K. (2018). Moving the science of team science forward: Collaboration and creativity. *American Journal of Preventive Medicine*, 54(6), S230–S239. PMID: 18619406

Halvorsen, A. L., & Kesler Lund, A. (2013). LS and history education. *Social Studies*, 104(3), 123–129. DOI: 10.1080/00377996.2012.698326

Hämäläinen, R., Nissinen, K., Mannonen, J., Lämsä, J., Leino, K., & Taajamo, M. (2021). Understanding teaching professionals' digital competence: What do PIAAC and TALIS reveal about technology-related skills, attitudes, and knowledge?. Computers in human behavior, 117, 106672. DOI: 10.1016/j.chb.2020.106672

Hamdan, H. A., Andersen, P. H., & De Boer, L. (2021). Stakeholder collaboration in sustainable neighborhood projects—A review and research agenda. *Sustainable Cities and Society*, 68, 102776. DOI: 10.1016/j.scs.2021.102776

Hameed, I., Hyder, Z., Imran, M., & Shafiq, K. (2021). Greenwash and green purchase behavior: An environmentally sustainable perspective. *Environment, Development and Sustainability*, 23(9), 1–22. DOI: 10.1007/s10668-020-01202-1

Hannafin, M. J., & Hannafin, K. M. (2010). Cognition and student-centered, web-based learning: Issues and implications for research and theory. In *Learning and instruction in the digital age* (pp. 11–23). Springer. DOI: 10.1007/978-1-4419-1551-1_2

Hannan, E., & Liu, S. (2023). AI: New source of competitiveness in higher education. . *Competitiveness Review*, 33(2), 265–279. DOI: 10.1108/CR-03-2021-0045

Hanson, E. M., & Henry, W. (1992). Strategic marketing for educational systems. *School Organization*, 12(3), 255–267. DOI: 10.1080/0260136920120302

Haram, M. H. S. M., Lee, J. W., Ramasamy, G., Ngu, E. E., Thiagarajah, S. P., & Lee, Y. H. (2021). Feasibility of utilising second life EV batteries: Applications, lifespan, economics, environmental impact, assessment, and challenges. Alexandria Engineering Journal, 60(5), 4517-4536. DOI: 10.1016/j.aej.2021.03.021

Hargie, O. (2016). The importance of communication for organisational effectiveness. In. Lobo, F. (Ed.) *Psicologia do Trabalho e das Organizações. Braga*, (pp. 15-32) Axioma.

Harrison, O. (2022, December 12). *Building a positive team climate for better performance: How to bring psychological safety to tech teams*. Forbes.https://www.forbes.com/sites/forbestechcouncil/2022/12/12/building-a-positive-team-climate-for-better-performance-how-to-bring-psychological-safety-to-tech-teams/?sh=7bd0258fdcc4

Harrison-Walker, L. J. (2009). Strategic positioning in higher education. *Academy of Educational Leadership Journal*, 13(1), 103.

Hart, R. (1999). The birth of the trade union movement in the English-speaking Caribbean area. *Social and Economic Studies*, 48(3), 173–196.

Hartwig, A., Clarke, S., Johnson, S., & Willis, S. (2020). Workplace team resilience: A systematic review and conceptual development. *Organizational Psychology Review*, 10(3-4), 169–200. DOI: 10.1177/2041386620919476

Hasal, M., Nowaková, J., Ahmed Saghair, K., Abdulla, H., Snášel, V., & Ogiela, L. (2021). Chatbots: Security, privacy, data protection, and social aspects. Concurrency and Computation: Practice and Experience, 33(19), e6426. DOI: 10.1002/cpe.6426

Hassini, E. (2006). Student instructor communication: The role of email, computers and education. *Computers & Education*, 47(1), 29–40. DOI: 10.1016/j.compedu.2004.08.014

Hatch, M. J., & Schultz, M. (2002). The dynamics of organizational identity. *Human Relations*, 55(8), 989–1018. DOI: 10.1177/0018726702055008181

Hawley, T. S. (2012). Purpose as content and pedagogy: Rationale-development as a core theme of social studies teacher education. *Journal of Inquiry and Action in Education*, 4(3), 1. https://digitalcommons.buffalostate.edu/cgi/viewcontent.cgi?article=1041&context=jiae

Haynes, C., Joseph, N. M., Patton, L. D., Stewart, S., & Allen, E. L. (2020). Toward an understanding of intersectionality methodology: A 30-year literature synthesis of black women's experiences in higher education. *Review of Educational Research*, 90(6), 751–787. DOI: 10.3102/0034654320946822

Heinze, A., Procter, C., & Scott, B. (2007). Use of conversation theory to underpin blended learning. *International Journal of Teaching and Case Studies*, 1(1-2), 108–120. DOI: 10.1504/IJTCS.2007.014213

Hemsley-Brown, J., & Oplatka, I. (2006). Universities in a competitive global marketplace: A systematic review of the literature on higher education marketing. *International Journal of Public Sector Management*, 19(4), 316–338. DOI: 10.1108/09513550610669176

Henao-Villa, C. F., García-Arango, D. A., Aguirre-Mesa, E. D., González-García, A., Bracho-Aconcha, R., Solorzano-Movilla, J. G., & Arboleda-Lopez, A. P. (2017). Multidisciplinariedad, interdisciplinariedad y transdisciplinariedad en la formación para la investigación en ingeniería. *Revista Lasallista de Investigacion*, 14(1), 179–197. DOI: 10.22507/rli.v14n1a16

Henderson, P. W., Cote, J. A., Leong, S. M., & Schmitt, B. (2003). Building strong brands in Asia: Selecting the visual components of image to maximize brand strength. *International Journal of Research in Marketing*, 20(4), 297–313. DOI: 10.1016/j.ijresmar.2003.03.001

Heng, K., Hamid, M. O., & Khan, A. (2020). Factors influencing academics' research engagement and productivity: A developing countries perspective. *Issues in Educational Research*, 30(3), 965–987.

Hennessy, S., D'Angelo, S., McIntyre, N., Koomar, S., Kreimeia, A., Cao, L., ... & Zubairi, A. (2022). Technology use for teacher professional development in low-and middle-income countries: A systematic review. Computers and Education Open, 3, 100080. DOI: 10.1016/j.caeo.2022.100080

Hennissen, P., Beckers, H., & Moerkerke, G. (2017). Linking practice to theory in teacher education: A growth in cognitive structures. *Teaching and Teacher Education*, 63, 314–325. DOI: 10.1016/j.tate.2017.01.008

Henschke, J. A. (2020). *Facilitating Adult and Organizational Learning Through Andragogy: A History, Philosophy, and Major Themes: A History, Philosophy, and Major Themes*. IGI Global. https://doi.org/https://doi.org/10.4018/978-1-7998-3937-8

Heracleous, L., & Werres, K. (2016). On the road to disaster: Strategic misalignments and corporate failure. *Long Range Planning*, 49(4), 491–506. DOI: 10.1016/j.lrp.2015.08.006

Herbert, D. (2001). Literary places, tourism and the heritage experience. *Annals of Tourism Research*, 28(2), 312–333. DOI: 10.1016/S0160-7383(00)00048-7

Herrera, J. (2006). El vínculo universidad – empresa en la formación de los profesionales universitarios. *Actualidades Investigativas en Educación*, 19(2), 1–30. DOI: 10.15517/aie.v6i2.9208

Herrera-Pavo, M. Á. (2021). Collaborative learning for virtual higher education. *Learning, Culture and Social Interaction*, 28, 100437. DOI: 10.1016/j.lcsi.2020.100437

Hervas, G. (2021). Lesson Study as a Faculty Development Initiative in Higher Education: A Systematic Review. *AERA Open*, 7, 2332858420982564. Advance online publication. DOI: 10.1177/2332858420982564

Hewlett, S. A. (2024, January 23). *The new rules of executive presence*. Harvard Business Review. https://hbr.org/2024/01/the-new-rules-of-executive-presence

Hidalgo, D. A. Z., & Román, F. Q. (2023). El aula invertida en el trabajo colaborativo en estudiantes de una universidad pública peruana. *Horizontes.Revista de Investigación en Ciencias de la Educación*, 7(31), 2433–2447. DOI: 10.33996/revistahorizontes.v7i31.675

Hiebert, J., Cai, J., Hwang, S., Morris, A., & Hohensee, C. (2022). What Is research, and why do people do it? In *Doing research: A new researcher's guide. Research in mathematics education* (pp. 1–15). Springer., DOI: 10.1007/978-3-031-19078-0_1

Hill, N. S., & Bartol, K. M. (2016). Empowering leadership and effective collaboration in geographically dispersed teams. *Personnel Psychology*, 69(1), 159–198. DOI: 10.1111/peps.12108

Hilton, A., Hilton, G., Dole, S., & Goos, M. (2015). School leaders as participants in teachers' professional development: The impact on teachers' and school leaders' professional growth. *The Australian Journal of Teacher Education*, 40(12), 8. DOI: 10.14221/ajte.2015v40n12.8

Hipni, A., Ramli, N. L., & Wan Ghopa, W. A. (2011). Motivation for research and publication: Experience as a researcher and an academic. *Procedia: Social and Behavioral Sciences*, 18, 213–219. DOI: 10.1016/j.sbspro.2011.05.030

Hirokawa, R. Y. (1983). Group communication and problem-solving effectiveness: An investigation of group phases. *Human Communication Research*, 9(4), 291–305. DOI: 10.1111/j.1468-2958.1983.tb00700.x

Hoang, D. T. N., & Hoang, T. (2022). Enhancing EFL students' academic writing skills in online learning via Google Docs-based collaboration: A mixed-methods study. *Computer Assisted Language Learning*, •••, 1–23. DOI: 10.1080/09588221.2022.2083176

Hoch, J. E., Bommer, W. H., Dulebohn, J. H., & Wu, D. (2016). Do ethical, authentic, and servant leadership explain variance above and beyond transformational leadership? A meta-analysis. *Journal of Management*, 44(2), 501–529. https://doi.org/10.1177/0149206316665461

Hoegl, M., & Gemuenden, H. G. (2001). Teamwork quality and the success of innovative projects: A theoretical concept and empirical evidence. *Organization Science*, 12(4), 435–449. https://doi.org/10.1287/orsc.12.4.435.10635

Hofstede, G. (1980). *Culture's consequences: International differences in work-related values*. Sage Publications.

Hogan, S., Almquist, E., & Glynn, S. E. (2005). Brand-building: Finding the touchpoints that count. *The Journal of Business Strategy*, 26(2), 11–18. DOI: 10.1108/02756660510586292

Hogg, M. A., Abrams, D., Otten, S., & Hinkle, S. (2004). The social identity perspective: Intergroup relations, self-conception, and small groups. *Small Group Research*, 35(3), 246–276. https://doi.org/10.1177/1046496404263424

Holmes, T. (2005). Ten characteristics of a high performance team. In Silberman, M. (Ed.), *The 2005 ASTD team and organization development sourcebook* (pp. 179–182). ASTD Press.

Homan, A. C., Gündemir, S., Buengeler, C., & van Kleef, G. A. (2020). Leading diversity: Towards a theory of functional leadership in diverse teams. *The Journal of Applied Psychology*, 105(10), 1101–1128. DOI: 10.1037/apl0000482 PMID: 31971407

Honebein, P. C. (1996). Seven goals for the design of constructivist learning environments. Constructivist learning environments: *Case studies in instructional design*, 11-24.

Hong, L., & Page, S. E. (2004). Groups of diverse problem solvers can outperform groups of high-ability problem solvers. *Proceedings of the National Academy of Sciences of the United States of America*, 101(46), 16385–16389. DOI: 10.1073/pnas.0403723101 PMID: 15534225

Hoorens, V. (2011). The social consequences of self-enhancement and self-protection. In Alicke, M., & Sedikides, C. (Eds.), *Handbook of self-enhancement and self-protection* (pp. 235–257). Guilford Press.

Hopkins, G. (2017). What makes effective teaching teams tick? Education World, https://www.educationworld.com/a admin/admin/admin408 a.shtml

Horner, M. (1997). Leadership theory: Past, present and future. *Team Performance Management*, 3(4), 270–287. DOI: 10.1108/13527599710195402

Horstmeyer, A. (2020). The generative role of curiosity in soft skills development for contemporary VUCA environments. *Journal of Organizational Change Management*, 33(5), 737–751. DOI: 10.1108/JOCM-08-2019-0250

Hosseini, E., Saeida Ardekani, S., Sabokro, M., & Salamzadeh, A. (2022). The study of knowledge employee voice among the knowledge-based companies: The case of an emerging economy. *Revista de Gestão*, 29(2), 117–138. DOI: 10.1108/REGE-03-2021-0037

Hostetler, A., Sengupta, P., & Hollett, T. (2018). Unsilencing critical conversations in social-studies teacher education using agent-based modeling. *Cognition and Instruction*, 36(2), 139–170. DOI: 10.1080/07370008.2017.1420653

Howard, B., Ilyashenko, N., & Jacobs, L. (2023). Cross-cultural collaboration through virtual learning in higher education. *Perspectives in Education*, 41(1), 74–87. DOI: 10.38140/pie.v41i1.6319

Howell, J. B., & Saye, J. W. (2016). Using LS to develop a shared professional teaching knowledge culture among 4th grade social studies teachers. *Journal of Social Studies Research*, 40(1), 25–37. DOI: 10.1016/j.jssr.2015.03.001

Howlett, M. (2022). Looking at the 'field'through a Zoom lens: Methodological reflections on conducting online research during a global pandemic. Qualitative Research. DOI: 10.1177/1468794120985691

Hrastinski, S. (2021). *Digital tools to support teacher professional development in lesson studies: a systematic literature review*. International Journal for Lesson and Learning Studies., DOI: 10.1108/IJLLS-09-2020-0062

Hrynchak, P., & Batty, H. (2012). The educational theory basis of team-based learning. *Medical Teacher*, 34(10), 796–801. DOI: 10.3109/0142159X.2012.687120 PMID: 22646301

Huang, R., Helgevold, N., & Lang, J. (2021). Digital technologies, online learning and lesson study. *International Journal for Lesson and Learning Studies*, 10(2), 105–117. DOI: 10.1108/IJLLS-03-2021-0018

Huang, X., & Lajoie, S. P. (2023). Social emotional interaction in collaborative learning: Why it matters and how can we measure it? *Social Sciences & Humanities Open*, 7(1), 100447. DOI: 10.1016/j.ssaho.2023.100447

Huang, Y. K., Chuang, N. K., & Kwok, L. (2023). To speak up or remain silent: The double-edged effects of trust and felt trust. *International Journal of Contemporary Hospitality Management*, 35(9), 3285–3304. DOI: 10.1108/IJCHM-05-2022-0676

Hubbard, J. (2007). LS: Teachers Collaborate in Lesson Development. *Social Studies and the Young Learner*, 19(4), 25–29.

Hudzik, J. (2015). Leading internationalisation in higher education. What matters most? *Journal of Studies in International Education*, 19(1), 6–21.

Hughes, J. E., & Roblyer, M. (2023). *Integrating educational technology into teaching: Transforming learning across disciplines* (9th ed.). Pearson Education, Inc.

Hunt, V., Layton, D., & Prince, S. (2015). *Why Diversity Matters*. McKinsey & Company. https://www.mckinsey.com/capabilities/people-and-organizational-performance/our-insights/why-diversity-matters

Hurst, E. J. (2020). Web conferencing and collaboration tools and trends. *Journal of Hospital Librarianship*, 20(3), 266–279. Advance online publication. DOI: 10.1080/15323269.2020.1780079

Hurtado, S., & Carter, D. F. (1997). Effects of college transition and perceptions of the campus racial climate on Latino college students' sense of belonging. *Sociology of Education*, 70(4), 324–345. DOI: 10.2307/2673270

Husami, K. (2022, May 10). *How can technology be a barrier to communication?* Inside telecom. https://insidetelecom.com/how-can-technology-be-a-barrier-to-communication/

Hussain, A., & Abalkhail, A. M. (2013). Determinants of library use, collections and services among the students of engineering: A case study of King Saud University. *Collection Building & Management*, 32(3), 100–110. DOI: 10.1108/CB-07-2012-0033

Hussin, W. N. T. W., Harun, J., & Shukor, N. A. (2019, July). Online tools for collaborative learning to enhance students' interaction. In *2019 7th International Conference on Information and Communication Technology (ICoICT)* (pp. 1-5). IEEE. https://doi.org/DOI: 10.1109/ICoICT.2019.8835197

IBM. (2019). *IBM Diversity & Inclusion Report*. Retrieved from https://www.ibm.com/annualreport/assets/downloads/IBM_2019_Annual_Report.pdf

Ignacio, J., Chen, H. C., & Roy, T. (2022). Advantages and challenges of fostering cognitive integration through virtual collaborative learning: A qualitative study. *BMC Nursing*, 21(1), 251. DOI: 10.1186/s12912-022-01026-6 PMID: 36076227

Ika, L. A., & Pinto, J. K. (2022). The "re-meaning" of project success: Updating and recalibrating for a modern project management. *International Journal of Project Management*, 40(7), 835–848. Advance online publication. DOI: 10.1016/j.ijproman.2022.08.001

Ikolo, V. E. (2015). User satisfaction with library services: A case study of Delta State University library. *International Journal of Information and Communication Technology Education*, 11(2), 80–89.

Indeed Editorial Team. (2024, June 28). *What are theories of performance management? (With benefits)*. Indeed Career Guide. https://uk.indeed.com/career-advice/career-development/theories-of-performance-management

Iñiguez Fuentes, M. S. (2016). *Influencia de la familia en el autoconcepto y la empatía de los adolescentes* [Doctoral thesis, Universitat de València, Spain]. https://www.educacion.gob.es/teseo/imprimirFicheroTesis.do?idFichero=v%2Bt%2FRFMi%2Fbc%3D

Ioannidis, S., & Kontis, A. P. (2023). The 4 Epochs of the Metaverse. Journal of Metaverse. DOI: 10.57019/jmv.1294970

Iqbal, M. Z., Mangina, E., & Campbell, A. G. (2022). Current challenges and future research directions in augmented reality for education. Multimodal Technologies and Interaction, 6(9), 75. DOI: 10.3390/mti6090075

Iqbal, M. Z., & Mahmood, A. (2011). Factors related to low research productivity at higher education level. *Asian Social Science*, 7(2), 188–193. DOI: 10.21522/TIJAR.2014.11.01.Art013

Ishtaiwa, F. F., & Aburezeq, I. M. (2015). The impact of Google Docs on student collaboration: A UAE case study. *Learning, Culture and Social Interaction*, 7, 85–96. DOI: 10.1016/j.lcsi.2015.07.004

Ivy, J. (2008). A new higher education marketing mix: The 7Ps for MBA marketing. *International Journal of Educational Management*, 22(4), 288–299. DOI: 10.1108/09513540810875635

Jain, P., & Brown, A. (2020). Using an Adapted Lesson Study with Early Childhood Undergraduate Students. *Teaching Education*, 33(2), 154–174. DOI: 10.1080/10476210.2020.1826424

Jamaica Teachers Association. (2024). History of the JTA. https://www.jta.org.jm/pages/history-jta Lafer, G. (2003). Graduate student unions: Organizing in a changed academic economy. *Labor Studies Journal, 28*(2), 25–43. https://doi.org/10.1353/lab.2003.0039

Jan-Mendoza, C. (2020). Communication and Communication Models. https://www.academia.edu/44018864/Communication_and_Communication_Models

Jantsch, E. (1970). Inter- and transdisciplinary university: A systems approach to education and innovation. *Policy Sciences*, 1(1), 403–428. DOI: 10.1007/BF00145222

Jelani, F., & Nordin, N. S. (2019). Barriers to effective communication at the workplace. *Universiti Teknologi MARA, 3*(2), 7-18 https://ir.uitm.edu.my/id/eprint/63597/1/63597.pdf

Jenifer, R. D., & Raman, G. P. (2015). Cross- cultural communication barriers in workplace. *International Journal of Management*, 6(1), 332–335. https://www.iaeme.com/IJM.asp

Jeong, K. O. (2016). A study on the integration of Google Docs as a web-based collaborative learning platform in EFL writing instruction. *Indian Journal of Science and Technology*, 9(39). Advance online publication. DOI: 10.17485/ijst/2016/v9i39/103239

Jeung, C. W., & Yoon, H. J. (2016). Leader humility and psychological empowerment: Investigating contingencies. *Journal of Managerial Psychology*, 31(7), 1122–1136. DOI: 10.1108/JMP-07-2015-0270

Jevons, C. (2006). Universities: A prime example of branding going wrong. *Journal of Product and Brand Management*, 15(7), 466–467. DOI: 10.1108/10610420610712856

Jiang, W., & Gu, Q. (2016). How abusive supervision and abusive supervisory climate influence salesperson creativity and sales team effectiveness in China. Mang. *Management Decision*, 54(2), 455–475. DOI: 10.1108/MD-07-2015-0302

Jimenez, A., Boehe, D. M., Taras, V., & Caprar, D. V. (2017). Working across boundaries: Current and future perspectives on global virtual teams. *Journal of International Management*, 23(4), 341–349. DOI: 10.1016/j.intman.2017.05.001

Jing, A., May, K., Lee, G., & Billinghurst, M. (2021). Eye see what you see: Exploring how bi-directional augmented reality gaze visualisation influences co-located symmetric collaboration. Frontiers in Virtual Reality. DOI: 10.3389/frvir.2021.697367

Jin, J. L., & Wang, L. (2024). Design and governance of international joint venture innovation strategy: Evidence from China. . *International Business Review*, 33(3), 102277. Advance online publication. DOI: 10.1016/j.ibusrev.2024.102277

Jlittle. (2023, May 1). *Ford's five day workweek. May 1st 1926. Today in Ford Motor Company history*. Gary Crossley Ford. https://www.garycrossleyford.com/blog/today-in-ford-history/fords-five-day-workweek-may-1st-1926/

Joachimsthaler, E., & Aaker, D. A. (2009). *Brand leadership: Building assets in an information economy*. Simon and Schuster.

Jogezai, N. A., Baloch, F. A., Jaffar, M., Shah, T., Khilji, G. K., & Bashir, S. (2021). Teachers' attitudes towards social media (SM) use in online learning amid the COVID-19 pandemic: the effects of SM use by teachers and religious scholars during physical distancing. Heliyon, 7(4). DOI: 10.1016/j.heliyon.2021.e06781

Johann, D., Neufeld, J., Thomas, K., Rathmann, J., & Rauhut, H. (2024). The impact of researchers' perceived pressure on their publication strategies. *Research Evaluation*, 00, 1–16. DOI: 10.1093/reseval/rvae011

Johari, A. B., Wahat, N., & Zaremohzzabieh, Z. (2021). Innovative work behavior among teachers in Malaysia: The effects of teamwork, principal support and humor. *Asian Journal of University Education*, 17(2), 72–84. DOI: 10.24191/ajue.v17i2.13387

Johnson, D. W., Johnson, R. T., & Smith, K. A. (1997). *El Aprendizaje Cooperativo regresa a la Universidad: ¿qué evidencia existe de que funciona?* Retrieved from: https://www.researchgate.net/publication/267940683_El_Aprendizaje_Cooperativo_regresa_a_la_Universidad_que_evidencia_existe_de_que_funciona#fullTextFileContent

Johnson, D. W., & Johnson, R. T. (2009). An educational psychology success story: Social interdependence theory and cooperative learning. *Educational Researcher*, 38(5), 365–379. DOI: 10.3102/0013189X09339057

Johnson, L. (2023). Black women and theoretical frameworks. *The Scholarship Without Borders Journal*, 1(2). Advance online publication. DOI: 10.57229/2834-2267.1018

Johnston, E., Burleigh, C., & Wilson, A. (2020). Interdisciplinary collaborative research for professional academic development in higher education. *Higher Learning Research Communications*, 10(1), 62–77. DOI: 10.18870/hlrc.v10i1.1175

Jony, A. I., & Serradell-López, E. (2021). Key factors that boost the effectiveness of virtual teamwork in online higher education. Research and Innovation Forum 2020: Disruptive Technologies in Times of Change, King, A. (1998). Transactive Peer Tutoring: Distributing Cognition and Metacognition. *Educational Psychology Review*, 10(1), 57–74. DOI: 10.1023/A:1022858115001

Jordan, K. (2022). Academics' perceptions of research impact and engagement through interactions on social media platforms. *Learning, Media and Technology*, 48(3), 415–428. https://doi.org/10.1080/17439884.2022.2065298

Josué, A., Bedoya-Flores, M., Mosquera-Quiñonez, E., Mesías-Simisterra, Á., & Bautista-Sánchez, J. (2023). Educational platforms: Digital tools for the teaching-learning process in education. *Ibero-American Journal of Education & Society Research*, 3(1), 259–263. DOI: 10.56183/iberoeds.v3i1.626

Joubert, J., Callaghan, R., & Engelbrecht, J. (2020). LS in a blended approach to support isolated teachers in teaching with technology. *ZDM Mathematics Education*, 52(5), 907–925. DOI: 10.1007/s11858-020-01161-x

Jovanović, A. & Milosavljević, A. (2022). VoRtex Metaverse platform for gamified collaborative learning. Electronics. DOI: 10.3390/electronics11030317

Judson, K. M., Aurand, T. W., Gorchels, L., & Gordon, G. L. (2008). Building a university brand from within: University administrators' perspectives of internal branding. *Services Marketing Quarterly*, 30(1), 54–68. DOI: 10.1080/15332960802467722

Judson, K. M., Gorchels, L., & Aurand, T. W. (2006). Building a university brand from within: A comparison of coaches' perspectives of internal branding. *Journal of Marketing for Higher Education*, 16(1), 97–114. DOI: 10.1300/J050v16n01_05

Juliana, C., Gani, L., & Jermias, J. (2021). Performance implications of misalignment among business strategy, leadership style, organizational culture and management accounting systems. *International Journal of Ethics and Systems*, 37(4), 509–525. DOI: 10.1108/IJOES-02-2021-0033

Kaendler, C., Wiedmann, M., Rummel, N., & Spada, H. (2015). Teacher competencies for the implementation of collaborative learning in the classroom: A framework and research review. *Educational Psychology Review*, 27(3), 505–536. DOI: 10.1007/s10648-014-9288-9

Kaimara, P., Fokides, E., Oikonomou, A., & Deliyannis, I. (2021). Potential barriers to the implementation of digital game-based learning in the classroom: Pre-service teachers' views. Technology, Knowledge and Learning, 26(4), 825-844. DOI: 10.1007/s10758-021-09512-7

Kaliisa, R., Rienties, B., Mørch, A. I., & Kluge, A. (2022). Social learning analytics in computer-supported collaborative learning environments: A systematic review of empirical studies. *Computers and Education Open*, 3, 100073. DOI: 10.1016/j.caeo.2022.100073

Kamath, B. (2018). An Empirical Study of the Brand Building of Engineering Institutions in Karnataka: A Strategic Framework (Doctoral dissertation, National Institute of Technology Karnataka, Surathkal).

Kanellopoulou, E.-M., & Darra, M. (2019). Benefits, Difficulties and Conditions of LS Implementation in Basic Teacher Education: A Review. *International Journal of Higher Education*, 8(18), 18. Advance online publication. DOI: 10.5430/ijhe.v8n4p18

Kannan, M., & Meenakshi, S. (2022). An analysis of the socio-psychological barriers in the course of communicative competence in the English language. *International Journal of Social Science and Humanities Research*, 10(2), 115–122.

Kapferer, J. N. (1997). *Strategic brand management: Creating and sustaining brand equity long term*. Kogan Page Publishers.

Kapur, R. (2018). *Barriers to effective communication*. Researchgate. https://www.researchgate.net/publication/323794732_barriers_to_effective_communication

Karakose, T., Polat, H., & Papadakis, S. (2021). Examining teachers' perspectives on school principals' digital leadership roles and technology capabilities during the COVID-19 pandemic. Sustainability. DOI: 10.3390/su132313448

Karam, M., Fares, H., & Al-Majeed, S. (2021). Quality assurance framework for the design and delivery of virtual, real-time courses. Information. DOI: 10.3390/info12020093

Kassim, N. (2009). Evaluating users' satisfaction on academic library performance. *Malaysian Journal of Library and Information Science*, 14(2), 101–115. https://ejournal.um.edu.my/index.php/MJLIS/article/view/6960

Katzenbach, J. R., & Smith, D. K. (2015). *The wisdom of teams: Creating the high-performance organization.* Harvard Business Review Press.

Kaufman, D., Felder, R., & Fuller, H. (2000). Accounting for individual effort in cooperative learning teams. *Journal of Engineering Education*, 89(2), 133–140. DOI: 10.1002/j.2168-9830.2000.tb00507.x

Keller, K. L. (2013). *Building.* Measuring, and Managing Brand Equity.

Keller, K. L., & Swaminathan, V. (2019). *Strategic brand management: Building, measuring, and managing brand equity.* Pearson.

Kelloway, E. K., Turner, N., Barling, J., & Loughlin, C. (2012). Transformational leadership and employee psychological well-being: The mediating role of employee trust in leadership. *Work and Stress*, 26(1), 39–55. DOI: 10.1080/02678373.2012.660774

Kennedy, M. M. (2016). How does professional development improve teaching? *Review of Educational Research*, 86(4), 945–980. DOI: 10.3102/0034654315626800

Kent, M. L. (2017). *Principles of dialogue and the history of Dialogic Theory in public relations. Researchgate.* https://www.researchgate.net/publication/318509024_Principles_of_Dialogue_and_the_ History_of_Dialogic_Theory_in_Public_Relations

Kent, M. L., & Taylor, M. (1998). Building dialogic relationships through the World Wide Web. *Public Relations Review*, 24(3), 321–334. DOI: 10.1016/S0363-8111(99)80143-X

Kent, M. L., & Taylor, M. (2002). Toward a dialogic theory of public relations. *Public Relations Review*, 28(1), 21–37. DOI: 10.1016/S0363-8111(02)00108-X

Kent, M. L., & Taylor, M. (2021). Fostering dialogic engagement: Toward an architecture of social media for social change. *Social Media + Society*, 7(1), 1–10. DOI: 10.1177/2056305120984462

Kern, S. (2011). Analytic model for academic research productivity having factors, interactions and implications. *Cancer Biology & Therapy*, 12(11), 949–956. DOI: 10.4161/cbt.12.11.18368

Keyton, J., Ford, D. J., & Smith, F. L. (2012). Communication, collaboration, and identification as facilitators and constraints of multiteam systems. In S. J. Zaccaro, M. A. Marks, & L. A. DeChurch (Eds.), *Multiteam systems: An organization form for dynamic and complex environments* (pp. 173–190). Routledge/Taylor & Francis Group.

Keyton, J. (2017). Communication in organizations. *Annual Review of Organizational Psychology and Organizational Behavior*, 4(1), 501–526. DOI: 10.1146/annurev-orgpsych-032516-113341

Keyton, J., Ford, D. J., & Smith, F. L. (2008). A Mesolevel Communicative Model of Collaboration. *Communication Theory*, 18(3), 376–406. DOI: 10.1111/j.1468-2885.2008.00327.x

Kezar, A., & Eckel, P. D. (2002). The effect of institutional culture on change strategies in higher education: Universal principles or culturally responsive concepts? *The Journal of Higher Education*, 73(4), 435–460. DOI: 10.1080/00221546.2002.11777159

Kiger, M. E., & Varpio, L. (2020). Thematic analysis of qualitative data: AMEE guide No 131. *Medical Teacher*, 42(8), 846–854. DOI: 10.1080/0142159X.2020.1755030 PMID: 32356468

Kilgo, C. A., Ezell Sheets, J. K., & Pascarella, E. T. (2015). The link between high-impact practices and student learning: Some longitudinal evidence. *Higher Education*, 69(4), 509–525. DOI: 10.1007/s10734-014-9788-z

Kim, B., Park, E., & Camero, G. T. (2017). Transparent communication efforts inspire confident, even greater, employee performance. *Asian Journal of Public Relations*, 1(1), 9–31.

Kim, S., Lee, H., & Connerton, T. P. (2020). How psychological safety affects team performance: Mediating role of efficacy and learning behavior. *Frontiers in Psychology*, 11, 1581. DOI: 10.3389/fpsyg.2020.01581 PMID: 32793037

Kıral, E., & Durdu, İ. (2021). The relationship between tendency to gossip and organizational commitment. *International Online Journal of Education & Teaching*, 8(3), 1833–1856.

Kirschner, P. A. (2001). Using integrated electronic environments for collaborative teaching/learning. *Learning and Instruction*, 10, 1–9. DOI: 10.1016/S0959-4752(00)00021-9

Kirschner, P., Strijbos, J. W., Kreijns, K., & Beers, P. J. (2004). Designing electronic collaborative learning environments. *Educational Technology Research and Development*, 52(3), 47–66. DOI: 10.1007/BF02504675

Kivimaki, M., & Elovainio, M. (1999). A short version of the team climate inventory: Development and psychometric properties. *Journal of Occupational and Organizational Psychology*, 72(2), 241–246. DOI: 10.1348/096317999166644

Klein, J. T., Häberli, R., Scholz, R. W., Grossenbacher-Mansuy, W., Bill, A., & Welti, M. (2001). Transdisciplinarity: Joint problem solving among science, technology, and society. In *Birkhäuser Basel eBooks*.

Klein, J. T. (2008). Evaluation of interdisciplinary and transdisciplinary research. *American Journal of Preventive Medicine*, 35(2), S116–S123. DOI: 10.1016/j.amepre.2008.05.010 PMID: 18619391

Klein, J. T. (2010). *Creating interdisciplinary campus cultures*. John Wiley & Sons.

Knopf, T., Stumpp, S., & Michelis, D. (2021). How online collaborative learning leads to improved online learning experience in higher education. In Karpasitis, C. (Ed.), *ECSM 2021 8th European Conference on Social Media 2021* (No. July, pp. 119-127).

Knowles, M. (1975). *Self-Directed Learning: A Guide for Learners and Teachers* (Vol. 2). Association Press., DOI: 10.1177/105960117700200220

Knowles, M. S., Holton, E., & Swanson, R. (2005). *The adult learner: the definitive classic in adult education and human resource development* (6th ed.). Elsevier. DOI: 10.4324/9780080481913

Kochan, & Kimball. (2019). Unions, worker voice, and management practices: Implications for a high-productivity, high-wage economy. *RSF: The Russell Sage Foundation Journal of the Social Sciences, 5*(5), 88–108. https://doi.org/10.7758/rsf.2019.5.5.05

Kohlmeier, J., Howell, J., Saye, J., McCormick, T., Shannon, D., Jones, C., & Brush, T. (2020). Investigating teacher adoption of authentic pedagogy through LS. *Theory and Research in Social Education*, 48(4), 492–528. DOI: 10.1080/00933104.2020.1751761

Kolb, D. (2014). *Experiential Learning: Experience as the Source of Learning and Development*. Pearson Education.

Kopelman, R. E., Brief, A. P., & Guzzo, R. A. (1990). The role of climate and culture in productivity. In Schneider, B. (Ed.), *Organizational climate and culture* (pp. 282–318). Jossey-Bass.

Kopelman, R. E., Prottas, D. J., & Davis, A. L. (2008). Douglas McGregor's theory X and Y: Toward a construct-valid measure. *Journal of Managerial Issues*, •••, 255–271.

Korkmaz, F., & Zorlu, K. (2021). *Organizational communication as an effective Communication Strategy in Organisation and the Role of the Leader. In book: Management strategies to survive in a competitive environment.* How to Improve Company Performance., DOI: 10.1007/978-3-030-72288-3_21

Kotler, P. (2009). *Marketing management: A south Asian perspective.* Pearson Education India.

Kotler, P., & Armstrong, G. (2010). *Principles of marketing.* Pearson education.

Kotler, P., & Fox, K. F. (1995). *Strategic marketing for educational institutions.* Prentice Hall.

Kottman, A., Huisman, J., Brockerhoff, L., Cremonini, L., & Mampaey, J. (2016). How can one create a culture for quality enhancement: Final report. Ghent University: Ghent, Belgium.

Kox, E. S., Kerstholt, J. H., Hueting, T. F., & de Vries, P. W. (2021). Trust repair in human-agent teams: the effectiveness of explanations and expressing regret. Autonomous agents and multi-agent systems, 35(2), 30. DOI: 10.1007/s10458-021-09515-9

Kozlowski, S. W. J., & Ilgen, D. R. (2006). Enhancing the effectiveness of work groups and teams. *Psychological Science in the Public Interest*, 7(3), 77–124. DOI: 10.1111/j.1529-1006.2006.00030.x PMID: 26158912

Krause, R., Withers, M. C., & Waller, M. J. (2024). Leading the board in a crisis: Strategy and performance implications of board chair directive leadership. *Journal of Management*, 50(2), 654–684. https://doi-org.trevecca.idm.oclc.org/10.1177/01492063221121584. DOI: 10.1177/01492063221121584

Kreijns, K., Kirschner, P. A., & Jochems, W. (2003). Identifying the pitfalls for social interaction in computer-supported collaborative learning environments: A review of the research. *Computers in Human Behavior*, 19(3), 335–353. DOI: 10.1016/S0747-5632(02)00057-2

Kruk, M. (2022). Dynamicity of perceived willingness to communicate, motivation, boredom and anxiety in Second Life: The case of two advanced learners of English. . *Computer Assisted Language Learning*, 35(1-2), 190–216. Advance online publication. DOI: 10.1080/09588221.2019.1677722

Kubo, K., Okazaki, H., Ichikawa, H., Nishihara, S., Nawa, H., Okazaki, M., Kawasaki, Y., Nakura, H., Matsunaga, H., & Sendo, T. (2011). Usefulness of group work as a teaching strategy for long-term practical training in the 6-year pharmaceutical education. Yakugaku Zasshi. *Journal of the Pharmaceutical Society of Japan*, 132(12), 1467–1476. PMID: 22986221

Kumako, S. K., & Asumeng, M. A. (2013). Transformational leadership as a moderator of the relationship between psychological safety and learning behaviour in work teams in Ghana. *SA Journal of Industrial Psychology*, 39(1). Advance online publication. https://doi.org/10.4102/sajip.v39i1.1036

Kumar, P. (2023). Organisational climate and its impact on job satisfaction. *International Journal of Advances in Engineering and Management*, 5(1), 1060–1071.

Kumi-Yeboah, A., Yuan, G., & Dogbey, J. (2017). Online collaborative learning activities: The perceptions of culturally diverse graduate students. *Online Learning : the Official Journal of the Online Learning Consortium*, 21(4), 5–28. DOI: 10.24059/olj.v21i4.1277

Kuna, P., Hašková, A., & Borza, Ľ (2023). Creation of virtual reality for education purposes. Sustainability. DOI: 10.3390/su15097153

Kurniawati, A. (2022). Google Docs to manage an EFL writing class: How it helps and what to prepare. [JEE]. *Journal of English and Education*, 8(2), 97–109. DOI: 10.20885/jee.v8i2.25740

Kushwaha, B. P., Singh, R. K., Varghese, N., & Singh, V. N. (2020). Integrating social media and digital media as new elements of integrated marketing communication for creating brand equity. Journal of Content. *Community & Communication*, 11(6), 52–64.

Kwak, N., & Ramirez, F. O. (2019). Is engineering harder to crack than science? A cross-national analysis of women's participation in male-dominated fields of study in higher education. *Annual Review of Comparative and International Education*, 2018(37), 159–183. DOI: 10.1108/S1479-367920190000037014

Laal, M., & Ghodsi, S. M. (2012). Benefits of collaborative Learning. *Social Behavioral Science*, 13, 486–490.

Laal, M., & Ghodsi, S. M. (2012). The effectiveness of collaborative learning on students' academic achievement: A meta-analysis. *Procedia: Social and Behavioral Sciences*, 46, 131–138.

Laal, M., & Laal, M. (2012). Collaborative learning: What is it? *Procedia: Social and Behavioral Sciences*, 31, 491–495. DOI: 10.1016/j.sbspro.2011.12.092

Labour Relations and Industrial Disputes Act. (1975). https://www.mlss.gov.jm/wp-content/uploads/2018/02/Laboour-Relations-and-Industrial-Disputes-Act5b15d.pdf

Lacka, E., Wong, T. C., & Haddoud, M. Y. (2021). Can digital technologies improve students' efficiency? Exploring the role of Virtual Learning Environment and Social Media use in Higher Education. *Computers & Education*, 163, 104099. https://doi.org/https://doi.org/10.1016/j.compedu.2020.104099. DOI: 10.1016/j.compedu.2020.104099

Ladson-Billings, G. (2014). Culturally relevant pedagogy 2.0: Aka the remix. *Harvard Educational Review*, 84(1), 74–84. DOI: 10.17763/haer.84.1.p2rj131485484751

Lafley, A. G., & Charan, R. (2008). *The game-changer: How you can drive revenue and profit growth with innovation*. Crown Business.

Lakkala, S., Galkienė, A., Navaitienė, J., Cierpiałowska, T., Tomecek, S., & Uusiautti, S. (2021). Teachers Supporting Students in Collaborative Ways—An Analysis of Collaborative Work Creating Supportive Learning Environments for Every Student in a School: Cases from Austria, Finland, Lithuania, and Poland. *Sustainability (Basel)*, 13(5), 2804. https://www.mdpi.com/2071-1050/13/5/2804. DOI: 10.3390/su13052804

Lambert, L. (2002). A framework for shared leadership. *Educational Leadership*, 59, 37–40. http://www.ascd.org/publications/educational-leadership/may02/vol59/num08/toc.aspx

Lammers, J. C. (2011). How institutions communicate: Institutional messages, institutional logics, and organizational communication. *Management Communication Quarterly*, 25(1), 154–182. DOI: 10.1177/0893318910389280

Lämsä, J., Hämäläinen, R., Koskinen, P., Viiri, J., & Lampi, E. (2021). What do we do when we analyse the temporal aspects of computer-supported collaborative learning? A systematic literature review. *Educational Research Review*, 33, 100387. DOI: 10.1016/j.edurev.2021.100387

Lan, Y. J. (2020). Immersion into virtual reality for language learning. Psychology of learning and motivation.

Landis, E. A., Hill, D., & Harvey, M. R. (2014). A synthesis of leadership theories and styles. *Journal of Management Policy and Practice*, 15(2), 97.

Lane, A. B., & Bartlett, J. (2016). Dialogic principles don't make it in Ppactice—And what we can do about It. *International Journal of Communication*, 10, 1–21.

Lantz-Wagner, S. (2022). Paths to Pathways: Exploring Lived Experiences of International Students to and Through Third-Party Pathway Programs.

Larson, L., & DeChurch, L. A. (2020). Leading teams in the digital age: Four perspectives on technology and what they mean for leading teams. *The Leadership Quarterly*, 31(1), 101377. DOI: 10.1016/j.leaqua.2019.101377 PMID: 32863679

Larsson, J. & Larsson, L. (2020). Integration, application and importance of collaboration in sustainable project management. Sustainability. DOI: 10.3390/su12020585

Lassoued, Z., Alhendawi, M., & Bashitialshaaer, R. (2020). An exploratory study of the obstacles for achieving quality in distance learning during the COVID-19 pandemic. Education sciences. DOI: 10.3390/educsci10090232

Lau, W. W., & Ngo, H. Y. (2019). Managing cultural diversity at work: The roles of diversity management and inclusive climate. *Asia Pacific Journal of Human Resources*, 57(2), 136–159. DOI: 10.1111/1744-7941.12173

LeaderFactor. (2023). *The complete guide to psychological safety*. https://www.leaderfactor.com/resources/what-is-psychological-safety

Leal Filho, W., Wall, T., Rayman-Bacchus, L., Mifsud, M., Pritchard, D. J., Lovren, V. O., ... & Balogun, A. L. (2021). Impacts of COVID-19 and social isolation on academic staff and students at universities: a cross-sectional study. BMC public health, 21(1), 1213. DOI: 10.1186/s12889-021-11040-z

Lea, S. J., Stephenson, D., & Troy, J. (2003). Higher education students' attitudes to student-centred learning: Beyond 'educational bulimia'? *Studies in Higher Education*, 28(3), 321–334. DOI: 10.1080/03075070309293

Lee, M. H., Wang, C., & Yu, M. C. (2023). A Multilevel Study of Change-Oriented Leadership and Commitment: The Moderating Effect of Group Emotional Contagion. Psychology Research and Behavior Management, 637-650. DOI: 10.2147/PRBM.S385385

Lee, J. Y., Kozlenkova, I. V., & Palmatier, R. W. (2015). Structural marketing: Using organizational structure to achieve marketing objectives. *Journal of the Academy of Marketing Science*, 43(1), 73–99. DOI: 10.1007/s11747-014-0402-9

Lee, L. H. J., & Tan, S. C. (2020). Teacher learning in Lesson Study: Affordances, disturbances, contradictions, and implications. *Teaching and Teacher Education*, 89, 102986. DOI: 10.1016/j.tate.2019.102986

Lee, M. Y. (2019). The development of elementary pre-service teachers' professional noticing of students' thinking through adapted LS. *Asia-Pacific Journal of Teacher Education*, 47(4), 383–398. DOI: 10.1080/1359866X.2019.1607253

Lee, Y., & Queenie Li, J. (2021). The role of communication transparency and organisational trust in publics' perception, attitudes and social distancing behaviour: A case study of the Covid 19 outbreak. *Journal of Contingencies and Crisis Management*, 29(4), 368–384. DOI: 10.1111/1468-5973.12354

Lei, M. & Medwell, J. (2021). … the COVID-19 pandemic on student teachers: How the shift to online collaborative learning affects student teachers' learning and future teaching in a Chinese …. Asia Pacific Education Review. DOI: 10.1007/s12564-021-09686-w

Lembke, S., & Wilson, M. G. (1998). Putting the "team" into teamwork: Alternative theoretical contributions for contemporary management practice. *Human Relations*, 51(7), 927–944. https://doi.org/10.1177/0018726798 05100704

Lencioni, P. M. (2002). *The five dysfunctions of a team: A Leadership Fable, 20th Anniversary Edition*. John Wiley & Sons.

Letsie, H., Nkhi, S. E., & Mncina, T. C. (2023). An investigation of the impact of non-formal education on sustainable development in Mafeteng, Lesotho. *Interdisciplinary Journal of Rural and Community Studies*, 5, 36–48. DOI: 10.38140/ijrcs-2023.vol5.04

Letsie, H., & Osunkule, O. (2024). An exploration of Pprticipatory communication practices in sustainable development and poverty alleviation: A case study of Lifajaneng village. *Journal of Asian and African Studies*, 00219096241235297. Advance online publication. DOI: 10.1177/00219096241235297

Levi, D., & Askay, D. (2020). *Group dynamics for teams* (6th ed.). SAGE Publications.

Levine, A., & Van Pelt, S. (2021). *The great upheaval: Higher education's past, present and uncertain future*. Johns Hopkins University Press.

Lewin, T. (2014, April 17). *Colleges increasing spending on sports faster than on academics, report finds*. The New York Times. https://www.nytimes.com/2014/04/07/education/colleges-increasing-spending-on-sports-faster-than-on-academics-report-finds.html

Lewis, C. (2016). How does LS improve mathematics instruction? *ZDM Mathematics Education*, 48(4), 571–580. DOI: 10.1007/s11858-016-0792-x

Lewis, C. C., Perry, R. R., Friedkin, S., & Roth, J. R. (2012). Improving Teaching Does Improve Teachers: Evidence from LS. *Journal of Teacher Education*, 63(5), 368–375. DOI: 10.1177/0022487112446633

Lewis, T. (2006). Creativity: A framework for the design/problem solving discourse in technology education. *Journal of Technology Education*, 17, 36–53.

Li, J., & Li, Y. (2021). The role of grit on students' academic success in experiential learning context. *Frontiers in Psychology*, 12, 774149. DOI: 10.3389/fpsyg.2021.774149 PMID: 34733225

Limeri, L. B., Carter, N. T., Choe, J., Harper, H. G., Martin, H. R., Benton, A., & Dolan, E. L. (2020). Growing a growth mindset: Characterizing how and why undergraduate students' mindsets change. International Journal of STEM Education, 7, 1-19. DOI: 10.1186/s40594-020-00227-2

Lim-Ratnam, C., Lee, C., Jiang, H., & Sudarshan, A. (2019). Lost in adaptation? Issues of adapting Japanese lesson study in non-Japanese contexts. *Educational Research for Policy and Practice*, 18(3), 263–278. DOI: 10.1007/s10671-019-09247-4

Lincoln, Y. S., & Guba, E. G. (1985). *Naturalistic Inquiry*. SAGE. DOI: 10.1016/0147-1767(85)90062-8

Lin, P. S., & Kennette, L. N. (2022). Creating an inclusive community for BIPOC faculty: Women of colour in academia. *SN Social Sciences*, 2(11), 246. DOI: 10.1007/s43545-022-00555-w PMID: 36339527

Lipponen, L. (2023). Exploring foundations for computer-supported collaborative learning. In Stahl, G. (Ed.), *Computer support for collaborative learning* (pp. 72–81). Routledge. DOI: 10.4324/9781315045467-12

Liu, W., Zhang, P., Liao, J., Hao, P., & Mao, J. (2016). Abusive supervision and employee creativity: The mediating of psychological safety and organisational identification. *Management Decision*, 54(1), 130–147. DOI: 10.1108/MD-09-2013-0443

Li, Y. (2023). The effect of online collaborative writing instruction on enhancing writing performance, writing motivation, and writing self-efficacy of Chinese EFL learners. *Frontiers in Psychology*, 14, 1165221. DOI: 10.3389/fpsyg.2023.1165221 PMID: 37441335

Llopis, G. (2013). *The innovation mentality: Six strategies to disrupt the status quo and reinvent the way we work*. Entrepreneur Press.

Lomas, C., Burke, M., & Page, C. L. (2008). Collaboration tools. *Educause Learning Initiative*, 2(11). http://www.ccti.colfinder.org/sites/default/files/PreService_International/resources/KD/M4/U4/Collaboration%20Tools.pdf

López Esquivel, N. G. (2021). Simulación clínica como método innovador de enseñanza-aprendizaje en las carreras de Medicina de la Universidad del Pacífico. *Revista Multidisciplinar UP, 2*(2), 13–23. https://www.upacifico.edu.py:8043/index.php/Rev_MUP/article/view/199

Lorenzo-Alvarez, R., Rudolphi-Solero, T., Ruiz-Gomez, M. J., & Sendra-Portero, F. (2020). Game-Based learning in virtual worlds: A multiuser online game for medical undergraduate radiology education within second life. . *Anatomical Sciences Education*, 13(5), 602–617. DOI: 10.1002/ase.1927 PMID: 31665564

Lou, Y., Abrami, P. C., & Spence, J. C. (2000). Effects of within-class grouping on student achievement: An exploratory model. *The Journal of Educational Research*, 94(2), 101–112. DOI: 10.1080/00220670009598748

Lueg, K., & Graf, A. (2021, June 10). *The organization of higher education: An overview of sociological research into universities as organizations.* Elgaronline https://www.elgaronline.com/edcollchap/book/9781839103261/book-part-9781839103261-10.xml

Luft, J. (1961). The johari window. *Human relations training news, 5*(1), 6-7.

Lu, J., Zhang, Z., & Jia, M. (2019). Does servant leadership affect employees' emotional labor? A social information-processing perspective. *Journal of Business Ethics*, 159(2), 507–518. DOI: 10.1007/s10551-018-3816-3

Lumpkin, A., Achen, R. M., & Dodd, R. K. (2015). Student perceptions of active learning. *College Student Journal*, 49(1), 121–133.

Luna, M., & Molero, D. (2013). Revisión teórica sobre el autoconcepto y su importancia en la adolescencia. (2013). *Revista Electrónica de Investigación y Docencia (REID), 10.*https://revistaselectronicas.ujaen.es/index.php/reid/article/view/991

Lune, H., & Berg, B. L. (2017). *Qualitative research methods for the social sciences.* Pearson.

Luthans, F., & Avolio, B. J. (2003). Authentic leadership development. In Cameron, K. S. (Ed.), *J. E.*

Lutz, G. (2021, May 4). *The world of research infrastructure.* https://forscenter.ch/wp-content/uploads/2021/05/presentation-research-infrastructures-4.5.2021_compressed.pdf

Mabelebele, J. (2015). *The Future of Higher Education in South Africa.Higher Education Conference, 1st September 2015*, Pricewaterhouse Cooper, Cape Town, South Africa.

MacGregor, J. (2000). Collaborative learning: Reframing the classroom. *Thought & Action*, 16(1), 9–16.

Macías, M. E., ... (2023). Proyecto de innovación y mejora de la calidad docente. Convocatoria 2022/2023. Diseño de micro vídeos para el profesorado sobre diversidad y buenas prácticas inclusivas para el alumnado universitario. https://docta.ucm.es/rest/api/core/bitstreams/3d46fb73-1da8-4aa5-9843-4f646ddd0e56/content

MacInnes, J., Gadsby, E., Reynolds, J., Mateu, N. C., Lette, M., Ristl, C., & Billings, J. (2020). Exploring the team climate of health and social care professionals implementing integrated care for older people in Europe. *International Journal of Integrated Care*, 20(4), 3. Advance online publication. DOI: 10.5334/ijic.5467 PMID: 33132788

MacLeod, M. (2016). What makes iterdisciplinarity difficult? Some consequences of domain specificity in interdisciplinary practice. https://link.springer.com/article/10.1007/s11229-016-1236-4

Macnamara, J., Lwin, M., Adi, A., & Zerfass, A. (2016). 'PESO' media strategy shifts to 'SOEP': Opportunities and ethical dilemmas. *Public Relations Review*, 42(3), 377–385. DOI: 10.1016/j.pubrev.2016.03.001

Madariaga, L., Allendes, C., Nussbaum, M., Barrios, G., & Acevedo, N. (2023). Offline and online user experience of gamified robotics for introducing computational thinking: Comparing engagement, game mechanics and coding motivation. . *Computers & Education*, 193, 104664. DOI: 10.1016/j.compedu.2022.104664

Madsen, S. R. (2012). Women and leadership in higher education: Learning and advancement in leadership programs. *Advances in Developing Human Resources*, 14(1), 3–10. DOI: 10.1177/1523422311429668

Madsen, S. R., & Longman, K. A. (2020). Women's leadership in higher education: Status, barriers, and motivators. *Journal of Higher Education Management*, 35(1), 13–24.

Maheshwari, G., & Nayak, R. (2022). Women leadership in Vietnamese higher education institutions: An exploratory study on barriers and enablers for career enhancement. *Educational Management Administration & Leadership*, 50(5), 758–775. DOI: 10.1177/1741143220945700

Makri, A., & Vlachopoulos, D. (2020). Applying adult learning theories in digital educational and training programs. EDULEARN20 Proceedings, Marcut, I. G., & Chisiu, C. M. (2018). Heutagogy–an appropriate framework for computer aided learning course with post-graduate teacher students. *Journal Plus Education*, 21, 203–215.

Malecka, B., Boud, D., & Carless, D. (2022). Eliciting, processing and enacting feedback: Mechanisms for embedding student feedback literacy within the curriculum. *Teaching in Higher Education*, 27(7), 908–922. DOI: 10.1080/13562517.2020.1754784

Mallik, D. M. A., & Achar, A. (2020). Comparative analysis of 7P's marketing mix in brand building among management institutes-An empirical. *International Journal of Scientific and Technology Research*, 9(3), 6691–6699.

Mantikayan, J. M., & Abdulgani, M. A. (2018). Factors affecting faculty research productivity: Conclusions from a critical review of the literature. *JPAIR Multidisciplinary Research*, 31, 1–21. DOI: 10.7719/jpair.v31i1.56

Mara, M., Stein, J. P., Latoschik, M. E., Lugrin, B., Schreiner, C., Hostettler, R., & Appel, M. (2021). User responses to a humanoid robot observed in real life, virtual reality, 3D and 2D. Frontiers in psychology, 12, 633178. DOI: 10.3389/fpsyg.2021.633178

Marbley, A. F., Wong, A., Santos-Hatchett, S. L., Pratt, C., & Jaddo, L. (2011). Women faculty of colour: Voices, gender, and the expression of our multiple identities within academia. *Advancing Women in Leadership*, 31(1), 166–174.

Marconi, J. (1999). *The complete guide to publicity: Maximize visibility for your product, service, or organization.* Contemporary Books.

Marconi, J. (2004). *Public relations: The complete guide.* South-Western Pub.

Marjaei, S., Ahmadianyazdi, F., & Chandrashekara, M. (2002). Awareness and satisfaction of research scholars using library resources and services in academic libraries. *Library Philosophy and Practice* (e-journal). 6898. https://digitalcommons.unl.edu/libphilprac/6898

Marjanović, J., Domazet, I., & Miljković, J. (2023). Higher Education Branding through Instrumental Values. *JWEE*, (3/4), 75–94.

Martens, J. (2020). 12. Vocalizations and Speciation of Palearctic Birds. Ecology and evolution of acoustic communication in birds, 221-240. DOI: 10.7591/9781501736957-019

Martínez Cantos, J. (2020). Políticas de igualdad y diversidad. In F. J. García Castaño, M. C. López Sánchez & C. Torrego Seco (dirs.), *Educación inclusiva* (pp. 727-745). Ediciones Pirámide.

Martinez, A., Bellody, K., & Smith, E. (2023). Collaborative communication with library student workers in unexpected places: digital reference analysis.

Matošková, J. (2020). Communication tools as drivers of employees' knowledge sharing: Evidence from the Czech Republic. *Problems and Perspectives in Management*, 18(1), 415–427. DOI: 10.21511/ppm.18(1).2020.36

Mattessich, P. W., & Johnson, K. M. (2018). *Collaboration: What makes it work* (3rd ed.). Fieldstone Alliance.

Maxwell, J. A. (2012). *Qualitative research design: An interactive approach*. Sage publications.

May, D. R., Gilson, R. L., & Harter, L. M. (2004). The psychological conditions of meaningfulness, safety and availability and the engagement of the human spirit at work. *Journal of Occupational and Organizational Psychology*, 77(1), 11–37. DOI: 10.1348/096317904322915892

Mayrhofer, E. (2019). LS and teachers' beliefs. *International Journal for Lesson and Learning Studies.*, 8(1), 19–33. DOI: 10.1108/IJLLS-11-2018-0091

McCollum, B. M. (2020). Online collaborative learning in STEM. Active learning in college science: The case for evidence-based practice, 621-637. DOI: 10.1007/978-3-030-33600-4_38

McConnell, J. (2007). Making intranets meaningful. *Communication World*, 24(3), 24–25.

McGill, M. M., & Settle, A. (2012). Institutional support for computing faculty research productivity: Does gender matter? *Proceedings of the Annual Southeast Conference*. doi:DOI: 10.1145/2184512.2184522

McGuire, A. L., Aulisio, M. P., Davis, F. D., Erwin, C., Harter, T. D., Jagsi, R., ... & COVID-19 Task Force of the Association of Bioethics Program Directors (ABPD). (2020). Ethical challenges arising in the COVID-19 pandemic: An overview from the Association of Bioethics Program Directors (ABPD) task force. The American Journal of Bioethics, 20(7), 15-27. DOI: 10.1080/15265161.2020.1764138

McIntosh, G. L., & Rima, S. D. (2007). *Overcoming the dark side of leadership: How to become an effective leader by confronting potential failures*. Baker Books.

McKay, P. F., Avery, D. R., & Morris, M. A. (2008). Mean racial-ethnic differences in employee sales performance: The moderating role of diversity climate. *Personnel Psychology*, 61(2), 349–374. DOI: 10.1111/j.1744-6570.2008.00116.x

McKinney, T. (2020). *Fostering psychological safety: What is a leader to do?* (Publication No. 2446975937). [doctoral dissertation, Benedictine University]. ProQuest Dissertations and Theses Global.

McKinney, J. C., & Gammie, C. F. (2004). A measurement of the electromagnetic luminosity of a Kerr black hole. *The Astrophysical Journal*, 611(2), 977–995. DOI: 10.1086/422244

McKinsey and Company. (2021, February 11). Psychological safety and the critical role of leadership development. https://www.mckinsey.com/capabilities/people-and-organizational-performance/our-insights/psychological-safety-and-the-critical-role-of-leadership-development

Mclean, M., Van Wyk, J., Peters-Futre, E., & Higgins-Opitz, S. (2006). The small group in problem-based learning: More than a cognitive learning experience for first year medical students in a diverse population. *Medical Teacher*, 28(4), e94–e103. DOI: 10.1080/01421590600726987 PMID: 16807164

Mcleod, S. (2024). Constructivism learning theory and philosophy of education. *Child Psychology*, 1(2), 211–223.

McLoughlin, C., Patel, K. D., O'Callaghan, T., & Reeves, S. (2018). The use of virtual communities of practice to improve interprofessional collaboration and education: Findings from an integrated review. *Journal of Interprofessional Care*, 32(2), 136–142. DOI: 10.1080/13561820.2017.1377692 PMID: 29161155

Mebert, L., Barnes, R., Dalley, J., Gawarecki, L., Ghazi-Nezami, F., Shafer, G., Yezbick, E. (2020). Fostering student engagement through a real-world, collaborative project across disciplines and institutions. *Higher Education Pedagogies*, 5(1),30–51.https://doi.org/. 2020. 1750306DOI: 10.1080/23752696

Mebert, M., Schultz, M., & Zimmermann, B. (2020). The impact of diversity on team performance: A review of the literature. *Journal of Management*, 46(1), 1–15.

Medium. (2024). *How can technology be a barrier to communication?* https://medium.com/@shaifulhoquetoha2004/how-can-technology-be-a-barrier-to-communication-f954ed06e684

Mehta, D., & Wang, X. (2020). COVID-19 and digital library services–a case study of a university library. *Digital Library Perspectives*, 36(4), 351–363. Advance online publication. DOI: 10.1108/DLP-05-2020-0030

Mehta, V., Chugh, C., & Perwez, A. (2017). Why should you do Research? *Journal of Medical Research and Innovation*, 1(1), 17.

Merriam, S. B., & Baumgartner, L. M. (2020). *Learning in adulthood: A comprehensive guide*. John Wiley & Sons.

Merriam, S. B., & Tisdell, E. J. (2015). *Qualitative research: A guide to design and implementation*. John Wiley & Sons.

Merrilees, B., & Miller, D. (2008). Principles of corporate rebranding. *European Journal of Marketing*, 42(5/6), 537–552. DOI: 10.1108/03090560810862499

Mezirow, J. (2018). Transformative learning theory. In *Contemporary theories of learning* (pp. 114–128). Routledge. DOI: 10.4324/9781315147277-8

Mickelson, J. J., Kaplan, W. E., & Macneily, A. E. (2009). Active learning: A resident's reflection on the impact of a student-centred curriculum. *Canadian Urological Association Journal*, 3(5), 399. DOI: 10.5489/cuaj.1154 PMID: 19829736

Mikula, K., Skrzypczak, D., Izydorczyk, G., Warchoł, J., Moustakas, K., Chojnacka, K., & Witek-Krowiak, A. (2021). 3D printing filament as a second life of waste plastics—a review. Environmental Science and Pollution Research, 28, 12321-12333. DOI: 10.1007/s11356-020-10657-8

Milem, J. F. (2003). The educational benefits of diversity: Evidence from multiple sectors. In *Compelling interest: Examining the evidence on racial dynamics in higher education* (pp. 126–169). Stanford University Press. DOI: 10.1515/9780804764537-009

Miles, Huberman & Saldaña (2014). Qualitative Data Analysis: A Methods Sourcebook and The Coding Manual for Qualitative Researchers, Thousand Oaks, CA: SAGE, 303 pp.

Miles, M. B., Huberman, A. M., & Saldana, J. (2014). *Qualitative data analysis: A method sourcebook*. Sage Publications.

Miller, J. (2018, October 6). *Are the traditional roles of teachers' unions changing?* https://errolmiller.com/traditional-roles-of-teachers-unions-changing/#google_vignette

Mills, G. E., & Gay, L. R. (2019). *Educational research: Competencies for analysis and applications* (12th ed.). Pearson.

Mills, M. S. (2013). Collaborative presentations using Google Docs. In *The Plugged-In Professor* (pp. 151–163). Chandos Publishing. DOI: 10.1016/B978-1-84334-694-4.50012-0

Miner, J. B. (2005). *Essential theories of motivation and leadership*. M.E. Sharpe.

Ming, C., Xiaoying, G., Huizhen, Z., & Bin, R. (2015). A review on psychological safety: Concepts, measurements, antecedents and consequences variables In *Proceedings of the 2015 International Conference on Social Science and Technology Education*, (pp.433-440) Atlantis Press. DOI: 10.2991/icsste-15.2015.118

Mishra, S. (2020). Social networks, social capital, social support and academic success in higher education: A systematic review with a special focus on 'underrepresented'students. . *Educational Research Review*, 29, 100307. Advance online publication. DOI: 10.1016/j.edurev.2019.100307

Misra, J., Smith-Doerr, L., Dasgupta, N., Weaver, G., & Normanly, J. (2017). Collaboration and gender equity among academic scientists. *Social Sciences (Basel, Switzerland)*, 6(1), 1–22. DOI: 10.3390/socsci6010025

MIT Media Lab. (n.d.). *About the Media Lab*. Retrieved from https://www.media.mit.edu/about/

Mitchell, T. R., Biglan, A., Oncken, G. R., & Fiedler, F. E. (1970). The contingency model: Criticism and suggestions. *Academy of Management Journal*, 13(3), 253–267. DOI: 10.2307/254963

Mkhize, Z. V. (2024). Teaching while black: Black women millennials' experiences of teaching in South African universities. *Journal of Women and Gender in Higher Education*, 1-18. https://doi.org/DOI: 10.1080/26379112.2023.2286990

Mlambo, M., Silén, C., & McGrath, C. (2021). Lifelong learning and nurses' continuing professional development, a metasynthesis of the literature. BMC nursing. DOI: 10.1186/s12912-021-00579-2

Mncina, T. C., Letsie, H., Nkhi, S. E., & Mofana, M. (2024). Effective communication in postgraduate supervision: Shaping experiences and overcoming challenges. *Interdisciplinary Journal of Education Research*, 6(13), 1–21. DOI: 10.38140/ijer-2024.vol6.13

Mohammed, M., & AL-Jaberi, M. A. (2021). Google Docs or Microsoft Word? Master's students' engagement with instructor written feedback on academic writing in a cross-cultural setting. *Computers and Composition*, 62, 102672. DOI: 10.1016/j.compcom.2021.102672

Mohrman, K., Ma, W., & Baker, D. (2008). The research university in transition: The emerging global model. *Higher Education Policy*, 21, 5–27. DOI: 10.1057/palgrave.hep.8300175

Moliner, L., & Alegre, F. (2020). Efectos de la tutoría entre iguales en el autoconcepto matemático de los estudiantes de secundaria. *PLoS One*, 15(4), E0231410. DOI: 10.1371/journal.pone.0231410 PMID: 32275730

Moonma, J. (2021). Comparing collaborative writing activity in EFL classroom: Face-to-face collaborative writing versus online collaborative writing using Google Docs. *Asian Journal of Education and Training*, 7(4), 204–215. DOI: 10.20448/journal.522.2021.74.204.215

Moore, J. Ind, N. (Ed.). (2003). Beyond branding. Kogan Page Publishers. pp 104-121

Moorhouse, B. L. (2023). Teachers' digital technology use after a period of online teaching. *ELT Journal*, 77(4), 445–457. DOI: 10.1093/elt/ccac050

Moorhouse, B. L., & Yan, L. (2023). Use of Digital Tools by English Language Schoolteachers. *Education Sciences*, 13(3), 226. https://www.mdpi.com/2227-7102/13/3/226. DOI: 10.3390/educsci13030226

Morgan, S., Ahn, S., Mosser, A., Harrison, T., Wang, J., Huang, Q., Ryan, A., Mao, B., & Bixby, J. (2021). The effect of Ttam communication behaviors and Ppocesses on interdisciplinary teams' research productivity and team satisfaction. Informing Science. *The International Journal of an Emerging Transdiscipline*. 24. 083-110. DOI: 10.28945/4857

Morgan, R. P. (2022). *Team work: Why some teams work, while others fail and how to build a team that succeeds. The awesome leader's guide*. Choose Awesome Company.

Morris, M., & Ogan, C. (2018). The Internet as mass medium. In The Media, Journalism and Democracy (pp. 389-400). Routledge. DOI: 10.4324/9781315189772-25

Morrison-Smith, S., & Ruiz, J. (2020). Challenges and barriers in virtual teams: A literature review. *SN Applied Sciences*, 2(6), 1–33. DOI: 10.1007/s42452-020-2801-5

Morton, B. C., & Gil, E. (2019). Not a solo ride: Co-constructed peer mentoring for early-career educational leadership faculty. *International Journal of Mentoring and Coaching in Education*, 8(4), 361–377. DOI: 10.1108/IJMCE-02-2019-0026

Mourad, M., Ennew, C., & Kortam, W. (2011). Brand equity in higher education. *Marketing Intelligence & Planning*, 29(4), 403–420. DOI: 10.1108/02634501111138563

Mpungose, C. B. (2023). Lecturers' reflections on use of Zoom video conferencing technology for e-learning at a South African university in the context of coronavirus. *African Identities*, 21(2), 266–282. DOI: 10.1080/14725843.2021.1902268

Mudaly, R., & Chirikure, T. (2023). STEM education in the Global North and Global South: Competition, conformity, and convenient collaborations. *Frontiers in Education*, 8. Advance online publication. https://doi.org/10.3389/feduc.2023.1144399

Muia, A. M., & Oringo, J. O. (2026). Constraints on research productivity in Kenyan universities: Case study of University of Nairobi, Kenya. *International Journal of Recent Advances in Multidisciplinary Research, 03*(08), 1785-1794.

Murata, A., & Takahashi, A. (2002). *Vehicle to Connect Theory, Research, and Practice: How Teacher Thinking Changes in District-Level LS in Japan.* Proceedings of the Annual Meeting [of the] North American Chapter of the International Group for the Psychology of Mathematics Education (24th, Athens, GA, October 26-29, 2002). Volumes 1-4; see SE 066887.

Murata, A. (2011). Introduction: Conceptual overview of lesson study. In Alston, A., Hart, L., & Murata, A. (Eds.), *Lesson-study research and practice in mathematics: Learning together* (pp. 1–12). Springer. DOI: 10.1007/978-90-481-9941-9_1

Musto, R. G. (2021). *The attack on higher education: The dissolution of the American university.* Cambridge University Press. DOI: 10.1017/9781108559355

Muszynska, K. (2018). A concept for measuring effectiveness of communication in project teams. *Journal of Economics and Management*, 33(3), 63–79. DOI: 10.22367/jem.2018.33.04

Muzyka, J. L., & Luker, C. S. (Eds.). (2016). The Flipped Classroom: Vol. 1. *Background and Challenges.* Oxford University Press.

Mystakidis, S. (2022). Metaverse. Encyclopedia. DOI: 10.3390/encyclopedia2010031

Mystakidis, S., Berki, E., & Valtanen, J. P. (2021). Deep and meaningful e-learning with social virtual reality environments in higher education: A systematic literature review. Applied Sciences. DOI: 10.3390/app11052412

Nadella, S. (2017). *Hit refresh: The quest to rediscover Microsoft's soul and imagine a better future for everyone.* Harper Business.

Naghdipour, B., & Manca, S. (2023). Teaching presence in students' WhatsApp groups: Affordances for language learning. *E-Learning and Digital Media*, 20(3), 282–299. DOI: 10.1177/20427530221107968

Nakajima, T. M., & Goode, J. (2019). Transformative learning for computer science teachers: Examining how educators learn e-textiles in professional development. *Teaching and Teacher Education*, 85, 148–159. DOI: 10.1016/j.tate.2019.05.004

National Research Council. (2015). Overview of the research on team effectiveness. In Cooke, N. J., & Hilton, M. L. (Eds.), *Enhancing the effectiveness of team science*. National Academies Press., https://www.ncbi.nlm.nih.gov/books/NBK310384/

Neal, S., Rhyne, R., Boatman, J., Watt, B., & Yeh, M. (2023). *Global leadership forecast 2023: DDI*. DDI. https://www.ddiworld.com/global-leadership-forecast-2023

Neuendorf, K. A. (2019). Content analysis and thematic analysis. In Brough, P. (Ed.), *Research methods for applied psychologists: Design analysis and reporting* (pp. 211–223). Routledge.

Nevenglosky, E. A., Cale, C., & Panesar Aguilar, S. (2019). Barriers to effective curriculum implementation. *Research in Higher Education*, 36, •••. https://files.eric.ed.gov/fulltext/EJ1203958.pdf

Newman, S. A. & Ford, R. C. (2021). Five steps to leading your team in the virtual COVID-19 workplace. Organizational Dynamics. DOI: 10.1016%2Fj.orgdyn.2020.100802

Niles, M. T., Schimanski, L. A., McKiernan, E. C., & Alperin, J. P. (2020). Why we publish where we do: Faculty publishing values and their relationship to review, promotion and tenure expectations. *PLoS One*, 15(3), e0228914. DOI: 10.1371/journal.pone.0228914

Nilsen, M., Kongsvik, T., & Almklov, P. G. (2022). Splintered structures and workers without a workplace: how should safety science address the fragmentation of organizations?. Safety science. DOI: 10.1016/j.ssci.2021.105644

Nilson, L. B. (2010). *Teaching at its best: A research-based resource for college instructors* (2nd ed.). Jossey-Bass.

Nishii, L. H., & Mayer, D. M. (2009). Do inclusive leaders help to reduce turnover in diverse groups? The moderating role of leader–member exchange in the diversity to turnover relationship. *The Journal of Applied Psychology*, 94(6), 1412–1426. DOI: 10.1037/a0017190 PMID: 19916652

Nkhi, S. E., & Shange, T. (2024). The impact of pedagogical translanguaging in enhancing communicative competence of university students in Lesotho. *International Journal of Language Studies*, 18(1), 25–52. DOI: 10.5281/zenodo.10468177

Noonan, J. (2019). An affinity for learning: Teacher identity and powerful professional development. *Journal of Teacher Education*, 70(5), 526–537. DOI: 10.1177/0022487118788838

Northouse, P. G. (2022). *Leadership: theory and practice* (9th ed.). SAGE Publications.

Norton, W. E. & Chambers, D. A. (2020). Unpacking the complexities of de-implementing inappropriate health interventions. Implementation Science. DOI: 10.1186/s13012-019-0960-9

Norwich, B. (2018). Making Sense of International Variations in LS and LS-like Practices: An Exploratory and Conceptual Perspective. *International Journal for Lesson and Learning Studies*, 7(3), 201–216. DOI: 10.1108/IJLLS-02-2018-0007

Novacek, G., Lee, J., & Krentz, M. (2021). *It's time to reimagine diversity, equity, and inclusion. Leading in the new reality. Resilience.* Boston Consulting Group. https://web-assets.bcg.com/0b/c4/c45a07e54f48ae0dc784667a66dd/bcg-its-time-to-reimagine-diversity-equity-and-inclusion-may-2021-r.pdf

NSDC (National Staff Development Council). (2011). *Standards for professional learning.* Scribbr. www.nsdc.org

O'Connor, K. (2022). Constructivism, curriculum and the knowledge question: Tensions and challenges for higher education. *Studies in Higher Education*, 47(2), 412–422. DOI: 10.1080/03075079.2020.1750585

O'donovan, R., & McAuliffe, E. (2020a). A systematic review exploring the content and outcomes of interventions to improve psychological safety, speaking up and voice behavior. *BMC Health Services Research*, 20(1), 1–11. DOI: 10.1186/s12913-020-4931-2 PMID: 32041595

O'donovan, R., & Mcauliffe, E. (2020b). A systematic review of factors that enable psychological safety in healthcare teams. *International Journal for Quality in Health Care : Journal of the International Society for Quality in Health Care*, 32(4), 240–250. DOI: 10.1093/intqhc/mzaa025 PMID: 32232323

O'Neill, T. A., & Salas, E. (2018). Creating high performance teamwork in organizations. *Human Resource Management Review*, 28(4), 325–331. DOI: 10.1016/j.hrmr.2017.09.001

Oates, M., Crichton, K., Cranor, L., Budwig, S., Weston, E. J., Bernagozzi, B. M., & Pagaduan, J. (2022). Audio, video, chat, email, or survey: How much does online interview mode matter? *PLoS One*, 17(2), e0263876. DOI: 10.1371/journal.pone.0263876 PMID: 35192659

O'Dowd, R. (2021). What do students learn in virtual exchange? A qualitative content analysis of learning outcomes across multiple exchanges. International Journal of Educational Research. DOI: 10.1016/j.ijer.2021.101804

Oh, J., Kim, D. H., & Kim, D. (2023). The impact of inclusive leadership and autocratic leadership on employees' job satisfaction and commitment In sport organizations: The mediating role of organizational trust and the moderating role of sport involvement. *Sustainability (Basel)*, 15(4), 3367. DOI: 10.3390/su15043367

Olaisen, J., & Revang, O. (2017). Working smarter and greener: Collaborative knowledge sharing in virtual global project teams. *International Journal of Information Management*, 37(1), 1441–1448. DOI: 10.1016/j.ijinfomgt.2016.10.002

Olesen, M. (2020). Cooperative collaboration in the hybrid space of Google Docs-based group work. *Education Sciences*, 10(10), 269. DOI: 10.3390/educsci10100269

Oliver, K. M. (2000). Methods for developing constructivism learning on the web. *Educational Technology*, 40(6), 231–25.

Oliver, R. (2000). The role of motivation in collaborative learning. *Educational Psychology Review*, 12(2), 135–154.

Oliver, R. (2001). Developing e-learning environments that support knowledge construction in higher education. Presented at the *2nd International We-B Conference*, p. 407 – 416. Perth, Western Australia.

Olugbo, M., Obienu, A. C., & Frank, A. (2023). Impact of effective communication on institutional performance: Case study in higher learning institutions. *Journal of Education. Society and Behavioural Science*, 36(10), 28–44. DOI: 10.9734/jesbs/2023/v36i101264

O'Neill, G., & McMahon, T. (2005). Student-centred learning: What does it mean for students and lecturers? Emerging issues in the practice of university learning and teaching, 1, 27-36.

Ong, C. H., Shi, C. H., Kowang, T. O., Fei, G. C., & Ping, L. L. (2020). Factors influencing job satisfaction among academic staffs. *International Journal of Evaluation and Research in Education*, 9(2), 285–291. DOI: 10.11591/ijere.v9i2.20509

Oni, T., Assah, F., Erzse, A., Foley, L., Govia, I., Hofman, K. J., ... & Wareham, N. J. (2020). The global diet and activity research (GDAR) network: a global public health partnership to address upstream NCD risk factors in urban low and middle-income contexts. Globalization and Health, 16, 1-11. DOI: 10.1186/s12992-020-00630-y

Onyefulu, C., & Johnson, H. (2009). A survey of lecturers' views on establishing research groups in a faculty in the University of Technology, Jamaica. In Ezenne, A. (Ed.), *Higher Education in the Caribbean: Research, Challenges and Prospects* (pp. 231–264). C & A Publishers Ltd.

Opfer, D. (2016). *Conditions and practices associated with teacher professional development and its impact on instruction in TALIS 2013.*

Opfer, V. D., & Pedder, D. (2011). The lost promise of teacher professional development in England. *European Journal of Teacher Education, 34*(1), 3e24. https://doi.org/DOI: 10.1080/02619768.2010.534131

Organización Mundial de la Salud. (20th May 2024). Salud mental. https://www.who.int/es/health-topics/mental-health

Osaze Patrick, I., Aghojare, B., & Ferdinand, O. A. (2015). Assess users' satisfaction on academic library performance: A study. *International Journal of Academic Research and Reflection,* 3(5), 67–77.

Ostad-Ali-Askari, K. (2022). Management of risks substances and sustainable development. Applied Water Science. DOI: 10.1007/s13201-021-01562-7

Ou, A. Y., Seo, J., Choi, D., & Hom, P. W. (2017). When can humble top executives retain middle managers? The moderating role of top management team faultiness. *Academy of Management Journal,* 60(5), 1915–1931. DOI: 10.5465/amj.2015.1072

Ovcharuk, O., Ivaniuk, I., Soroko, N., Gritsenchuk, O., & Kravchyna, O. (2020). The use of digital learning tools in the teachers' professional activities to ensure sustainable development and democratization of education in European countries. *EDP Sciences, E3S Web of Conferences.* https://doi.org/https://doi.org/10.1051/e3sconf/202016610019

Owens, B. P., & Hekman, D. R. (2012). Modelling how to grow: An examination of humble leader behaviours, contingencies and outcomes. *Academy of Management Journal,* 55(4), 787–818. DOI: 10.5465/amj.2010.0441

Owens, B. P., Johnson, M. D., & Mitchell, T. R. (2013). Expressed humility in organisations: Implications for performance, teams and leadership. *Organization Science,* 24(5), 1517–1538. DOI: 10.1287/orsc.1120.0795

Owusu-Agyeman, Y. (2019). An analysis of theoretical perspectives that define adult learners for effective and inclusive adult education policies. *International Review of Education,* 65(6), 929–953. DOI: 10.1007/s11159-019-09811-3

Özdemir, O. (2021). A case study regarding the comparison of collaborative writing in digital and face-to-face environments. *International Journal of Psychology and Educational Studies,* 8(2), 246–258. DOI: 10.52380/ijpes.2021.8.2.425

Ozdem-Yilmaz, Y., & Bilican, K. (2020). Discovery Learning—Jerome Bruner. *Science education in theory and practice: An introductory guide to learning theory*, 177-190.

Ozigbo, A. M., Idegbesor, M., Ngige, C. D., & Nwakoby, N. P. (2020). Team building and performance in organizations: An exploration of issues. *International Journal of Management and Entrepreneurship*, 2(1), 184–199.

Paais, M., & Pattiruhu, J. R. (2020). Effect of motivation, leadership, and organizational culture on satisfaction and employee performance. *The Journal of Asian Finance. Economics and Business*, 7(8), 577–588. DOI: 10.13106/jafeb.2020.vol7.no8.577

Pacia, D. R., & Guevarra, P. M. (2023). Influence of path-goal theory of leadership styles and the moderating role of task structure in leadership on teachers' satisfaction, motivation, and performance. *International Journal of Multidisciplinary: Applied Business & Education Research*, 4(7), 2330–2345. https://doi-org.trevecca.idm.oclc.org/10.11594/ijmaber.04.07.15. DOI: 10.11594/ijmaber.04.07.15

Paek, J. (2004). A systems approach to mentoring: A review of literature. Paper presented at the *Academy of Human Resource Development International Conference* (AHRD), Austin, TX, 367- 374.

Page Group. (20th May 2024). *Estudio sobre diversidad e inclusión 2022*. https://www.michaelpage.es/sites/michaelpage.es/files/2022-06/MP_ES_Estudio_Diversidad_Inclusi%C3%B3n_2022.pdf

Page, S. E. (2007). *The Difference: How the Power of Diversity Creates Better Groups, Firms, Schools, and Societies*. Princeton University Press.

Palamidessi, M., & Legarralde, M. (2006). *Teachers' unions, governments and educational reforms in Latin America and the Caribbean: Conditions for dialogue*. Inter-American Bank Regional Policy Dialogue.

Palincsar, A. S. (1998). Social constructivist perspectives on teaching and learning. *Annual Review of Psychology*, 49(1), 345–375. DOI: 10.1146/annurev.psych.49.1.345 PMID: 15012472

Palmer, R. (2021). Building a culture of trust: An imperative for effective school leadership. Faculty Publications, 4246 https://digitalcommons.anderws.edu/pubs/4246

Pardee, J. W., Fothergill, A., Weber, L., & Peek, L. (2017). The collective method: Collaborative social science research and scholarly accountability. *Qualitative Research*, 18(6), 671–688. DOI: 10.1177/1468794117743461

Parker, S. K. & Grote, G. (2022). Automation, algorithms, and beyond: Why work design matters more than ever in a digital world. *Applied Psychology*. DOI: 10.1111/apps.12241

Park, Y. S., Konge, L., & Artino, A. (2019). The positivism paradigm of research. *Academic Medicine*, 95(5), 1. DOI: 10.1097/ACM.0000000000003093 PMID: 31789841

Patel, L. (2015). *Decolonizing educational research: From ownership to answerability*. Routledge. DOI: 10.4324/9781315658551

Patil, R., Raheja, D. K., Nair, L., Deshpande, A., & Mittal, A. (2023). The power of psychological safety: Investigating its impact on team learning, team efficacy, and team productivity. *The Open Psychology Journal*, 16(1).

Patton, M. Q. (2002). *Qualitative research and evaluation methods* (3rd ed.). Sage.

Pearson, M. L., Albon, S. P., & Hubball, H. (2015). Case study methodology: Flexibility, rigour, and ethical considerations for the scholarship of teaching and learning. *The Canadian Journal for the Scholarship of Teaching and Learning*, 6(3), 12. DOI: 10.5206/cjsotl-rcacea.2015.3.12

Peate, L. (2021). *The Nursing Associate's Handbook of Clinical Skills* (1st ed.). John Wiley & Sons Ltd., www.wiley.com/nursingassociate

Pellitteri, J. (2021). Emotional intelligence and leadership styles in education. *Psychology & its Contexts/Psychologie a Její Kontexty, 12*(2).

Pendones, J. A., Flores, Y., Espino, G., & Durán, F. A. (2021). Autoconcepto, autoestima, motivación y su influencia en el desempeño académico. Caso: Alumnos de la carrera de Contador Público. *RIDE Revista Iberoamericana para la Investigación y el Desarrollo Educativo*, 12(23). Advance online publication. DOI: 10.23913/ride.v12i23.1008

Penner-Williams, J., Diaz, E. I., & Worthen, D. G. (2019). Sustainability of teacher growth from professional development in culturally and linguistically responsive instructional practices. *Teaching and Teacher Education*, 86, 102891. DOI: 10.1016/j.tate.2019.102891

Pérez-Tejero, J., Ocete, C., Ortega-Vila, G., & Coterón, J. (2012). Diseño y aplicación de un programa de intervención de práctica deportiva inclusiva y su efecto sobre la actitud hacia la discapacidad: El Campus Inclusivo de Baloncesto. *Revista Internacional de Ciencias del Deporte, 8*(29), 258– 271. https://doi.org/http://dx.doi.org/10.5232/ricyde2012.0 2905

Perry, M. (2003). Distributed cognition. *HCI models, theories, and frameworks: Toward a multidisciplinary science*, 193-223.

Peters, L. H., Hartke, D. D., & Pohlmann, J. T. (1985). Fiedler's contingency theory of leadership: An application of the meta-analysis procedures of Schmidt and Hunter. *Psychological Bulletin*, 97(2), 274–285. https://doi-org.trevecca.idm.oclc.org/10.1037/0033-2909.97.2.274. DOI: 10.1037/0033-2909.97.2.274

Pham, V. P. H. (2021). The effects of collaborative writing on students' writing fluency: An efficient framework for collaborative writing. Sage Open. DOI: 10.1177/2158244021998363

Phelps, O. W. (1960). Rise of the labour movement in Jamaica. *Social and Economic Studies*, 9(4), 417–468.

Phillips, D. C. (1995). The good, the bad and the ugly: The many faces of constructivism. *Educational Researcher*, 24(7), 5–12. DOI: 10.3102/0013189X024007005

Phiri, V. (2021). *Effective speaking and effective listening*. DOI: 10.13140/RG.2.2.31707.69922

Pink, D. H. (2009). *Drive: The Surprising Truth About What Motivates Us*. Riverhead Books.

Pizzolitto, E., Verna, I., & Venditti, M. (2023). Authoritarian leadership styles and performance: A systematic literature review and research agenda. *Management Review Quarterly*, 73(2), 841–871. DOI: 10.1007/s11301-022-00263-y

Polly, D., Martin, F., & Guilbaud, T. C. (2021). Examining barriers and desired supports to increase faculty members' use of digital technologies: Perspectives of faculty, staff and administrators. . *Journal of Computing in Higher Education*, 33(1), 135–156. Advance online publication. DOI: 10.1007/s12528-020-09259-7

Pontefract, D. (2023, February 8). New research suggests an alarming decline in high-quality leaders. *Forbes*. https://www.forbes.com/sites/danpontefract/2023/02/08/new-research-suggests-an-alarming-decline-in-high-quality-leaders/

Posthuma, R., & Al-Riyami, S. (2012). Leading teams of higher education administrators: Integrating goal setting, team role, and team life cycle theories. *Higher Education Studies*, 2(3), 44–54. DOI: 10.5539/hes.v2n3p44

Prakash, D., Bisla, M., & Rastogi, S. G. (2021). Understanding authentic leadership style: The Satya Nadella Microsoft approach. *Open Journal of Leadership*, 10(2), 95–109. DOI: 10.4236/ojl.2021.102007

Prince, T., Snowden, E., & Matthews, B. (2010). Utilising peer coaching as a tool to improve student-teacher confidence and support the development of classroom

Probert, B., & Sachs, J. (2015). The Rise of Teaching Focused Academics in Universities. *International Journal of Chinese Education*, 4(1), 48–67. DOI: 10.1163/22125868-12340044

Qian, X., Zhang, M., & Jiang, Q. (2020). Leader humility and subordinates' organisational citizenship behaviour and withdrawal behaviour: Exploring the mediating mechanisms of subordinates' psychological capital. *International Journal of Environmental Research and Public Health*, 17(7), 1–14. DOI: 10.3390/ijerph17072544

Qin, M. (2022). The impact of middle and senior leadership styles on employee performance--evidence from Chinese enterprises. *Informing Science: The International Journal of an Emerging Transdiscipline, 25*, 123-142. https://doi-org.trevecca.idm.oclc.org/10.28945/4936

Quinn, R. (2023, August 29). Higher Ed unionization has surged since 2012, bucking U.S. labor trends. Insider Higher Ed. https://www.insidehighered.com/news/faculty-issues/labor-unionization/2024/08/29/higher-ed-unionization-bucks-labor-trends-surged

Rabiul, M. K., Karatepe, O. M., Karim, R. A., & Panha, I. (2023). An investigation of the interrelationships of leadership styles, psychological safety, thriving at work, and work engagement in the hotel industry: A sequential mediation model. *International Journal of Hospitality Management*, 113, 103508. https://doi.org/10.1016/j.ijhm.2023.103508

Rabiul, M. K., Rashed, K., & Rashid, H. O. (2024). Transformational leadership style and psychological safety to meaningful work: Moderating role customer incivility. *Journal of Management Development*, 43(1), 49–67. DOI: 10.1108/JMD-09-2023-0292

Rådberg, K. K. & Löfsten, H. (2023). The entrepreneurial university and development of large-scale research infrastructure: exploring the emerging university function of collaboration and …. The Journal of Technology Transfer. DOI: 10.1007/s10961-023-10033-x

Radha, P., & Aithal, P. S. (2023). A study on the performance of employees in the banking sector and its impact on the organizational health. *International Journal of Management* [IJMTS]. *Technology and Social Sciences*, 8(4), 119–127.

Radicioni, B. (2023, December 15). *What is inclusive leadership?* Babson Thought & Action. https://entrepreneurship.babson.edu/what-is-inclusive-leadership/

Rahmadi, F. (2020). WhatsApp Group for Teaching and Learning in Indonesian Higher Education: What's Up? Rasiah, R. R. V. (2014). Transformative higher education teaching and learning: Using social media in a team-based learning environment. *Procedia: Social and Behavioral Sciences*, 123, 369–379.

Rahman, S., & Alam, M. (2019). Leadership style and its impact on employee performance: An empirical study on private commercial banks in Bangladesh. *International Journal of Human Resource Management*, 8(3), 1–10.

Rambe, P. (2017). Spaces for interactive engagement or technology for differential academic participation? Google Groups for collaborative learning at a South African University. *Journal of Computing in Higher Education*, 29(2), 353–387. DOI: 10.1007/s12528-017-9141-5

Ramsay, P. A. (2011). Much writing begets good writing: Some considerations for teaching writing in an Anglophone Creole context. *Caribbean Curriculum, 18*, 27-42. https://journals.sta.uwi.edu/ojs/index.php/cc/article/view/577

Rappleye, J., & Komatsu, H. (2017). How to make LS work in America and worldwide: A Japanese perspective on the onto-cultural basis of (teacher) education. *Research in Comparative and International Education*, 12(4), 398–430. DOI: 10.1177/1745499917740656

Rasiah, R., Kaur, H., & Guptan, V. (2020). Business continuity plan in the higher education industry: University students' perceptions of the effectiveness of academic continuity plans during COVID-19 …. Applied System Innovation. DOI: 10.3390/asi3040051

Ravitch, S. M., & Riggan, M. (2017). Reason & rigor: How theoretical frameworks guide. *The Qualitative Report*, 21(9), 1708.

Ray, P. P. (2023). ChatGPT: A comprehensive review on background, applications, key challenges, bias, ethics, limitations and future scope. Internet of Things and Cyber-Physical Systems. DOI: 10.1016/j.iotcps.2023.04.003

Razali, S. N., Shahbodin, F., Hussin, H., & Bakar, N. (2015). Factors affecting the effective online collaborative learning environment. In Abraham, A., Muda, A., & Choo, Y. H. (Eds.), *Pattern analysis, intelligent security and the Internet of Things: Advances in intelligent systems and computing* (Vol. 355). Springer., DOI: 10.1007/978-3-319-17398-6_20

Redondo- Duarte. S. (2012). *Evaluación de la aplicación del modelo pedagógico de UEM personal a estudios universitarios de grado y postgrado en modalidad online* [Doctoral dissertation, Universidad Europea de Madrid, Spain]. https://abacus.universidadeuropea.com/handle/11268/1342

Reeves, D. B. (2010). Transforming Professional Development into Student Results (Alexandria, VA: Association for Supervision and Curriculum Development, 2010). (Washington, DC: Council of Chief State School Officers, April 2011). *Journal of School Psychology*, 38(3), 277–298.

Rehman, S. U., & Cao, Q. (2017). Rise in level of trust and trustworthiness with trust building measures: A mathematical model. *Journal of Modelling in Management*, 12(3), 17–34. DOI: 10.1108/JM2-09-2015-0076

Revere, L., & Kovach, J. V. (2011). Online technologies for engaged learning: A meaningful synthesis for educators. *Quarterly Review of Distance Education*, 12(2), 13–124, 149–150. https://www.proquest.com/openview/ee56bfc90cac37ad96a4f6be61918f02/1?pq-origsite=gscholar&cbl=29705

Rice, P. (2000). *Adolescencia. Desarrollo, relaciones y cultura*. Prentice Hall.

Richardson, L., & Adams St. Pierre, E. (2018). Writing: A Method of Inquiry. In Denzin, N. K., & Lincoln, Y. S. (Eds.), *The SAGE handbook of qualitative research* (p. 1417). SAGE Publications Inc.

Richter, S. & Richter, A. (2023). What is novel about the Metaverse?. International Journal of Information Management. DOI: 10.1016/j.ijinfomgt.2023.102684

Richter, N. F., Martin, J., Hansen, S. V., Taras, V., & Alon, I. (2021). Motivational configurations of cultural intelligence, social integration, and performance in global virtual teams. *Journal of Business Research*, 129, 351–367. DOI: 10.1016/j.jbusres.2021.03.012

Rivaldo, Y., & Nabella, S. D. (2023). Employee performance: Education, training, experience and work discipline. *Calitatea*, 24(193), 182–188.

Roberts, J. K., Pavlakis, A. E., & Richards, M. P. (2021). It's more complicated than it seems: Virtual qualitative research in the COVID-19 era. International journal of qualitative methods, 20, 16094069211002959. DOI: 10.1177/16094069211002959

Robinson, B., & Schaible, R. M. (1995). Collaborative teaching: Reaping the benefits. *College Teaching*, 43(2), 57–59. DOI: 10.1080/87567555.1995.9925515

Robinson, E. T., Jones, C., & Brazeau, G. A. (2023). Addressing an uncertain future with a culture of psychological safety. *American Journal of Pharmaceutical Education*, 87(7), 100032. Advance online publication. DOI: 10.1016/j.ajpe.2022.11.005 PMID: 37380278

Røed, R. K., Powell, M. B., Riegler, M. A., & Baugerud, G. A. (2023). A field assessment of child abuse investigators' engagement with a child-avatar to develop interviewing skills. Child Abuse & Neglect. DOI: 10.1016/j.chiabu.2023.106324

Rogers, Y. (2006). Distributed Cognition and Communication. In Brown, K. (Ed.), *Encyclopedia of Language & Linguistics* (2nd ed., pp. 731–733). Elsevier., https://doi.org/https://doi.org/10.1016/B0-08-044854-2/00862-2 DOI: 10.1016/B0-08-044854-2/00862-2

Rogoff, B. (1994). Developing understanding of the idea of communities of learners. In Resnick, L. B., Levine, J. M., & Teasley, S. D. (Eds.), *Perspectives on socially shared cognition* (pp. 185–210). American Psychological Association.

Román, M. O., Justice, C., Paynter, I., Boucher, P. B., Devadiga, S., Endsley, A., ... & Wolfe, R. (2024). Continuity between NASA MODIS Collection 6.1 and VIIRS Collection 2 land products. Remote Sensing of Environment, 302, 113963. DOI: 10.1016/j.rse.2023.113963

Romero Carrión, V.L., Bedón Soria, Y.T., & Franco Medina, J. L. (2022). Meta-análisis de competencias transversales en la empleabilidad de los universitarios. *Revista gestión de las personas y tecnología, 15*(43), 20-42. http://dx.doi.org/DOI: 10.35588/gpt.v15i43.5464

Roschelle, J., & Teasley, S. D. (1995). The construction of shared knowledge in collaborative learning. *Journal of the Learning Sciences*, 4(1), 59–129.

Rossiter, M. P., & Bale, R. (2023). Cultural and linguistic dimensions of feedback: A model of intercultural feedback literacy. *Innovations in Education and Teaching International*, 60(3), 368–378. DOI: 10.1080/14703297.2023.2175017

Roussin, C. J., & Webber, S. S. (2012). Impact of organisational identification and psychological safety on initial perceptions of coworker trustworthiness. *Journal of Business and Psychology*, 27(3), 317–329. DOI: 10.1007/s10869-011-9245-2

Roy, R., & El Marsafawy, H. (2020). *Organizational structure for 21st century higher education institutions: Meeting expectations and crossing hallenges.*https://www.researchgate.net/publication/340685039_ORGANIZATIONAL_STRUCTURE_FOR_21ST_CENTURY_HIGHER_EDUCATION_INSTITUTIONS_MEETING_EXPECTATIONS_AND_CROSSING_CHALLENGES

Roy, E. D., Morzillo, A. T., Seijo, F., Reddy, S. M., Rhemtulla, J. M., Milder, J. C., Kuemmerle, T., & Martin, S. L. (2013). The elusive pursuit of interdisciplinarity at the human-environment interface. *Bioscience*, 63(9), 745–753. DOI: 10.1093/bioscience/63.9.745

Runyan, A. S. (2018). What is intersectionality and why it is important. *American Association of University Professors*, 104(6), 10–14.

Ruoslahti, H. (2018). Co-creation of knowledge for innovation requires multi-stakeholder public relations. In *Public relations and the power of creativity: Strategic opportunities, innovation and critical challenges* (pp. 115–133). Emerald Publishing Limited. DOI: 10.1108/S2398-391420180000003007

Rupal, J. (nd). The barriers to effective communication https://www.peakwriting.com/UMUC/barriers_effective.pdf

Rus-Calafell, M., Ward, T., Zhang, X. C., Edwards, C. J., Garety, P., & Craig, T. (2020). The role of sense of voice presence and anxiety reduction in AVATAR therapy. Journal of Clinical Medicine, 9(9), 2748. DOI: 10.3390/jcm9092748

Rysavy, M. D. T. & Michalak, R. (2020). Working from home: How we managed our team remotely with technology. Journal of Library Administration.

Sääksjärvi, M., & Samiee, S. (2011). Relationships among brand identity, brand image and brand preference: Differences between cyber and extension retail brands over time. *Journal of Interactive Marketing*, 25(3), 169–177. DOI: 10.1016/j.intmar.2011.04.002

Sahin, F. (2012). The mediating effect of leader–member exchange on the relationship between Theory X and Y management styles and affective commitment: A multilevel analysis. *Journal of Management & Organization*, 18(2), 159–174. DOI: 10.5172/jmo.2012.18.2.159

Sahito, Z., & Vaisanen, P. (2017). Factors affecting job satisfaction of teacher educators: Empirical evidence from the Universities of Sindh Province of Pakistan. *Journal of Teacher Education and Educators*, 6(1), 5–30. DOI: 10.5430/ijhe.v6n4p122

Saika, M., & Gohain, A. (2013). Use and user's satisfaction in library resources and services: A study in Tezpur University (India). *International Journal of Library and Information Science*, 5(6), 167–175.

Salas, E., Sims, D. E., & Burke, C. S. (2005). Is there a "big five" in teamwork? *Small Group Research*, 36(5), 555–599. https://doi.org/10.1177/1046496405277134

Saldaña, J. (2013). The Coding Manual for Qualitative Researchers. *Sage (Atlanta, Ga.)*.

Salma, N. (2020). Collaborative Learning: An Effective Approach to Promote Language Development. *International Journal of Social Sciences and Educational Studies*, 7(2), 5.

Sanahuja Ribés, A., Cantos Aldaz, F. J., & Moliner Miravet, L. (2023). *¿Trabajamos en equipos cooperativos? Percepciones de estudiantes de bachillerato*. Proceedings 2nd International Congress: Education and Knowledge. Universitat Jaume I. Octaedro.

Sattar, M., Palaniappan, S., Lokman, A., Shah, N., Khalid, U., & Hasan, R. (2020). Motivating medical students using virtual reality based education. International Journal of Emerging Technologies in Learning (iJET), 15(2), 160-174. DOI: 10.3991/ijet.v15i02.11394

Sawyer, J., & Obeid, R. (2017). Cooperative and collaborative learning: Getting the best of both words. In Obeid, R., Schwartz, A., Shane-Simpson, C., & Brooks, P. J. (Eds.), *How we teach now: The GSTA guide to student-centered teaching* (pp. 163–177). Society for the Teaching of Psychology.

Sawyer, R. K., & Obeid, N. (2017). *Collaborative learning in the 21st century: A handbook for educators*. Routledge.

Sax, L. J., Hagedorn, L. S., Arredondo, M., & Dicrisi, F. A.III. (2002). Faculty research productivity: Exploring the role of gender and family-related factors. *Research in Higher Education*, 43(4), 423–446. DOI: 10.1023/A:1015575616285

Sayyed, K. (2024). Assessing research productivity and quality across disciplines in the School of Arts and Sciences at the Lebanese American University. *SAGE Open*, •••, 1–21. DOI: 10.1177/21582440241237050

Schensul, S. L., Schensul, J. J., & LeCompte, M. D. (1999). *Essential ethnographic methods, observations, interviews and questionnaire*. Rowan Altanura Publishers.

Schipper, T. M., van der Lans, R. M., de Vries, S., Goei, S. L., & van Veen, K. (2020). Becoming a more adaptive teacher through collaborating in Lesson Study? Examining the influence of Lesson Study on teachers' adaptive teaching practices in mainstream secondary education. *Teaching and Teacher Education*, 88, 102961. DOI: 10.1016/j.tate.2019.102961

Schipper, T., Goei, S. L., de Vries, S., & van Veen, K. (2017). Professional growth in adaptive teaching competence as a result of Lesson Study. *Teaching and Teacher Education*, 68, 289–303. DOI: 10.1016/j.tate.2017.09.015

Schmidtke, J. M., & Cummings, A. (2017). The effects of virtualness on teamwork behavioral components: The role of shared mental models. *Human Resource Management Review*, 27(4), 660–677. https://doi.org/10.1016/j.hrmr.2016.12.011

Schultz, M., & De Chernatony, L. (2002). Introduction: The challenges of corporate branding. *Corporate Reputation Review*, 5(2-3), 105–105. DOI: 10.1057/palgrave.crr.1540168

Schunk, D. H. (2012). *Learning theories an educational perspective*. Pearson Education, Inc.

Schurr, N., Okamoto, S., Maheswaran, R. T., Scerri, P., & Tambe, M. (2005). Evolution of a teamwork model. In Sun, R. (Ed.), *Cognition and multi-agent interaction: From cognitive modeling to social simulation* (pp. 307–327). Cambridge University Press., https://doi.org/10.1017/cbo9780511610721.013

Schwab, K. World Economic Forum, & Sala-i-Martín, X. (2013). *The Global Competitiveness Report 2013–2014: Full Data Edition*. World Economic Forum.

Selander, K., Korkiakangas, E., Toivanen, M., Yli-Kaitala, K., Kangas, H., Nevanperä, N., & Laitinen, J. (2023). Engaging leadership and psychological safety as moderators of the relationship between strain and work recovery: A cross-sectional study of HSS employees. *Health Care*, 11(7), 1045. DOI: 10.3390/healthcare11071045 PMID: 37046972

Seo, H. J., Park, G. M., Son, M., & Hong, A. J. (2021). Establishment of virtual-reality-based safety education and training system for safety engagement. Education Sciences. DOI: 10.3390/educsci11120786

Sezer, B. (2024). The effects of group-based personalized online teaching on learners' community of inquiry and achievement of a course. *Turkish Online Journal of Distance Education*, 25(2), 130–143. https://doi.org/https://doi.org/10.17718/tojde.1310963. DOI: 10.17718/tojde.1310963

Shahid, S., & Din, M. (2021). Fostering psychological safety in teachers: The role of school leadership, team effectiveness and organisational culture. *International Journal of Educational Leadership and Management*, 9(2), 122–149. DOI: 10.17583/ijelm.2021.6317

Sharp, G., Bourke, L., & Rickard, M. J. F. X. (2020). Review of emotional intelligence in health care: An introduction to emotional intelligence for surgeons. . *ANZ Journal of Surgery*, 90(4), 433–440. Advance online publication. DOI: 10.1111/ans.15671 PMID: 31965690

Shava, G., Hleza, S., Tlou, F., Shonhiwa, S., & Mathonsi, E. (2021). Qualitative content analysis. *International Journal of Research and Innovation in Social Science*, V(VII).

Sher, A., Gul, S., Riaz, M. K., & Naeem, M. (2019). Psychological safety: A cross-level study of a higher educational institute (HEI). *Journal of Management Sciences*, 6(1), 30–49. DOI: 10.20547/jms.2014.1906103

Shore, L. M., Randel, A. E., Chung, B. G., Dean, M. A., Ehrhart, K. H., & Singh, G. (2011). Inclusion and diversity in work groups: A review and model for future research. *Journal of Management*, 37(4), 1262–1289. DOI: 10.1177/0149206310385943

Shuffler, M. L., Kramer, W. S., Carter, D. R., Thayer, A. L., & Rosen, M. A. (2018). Leveraging a team-centric approach to diagnosing multiteam system functioning: The role of intrateam state profiles. *Human Resource Management Review, 28* (4), 361-377.FRENCH https://doi.org/DOI: 10.1016/j.hrmr.2017.08.003

Shulman, L. S. (1987). Knowledge and teaching: Foundations of the new reform. *Harvard Educational Review*, 57(1), 61–77. https://eric.ed.gov/. DOI: 10.17763/haer.57.1.j463w79r56455411

Shurygin, V., Saenko, N., Zekiy, A., Klochko, E., & Kulapov, M. (2021). Learning management systems in academic and corporate distance education. [iJET]. *International Journal of Emerging Technologies in Learning*, 16(11), 121–139. DOI: 10.3991/ijet.v16i11.20701

Simon, N., & Fierro, A. S. (2023). Information technology tools for coil virtual exchange. In *Implementing Sustainable Change in Higher Education* (pp. 312–332). Routledge. DOI: 10.4324/9781003445227-21

Sims, L., & Walsh, D. (2009). Lesson Study with preservice teachers: Lessons from lessons. *Teaching and Teacher Education*, 25(5), 724–733. DOI: 10.1016/j.tate.2008.10.005

Sinek, S. (2009). *Start with Why: How Great Leaders Inspire Everyone to Take Action*. Portfolio.

Singh, S., & Sonnenburg, S. (2012). Brand performances in social media. *Journal of Interactive Marketing*, 26(4), 189–197. DOI: 10.1016/j.intmar.2012.04.001

Singh-Wilmot, M. (2024, May 13). *Jamaica the 'STEM Island' – A dream that can come true*. The Gleaner. https://jamaica-gleaner.com/article/news/20240513/dr-marvadeen-singh-wilmot-jamaica-stem-island-dream-can-come-true

Sinha, S., & Sinha, D. (2007). Emotional intelligence and effective communication. In Kaul, A., & Kumar Gupta, S. (Eds.), *Management communication: Trends & strategies*. McGraw Hill.

Skott, C. K., & Møller, H. (2020). Adaptation of lesson study in a Danish context: Displacements of teachers' work and power relations. *Teaching and Teacher Education*, 87, 102945. DOI: 10.1016/j.tate.2019.102945

Skrtic, T. M., Sailor, W., & Gee, K. (1996). Voice, collaboration, and inclusion: Democratic themes in educational and social reform initiatives. *Remedial and Special Education*, 17(3), 142–157. DOI: 10.1177/074193259601700304

Smith, B. L., & MacGregor, J. T. (1992). What is collaborative learning? Collaborative learning: A sourcebook for higher education, 10(2), 1-11.

Smith, K., Mansfield, J., & Adams, M. (2024). Learning from a dilemma: The opportunities online teaching provided for teacher growth and development. The Australian Educational Researcher. DOI: 10.1007/s13384-024-00704-5

Smith, D. G. (2024). *Diversity's promise for higher education: Making it work*. JHU Press. DOI: 10.56021/9781421449241

Smith, D. G., & Turner, C. S. V. (2015). *The Radical Transformation of Diversity and Inclusion: The Millennial Influence*. Deloitte University Leadership Center for Inclusion.

Smith, H. R. (2013). The role of trust in religious education. *Religious Education (Chicago, Ill.)*, 14(2). https://rsc.byu.edu/vol-14.no-2-2013/role-trust-religious-education

Smith, L. T. (2021). *Decolonizing methodologies: Research and indigenous peoples*. Bloomsbury Publishing. DOI: 10.5040/9781350225282

Smith, M. K., Wood, W. B., Adams, W. K., Wieman, C., Knight, J. K., Guild, N., & Su, T. T. (2009). Why peer discussion improves student performance on in-class concept questions. *Science*, 323(5910), 122–124. DOI: 10.1126/science.1165919 PMID: 19119232

Smith, R. D. (2020). *Strategic planning for public relations*. Routledge. DOI: 10.4324/9781003024071

Smooth, W. G. (2016). Intersectionality and women's advancement in the discipline and across the academy. *Politics, Groups & Identities*, 4(3), 513–528. Advance online publication. DOI: 10.1080/21565503.2016.1170706

Soares, A. E., & Lopez, M. P. (2020). Are students safe to learn? The role of lecturer's authentic leadership in the creation of psychologically safe environments and their impact on academic performance. *Active Learning in Higher Education*, 21(1), 65–78. DOI: 10.1177/1469787417742023

Sobaih, A. E. E., Hasanein, A. M., & Abu Elnasr, A. E. (2020). Responses to COVID-19 in higher education: Social media usage for sustaining formal academic communication in developing countries. Sustainability. DOI: 10.3390/su12166520

Soemitra, A., Lubis, A. S., Dewi, R. S., & Ovami, D. C. (2023). Essential Hard skill For Students in VUCA Era: Literature Study. *Journal of Trends Economics and Accounting Research*, 3(4), 605–610. DOI: 10.47065/jtear.v3i4.634

Soliman, A., & Shaikh, A. (2015). Collaborative learning: A pedagogical approach for enhancing student engagement and learning outcomes. *International Journal of Educational Development*, 35(1), 1–10.

Solomon, C., Harvey, B., Kahn, K., Lieberman, H., Miller, M. L., Minsky, M., . . . Silverman, B. (2020). History of logo. Proceedings of the ACM on Programming Languages, 4(HOPL), 1-66. DOI: 10.1145/3386329

Solomon, G. E., Carley, S., & Porter, A. L. (2016). How multidisciplinary are the multidisciplinary journals science and nature? *PLoS One*, 11(4), e0152637. DOI: 10.1371/journal.pone.0152637

Somech, A. (2005). Teachers' personal and team empowerment and their relations to organizational outcomes: Contradictory or compatible constructs? *Educational Administration Quarterly*, 41(2), 237–266. DOI: 10.1177/0013161X04269592

Sosna, M., Trevinyo-Rodríguez, R. N., & Velamuri, S. R. (2010). Business model innovation through trial-and-error learning: The Naturhouse case. *Long Range Planning*, 43(2-3), 383–407. DOI: 10.1016/j.lrp.2010.02.003

Sotodeh Asl, N., Ghorbani, R., & Rashidy-Pour, A. (2014). Viewpoints of faculty members of Semnan University of Medical Sciences about research barriers. *Koomesh*, ●●●, 1–7. http://eprints.semums.ac.ir/346/

Springer, L., Stanne, M., & Donovan, S. (1999). Effects of small-group learning on undergraduates in science, mathematics, engineering and technology: A meta-analysis. *Review of Educational Research*, 69(1), 21–52. DOI: 10.3102/00346543069001021

Stachowski, C. A. (2011). Educational marketing: A review and implications for supporting practice in tertiary education. *Educational Management Administration & Leadership*, 39(2), 186–204. DOI: 10.1177/1741143210390056

Stadnick, N. A., Poth, C. N., Guetterman, T. C., & Gallo, J. J. (2021). Advancing discussion of ethics in mixed methods health services research. *BMC Health Services Research*, 21(577). Advance online publication. DOI: 10.1186/s12913-021-06583-1

Staley, D., & Trinkle, D. (2011, February 11). *The changing landscape of higher education*. EDUCASE Review. https://er.educause.edu/articles/2011/2/the-changing-landscape-of-higher-education

Stanford Virtual Human Interaction Lab. (n.d.). Retrieved from https://vhil.stanford.edu/

Stanley, W. B. (2015). Social studies and the social order: Transmission or transformation? In *Social studies today* (pp. 17–24). Routledge.

State of the global workplace: 2024 report. (n.d.). Gallup, Inc. https://www.gallup.com/workplace/349484/state-of-the-global-workplace.aspx

Steen, J. L. (2020). Branding in Higher Education: How Meaning-Making Efforts Lead to Successful Branding Outcomes that Positively Influence Reputation and a Strong Institutional Culture (Doctoral dissertation, Azusa Pacific University).

Steigerwald, E., Ramírez-Castañeda, V., Brandt, D., Báldi, A., Shapiro, J., Bowker, L. & Tarvin, R. (2022). Overcoming language barriers in academia: Machine translation tools and a vision for a multilingual future. *Bio Science, 72*. htps://.DOI: 10.1093/biosci/biac062

Stern, B. S. (2013). *Social studies: Standards, meaning, and understanding*. Routledge. DOI: 10.4324/9781315851204

Stigler, J. W., & Hiebert, J. (2016). LS, improvement, and the importing of cultural routines. *ZDM Mathematics Education*, 48(4), 581–587. DOI: 10.1007/s11858-016-0787-7

Stock, R., Mahoney, E., & Carney, P. A. (2013). Measuring team development in clinical care settings. *Family Medicine*, 45(10), 691–700.

Stokols, D., Hall, K. L., Taylor, B. K., & Moser, R. P. (2008). The science of team science: Overview of the field and introduction to the supplement. *American Journal of Preventive Medicine*, 35(2), S77–S89. DOI: 10.1016/j.amepre.2008.05.002 PMID: 18619407

Storch, N. (2019). Collaborative writing as peer feedback. In Hyland, K., & Hyland, F. (Eds.), *Feedback in second language writing: Contexts and issues* (pp. 143–161). Cambridge University Press. DOI: 10.1017/9781108635547.010

Sudhagar, R., & Pradeep, S. (2018). Most common barriers to effective communication in the skill- based challenges about the lassroom situation. *International Journal of Trend in Research and Development*, 86-87, c.

Sugiharjo, R. J., Purbasari, R. N., Rahmat, A., & Paijan, P. (2023). The role of the work environment as a mediation for the effect of leadership style on the performance of banking institution employees. *Dinasti International Journal of Management Science*, 5(1), 1–14. DOI: 10.31933/dijms.v4i6.1976

Sugiyama, K., Cavanagh, K. V., van Esch, C., Bilimoria, D., & Brown, C. (2016). Inclusive leadership development. *Journal of Management Education*, 40(3), 253–292. DOI: 10.1177/1052562916632553

Su, J., & Tong, X. (2015). Brand personality and brand equity: Evidence from the sportswear industry. *Journal of Product and Brand Management*, 24(2), 124–133. DOI: 10.1108/JPBM-01-2014-0482

Sunzuma, G., & Kakoma, L. (2023). Zimbabwean mathematics pre-service teachers' implementation of the learner-centred curriculum during teaching practice. *Eurasia Journal of Mathematics, Science and Technology Education*, 19(5), em2258. Advance online publication. DOI: 10.29333/ejmste/13131

Susilawati, S., Fajriah, Y. N., & Yunita, S. (2023, July). Google Docs in English for Business Purposes courses: The exploration of students' acceptance. In *ELT Forum: Journal of English Language Teaching* (Vol. 12, No. 2, pp. 98-109). https://doi.org/ DOI: 10.15294/elt.v12i2.67253

Suzuki, S. N., Kanematsu, H., Barry, D. M., Ogawa, N., Yajima, K., Nakahira, K. T., ... & Yoshitake, M. (2020). Virtual Experiments in Metaverse and their Applications to Collaborative Projects: The framework and its significance. Procedia Computer Science, 176, 2125-2132. DOI: 10.1016/j.procs.2020.09.249

Sykes, G., Bird, T., & Kennedy, M. (2010). Teacher education: Its problems and some prospects. *Journal of Teacher Education*, 61(5), 464–476. DOI: 10.1177/0022487110375804

Taherdoost, H. (2017). Validity and reliability of the research instrument: How to test the validation of a questionnaire/survey in a research. *International Journal of Academic Research in Management*, 5(3), 28-36. United Nations Educational, Scientific and Cultural Organization. (2024). *What you need to know about higher education*https://www.unesco.org/en/higher-education/need-know

Takahashi, A., & McDougal, T. (2016). Collaborative lesson research: Maximizing the impact of LS. *ZDM Mathematics Education*, 48(4), 513–526. DOI: 10.1007/s11858-015-0752-x

Talan, T. (2021). The effect of computer-supported collaborative learning on academic achievement: A meta-analysis study. [IJEMST]. *International Journal of Education in Mathematics, Science, and Technology*, 9(3), 426–448. DOI: 10.46328/ijemst.1243

Tamiru, N. (2023, June). *Team dynamics: Five keys to building effective teams.* https://www.thinkwithgoogle.com/intl/en-emea/consumer-insights/consumer-trends/five-dynamics-effective-team/

Tan, J. S., & Chen, W. (2022). Peer feedback to support collaborative knowledge improvement: What kind of feedback feed-forward? *Computers & Education*, 187, 104467. DOI: 10.1016/j.compedu.2022.104467

Taras, V., Kirkman, B. L., & Steel, P. (2010). Examining the impact of culture's consequences: A three-decade, multilevel, meta-analytic review of Hofstede's cultural value dimensions. *The Journal of Applied Psychology*, 95(3), 405–439. DOI: 10.1037/a0018938 PMID: 20476824

Tariq, A. (2023, June 8). *Implementing the transactional model of Communication for better collaboration.* Chanty. https://www.chanty.com/blog/transactional-model-of-communication/

Tariq, M. U. (2024). Harnessing Persuasive Technologies for Enhanced Learner Engagement and Motivation. In M. Sanmugam, D. Lim, N. Mohd Barkhaya, W. Wan Yahaya, & Z. Khlaif (Eds.), *Power of Persuasive Educational Technologies in Enhancing Learning* (pp. 30-62). IGI Global. https://doi.org/DOI: 10.4018/979-8-3693-6397-3.ch002

Tariq, M. U. (2024). Multidisciplinary service learning in higher education: Concepts, implementation, and impact. In S. Watson (Ed.), *Applications of service learning in higher education* (pp. 1-19). IGI Global. https://doi.org/DOI: 10.4018/979-8-3693-2133-1.ch001

Tariq, M. U. (2024). Neurodiversity inclusion and belonging strategies in the workplace. In J. Vázquez de Príncipe (Ed.), *Resilience of multicultural and multigenerational leadership and workplace experience* (pp. 182-201). IGI Global. https://doi.org/DOI: 10.4018/979-8-3693-1802-7.ch009

Tariq, M. U. (2024). AI and IoT in flood forecasting and mitigation: A comprehensive approach. In Ouaissa, M., Ouaissa, M., Boulouard, Z., Iwendi, C., & Krichen, M. (Eds.), *AI and IoT for proactive disaster management* (pp. 26–60). IGI Global., DOI: 10.4018/979-8-3693-3896-4.ch003

Tariq, M. U. (2024). AI and the future of talent management: Transforming recruitment and retention with machine learning. In Christiansen, B., Aziz, M., & O'Keeffe, E. (Eds.), *Global practices on effective talent acquisition and retention* (pp. 1–16). IGI Global., DOI: 10.4018/979-8-3693-1938-3.ch001

Tariq, M. U. (2024). Application of blockchain and Internet of Things (IoT) in modern business. In Sinha, M., Bhandari, A., Priya, S., & Kabiraj, S. (Eds.), *Future of customer engagement through marketing intelligence* (pp. 66–94). IGI Global., DOI: 10.4018/979-8-3693-2367-0.ch004

Tariq, M. U. (2024). Challenges of a metaverse shaping the future of entrepreneurship. In Inder, S., Dawra, S., Tennin, K., & Sharma, S. (Eds.), *New business frontiers in the metaverse* (pp. 155–173). IGI Global., DOI: 10.4018/979-8-3693-2422-6.ch011

Tariq, M. U. (2024). Cybersecurity Risk Assessment Models and Theories in the Travel and Tourism Industry. In Thealla, P., Nadda, V., Dadwal, S., Oztosun, L., & Cantafio, G. (Eds.), *Corporate Cybersecurity in the Aviation, Tourism, and Hospitality Sector* (pp. 1–17). IGI Global., DOI: 10.4018/979-8-3693-2715-9.ch001

Tariq, M. U. (2024). Emerging trends and innovations in blockchain-digital twin integration for green investments: A case study perspective. In Jafar, S., Rodriguez, R., Kannan, H., Akhtar, S., & Plugmann, P. (Eds.), *Harnessing blockchain-digital twin fusion for sustainable investments* (pp. 148–175). IGI Global., DOI: 10.4018/979-8-3693-1878-2.ch007

Tariq, M. U. (2024). Emotional intelligence in understanding and influencing consumer behavior. In Musiolik, T., Rodriguez, R., & Kannan, H. (Eds.), *AI impacts in digital consumer behavior* (pp. 56–81). IGI Global., DOI: 10.4018/979-8-3693-1918-5.ch003

Tariq, M. U. (2024). Empowering student entrepreneurs: From idea to execution. In Cantafio, G., & Munna, A. (Eds.), *Empowering students and elevating universities with innovation centers* (pp. 83–111). IGI Global., DOI: 10.4018/979-8-3693-1467-8.ch005

Tariq, M. U. (2024). Enhancing cybersecurity protocols in modern healthcare systems: Strategies and best practices. In Garcia, M., & de Almeida, R. (Eds.), *Transformative approaches to patient literacy and healthcare innovation* (pp. 223–241). IGI Global., DOI: 10.4018/979-8-3693-3661-8.ch011

Tariq, M. U. (2024). Enhancing Students and Learning Achievement as 21st-Century Skills Through Transdisciplinary Approaches. In Kumar, R., Ong, E., Anggoro, S., & Toh, T. (Eds.), *Transdisciplinary Approaches to Learning Outcomes in Higher Education* (pp. 220–257). IGI Global., DOI: 10.4018/979-8-3693-3699-1.ch007

Tariq, M. U. (2024). Equity and inclusion in learning ecosystems. In Al Husseiny, F., & Munna, A. (Eds.), *Preparing students for the future educational paradigm* (pp. 155–176). IGI Global., DOI: 10.4018/979-8-3693-1536-1.ch007

Tariq, M. U. (2024). Fintech startups and cryptocurrency in business: Revolutionizing entrepreneurship. In Kankaew, K., Nakpathom, P., Chnitphattana, A., Pitchayadejanant, K., & Kunnapapdeelert, S. (Eds.), *Applying business intelligence and innovation to entrepreneurship* (pp. 106–124). IGI Global., DOI: 10.4018/979-8-3693-1846-1.ch006

Tariq, M. U. (2024). Generative AI in Curriculum Development in Higher Education. In Fields, Z. (Ed.), *Impacts of Generative AI on Creativity in Higher Education* (pp. 227–258). IGI Global., DOI: 10.4018/979-8-3693-2418-9.ch009

Tariq, M. U. (2024). Integrating ESG Principles Into Corporate Governance for Sustainable Ecosystem Services. In Castanho, R. (Ed.), *ESG and Ecosystem Services for Sustainability* (pp. 89–118). IGI Global., DOI: 10.4018/979-8-3693-3771-4.ch004

Tariq, M. U. (2024). Integration of IoMT for Enhanced Healthcare: Sleep Monitoring, Body Movement Detection, and Rehabilitation Evaluation. In Liu, H., Tripathy, R., & Bhattacharya, P. (Eds.), *Clinical Practice and Unmet Challenges in AI-Enhanced Healthcare Systems* (pp. 70–95). IGI Global., DOI: 10.4018/979-8-3693-2703-6.ch004

Tariq, M. U. (2024). Leveraging artificial intelligence for a sustainable and climate-neutral economy in Asia. In Ordóñez de Pablos, P., Almunawar, M., & Anshari, M. (Eds.), *Strengthening sustainable digitalization of Asian economy and society* (pp. 1–21). IGI Global., DOI: 10.4018/979-8-3693-1942-0.ch001

Tariq, M. U. (2024). Metaverse in business and commerce. In Kumar, J., Arora, M., & Erkol Bayram, G. (Eds.), *Exploring the use of metaverse in business and education* (pp. 47–72). IGI Global., DOI: 10.4018/979-8-3693-5868-9.ch004

Tariq, M. U. (2024). Navigating the Personalization Pathway: Implementing Adaptive Learning Technologies in Higher Education. In Minh Tung, T. (Ed.), *Adaptive Learning Technologies for Higher Education* (pp. 265–291). IGI Global., DOI: 10.4018/979-8-3693-3641-0.ch012

Tariq, M. U. (2024). Revolutionizing health data management with blockchain technology: Enhancing security and efficiency in a digital era. In Garcia, M., & de Almeida, R. (Eds.), *Emerging technologies for health literacy and medical practice* (pp. 153–175). IGI Global., DOI: 10.4018/979-8-3693-1214-8.ch008

Tariq, M. U. (2024). Smart Transportation Systems: Paving the Way for Sustainable Urban Mobility. In Munuhwa, S. (Ed.), *Contemporary Solutions for Sustainable Transportation Practices* (pp. 254–283). IGI Global., DOI: 10.4018/979-8-3693-3755-4.ch010

Tariq, M. U. (2024). Streamlining Operations Insights and Innovations From the Gulf Cooperation Council (GCC). In Ayed, T., Ali, I., Abdelhamid, H., & Mohamed, A. (Eds.), *Utilizing Case Studies in Business Education* (pp. 188–216). IGI Global., DOI: 10.4018/979-8-3693-3779-0.ch010

Tariq, M. U. (2024). The role of AI ethics in cost and complexity reduction. In Tennin, K., Ray, S., & Sorg, J. (Eds.), *Cases on AI ethics in business* (pp. 59–78). IGI Global., DOI: 10.4018/979-8-3693-2643-5.ch004

Tariq, M. U. (2024). The role of AI in skilling, upskilling, and reskilling the workforce. In Doshi, R., Dadhich, M., Poddar, S., & Hiran, K. (Eds.), *Integrating generative AI in education to achieve sustainable development goals* (pp. 421–433). IGI Global., DOI: 10.4018/979-8-3693-2440-0.ch023

Tariq, M. U. (2024). The role of emerging technologies in shaping the global digital government landscape. In Guo, Y. (Ed.), *Emerging developments and technologies in digital government* (pp. 160–180). IGI Global., DOI: 10.4018/979-8-3693-2363-2.ch009

Tariq, M. U. (2024). The transformation of healthcare through AI-driven diagnostics. In Sharma, A., Chanderwal, N., Tyagi, S., Upadhyay, P., & Tyagi, A. (Eds.), *Enhancing medical imaging with emerging technologies* (pp. 250–264). IGI Global., DOI: 10.4018/979-8-3693-5261-8.ch015

Tariq, M. U. (2025). Cultivating Cultural Intelligence for the Global Workforce. In Huzooree, G., & Chandan, H. (Eds.), *Revitalizing Student Skills for Workforce Preparation* (pp. 297–332). IGI Global., DOI: 10.4018/979-8-3693-3856-8.ch010

Tariq, M. U. (2025). Vision and Strategy: Steering Modern Enterprises Towards Long-Term Success. In Sedky, A. (Ed.), *Resiliency Strategies for Long-Term Business Success* (pp. 51–78). IGI Global., DOI: 10.4018/979-8-3693-9168-6.ch003

Taylor, L. D.Jr, & Brownell, E. (2017). Building inclusive leaders: A critical framework for leadership education. In Boitano, A., Schockman, H. E., & Dutra, R. L. (Eds.), *Breaking the zero-sum game: Transforming societies through inclusive leadership* (pp. 323–340). Emerald Publishing Limited. DOI: 10.1108/978-1-78743-185-020171033

Tegally, H., San, J. E., Cotten, M., Moir, M., Tegomoh, B., Mboowa, G., ... & Schubert, G. (2022). The evolving SARS-CoV-2 epidemic in Africa: Insights from rapidly expanding genomic surveillance. Science, 378(6615), eabq5358. DOI: 10.1126/science.abq5358

Teng, M. F. (2021). The effectiveness of incorporating metacognitive prompts in collaborative writing on academic English writing skills. *Applied Cognitive Psychology*, 35(3), 659–673. DOI: 10.1002/acp.3789

Terzić, E. (2018). The significance of vertical and horizontal communication for business effectiveness in sports organizations. *Sport Science (Travnik)*, 11, 110–118.

Thau, S., Bennett, J., Mitchel, M. S., & Marrs, M. B. (2009). How management style moderates the relationship between abusive supervision and workplace deviance: An uncertainty management theory perspective. *Organizational Behavior and Human Decision Processes*, 108(10), 79–92. DOI: 10.1016/j.obhdp.2008.06.003

Thompson, A., Elahi, F., Realpe, A., Birchwood, M., Taylor, D., Vlaev, I., ... & Bucci, S. (2020). A feasibility and acceptability trial of social cognitive therapy in early psychosis delivered through a virtual world: the VEEP study. Frontiers in Psychiatry, 11, 219. DOI: 10.3389/fpsyt.2020.00219

Tierney, W. (2006). *Trust and the public good*. Peter Lang.

Ting-Toomey, S. (1999). *Communicating Across Cultures*. The Guilford Press.

Tlili, A., Huang, R., Shehata, B., Liu, D., Zhao, J., Metwally, A. H. S., ... & Burgos, D. (2022). Is Metaverse in education a blessing or a curse: a combined content and bibliometric analysis. Smart Learning Environments, 9(1), 1-31. DOI: 10.1186/s40561-022-00205-x

Tortosa, A. J. P., & Pineda, J. A. S. (2021). *Challenge-Based Learning: un puente metodológico entre la Educación Superior y el mundo profesional*. ARANZADI/CIVITAS.

Towaf, S. M. (2016). Integration of LS in Teaching Practice of Social Study Student Teachers to Improve the Quality of Learning and Promote a Sustainable LS. *Journal of Education and Practice*, 7(18), 83–91. https://iiste.org/Journals/index.php/JEP

Trade Union Act. (1919). htttps://laws.moj.gov.jm/library/statute/the-trade-union-act

Travis, T. A. (2016). Four ways to approach difficult conversations and build trust. TrustED: The bridge to school improvement. https://trustedschool.org/2016/05/14/4-ways-to-approach-difficult-converstations-build-trust/

Trengove, E. (2017). Peer interaction as mechanism for providing timely and accessible feedback to a large undergraduate class. *International Journal of Electrical Engineering Education*, 54(2), 119–130. DOI: 10.1177/0020720916688486

Troise, C., Corvello, V., Ghobadian, A., & O'Regan, N. (2022). How can SMEs successfully navigate VUCA environment: The role of agility in the digital transformation era. *Technological Forecasting and Social Change*, 174, 121227. DOI: 10.1016/j.techfore.2021.121227

Tsui, L. (1999). Courses and instruction affecting critical thinking. *Research in Higher Education*, 40(2), 185–200. DOI: 10.1023/A:1018734630124

Tsui, L. (2002). Fostering critical thinking through effective pedagogy: Evidence from four institutional case studies. *The Journal of Higher Education*, 73(6), 740–763. DOI: 10.1080/00221546.2002.11777179

Tuanaya, R., Manggaberani, A., Safitri, R., & Ramadan, S. (2022). Meta-analysis study: Analysis of the Effect of Digital Platforms on Learning Outcomes. *Materials of International Practical Internet Conference "Challenges of Science"*. https://doi.org/DOI: 10.31643/2022.17

Turnbull, D., Chugh, R., & Luck, J. (2021). Transitioning to E-Learning during the COVID-19 pandemic: How have Higher Education Institutions responded to the challenge?. Education and Information Technologies. DOI: 10.1007/s10639-021-10633-w

Turner, J. N. (2020). Communicating for change. In J, Tacchi & T. Tufte (Eds.), *Studies in communication for social change*. Palgrave. https://doi.org/DOI: 10.1007.978-3-030-42513-5_4

Turner, J. C., Hogg, M. A., Oakes, P. J., Reicher, S. D., & Wetherell, M. S. (1987). *Rediscovering the Social Group: A Self-Categorization Theory*. Basil Blackwell.

Uhl-Bien, M., & Arena, M. (2018). Leadership for organizational adaptability: A theoretical synthesis and integrative framework. *The Leadership Quarterly*, 29(1), 89–104. DOI: 10.1016/j.leaqua.2017.12.009

Ukoha, C. (2022). As simple as pressing a button? A review of the literature on BigBlueButton. Procedia Computer Science. DOI: 10.1016/j.procs.2021.12.167

Ullal, M. S., Hawaldar, I. T., Samartha, V., Suhan, M., Padmanabha Achar, A., & Srivastava, D. (2021). How to build a brand: Inside an Indian customers' mind? *Academy of Strategic Management Journal*, ●●●, 20.

Umar, M. & Ko, I. (2022). E-learning: Direct effect of student learning effectiveness and engagement through project-based learning, team cohesion, and flipped learning during the .... Sustainability. DOI: 10.3390/su14031724

University of Technology. Jamaica. (2019). *Student Handbook for graduate and undergraduate students: 2019-2020*. PeartreeXpress. University of Technology, Jamaica. (n.d.). *University's annual research productivity reports*. SGRE.

Urde, M. (2003). Core value-based corporate brand building. *European Journal of Marketing*, 37(7/8), 1017–1040. DOI: 10.1108/03090560310477645

Usha, R. K. (2016). Communication barriers. *Journal of English Language and Literature*, 3(2), 74–76.

Valenzano, A., Scarinci, A., Monda, V., Sessa, F., Messina, A., Monda, M., ... & Cibelli, G. (2020). The social brain and emotional contagion: COVID-19 effects. Medicina, 56(12), 640. DOI: 10.3390/medicina56120640

Van den Beemt, A., Groothuijsen, S., Ozkan, L., & Hendrix, W. (2023). Remote labs in higher engineering education: engaging students with active learning pedagogy. Journal of Computing in Higher Education, 35(2), 320-340. DOI: 10.1007/s12528-022-09331-4

Van den Beemt, A., MacLeod, M., Van der Veen, J., Van de Ven, A., Van Baalen, S., Klaassen, R., & Boon, M. (2020). Interdisciplinary engineering education: A review of vision, teaching, and support. Journal of engineering education, 109(3), 508-555. DOI: 10.1002/jee.20347

Van Dijk, J. A. (2020). The digital divide. *Polity*.

Van Driel, J. H., Meirink, J. A., van Veen, K., & Zwart, R. C. (2012). Current trends and missing links in studies on teacher professional development in science education: A review of design features and quality of research. *Studies in Science Education*, 48(2), 129–160. DOI: 10.1080/03057267.2012.738020

Van Houtte, M. (2007). Exploring teacher trust in technical/vocational secondary schools. *Teaching and Teacher Education*, 23(6), 826–839. DOI: 10.1016/j.tate.2006.03.001

Van Knippenberg, D., De Dreu, C. K. W., & Homan, A. C. (2004). Work group diversity and group performance: An integrative model and research agenda. *The Journal of Applied Psychology*, 89(6), 1008–1022. DOI: 10.1037/0021-9010.89.6.1008 PMID: 15584838

Varhelahti, M., & Turnquist, T. (2021). Diversity and Communication in Virtual Project Teams. *IEEE Transactions on Professional Communication*, 64(2), 201–214. DOI: 10.1109/TPC.2021.3064404

Vauterin, J. J. & Virkki-Hatakka, T. (2021). Mentoring PhD students working in industry: Using hermeneutics as a critical approach to the experience. Industry and Higher Education. DOI: 10.1177/0950422220959233

Venter, A. (2020). Synchronising Informal and Formal Learning Spaces to Facilitate Collaborative Online Learning. *Africa Education Review*, 17(6), 1–15. DOI: 10.1080/18146627.2021.1954536

Vermunt, J. D., Vrikki, M., van Halem, N., Warwick, P., & Mercer, N. (2019). The impact of Lesson Study professional development on the quality of teacher learning. *Teaching and Teacher Education*, 81, 61–73. DOI: 10.1016/j.tate.2019.02.009

Vidovich, L., & Currie, J. (2011). Governance and trust in higher education. *Studies in Higher Education*, 36(1), 43–56. DOI: 10.1080/03075070903469580

Villalon, J. J.Julio J. Villalon. (2016). LS: Its influence on planning, instruction, and self-confidence of pre- service mathematics teachers. *US-China Education Review B*, 6(7), 429–439. DOI: 10.17265/2161-6248/2016.07.003

Von Glasersfeld, E. (2013). *Radical constructivism* (Vol. 6). Routledge. DOI: 10.4324/9780203454220

Voogt, J., & Roblin, N. P. (2012). A comparative analysis of international frameworks for 21st century competences: Implications for national curriculum policies. *Journal of Curriculum Studies*, 44(3), 299–321. DOI: 10.1080/00220272.2012.668938

Vrikki, M., Warwick, P., Vermunt, J. D., Mercer, N., & Van Halem, N. (2017). Teacher learning in the context of LS: A video-based analysis of teacher discussions. *Teaching and Teacher Education*, 61, 211–224. DOI: 10.1016/j.tate.2016.10.014

Vygotsky, L. (1962). Thought and language. In *MIT Press eBooks*. DOI: 10.1037/11193-000

Vygotsky, L. S. (1978). *Mind in society: The development of higher psychological processes*. Harvard University Press.

Wadi, H., Suryanti, N. M. N., & Sukardi, S. (2020, August). *The Collaborative Learning for Multicultural of Social Science with LS Pattern for Strengthening Student Character Education*. In 1st Annual Conference on Education and Social Sciences (ACCESS 2019) (322-326). Atlantis Press.

Wagner, C., Garner, M., & Kawulich, B. (2011). The state of the art of teaching research methods in the social sciences: Towards a pedagogical culture. *Studies in Higher Education*, 36(1), 75–88. DOI: 10.1080/03075070903452594

Wahdiniawati, S. A., & Sarinastiti, N. (2023). Employee development: Analysis organization culture, competence and mentoring: A literature review. *International Journal of Business and Applied Economics*, 2(2), 295–308. DOI: 10.55927/ijbae.v2i2.2798

Wake, G., Foster, C., & Swan, M. (2013, July). A theoretical lens on LS: Professional learning across boundaries. In *Proceedings of the 37th Conference of the International Group for the Psychology of Mathematics Education* (Vol. 4, 369-376).

Walker, E. (2011). How "Language-Aware" Are Lesson Studies İn An East Asian High School Context. *Language and Education*, 25(3), 187–202. DOI: 10.1080/09500782.2011.555557

Wang, C. L. (2021). New frontiers and future directions in interactive marketing: Inaugural Editorial. *Journal of Research in Interactive Marketing*, 15(1), 1–9. DOI: 10.1108/JRIM-03-2021-270

Wang, D., Wang, L., Wei, S., Yu, P., Sun, H., Jiang, X., & Hu, Y. (2022). Effects of authoritarian leadership on employees' safety behavior: A moderated mediation model. *Frontiers in Public Health*, 10, 846842. Advance online publication. DOI: 10.3389/fpubh.2022.846842 PMID: 35655454

Wang, S. (2020). The role and path of university academic journals in research integrity building. *Advances in Social Science, Education and Humanities Research*, 505, 401–407.

Wang, Y., Liu, J., & Zhu, Y. (2018). Humble leadership, psychological safety, knowledge sharing and follower creativity: A cross-level investigation. *Frontiers in Psychology*, 9, 1727. DOI: 10.3389/fpsyg.2018.01727 PMID: 30283379

Wang, Z., Liu, Y., & Liu, S. (2019). Authoritarian leadership and task performance: The effects of leader-member exchange and dependence on leader. *Frontiers of Business Research in China*, 13(1), 19. Advance online publication. DOI: 10.1186/s11782-019-0066-x

Ward, M. E. (2013). *Tools of the blogging trade: A study of how dialogic principles help organizations structure blogs to build relationships. Athens* [Masters dissertation, University of Georgia] Georgia

Warrican, S. J. (2015). Fostering true literacy in the Commonwealth Caribbean: Bridging the cultures of home and school. In Smith, P., & Kumi-Yeboah, A. (Eds.), *Handbook of research on cross-cultural approaches to language and literacy development* (pp. 367–392). IGI Global. DOI: 10.4018/978-1-4666-8668-7.ch015

Warrican, S. J., Alleyne, M. L., Smith, P., Cheema, J., & King, J. R. (2019). Peer effects in the individual and group literacy achievement of high-school students in a bi-dialectal context. *Reading Psychology*, 40(2), 117–148. DOI: 10.1080/02702711.2019.1571545

Weaver, J., Matney, G., Goedde, A., Nadler, J., & Patterson, N. (2021). *Digital tools to promote remote lesson study*. International Journal for Lesson and Learning Studies., DOI: 10.1108/IJLLS-09-2020-0072

Weber-Main, A. M., Finstad, D. A., Center, B. A., & Bland, C. J. (2013). An adaptive approach to facilitating research productivity in a primary care clinical department. *Academic Medicine*, 88(7), 929–938. DOI: 10.1097/ACM.0b013e318295005f

Weerasinghe, I. M. S., Lalitha, R., & Fernando, S. (2017). Students' satisfaction in higher education literature review. *American Journal of Educational Research*, 5(5), 533–539. DOI: 10.12691/education-5-5-9

Weimer, M. (2013). *Learner-centered teaching: Five key changes to practice* (2nd ed.). Jossey-Bass.

Wei, R. C., Darling-Hammond, L., & Adamson, F. (2010). *Professional development in the United States: Trends and challenges* (Vol. 28). National Staff Development Council.

Welch, M., & Jackson, P. R. (2007). Rethinking internal communication: A stakeholder approach. *Corporate Communications*, 12(2), 177–198. DOI: 10.1108/13563280710744847

Weller, P. (2013). *Dialogue theories. Dialogue society.* London Great Britain. https://www.dialoguesociety.org/publications/Dialogue-Theories-Preview.pdf

Wenger, E. (1998). Communities of practice: Learning as a social system. *The Systems Thinker*, 9(5), 2–3.

Wessels, H. (2018). *Noticing in Pre-service Teacher Education: Research Lessons as a Context for Reflection on Learners' Mathematical Reasoning and Sense-Making*. In G. Kaiser et al. (Eds.), Invited Lectures from the 13th International Congress on Mathematical Education. ICME-13 Monographs. DOI: 10.1007/978-3-319-72170-5_41

West Indies Group of University Teachers. (2024). The origin. http://wigut.uwimona.edu.jm/content/about

Westbury, I., Hansen, S.-E., Kansanen, P., & Björkvist, O. (2005). Teacher Education for Research-Based Practice in Expanded Roles: Finland's Experience. *Scandinavian Journal of Educational Research*, 5(5), 475–485. DOI: 10.1080/00313830500267937

West, J. D., Jacquet, J., King, M. M., Correll, S. J., & Bergstrom, C. T. (2013). The Role of Gender in Scholarly Authorship. *PLoS One*, 8(7), e66212. DOI: 10.1371/journal.pone.0066212 PMID: 23894278

Wheeler, A. (2017). *Designing brand identity: an essential guide for the whole branding team*. John Wiley & Sons.

Whillans, A., Perlow, L., & Turek, A. (2021). Experimenting during the shift to virtual team work: Learnings from how teams adapted their activities during the COVID-19 pandemic. Information and Organization. DOI: 10.1016%2Fj.infoandorg.2021.100343

Whitaker, M., & Denise, E. J. (Eds.). (2018). *Counternarratives from women of colour academics: Bravery, vulnerability, and resistance*. Routledge. DOI: 10.4324/9780429465505

Wickens, C. M. (2008). The organizational impact of university labor unions. *Higher Education*, 56(5), 545–564. https://doi.org/10.1007/s10734-008-9110-z

Williams, D. A. (2013). *Strategic diversity leadership: Activating change and transformation in higher education*. Stylus Publishing, LLC.

Williams, D. A., Wade-Golden, K. C., & Stevens, F. I. (2020). *Making diversity work on campus: A research-based perspective*. Stylus Publishing, LLC.

Williams, K. Y., & O'Reilly, C. A. (1998). Demography and diversity in organizations: A review of 40 years of research. *Research in Organizational Behavior*, 20, 77–140.

Wilson, V. (2011). Research methods: Content analysis. *Evidence Based Library and Information Practice*, 6(4), 177–179. DOI: 10.18438/B8CG9D

Winton, B. G. (2022). Emotional intelligence congruence: The influence of leader and follower emotional abilities on job satisfaction. . *Leadership and Organization Development Journal*, 43(5), 788–801. Advance online publication. DOI: 10.1108/LODJ-04-2021-0163

Wirtz, J., & Chew, P. (2002). The effects of incentives, deal proneness, satisfaction and tie strength on word-of-mouth behaviour. *International Journal of Service Industry Management*, 13(2), 141–162. DOI: 10.1108/09564230210425340

Witherspoon, D. P., White, R. M., Bámaca, M. Y., Browning, C. R., Leech, T. G., Leventhal, T., Matthews, S. A., Pinchak, N., Roy, A. L., Sugie, N., & Winkler, E. N. (2023). Place-based developmental research: Conceptual and methodological advances in studying youth development in context. *Monographs of the Society for Research in Child Development*, 88(3), 7–130. DOI: 10.1111/mono.12472 PMID: 37953661

Witting, M. (2006). Relations between organizational identity, identification and organizational objectives: An empirical study in municipalities (Master's thesis, University of Twente).

Wollny, A., Jacobs, I., & Pabel, L. (2020). Trait emotional intelligence and relationship satisfaction: The mediating role of dyadic coping. *The Journal of Psychology*, 154(1), 75–93. DOI: 10.1080/00223980.2019.1661343 PMID: 31524567

Wood, K. (2018). The many faces of LS and learning study. *International journal for lesson and learning studies*. 7(1), 2018. 2-7. https://doi.org/DOI: 10.1108/IJLLS-10-2017-0047

Woodard, R., & Babcock, A. (2014). Designing writing tasks in Google Docs that encourage conversation: An inquiry into feedback and revision. In Anderson, R., & Mims, C. (Eds.), *Handbook of research on digital tools for writing instruction in K-12 settings* (pp. 1–29). IGI Global. DOI: 10.4018/978-1-4666-5982-7.ch001

Woodrich, M. P., & Fan, Y. (2017). Google Docs as a tool for collaborative writing in the middle school classroom. *Journal of Information Technology Education*, 16, 391–410. http://jite.informingscience.org/documents/Vol16/JITEv16ResearchP391-410Woodrich3331.pdf. DOI: 10.28945/3870

Woolf, J. (2024, March 25). How Pixar fosters a culture of vulnerability at work. *Harvard Business Review*. https://hbr.org/2024/03/how-pixar-fosters-a-culture-of-vulnerability-at-work

Wreden, N. (2007). *Profit Brand: How to Increase the Profitability Accountability and Sustainability of Brands*. Kogan Page Publishers.

Wu, A., Roemer, E. C., Kent, K. B., Ballard, D. W., & Goetzel, R. Z. (2021). Mejores prácticas organizacionales que apoyan la salud mental en el lugar de trabajo. *Journal of Occupational and Environmental Medicine*, 63(12), E925–E931. DOI: 10.1097/JOM.0000000000002407 PMID: 34840320

Wuchty, S., Jones, B. F., & Uzzi, B. (2007). The increasing dominance of teams in production of knowledge. *Science*, 316(5827), 1036–1039. DOI: 10.1126/science.1136099 PMID: 17431139

Wu, M.-J., Zhao, K., & Fils-Aime, F. (2022). Response rates of online surveys in published research: A meta-analysis. [Zain, S. M., Ab-Rahman, M. S., Mohd Ihsan, A. K. A., Zahrim, A., Mohd Nor, M. J., Mohd Zain, M. F.]. *Computers in Human Behavior Reports*, 7, 100206. DOI: 10.1016/j.chbr.2022.100206

Wu, T. (2022). Digital project management: Rapid changes define new working environments. . *The Journal of Business Strategy*, 43(5), 323–331. Advance online publication. DOI: 10.1108/JBS-03-2021-0047

Wu, T., Liu, Y., Hua, C., Lo, H., & Yeh, Y. (2019). Too unsafe to voice? Authoritarian leadership and employee voice in Chinese organizations. *Asia Pacific Journal of Human Resources*, 58(4), 527–554. DOI: 10.1111/1744-7941.12247

Wyk, J. V., & Haffee, V. (2017). Collaborative learning in higher education: A review of the literature. *The Journal of Higher Education*, 88(3), 465–494.

Wyk, M. M. V., & Haffee, T. (2017). Collaborative learning in higher education: Exploring the use of collaboration platforms. *Journal of Communication*, 8(1), 19–31.

Yaffe, T., & Kark, R. (2011). Leading by example: The case of leader OCB. *The Journal of Applied Psychology*, 96(4), 806–826. DOI: 10.1037/a0022464 PMID: 21443315

Yegros-Yegros, A., Rafols, I., & D'Este, P. (2015). Does interdisciplinary research lead to higher citation impact? The different effect of proximal and distal interdisciplinarity. *PLoS One*, 10(8), e0135095. DOI: 10.1371/journal.pone.0135095 PMID: 26266805

Yousaf, R., & Schmiede, R. (2017). Barriers to women's representation in academic excellence and positions of power. *Asian Journal of German and European Studies*, 2(1), 1–13. DOI: 10.1186/s40856-017-0013-6

Yurkofsky, M. M., Blum-Smith, S., & Brennan, K. (2019). Expanding outcomes: Exploring varied conceptions of teacher learning in an online Professional development experience. *Teaching and Teacher Education, 82*, 1e13. https://doi.org/DOI: 10.1016/j.tate.2019.03.002

Zackrison, E. (2021, March 10). Leading Strategically [Video]. LinkedIn Learning. https://www.linkedin.com/learning/leading-strategically/aligning-needs?u=43761300

Zakaria, N. (2017). Emergent patterns of switching behaviors and intercultural communication styles of global virtual teams during distributed decision making. *Journal of International Management*, 23(4), 350–366. DOI: 10.1016/j.intman.2016.09.002

Zeichner, K. M. (1983). Alternative Paradigms of Teacher Education. *Journal of Teacher Education*, 34(3), 3–9. https://eric.ed.gov/. DOI: 10.1177/002248718303400302

Zeng, Y., & Day, C. (2019). Collaborative teacher professional development in schools in England (UK) and Shanghai (China): Cultures, contexts and tensions. *Teachers and Teaching*, 25(3), 379–397. DOI: 10.1080/13540602.2019.1593822

Zhang, M., Ding, H., Naumceska, M., & Zhang, Y. (2022). Virtual reality technology as an educational and intervention tool for children with autism spectrum disorder: current perspectives and future directions. Behavioral Sciences. DOI: 10.3390/bs12050138

Zhang, T., Shaikh, Z. A., Yumashev, A. V., & Chłąd, M. (2020). Applied model of E-learning in the framework of education for sustainable development. Sustainability. DOI: 10.3390/su12166420

Zhang, L., Basham, J. D., Carter, R. A.Jr, & Zhang, J. (2021). Exploring Factors associated with the implementation of student-centered instructional practices in US classrooms. *Teaching and Teacher Education*, 99, 103273. DOI: 10.1016/j.tate.2020.103273

Zhang, Y., Zhao, R., & Yu, X. (2022). Enhancing virtual team performance via high-quality interpersonal relationships: Effects of authentic leadership. *International Journal of Manpower*, 43(4), 982–1000. Advance online publication. DOI: 10.1108/IJM-08-2020-0378

Zhao, Y., Pohl, O., Bhatt, A. I., Collis, G. E., Mahon, P. J., Rüther, T., & Hollenkamp, A. F. (2021). A review on battery market trends, second-life reuse, and recycling. Sustainable Chemistry, 2(1), 167-205. DOI: 10.3390/suschem2010011

Zhao, L. (2012). Investigation into motivation types and influences on motivation: The case of Chinese non-English majors. *English Language Teaching*, 5(3), 100–122.

Zheng, W., Kim, J., Kark, R., & Mascolo, L. (2023, September 28). *What makes an inclusive leader?* Harvard Business Review. https://hbr.org/2023/09/what-makes-an-inclusive-leader

Zhu, C. (2012). Collaborative learning in higher education: A review of the literature. *Educational Research Review*, 7(1), 1–12.

Zhu, J., Yao, J., & Zhang, L. (2019). Linking empowering leadership to innovative behaviour in professional learning communities: The role of psychological empowerment and team psychological safety. *Asia Pacific Education Review*, 20(4), 657–671. DOI: 10.1007/s12564-019-09584-2

Zulch, B. G. (2014). Communication: The foundation of project management. *Procedia Technology*, 16, 1000–1009. DOI: 10.1016/j.protcy.2014.10.054

About the Contributors

Tashieka S. Burris-Melville is a lecturer in the Faculty of Education and Liberal Studies at the University of Technology, Jamaica. She currently serves as programme leader for the M.Ed. and Ph.D. in Educational Leadership and Management in the faculty. She holds a Doctor of Education specializing in Leadership and Professional Practice from Trevecca Nazarene University and a Master of Arts in Linguistics from the University of the West Indies, Mona. Dr. Burris-Melville has taught courses in academic writing, linguistics, and leadership at the undergraduate and graduate levels. Her research interests include sociolinguistics, applied linguistics, writing in higher education, teamwork development, collaborative and inclusive leadership, transformational leadership, and online teaching and learning.

Shalieka T. Burris, a seasoned practitioner in higher education, is a lecturer in the Faculty of Education and Liberal Studies at the University of Technology, Jamaica. Boasting nearly a decade of experience shaping minds in academic institutions, her pedagogical journey began with a rigorous teaching diploma from the esteemed Shortwood Teachers' College in Kingston. Further enriching her expertise, Ms. Burris pursued and attained her bachelor's and master's degrees in linguistics at the renowned University of the West Indies, Mona. Currently, she is pursuing doctoral knowledge in Leadership and Organizational Intelligence at Trevecca Nazarene University, Nashville. Ms. Burris's scholarly contributions extend beyond the classroom, evidenced by her peer-reviewed publications on themes of collaborative learning and academic writing. Her research pursuits encapsulate adult education, emotional intelligence, team dynamics, followership, leadership, academic literacy, online pedagogy, and applied linguistics.

Adhwaa Alahmari is an associate professor in special education at King Khalid University. I graduated from the University of South Florida. My areas of interest include learning disability, RTI, and qualitative research.

Clavery Allen is a Senior Lecturer in Accounting at the University of Technology, Jamaica (UTech, Ja). He holds a PhD from the University of Bradford and a MSc in Finance and Accounting from the London South Bank University in the United Kingdom. He has held senior academic leadership posts including Head of the School of Business Administration at UTech. Ja. and President of the Academic Staff Union. His research interests include, Leadership, corporate debt, product recall, environmental protection and corporate governance.

Denise Allen is a lecturer and subject leader in the School of Computing and Information Technology at the University of Technology, Jamaica. She serves as the secretary of the University of Technology Academic Staff Union (UTASU) and is a practising attorney-at-law. Denise holds a Legal Education Certificate from the Norman Manley Law School, an LLB (Hons) from UTech, Jamaica, an MSc in Advanced Computer Science (AI specialization) from the University of Manchester, and a BSc in Computing and Management Studies (Hons) from UTech, Jamaica. Additionally, she has a Post-Graduate Diploma in Education from UTech, Jamaica. Her most recent research was a conference paper on leadership in Higher Educational Institutions. She has supervised numerous undergraduate research projects in Computing and delivered presentations on Technology in Education and Data Protection Readiness. Her research interests include leadership in education, artificial intelligence, information security, and technological solutions in law.

Andi Asrifan, S.Pd, M.Pd, a distinguished figure in the realm of education, particularly in English Language Education, has made significant contributions through his extensive research, teaching, and leadership roles. As the Head of the Institute for Cooperation and International Affairs at Universitas Muhammadiyah Sidenreng Rappang, Dr. Asrifan's academic journey is marked by a rich tapestry of achievements, including a Doctor of Education in English Language Education. His work spans various facets of education, language, and technology, reflecting the diverse range of topics covered in his publications and research endeavors. These include, but are not limited to, the impact of the COVID-19 pandemic on educational practices, methodologies in English as a Foreign Language (EFL) classrooms, and the integration of technology in teaching and learning processes. Dr. Asrifan's commitment to advancing educational standards and practices is further evidenced by his active participation in international conferences, webinars, and workshops across countries like India, the Philippines, and Pakistan. These events, organized by various institutions and associations, underscore his role as a global educator and thought leader. His dedication to professional development is also highlighted through his involvement in numerous courses and certifications in personal branding, public speaking, and literacy teaching. Moreover, Dr. Asrifan's leadership extends beyond academia into organizational and educational development, where he has served in various capacities, including as an external examiner for Ph.D. dissertations and a reviewer for scientific journals. His accolades, memberships in professional organizations, and roles as an ambassador for international associations speak volumes of his influence and commitment to fostering educational excellence and sustainable development goals globally.

Tolgahan Ayantaş, born in 1992 in Ankara, Turkey, Tolgahan Ayantaş completed his primary and secondary education in Ankara. He graduated from the Social Studies Teaching programme at the Faculty of Educational Sciences, Ankara University, in 2014. Following his graduation, he taught at public schools and a private institution. Additionally, he worked as an educational content designer, a subject matter expert for exam questions, and a textbook author. In 2018, he was appointed as a research assistant in the Social Studies Education Department at the Faculty of Educational Sciences, Ankara University. He completed his master's degree in social studies education at the Graduate School of Educational Sciences, Ankara University, in 2019. He completed his PhD degree in Social Studies Education at the Graduate School of Educational Sciences, Gazi University, in 2024. His research interests include Social Studies education, the training of Social Studies teachers, professional development models for teachers, the teaching of History topics within Social Studies, History education, digitalisation in education, computational thinking, and textbook analysis. Tolgahan Ayantaş teaches courses such as "Science, Technology, and Society," "History of the First Turkish-Islamic States," "History of Civilization," "Medieval History," "Globalisation and Society," and "Teaching Practice" within the Social Studies Teaching undergraduate programme at the Faculty of Educational Sciences, Ankara University. He has also authored two textbooks currently used at the 4th-grade level in primary schools. Tolgahan Ayantaş is an accomplished researcher in Social Studies education, focusing on teacher development, History education, digitalisation in education, and textbook analysis. He is currently engaged in two EU Erasmus projects aimed at enhancing educational practices across Europe. His work regularly features at national and international conferences, where he shares insights on effective teaching methodologies, the integration of digital tools in education, and the alignment of educational materials with standards. Ayantaş remains committed to advancing education through innovative research and cross-cultural collaboration.

Nadine Barrett-Maitland is a senior Lecturer in the School of Computing and Information Technology at the University of Technology, Jamaica. She holds a PhD. in Computer Science from the University of the West Indies Mona; a MSc in Computer Science from the UWI, Mona and a B.Sc. in Computer Studies with

Management from the University of Technology Jamaica. Her research area is Information Security, Artificial Intelligence, Leadership and issues related to the use of Information Technology to improve lives. Doctor Barrett-Maitland has several published works in peer review Journals, Conferences proceedings and Book Chapters. She is a guest columnist in the Jamaica Gleaner. She is a Christian and enjoys learning, writing, teaching and conducting research. Dr Barrett has been engaged as guest speaker on several occasions to address many topics relating to computer science, information technology and artificial intelligence among other areas.

Oprah Burris is an experienced educator with seven years of dedicated service in the fields of Religious Education and Social Studies. Passionate about fostering teamwork and promoting a love of learning among her students, Ms. Burris takes great joy in seeing her students thrive academically and personally. Her commitment to education took her to China, where she had the rewarding experience of teaching English, further enriching her teaching practice and global perspective. Her enthusiasm and dedication make her a cherished and inspiring presence in the classroom.

Anita Candra Dewi has established herself as a prominent figure in the educational sector, particularly in Makassar, where she has contributed significantly as a civil servant, lecturer, and teacher across various educational institutions. With a profound academic background, Dr. Dewi holds a doctoral degree (S-3) in Indonesian Language Education, showcasing her deep commitment and expertise in language and education. Her academic journey is a testament to her dedication to advancing the study and teaching of the Indonesian language and literature. Beyond her formal teaching roles, Dr. Dewi is actively involved in the broader educational community by participating in numerous seminars, workshops, and training sessions. These activities highlight her eagerness to stay at the forefront of educational methodologies and pedagogical innovations, particularly in the realm of language education. Her involvement in these events allows her to share her insights and expertise with fellow educators and students and enables her to learn and adapt to the evolving educational landscape continuously. Dr. Dewi's contributions to the field extend into scholarly work as well. She has authored several academic papers and books on language learning and literature. These publications serve as valuable resources for students, educators, and researchers, offering fresh perspectives and practical strategies for teaching and learning the Indonesian language and exploring its rich literary traditions. Through her multifaceted career, Dr. Anita Candra Dewi exemplifies the role of an educator who is deeply invested in both the theoretical and practical aspects of language education, making significant strides in enhancing the quality and accessibility of language learning in Indonesia.

Memory Deredzai is an Educational Psychology PhD student in the Department of Educational Foundations, Faculty of Education at the University of Zimbabwe. She holds a Master of Science Degree in Counselling Psychology (Great Zimbabwe University), a Bachelor of Science in Monitoring and Evaluation (Lupane State University), a Bachelor of Education Degree in Psychology (Great Zimbabwe University) and a Diploma in Education (University of Zimbabwe). Currently, she is a lecturer of Psychology at Madziwa Teachers' College, Mashonaland Central Province Zimbabwe which falls under the Scheme of the Association of the University of Zimbabwe. She also has vast primary school teaching experience spanning more than a decade. Ms Memory Deredzai is an upcoming scholar and academic who has an urge for academic and professional growth. Her research interests are domiciled in the areas of guidance and counselling, social and emotional intelligence, gender and resilience in marginalised populations. To Ms Memory, the sky is the limit.

Sonia Escorial Santa-Marina Early Childhood Education Teacher and Degree in Psychopedagogy with a specialisation in Special Education from the Complutense University of Madrid (Spain). Currently pursuing a PhD in Education with a clear line of research: inclusive education, more specifically Universal Design for Learning (UDL). Experience as a teacher and researcher for more than 10 years at university level, previously experience as a psychopedagogue in nursery schools, teacher and counsellor in private and public schools and consultant for different educational projects. She has been a speaker on issues related to attention to diversity. She currently directs the Diversity and Inclusion Unit at Unie Universidad, EAE Business School and The Core (part of Grupo Planeta, Formación y Universidades), and has been an expert in attention to diversity in universities for more than 10 years in different educational institutions.

Sanchita Ghosh is a highly driven worker who holds a Master of Computer Applications degree. Her current position as a Technical Assistant at Brainware University allows her to specialize on IoT, AI, networking, cybersecurity, and cloud computing. Sanchita is passionate about using technology to solve complicated challenges, and she actively participates in projects and activities that promote innovation and progress the digital transformation. Her diversified skill set and dedication to continual learning make her an invaluable asset in the ever-changing field of information technology.

Pedzisai Goronga is a Senior Lecturer and Chairperson of the Department of Educational Foundations, Faculty of Education at the University of Zimbabwe. He teaches both undergraduate and postgraduate modules in Educational Psychology and coordinates Faculty-wide modules. He holds a Doctor of Philosophy (PhD) Degree in Educational Psychology from the University of Pretoria, South Africa, M Ed in Educational Psychology from the University of Zimbabwe, B Ed in Primary Education and a Diploma in Education from the same university. His areas of research interest include among many other issues; resilience studies, gender and education, human learning and performance, guidance and counselling and emotional intelligence. Dr Pedzisai Goronga has vast teaching experience at the primary school level and more than close to two decades of teaching experience at the university level. Dr Pedzisai Goronga is a visionary leader, an honest follower and a team player who thrives on collaboration to meet set goals.

Robert Johnson holds a first degree in Pure & Applied Chemistry (UWI, Mona), a M.Sc in Analytical Chemistry (Dalhousie University), and a Post graduate Diploma in Education (UTech, Ja). Curretly, I am a Senior Lecturer in General and Analytical Chemistry.

Badruddin Kaddas, S.Ag., M.Ag., Ph.D, is a highly respected academic and leader in Islamic education, with a career spanning over two decades. Born in Timurung, he pursued his undergraduate and master's degrees at Universitas Muslim Indonesia, focusing on Islamic Communication and Broadcasting. He later earned his Ph.D. in Islamic Communication from Universiti Utara Malaysia, further solidifying his expertise in the field. Throughout his career, Dr. Badruddin has held various significant academic and administrative roles at Universitas Islam Makassar, where he has been instrumental in shaping the institution's educational landscape. His roles have included serving as the Dean of the Faculty of Teacher Training and Education and currently as Vice Rector II. In these capacities, he has overseen numerous initiatives aimed at improving the quality of education, enhancing faculty capabilities, and integrating modern educational technologies. Beyond his institutional responsibilities, Dr. Badruddin is deeply involved in professional organizations, particularly within Nahdlatul Ulama, where he has served in leadership roles such as Vice Secretary and Vice Chairman at both regional and national levels. His involvement in these organizations reflects his commitment to community development and his dedication to promoting inclusive and accessible education. Dr. Badruddin's contributions extend to research and publication as well. He has been involved in various research projects focused on empowering Islamic institutions and has published works on the effectiveness of Islamic communication strategies. His research interests include the role of communication in Islamic education, the development of Islamic broadcasting, and the application of technology in educational settings. In recognition of his contributions, Dr. Badruddin has received several awards, including being named the Best Lecturer at Universitas Islam Makassar. His ongoing work continues to impact the field of Islamic education, making significant strides in fostering a more inclusive and innovative educational environment.

Tara Knight is a doctoral candidate in the School of Leadership and Interdisciplinary Studies at Trevecca Nazarene University in Nashville, TN. She holds a Master of Business Administration degree from the University of Arizona Global Campus and a Bachelor of Science in Business Management from Saint Joseph's College in Brooklyn, NY. Her research interests include women in ministry leadership, women in corporate leadership, emotional intelligence, mentorship, professional development, career progression, employee satisfaction, and employee work environment.

Joan Lawla is a retired Senior Lecturer in Business - with a focus on Marketing, Consumer Behaviour and Research. She is the former Head, School of Business Administration at the University of Technology, Jamaica. She holds a MBA in Marketing and Hospitality Management and is ABD for a PhD in Ethics from the University of the West Indies, Mona, a LLB from the University of Technology, Jamaica and a LEC from the Norman Manley Law School She is a practicing attorney at law and is the immediate past president of the University of Technology Academic Staff Union. Her research interests are ethics, consumer bahaviour and political marketing.

Hlompho Cynthia Letsie is a lecturer of Communication and Advertising at the Limkokwing University of Creative Technology-Lesotho in the Faculty of Communication and Media Broadcasting. She holds Masters in Development Studies and Masters in Applied Communication Management. Her interests are in Advertising and Communication development.

Morine Matongo is a lecturer in the Department of Educational Foundations, Faculty of Education, University of Zimbabwe. She holds a PhD in Sociology of Education which she teaches to both undergraduate and post graduate students. She also holds a Master of Education degree in Sociology of Education. Her areas of research interest include among others, Gender and Education, equality of educational opportunities, Social Change, ICT and pedagogy and Indigenous Knowledge Systems (IKSs). Her primary school teaching experience spans 18 years..

Hope Mayne is an Associate Professor of Curriculum and Instruction, and the Acting Associate Vice President for Teaching and Learning at the University of Technology, Jamaica. Her scholarly work focuses on: STEM TVET integration, curriculum implementation and reform, curriculum as lived experiences, curriculum as social reconstruction, decolonizing the curriculum and the integration of Artificial Intelligence in the teaching and learning environment.

Tsepiso Mncina is a lecturer of Communication, Journalism and Public Relation at the Limkokwing University of Creative Technology-Lesotho in the Faculty of Communication and Media Broadcasting. She holds a Masters of Communication with a major in Public Relation. Her interests are in Journalism, Public Relations, Communication and Educational technologies.

Mofana is a lecturer of Communication and Advertising at the Limkokwing University of Creative Technology-Lesotho in the Faculty of Communication and Media Broadcast. He holds a Masters in Advertising Communication. His interests are Advertising, Communication and Higher Education Studies.

Mulyadi, an academic professional with a significant background in educational management, has cultivated an extensive career in teaching and research. Born on November 4, 1973, in Bone, he pursued his higher education at Universitas Muslim Indonesia (UMI), earning his bachelor's degree in Ushuluddin in 1997. He furthered his education by obtaining a master's degree in Educational Management from PPS UNM in 2002 and a doctorate in Educational Science from the same institution in 2018. Over the years, Dr. Mulyadi has actively contributed to the academic community through teaching various subjects in educational foundations, evaluation, and counseling at Universitas Islam Makassar. His professional development includes participating in numerous workshops, seminars, and training sessions, both as a participant and a contributor, enhancing his expertise in educational methodologies and Islamic education. In addition to his academic duties, he has played a pivotal role in organizational activities, including serving as a secretary for the Nahdlatul Ulama in Makassar and contributing to educational development programs at various levels. His research interests are diverse, encompassing the evaluation of teacher performance post-certification, the development of educational models for marginalized communities, and the social-emotional development of early childhood education.

Sekoai Nkhi is a Senior Lecturer in the Faculty of Communications, Media and Broadcasting at the Limkokwing University of Creative Technology-Lesotho. He holds a PhD in Language, Linguistics and Literature from the University of South Africa. His research interests are in Applied Linguistics, Communications,

Curriculum and Development, Language Education and the Minority Language Media.

Cynthia Onyefulu is a Professor of Educational Assessment specialising in Psychometrics. She is a Visiting Fellow in Educational Development at the University of Windsor in Canada. She has authored and co-authored several peer-reviewed journal articles, books, book chapters, and instructional manuals. She has also published several technical reports on commissioned studies. She has served as an Editor-in-Chief for the Journal of Arts, Science and Technology, and a reviewer for the American Educational Research Association, the Continental Journal of Education Research, the Caribbean Education Research Journal, the Collected Essays on Learning and Teaching, and the World Education Research Association, among others. She is a member of the Assessment in Higher Education Network (AHE), the American Educational Research Association (AERA), the Caribbean Case Researchers' Association (CCRA), the Bioethics Society of the English-Speaking Caribbean (BSESC), and the Mixed Methods International Research Association Caribbean Chapter (MMIRA-CC).

Sara Redondo Duarte is currently a full-time professor at the Faculty of Education (Department of Educational Studies) at Complutense University of Madrid (Spain). She holds a PhD in Education, a Master's degree in Educational Technology and a Master's degree in Business Administration and Management. She enjoyed a research fellowship at the Educational Research and Documentation Center of the Ministry of Education in Spain from 2005 to 2008. Most of her professional career has been devoted to faculty development and management of educational innovation projects. She is a member of the consolidated research group Innovation, Selection and Practice of Teaching Researchers at the Complutense University. Her lines of research focus on faculty development, educational project management and the didactic use of technologies. Previously, she has held university management positions as Director of Educational Innovation and Faculty Development and Director of Student Experience (among other positions) at Universidad Europea. She is co-author of several publications of the Eurydice Network (European Commission), the Spanish Ministry of Education and papers in educational research journals. She has received recognition for good practices in university leadership and management from Universitat Politècnica de Catalunya (2021) and the Management Excellence Club (2019) in Spain. She has been honored at the International e-learning Awards in the 2018, 2019 and 2022 editions.

Nekiesha C. Reid is a dedicated educator and lecturer and, with a strong passion for language and communication, she has been actively engaged in the academic sphere, contributing to both teaching and research. Nekiesha holds a Postgraduate Diploma in Higher Education from the University of Guyana, an MA in English Language from the University of the West Indies, Mona, and a BA in Media & Communication from the same institution. Currently serving as a lecturer within the Department of Language & Cultural Studies at the University of Guyana, Nekiesha imparts her knowledge and expertise to her students, fostering an environment of learning and growth. Beyond her academic roles, Nekiesha is known for her mentoring and advising skills. She served as a Senior Resident Advisor at the Office of Student Services and Development through the Elsa Leo- Rhynie Hall of residence at the University of the West Indies at Mona, contributing to the holistic development of students. In that role, she created the Towers Performing Arts and Cultural Kaleidoscope (T-PACK) as well as the Towers Mentorship Network and served as head of the Towers disciplinary committee. Nekiesha's diverse background also includes media experience, having worked as a Production Assistant at Nationwide News Network and as a Business Reporter at Jamaica Observer, Ltd. Her skills extend to public speaking, presentation, and event management, making her a well-rounded educator and professional.

Leesha Roberts, an Assistant Professor at the Center of Education Programmes at The University of Trinidad and Tobago, is a leader in her field. With twenty-two years of experience in education and computing, she currently leads as the Discipline Leader for Educational Technology/Instructional Design and TVET subjects for the University's undergraduate and postgraduate programs. Her research focuses on ICT integration in Caribbean Education, where she not only supervises postgraduate students' research in these areas but also guides them to excel. She began her career in the public service, particularly at the Ministry of Education, from 2002 to 2006, where her responsibilities included leading projects to implement technology-based solutions. Her work involved acquiring, evaluating, and implementing ICTs in primary schools throughout Trinidad and Tobago, designing and developing various user applications, and re-engineering the I.T. unit to align with 21st-century education. She has also participated in various international and regional programmes for the Ministry of Education, such as PIRLS, TIMSS, and Microsoft Partners in Learning, showcasing her leadership skills. Leesha's impact extends beyond the classroom. She has trained staff and lectured extensively on various ICT-related subjects at major local higher education institutions in Trinidad and Tobago. Her PhD in Education, focused on ICT integration and instructional design, is a testament to her dedication to her field. Her work, which aims to equip students with the necessary technology integration skills for teaching and learning, has significant implications for the future of education. It also contributes to research in ICT integration at the educational level in Trinidad and Tobago and the Caribbean, underscoring the importance of her contributions.

Vivit Rosmayanti, S.Pd.I., M.Pd was born in Botta on June 26, 1987. She has over 10 years of experience teaching at the University. She obtained a bachelor's degree in English Education from Alauddin State Islamic University. She completed her master's and doctoral degrees in English Education from Makassar State University. She is currently a lecturer in the Post Graduate Program, Department of English Education at Makassar State University, South Sulawesi, Indonesia. She is also actively writing research articles to be published in nationally and internationally accredited journals. She has written in some chapter books, monographs, and reference books. She is interested in teaching methods for teaching English. Her research interests include language teaching methodology, ICT instruction, and ESP teaching. She can be contacted at email: rosmayantivivit@gmail.com

Piyal Roy is an accomplished academician in the field of Computer Science & Engineering. He has completed his BSc in Computer Science, MSc in Computer Science and MTech in Computer Science & Engineering. Currently, he is working as an Assistant Professor at Computer Science & Engineering department at Brainware University, India.

Nobhonil Roy Choudhury An Assistant Professor with 9 years of experience in Computer Science and BCA curriculum development, known for fostering student engagement and supporting learning objectives. With expertise in PC programming and subjects like C, Java, and Cyber Security, they have a proven track record in academic advisement and technology integration in education. Career Highlights: Current role at Brainware University, focusing on up-to-date technology curriculum and NAAC work. Previous position at GitaRam Institute of Management, where they enhanced computer literacy and monitored industry trends. Started as a Teaching Assistant at Narula Institute of Technology, providing personalized student support. This educator is dedicated to technological proficiency and academic excellence, continually advancing student success.

Atherine Salmon is a distinguished educator in finance and business education, currently lecturing at the University of Technology, Jamaica. She holds a Doctor of Business Administration from Edinburgh Napier University and an MBA with a Finance emphasis. Her academic journey also includes a B.Sc. in Accounting (Honours) and a Diploma in Business Education. Atherine serves as VP Communications for the North America Case Researchers Association and supervises graduate research at UTech. She co-facilitates case research training, mentors case writers, and co-chaired the Formation of the Caribbean Case

Researchers Association. She has held leadership roles, including Program Director at UTech, Ja Western Campus, and various adjunct lecturer positions. Her dedication extends to community development, having served as a Community Development Officer and held leadership positions at the Westmoreland Cooperative Credit Union. Atherine's commitment to education and community development underscores her significant contributions to her field.

SyamsuardiSaodi was born in Bulu, Lappariaja District, on February 10, 1983. He is the second child of H. Saodi Nuntung and Hj. Haneria Haddaning. He began his elementary education at State Elementary School 146 Bengo and continued to SLTP Negeri 2 Lappariaja and SMA Negeri 1 Lappariaja. He earned his bachelor's degree from the State University of Makassar in Automotive Engineering Education in 2000 and completed his master's degree in Language Studies with a concentration in Early Childhood Education at the same university in 2006. Dr. Syamsuardi completed his Ph.D. in Educational Sciences at the State University of Makassar in 2021. Dr. Syamsuardi is a permanent lecturer in the Early Childhood Teacher Education Study Program at the Faculty of Education, State University of Makassar. He has held various significant positions, including Head of the Early Childhood Teacher Education Study Program (2014-2018), Coordinator of the Center for Cooperation and Innovation Development in Education (2021-2022), and Head of the Curriculum and Entrepreneurship Module Center at the Institute for Innovation and Entrepreneurship Development (LIPK) from 2021 to 2025.

Saptarshi Kumar Sarkar is an Assistant Professor at Brainware University. With a dedication to academic excellence, he brings a wealth of knowledge and experience to his students. His research interests include AI, ML and Social Networking, contributing significantly to advancements in his field.

Madhuri Sawant Nationality: Indian Present Designation: Director Parent Organization: Department of Tourism Administration, Dr. Babasaheb Ambedkar Marathwada University, Aurangabad – 431 004 (M.S), India. Other Positions: Director, International Centre for Buddhist Tourism Coordinator, Research & Consultancy Cell Coordinator, Vocational Programme in Travel & Tourism Management International Position: Executive Secretary, Euro-Asia Tourism Studies Association

Sharlene Smith has an earned doctorate degree in Curriculum & Instruction with focus in Adult Education and Autism Spectrum Disorder from the University of South Florida in Tampa, Florida. She also has a Master of Arts degree in Adult Education and Human Resource Development; and two Graduate Certificates in Autism Spectrum Disorder, and Leadership in Developing Human Resources from the University of South Florida; a Graduate Certificate in Applied Behavior Analysis from Monmouth University in New Jersey; and a Bachelor of Science degree in Professional Management from Nova Southeastern University in Fort Lauderdale. Dr. Smith is a special educator, behavior analyst, and autism consultant. She presently serves as the Operational Director and Instructor for the Transition and Career Studies program for students with intellectual and developmental disabilities at Georgian Court University (GCU) in New Jersey. Additionally, she is an Adjunct Professor for the School of Education special education program at GCU. Dr. Smith is also a scholar and co-author of several published research publications, including two book chapters.

Natasha Swann is a 25-year veteran educator, working as an assistant professor of Education at the University of The Bahamas for the past thirteen years. She works as the Chair of the School of Education. As a teacher educator, Dr. Swann teaches Language Arts and Literacy Methods. She also works in the capacity of Teaching Practice Supervisor. Dr. Swann is a Senator on the Academic Senate at the University of The Bahamas where she currently serves as chair of the Research and Creative Works Committee. She is a published dramatist, playwright and producer, where she systematically integrates the performing arts in her teaching. Dr. Swann is a proud critical theorist who understands the role of empowerment and emancipation through her work with marginalized populations in education. Dr. Swann's research interests pertain to arts-based, critical and multiliteracies theories.

Muhammad Usman Tariq has more than 16+ year's experience in industry and academia. He has authored more than 200+ research articles, 100+ case studies, 50+ book chapters and several books other than 4 patents. He is founder and CEO of The Case HQ, a unique repository for courses, narrative and video case studies. He has been working as a consultant and trainer for industries representing six sigma, quality, health and safety, environmental systems, project management, and information security standards. His work has encompassed sectors in aviation, manufacturing, food, hospitality, education, finance, research, software and transportation. He has diverse and significant experience working with accreditation agencies of ABET, ACBSP, AACSB, WASC, CAA, EFQM and NCEAC. Additionally, Dr. Tariq has operational experience in incubators, research labs, government research projects, private sector startups, program creation and management at various industrial and academic levels. He is Certified Higher Education Teacher from Harvard University, USA, Certified Online Educator from HMBSU, Certified Six Sigma Master Black Belt, Lead Auditor ISO 9001 Certified, ISO 14001, IOSH MS, OSHA 30,

Joyce Esi Tawiah-Mensah obtained her Ph.D. in Curriculum and Instruction in Early Childhood Education with cognate in Literacy, and a Graduate Certificate in Program Evaluation from University of South Florida, USA. She holds M. Phil. in Applied Linguistics and B.Ed. in Ghanaian Language from University of Education, Winneba, Ghana. Dr. Tawiah-Mensah is currently a Senior lecturer at the Department of Basic Education, University of Cape Coast (UCC), Ghana and a course coordinator mentoring Early Childhood Education (ECE) Course Tutors as well as those in the field of Ghanaian Language for the new B.Ed. programme being implemented at the Colleges of Education in Ghana. Dr. Tawiah-Mensah has expertise in ECE, play-based pedagogies, language and literacy pedagogies, curriculum design and implementation as well as programme evaluation. Her research interest centres on issues relating to ECE, teacher preparation, interactive and culturally responsive pedagogies that promote language and literacy acquisition, multivocal studies involving learners, parents and teachers. She has also engaged in an international research project and co-authored refereed articles and book chapters

Remi Thomas I have been working towards guiding my students using my diverse experience to ensure their intellectual assets & potential can be effectively channelized. Having built industrial expertise over 12 years, I bring to the table a fusion of knowledge & skills in domains such as Marketing, Business Development, Ed-Tech, Operations Management, Tourism, Communication & Entrepreneurship. I have 4 published research papers in my name and have been a part of several National & International Conferences on Tourism & Management. I am planning to explore & contribute to the field of research with my experience to guide students in their pursuit to becoming passionate & talented professionals, true to the words of being 'student-centric'.

Meredith Williams is a Lecturer in Medical Technology at the University of Technology, Jamaica. He holds a MSc in Cellular Pathology from the University of Westminster London. He has been actively engaged in academic unions for over 20 years. His research interests are endometriosis, polycystic ovarian syndrome, and ovarian cancer.

Eraldine Williams-Shakespeare is an Associate Professor in Education at the University of Technology, Jamaica. She holds a PhD. in Curriculum and Instruction, Instructional Technology emphasis from the University of South Florida, Tampa and a MA in Open. Distance and Flexible Learning from the University of London, External College. She is a certified instructional designer and evaluator with over 24 years of experience in education. An avid researcher, she has published in several local and international peer reviewed journals and has research interests in distance and online learning, teacher education, technologies in teacher education, curriculum development and planning, online curricula and women in academia.

Taneisha Wright-Cameron holds two Master of Education degrees in Educational Measurement and Curriculum, Teaching, and Learning Studies from the University of West Indies, Mona, Jamaica, and the Memorial University of Newfoundland, St. John's respectively. Her research interests include educational measurement, assessment, curriculum development and evaluation, research approaches, and restorative justice education. She has participated in conferences with poster presentations focused on investigating the effects of CSEC Mathematical ability on the performance of CAPE Cost and Management Accounting students and delivered a workshop presentation on the impact of Restorative Justice Circle Pedagogy for International Graduate Students. Taneisha's career spans the Secondary level of Education, where she was a Senior Teacher with special responsibilities as an External Examination Coordinator and a Business Educator, and the Post-Secondary level as an Adjunct Lecturer in Research Methods and Research Supervisor. She desires to improve the quality of decision-making and the credibility of outcomes in Education.

Index

A

academic unions 422, 423, 424, 425, 428, 429
Academic Writing Instruction 217, 218, 219, 220, 231, 238, 239, 248
Adult Learning 252, 255, 256, 257, 258, 260, 272, 273, 275, 277, 278, 280
Artificial Intelligence 135, 275, 285, 286, 297, 298, 300, 302, 396, 511
Asynchronous Collaboration 248, 253
attitudes 3, 14, 39, 51, 76, 114, 124, 131, 147, 186, 208, 212, 241, 298, 304, 305, 321, 322, 323, 326, 327, 328, 332, 369, 383, 390, 412, 491
Authoritarian 12, 26, 27, 37, 48, 115, 129, 130, 137, 140, 141, 430
Autocratic 115, 129, 130, 131, 132, 136, 139

B

Brand Equity 449, 467, 471, 473, 474, 475, 476
Branding 449, 450, 451, 453, 454, 455, 456, 457, 460, 467, 469, 470, 473, 474, 475, 476

C

Collaboration 2, 3, 5, 8, 14, 20, 30, 32, 34, 35, 38, 41, 42, 43, 44, 45, 46, 47, 49, 50, 59, 60, 62, 70, 74, 78, 86, 88, 92, 93, 94, 96, 97, 102, 103, 104, 109, 110, 111, 129, 134, 135, 145, 148, 149, 150, 152, 153, 154, 156, 157, 168, 171, 173, 188, 189, 192, 193, 194, 195, 196, 197, 198, 199, 202, 203, 205, 206, 207, 208, 215, 217, 219, 220, 221, 222, 223, 224, 225, 226, 227, 228, 229, 230, 235, 236, 237, 238, 239, 240, 243, 244, 245, 246, 248, 251, 252, 253, 254, 255, 256, 257, 259, 260, 263, 268, 269, 272, 274, 275, 285, 286, 287, 288, 289, 290, 293, 295, 296, 297, 298, 299, 302, 304, 305, 306, 309, 316, 319, 322, 330, 334, 339, 342, 343, 345, 348, 349, 350, 358, 359, 360, 367, 368, 369, 370, 371, 372, 373, 374, 375, 376, 378, 379, 380, 381, 382, 383, 384, 385, 386, 388, 390, 391, 392, 393, 394, 395, 396, 397, 398, 402, 403, 404, 405, 410, 411, 412, 413, 414, 419, 420, 422, 427, 428, 433, 438, 441, 444, 450, 451, 453, 472, 479, 480, 481, 483, 484, 485, 487, 489, 490, 491, 492, 493, 494, 495, 496, 497, 499, 500, 501, 502, 503
collaborative learning 60, 68, 80, 84, 152, 154, 183, 187, 188, 189, 190, 191, 192, 193, 195, 196, 199, 202, 203, 204, 205, 206, 207, 208, 209, 210, 212, 213, 214, 215, 217, 218, 219, 220, 221, 223, 225, 226, 227, 228, 229, 230, 231, 233, 238, 239, 240, 241, 242, 243, 244, 245, 246, 247, 248, 249, 259, 260, 263, 265, 270, 272, 283, 285, 289, 297, 298, 303, 305, 306, 307, 394, 397, 414
Collaborative Writing 217, 218, 219, 220, 221, 222, 224, 225, 226, 229, 231, 233, 234, 237, 241, 245, 246, 247, 248, 295, 308
Communication Barriers 241, 318, 322, 331, 335
Community of Inquiry 255, 256, 258, 273, 281
Computer-Supported Collaborative Learning 84, 219, 221, 244, 245, 247, 248, 303, 394
Connectivism 255, 258, 272, 277, 282
constructivism 59, 190, 191, 210, 211, 213, 214, 215, 228, 246
cooperative learning 187, 188, 194, 209, 212, 243, 330
critical narrative inquiry 401

D

Digital Literacy 157, 221, 248, 275, 302
Digital Tools 154, 156, 157, 179, 184, 247, 251, 252, 253, 255, 256, 257, 258, 259, 260, 261, 263, 264, 265, 267, 268, 269, 270, 271, 272, 273, 274, 275, 276, 280, 331, 495
Digital Transformation 86, 275, 279, 300, 302
Directive 95, 99, 115, 124, 125, 129, 130, 139, 161
Distributed Cognition 251, 253, 255, 259, 273, 281, 282
diversity 9, 23, 25, 37, 47, 48, 57, 58, 62, 63, 64, 65, 66, 73, 74, 76, 79, 80, 83, 84, 86, 87, 98, 124, 133, 135, 191, 193, 196, 197, 198, 205, 206, 212, 213, 235, 253, 279, 282, 301, 348, 369, 374, 377, 383, 390, 392, 393, 411, 450, 451, 475, 476, 479, 480, 482, 501, 503, 504, 505, 506, 507, 511

E

Educational Technology 51, 211, 213, 243, 244, 251, 252, 255, 261, 273, 274, 277, 279, 282, 302
Effective Communication 32, 33, 35, 42, 45, 47, 48, 49, 87, 99, 126, 146, 189, 196, 205, 264, 295, 313, 314, 315, 316, 318, 319, 320, 321, 322, 323, 324, 325, 326, 327, 328, 329, 331, 332, 333, 334, 335, 382, 392, 453
Emerging Trends 275, 379, 501, 510
emotions 8, 23, 32, 36, 52, 129, 137, 318, 322, 323, 324, 326, 327, 328
employee development 115, 141
employee performance 115, 118, 121, 128, 137, 139, 140, 141, 331
experiential learning 57, 58, 59, 60, 61, 62, 63, 75, 83, 84, 110, 178, 195, 210, 248, 276, 300, 453

F

feedback strategies 57, 71

Framework 3, 9, 20, 23, 26, 59, 62, 64, 65, 68, 70, 78, 87, 93, 96, 97, 98, 118, 125, 131, 151, 158, 173, 189, 190, 191, 207, 208, 244, 255, 256, 258, 259, 260, 264, 273, 275, 280, 282, 305, 308, 310, 312, 321, 334, 361, 371, 373, 390, 404, 405, 406, 410, 413, 414, 423, 427, 428, 449, 455, 456, 457, 464, 467, 469, 473, 502

H

higher education 1, 2, 3, 12, 13, 14, 15, 18, 20, 21, 24, 30, 36, 51, 52, 53, 54, 56, 61, 65, 73, 79, 80, 135, 136, 140, 145, 168, 171, 172, 179, 180, 185, 187, 188, 192, 193, 194, 199, 200, 201, 202, 203, 208, 209, 210, 212, 213, 214, 215, 242, 243, 244, 245, 246, 248, 251, 252, 254, 257, 258, 259, 260, 263, 268, 270, 274, 275, 277, 278, 279, 280, 281, 282, 283, 300, 304, 307, 308, 309, 310, 311, 313, 314, 315, 316, 318, 319, 320, 321, 324, 328, 332, 334, 339, 340, 346, 348, 359, 360, 361, 363, 364, 366, 371, 372, 373, 374, 375, 376, 377, 379, 380, 381, 388, 391, 394, 396, 397, 398, 415, 425, 443, 446, 447, 449, 450, 451, 452, 453, 454, 455, 457, 458, 459, 460, 465, 466, 467, 469, 470, 471, 472, 473, 474, 475, 476, 479, 484, 486, 492, 495, 501, 503, 504, 505, 506, 507, 508, 510
Higher Education Institutes 457, 458, 460
high-performing teams 4, 5, 8, 13, 21, 94, 95, 98, 99, 315, 316, 328
Humble Leadership 39, 56

I

Inclusion 9, 10, 12, 23, 37, 38, 45, 46, 47, 48, 57, 58, 62, 63, 64, 65, 73, 75, 76, 77, 80, 84, 86, 87, 124, 133, 135, 137, 196, 374, 450, 479, 501, 503, 504, 506, 507, 509, 510
Inclusive Governance 29

Innovation 5, 9, 14, 17, 18, 19, 20, 21, 23, 24, 31, 32, 38, 41, 42, 43, 45, 46, 47, 49, 53, 59, 63, 64, 74, 80, 92, 93, 95, 100, 101, 102, 107, 109, 110, 111, 117, 127, 129, 134, 147, 151, 192, 197, 198, 199, 263, 279, 301, 305, 309, 319, 334, 340, 347, 349, 364, 367, 368, 377, 380, 390, 396, 406, 414, 429, 471, 475, 476, 479, 493, 494, 495, 496, 497, 503, 504, 506, 509, 510, 511

L

labor market 58, 62, 65, 86
leadership 3, 6, 12, 19, 20, 21, 24, 25, 26, 27, 32, 33, 34, 35, 36, 37, 38, 39, 41, 45, 46, 47, 48, 49, 50, 51, 52, 53, 54, 55, 56, 68, 87, 91, 92, 93, 94, 95, 98, 99, 100, 101, 102, 103, 104, 105, 106, 107, 108, 109, 110, 111, 112, 113, 114, 115, 116, 117, 118, 119, 120, 121, 122, 123, 124, 125, 126, 127, 128, 129, 130, 131, 132, 133, 134, 135, 136, 137, 138, 139, 140, 141, 142, 176, 192, 193, 194, 195, 255, 279, 285, 301, 305, 306, 312, 334, 346, 347, 353, 358, 367, 368, 369, 370, 371, 372, 373, 376, 377, 378, 380, 381, 382, 386, 387, 388, 389, 390, 391, 392, 393, 394, 395, 396, 397, 398, 405, 414, 420, 421, 422, 426, 429, 430, 432, 433, 434, 435, 438, 439, 440, 441, 442, 443, 444, 445, 446, 452, 472, 473, 476, 479, 491, 503, 506, 507, 509
Leadership development programs 21, 93, 105, 106, 107, 110, 111, 136
leadership style 3, 26, 95, 99, 101, 115, 116, 118, 119, 120, 121, 123, 124, 125, 127, 128, 129, 130, 131, 133, 136, 137, 138, 139, 140, 141, 142, 430
Leadership styles 12, 19, 91, 92, 93, 94, 95, 99, 100, 101, 102, 104, 105, 107, 109, 110, 111, 115, 119, 121, 122, 123, 124, 125, 126, 127, 128, 129, 130, 133, 135, 136, 138, 140, 429, 430, 446
lesson study 145, 148, 149, 150, 151, 153, 154, 155, 156, 157, 158, 160, 166, 168, 173, 175, 176, 177, 178, 179, 180, 181, 182, 183, 184, 185

M

Mentorship 36, 45, 46, 93, 94, 186, 196, 197, 198, 339, 342, 343, 349, 353, 358, 359, 367, 368, 369, 370, 372, 381, 384, 385, 387, 389, 390, 391, 392, 393, 440, 487, 488, 491, 498
Motivation 3, 36, 59, 60, 67, 87, 91, 92, 93, 96, 104, 105, 109, 116, 117, 119, 121, 124, 125, 129, 130, 131, 137, 138, 139, 140, 170, 177, 189, 191, 196, 200, 213, 219, 245, 252, 257, 298, 302, 306, 307, 339, 343, 344, 345, 346, 354, 355, 356, 359, 362, 363, 366, 379, 390, 391, 428, 508
multidisciplinary collaboration 286

O

Organizational culture 18, 19, 20, 21, 23, 79, 101, 107, 108, 110, 111, 116, 117, 128, 139, 444, 451, 459, 501
Organizational success 5, 35, 105, 106, 109, 111, 314

P

Paternalistic Leadership 115, 130
practices 3, 8, 11, 13, 14, 33, 39, 57, 63, 64, 68, 87, 91, 92, 93, 95, 107, 108, 111, 132, 134, 146, 147, 148, 149, 150, 151, 152, 154, 155, 156, 157, 158, 159, 160, 161, 162, 167, 169, 172, 173, 176, 181, 182, 184, 186, 191, 198, 201, 202, 203, 205, 212, 217, 231, 252, 255, 260, 278, 289, 298, 299, 332, 343, 344, 361, 362, 369, 370, 376, 379, 391, 404, 412, 428, 437, 441, 445, 465, 469, 479, 483, 490, 491, 492, 503, 508, 509, 510
professional development 21, 46, 58, 104, 106, 146, 147, 149, 151, 152, 153, 155,

156, 157, 158, 160, 170, 171, 176, 177, 178, 179, 180, 181, 182, 183, 184, 185, 186, 194, 202, 203, 252, 271, 291, 299, 304, 307, 374, 379, 387, 388, 389, 392, 441, 504

psychological safety 1, 2, 3, 4, 5, 6, 8, 9, 10, 11, 12, 13, 14, 15, 16, 17, 18, 19, 20, 21, 22, 23, 24, 25, 26, 29, 30, 31, 32, 33, 34, 35, 36, 37, 38, 39, 40, 41, 42, 43, 44, 45, 46, 47, 48, 49, 50, 51, 52, 53, 54, 55, 56, 66, 67, 68, 69, 70, 71, 79, 83, 85, 97, 134, 382, 391, 421, 429, 430, 439, 443, 444, 445, 446

R

research 1, 3, 5, 8, 13, 14, 15, 16, 17, 18, 19, 20, 23, 24, 25, 39, 40, 51, 52, 53, 54, 55, 58, 65, 68, 69, 81, 85, 86, 92, 94, 100, 102, 103, 105, 109, 110, 111, 112, 113, 115, 116, 118, 120, 122, 123, 125, 126, 127, 128, 129, 130, 131, 136, 138, 140, 141, 145, 146, 147, 148, 149, 151, 152, 154, 155, 159, 160, 161, 162, 163, 164, 165, 166, 168, 169, 170, 171, 172, 175, 176, 177, 178, 179, 180, 181, 182, 183, 184, 185, 188, 189, 192, 193, 194, 195, 199, 200, 201, 202, 203, 209, 210, 211, 212, 213, 214, 215, 217, 219, 220, 221, 225, 230, 231, 232, 233, 238, 239, 241, 242, 243, 244, 245, 247, 248, 255, 259, 260, 261, 262, 263, 265, 268, 269, 270, 274, 275, 277, 278, 279, 281, 282, 286, 287, 288, 289, 290, 291, 297, 300, 301, 302, 303, 304, 305, 306, 307, 308, 309, 311, 312, 315, 329, 331, 332, 333, 334, 339, 340, 341, 342, 343, 344, 345, 346, 347, 348, 349, 350, 351, 352, 353, 354, 355, 356, 357, 358, 359, 360, 361, 362, 363, 364, 365, 366, 367, 368, 369, 370, 371, 372, 373, 374, 375, 376, 377, 378, 379, 380, 381, 382, 385, 386, 387, 388, 389, 390, 391, 392, 394, 395, 396, 397, 398, 401, 402, 403, 404, 405, 406, 407, 408, 409, 410, 411, 412, 413, 414, 415, 419, 421, 422, 425, 426, 428, 429, 443, 444, 445, 446, 449, 455, 456, 457, 472, 473, 474, 479, 493, 494, 504, 505, 506, 507, 511

Research Productivity 333, 339, 340, 341, 342, 343, 344, 345, 346, 347, 348, 349, 350, 351, 352, 353, 354, 358, 359, 360, 361, 363, 364, 365, 366, 373, 375, 376, 379, 392, 394, 398

role model 68, 69

S

Safe Environment 8, 9, 12, 14, 31, 39, 43, 45, 57, 67, 429

Servant 12, 51, 52, 54, 92, 93, 95, 101, 102, 103, 104, 105, 107, 108, 109, 110, 111, 113, 114, 115, 122, 127, 131, 132, 133, 137, 430, 444, 445

Servant leadership 12, 51, 52, 54, 92, 93, 95, 101, 104, 105, 107, 108, 109, 110, 111, 113, 114, 115, 131, 132, 137, 430, 444, 445

skills 4, 33, 34, 35, 36, 52, 58, 59, 60, 62, 64, 66, 68, 70, 75, 79, 83, 86, 87, 88, 98, 103, 105, 106, 115, 117, 122, 130, 141, 142, 146, 147, 148, 151, 154, 155, 159, 161, 162, 165, 167, 169, 170, 172, 173, 186, 187, 188, 189, 192, 193, 194, 195, 196, 197, 198, 199, 200, 201, 202, 203, 205, 207, 208, 209, 218, 219, 220, 221, 224, 225, 226, 231, 239, 242, 243, 247, 248, 254, 257, 258, 259, 277, 292, 304, 309, 314, 320, 324, 325, 327, 330, 333, 345, 346, 347, 368, 369, 378, 380, 383, 387, 390, 392, 404, 412, 413, 433, 435, 436, 439, 441, 453, 459, 472, 493, 508, 511

social studies 145, 159, 160, 161, 162, 163, 165, 166, 169, 170, 171, 172, 173, 175, 176, 177, 179, 180, 182, 186, 413, 444

student teams 57, 66, 68, 69, 71, 79

T

teaching excellence 367, 368, 370, 371, 381
team development 91, 92, 93, 94, 95, 96, 98, 99, 101, 102, 103, 109, 110, 111, 115, 116, 118, 119, 120, 127, 136, 426, 427, 432, 433, 434, 447
team dynamics 14, 20, 26, 29, 91, 92, 93, 94, 95, 96, 97, 99, 100, 102, 104, 105, 109, 110, 111, 126, 195, 274, 282, 313, 314, 382, 383, 388, 413, 419, 420, 433, 434, 438, 441
team effectiveness 13, 45, 46, 47, 53, 55, 93, 98, 101, 358, 364, 422, 428, 429, 432, 433, 435, 440, 442
teams 1, 2, 4, 5, 6, 8, 9, 10, 11, 12, 13, 15, 18, 19, 20, 21, 23, 24, 25, 26, 32, 34, 35, 37, 38, 41, 50, 52, 53, 55, 57, 58, 59, 64, 66, 67, 68, 69, 71, 73, 74, 79, 85, 92, 93, 94, 95, 96, 97, 98, 99, 100, 101, 102, 103, 104, 105, 107, 108, 109, 110, 111, 114, 117, 118, 119, 120, 121, 124, 125, 126, 127, 129, 131, 132, 133, 134, 135, 136, 140, 145, 149, 152, 161, 162, 165, 166, 167, 168, 169, 170, 171, 172, 173, 192, 193, 194, 197, 212, 253, 256, 274, 279, 282, 285, 287, 294, 299, 305, 311, 313, 314, 315, 316, 317, 318, 322, 324, 326, 327, 328, 333, 341, 348, 349, 361, 369, 371, 377, 378, 379, 382, 392, 393, 396, 397, 398, 399, 402, 404, 405, 415, 421, 426, 428, 429, 430, 433, 439, 443, 444, 445, 450, 453, 479, 480, 484, 486, 487, 490, 491, 492, 497, 503, 504, 506
Teamwork 2, 29, 30, 37, 41, 42, 61, 68, 71, 93, 94, 97, 99, 107, 108, 109, 130, 150, 151, 168, 171, 172, 173, 174, 186, 187, 188, 189, 192, 193, 194, 195, 196, 197, 198, 199, 203, 205, 206, 207, 208, 209, 239, 251, 252, 253, 254, 255, 256, 257, 258, 259, 260, 261, 263, 265, 266, 268, 269, 274, 276, 277, 278, 279, 285, 320, 321, 324, 339, 342, 343, 348, 349, 350, 358, 359, 364, 367, 368, 370, 372, 373, 377, 378, 380, 381, 382, 389, 391, 395, 396, 404, 419, 420, 421, 422, 424, 425, 426, 428, 429, 435, 437, 439, 444, 445, 446, 447, 450, 453, 471, 472, 487, 501
teamwork skills 187, 193, 194, 195, 196, 197, 198, 199, 203, 209, 257, 277, 453
third space 401, 402, 403, 405, 406, 410, 411, 412
Transactional 92, 95, 101, 102, 103, 104, 105, 109, 110, 111, 112, 113, 115, 119, 127, 128, 136, 316, 317, 318, 319, 323, 325, 326, 327, 329, 334
Transformational 12, 26, 54, 92, 95, 100, 101, 102, 104, 105, 107, 109, 110, 111, 112, 113, 114, 115, 117, 119, 122, 127, 128, 396, 411, 430, 445
Trust 3, 4, 8, 9, 10, 11, 12, 13, 20, 21, 29, 30, 31, 32, 33, 34, 35, 36, 37, 38, 39, 40, 41, 42, 43, 44, 45, 46, 47, 48, 49, 50, 51, 52, 53, 54, 55, 56, 66, 67, 70, 73, 79, 92, 95, 97, 101, 103, 104, 108, 113, 114, 117, 121, 124, 128, 130, 131, 133, 139, 156, 194, 230, 257, 283, 303, 304, 305, 315, 316, 332, 372, 378, 379, 380, 382, 387, 388, 390, 393, 404, 409, 410, 411, 421, 426, 429, 439, 441, 451, 462, 467, 469

U

university 1, 15, 18, 23, 24, 29, 30, 31, 32, 33, 36, 37, 40, 41, 42, 43, 44, 45, 46, 47, 48, 49, 50, 51, 52, 54, 57, 58, 59, 62, 63, 64, 65, 66, 68, 73, 74, 75, 76, 77, 78, 80, 82, 91, 113, 115, 133, 137, 145, 161, 162, 169, 175, 187, 211, 213, 215, 217, 218, 219, 220, 225, 231, 232, 241, 246, 251, 252, 255, 260, 263, 264, 277, 278, 280, 287, 298, 300, 303, 307, 309, 313, 320, 329, 333, 335, 339, 341, 342, 343, 344, 345, 346, 347, 348, 349, 350, 351, 352, 353, 355, 356, 357, 358, 359, 362, 363, 364, 365, 366, 367, 372, 373, 381, 396, 398, 401, 409, 414, 419, 420, 421, 423, 424,

425, 433, 443, 446, 447, 449, 466, 471, 472, 473, 476, 479, 505, 506, 507

V

Virtual Reality 248, 285, 286, 287, 296, 297, 298, 300, 302, 303, 305, 306, 307, 308, 310, 312, 493, 494
Virtual Teamwork 207, 251, 252, 253, 254, 256, 257, 266, 279, 367, 378, 389

VUCA 57, 58, 59, 80, 83, 86

W

women of color 135, 395
work environment 3, 11, 14, 16, 21, 31, 35, 36, 43, 61, 64, 66, 67, 86, 103, 108, 109, 115, 116, 118, 121, 125, 141, 302, 382, 430, 483, 492

Milton Keynes UK
Ingram Content Group UK Ltd.
UKHW051612021124
450590UK00001B/4